Trial Practice Series

ENGINEERING EVIDENCE

Max Schwartz
Civil and Mechanical Engineer

Neil Forrest Schwartz
Member, California Bar

SHEPARD'S/McGRAW-HILL
P.O. Box 1235
Colorado Springs, CO 80901

McGRAW-HILL BOOK COMPANY

New York • St. Louis • San Francisco • Colorado Springs • Auckland • Bogota Hamburg • Johannesburg • London • Madrid • Mexico • Montreal • New Delhi • Panama • Paris • São Paulo • Singapore • Sydney • Tokyo • Toronto

12345678910 SHHA 8987654321

Library of Congress Cataloging in Publication Data

Schwartz, Max, 1922–
Engineering evidence.
(Trial practice series)
Includes index.
1. Evidence, Expert—United States.
2. Evidence, Demonstrative—United States.
3. Forensic engineering—United States.
I. Schwartz, Neil Forrest, joint author. II. Title.
III. Series.
KF8961.S38 347.73'64 80-23236

ISBN 0-07-055740-3

To Clara, wife and mother of the authors, whose patience, strength, encouragement, and loving support made our goal achievable

Acknowledgments

We would like to thank Jeremy Robinson, Senior Editor of McGraw-Hill Book Company, who initiated this project. We appreciate the inspiration given us by Louis M. Brown, Professor of Law Emeritus, University of Southern California, to incorporate the philosophy of preventive law in this work. We are grateful, too, to David S. Ament, our sponsoring editor at Shepard's/McGraw-Hill, for his help throughout the writing of this book.

Preface

This work is a comprehensive effort to cover engineering evidence as it relates to the expanding field of civil litigation. Inasmuch as engineering evidence is the backbone of litigation involving design, construction and manufacturing, the authors have included in this work general discussion of the various engineering disciplines, engineering terminology and symbols, and the laws of physics and mechanics. In addition, the authors have attempted to take a chronological approach to locating, obtaining, evaluating, preparing and presenting engineering evidence for litigation.

Max Schwartz
Neil Forrest Schwartz

June 30, 1980
Los Angeles, California

Contents

Summary

Detailed

3 Discovering Evidence in Products Liability Cases

4 Discovering Evidence in Construction Litigation

5 Discovering Evidence in Catastrophic, Natural Disasters

6 Discovering Evidence in Transportation Accidents

1 Introduction

§1.01 A. Preamble

Each day, mankind's dependence on things beyond its control and understanding increases. The basic character of rural society has been replaced with technological systems which dominate all areas of human affairs. Manufacturing, husbandry, textile production, construction, transportation, communication, and harnessing of energy comprise a large portion of such complicated systems.

As science and technology continue to develop, the gap between the layperson's comprehension of this technology and the technology itself expands. Mankind is directly or indirectly making itself vulnerable to circumstances beyond its control. We need only consider the products we use, the dwellings in which we live, the food which we consume, the transportation vehicles which we utilize, and the sources of energy that we tap to appreciate the general state of ignorance and dependence in which we live.

In addition to this scientific development there is spiraling inflation, exhaustion of livable land, and scarcity of materials and energy supplies. These factors, in turn, provide incentive for technological development to follow a path which does not always coincide with the interests of human beings in health or safety. Inflation has put great pressures on designers, builders, and manufacturers to offer marketable products. The result is often lowered standards in materials and workmanship. New construction continues on available but marginal land. The consequences are flooding, mudslides, landslides, and foundation settlements. In either situation, manufacturing and construction become more complex and diversified and quality control is reduced. Whatever the reason, cases of a gasoline tank which explodes after impact, an aviation pylon which causes an engine dismount, a nuclear facility which malfunctions and has its cooling supply system inadvertently shut off, an off-site plutonium contamination, or a construction project utilizing inferior materials on a shoddy site, all have one thing in common: someone has suffered damages for which compensation may be sought through civil litigation.

Civil litigation, like technology, is becoming more complex. The trier of fact, whether jury, judge, or arbitrator, is often in need of special assistance when the matter at issue is beyond common experience. In such a case, an expert may testify on that issue if that witness has special knowledge, skill, experience, training, or education on the matter in controversy.

The purpose of this book is to aid the attorney in the accumulation, preparation, and presentation of engineering evidence in trial. Engineering evidence is the backbone of litigation involving design, construction, and manufacturing. The means of determining what kind of evidence is required in view of the specific nature of the case, where to obtain this evidence, and how to effectively introduce admissible evidence is the subject of this work.

B. Chapter Summaries

§1.02 1. Selection of an Engineering Expert

Chapter 2 deals generally with selection of an engineering expert. A detailed discussion focuses on types of experts available to the attorney where particular issues are involved. There is also an in-depth treatment of methods of locating and using a particular kind of expert.

When an engineering expert is sought, counsel should be able to distinguish between a professional and a nonprofessional engineer. The characteristics differentiating these experts and their respective qualifications are covered in that chapter.

§1.03 2. Discovering Evidence in Products Liability Cases

Discovering evidence in a products liability case is the subject of chapter 3. To familiarize the reader with basic product parts, the chapter identifies and discusses the dynamic and static components of a product. After examining the mechanics of a typical product, various possible sources of relevant manufacturing evidence are identified. In addition, testing procedures and methods and a suggested check list for discovery are covered. Finally, there is a comprehensive consideration of the issue of damages as it relates to evidentiary techniques, estimates, and liability.

§1.04 3. Discovering Evidence in Construction Litigation

The fourth chapter is very broad, and deals with discovering evidence for construction litigation. Architects, engineers, owners, contractors, subcontractors, material suppliers and others are discussed in terms of both their theoretical and practical contributions. Construction contract documents, plans, maps, and calculations are described and explained, and a document check list is suggested. The chapter presents codes and standards which cover construction, safety, fire, electrical work, plumbing, zoning, and building. In addition, construction damages are identified and considered in the context of evidence, estimation, and liability. Finally, there are typical construction cases, with emphasis on sources of construction evidence.

§1.05 4. Discovering Evidence in Catastrophic, Natural Disasters

Discovering evidence in cases arising out of various kinds of natural disasters, such as earthquakes and floods, is dealt with in chapter 5. There is discussion of identifying, locating, and acquiring historical documents such as topographic maps, weather records, earthquake records, and soil and geological reports. Also, the chapter describes the responsibilities of the numerous federal, state, county, and municipal agencies which aim at preventing catastrophic occurrences. In addition to a suggested check list for the discovery of relevant evidence in catastrophic or natural disaster litigation, this chapter considers subjects relating to damages, including evidence, estimates, and liability.

§1.06 5. Discovering Evidence in Transportation Accidents

Chapter 6 is about discovering evidence in road and rail transportation cases. There are descriptions and explanations of roadway vehicles such as automobiles and trucks and rail vehicles such as locomotives and railroad cars, as well as of roadway safety devices and railway safety devices and structures. The federal, state, local, and professional organizations which regulate roadway and railroad transportation are discussed. The chapter includes a presentation of the laws of physics which affect roadway and railway vehicles, with an explanation of the concepts of dynamic and static forces and energy.

Finally, the chapter contains a check list of relevant evidence applicable to transportation accidents.

§1.07 6. Preparation of Expert and Evidence for Trial

Chapter 7 covers the practical aspects of preparing the expert and the evidence for litigation. Various factors which must be considered by the attorney in determining the desirability of an expert witness are discussed. Pretestimony guidelines for the expert witness including objectivity, tenacity, self-restraint, humility, and motivation are treated. In addition, the chapter examines trial preparation considerations which relate to tactics and pitfalls, as well as discovery subjects pertaining to partisan and adverse experts' qualifications, analyses, and findings. Finally, the preparation of exhibits including photographs, models, diagrams, and outside-courtroom examinations is dealt with in this chapter.

§1.08 7. Presenting Engineering Evidence for Trial

Presentation of demonstrative engineering evidence in litigation is the subject of chapter 8 as the development of this book continues to follow a basic chronological order. This chapter discusses various types of demonstrative evidence and applicable admissibility requirements. Photographic evidence and photographic distortion are covered in detail. In addition, there are descriptions of numerous presentation methods, procedures, tactics, and problems.

§1.09 8. Examining Experts in Trial

Direct and cross-examination of experts at trial are discussed in the ninth chapter. On direct examination of an expert, the chapter examines the subjects of expert testimony and the qualification criteria, as well as other tactics and considerations.

With respect to the cross-examination of an adverse expert, nine potential situations are treated. In addition, chapter 9 deals with examination of expert witnesses on real and illustrative evidence.

§1.10 9. Statutory and Case Law on Expert Evidence

Chapter 10 comprehensively presents the statutory and case law on expert evidence. The chapter discusses, among other things: what expert evidence is; how it is used; the weight of expert evidence; and the basis of expert testimony. The work product doctrine and the attorney-client privilege is analyzed in terms of the legal distinction between an expert witness and an expert consultant. There is also a detailed treatment of the law pertaining to court-appointed experts, compensation of experts, and examination of experts. Finally, the chapter examines expert evidence as it relates to safety codes, learned treatises, common practice, experiments, and arbitration proceedings.

§1.11 10. Sources of Experts

The first appendix contains names and addresses of professional societies which can serve as resources to counsel in selecting an expert.

§1.12 11. Governing Regulations of Safety and Materials

Appendixes B, C, and D deal with governing regulations of safety and materials. They discuss various federal, state, county, municipal, and professional associations' regulations as they pertain to: construction and buildings; industry and machinery; and roadway vehicles and trains. They also correlate specific governing regulations with identified subject matters.

§1.13 12. Engineering Terminology and Glossary

Appendix E presents engineering and legal terminology as it relates to engineering evidence. The technical engineering terms which are used in products, construction, transportation, and catastrophic litigation cases are explained in simplified and comprehensible language. In addition, the appendix includes a section on the standard letter symbols which represent common engineering terms.

C. Overview of the Use of Engineering Evidence

§1.14 1. Generally

Most legal disputes are eventually resolved by way of settlement. Settlement frequently can be expedited and dramatically strengthened with the backing of an engineering expert consultant.

The expert can illuminate the intricacies of construction and products liability cases from the firsthand perspective of standard practice. In addition, the consultant is in a position to expose the camouflage which may obscure issues in a case. As in any profession, an expert from a particular field is able to recognize and fully utilize the data on hand, which capacity, in turn, enhances settlement possibilities.

§1.15 2. Importance of Retaining an Expert

Retaining an engineering expert is frequently vital to satisfactory conclusion of a disputed matter.

Too often, the engineering expert is retained shortly before trial and only after all hope for settlement has been lost. This happens because of reluctance on the part of attorneys to spend money on an expert even though an attorney may be fully aware of the need for such service.

Delays in obtaining an expert's services often handicap proper technical studies. Critical evidence may no longer be available; site conditions may have radically changed. A meritless lawsuit may be submerged in litigation for five years.

Since most actions which involve engineering evidence are settled out of court, proper professional investigation and reporting can tip the scales toward satisfactory negotiation and settlement.

It is often said that the most important time spent in winning a lawsuit is that spent in initially preparing the case. This is why it is important for the attorney to understand the engineering evidence available and relevant to the issues in controversy.[1]

Selective use of an objective and reputable engineering expert can frequently prevent unnecessary lawsuits between parties. In one case, an expert was brought in to resolve a dispute between an owner and contractor over cracking in the plaster of a newly constructed swimming pool. The owner, believing the contractor to be at fault, demanded remedial work. The contractor denied responsibility and requested compensation for the extra work. Litigation was avoided when both parties submitted the matter to an independent engineer who investigated the site, reviewed the plans and specifications, and determined that the cracking had been caused by the owner's last-minute desire to have a jacuzzi constructed adjacent to the pool so that they shared a common wall. The wall had turned out to be inadequate to withstand the water pressure exerted on it.

§1.16 3. Importance of Identifying Chain of Custody

When certain samples, materials, or items are obtained by the expert or any other person, the object should be securely maintained so that the *chain of custody* can be established to show that: (1) it is the object which was involved in the incident; and (2) its condition is substantially unchanged.

If the chain of custody of relevant evidence could not be verified, substituted or tampered with objects could contaminate and distort the facts. In addition, it is doubtful whether such evidence would even be admissible, since it would lack a proper foundation.

---

[1]§§7.01-.11.

D. Pre-Expert Investigation

§1.17 1. Preliminary Investigation

Before retaining an engineering expert, counsel can save time and costs by personally conducting a preliminary investigation to obtain pertinent and vital information which can eventually be used by the expert. This will serve to educate counsel and reduce the amount of investigation that would be required of the expert.

Following is a brief outline of suggested steps to be taken by counsel in the preliminary investigation of a case:

A. Review of available data
   1. Conference with client
   2. Review of client's files
   3. Review of drawings,[2] specifications,[3] and other data
   4. Review of contract documents[4]
   5. Review of advertisements, brochures,[5] offers for sale[6]

B. Inspection of site or subject product
   1. Measurements, sketches, and photographs[7]
   2. Sample collection of subject product
   3. Sample collection of similar products

C. Review of governing regulations dealing with subject of litigation
   1. Building codes[8]
   2. Safety regulations[9]
   3. Industry standards[10]
   4. Design standards
   5. Case law
   6. Other regulations

D. Determination of the issues involved
   1. Plaintiff's point of view
   2. Defendant's point of view

---

[2]**§4.04.**
[3]**§§3.17, 4.09.**
[4]**§§4.03, 4.18.**
[5]**§3.13.**
[6]**§3.19.**
[7]**§8.09.**
[8]**§4.37.**
[9]**§4.46.**
[10]**§2.36.**

E. Determination of approximate damages
  1. Damages to the plaintiff
  2. Damages to the defendant
F. Identification of all parties
  1. Determination of necessary parties
  2. Responsibility between parties
G. Case evaluation
  1. Likelihood of success
  2. Cost of litigation
  3. Time involved

§1.18 2. Secondary Investigation

Following preliminary investigation of the case, counsel may continue to personally investigate and prepare the case by going more deeply into the case history, related documents, financial summaries, and computation of damages.

The following brief outline details basic subjects that can be documented by counsel during the preliminary preparation of products liability, construction, castastrophic, or transportation accident cases:

A. Preparation of history of case
  1. Products liability cases
    a. Manufacturer
    b. Distributor
      (1) Retailer
      (2) Wholesaler
    c. Consumer
    d. Repairs
    e. Modification
    f. Accident
  2. Construction cases
    a. Preparation of plans
    b. Specifications
    c. Construction contracts
    d. Permits
    e. Inspections
    f. Construction
  3. Catastrophic cases
    a. History of natural events
    b. Design of improvements

c. Construction
d. Catastrophe
4. Transportation accident cases
a. Design
b. Construction
c. Maintenance of facilities
d. Accident

B. Review of related documents
1. Products liability cases
a. Advertisements[11]
b. Brochures[12]
c. Sales documents[13]
d. Manuals[14]
e. Data on components[15]
f. Manufacturer's drawings[16]
g. Certified prints[17]
h. Specifications[18]
2. Construction cases
a. Preliminary plans[19]
b. Working drawings[20]
c. Specifications[21]
d. Bidding documents
e. Construction contract[22]
f. Building permits[23]
g. Inspection reports[24]

---

[11] **§3.13.**
[12] *Id.*
[13] **§3.19.**
[14] **§3.14.**
[15] **§3.15.**
[16] **§3.16.**
[17] *Id.*
[18] **§§3.17, 4.09.**
[19] **§4.22.**
[20] **§4.04.**
[21] **§§3.17, 4.09.**
[22] **§4.20.**
[23] **§4.22.**
[24] **§4.26.**

h. Field notes
i. Change orders[25]
3. Catastrophic cases
a. Preliminary plans[26]
b. Historic documents of natural events
c. Working drawings[27]
d. Specifications[28]
e. Bidding documents
f. Construction contract[29]
g. Permits[30]
h. Inspection reports
i. Field notes
j. Change orders
4. Transportation accidents
a. Plans of transportation facility
b. Maps[31]
c. Signal and communication devices
d. Safety devices
e. Design standards
f. Operators' standards

C. Financial summary
1. Contract price
2. Extras[32]
3. Schedule of payments
4. Penalties

D. Computation of damages
1. Repair costs[33]
2. Related expenses
3. Costs due to delays

---

[25] **§4.21.**
[26] **§4.22.**
[27] **§4.04.**
[28] **§§3.17, 4.09.**
[29] **§4.20.**
[30] **§4.22.**
[31] **§4.10.**
[32] **§4.22.**
[33] **§4.60.**

4. Extended overhead[34]
5. Loss of productivity[35]
6. Interest on loans

§1.19 E. Importance of Early Investigation

The importance of conducting an expeditious investigation of the available evidence relating to a particular incident cannot be overemphasized. Failure to investigate, locate, and preserve tangible evidence involved in a litigable event usually prejudices, if it does not preclude, successful prosecution of a lawsuit.

§1.20 1. Preservation of Evidence

A contractor fell to the ground while ascending a wooden ladder.[36] One side rail of the ladder had allegedly snapped while the contractor was in the process of carrying tools and supplies to the roof. The contractor sued the manufacturer of the ladder for damages. More than four years after the incident, and while the case was deep in litigation, the contractor retained an engineering expert to inspect, test, and analyze the subject side rail for any defect. Unfortunately, the parts of the ladder had not been well preserved. The contractor had kept the side rail and the rest of the ladder outside in his construction yard. For more than four years the sun and rain had battered the evidence. The side rail and ladder had weathered, dried out, and splintered considerably. This made it difficult for the expert to ascertain the condition that the ladder had been in four years before. Obviously, the ultimate result could have been easier to determine if the side rail and ladder had been properly preserved indoors, under conditions which would have sustained their condition as of the date of the incident.

In another case, involving an international contract to bore a tunnel through a European mountain, a lawsuit developed when the contractor failed to complete operations as scheduled. One issue in this multiparty litigation was whether the tunnel boring machine was designed adequately to meet geological specifications. The contractor, who personally designed and constructed the tunnel boring machine,[37] was forced to scrap the machine after completion of the tunnel to pay off various obligations to subcontractors. Years later, when the capability of the subject machine began to crystallize as an issue, an engineering expert was retained to investigate and report. Unfortunately, no photographs had been taken of the machine, the contractor did not have any design plans, and the components which had made up the machine had long been dispersed and resold. In other words, the contractor was unable to identify the individual components of the machine. Therefore, it was impossible to accurately reconstruct the machine or to determine its tunnel boring capability in terms of torque

---

[34] §§4.64, 4.66.
[35] §4.65.
[36] §§3.27, 3.49.
[37] §§3.06, 3.29.

and horsepower. The results would have been different had early investigation preserved the critical data which described the component parts of the machine.[38]

§1.21 2. Change of Character of Evidence

Many conditions which result in litigation are subject to rapid change. For this reason, it is essential that the original character of conditions somehow be preserved. This is particularly true in construction accidents, transportation accidents, and catastrophic accidents.

In one case, a 70-year-old woman tripped and injured herself when she allegedly stepped into a pothole in the middle of a small supermarket parking lot. The next week, the entire lot was resurfaced with asphalt according to the market's normal yearly maintenance policy. No photographs had been taken; no witnesses were present. Negligence became basically a question of credibility.

Similarly, evidence relating to scaffolding or shoring accidents, or flooding or fire incidents, is particularly subject to change. In addition, reconstruction of transportation accidents requires that the evidence be memorialized for subsequent interpretation. Where vehicles are to be repaired or salvaged, care must be taken to insure that sufficient data will be available for eventual analysis. Of course, the ideal situation would be to have an engineering expert on the scene immediately to investigate from the original sources of evidence.

§1.22 3. Loss of Evidence

The loss of real evidence not only frequently makes it difficult to prove certain critical issues, but may sometimes give rise to an adverse inference. This inference is that if weaker and less satisfactory evidence is offered when it appears that stronger and more satisfactory evidence was within the power of the party to produce, the evidence offered should be viewed with distrust.

While a good faith loss of evidence would not necessarily create any adverse evidentiary inference, the requirements of proof would often be impossible to satisfy. In one case, an employee was performing unloading operations inside a disconnected semitrailer.[39] While the employee was operating a forklift at the front end of the trailer, the trailer nose-dived. This caused the forklift to topple over and injure the employee.

Litigation was commenced against the alleged manufacturer of the semitrailer for negligent design and construction of the landing gears. Another theory of liability was the manufacturer's failure to advise the use of safety jacks to insure stability during loading operations.

Two weeks before trial, many years after the original incident, an engineering expert was retained to gather evidence, determine liability, and identify the manufacturer. It appeared that the trailer had been hitched and then taken from the loading dock soon after the accident. The total evidence relating to the trailer itself was one

---

[38] §3.01.

[39] §6.02.

unclear photographic[40] print of unknown origin. No evidence related to the named defendant manufacturer other than that tenuous photograph. Based solely on the photograph, the expert was able to reconstruct the accident and the mechanics of the defect in the landing gear. Unfortunately, the plaintiff was unable to present sufficient evidence to connect the named defendant with the subject semitrailer. Had an early investigation located and identified the particular semitrailer involved in the incident, litigation would have been successful.

F. Preventive Law

§1.23 1. Generally

Much can be said about the role of the engineering expert in a preventive law context.[41] Some legal commentators[42] describe the preventive law approach as emphasizing the structuring and planning of events to avoid litigation while maximizing the benefit to the client. To make this feasible, it is necessary for counsel to be familiar with, among other matters, relevant case and statutory law on the particular subject of inquiry. By understanding and anticipating the law, the trends, and the practical consequences and outcome of litigation, counsel is in a position to advise a client. In practice, this may take the form of recommending: redesign of a machine or vehicle; relocation of a dangerous or obnoxious facility; installation of permanent warning signs or safety devices on products; use of specifically designated conditions, terms, procedures, and responsibilities in construction documents; or economic advantages of resolving a matter with little or no litigation.

Timing in the preventive law context is crucial. The earlier counsel becomes involved in a client's situation, the greater the number of options available to counsel in structuring the client's activities. Once a client's activities are planned, preventive law considerations continue. A change in the law, in facts, or in new engineering concepts or knowledge may well require re-evaluation, if not modification, of the original advice, in order to protect the current rights and liabilities of a client.

An important problem in the field of preventive law is the architect's role in inspecting construction work and its relation to the owner and contractor. In a recent federal district court case,[43] an architect's letter to a contractor, with copies to the owner and to the surety for the contractor, was found to be defamatory. The verdict returned against the architect was $20,000 compensatory damages and $5,000 punitive damages.

Although the architect contended that his complaints were true and that he had a professional responsibility to advise all parties concerned with the construction of the

---

[40] **§§8.13, 8.15.**

[41] **§4.73.**

[42] Brown & Brown, *What Counsels the Counselor? The Code of Professional Responsibility's Ethical Considerations: A Preventive Law Analysis,* 10 Vill L Rev 453 (1976).

[43] G-K Constr Co v Bradfield (WD Tenn), discussed in Ostrower & Lee, *Design Professional's Critical Letter Held Defamatory,* May 1980 Consulting Engineer 42.

contractor's alleged defective performance, the jury found that the architect had not acted in good faith in writing the letter.

For this reason, it would appear that an architect who is retained to inspect certain construction must scrutinize performance letters and reports to the parties to insure that the contents of the letter and reports do not go beyond what is reasonably necessary to protect the owner's interests. Apparently, an architect who states that the contractor was intentionally "attempting to hide defective materials and workmanship" has gone beyond the point reasonably necessary to protect the owner's interest and may therefore be liable for damages.

§1.24 2. Design and Construction

Preventive law[44] concepts can be applied to define the relationship between the owner and the architect/engineer, contractor, or vendor. By understanding potential areas of dispute, steps can be taken to reduce opportunities for conflict before they materialize.

Prior to issuance of a purchase order or completion of the contract documents, the conditions, scope, and schedule of professional services as well as the compensation to the architect/engineer should be established. Compensation may take the form of a lump sum, percentage of the total cost of construction, payroll times a multiplier, retainer, or any combination.

The nature of a project normally influences the form of compensation. Lump sum fees are used when the job is of standard nature, without requiring extensive research in unusual areas. When the scope of necessary design services cannot readily be defined, the cost plus a fixed fee or the payroll times a multiplier is commonly used. Retainer fees or per diem basis are normally used for a consultant. Matching the form of compensation to the nature of the job will eliminate a large area of potential conflict.

The range of professional services furnished by an architect/engineer can be broad. Most owners are not aware of how narrow or how extensive these services can be. Frequently, owners may expect more than the design professional had intended. It is thus necessary to define the extent of services early and before any contract documents are signed.

§1.25 a. Basic Services

Following is a general description of the basic services, including design, available from the architect/engineer:

1. Schematic and preliminary drawings, estimates, and specifications
2. Final working drawings and specifications
3. Assistance in preparation of bid and contract documents
4. Shop drawings
5. Supervision of construction

---

[44]§4.73.

6. Interpretation of drawings and specifications during construction
7. Contract payment certificates
8. As-built drawings
9. Renderings and industrial illustrations
10. Selection of colors, textures, and finishes
11. Reproduction of documents during construction
12. Surveys

Final working drawings and specifications may include some or all of the following disciplines:

1. Architecture[45]
2. Civil engineering[46]
3. Structural engineering[47]
4. Mechanical engineering[48]
5. Electrical engineering[49]
6. Chemical or process engineering
7. Industrial engineering
8. Landscape architecture

The contract documents should list the disciplines included in the professional services.

Supervision of construction[50] can range from being on call to clarify plans and specifications, to periodic observations, to continuous eight-hour-daily inspection. Without clear definition, supervision can be another area of disagreement.

These basic services are only a few of those which may apply to the various parts of the project. In addition, since not all specified services may be applicable to the entire job, they all should be clearly expressed in the contract documents.

§1.26 b. Scope of Work

Once the owner and the architect/engineer have established the scope of work, both parties should take care to adhere to that scope. The owner should not request that the architect/engineer perform additional studies outside the initial scope of the work. Similarly, the architect/engineer should not offer additional studies unless an addendum to the contract is agreed upon.

An increase in the scope of the project is a major source of conflicts between the

---

[45] **§4.22.**
[46] **§§4.10, 5.05.**
[47] **§4.22.**
[48] *Id.*
[49] *Id.*
[50] **§1.28.**

parties. This change in scope is difficult to avoid because of the familiarity and informality that develop between the parties during the design stage of the work.

Soon after the contract is signed, the owner should meet with the architect/engineer to provide the architect/engineer with all available data on the property, facilities, soil reports, surveys, existing plans, company standards, and operations of the facilities, and with a schedule for performing the work. The schedule should include the dates for the completion of the schematics, preliminary and final drawings, and specifications.

The parties should decide in the beginning how control should be exercised over the project. Periodic reviews of plans and specifications by the owner at specified times are advisable. Many design firms demand such reviews, approvals, or corrections before they will go on to the next phase of work. One suggested method of review is to have the architect/engineer submit plans and specifications to the owner when they are 10 per cent, 50 per cent, and 90 per cent complete. Firm dates should be established for these submittals. It is the owner's duty to review within the maximum number of days within which the submittals must be returned to the architect/engineer. This method of review promotes full control of progress, scope, and cost of the project.

Once the guidelines for continuous review and approval have been established, steps should be taken to set up effective liaison between the parties. Representatives of both the owner and the architect/engineer should be selected and assigned as sole representatives of the two parties for all communications. Each person gathers information, requirements, questions, and answers from the various divisions of his or her respective company. The owner's agent should be in close contact with management, production, operation, maintenance, quality control, and purchasing. In addition, the owner's agent should see that the requirements of each department are integrated into the project. The agent for the design firm should provide the correct data and answers to the supervisors of the architectural, mechanical, structural, and other design groups. The two representatives should encourage frequent dialogues, conferences, and communication between the owner and the architect/engineer, but should be sure that all such communication occurs through those representatives. This will reduce the incidence of confusion and conflict in instructions which often plagues design projects and precipitates litigation.

§1.27 c. Communication

Once the groundwork has been laid for communication, there are methods of ensuring effective exchange. The most generally accepted medium of communication in these circumstances is graphic representation. Such representation may take the form of flow diagrams, plans, sketches, bar charts, and tabulations. However, as in any language, a glossary or legend is necessary. Mutual understanding of terms of art, abbreviations, and symbols is important. Each engineering discipline has its own recognized symbols and nomenclature. The owner's representative should include in the project file the standard symbols for each engineering field. A single symbol on an engineering drawing can mean more than a written paragraph.

There is frequently a need to transmit drawings, specifications, cost estimates, and other documents between the client and the architect/engineer. The *letter of transmittal* can be handwritten or typed on NCR paper (no carbon is required). The original and one copy are generally sent to the recipient and one copy is retained in the sender's file. The recipient signs one copy, adds any comments, and returns that copy to the sender. In this manner, all transmittal of information and documents is easily recorded, reviewed, and commented on. Approvals or changes can be made at this time. The *message reply* is also on NCR paper, and is used mainly to forward information, confirm telephone conversations, record questions and answers, serve as a *tickler file,* and establish a chronology of the project. The message reply forms can confirm responsibility for changes or increases in the scope of the job and warn against potential problems.

A basic rule in coordinating a project is always to confirm instructions and commitments in writing. It is risky to assume that the job will be done according to oral agreement. Many busy people have poor memories, and almost everyone will take something more seriously when it is in writing. On critical items it is wise to send a copy of the memo to a third party who can serve as a witness. Every sketch, note, or memo should be dated and signed or initialled.

The representative should always strive for conciseness and clarity in oral and written reports and instructions. Memos and letters should be kept to a single subject. Representatives should never invade the internal organization of the owner or the architect/engineer without the knowledge and consent of the person in charge. In any transaction, the writer should be careful to send copies to everyone with the right to be notified of that transaction.

§1.28 d. Supervision and Inspection

The architect/engineer's role during construction is often misunderstood.[51] It is important for the owner to know what level of supervision or inspection services is required, and to recognize that the more complete the service the more it will cost. If the architect/engineer is to have complete control and supervision over construction of the project, the architect/engineer must have authority, usually monetary, over the contractors. To be held liable for the construction, the architect/engineer must have the authority to have the plans and specifications followed exactly. Continuous inspection can cost more than design of the project when it includes compaction tests of the soil, field surveying to assure alignment and plumbness of structures, and laboratory testing of steel, concrete, masonry, and other components of the project. These are considered predictable special services.

When the client does not specifically require the architect/engineer to take full responsibility for construction, most design firms will simply provide adequate inspection or observing services. The great difference between observing services and continuous inspection must be understood by the owner. Although most serious construction errors or problems can be spotted by such inspection or observation, it is not a risk-free service.

§1.29 e. Special Services

Predictable special services should be arranged for by explicit notation in the contract. They may require compensation far in excess of the original engineering fee;

---

[51]§1.25.

such services may include land surveys, soil investigation, and technical inspection of the project by a full-time resident engineer and supporting staff. Such personnel may review and approve requests for monthly or final payments to the contractors, issue certificates of completion, provide as-built drawings, make field measurements to verify exiting conditions, or prepare shop details.

Unpredicted special services are usually not included in the contract. These services fall outside the lump sum contract, and are usually viewed as justifiable extras. Examples of extras could include excessive preliminary design, preparation of alternate designs, abandoned design work, redesign for major changes after approval of preliminary plans, evaluations and recommendations on contractor's claims, assistance to the owner as an expert witness in litigation arising out of the project, and observation of the project for a period longer than the period of services.

2 Selection of an Engineering Expert

§2.01 A. What Is an Engineer

Assume that owner of a multistory office building seeks legal assistance. The building is only one year old, yet it has been plagued continually with serious problems. The elevators operate erratically, stopping three feet above floor levels, making sudden drops, and having their doors close prematurely. Not only have some of the glass plates been popping out of the curtain walls, but two floors have sagged so badly that doors have jammed closed and windows have cracked.

At this point an attorney may be retained by the owner. Should counsel accept the owner's case, it will be necessary to determine the causes of the defects and the persons at fault. Since many different engineering disciplines are involved in construction of a building, counsel is likely to have to rely on expert advice.

The intricacies of building construction are frequently so great that the first steps in identifying responsibility for construction mishaps may appear difficult. The attorney's first determination is what kind of expert to consult to investigate, report, and, if necessary, testify in litigation.

It might be said that complaints arising out of building construction are analogous to complaints relating to the human body. As knowledge of the human bone structure, for instance, is within the expertise of the orthopedic surgeon, so knowledge of a steel frame of a building is within the expertise of the structural engineer.[1] Similarly, as a neurosurgeon may be called on to testify about the nature of a nervous disorder, so may an electrical engineer[2] be deemed qualified to testify when the subject matter is an erratic elevator or a defective electrical distribution system.

Beyond these simple analogies, it can be noted that the components of a machine, building, or industrial plant reflect the expertise of various engineering specialties which have been integrated to provide a composite and complete product.

When potential for litigation develops as a result of complaints, engineering specialists are essential to a proper diagnosis, prognosis, and treatment of the problem.

§2.02 1. Professional Engineers

There has been considerable controversy over the proper use of the terms *engineer* and *professional engineer.* At times, each term has been used loosely to add dignity or imply education and experience with respect to persons who may be involved in sales, maintenance, or other unscientific or nontechnical activities. For purposes of this book, the definitions used by the governmental agencies responsible for licensing and administration of engineers will be adopted.

The National Council of Engineering Examiners (NCEE) generally defines an engineer as a person with special knowledge, education, and experience of mathematics, physics, and engineering sciences, and of methods of engineering analysis and design.[3]

The NCEE distinguishes a professional engineer as an engineering specialist, duly registered and licensed as a professional engineer.[4] Some of the recognized professional engineering specialties are: control systems engineers;[5] corrosion engineers; fire protection engineers; manufacturing engineers;[6] safety engineers;[7] and traffic engineers.[8] Numbers and types of engineering specialties vary from state to state, and depend on the particular needs of the area.

Another term often used indiscriminately is *consulting engineer.* Most state engineering registration laws define a consulting engineer as one who provides a professional-level engineering service in an individual capacity for a specific client with who the engineer has a commission for consulting engineering services, and from whom a fee is received.[9]

This consulting engineering service must be in a recognized engineering specialty for which there is an approved university-level curriculum accredited by the Engineers' Council for Professional Development.

---

[1]**§2.05.**

[2]**§2.08.**

[3]NCEE, *The Practice of Engineering in the United States* (1973).

[4]*Id.*

[5]**§2.22.**

[6]**§2.15.**

[7]*Id.*

[8]**§2.14.**

[9]Cal Bus & Prof Code, §6730.1 (West 1975).

In addition, this service requires training in theory and practical application of engineering knowledge at a professional level. It is thus distinguishable from the manual skill of an artisan or craftsworker or from the abilities required for use of engineering devices as ordinarily exercised by a technician under the continuing direction of a professional engineer. Examples of those with these last skills are laboratory technicians or architectural draftsmen.

§2.03 a. Civil Engineers

The oldest engineering profession is considered to be that of *civil engineering.* Predecessors of members of this profession were primarily responsible for the design and construction of ancient fortresses, aquaducts, temples, and harbor facilities. The pyramid of Cheops, the temple at Karnak, and Solomon's temple in Jerusalem were such ancient projects, as was the Roman aquaduct in Caesarea. The Great Wall of China—1500 miles long—was built in the third century B.C. In the course of thousands of years of carrying out similar construction, this activity evolved into what is now recognized as civil engineering. Due to the nature of such construction and its relationship to public safety, the first state registration laws were directed toward civil engineering.

As it is the oldest group in recognized professional engineering, the body of knowledge attributed to civil engineering is extensive. It is generally understood to embrace all studies and activities connected with fixed waterworks, such as water power, drainage,[10] irrigation, water supply, inland waterways, and harbors. It also has to do with other fixed works related to transportation, including railroads,[11] highways, tunnels, and airports. In the area of municipal improvements, civil engineering covers purification of water, sewerage, sewage disposal, and refuse disposal. It also incorporates design and supervision of construction of foundations, framed and homogeneous structures, and buildings and bridges.[12]

§2.04 (1) Soils Engineers

One specialty which evolved out of the field of civil engineering[13] is that of the *soils engineer.* The soils engineer is qualified and experienced in soils mechanics and is capable of performing laboratory tests on soil samples for analysis.

The primary duty of the soils engineer is to investigate soil for proposed building foundations and site grading for housing, industry, and municipal improvements. The soils engineer is especially interested in the presence of ground water and in the stability of cuts and fills of earthen structures.

In some states, the soils engineer must be a registered civil engineer with control of an approved soil testing laboratory. The soils engineer often must coordinate studies and recommendations with those of a geologist. A geologist's expertise generally en-

---

[10]**§5.08.**

[11]**§6.14.**

[12]Cal Bus & Prof Code §6731 (West 1975).

[13]**§2.03.**

compasses a broader and deeper knowledge of the earth's crust than does the expertise of the soils engineer. The soils engineer may be called in as a consultant to a structural engineer in the design of foundations, or to a highway engineer in the design of roadways and bridges.[14]

§2.05 (2) Structural Engineers

Another important branch of civil engineering[15] which has developed into a fully recognized profession is *structural engineering.* In California, structural engineer refers to a registered civil engineer who by examination and experience has been found qualified in the field of structural engineering.[16]

A structural engineer's work is essentially the investigation and design of force-resisting and load-supporting structural members. These may include foundations, walls, beams, columns, trusses, and other framing portions of buildings and structures. The professional activity of the structural engineer also requires familiarity with engineering laws, knowledge of the formulae for the physical properties of the materials used in structural members, and proficiency in the various methods of construction.

Where the state does not recognize structural engineering as a separate and distinct specialty,[17] civil engineering is considered to encompass the discipline of structural design. Even in states where a title of structural engineer is granted, the registered civil engineer can perform almost all the functions of a structural engineer.[18]

§2.06 b. Architects

The prime design professional of commercial, residential, and public buildings is the *architect.* The architect plans and designs buildings, identifies construction problems, and gathers background information. The architect evaluates this information and creates a design that satisfies the client's requirements. Another important responsibility of the architect is to organize all the services needed for construction, by preparing plans, specifications, and other contract documents for the builder and craft workers. The architect also coordinates the engineering consultants on the project.

In most states, the architect is simply defined as a holder of a certificate which permits that person to engage in the practice of architecture. Practice of architecture is generally understood to mean the planning and design of building sites and their related facilities. It includes consultation, investigation, evaluation, preparation of instruments of service such as drawings and specification, and supervision of construction.[19]

Historically, the architect evolved from the old master builder who was charged

---

[14]**§6.04.**

[15]**§2.03.**

[16]§16 Cal Adm Code §404(s) (1969).

[17]Cal Bus & Prof Code §6702 (West 1975).

[18]16 Cal Adm Code §404(e-e) (1976).

[19]Registration Act 240, Mich Comp Laws, vol III, §338.552 (1970); Cal Bus & Prof Code §§5550 (West 1974).

with responsibility for designing and supervising construction of palaces, temples, and cathedrals, and who was retained by the nobility and religious leaders.

Some of the more renowned master builders are Sir Christopher Wren (1632-1723), principally known as the architect of St. Paul's Cathedral in London, and Sir Charles Barry, the architect of the Houses of Parliament in Westminster (begun 1839).

§2.07 c. Mechanical Engineers

Mechanical engineering is another broad profession which takes in many specialties. The principal concerns of this field are the utilization and conversion of various sources of energy to perform work.

This branch of professional engineering deals with the generation, transmission, and utilization of energy in electrical, thermal, and mechanical form.[20] Mechanical engineering also encompasses design relating to production of tools and machinery. In addition, this area has an important function in building and facility design, since it includes responsibility for planning of heating, ventilation, refrigeration, and plumbing systems. The mechanical engineer is usually a consultant to the architect, and provides the architect with plans and specifications on the above-noted specialties. The mechanical engineer also supervises installation of these mechanical components in buildings.

In industrial projects, the mechanical engineer is usually the prime design engineer, responsible for the major planning of the manufacturing facility. In this respect, the mechanical engineer's responsibility is similar to an architect's responsibility for a building.

A number of disciplines have evolved out of mechanical engineering. These include material handling, fire protection, process piping, pressure vessels, pumps, and compressors.

§2.08 d. Electrical Engineers

An *electrical engineer* designs, develops, and supervises the manufacturing of electrical and electronic equipment, and prepares plans and specifications for electrical services and wiring in construction projects. In addition, the electrical engineer assists in the operation of electrical power generation and distribution facilities.[21]

Electrical engineering is described in most states as that branch of professional engineering which involves studies and activities relating to the generation, transmission, and utilization of electrical energy.[22] This body of knowledge includes the design of electrical, electronic, and magnetic circuits, and the technical control of their operations. The area also takes in the subjects of illumination, protective devices, instrumentation, control, electrical machinery, and communication.

As happened in the fields of mechanical and civil engineering, electrical engineering has expanded to become many specialties. Each has now become recognized as a separate and distinct discipline, concentrated in one of the areas listed above.

---

[20] 16 Cal Adm Code §4O4(y); Cal Bus & Prof Code, §6734.2 (West 1975).

[21] 16 Cal Adm Code §404(t); Cal Bus & Prof Code §6735.1 (West 1975).

[22] *Id.*

§2.09 e. Chemical Engineers

The expansion of petrochemical and other chemical process industries has been instrumental in making chemical engineering a recognized engineering profession. In essence, *chemical engineering* is that branch of engineering which deals with the industrial uses of chemistry.

Specifically, chemical engineering is defined as that branch of professional engineering relating to development and application of processes involving chemical or physical changes of materials. These processes are usually resolved into a coordinated series of unit[23] physical operations and chemical processes.[24] The chemical engineer is concerned with the research, design, production, operation, organization, and economics of such activities.

§2.10 f. Nuclear Engineers

Due to the energy crisis which became more intense after 1973, *nuclear engineering* has become an important yet controversial field. In cases based on accidents involving nuclear power plants and their equipment, the most qualified engineering expert would be the nuclear engineer.

Nuclear engineering relates to the principles of nuclear physics generally and the engineering utilization of nuclear phenomena to benefit mankind.[25] It is concerned with protecting the public from the potential hazards of radiation and radioactive materials, and with the safe operation of the nuclear reaction process.

Nuclear engineering is mainly concerned with the relationship of radiation and nuclear particles to matter, and encompasses planning and design of specialized equipment and process systems of nuclear facilities.

§2.11 g. Metallurgical Engineers

When the quality of a metal machine part is in question, or the cause of failure of such a part must be determined, a qualified expert would be the *metallurgical engineer.*

Metallurgical engineering is that branch of professional engineering which involves the research, understanding, and application of principles of the properties and behavior of metals.[26] This may occur in the course of extracting, refining, and processing of metals from the original ore to the final alloy. The field also relates to the stability of metal when exposed to stress, corrosion, and other outside influences.

Metallurgical engineers usually work with laboratories which specialize in the testing and analysis of all types of metals and alloys.[27]

§2.12 h. Quality Engineers

Generally in products liability cases there is some question about the quality of material and manufacture of a particular product. The engineering discipline dedi-

---

[23] 16 Cal Adm Code §404(p) (1977).

[24] *Id.*

[25] 16 Cal Adm Code §404(a-a) (1977).

[26] 16 Cal Adm Code §404(z) (1977).

[27] §3.30.

cated to the maintenance of quality in materials and production methods is known as *quality engineering.*

Quality engineering involves the planning, development, and operation of quality control systems, and the application and analysis of testing[28] and inspection procedures. An engineer with this specialty needs the ability to apply metrology[29] and statistical methods to diagnose and correct improper quality control practices.

§2.13 i. Fire Protection Engineers

In cases of destruction by fire, the expert qualified to determine adequacy of fire protection equipment and construction is the *fire protection engineer.*

Fire protection engineering is a specialty branch of engineering aimed at the safeguarding of life and property from fire and fire-related disasters. This area of expertise includes the identification, evaluation, correction, and prevention of present and potential fire and fire-related panic hazards. These functions are especially important in buildings, groups of buildings, and communities. In addition, this field encompasses arrangement of fire resistive building materials, fire detection, and extinguishing systems and devices.

The fire protection engineer is a consultant to fire insurance companies, fire departments, and building and safety departments. Such engineers' recommendations become part of the fire codes[30] as well as building and safety codes.[31]

§2.14 j. Traffic Engineers

Many personal injury cases relate to motor vehicle accidents in which not only the drivers and motor vehicles, but also the street and traffic control devices, may be at fault. The engineering expert most closely concerned with this latter area of expertise is the *traffic engineer.*

Traffic engineering can be defined as the science of measuring traffic, travel, and human factors which affect traffic generation and flow. The traffic engineer must apply this knowledge to the planning, operation, and evaluation of streets, highways, and their networks. The field is also concerned with lands abutting on highways, and with the interrelationships of modes of travel. The main goal of traffic engineering is to insure safe and most effective movement of people and goods.[32]

The traffic engineer also is involved with the development of highway lighting and signaling systems. These include standards for signing, delineation, warning devices, and pavement markings. The traffic engineer also makes field inspections of traffic control and safety devices,[33] and correlates geometric design and directional signing.

---

[28] **§3.30.**

[29] 16 Cal Adm Code §404(c-c) (1977); Metrology is the science of measures and weights; *The Living Webster Encyclopedic Dictionary* 601 (1977).

[30] **§4.45.**

[31] 16 Cal Adm Code §404(u) (1977). See **§4.37.**

[32] 16 Cal Adm Code §404(f-f) (1977).

[33] **§6.08.**

§2.15 k. Manufacturing Engineers

Consumer products liability claims are usually based on one or more of the following deficiencies: design error; improper materials; poor workmanship; or failure to warn of possible danger in use of the product. The engineering expert with overall responsibility for the manufacturing process of a product is the *manufacturing engineer.*

Manufacturing engineering is concerned with engineering procedures in manufacturing processes and with production methods for industrial commodities and products. In addition, this field takes in planning of the practices of manufacturing, research, and development, and integration of tools, processes, machines, and equipment in facilities for producing quality products with optimal expenditure.[34]

§2.16 l. Safety Engineers

In cases where the issue is the adequacy of safety in the workplace, in public facilities, or in areas where there is uncertainty about the inherent safety of equipment, the engineering expert who may be best suited to handle the situation is the *safety engineer.*

Safety engineering is the specialty concerned mainly with engineering principles essential to the identification, elimination, and control of hazards to persons and property. This area of expertise embraces the development, analysis, production, construction, testing,[35] and utilization of systems, products, and procedures to eliminate hazards.

Safety engineers are part of management in most industrial facilities as well as on large construction projects. Their recommendations and standards are frequently written into federal and state regulations which have to do with safety.[36]

§2.17 m. Ceramic Engineers

One of the many new specialties developed as a result of the space age is *ceramic engineering.* Many sophisticated products which have entered the consumer market are made entirely or in part from ceramics.[37] In products liability cases, where these items are involved, the necessary expert would be the ceramic engineer.

Ceramic engineering is that branch of engineering relating to the design, manufacturing, and testing of ceramic products. Ceramics itself is the shaping and baking of clay articles such as cooking utensils, roof tiles, or procelain. The expertise of such an engineer also includes the design, operation, and control of specialized manufacturing processes for the production of ceramic products.

The body of knowledge of the ceramic engineer encompasses an understanding of the properties of ceramic raw materials, including mining, processing, beneficiation,

---

[34]16 Cal Adm Code §404(x) (1977).

[35]**§3.30.**

[36]16 Cal Adm Code §404(d-d) (1977); American Society of Safety Engineers, *The Scope and Functions of the Professional Safety Position* (1973).

[37]Petition Requesting Approval of the Discipline of Ceramic Engineering for Regulation under the California Professional Engineering Act (1972).

and preparation for ceramic fabrication. Other areas of specialized knowledge include high temperature processing, design and operation of kilns, measurement and regulation of high temperatures, and principles of heating technology.

§2.18 n. Petroleum Engineers

The international oil crisis has brought to prominence the functions of the *petroleum engineer.*

Petroleum engineering is that branch of professional engineering concerning the exploration, exploitation, location, and recovery of natural fluid hydrocarbons. It embraces the research, design, production, and operation of refineries and their economic aspects.[38]

§2.19 o. Land Surveyors

A common source of litigation is disputes over the location of property lines. Such controversies may arise in connection with adjoining property owners, right of ways, easements, and other real property problems. The acknowledged expert in this field is the licensed *land surveyor.*

Land surveying is an ancient branch of engineering, involving measurement of land through the use of basic principles of mathematics and the related physical and applied sciences. It also requires an understanding of the law of evidence necessary to establish property lines.

Land surveying includes measuring and locating lines, angles, elevations, and natural and manmade features.[39] The process of measuring can take place in the air, on the surface of the earth, within underground workings, and on the beds of bodies of waters.

Land surveying is the initial part of construction, central to such activities as staking or monumenting property boundaries, aligning and grading streets or railroads, and establishing corners of buildings. Other activities of the land surveyor include preparation of maps,[40] record plats, field note records and property descriptions that represent the surveys.[41]

§2.20 2. Nonprofessional Engineers

Modern industry; especially industry associated with aerospace and electronics, has become so highly specialized that many new engineering disciplines have been created. Most of these are subdivisions of the basic civil, mechanical, and electrical engineering fields which have become independent and highly sophisticated specialties. This development is due to, among other things, new materials and sciences, expanded methods

---

[38] 16 Cal Adm Code §404(b-b) (1977).

[39] **§4.17.**

[40] **§4.10.**

[41] Cal Bus & Prof Code §8761 (West 1975).

of computation, and the dynamic explosion of growth in many industries. There are now engineers who devote their full professional lives to items such as aircraft structures, hydraulic systems, or telemetry. These engineers can be considered as *nonprofessional engineers* since they are exempt under the engineering registration laws.[42]

Surveying,[43] which was once associated only with land measurement and distances figured in hundreds of feet, has developed into a science of measurement of distances of millions of miles for navigation through space.

Mechanical engineers[44] who originally designed steam boilers have developed into designers of rocket engines for space vehicles using exotic fuels.

To appreciate how these new disciplines have expanded, it is only necessary to stroll through a university bookstore. Shelves full of books on computer science, astronomics, and electronics far outnumber books on basic engineering subjects. Technicians are now performing work so complex and skill-demanding that industry has recognized these technical specialists as engineers. In fact, nonprofessional engineers currently outnumber the registered professionals.

No matter whether members of this large group of nonprofessional engineers are registered, they serve a necessary function in the development of spacecraft, supersonic aircraft, computers, communication equipment, and other important products of modern society. Thus they are an important source of expert witnesses on those particular subjects.[45]

§2.21 a. Automotive Industry

Some of the responsibilities of nonprofessional engineers in the automotive industry are discussed below:

1. Metallographic technicians analyze metals and alloys
2. Tooling engineers plan production processes for the manufacturing of mechanical products and the providing of proper machinery and tools
3. Welding engineers deal with the mechanics of metals fusion
4. Stress analysts look at the forces tending to produce stress and strain on components of machines and products
5. Die cast engineers plan and design machines for cutting or shaping materials
6. Hydraulics engineers work in the science of utilizing fluids in motion and under pressure in the operation of machinery

§2.22 b. Control Systems Industry

Some of the responsibilities of nonprofessional engineers in the control systems industry are:

---

[42]Cal Bus & Prof Code §6747 (West 1975).

[43]**§2.19.**

[44]**§2.07.**

[45]Industrial News (Los Angeles), Apr 26, 1976.

1. Computer program engineers/software engineers design the instructions necessary for a computer to find the solution to a problem
2. Control systems engineers design the system for regulating mechanisms of the computer
3. Computer operators operate the computer
4. Computer design engineers design the electronic contrivance which solves problems and performs complicated calculations by processing data according to prescribed and programmed instructions.

§2.23 c. Aerospace Industry

Aerospace is probably the industry most responsible for creation of new engineering disciplines. Some of the responsibilities of typical nonprofessional aerospace engineers are:

1. Navigation and guidance engineers determine the location, speed, destination, and direction of aircraft and spacecraft
2. Avionics systems engineers design systems which activate electronic and electrical devices for use in aircraft and spacecraft
3. Communication engineers design and operate systems used for transmission and communication of messages and information
4. Telemetry engineers design and operate the transmitters and receivers of radio communications of coded data between a ground station and a spacecraft or satellite
5. Flight control engineers control the spacecraft in flight by means of radio communications and electronic devices
6. Reliability engineers insure the standard of quality necessary for proper functioning of the spacecraft
7. Test engineers examine and probe a spacecraft's capability to function

§2.24 d. Others

There are companies whose sole activity is to serve as experts in litigation. They provide expert witnesses for hire. Colloquially, they are often referred to as *hired guns*.

These companies usually employ many engineers of different specialties who are available to perform investigations and testify in court. The fee paid by the attorney to the expert may also include an allowance for supervision, review, expert back-up, administration, and profit to the company offering this service.

The expert agencies may use more than one expert on a case, one expert reviewing the findings of another. In addition, these agencies have experts in such diverse fields of law as products, the environment, admiralty, metallurgy, and aviation.

B. Sources of Experts

1. Academic

§2.25 a. Universities

Many universities which have schools of engineering, chemistry, or other sciences have *consultant bureaus* through which faculty members may be retained for consultation and expert testimony services. Sometimes, certain faculty personnel will associate informally and offer their services as consultants to the public or the government. Individuals in these groups may include chairpersons of departments, professors, assistant professors, and laboratory specialists.

Some of the subjects which these highly qualified experts typically investigate or testify about include: fractures of structural materials; failure of aircraft components; accident reconstruction; physical metallurgy; corrosion or failure of automotive parts.

In addition to personal qualifications which command respect, such academic experts usually have access to modern, well-equipped university laboratories,[46] as well as to large, complete technical libraries.

Most universities maintain rosters of their faculty members which include descriptions of each member's education, areas of specialization, subjects of books and articles written, and courses taught or lectured in. An attorney may find these rosters a valuable source of information in the search for a qualified expert. A more direct method may be to get in touch with the dean of a particular school which offers the specialty required. The dean would normally have firsthand knowledge of the background and capabilities of the entire faculty. In addition, the dean may know who would be available to serve as a consultant or expert.

§2.26 b. Research Organizations

An additional source of experts is *think tanks*. These research and development organizations are normally staffed with highly qualified research personnel who offer their services to the public as well as to the government. The organizations themselves depend on outside consultants.

The procedure for locating the proper expert within a research organization would be similar to that used within a university, discussed in the previous section.

§2.27 2. Professional Engineering Societies

Due to rapid technological change in the engineering field, the role of professional societies is very significant in an engineer's professional life. Active membership in one or more such societies may be considered essential.

---

[46]§2.29.

Most of the professional engineering disciplines have organized professional societies and associations. These are national organizations with local chapters in major cities. As with other professional groups, their purpose is to:

1. Promote the welfare of the profession
2. Provide a forum for discussion of common problems
3. Advance the technical level of the field

The local chapter of the professional society representing the specialty needed by the attorney is an ideal source of engineering experts. If greater selectivity must be exercised in choosing an expert, counsel can contact the national headquarters of that association. In either case, rosters would be available listing the background, qualifications, and specialty fields of each member.

Various professional architectural and engineering societies located throughout the United States are listed at Appendix A by discipline and location.

§2.28 3. Testing Laboratories

Laboratories generally fall into categories of physical testing and chemical testing laboratories. Most laboratories specialize in specific areas such as soils, concrete, masonry, bacteriology, chemistry, water quality, air quality, fire resistance, electricity, and electronics. In cases of defective buildings, machinery, or other products, laboratories can determine the extent of fatigue, creep, stress, rupture, chemical deterioration, or other possible cause of failure. Their findings can augment the testimony of the engineering expert.

Most consulting engineers lack in-house laboratory equipment facilities. Therefore, they rely mainly on mathematical analysis for determining strength of materials, products, and structures. Use of testing laboratories to support mathematical proof is of great value.

Some large engineering firms and most engineering professors do have access to laboratory equipment. There are also engineering firms which specialize in laboratory testing of products rather than in design services. Most states require that testing laboratories be supervised by registered engineers who specialize in the particular field.

A testing laboratory can perform tests specified by quality control organizations such as the American Society of Testing and Materials, the American National Standards Institute, and the Underwriters' Laboratories, Inc. It may be wise to have a consulting engineer advise the attorney as to the type of laboratory to use and the specific test to perform.

When searching for a laboratory to run specific tests, it is recommended that the attorney contact the American Council of Independent Laboratories, Inc., 1725 K Street, N.W., Washington D.C., 20006. This national organization can help in locating a local laboratory staffed and equipped to meet any specified need.

In addition, the following two national publications provide a listing of testing and research laboratories:

Directory of Testing Laboratories
American Society for Testing and Materials
1916 Race Street
Philadelphia, PA 19103

Industrial Research Laboratories of the United States
Bowker Associates
1180 Avenue of the Americas
New York, NY 10036

§2.29 a. Qualifying Testing Laboratories

Reports issued from most testing laboratories must be prepared by or under the supervision of the appropriate registered civil, electrical, or mechanical engineer. A report must be signed and sealed by the registered engineer when it goes beyond tabulation of test data. This might include: interpretation of data to draw conclusions; expressing engineering judgment or recommendations as resulting from test data; and performing design work in the preparation of plans, specifications, or other documents requiring the preparer's registration as a civil, mechanical, or electrical engineer.

Generally, testing activities of laboratories are classified as either physical or chemical. Some laboratories specialize in testing of soils, concrete, masonry, metal, and other construction materials. These laboratories can provide the construction inspection services which are required by codes. In the field of environmental and chemical analysis, many specialize in the areas of water supply, waste water, air, and solid wastes.

For very specific analysis and testing, the laboratories selected should have the latest sophisticated apparatus for such processes as atomic absorption, spectrophotometry, mass spectrometry, gas chromotography, and thermogravimetric analysis.

Many laboratories perform analysis, testing, and sampling or inspection of construction materials. A majority of them do research and development in the fields of their specialty. Most laboratories also provide consulting services.

Litigation over building construction or machinery often centers on defective or overstressed materials. Use of such materials may result in damage caused by tension, compression, breakage, bending, cracking, or excessive wear from physical or chemical destruction. Samples of the subject components should be saved for testing and analysis. If the material is susceptible to additional changes due to atmospheric or other natural conditions, the sample should be preserved as well as it can. This would include protecting it from excessive changes of temperature or moisture content.

It is important to obtain the samples as soon as possible after the problem has occurred. They should be tagged to identify the date and location of their taking.

§2.30 b. Physical Testing

Most physical testing laboratories are staffed with qualified and experienced engineers, scientists, and technicians. These include metallographers, mining engineers, petroleum engineers, radiographers, microbiologists, spectrographers, and wood technologists.

Staff members of the testing laboratories belong to many professional associations relating to particular materials and industry. Some of the representative professional associations are listed below:

1. American Council of Independent Laboratories
2. American National Standards Institute
3. American Society of Testing and Materials
4. Institute of Environmental Sciences
5. National Society of Professional Engineers

§2.31 c. Chemical Testing

Potential experts who may be found in chemical testing laboratories are scientists who hold a master's degree or doctorate in chemistry or biology, analytical chemists, pharmacologists, laboratory technicians, and resin and coating specialists.

§2.32 d. Soils Testing

Soils testing laboratories are staffed by such professionals as geologists, civil engineers with a major in soils[47] and foundation engineering, specialists in applied earth science, geophysical engineers, and researchers in soil mechanics.

§2.33 4. Industry

Manufacturers of construction materials, mechanical components, and electrical devices have formed national organizations[48] to standardize and maintain the quality of their products. These organizations by their very nature are a good source of experts for a particular product. They are also helpful in establishing the state of the art and the standard practice for any period of time or locality.

In addition to the manufacturers' associations, standards associations establish recognized standards for quality of materials and workmanship.[49] These associations are usually staffed either by highly qualified personnel or by retained experts who prepare tests and write standards.

Manufacturers of building materials are the group of experts who are usually most familiar with their products' chemical, structural, and physical properties and limitations.

In reference to manufacturers of a complex product, such as an elevator, it must be understood that this would include manufacturers of all component parts. Elevator

---

[47]**§2.04.**

[48]Safety in the Market Place, Sub-council on Product Safety of the National Business Council for Consumer Affairs, Apr 1973.

[49]*Id.*

manufacturing companies must purchase motors,[50] pumps, valves, electrical controls,[51] and many other components from other manufacturers before they can assemble and install the final product.

§2.34 a. Material Associations

The industrial associations, which are divided into construction material associations and manufacturers' associations, are listed in this section and the next:

Metal and Steel

American Institute of Steel Construction
101 Park Avenue
New York, NY 10017

Aluminum Association
750 Third Avenue
New York, NY 10017

American Iron and Steel Institute
150 East 42nd Street
New York, NY 10017

American Welding Society, Inc.
United Engineering Center
345 East 47th Street
New York, NY 10017

Architectural Aluminum Manufacturers Association
35 East Wacker Drive
Chicago, IL 60601

Cast Iron Pipe Institute
2029 K Street NW
Washington, D.C. 20006

Concrete Reinforcing Steel Institute
228 North LaSalle Street
Chicago, IL 60601

Metal Building Manufacturers Association
2130 Keith Building
Cleveland, OH 44115

Wood and Wood Products

American Institute of Timber Construction
1700 K Street NW
Washington, D.C. 20006

American Wood Council
7216 Via Vista
San Jose, CA 95139

---

[50] **§3.03.**
[51] **§3.07.**

American Plywood Association
1119 A Street
Tacoma, WA 98401

§2.35 b. Manufacturing Associations

The industrial associations listed below are organized within particular industries:

Crane Manufacturers Association of America
1326 Freeport Road
Pittsburgh, PA 15238

National Electrical Manufacturers Association
155 East 44th Street
New York, NY 10017

National Elevator Industry Institute
2417 Beverly Boulevard
Los Angeles, CA 90057

National Electric Sign Association
10922 South Western Avenue
Chicago, IL 60642

Institute of Boiler and Radiator Manufacturers
393 Seventh Avenue
New York, NY 10001

National Elevator Manufacturers Industry, Inc.
101 Park Avenue
New York, NY 10017

National Automatic Sprinkler and Fire Control Association, Inc.
2 Holland Avenue
White Plains, NY 10603

§2.36 c. Standards Associations

The goals of standards associations are, generally, to investigate and research safety factors in constructed and manufactured products. In addition, their goal is to develop and promulgate uniformity in regulations which pertain to building construction and consumer goods, and to educate professionals in the manufacturing and design industries.

Some representative standards associations are listed below:

American National Standards Institute
1430 Broadway
New York, NY 10018

American Society for Testing and Materials
1916 Race Street
Philadelphia, PA 19103

Building Officials and Code Administrators International
1313 East 60th Street
Chicago, IL 60637

International Association of Plumbing and Mechanical Officials
5032 Alhambra Avenue
Los Angeles, CA 90032

International Conference of Building Officials
5360 Workman Mill Road
Whittier, CA 90601

National Bureau of Standards
United States Department of Commerce
Washington, D.C. 20234

National Fire Protection Association
470 Atlantic Avenue
Boston, MA 02210

Southern Building Code Congress
3617 Eighth Avenue, South
Birmingham, AL 35221

Factory Mutual Engineering Division
Standards-Laboratories Department
1151 Boston-Providence Turnpike
Norwood, MA 02062

Underwriters' Laboratories, Inc.
207 Ohio Street
Chicago, IL 60611

§2.37 5. Construction

There are a great many nonprofessional experts in the construction industry. They include general contractors,[52] construction superintendents, deputy inspectors, and subcontractors.[53] Other potential experts are craft journeymen, clerks of the works, and field engineers. Contractors and superintendents have the greatest expertise in coordinating the many trades and materials into an orderly and efficient construction effort. Their principal strengths are knowledge and experienced judgment. In addition, they must be fully conversant with the language of all the engineering disciplines shown on the plans and specifications, as well as with the business end of construction. These persons also must be aware of the safety laws governing the work, and abide by the various union contracts in effect on the job.

Where nonprofessional experts are required for construction litigation, there are three major sources for finding such an expert. These include the following:

1. Associations for general contractors

---

[52] **§4.35.**

[53] **§4.36.**

2. Associations of craft contractors or subcontractors
3. Craft labor organizations

§2.38 a. Contractors' Associations

The contractors' associations listed below are both national and regional. Similar but varying titles may be used in different jurisdictions:

American Building Contractors Association
Associated General Contractors of America
Engineering Grading Contractors Association
National Association of Home Builders

§2.39 b. Craft Contractors' Associations

When an issue arises as to the standard practice or cost estimate for certain construction craft work, an expert may be found within the ranks of the craft subcontractors' associations listed below:

American Concrete Pumping Association
Masonry Institute of America
National Association of Plumbing Contractors
National Electrical Contractors Association
Institute of Heating and Air Conditioning Industries
Sheet Metal, Air Conditioning, Heating Contractors Association
United Sheet Metal Contractors Association
Underground Engineering Contractors Association
National Electrical Contractors Association
Contractors Plasterers Association
Painting and Decorating Contractors Association

§2.40 c. Craft Labor Organizations

Craft labor organizations grew out of the craft guilds, groups of crafts workers banded together for the mutual improvement of their work and the training of new workers in the craft. Many craft unions have training programs for their apprentices.

However, since the advent of industrialization, some unions have come to include all wage earners in a given industry. In such a case, they are less inclined to work for improvement of a craft than to seek economic power. This distinction must be recognized in the search for an expert craftsman.

Following are the predominant craft unions in the construction industry:

Building and Construction Trades Department
AFL-CIO
815 16th Street NW
Washington, D.C. 20006

Bricklayers & Stonemasons Union

Carpenters Union

Cement Masons Union

International Brotherhood of Electrical Workers

International Union of Elevator Constructors

Glazers and Glassworkers Union

Iron Workers Union

International Brotherhood of Machinists

Millwrights and Machinery Erectors Union

Oil Chemical and Atomic Workers International

Operating Engineers

Painters and Allied Trades

Sheet Metal Workers Inernational Association

Steam-Refrigeration-Air Conditioning & Pipe Fitters

§2.41 6. Government

Many professional as well as nonprofessional experts are employed by the government. Consequently, government agencies are a source of experts required by an attorney, and such experts are to be found in various departments of the federal, state, and county governments.

Most governmental agencies do their own design work and have enormous information resources at their disposal. Such data is not easily available to the private professional consultant. Major projects such as dams, harbors, and flood control facilities are designed mainly by governmental agencies. Therefore, the government frequently may be the most expedient source of qualified experts. Another possible source would be a retired government engineer.

§2.42 a. Federal

Following are some of the federal agencies which may serve as sources of engineering experts:

Army Department-Corps of Engineers

Civil Aeronautics Board

Consumer Products Safety Commission

Department of Defense

Department of the Air Force

Department of Transportation
Federal Aviation Administration
Federal Maritime Commission
General Services Administration
Geological Survey-Department of the Interior
National Aeronautics and Space Administration
National Transportation Safety Board
Navy Department
Occupational Safety and Health Administration-Department of Labor

§2.43 b. State

Titles of particular state agencies may vary from state to state. Following is a suggestion of titles of potential sources of engineering experts:

Board of Achitectural Examiners
Board of Registration for Geologists and Geophysicists
Board of Registration of Professional Engineers
Contractors State License Board
Department of Consumer Affairs
Division of Mines and Geology
Fire Marshall
Industrial Relations Department-Division of Industrial Safety
Transportation Department
Water Resources Control Board

§2.44 c. Local Government

The titles of various county, city, and local governmental agencies and departments vary depending on the particular locality. However, their area of responsibility is similar. Experts may be found in departments such as the following:

Air Pollution Control
Building and Safety
Engineering Department
Fire Department
Flood Control District
Road Department
Sanitation District
Traffic Department
Waterworks District

§2.45 C. Qualifications of Experts

The attorney who seeks the aid of an engineering expert must first qualify the potential expert, looking to a combination of qualities. These include the expert's academic, experience, and personal qualifications. Since these are similar to the factors considered by state boards of registration, the guidelines of these agencies may be helpful in the attorney's finding of a qualified expert. See the chart, Figure 2-1.

On the matter of education, the attorney should inquire whether the person being considered as a potential expert has graduated from an Engineering Council for Professional Development (ECPD)-approved school. A foreign school is considered a non-ECPD-approved school.

As to the expert's field of specialty, the attorney must determine whether the engineer who will be asked to act as an expert in road design, for example, graduated in the field of civil engineering. Additional questions may include:

> What type of degree did the engineer earn? Was the degree a bachelor's, master's, or doctorate?
>
> Has the engineer updated his or her engineering education since leaving school?
>
> If so, in what type of program?

The expert's experience must be determined based on more than the number of years of practice since graduation. Important issues may be the types of specialties the engineer worked in and the extent of participation in responsible, decision-making positions. The nature and location of engineering experience is also relevant. The fact that an engineer worked in a foreign country, for example, may not particularly qualify that engineer to meet professional standards in the United States. In addition, employment in a particular state or city within the United States may have considerable effect on the qualifications of the engineer to express a professional opinion on questions that may be local in nature.

Military service may be another important form of experience when it is present in addition to the general background of an engineer. If the engineer has served with the Army Corps of Engineers or the Navy Construction Battalion, such service would increase experience in general engineering projects such as building of roadways or earthworks. In the area of military service, an engineer should be questioned not only about military training in the field in question, but also about any service in a responsible decision-making position.

Another factor in qualifying an engineer would be whether the expert has ever taught the particular specialty at a university or in the military.

§2.46 1. Registration of Professional Engineers

Two major approaches to the registration of professional engineers are taken by the various states. One method is to license all qualified and tested applicants as registered professional engineers. The second method is to qualify and test registrants in a particular discipline of engineering and award a title designating that specialty, such as registered civil engineer, registered mechanical engineer, or whatever branch of engineering is the field of expertise.

Figure 2-1 Qualification Requirements of a Professional Engineer

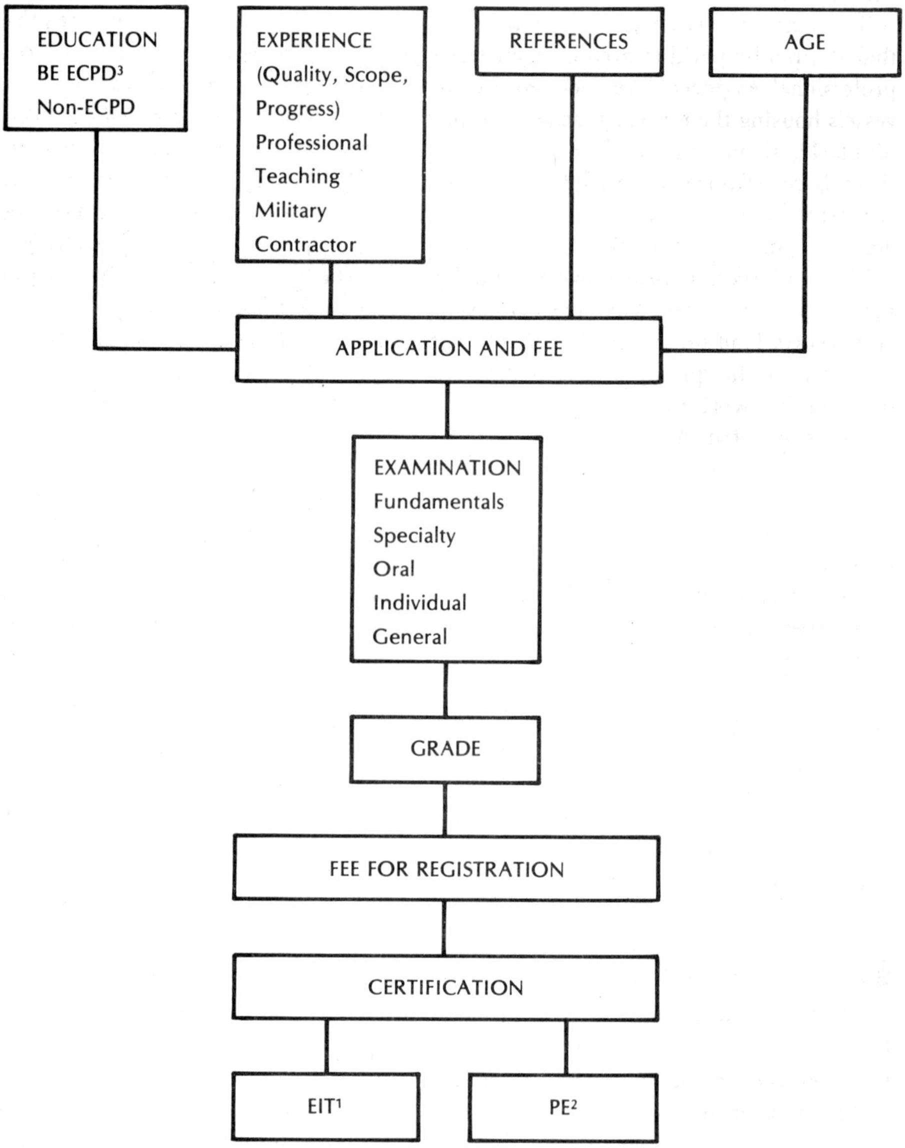

[1]Engineer-in-Training

[2]Professional Engineer

[3]Engineers' Council for Professional Development

Most states require that any person practicing engineering be registered. This includes persons professing to be engineers and those in responsible charge of engineering work.

There are inconsistencies in the licensing laws. For instance, a state may require that the public parking area of a nuclear power plant be designed by a registered professional engineer,[54] yet not require that the electrical controls or the pressure vessels housing the nuclear reactor be approved by a registered professional engineer. Similarly, airport runways must be designed by registered civil engineers; however, there is no requirement that the aircraft carrying 300 passengers be designed by registered engineers.[55] School buildings must be designed by registered architects or engineers, but school buses are not required to be designed by registered engineers.[56]

The conflicts described above are due largely to the exemptions which are part of most registration laws. The laws may exempt such persons as architects, professional engineers or land surveyors who are employed by a railroad, designers of manufactured products for the quality of which the manufacturer assumes responsibility, owners doing design work in connection with their own property, and persons working on certain small structures.[57]

The present situation in the engineering licensing laws is somewhat anomalous. Licensing of engineers in California started in 1929, at which time only civil engineers were required to be registered. This requirement was mainly a response to the collapse of St. Francis Dam, near Newhall, on March 12, 1928 which resulted in 400 deaths and destruction of 600 homes. The primary purpose of registering engineers has always been the establishment of minimum standards to protect public health, welfare, and safety.

Those engineers who qualify for registration as professional engineers must have adequate familiarity with the technical and nontechnical areas which are considered important in their special field of competence. These may include biological systems, business administration, communication arts, design and applications, economics, engineering science, humanities and history, law, multidisciplinary engineering, political science, physical science, professional ethics, social and behavioral science, and systems management.

§2.47 2. Academic Background

Most states have a minimum requirement for registration of professional engineers, based on whether the applicant is a graduate of a school approved or accredited by the Engineering Council for Professional Development (ECPD).[58]

An applicant who has passed the written examination on graduation from an accredited engineering school qualifies for an *intern engineer* or an *engineer in train-*

---

[54]California is one of the states that has inconsistencies in licensing laws, as discussed in Industrial News (Los Angeles), Apr 26, 1976.

[55]*Id.*

[56]*Id.*

[57]Registration Act 240, Mich Comp Laws, vol III, §338.569 (1970).

[58]Industrial News (Los Angeles), Apr 26, 1976.

ing certificate. Following a specified number of years of acceptable engineering experience, the engineer qualifies to take a second written examination for the *professional engineer* license.

The license applicant who graduated from an ECPD-approved school and who has 12 years of professional experience is usually required to pass a 16-hour written test. The applicant who is a non-ECPD school graduate may be required to have at least 20 years of professional experience before taking the examination. Special consideration may be given to the applicant who is 40 years of age or older or who is a graduate of an ECPD-approved school with 20 years of professional experience. Such an applicant may be required only to take an eight-hour written examination.[59]

An applicant who has completed engineering education in a country other than the United States may have to meet the same requirements as the applicant who graduated from a non-ECPD school.

State registration laws may not be uniform because they are frequently drawn to meet local conditions.

§2.48 3. Experience—Public/Private Sector

Because of the vast quantity of specialized knowledge required for any one engineering discipline, the engineer's work experience, as it relates to any particular issue, is of great relevance to that engineer's usefulness as an expert.

The expert who has successfully carried out projects similar to the one in the subject case will usually prove to have more practical knowledge than the expert who has achieved only scholarly distinction in that field of expertise.

Experience must demonstrate that the engineer has acquired through practice the professional judgment, capacity, and competence essential to the expert application of the engineering sciences.

Depending on the litigated issue, the engineer's experience may have to have been broad enough to assure the attainment of a reasonably well-rounded professional competence in the basic engineering field, rather than some highly specialized and narrow skill.

The ideal record of an engineer's professional work experience should indicate successive and continued progress from initial work of a relatively simple character to work of greater complexity and carrying a higher degree of responsibility.

§2.49 4. Publishing

Publication of books and articles in technical engineering journals is a significant element in determining an engineer's level of professional recognition. An expert widely recognized and respected in a particular field of specialty is usually more persuasive than one equally expert but less well-known.

§2.50 5. Teaching

Teaching in engineering colleges and in professional continuing education programs lets the engineer develop essential skills of communication. Such oratorical skill is

---

[59] *Id.*

important in a courtroom. Effective spoken expression of an expert witness is crucial in explaining a complex technical issue to the trier of fact.

§2.51 6. Membership in Professional or Other Associations

A professional society's committee members are likely candidates for professional experts. The official registers or directories published by these professional societies list the members of various technical committees.

The National Society of Professional Engineers, 2092 K Street NW, Washington, D.C. 20006, publishes a *Directory of Engineers in Private Practice* which is organized by state and county.

The American Consulting Engineers Council, 1155 15th Street NW, Washington, D.C. 20005, publishes a directory of *Engineering Consultants,* listing engineers alphabetically, geographically, and by area of specialized expertise.

§2.52 7. Cost Estimating Capabilities

An important point of contention in construction disputes is financial damages. This is also true in litigation arising out of catastrophic accidents and products liability. A frequent question arises as to what would have been the cost of a safer product.

Historically, engineers are required to be strong in three areas, safety, integrity, and economics. Many engineers seem to concentrate on the first two areas while paying little attention to the third item. However, in order to deliver effective testimony in court, the engineering expert must be qualified to determine the economics, or costs, which relate to matters within the expert's field of specialty.

Many cases will involve the testimony of two opposing estimates as to the amount of damages. These damages may have been caused by overruns, delays, expansion of scope of work, or substitution of materials. There is currently a demand for estimators and cost engineers, due to the increasing size and complexity of projects under construction today. Such projects are far more sophisticated than they were ever in the recent past. Cost estimates for such projects are beyond the capability of the engineer who is concerned only with design.

The modern estimator must use control systems and computerized *critical path methods*[60] in preparing estimates for proposals, recording changes, delays, reschedules, and in taking care of all the other contingencies which have financial impact on a construction project.

There is a special branch of engineering called *cost engineering* which employs construction estimating engineers. These engineers have formed professional organizations. One such organization is the American Association of Cost Engineers located in Morgantown, West Virginia. Another organization is the American Society of Professional Estimators.

Finally, it should be emphasized that the engineering expert must be able to understand, produce, and evaluate the many tools and documents used in cost estimating and cost control.

---

[60] J. Antil & R. Woodhead, Critical Path Methods in Construction Practice (2d ed 1970).

§2.53 D. Additional Readings

American Society of Safety Engineers, *Scope and Functions of the Professional Safety Position,* American Society of Safety Engineers, Park Ridge, Ill, 1973.

California Board of Architectural Examiners, An Act Regulating the Practice of Architecture in the State of California with Rules and Regulations. Excerpt from Government Code, ch 2, State Documents, div 3, ch 3, Business and Professions Code, ch 3, arts 1-3, 1975.

California Board of Registration for Professional Engineers, *Bulletin 3-75, Information for Registration as a Professional Engineer During the Initial (Grandfather) Period,* Department of Consumer Affairs, Agriculture and Service Agency.

California Administrative Code, *Rules and Regulations* of the Board of Registration for Professional Engineers, tit 16, ch 5.

California Board of Registration for Professional Engineers, *Bulletin 75-5(b), Safety Engineer.*

California Business & Professions Code, *The Land Surveyors' Act, Div 3, Ch 7,* Board of Registration for Professional Engineers, 1977.

California Business & Professions Code, *The Professional Engineer Act, div 3, ch 7.*

California Business & Professions Code, Preprint Senate Bill No 17, proposed by Senator Rodda, *An Act to Repeal and Add Chapter 7 of Division 3 of the Business & Professions Code, Relating to Professional Engineers, California,* July 14, 1976.

Engineering & Land Surveying Article 145, New York.

Industrial News of California, State Aims to Clear up Inconsistencies, April 26, 1976.

Los Angeles County Building & Construction Trades Council, *Roster,* October 1978.

Michigan Department of Licensing & Regulations, *Rules & Regulations.*

Michigan Department of Licensing & Regulations, *Registration Act 240 of 1937 for Architects, Professional Engineers and Land Surveyors,* Board of Registration for Architects, Professional Engineers & Land Surveyors, Lansing, Mich, 1938.

Michigan Society of Professional Engineers, *The Michigan Professional Engineer.*

National Council of Engineering Examiners (NCEE), *Model Rules Professional Conduct,* 1972.

National Council of Engineering Examiners (NCEE), *The Practice of Engineering in the United States,* Seneca, SC, 1973.

National Council of Engineering Examiners (NCEE), *Regarding NCEE Services; Council Records and Certification,* Seneca, SC.

Professional Engineers Registration Law No 367, *an Act,* Pennsylvania.

State Board of Engineering & Land Surveying, *Handbook 36: Professional Education, Engineering and Land Surveying, Laws, Rules, Information,* New York.

Structural Engineers Association of Southern California, *By-Laws, Code of Ethics, Code of Standard Practice,* 1968.

3 Discovering Evidence in Products Liability Cases

§3.01 A. Identification of Components

This chapter will concentrate on products liability cases which have to do with machines. A machine is a more complex apparatus than a static product such as a ladder, pipe, or structure. Nonetheless, the suggested discovery procedures may be just as applicable to cases involving simpler products. An attorney understanding the components of machinery would have little difficulty in the discovery process of cases relating to other products.

Products can be generally divided into consumer and industrial products. Consumer products are familiar to laypersons, and would include such items as electric razors, food blenders, and lawn mowers. Industrial products are generally divided into two distinct categories: (1) products which process or handle dry materials; and (2) products which process or handle liquids.

The first industrial product category includes the following:

Material handling equipment, such as belt conveyors, bucket elevators, etc.

Feeders, including belt, pan, vibratory, pneumatic, and apron feeders

Screening and classification equipment, like vibratory screens and classifiers

Size reduction equipment, such as rock crushers, breakers, mills, and impactors
Mixers, which include agitators and blenders
Fans and blowers
Dust collectors, collection systems bins, and silos

The second category might contain the following:

Filters and liquid-solid separators, such as centrifuge and vibrating screens
Pumps and ejectors
Compressors
Air driers and filters
Storage equipment, which includes tanks and vessels

A typical machine can be reduced to a definite number of dynamic and static components. The dynamic components are arranged to transmit and modify energy to perform desired work. Electric razors, motorcycles, and tunnel-boring moles[1] are all examples of machines. Each has a motor,[2] which may be electric, diesel, or gasoline powered. The power from the motor, a prime mover, is transmitted by a series of devices, a power train, to perform useful work. The transmission[3] of energy may culminate in the oscillation of clipper blades in an electric razor, in the rotation of the drive wheel of a motorcycle, or in the thrusting and turning of the cutter head in a tunnel-boring machine.

The static parts of a machine[4] consist of the base, frame, enclosure, and all other components which support, protect, and house the dynamic parts.

Products liability cases tend to be the result when one or more of a machine's components in their individual capacities, or as part of the power train, fail to perform in a proper manner.

The attorney in products liability cases should become familiar with the entire machine and with its individual components in order to understand and be able to discuss the pertinent issues.

§3.02 1. Dynamic Components

The basic dynamic components of a machine include a motor, a transmission, drive parts, and controls.

The type of motor,[5] or prime mover, used in a particular machine is classified according to form of energy source. Where the energy is supplied by electrical current, the prime mover is an electric motor. When the energy source is liquid or gaseous fuel, the drive unit is either reciprocating or rotary combustion engine.

---

[1] §3.29.
[2] §3.03.
[3] §3.05.
[4] §3.09.
[5] §3.03.

Almost every motor or engine delivers its power[6] output by means of a rotating shaft. The energy[7] of the rotating shaft is rated at a particular horsepower[8] and is translated into a combination of torque (T)[9] and rotation (rpm). For a given horsepower, the torque is inversely proportional to rpm and vice versa. By formula, it would appear as follows:

$$\text{hp} = \text{T} \times \text{rpm} \ \textit{or} \ \text{T} = \text{hp} \div \text{rpm}$$

The general term for a device designed to transmit rotating energy from a motor to the parts performing the useful work is the transmission.[10] The transmission may maintain, increase, or decrease the rate of rotation of the motor, as well as change the direction of the axis of rotation. Some popular methods of power transmission are the gear box, chain drive, gear reducer, V-belt drive, or hydraulic torque drive. Each of these drives must be capable of absorbing the forces[11] imposed by the prime mover.

§3.03 a. Electric Motors Generally

The commonest type of motor is the electric motor, which converts electrical energy[12] into mechanical work. This conversion depends on the horsepower rating[13] and rpm of the motor. The higher the horsepower, the greater the torque the motor can deliver at a given rpm.

A variable characteristic of an electric motor is the form of electrical energy it receives. Electrical energy is available in a variety of forms.[14] It may be available in the form of direct current (dc) or alternating current (ac). Alternating current may be single-phased or multiphased. Use and power requirements of the machine determine the most efficient form in which the electrical energy is to be received.

An important feature of an electric motor is its need for protection from the environment. As a result, the motor frame, or housing, is manufactured taking into account the environmental conditions to which the motor may be subjected. Some of the more typical motor frame types are the drip-tight, totally enclosed fan-cooled, explosion-proof, and general purpose motors.

---

[6] **§6.26.**

[7] **§6.27.**

[8] In its simplest form, horsepower can be defined as the rate at which work is done. It is the result of the work done (stated in ft-lbs) divided by the time involved.

[9] Torque is that force which tends to produce torsion or rotation. In motors, it is considered to be the amount of force produced by a motor to turn the load (measured in ft-lbs).

[10] **§3.05.**

[11] **§6.24.**

[12] **§6.26.**

[13] *Id.*

[14] Voltage is a unit of electromotive force. Simply defined, it is a force which when applied to a conductor (such as a wire) will produce a current in the conductor.

§3.04 (1) Enclosures for Controls

The National Electrical Manufacturers Association (NEMA)[15] describes the various enclosures for electrical controls as follows:

> NEMA Type 1, general purpose, is used to prevent accidental contact with enclosed apparatus. This type is suitable for application indoors where not exposed to unusual service conditions
>
> NEMA Type 2, driptight, is to prevent accidental contact, and, in addition, to exclude falling moisture or dirt
>
> NEMA Type 3, weatherproof, (weather resistant) protects against specified hazard, and is suitable for use outdoors
>
> NEMA Type 3R, raintight, is used to protect against entrance of water from a beating rain, and is suitable for general outdoor application not requiring sleetproof
>
> NEMA Type 4, watertight, is designed to exclude water applied from hose stream. This type is used to protect against stream of water during cleaning operations
>
> NEMA Type 5, dust-tight, is constructed so that dust will not enter the enclosed case, and is being replaced in some equipment by NEMA Type 12
>
> NEMA Type 6, submersible, is intended to permit enclosed apparatus to be operated successfully when submerged in water under specified pressure and time
>
> NEMA Type 7 (Class I), hazardous locations, is designed to meet application requirements of National Electrical Code for Class I, hazardous locations (explosive atmospheres)
>
> NEMA Type 8, hazardous locations, is identical to Type 7, except that the apparatus is immersed in oil
>
> NEMA Type 9 (Group E, F or G, Class II), hazardous locations, is designed to meet application requirements of National Electrical Code for Class II hazardous locations (combustible dusts, etc.)
>
> NEMA Type 10, meets requirements of the United States Bureau of Mines, and is suitable for use in coal mines
>
> NEMA Type 11, acid and fume resistant, oil immersed, provides oil immersion of apparatus making it suitable for application where equipment is subject to acid or other corrosive fumes
>
> NEMA Type 12, industrial use, is for those industries where the user desires to exclude dust, lint, fibers, flyings, oil, or coolant seepage

As required by the National Electrical Manufacturers Association (NEMA, most

---

[15] National Electrical Manufacturers Association, 155 East 44th Street, New York, NY 10017. The organization establishes certain voluntary industry standards relating to motors, e.g.: operating characteristics; terminology; basic dimensions; ratings; and testing.

of the critical information concerning a motor appears on the nameplate attached to that motor. See Figure 3-1. This data includes the manufacturer's name, serial number of the motor, horsepower, rpm,[16] frequency of current, frame type, voltage, full-load amperage,[17] and any limiting environmental conditions.

In some cases, an electric motor is used to drive a hydraulic pump, which in turn transmits energy in the form of fluid-in-motion to a hydraulic motor or cylinder. The hydraulic motor receives the fluid and converts the hydraulic energy into mechanical energy. The hydraulic motor is similar to the hydraulic pump except that it operates in reverse. Gear-type hydraulic motors are propelled by the force exerted by the oil under pressure against the gear teeth.

The speed of a hydraulic motor is directly proportional to the volume of oil delivered to the motor during an increment of time. This is commonly expressed as rpm per gallon per minute. The torque output is proportional to the difference in pressure between the intake and exhaust ports of the hydraulic motor. In addition to gear-type hydraulic motors, there are piston-type and vane-type motors. All of these translate fluid energy into mechanical energy.

The following common electrical formulas illustrate the relationships among electrical terms which are associated with use of electric motors.

Electrical Formulas

To Find	Alternating Current	
	Single-phase	Three-phase
Amperes when horsepower is known	$\frac{\text{hp} \times 746}{\text{E} \times \text{Eff} \times \text{pf}}$	$\frac{\text{hp} \times 746}{1.73 \times \text{E} \times \text{Eff} \times \text{pf}}$
Amperes when kilowatts are known	$\frac{\text{Kw} \times 1000}{\text{E} \times \text{pf}}$	$\frac{\text{Kw} \times 1000}{1.73 \times \text{E} \times \text{pf}}$
Amperes when kilovolt-amperes are known	$\frac{\text{Kva} \times 1000}{\text{E}}$	$\frac{\text{Kva} \times 1000}{1.73 \times \text{E}}$
Kilowatts	$\frac{\text{I} \times \text{E} \times \text{pf}}{1000}$	$\frac{1.73 \times \text{I} \times \text{E} \times \text{pf}}{1000}$
Kilovolt-amperes	$\frac{\text{I} \times \text{E}}{1000}$	$\frac{1.73 \times \text{I} \times \text{E}}{1000}$
Horsepower (output)	$\frac{\text{I} \times \text{E} \times \text{Eff} \times \text{pf}}{746}$	$\frac{1.73 \times \text{I} \times \text{E} \times \text{Eff} \times \text{pf}}{746}$

I = Amperes; E = Volts; Eff = Efficiency; pf = Power factor; Kva = Kilovolt-amperes; Kw = Kilowatts; hp = Horsepower.

[16]rpm is the number of shaft revolutions performed per minute.

[17]Amperage is a unit of intensity of electric current being produced in a conductor by the applied voltage.

Figure 3-1 Electric Motor Nameplate

Nameplate data includes model and serial number, horsepower rating, type of service, full-load amperes, full-load rpm, voltage, cycles, phase and frame information. In addition, user is advised as to the maximum temperature at which motor can be used.

ABC INDUCTION MOTOR
MODEL 123ABC SER. NO. AB 12345
HP 15 SERVICE FACTOR 1.15
FL RPM 1750 TIME FACTOR CONT
VOLTS 230/460 CYCLES 60 PHASE 3
FL AMP 38.6/19.3
TYPE K FRAME 254 NEMA CL B CODE G
INSULATION CLASS B MAX. AMBIENT 40°C

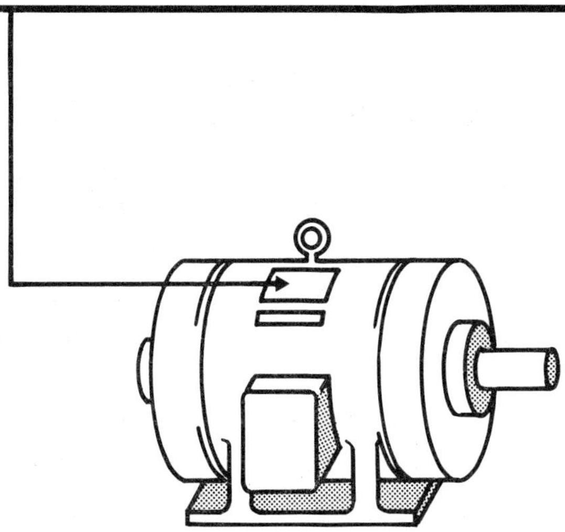

§3.05 b. Transmissions

A relatively simple type of transmission is the roller chain and sprockets. The chain and sprockets are manufactured to match in width and pitch, or spacing of teeth; they are identified by an American Standards Association (ASA) number. This number indicates the dimensions of the sprocket tooth and the link of the chain. In the case of the sprocket, the number of teeth is part of the description. There may be as few as 8 or as many as 112 teeth in a sprocket. A sprocket is also described by the shape of its hub, and by whether it is to be used with a single-, double-, or triple-width chain.

Operating capacity is the horsepower rating of a chain and sprocket set. This rating is based on the ASA number, the rpm, and the number of teeth in the smaller sprocket of the set. Multiple chains would increase the horsepower rating.

The main advantage of the chain and sprocket drive is the ease with which the rpm and torque of the driven part can be changed. The speed ratio of the driven sprocket to the driver sprocket is inversely proportional to the number of teeth in each sprocket. A driver sprocket with 22 teeth attached to an electric motor rotating at 1800 rpm will rotate a driven sprocket which has 11 teeth at the rate of 3600 rpm. The reverse is also true; a 44-tooth driven sprocket will rotate at 900 rpm.

The primary purpose of the transmission device is to transfer energy from the prime mover to the driven part with as little efficiency loss as possible. With the exception of the inevitable loss of efficiency from friction, the horsepower through the power train remains nearly constant. The basic formulas for the relationship between horsepower, torque, and rpm in various units of measurement are as follows:

$$\text{hp} = \text{Torque (in lb-inches)} \times \text{rpm} \div 63025 \textit{ or}$$

$$\text{Torque (in lb-inches)} = 63025 \times \text{hp} \div \text{rpm}$$

For example, a 100-horsepower motor rotating at 1800 rpm will theoretically deliver the following torque:

$$T = 63025 \times 100 \div 1800 = 3501.39 \text{ lb-inches Torque}$$

If through the transmission the speed of rotation is doubled to 3600 rpm, the resulting torque will be:

$$T = 63025 \times 100 \div 3600 = 1750.7 \text{ lb-inches}$$

Reducing the rpm by one-half will increase the torque to 7002.8 lb-inches.

Since a torque is expressed as a force times a distance, the force in pounds is considered to be exerted at the outer perimeter of the gear, sprocket, or pulley, and is equal to the torque divided by the distance between the axis of the shaft and the effective perimeter of the device. For example, a sprocket with a pitch diameter of 2.66 inches and a torque of 3501.4 lb-inches will exert a pull on the chain equal to:

$$\text{Force} = 3501.4 \div 2.66/2 = 2632.63 \text{ lbs.}$$

Therefore, for a given torque, the larger the diameter of the sprocket, gear, or pulley, the less will be the force at the perimeter. The smaller the diameter, the greater the force.

§3.06 c. Power Train

As stated at the beginning of this chapter, the purpose of every machine is to produce useful work. The driven parts which perform this work may be a complex power train, which rotates the drive wheels of a motor vehicle, or may be a simple device such as happens with the rotation of the impeller of a pump.

Since the horsepower[18] available to the driven part is the horsepower of the motor less all energy lost in friction,[19] heat, leakage, and slippage, the ratio of output to input energy represents the efficiency of the machine.

Since loss of energy is not constant with any machine but increases with age, wear of each moving part, and lack of lubrication, most machines are designated by the horsepower of their prime mover rather than by that of the final driven parts. The horsepower rating of an automobile is normally defined as the horsepower of the engine alone without any of the accessories, and not that of the drive wheels of the vehicle. See chapter 6 on transportation for discussion of different horsepower ratings of motor vehicles.

It is important to take into account this difference in power in litigation dealing with apparent lack of adequate power or misrepresentation of horsepower.

A machine is normally designed and manufactured to produce a specified amount of useful work. The purchaser of an electric hoist is more interested in the speed and lifting capacity of a hoist than in the horsepower of its electric motor.

The driven parts may consist of a chain of components, each intended to carry energy from the prime mover. In an improperly designed machine one or more of the components in the power train may be undersized and incapable of carrying the torque or other forces to the next component of the train. In such a case, there are failures in the components of the driven parts.

One of the tasks of the investigating expert engineer is to analyze this power train to determine whether each part is capable of receiving and transmitting the energy required. Such an analysis should take into consideration the impact forces involved in machinery operation.

An example of failure in the components of a machine is presented in the following case of a tunnel-boring mole.

A contractor who purchased a mole to drill a three-mile-long tunnel[20] claimed that since the main gear and other parts of the machine failed on the job, it was necessary to resort to the more expensive and time-consuming method of tunneling with explosives. The manufacturer of the mole contended that the soil encountered in the drilling was not as described prior to sale of the unit, and that had the soil been as specified, the unit would not have failed.

In the investigation, the expert used as evidence the manufacturer's certified drawings, operating manual, and records of repair work and replacement of equipment. Also used were photographs of defective parts, the geologist's report, data from the various manufacturers of the individual machine components, and the metallurgical analysis[21] of the broken gear. The mole itself was not accessible for inspection since it was located over a mile deep in a tunnel. The unit was covered with mud and was stored in a poorly illuminated opening cut adjacent to the main tunnel, all of which impeded inspection of the mechanical components.

---

[18] **§6.28.**

[19] *Id.*

[20] **§3.29.**

[21] **§3.33.**

By reliance on the information obtained from the drawings and specifications, it was determined that there were components in the power train[22] which were rated by their respective manufacturers as incapable of carrying the forces induced by cocomponents on the machine. It was also found that there had been no provision for eccentric loading of the cutting wheel, which tended to overload the shaft bearings. In addition, inadequate provisions for cooling and filtering the hydraulic fluid led to a loss of power.

The tunnel-boring mole investigation was typical of how an expert researches a machine made up of components which have been manufactured by many different companies. By identifying each component and obtaining all pertinent data from the respective manufacturers, the expert was able to reasonably determine the capacity of the entire machine in its operation as a single unit.

§3.07 d. Controls

Almost every machine must be regulated as to the amount of energy received and transmitted to its various components. Some machines require a starting force greater than the force required during normal operation. A larger force is needed to overcome the inertia of the machine at rest. Acceleration and deceleration also necessitate some type of control on the energy expended. Controls serve to limit the amount of electric current entering a motor to prevent overheating of the conductors and the windings of the motor.

Hydraulic systems, for instance, have pressure reducers and relief valves that dissipate sudden surges of high pressure which otherwise might burst the pipes, seals, gaskets, or other parts containing fluid. The flow of fluid in the system must be regulated to increase or decrease the speed of hydraulic motors. This is accomplished by directional control valves which divert the flow to different parts of the system.

Controls also serve as indicators of various conditions of the components. In hydraulic systems, there are gauges and assorted types of indicators to signal the pressure, flow, temperature, or liquid level of the fluid in the overall unit. If a record of this information is required, the controls may include some type of recording device. The recorder usually consists of circular charts or strips on which a pen continuously marks the status of the information picked up by a sensor.

An indicator and recording device receives information in the form of a signal from the transmitter. A sensor transmitter reacts to differences in temperature, pressure, flow, or liquid level. It signals these changes by means of varying air pressure or electric current within a tube or conductor. A receiver may indicate, record, or do both.

The most important function of some instruments is to control the system automatically. This is accomplished by means of a device generally known as a controller. A controller may be combined with an indicator or recorder. It reacts to the signal received and, in turn, transmits another signal to activate a control valve, an electronic relay, or some similar actuating device. It is by means of such a controller that the liquid in a tank can be maintained at a specified height or the temperature in a water system can be kept at a predetermined level.[23]

---

[22] §3.06.

[23] Examples of highly controlled machines are the household clothes washer and dishwasher.

The control system can be referred to as the "brains" of the machine. It senses the information, reports it, records it, and initiates an activity which results in the desired operation. The control system of an elevator, for example, receives the signal from the push button on any floor. The signal is indicated with a light. The controller, then, starts the electric motor and hoist which moves the elevator cab. A signal from a second push button within the cab will activate the stopping sequence at the selected floor level and, subsequently, initiate the opening of the doors.

§3.08 e. Energy Sources

Every machine which does work needs an energy source input of some form. The commonest sources of energy are electricity, liquid fuel, gaseous fuel, compressed air, or steam.

Some machines convert the medium of energy from one form to another. An emergency generator which is operated by a gasoline engine creates electricity. A hydraulic elevator converts electrical energy to pressurized fluid, which raises the cab by means of a hydraulic ram. A motor vehicle engine is powered by gasoline, but generates electrical energy for the lights and ignition, and compresses fluid for the brakes.

§3.09 2. Static Components

Every machine, whether it is a small electric razor or a tunnel-boring mole, requires a frame to hold its moving parts and a housing to protect these parts from the environment. The housing also safeguards the user from the moving parts. The frame must be strong enough to resist all shocks caused by outside forces and dynamic components while the machine is in operation. The housing must be made of materials which are resistant to wear and chemical deterioration. In some cases, the housing must be insulated against temperature, moisture, or electricity. Some housings resist atmospheric pressures while others have high internal pressures.

Where moving parts are supported by a frame, the interface can be bearings or bushings for rotating parts, and springs or shock absorbers for oscillating parts.

All of the above components constitute the static portion of a machine. Products liability cases may arise out of defects in these static components just as frequently as they result from defective dynamic parts.[24]

§3.10 a. Materials

The parts of a machine must be designed to carry all loads without failure. Proper design takes into account the following:

1. Determination of the general shape or form of the parts
2. Evaluation of the forces which the part is expected to carry during its useful life

---

[24]Examples include such defects as an absent chain guard or exposed fuel tank in a motor vehicle.

3. Expression of maximum stress in terms of the forces and dimensions of the parts
4. Adjustment of the dimensions to meet strength, space, and fabrication requirements
5. Selection of suitable materials and maximum allowable stresses

A machine is said to have failed whenever it no longer functions properly in its intended use. Yet, improper function is a relative concept. Deformation, which may be considered satisfactory in one use, may be entirely unsatisfactory in another use. For practically all machine parts, a value of limiting distortion or deformation for satisfactory usage must be established. Four types of failure which can occur due to excessive deformation are discussed in the subsections which follow.

Excessive Elastic Deformation·

This type of failure entails no damage to the material, and is fundamentally one of design. There may be plenty of material to carry the load without collapse, but not enough material to prevent objectionable distortion. Thus, when a member fails due to excessive elastic deformation, the design may be improved by increasing the amount of material or using a different, less flexible material.

Slip

This type of failure is due to inelastic or plastic action. A material is said to be elastic when it returns to its original dimensions after a cycle of loading and unloading, and when the amount of strain developed during loading is relatively small. A material is inelastic or plastic when the strain developed during loading prevents the material from resuming its original dimensions. The change in dimensions may be sufficient in the case of a closefitting machine part to render the part unfit for further use, even though the part may have remained whole.

Fracture

This term denotes the complete separation of the material into two or more portions, rendering the original part unfit for further use.

The first two modes of fracture failure are yielding and fracture in the absence of buckling. These types of failure can be caused by stresses due to tension, compression, bearing, bending, shear, torsion, combined stress, creep, and fatigue.

A member under axial tension will begin to yield or take a permanent set; then, if the tensile force is increased, fracture will occur. During the yielding phase the member both elongates and *necks down*, thus reducing its cross-sectional area. Fracture may be expected to occur when the stress on the minimum net section is equal to the tensile strength of the material.

Generally, the strength of compression members is controlled by buckling. In cases of short, compact compression members, in which there is no possibility of buckling, yielding will occur until the compressive strength of the material is exceeded.

Creep

This is a continuing deformation over a period of time in a material subjected to a constant load. The tendency of a material to creep usually becomes greater with an increase in pressure, stress, or temperature.[25]

Certain mechanical stresses are relatively easy to determine by mathematics while others are very difficult. One stress which is difficult to calculate is impact stress. The impact stress[26] within a material is inversely proportional to the time that motion is stopped or changed.

The whole area of impact stresses evolved from the equation:

$$F = ma$$

where:

F = resulting force[27]
m = mass of the object
a = rate of acceleration or deceleration of mass[28]

Therefore, the faster an object is stopped, the greater the force and resulting stress. This is the most common cause of failure in a machine.

§3.11 b. Connections

Of the many components in a machine or structure, the connections are the most critical in keeping the entire assembly together. These devices, also called fasteners, are used to hold one part of the machine to another. In doing so, they transfer forces through the machine. Fasteners include nuts, bolts, screws, nails, spikes, clamps, locking devices, keys, cotters, rivets, and welds. See Figure 3-2.

Many machine failures occur in the connections. See Figure 3-3. The connections must absorb sudden stops which can cause impact and high stresses, resulting in failure of the fasteners. Similarly, misalignment in the various parts of a machine may cause a connection to fail. This can occur in the coupling or flange connection of a drive shaft.

Because of constant movement and exposure to stress, fasteners of all kinds must be periodically inspected, tightened, adjusted, and lubricated. Failure to properly maintain them may result in wear, fatigue, creep, deformation, or crystallization of the metal.[29]

B. Products Documents

§3.12 1. Manufacturer's Information

A valuable source of information on any product is the manufacturer's publications. The numerous documents published by the manufacturer include sales brochures,[30]

---

[25] G. Murphy, Properties of Engineering Materials at 3-5 (2d ed 1946).

[26] **§6.24.**

[27] *Id.*

[28] **§6.22.**

[29] **§3.10.**

[30] **§3.13.**

Figure 3-2 Types of Structural Welds and Their Symbols

From *Civil Engineering for the Plant Engineer* by Max Schwartz. Copyright © 1972 by McGraw-Hill, Inc. Used with the permission of McGraw-Hill Book Company.

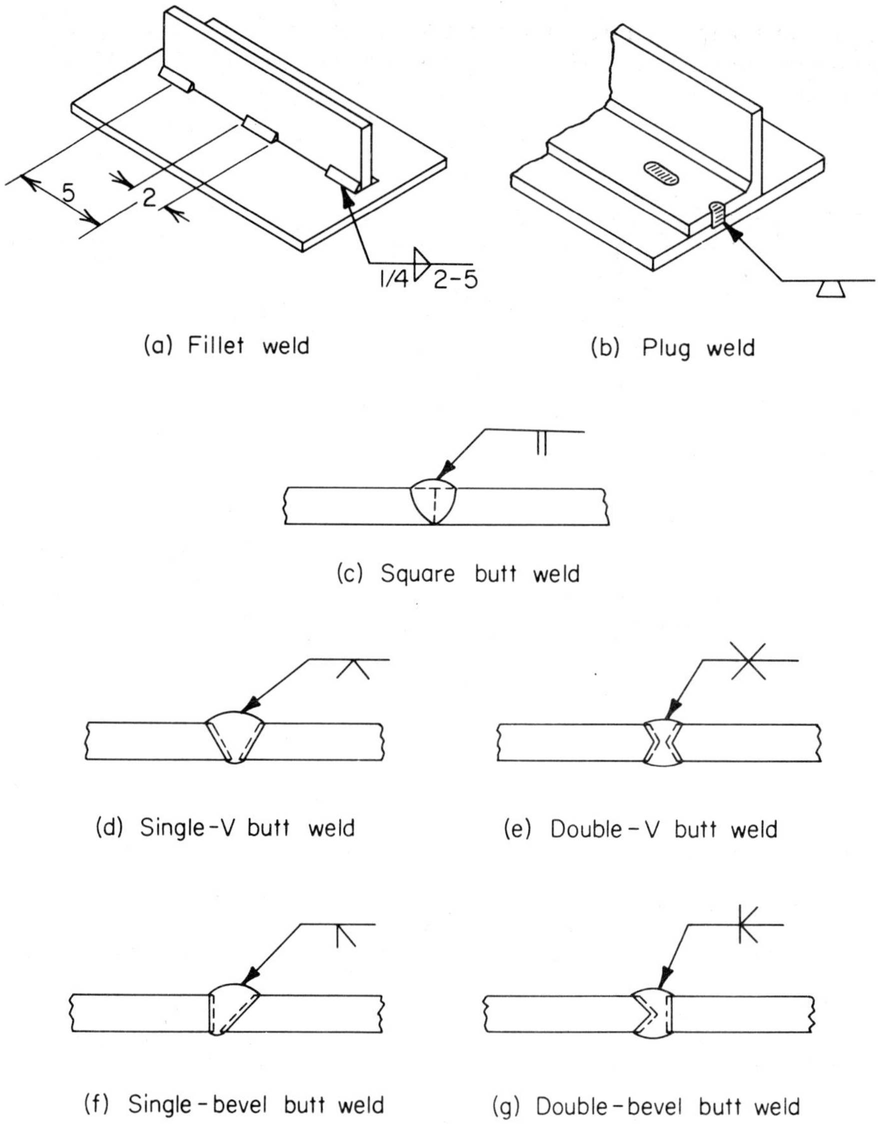

Figure 3-3 Conditions of Failure in Bolted Connections

(a) bolt in single shear, (b) bolt in double shear, (c) bolt in bending, (d) bolt in tension, (e) plate in bearing, (f) plate in tension, (g) bolt in bearing, (h) plate in shear

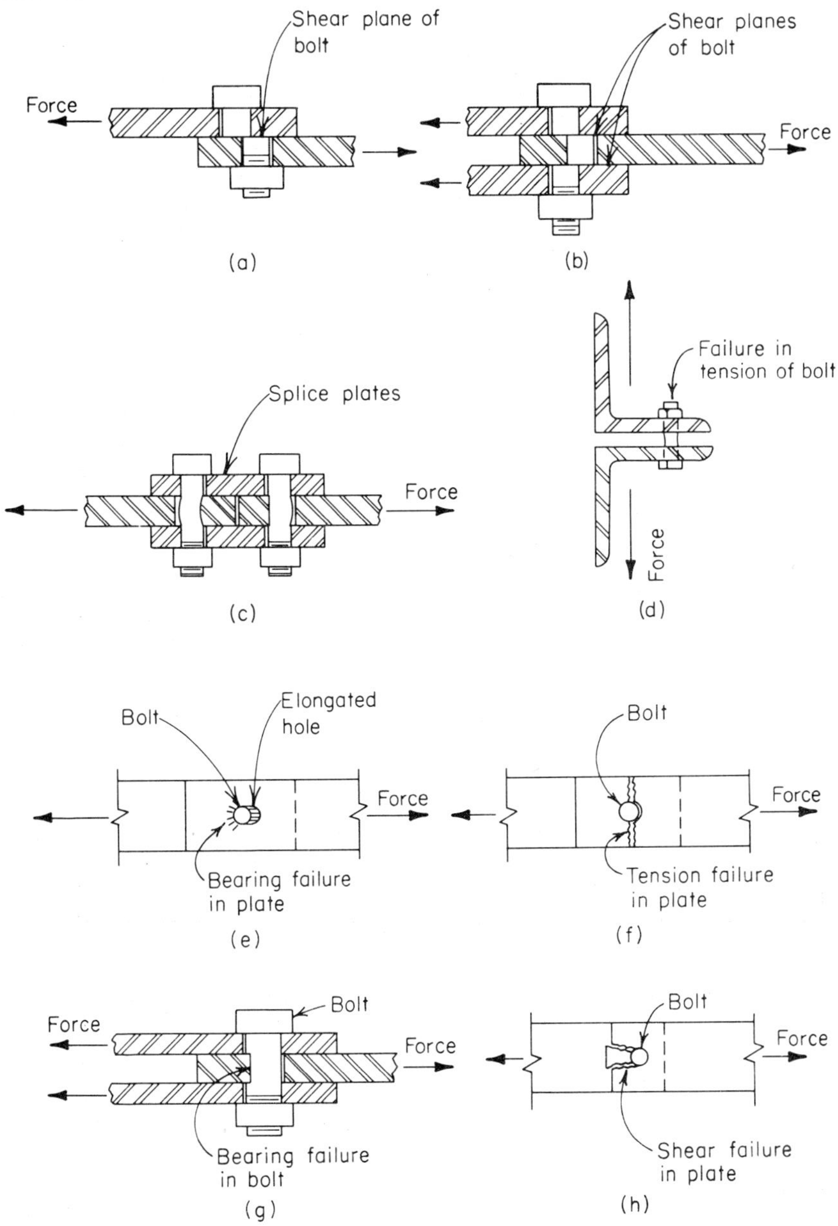

manuals,[31] data sheets,[32] certified drawings,[33] parts lists,[34] specifications, warranties,[35] and terms of sale.[36] In addition, there are quotations and proposals, invoices, documents, labels, warnings, and various forms of public advertisement.

The sections which follow will discuss in greater detail the information obtainable from the manufacturer.[37]

§3.13 a. Sales Brochures

Sales brochures provide a general description of the product and disclose the capabilities of various models.

Brochures or catalogs are usually prepared by professional copywriters, photographers, commercial artists, advertising experts, and layout designers. Their main purpose is to create something attractive which will draw attention to the particular product. The data in such brochures is general rather than technical in nature.

The cost of producing a sales brochure is relatively high due to the professional artwork, photography, and the printing process. Therefore, brochures are published infrequently and in large quantities. Often this means that a brochure will include obsolete information about the product. Most products are modified continuously due to revisions in design, fabrication, material cost, and substitution.

Use of a sales brochure should be scrutinized closely and approached with care, since it is well known among technical people that a brochure is basically an advertising piece with little dependability for engineering purposes.

Many sales brochures contain a disclaimer clause which reflects on the accuracy of the technical data printed. A typical clause is as follows:

> The information herein is to assist customers in determining whether our products are suitable for their applications. We request that customers inspect and test our products before use and satisfy themselves as to contents and suitability. Nothing herein shall constitute a warranty, express or implied, including any warranty of merchantability or fitness, nor is protection from any law or patent to be inferred. All patent rights reserved. The exclusive remedy for all proven claims is replacement of our materials and in no event shall we be liable for special, incidental, or consequential damages.

§3.14 b. Manuals

The operating or service manual is an important manufacturer's publication. It normally accompanies the product on delivery.

The manual basically describes recommended operation and maintenance proce-

---

[31]§3.14.

[32]§3.15.

[33]§3.16.

[34]§3.20.

[35]§3.18.

[36]§3.19.

[37]§7.29.

dures for competent use of a particular product. It describes the type of lubricating oils to be used, details frequency of lubrication, and specifies the location of parts to be lubricated or adjusted during the life of the product. In addition, the manual explains the procedure for assembling or disassembling.

Not only is the manual an important document for the user, but it is also an invaluable piece of evidence in a products liability claim. It may put the manufacturer in a position to prove that damages resulted from improper maintenance or use of the product rather than from defective design or manufacture. The manual may instruct the user about the limitations of the product. For example, it may contain warnings against use under certain conditions of temperature, humidity, altitude, and air quality. Consequently, the manual has been recognized as an essential document in products liability cases, both for the plaintiff consumer and defendant manufacturer.

§3.15 c. Data Sheets

Another type of publication intended for the technical user of a product is the data sheet. By definition, such a publication provides technical information on the product. In the case of an electric motor, the data sheet will include a description not only of the electrical characteristics of the motor, but also of the materials and dimensions of the frame, shaft, base, and possible mounting arrangements. The data sheet gives engineering information on the whole range of models similar to the particular type described.

The user or engineer may rely on the data sheet in determining the final use of the product and its relationship to other parts of the entire machine or assembly.

§3.16 d. Certified Drawings

A certified drawing is a legal document issued by the manufacturer to the purchaser after receipt and acceptance of the purchase order.

A certified drawing sets forth the dimensions and key data regarding the unit as it will be manufactured and delivered to the buyer. This drawing is very important to the user, who must prepare the mounting of the unit in advance in order to accurately match that unit to the adjoining parts of another machine.

A certified drawing, as its name implies, is guaranteed by the manufacturer to be accurate in the information it provides. For that reason, the user may safely rely on that information in the design of the assembly. Should the product delivered differ from the one shown on the certified drawing, the user would have a claim against the manufacturer for damages sustained as a result of the error.

The description of the product shown on the certified drawing is not necessarily the same as the description in the sales brochure. As described in §3.13, a brochure may be used for years while the product is continuously being modified. Therefore, great reliance is placed on the certified drawing, which constitutes the most accurate source of information on the product.

§3.17 e. Specifications

Specifications printed on sales brochures are intended to influence architects, engineers, or purchasing agents in writing their particular job specifications.

These specifications are usually closely tied to the manufacturer's product and, if followed verbatim, may not be capable of being complied with by other manufacturers. Although more convenient, it may be ill-advised for the buyer or buyer's agent's specifications writer to blindly copy the manufacturer's recommended specifications.

The specifications, like the sales brochures,[38] are part of the manufacturer's sales effort. Their main purpose is to make it easy for the job specifications writer, and in so doing, lock the writer into a particular manufacturer. Rather than researching and creating a completely independent set of specifications, the writer is encouraged to merely copy the recommended specifications printed in the sales brochure.

Prewritten specifications often contain disclaimers and boiler plate language which attempt to waive the manufacturer's responsibility for the product. For instance, a thermal window manufacturer may indicate in the specifications that the product is warranted for 20 years. However, such warranty is conditional on the gasket, which is made by another manufacturer, also being guaranteed for 20 years. In addition, the manufacturer may require that the windows be protected from outside strains and stresses.

A specifications writer who copies prewritten specifications has little control over the quality of the product, since such prewritten specifications may not cover the product's weaknesses. Custom-designed specifications by a specifications writer are far more useful and reliable.

Many materials associations publish recommended specifications aimed at maintaining a minimum acceptable quality, and not directed to a single manufacturer. See chapter 11 on manufacturing standards.

§3.18 f. Warranty

Warranty conditions, which are usually an integral part of a purchase agreement, are often to be found on the reverse side of the sales agreement. The conditions are frequently written in small type, and are so complex that the consumer may have difficulty following their contents and meaning.

As noted in the previous section, some warranties are conditional on the warranties of other manufacturers. This permits the manufacturer to effectively limit its warranty, since the possibility that all conditions will be met is minimal.

The typical warranty provides for the following exclusions:

1. Product damaged or abused in shipment
2. Defects or failure due to operation above or beyond rated capacity
3. Use with other equipment not recommended by seller
4. Use in improper manner
5. Defects or failure due to misapplication, abuse, improper installation, abnormal conditions of temperature, humidity, abrasives, dirt, or corrosive material
6. Defects due to tampering or alteration by unauthorized personnel
7. Defects in any product designed by the buyer

---

[38] §3.13.

8. Defects in any product used by a party other than the buyer
9. Cost of assembly or disassembly of any equipment in connection with the repair or replacement of the product sold by the seller

The typical warranty also will include the following:

1. Seller warrants product to be free of defects of material and workmanship
2. Period of warranty
3. Conditions for replacement and repair
4. Liability of seller for direct or consequential damage to property or person
5. References to express, implied, or statutory warranties

§3.19 g. Terms of Sale

A nontechnical but important product document is the terms and conditions of sale. This document may accompany the proposal for sale. Some typical provisions deal with the following topics:

1. Quotations and acceptance, sale price, duration of offer, and F.O.B. location
2. Prices, the effect of changes, cancellation, or suspension by buyer
3. Credit terms, conditions for payment for the product by the buyer
4. Dimensions, accuracy of the product's dimensions
5. Samples, availability and cost of samples
6. Taxes, liability for payment of local, state, and federal taxes
7. Shipment, cost and liability of shipment
8. Refusal of shipment, buyer's liability for costs
9. Delay, liability of seller for damages
10. Nonperformance, liability of seller for damages
11. Claims, conditions of acceptance of claims by seller
12. Rejected material, responsibility for the damaged product
13. Warranty, conditions and limitations of warranty by seller
14. Waiver of breach, limitation of waiver of breach by seller
15. Consequential damages, liability for damages caused by product failure
16. Laws, compliance with local, state, and federal statutes
17. General, resolution of conflicts between buyer's and seller's conditions

§3.20 h. Parts List

A list of replacement parts is usually incorporated into or attached to the maintenance manual. Since most machine parts have a limited life span, manufacturers provide a parts list to enable the user to order replacement parts. This insures the manufacturer of a continuous market for the replacement components and thus provides a source of additional income.

Most parts lists describe each component by a part number rather than including a full description which would otherwise allow the user to purchase the component in the open market. Many parts used in a product are not manufactured by that product's manufacturer but are purchased from other sources.

It is imperative for the engineering expert to identify those parts which are not manufactured by the assembler of the final product. Once their identities have been established, the investigating expert can commence the search for technical data from the respective parts' manufacturers, and will then be able to determine whether the parts in question are compatible with the product as a whole. In addition, the expert will be able to find out about the limitations specified by the parts manufacturer. Since the parts manufacturer has little control over the use of its product by others, it is possible that the part is being misused. Thus the replacement parts list opens up a new area of research for the engineering expert in determining the subject product's quality.

§3.21 2. Competitive Manufacturer's Information

One of the first steps that any expert must take in analyzing a particular product, whether it be a machine, a construction component, or an electrical device, is to obtain data on as many competitive products as possible for comparison purposes. Some of the sources that the expert can take advantage of in obtaining this information are:

1. *Thomas Register of American Manufacturers*[39] which includes most machinery products and components
2. *Sweets Catalogs Files*[40] which cover architectural and construction products
3. Local manufacturers' registers

These registers are customarily subdivided by product, manufacturer, and industry. Another source is the yellow pages of the telephone book. Many manufacturers' guides are published by the individual industries, which list all the products and manufacturers which serve that industry.

The expert who has obtained a good-sized list of competitive manufacturers of similar products then should contact those manufacturers to acquire technical data, including the sales price, on the products. The competitive products should be similar in capacity, configuration, and purpose to the subject product. Such a review will provide the expert and the attorney with a good foundation for establishing the level of quality in the industry.

A good method of comparing similar products manufactured to perform the same function is to check and compare their total weight, horsepower, rotational speed, dynamic properties, and types of materials used in manufacture. Consideration should also be given to properties which resist environmental conditions, period of warranty, and price. It is not unusual for the expert witness to be cross-examined on familiarity with such products; therefore, the expert should be able to recite the names and comparative qualities of other, similar products.

---

[39]Thomas Register of American Manufacturers (Thomas Publishing Co 1974).

[40]Sweets Catalog File (McGraw-Hill Information Services 1978).

After collecting the data sheets, manuals, and other pertinent information on such products, the expert should include them in the investigation report.

In cases where the issue is the safety of a product, it would be valuable to compare the product's safety features to those of a competitive product. In this way, the expert can determine whether the safety provisions of the subject product are at the level of the state of the art as represented by similar products on the market.

§3.22 3. Check List for Documents

Following is a summary check list of products documents:

1. Advertisements in media
   a. Industrial newspapers
   b. Magazines
2. Assembly drawings
3. Calculations and computations
4. Certified drawings
5. Electrical single-line diagrams
6. Engineering data
7. Hydraulic schematics
8. Manuals
   a. Operating manuals
   b. Service manuals
9. Operating instructions
10. Outline drawings
11. Parts lists
12. Performance data
13. Photographs
14. Purchase orders
15. Quotations
16. Sales brochures
   a. Catalogs
17. Specifications
18. Technical bulletins
19. Test results

C. Acquisition of Parts and Specimens

§3.23 1. Subject Product

The ideal situation in products liability cases is to have the subject product available for actual examination by the expert and presentation as evidence in court. It is essential to determine whether the product is still available. It is important to get possession of the product, and it may have to be purchased. If it cannot be purchased, there must be a request to maintain it in its present condition. Unfortunately, many products are destroyed in the subject incident itself or some time prior to the expert's investigation.

It is very important to safeguard and preserve the product as it was at the time of the incident. If the entire product cannot be retained, at least the part which failed should be preserved. Any such portion is still a valuable piece of evidence. The preserved component may be a shaft, bolt, or some type of fitting which may be sufficient to help the investigating expert determine the cause of failure.

Care must be taken to safeguard certain products from deterioration caused by environmental conditions. In the case of a cracked wood ladder[41] which was stored in an open shed exposed to the elements, the wood dried, split, and changed in its overall composition. It is not unusual for an item of evidence to be stored for a period of four or five years prior to trial. Consequently, at the time of the examination, the evidence may no longer be in the condition it was in at the time of the incident.

If the product is vulnerable to dehydration, it should be sealed in vapor-tight material or kept in a room where there is a minimum loss of moisture. Similar precautions must be taken with items made of unprotected ferrous materials which may corrode and change their metallurgical composition. Other materials may deform on exposure to environmental changes.

In order to safeguard against accidental loss of the product, the item should be photographed soon after the incident, preferably in the position and condition it was in at the time of the failure. The photographs should be of high enough quality to be enlarged for study and presentation into evidence. A blurry or out-of-focus photograph is almost useless for a technical analysis.

The factual situations presented in the next six sections illustrate the analysis involved in the investigation of a particular product.

2. Typical Cases

§3.24 a. Case of the Broken Axle

A loaded trailer was being pulled by a motor vehicle. One axle of the trailer broke, which caused damage to the trailer and its cargo. The actual axle was retained and submitted to a physical laboratory for microscopic examination[42] of its metallurgy for purposes of finding out the possible causes of failure. In addition, the physical dimensions of the axle were measured so that a mathematical analysis of the stresses on that part could be carried out. By means of these two methods of analysis, it was possible to determine whether the cause of failure was a metallurgical defect or an overstressed condition in the axle. When the failure was found to be due to overstress, there was an analysis as to whether the overstress was due to faulty design or overloading of the trailer.

---

[41]§3.27.

[42]§3.33.

§3.25 b. Case of the Broken Swivel Chair

The plastic base of a swivel-type chair cracked, causing its user to fall and suffer injuries. The base of the chair was salvaged and examined in the laboratory. The base of a similar chair, made by the same manufacturer, was put through a destructive test[43] to determine its structural strength. The testing was not performed on the subject chair for fear of destroying it. It was determined in testing the equivalent chair that it was impossible for any person sitting on the chair, in any position, to cause the chair to break. A deductive analysis concluded that there was no faulty design in the product. Rather, the accident was probably caused by a defect in the particular plastic base, due either to material defect in the manufacture or abuse in shipment. Factors which made it difficult to determine the exact reason for failure were that: (1) the chair was several years old and had been subjected to various environmental changes; and (2) the fractured surface was altered by wear.

§3.26 c. Case of the Unstable Secretarial Chair

This case involved a secretarial chair, which overturned backwards, causing its user to fall to the floor and be injured. The expert attempted to ascertain the cause of the accident by taking measurements of the chair and analyzing its swivel wheels. The expert determined mathematically and by experimentation that the legs of the chair were too close relative to its center of gravity. It was possible for a user to overturn the chair by pushing backwards with the hands or feet. The particular chair was compared to similar secretarial chairs on the market. Various configurations were noted; these indicated that the center of gravity of the subject chair should have been placed in a more stable position.

§3.27 d. Case of the Cracked Wooden Ladder

A wooden extension ladder being used by a roofer on a two-story building failed when one of its rails broke, which caused the roofer to fall and sustain injuries.[44] The damaged section of the ladder was retained, but the undamaged section was put to use on another ladder and, eventually, lost.

The portion which was retained was kept in an open shed. By the time that portion of the ladder was examined by the expert, just prior to trial, the wood rails and rungs had dried out to such an extent that they were split. This condition could have been due either to dehydration or to defects in the original material. The nature of the cracks or splits was obscured by aging.

A noticeable feature of the ladder which was helpful to the expert was that the grain in the rails was diagonal to the axis of the rail. This indicated apparent violation of safety regulations by the manufacturer who produced the ladder. In addition, it was discovered that the manner of installing the nails and guides weakened the ladder. General deterioration of the ladder made it difficult to positively identify the cause of the accident.

---

[43]§3.30.

[44]For further discussion of this case, see §3.49.

Wood products may be protected by wrapping them in plastic membrane. Since moisture, due to condensation within the plastic, may cause variations in the wood, periodic uncovering is necessary. All items made of wood should be kept out of the sun and safeguarded against bruising.

§3.28 e. Case of the Runaway Ladder Stand

The product in this case was a movable aluminum ladder stand used in a parts warehouse. The accident was caused by failure of the wheels to lock when the ladder was used. The whole stand was intact and in use at the time of investigation. No changes occurred in its physical features from the time of the accident to the trial date. There had been no deterioration which could have caused the ineffectiveness of the locking device. The manufacturer which produced the subject stand made similar but more effective and expensive locking devices. Competitive manufacturers also made more effective locking mechanisms. In this case, the engineering expert testified that he did not advise the present users that the ladder stand was still unsafe or that its use should be discontinued.

§3.29 f. Case of the Tunnel-Boring Mole

Sometimes a product is so large and complex that there is difficulty in inspection even though the product is theoretically available for examination. In a case involving a tunnel-boring mole,[45] the particular machine was two miles deep inside the tunnel when available for investigation. Within the tunnel, there was no light except for the lamps on the hard hats of the investigators. The machine was covered with mud and, because of its structural complexity, it was difficult thoroughly to examine its condition. Since it was impossible to move the machine out of the tunnel for full inspection, reliance on the design drawings and data sheets was essential.

In addition to investigating the machine, the expert needed to identify and analyze its relevant components. The expert was required to obtain data from the respective manufacturers of the separate parts and compare that data with that of the ultimate manufacturer who assembled the components into the complete tunnel-boring mole. Ultimately, it was determined that some of the component parts were inadequate for the forces created by the tunneling operation.

§3.30 D. Data Obtained from Testing

Most manufactured products are affected by one or more controlling standards.[46] The purpose of these standards is to provide a uniform level of performance, dimensional characteristics, and factors bearing on the safety of the product.

The standards can have various sources. There are voluntary standards-writing and promulgating organizations, professional societies, trade associations, product-testing

---

[45] See **§§1.20, 3.06** for other discussions of this case.

[46] **App C.**

and certifying agencies, and governmental departments. Over 400 standards-writing organizations produce more than 20,000 standards.

Such standards incorporate testing procedures in order to establish the minimum quality and performance requirements for materials and products. For this reason, test results are valuable engineering evidence.

§3.31 1. Physical Testing

In the physical testing of a product, either of two methods can be used. First, *destructive testing* involves testing of a material until failure occurs. Second, *nondestructive testing*[47] is the testing of a material to identify its weaknesses without causing destruction of the material.

There are standard tests for every type of material which determine its limits of compression, shear, tension, flexure, elongation, deformation, and rate of deterioration under different kinds of loading and environmental conditions.

In the case of construction components, for instance, tests are performed on concrete, steel reinforcing bars, structural steel, timber, and a multitude of fasteners such as bolts, nails, and welds. For machinery components, there are tests designed for all types of steel, cast iron, aluminum, wrought iron, and other such metallic materials.

Tests are also performed to determine how particular properties function under varying environmental conditions such as high temperatures, cryogenic temperatures, excess moisture, lack of moisture, and exposure to corrosive atmospheres and liquids.

Certain recognized physical properties of each material are determined by accepted test procedures. These properties include *modulus of elasticity, tensile strength, yield strength, ultimate strength,* and *coefficient of thermal expansion,*[48] and are valuable in the design of all products.

Results of laboratory tests are usually illustrated on diagrams. A very common diagram is the *stress-strain diagram.* See Figure 3-4.

§3.32 a. Stress-Strain Diagrams

The most important properties of machinery and construction materials can be plotted on a stress-strain diagram (see Figure 3-4), which indicates by a series of points the unit strain or deformation per inch of length versus the unit stress the material is subjected to. Unit stress, which may be expressed in pounds per square inch, increases toward the top of the chart from zero at the bottom. The unit strain increases from left to right. When a line is drawn through the points plotted on this diagram for either tensile or compressive stresses, the points discussed next become obvious.

The slope of the straight portion of the line indicates the modulus of elasticity of the material, which can also be defined as the ratio of the unit strain to unit stress. Another term for the modulus of elasticity is *Young's modulus.*[49] When the plotted

---

[47]§3.35.

[48]App E.

[49]App E.

Figure 3-4 Stress-Strain Curve for Ductile Material

From *Civil Engineering for the Plant Engineer* by Max Schwartz. Copyright © 1972 by McGraw-Hill, Inc. Used with the permission of McGraw-Hill Book Company.

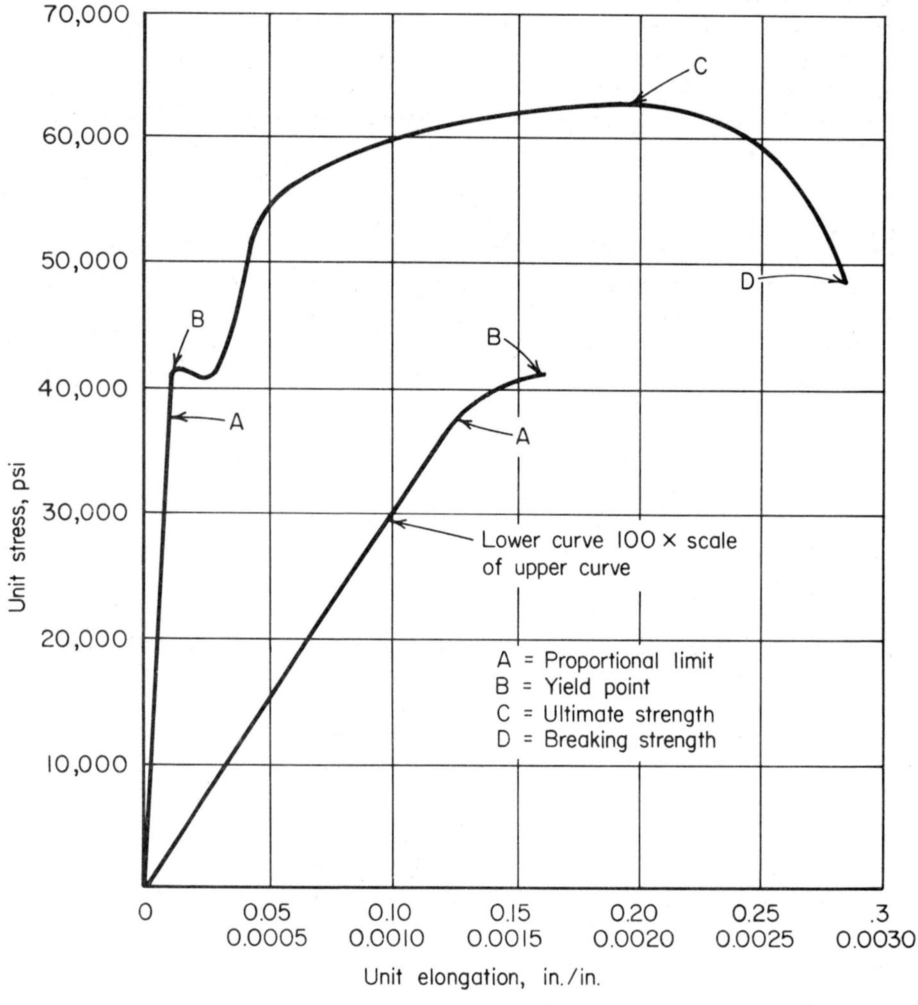

line is straight, it is said that deformation is proportional to stress. The point on the line where there is a sudden change of direction is called the *elastic limit* or *yield point,* and the unit stress at that point is called the *yield strength*[50] of the material.

---

[50] *Id.*

Beyond the yield point, the curve follows a more or less erratic course and may eventually even drop down before complete failure of the material.

Another way of defining the elastic limit is as the maximum unit stress to which a body can be subjected without permanent deformation. Within the straight portion of the elastic curve, the strain will go down to zero when stress is relieved to zero. If the stress is relieved after the yield point has been reached, there will be a permanent deformation, or set, in the material. Consequently, the yield strength is the key point on which allowable stresses are based.

Relatively rigid and brittle material will have a very steep line, while flexible or elastic material will tend to have a rather flat curve.

§3.33 2. Metallurgical Testing

Metallurgical testing is a specialty within physical testing, confined to the analysis of properties of metals. These tests are particularly important in litigation over the quality of machine parts. There are many recognized tests which are designed to determine the crystalline structure, brittleness, hardness, tensile, shear, and compressive strengths of metals. Some well-known tests include:

1. Brinell Hardness Test[51]
2. Rockwell Hardness Test[52]
3. Charpy Impact Hardness Test[53]
4. Izod Test[54]

Since material failure may result from any of a number of causes, the results of metallurgical tests have great value. These tests can indicate whether a metal part is substandard in quality, improper in design or manufacture, weakened by fatigue, overstressed, deteriorated, or affected by any combination of the above conditions which might have caused the failure.

Most manufacturers require their suppliers of raw materials to provide certified records of test results. Steel structural shapes, plates, and rods, for example, would be subjected to mill tests. Test results would indicate the condition of the particular melt of steel which produced the item. In addition, some manufacturers perform sample tests on raw materials to confirm their quality. These tests are done either by in-house laboratories or by outside testing facilities.

---

[51] *The Brinell Hardness Test* consists of forcing a ball of standard diameter into the specimen being tested under a stand and pressure, and judging the hardness of the material by the amount of metal displaced.

[52] *The Rockwell Hardness Test* is a test in which the hardness of a material is determined by the depth of penetration of an indenter under certain arbitrary conditions. The indenter may be either a steel ball of some specified diameter or a spherical-tipped, conical diamond.

[53] This test is made to determine the notched toughness, or impact strength, of a material. The test gives the energy required to break a standard notched specimen supported at the two ends.

[54] This is another test to determine the notched toughness of a material. The test gives the energy required to break a standard notched specimen supported as a cantilever beam.

The above metallurgical tests were sources of expert evidence in the following factual situations:

1. A broken motor shaft which was found to have failed because of progressive fatigue rather than overloading
2. A pinion gear of an earth-moving machine was found to have deteriorated due to abrasion from sand and dirt rather than because of substandard quality
3. A large drive shaft of a tunnel drilling machine[55] which sheared off was found to have been improperly tempered rather than improperly designed
4. A steel cable used in a gantry crane at a power plant failed, dropping the generator rotor.[56] It was determined that failure was due to corrosion, not overloading

§3.34 3. Chemical Testing

Chemical testing of liquid or gaseous materials is generally classified as qualitative or quantitative. These tests are designed to identify and determine the proportions of various elements or compounds in each material. They are also useful in determining the presence of impurities, deterioration, or change of character in a product.

Some of the specific chemical tests generally employed are:[57]

1. Differential thermal analysis
2. Differential scanning calorimetry
3. Atomic absorption spectrophotometry
4. Mass spectrometry
5. Gas chromatography
6. Infrared spectrophotometry
7. Thermogravimetric analysis

For example, in a case involving a defective roof, a sample of built-up roofing can be reduced by differential thermal analysis to determine the relative proportions of asphalt, fiber, gravel, and other components which make up the material.

§3.35 4. Nondestructive Testing

Nondestructive testing, as its name implies, is the technique of testing the quality of materials without applying stress to the point of destruction. Historically, the function of such testing was to assure that materials shipped out by the manufacturer met the proprietory standards. Today, such testing may be a valuable tool in determining defects in products liability litigation.

---

[55] **§3.29.**

[56] **§3.47.**

[57] **App E.**

Nondestructive testing can be accomplished by a number of methods, including magnetic particle,[58] dye penetrant,[59] ultrasonic,[60] eddy current,[61] radiography,[62] and stress analysis. Originally, such testing methods were applicable to ferrous, or iron-bearing, materials only. Today, they may be used in testing aluminum, titanium, stainless steel, uranium, tungsten, magnesium, and other nonferrous metals. They are also used on nonmetals such as glass, plastics, and ceramic materials.

The principal nondestructive testing methods are described in the five sections following this one.

§3.36 a. Magnetic Particle Testing

This method detects surface and slightly subsurface fissures, weld cracks, lack of penetration of weld, lack of fusion, and similar irregularities in ferrous materials. The piece to be tested is covered with magnetic particles and the tester sets up a magnetic field. The surface cracks crowd some of the magnetic lines of force outside, which attracts and holds the magnetic particles that can be seen. Some types of magnetic particles are treated to glow under an ultraviolet light.

§3.37 b. Dye Penetrant Testing

Dye penetrant is related to magnetic particle testing. However, it needs no ultraviolet light, but rather a chemical developer. By capillary action, a dye penetrates and infiltrates most cracks, seams, and porosity which are open to the surface. Both color contrasts and fluorescent dyes make defects stand out from the parent surface.

§3.38 c. Ultrasonic Testing

This method tests the material beneath the surface. Ultrasonic testing is used to detect subsurface cracks, voids, inclusions, lack of fusion, and porosity. It is also used to measure material thickness. As ultrasonic pulsed waves enter the sample, irregularities reflect back and appear as pips on a cathode ray tube.

§3.39 d. Eddy Current Testing

Electromagnetic testing methods are applied to detect surface and near-surface cracks and seams, to measure alloy contents and heat treatment, and to gauge wall thickness. A coil carrying alternating current induces an eddy current of the same frequency in the sample. The conditions are expressed in magnitude differences and phase differences, and are displayed on a cathode ray tube.

---

[58]§3.36.

[59]§3.37.

[60]§3.38.

[61]§3.39.

[62]§3.40.

§3.40 e. Radiographic Testing

Testing using gamma ray and x-ray can detect internal defects and lack of fusion in metals and nonmetals because radiographic techniques are highly sensitive. With variable penetration, these methods are ideal for testing thin or odd-shaped parts. Test films provide a permanent record of the results. Their only limitation is the possibility of improperly contained radiation.

§3.41 5. Other Tests

Additional types of testing relate to a product's susceptibility to fire or explosion. Such testing methods investigate the flammability, fire resistence, and flashpoint propensity of the subject product or its components. The pertinent tests are set forth in the publications of the Underwriters' Laboratories, Inc. and the National Fire Codes, as well as in the standards printed by the National Fire Prevention Association.

Laboratory testing of suspected faulty materials is truly forensic engineering. Every material used in a product is affected to some degree by external forces and environmental conditions. The aim of proper product design is selection of a material with particular properties and configuration which would adequately withstand the anticipated outside forces.

Whereas the stresses and strains on a product can be approximately determined by mathematical analysis, the internal properties of the materials making up the product can only be investigated by laboratory testing procedures. Generally, all manufacturers' data sheets and technical publications will refer to certain tests in describing the properties of their products. The expert involved in the research of a product will then have available the list of tests to which the product may be subjected. An additional source for description of applicable testing methods is the industrial or government standards for testing procedures, which sets up a basis for deciding whether a product conforms to accepted standards.

E. Check List for Discovery

§3.42 1. Interrogatories

The vital knowledge necessary to a products liability case may be obtained by interrogatories. The information required may be in-house data, within the exclusive custody and control of the manufacturer. This makes discovery of information more difficult, in that the inquiring party must know specifically what facts and documents should be sought. The following interrogatories illustrate types of questions which will be useful in gathering data on the identity and background of a particular product:

1. Were you directly or indirectly involved in the manufacture, distribution, or sale of the subject product?
2. If so, state your capacity fully.
3. Indicate whether you maintain production records that show when the subject product was manufactured and distributed.

4. If you do, state:
   a. When you began manufacturing the same model as the subject product;
   b. When the subject was manufactured;
   c. When the subject product was shipped to a retail distributor;
   d. A description of the chain of distribution.
5. Do you presently manufacture the same model as the subject product?
6. If not, state:
   a. When you discontinued production of said model;
   b. Why you discontinued production of said model;
   c. The changes or modifications in design made in all subsequent models;
   d. The reasons for each such change or modification;
   e. A description of each writing which documents any such change or modification.
7. Give the name, address, and telephone number of each person employed by you who participated in the original design of the subject product.
8. Do you contend that any patents exist which cover any of the design features of the subject product?
9. If so, describe each patent, including but not limited to:
   a. When it was issued;
   b. A description and date of each pending patent application.
10. Do you claim to be the original holder of any patents related to the subject product?
11. If not, state:
    a. The name, address, and telephone number of each person through whom you claim the patent;
    b. A description of the facts on which you make this claim.
12. Give the name, address, and telephone number of each person who prepared any plans or specifications for the materials used in the manufacture of the subject product.
13. Did you employ any stress analysis engineers to assist in the preparation of plans and specifications for the subject product?
14. If so, state:
    a. The name, address, and telephone number of each such person;
    b. The title, date, and description of each report, diagram, blueprint, or drawing prepared by each such person.
15. Were any tests performed or calculations made to find out about any particular components parts of the subject product that would be subjected to stress?
16. If they were, include:
    a. A description of each test or calculation;
    b. The results of each such test or calculation.

17. Disclose the safety factor incorporated into the design of the subject product for those parts that were subjected to stress.

18. Indicate the design capacity of the subject product as contrasted to its rated capacity.

19. State whether you conducted any tests to determine adequacy of the safety factor adopted for the design of the subject product.

20. If so, disclose:

    a. When each test was performed;

    b. The name, address, and telephone number of each person in charge of each such test;

    c. A description of the procedures employed;

    d. A description of the information sought;

    e. Each limit that the particular product was subjected to;

    f. The information obtained from each test.

21. Did you make any design changes as a result of information obtained from any test?

22. If so, state:

    a. A description of each change that was made;

    b. The results sought to be achieved by each change.

23. Did you fabricate all the component parts that are assembled into the subject product that you manufactured?

24. If not, disclose:

    a. Each component part that you purchase;

    b. The name, address, and telephone number of the person or entity from whom each part is obtained;

    c. The specifications, including material and tolerances, for each such part.

25. Do you test or inspect any of these parts?

26. If so, indicate:

    a. The procedure employed in each test or inspection;

    b. The name, address, and telephone number of each person who participated in the inspection or testing of these parts during the two-year period before and after the manufacture of the subject product.

27. Do the persons who perform the tests and inspections prepare written reports of the results of their tests or inspections?

28. If so, give:

    a. The name, address, and telephone number of the person who has present custody of each of these reports;

    b. The date of each report during the past two years that reveals any defects or any failure to meet specifications.

29. Do you maintain a foundry which produces any of the component parts of the subject product that you manufacture?

30. Do you machine any of the parts assembled in the subject product that you manufacture?
31. Within two years of manufacturing the subject product, did you publish and distribute any brochures, pamphlets, or other printed material that contained any warnings about possible injuries from the operation of the subject product that you manufactured and distributed?
32. If so, state:
    a. Descriptions of any such printed matter;
    b. The method employed to distribute the warnings to persons who were likely to operate these machines;
    c. The wording of the warning statements;
    d. Whether the warning was emphasized.
33. Have you supplemented, or otherwise amended, any such printed warnings in any publication subsequent to the date of manufacture of the subject product?
34. If you have done so, give:
    a. The wording of each supplemental statement that was intended to constitute a warning;
    b. The wording of each statement that amended any prior warning.
35. If you did not distribute any printed warnings about the possibility of injury resulting from use or operation of the subject product prior to the date of manufacture, do you do so at the present time?
36. If so, provide:
    a. The description of each printed instrument that contains any warning;
    b. An account of the method you employ to distribute the warning to persons likely to use the subject product;
    c. When you began to distribute such printed matter.
37. Within the last 10 years, have you received notice of injury to any other person, as a result of the use of a product that you manufactured, that was similar to the subject product that caused the injuries involved in the instant lawsuit?
38. If so, state:
    a. The name, address, and telephone number of each such injured person;
    b. The date and time of the named incident;
    c. The location of the named incident;
    d. Whether any sort of claim was made pursuant to any such incident;
    e. The jurisdictional location of the claim, including the legal and/or administrative entity before which this claim was presented;
    f. Any identifying number of the claim, i.e., file number.
39. What regulatory standards of the industry, company, or governmental agency are there regarding the design, manufacture, fabrication, or assembly of the subject product?
40. If any such guidelines or standards have been published or exist in written form, identify them.

41. Are you aware of any abnormalities, defects, or unconventional characteristics in the subject product?
    a. If so, explain in detail.
42. Was any procedure used for quality control or product safety of the subject product?
43. When did you first lose possession of the subject product or a component thereof?
44. Identify the purchaser of said product.
45. Give names and all other available information concerning all persons known to you who might have or claim to have knowledge of the subject incident or the resulting injuries claimed by plaintiff.
46. Specify whether the subject product contained components supplied or manufactured by others than yourself.
47. If it did, state the name of the manufacturer and designate the nature of the component.
48. Were any changes or modifications made in the design, manufacture, or assembly of subject product in the past five years?
49. If so, indicate:
    a. Type of changes or modifications;
    b. When made;
    c. Names and addresses of persons who authorized changes or modifications;
    d. Identity of persons who inspected, supervised, and performed changes;
    e. Reasons for making these changes.
50. In the last 10 years, have you or any of your agents or employees been informed by any person, firm, or government agency that the subject product was or might be in any way unsafe, hazardous, or dangerous?
51. If so, disclose:
    a. The name of the person or entity;
    b. The nature of the warning;
    c. The date of warning;
    d. Whether steps have been taken to rectify the unsafe condition.
52. Describe the procedure involved in the design, manufacture, fabrication, and assembly of subject product:
    a. Raw materials used;
    b. Machinery used;
    c. Nature, serial number, model number, and manufacturer name of component parts;
    d. Condition of product which left your company, whether subject product or a component thereof;
    e. Nature and method of inspecting for quality and safety of the subject product;
    f. Whether inspection was made on each individual unit or by way of spot-checking;

g. Form and packaging in which subject product or a component thereof leaves your control;

h. Name of the person in charge of supervising any of the above activities.

53. Do you possess or are you capable of obtaining any shop drawings, detail drawings, or blueprints covering the subject product?

54. If so, give:

a. Identity number of drawings;

b. Date;

c. Location.

55. Indicate any procedures for consumer complaint handling.

§3.43 2. Investigation of Electrical Accidents

Electrical devices improperly installed or used may cause overheating, which can result in fires, arcing in an inflammable atmosphere causing explosions, accidental shorting, or grounding causing electrocution. It is one of the greatest sources of injury and destruction.

Excessive current passing through an undersized conductor will heat up the conductor to an ignition temperature, causing the insulation and surrounding material to burn. Current jumping from one conductor to another with enough voltage behind it can make an arc hot enough to melt steel. This happens in the case of an unwanted shortage. The conduit itself provides a channel for the spreading of a fire or explosion when the air within the conduit contains combustible gases.

Not only do inflammable gases explode, but so does dust from combustible materials such as coal, flour, wood chips, and polystyrene. Nineteen per cent of all industrial fires are caused by electrical equipment which is improperly maintained, or which is equipped improperly and used in hazardous areas.

A suggested check list for obtaining evidence relating to the cause of an electrical fire follows:

A. Motors[63]

1. Were windings, ventilating ducts, commutators, and brushes clean, or dirty and plugged up?
2. Were motors lubricated regularly and properly?
3. Were bearings regularly inspected?
4. Was the air gap between rotor and stator[64] checked regularly?
5. Were motor lead connections tight, free of oil, and with their insulation in good condition?
6. Were there good ground connections?
7. Were motors regularly overhauled in keeping with operating conditions?

---

[63]§§3.03-.04.

[64]The stationary part, also known as the armature, is called the *stator*; the rotating part is called the *rotor*.

B. Control equipment[65]

1. Were starter switches, compensators, and air circuit breakers clean?
2. Were contacts in smooth conditions?
3. Were worn parts replaced?
4. Were all electrical and mechanical connections tight?
5. Were tripping points of circuit breakers checked regularly?

C. Wiring

1. Was insulation in good condition?
2. Were locknuts and bushings on conduit and armored cable tight, especially where vibration is severe?
3. Were extensions in good shape?
4. Were switch boxes, function boxes, and panel boxes clean and tightly covered?
5. Was open wiring clear of pipes and beams and properly supported on insulators?

D. Fuses

1. Were circuits not overfused?
2. Were fuse clips clean and tight?
3. Were fuse assemblies in refillable fuses tight?
4. Was ampere rating of "refills" not in excess of rating of fuse case?

E. Transformers

1. Was oil in transformer in good condition and at proper level?
2. Was operating temperature of transformer not in excess of 90°C?

F. Lightning arresters

1. Were ground connections checked regularly?
2. Was resistance of ground connection under 5 ohms?
3. Were ground wires properly bonded to pipes?

Fires involving fluorescent lamps have tended to be due to electric failure of the *ballast.* Combustibility of the ceiling, walls, or other surroundings is a major factor in the amount of damage caused by failure of the ballast.

When the ballast breaks down and arcing starts, the wiring insulation starts to burn, followed by wood and other combustible material.

§3.44 F. Safe Design vs Cost

One of the most important determinations in a products liability case is whether a product was negligently designed. The search for negligence raises questions as to the meaning of such terms as margin of safety, factor of safety, and factor of ignorance.

---

[65]§3.07.

Other pertinent considerations are industry standards, law of probability, and gravity of damages.

Every material has certain recognized properties that are considered standard for that particular composition. It is understood by engineers that these standard properties may vary within an acceptable range, depending on the source of raw material from which the subject material is made, method of manufacture, environmental conditions, and changes which result from usage.

Professionals who write and determine standards are presumed to agree on certain factors of safety governing the design of every product. These factors of safety are influenced by the degree of ignorance about the properties of the material, possible future usage of the product, and the extent of injury or loss which can be caused by failure.

§3.45 1. Factor of Safety

A factor of safety may be achieved either by designing for loads higher than expected or by scaling down the stresses representing the strength of a member to allowable or design stress value. The ratio of the ultimate strength stress to the allowable design stress is frequently referred to as the *factor of safety.*

The magnitude of the factor of safety is influenced by such considerations as:

1. Precision with which the assumed loadings (including impact and repeated as well as static loads) represent the actual service load, both present and future
2. Precision with which the strength of the structure can be calculated for various types of loading
3. Importance of the structure being designed and the consequences of failure
4. Precedent established by generally accepted specifications which apply to the type of structure being designed

Safety factors are generally based on a percentage of the expected ultimate strength or on the anticipated yield strength of the material. Such yield strength is the point at which permanent deformation occurs while the material is under stress. The ratio between the ultimate strength (yield strength) of the material and the recommended allowable strength is the *factor of safety.*

The consequences which failure would have influence the amount of safety factor. Therefore, the greater the catastrophic result of failure, the higher the recommended factor of safety.

Elements which determine reduction or increase of the factor of safety may be the product's weight, manufacturing cost, pressure from competitive prices, and ultimate foreseeable use. In addition, lack of time or funds for adequate engineering testing may preclude proper safety design.

It is the responsibility of the engineering expert to find out whether the product complies with industrial standards, to determine by mathematical analysis and professional judgment whether the product was properly designed and manufactured for its intended purpose.

To avoid failure, a fail-safe design may be incorporated into a product, as by building into the product a *weak link* that would prevent a major failure. Electric fuses, for example, are common weak links in an electric circuit. Numerous devices in mechanical systems are designed to fail with a minimum of damage to the product. Pressure relief valves, slip joints, and shear pins are typical safety devices.

Similarly, a margin of safety may be put into a product by either designing for a higher working stress than is expected or assuming a lower allowable stress than that normally allowed for in the particular material.

In addition to the safe mechanical design of a product, special devices may be installed to prevent injury to the operator. Such devices include chain guards and enclosure over electric components. These devices are governed by Occupational Safety and Health Administration regulations.

Some manufacturers tend to substitute printed warnings, either on the product itself or in the operation manual, for safety devices. Printed warnings often appear for example, on aluminum extension ladders. Such warnings appear on labels, and caution the user about maximum climbing height, maximum angle of inclination, and dangers of electrical contact.

Once a product has been manufactured, modification for safety purposes would require the taking into account of economic consequences. Making a manufacturing change is difficult unless the expert is versed in the machinery and tooling involved. A change of material or design may have an impact on the entire assembly line. The size of a bolt is relatively simple to modify, and its cost is ascertainable. However, the change in the configuration of a product component may involve new dies for casting and alterations in tooling, which may call for a completely different manufacturing procedure. In some cases, the cost of the change would be difficult to ascertain since manufacturing operations are usually proprietory and outside investigation is restricted. Consequently, the attorney should be familiar with elements affecting the design and safety factors of a product.

§3.46 G. Determining Liability for Damages

The National Commission on Product Safety Report states the following views in the area of products liability:

1. Safety begins at home in the behavior of the family, e.g., steadying ladders, storing knives, and supervising children
2. Safety begins with the home itself, as in good lighting, well-insulated wiring, slip-proof bathtubs and rugs, and latched cabinets for medicine and household chemicals
3. Safety begins in the factory, with design, construction, hazard analysis, and quality control

Liability can be attributed to all three factors, users, environment, and the product itself. Examination of each factor reveals subsidiary influences: users of different capacities and habits; environments encompassing differing social, political, and psychological conditions; and products acting in varying combination.[66]

---

[66]Advisory Comm of the Natl Business Council for Consumer Affairs, Report on Safety in the Market Place, at 2 (Apr 1973).

Therefore, evidence for products liability cases should be obtained looking to the same three bases, the activity of the user, the conditions of the environment and the product itself.

After a two-year inquiry into the extent of safety reasonably required in the manufacture of a product, the National Commission on Product Safety concluded:

> Risks of bodily harm to users are not unreasonable when consumers understand that risks exist, can appraise their probability and severity, know how to cope with them, and voluntarily accept them to get benefits that could not be obtained in less risky ways. When there is a risk of this character, consumers have reasonable opportunity to protect themselves; and public authorities should hesitate to substitute their value judgment about the desirability of the risk for those of the consumers who choose to incur it.
>
> But preventable risk is not reasonable (a) when consumers do not know that it exists; (b) when, though aware of it, consumers are unable to estimate its frequency and severity; (c) when consumers do not know how to cope with it and, hence, are likely to incur harm unnecessarily; or (d) when risk is unnecessary in . . . that it could be reduced or eliminated at a cost in money or in performance of the product that consumers would willingly incur if they knew the facts and were given the choice.[67]

H. Typical Products Liability Cases

§3.47 1. Case of the Falling Turbine Generator

The plaintiff, a major power company, sued the defendants, a crane manufacturer, a cable manufacturer, and a crane service company, alleging a product liability cause of action. Loss of electric generating capabilities by the plaintiff was said to have been caused by damage to the power company's turbine generator.

The alleged damage occurred while the power company was in process of maintaining its turbine generator. A rotor was being placed in the generator by means of a traveling gantry crane when the wire cable supporting the rotor broke, causing serious damage to both the rotor and the turbine.

The plaintiff claimed that the cable's failure to support the rotor was caused by corrosion in the wires which made up the cable. The defendants argued that the proximate cause of failure was not a physical defect, but rather misuse of the crane by overloading.

As a direct result of the serious damage to both the rotor and the turbine, the power company was forced to shut down its power producing activities for six months. During that period the company sustained substantial income loss, due to restraint in sale of electricity.

The plaintiff power company retained an engineering expert to determine the reasons for the cable's failure, including whether the cable broke because of either misuse of the crane, defective design and manufacture of the cable, or possibly improper maintenance of the crane and its components.

---

[67] *Id* at 8.

The expert inspected the crane, the broken portion of the cable,[68] and the plans and calculations prepared by the crane's manufacturer. In addition, the expert studied the technical data provided by the manufacturer of the cable.

The frayed section of cable was analysed in a metallurgical laboratory.[69] Its properties were compared to its manufacturer's specifications, industry standards, and the crane designer's specifications. Individual wires which made up the cable were tested to determine their ultimate strength. Many of the wire strands in the cable were found to be corroded.

The crane's maintenance records were reviewed, especially as they related to lubrication of the cable. It was determined that the crane had been maintained originally by a crane company, but that in the year preceding the failure, it was serviced by the power company.

By means of interviews with personnel involved in the accident, the engineering expert found out what occurred at the time the cable broke. The expert established the weight of the rotor as well as the speed at which it was being moved at the time.

The engineering expert prepared calculations to arrive at the stress which would be present in the subject cable at the time of the lifting of the rotor and with the type of reeving involved with the crane.

The break in the cable was found to be located in the equalizing sheave directly below the hoist. That sheave was fully covered except for the openings for the cable. The expert noted that it was impossible to see inside the sheave, much less to lubricate the cable within the cover of the sheave, and, most importantly, that the rope remained stationary within this sheave even though the balance of the rope was in motion during the lifting or lowering operation.

The expert found that with special effort, the rope could be pulled manually through the equalizing sheave while the hook was resting on the ground, thus exposing the hidden portion of the rope.

Once exposed, the rope could be inspected and lubricated.

The engineering expert presented these facts in an investigation report, which stated that there had been a combination of errors: the design of the crane did not allow for easy inspection or lubrication of the entire rope; the type of pulley used as an equalizer sheave did not permit inspection or access to the rope; and there was negligence in servicing of the crane in that a portion of the rope was never lubricated or inspected.

§3.48 2. Case of the Bursting Glass Bottle

The plaintiff, blinded by a flying piece of glass from a burst bottle, sued the defendant, manufacturer of the glass bottle. Plaintiff's product liability action was premised on his allegation that his injury occurred because the subject bottle was defective. The plaintiff's injury occurred while he was attempting to fill a glass bottle with water by inserting the end of a garden hose into the mouth of the bottle.

The issue in the case was proximate cause. The plaintiff argued that but for the defect in the bottle it would not have burst. The defendant contended that plaintiff's unsafe action was the proximate cause of injury.

---

[68] §3.22.

[69] §3.33.

The engineering expert duplicated the event by using a similar bottle from the same manufacturer, which was filled with the aid of a garden hose. The expert took necessary precautions by staying at a distance, but recorded the sequence of events on film. The experiment determined that when the bottle was lying on its side, an air bubble was created within the bottle; this was apparently compressed by the incoming water, causing the bottle to burst.

The expert prepared calculations to measure the volume of contained air, the resulting increase in air pressure due to water pressure, and the stresses in the glass shell of the bottle. The resulting stresses were found to be beyond the strength of the glass used in the subject bottle. This conclusion was reached by also measuring the water pressure at the end of the garden hose.

Evidence actually submitted into the trial record included a similar bottle, partially filled with water, the nozzle of the hose, the motion picture of the experiment, and still pictures from that simulated experiment.

§3.49 3. Case of the Collapsed Ladder

The plaintiff, a roofer, sued the defendant, the manufacturer of a ladder, on a product liability cause of action based on permanent injuries to plaintiff's back caused by a failure in defendant's product.[70]

The plaintiff fell to the ground while descending from the roof of a two-story building. His fall occurred when the wood extension ladder he was using for that purpose broke and collapsed. The plaintiff contended that the direct cause of his accident was a defect in the ladder, and retained an engineering expert to find out the actual cause of the ladder's failure and to inquire into the possibility of manufacturer defect or misuse.

The expert inspected, measured, photographed, and removed a portion of the ladder for laboratory analysis. The direction and nature of the wood grain in the rails and rungs of the ladder were measured and recorded.

Through interviews with the plaintiff and witnesses, the expert determined:

1. The location and angle of the ladder at the time of the accident
2. The plaintiff's weight
3. The position of the plaintiff on the ladder
4. The amount of extension of the ladder

The expert also inspected the building site to confirm the information regarding the building and also to better understand environmental conditions at that location.

The expert prepared a structural analysis of the stresses and strains which could occur in such a ladder, taking into account the load caused by a person of plaintiff's weight and position on the ladder. There was a study to see whether there was any sign of disease or decay in the wood.

The expert compared these findings with industrial standards for the manufacture of ladders, which included the American National Standards, the California Industrial

[70]Also discussed at **§3.27**.

Safety Orders, and the Standard Grading Rules for West Coast Lumber Inspection Bureau.

The expert found that there were *dip grains* in the side rails of the ladder which caused local weakening of the side rails. Further weakening had resulted from the manner in which the hardware was installed to lock the two sections of the extension ladder. The two side rails were cut from the same piece of wood; therefore, the same dip rail condition occurred at the same relative location. The holes that were drilled into the side rails to hold the rungs were close to the location of the dip grain, further weakening that location. In addition, the slope of grain in the balance of the rails exceeded the industry standards requirements.

The evidence presented on trial included the expert's testimony as to stresses, grain slope, and industry standards. A second expert, a certified wood grading inspector, confirmed use of a substandard grade of wood. Large photographs of the fractured portion of the ladder were presented in evidence, as were drawings depicting the position of the plaintiff on the ladder when the accident occurred, and illustrating the location of the high stresses and point of failure. A portion of the extension ladder was also offered in evidence.

§3.50 I. Additional Readings

Theodore Baumeister, *Mark's Mechanical Engineers Handbook,* McGraw-Hill Book Co, New York, NY, 6th ed 1964.

Boston Gear Works, *Boston Gear, Electrical Drive Systems,* Catalog M-C, Boston, 1970.

Herbert Herkiner, *The Engineer's Illustrated Thesaurus,* Chemical Publishing Co, New York, NY, 1952.

Peter S. Hopf, *Designer's Guide to OSHA,* McGraw-Hill Book Co, New York, NY, 1975.

Process Plant Construction Estimating Standards, Richardson Engineering Services, Inc, San Marcos, Cal, 1979.

Sub-council on Product Safety of the National Business Council for Consumer Affairs, *Safety in the Market Place,* 1973.

Codes & Standards

An Index to the Hazardous Materials Regulations, *Title 49 Code of Federal Regulations,* October 1, 1974.

General Industrial Safety Orders, *Title 17 California Administrative Code* §14, July 17, 1976.

Donald G. Fink, *Standard Handbook for Electrical Engineers,* McGraw-Hill Book Co, New York, NY, 10th ed 1968.

General Industry Guide for Applying Safety and Health Standards 29 CFR 1910, United States Department of Labor, October 1972.

Uniform Building Code Standards, International Council of Building Officials, Whittier, Cal, 1976.

4 Discovering Evidence in Construction Litigation

§4.01 A. Generally

Unlike products liability cases, construction litigation calls for a distinct type of evidence. Most construction of buildings or facilities is custom-made. That is, plans are prepared for an individual owner to meet specific requirements on a particular site. In addition, the relationship between the parties, the architect/engineer, owner, contractors, and others, is usually a one-time affair.

Figure 4-1 is a simple chart illustrating types of experts usually required for specific construction problems. More detailed information about these experts is given in chapter 2. Figure 4-2 is a suggested check list of sources of these experts in construction litigation.

§4.02 B. Function of the Expert in Construction Cases

The newly retained engineering expert will need access to the following documents:

1. Design plans,[1] also known as blueprints or working drawings
2. Specifications,[2] including both general conditions and technical sections
3. Addenda[3] for all changes to specifications
4. Field notes by job superintendent, clerk of the works, field engineers, etc.
5. Miscellaneous notes by architect, engineer, and superintendent
6. Contract documents[4]

The expert will want to inspect and photograph[5] the site to clarify the nature of the complaint. In addition, the expert will find out about changes made to the structure since the incident.

Testing samples of materials[6] involved in failure may be taken or requested by the expert. These may be in the form of wood beams, concrete cores, steel coupons, brick cubes, or soil test cores.

---

[1] §4.04.
[2] §§3.17, 4.09.
[3] §4.21.
[4] §4.20.
[5] §5.32.
[6] §4.63.

Figure 4-1 Experts on Specific Building Components

PROBLEM AREA	Architect	Civil Engineer	Structural Engineer	Mechanical Engineer	Soils Engineer	Electrical Engineer	Physical Laboratory	Soil Laboratory	Chemistry Laboratory	Electrical Laboratory
Soil Condition		●	●		●			●		
Demolition		●	●							
Earthwork		●			●			●		
Subsoil Drains		●		●						
Foundations		●	●		●			●		
Shoring		●	●		●			●		
Concrete Structure		●	●				●			
Steel Structure		●	●				●			
Wood Framing	●	●	●				●			
Masonry	●	●	●				●			
Roofing	●						●		●	
Plumbing	●			●						
Electrical						●				●
Fire Protection				●			●			
Heating	●			●			●			
Ventilation	●			●						
Air Conditioning	●			●						
Pavement		●			●		●			
Doors/Windows	●									
Painting	●						●		●	
Equipment				●						●

Figure 4-2 Finding an Expert in Construction Litigation

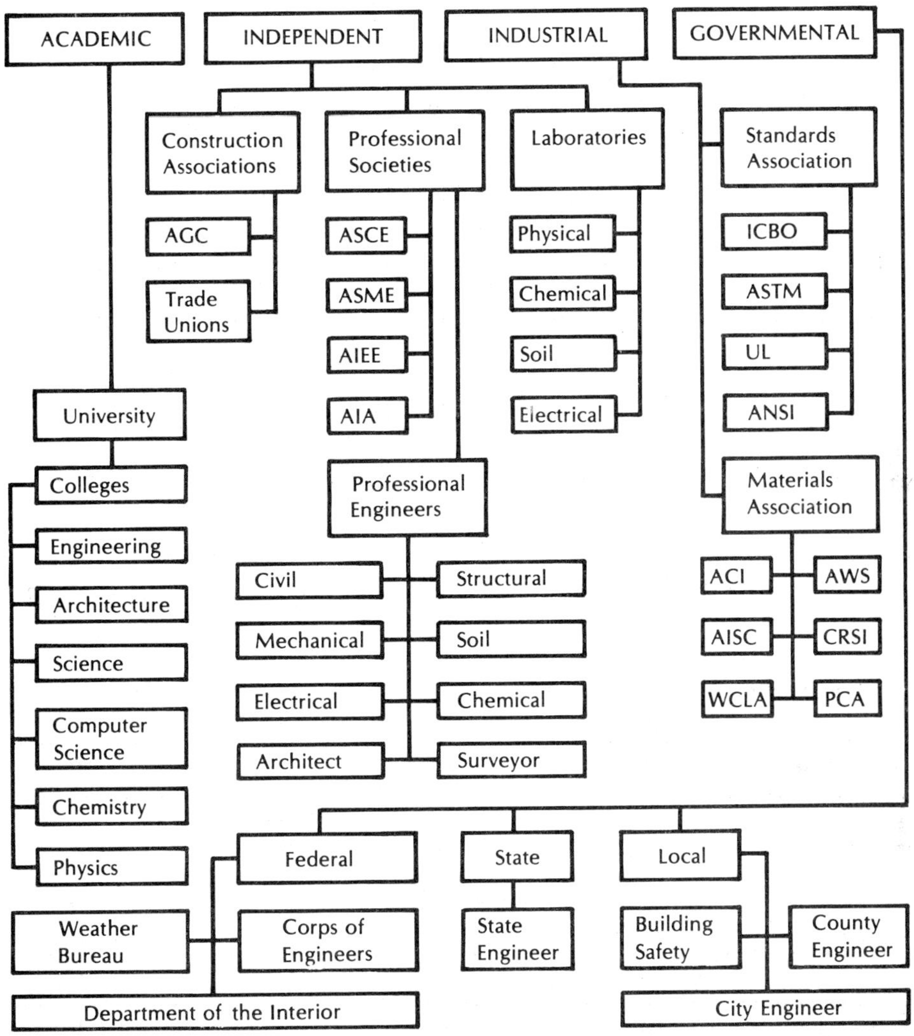

Abbreviations: ICBO = International Conference of Building Officials; ASTM = American Society for Testing and Materials; UL = Underwriters' Laboratories, Inc.; ANSI = American National Standards Institute; ACI = American Concrete Institute; AISC = American Institute of Steel Construction; WCLA = West Coast Lumbermen's Association; AWS = American Welding Society; CRSI = Concrete Reinforcing Steel Institute; PCA = Portland Cement Association; AGC = Association of General Contractors; ASCE = American Society of Civil Engineers; ASME = American Society of Mechanical Engineers; AIEE = American Institute of Electrical Engineers; AIA = American Institute of Architects

The expert should also evaluate plans, specifications, and other documents. Such evaluation would focus on the existence of proper design and consistency of data. In addition, the expert should examine the construction and determine whether it conforms to the design documents.

The expert would be interested in answers to the following questions: (1) whether the design conformed to the governing codes;[7] and (2) whether the design conformed to the manufacturer's recommendations or standard practice. These issues will suggest a multitude of others.

Was standard practice in this case good practice or was it less than a proper and professional job? Due to economic factors, the state of the art of construction has undergone deterioration in its level of professionalism and responsibility. Common use of design or construction does not necessarily make it good, safe, or durable.

§4.03 C. Architectural and Engineering Documents

Obtaining architectural and engineering documents requires patience and a lot of "dusty" work. Superseded drawings and memos are often thrown away, or, at best, not filed in any order. Disinterested parties do not have the time or patience to search for old records, and often claim that everything has been thrown away. However a quiet search will often yield enough data to recreate the situation at a particular period of the project in question.

Dating of the documents is most important. In addition to the architects' and engineers' formal reports, these persons may have personal diaries and notebooks which may help provide the dates of certain occurrences.

Documentary evidence includes the plans and related details, revisions to the plans, specifications,[8] addenda,[9] vendor's drawings, [10] shop drawings,[11] and other data relating to that specific job.

In addition to technical data on the project, an enormous amount of evidence is available in the form of business letters, applications for permits,[12] credit or loan applications, cancelled checks, signed receipts for registered and certified mail, special delivery letters, purchase orders, invoices, agreements, contracts, and interoffice memos.

These documents should naturally be scrutinized to determine authenticity. The most important factors to consider are the name of the author of the document, the date it was written, and the job name or number. Also, examination of documents should turn up any erasures, alterations, deletions, additions, substitutions, overwriting, misalignment of typewritten material, changes in handwriting characteristics, or other signs of tampering.

In addition to the above, pertinent data generated during a construction project is found in other written communication between the parties. These may include con-

---

[7] **§4.37.**

[8] **§3.17.**

[9] **§4.21.**

[10] **§4.06.**

[11] **§4.22.**

[12] *Id.*

struction status reports, construction inspection reports, minutes of building committee meetings, proposals by contractors, addenda to original bid documents, manpower logs, schedules, bulletins from architect or engineer notifying contractor and owner of proposed changes, and change orders to contract documents.

§4.04 1. Plans

Plans are graphic representations of a construction project. The project may be a building, a bridge, or an entire industrial facility. The plans give information about the project as a whole and in detail.

Standard symbols for use in plans have been developed for each construction discipline.

A complete set of plans for a building would normally include the following architectural drawings:

1. Plot plan
2. Foundation plan
3. Floor plan
4. Roof plan
5. Elevations, exterior and interior
6. Sections and details

In addition to the architectural drawings listed above, plans could include drawings relating to other disciplines such as:

1. Civil engineering[13]
2. Structural engineering[14]
3. Electrical engineering[15]
4. Mechanical engineering (heating, ventilating and air conditioning)[16]
5. Plumbing
6. Landscaping
7. Fire sprinklers

Plans are normally scale drawings which are capable of being scaled by the reader. *Scale drawing* means that smaller units of measurements in the plans represent full-size dimensions. For example, ¼ inch on the plans may represent 1 foot of the full-size dimension. This would be indicated on the plans as:

1/4″ = 1′-0″

---

[13] **§2.03.**

[14] *Id.*

[15] **§2.05.**

[16] **§2.07.**

The commonest scales for plans are 1/8″ = 1′-0″ and 1/4″ = 1′-0″. The commonest scales for details are 1/2″ = 1′-0″ and 1″ = 1′-0″.

Land surveys generally use engineer's measurements and scales. A foot of length is divided into tenths, rather than twelfths (inches). For example, 1″ = 10′-0″.

In case of conflict within a plan, the generally accepted practice of precedence is that figured dimensions govern over scale dimensions, and details govern over general drawings. The next section contains further rules of interpretation.

§4.05 a. Interpretation of Drawings

It is important to note several other rules on the interpretation of drawings.

Where notes on the drawings regarding materials or methods of installation conflict with the pertinent specification, the notes govern.

When specifications refer to construction methods by name, make, or catalog number, such reference should be interpreted as establishing a *standard of quality.* It should not be construed as limiting competition. The contractor may generally use any material or type of construction approved by the architect/engineer.

For purposes of clarity and legibility, drawings are essentially diagrammatic. Although the size and location of equipment are drawn to scale wherever possible, the contractor should make use of all data in all of the contract documents, and verify this data at the building site.

In some cases, where the design professional is hired by an owner/contractor, there is intentionally a minimum of reference to standard of quality. Use of generic names in place of specific brand names, or use of quality designations, is prevalent on the plans. An example would be to refer to the membrane under the slab or outside a basement wall only as "waterproof membrane." This leaves up to the owner/contractor the choice of whether to use a thin plastic film, good for a few years, or a heavy coat of fiber glass-reinforced asphalt, which may be watertight for 20 years or more.

§4.06 b. Vendor's Drawings

Vendors' and subcontractors' drawings are a great source of evidence about construction. These drawings cover a wide range of material and nature of work. They go far beyond the information given in the architectural or engineering design drawings. Steel-fabricating subcontractors prepare shop and erection drawings [17] which give the dimensions of each individual steel member, whether a 50-foot-long girder or a small clip angle. These drawings are made primarily for fabrication and erection, and accurately represent the work as installed.

Other vendors' drawings include elevators, air conditioning equipment, process machinery, pumps, fans, and other items which are prefabricated before delivery to the job site.

---

[17] §§4.03, 4.22.

§4.07 c. Certified Drawings

One class of vendor's drawings is extremely critical. These are *certified drawings*,[18] the final drawings submitted by the vendor to the architect/engineer for approval before beginning fabrication. These drawings are certified by the vendor, and are guaranteed to be true representations of the size, character, and material of the items to be delivered. The vendor commences fabrication only after the owner's acceptance of the certified drawings.

If the items delivered are not in accordance with the certified drawings, the owner may refuse to accept the items.

§4.08 d. As-Built Drawings

No matter how carefully architects/engineers prepare work drawings, changes are often made to the original concept during construction. In addition, errors and unexpected conditions often make revisions necessary.

Since it is essential to have accurate plans for historical record of the work, *as-built drawings* are usually required. These may be the original plans with modifications noted, or drawings partially or completely revised.

Changes in plans made before actual construction but after bidding are usually due to design changes, material substitution, building department corrections, and cost reduction. The original bid documents rarely specify the actual make and model of major pieces of equipment such as steam boilers, air compressors, or power transformers. These are usually ordered after the award of contract.

Manufacturer's drawings for equipment are referred to as *certified drawings*,[19] since they are certified by the manufacturer in the areas of outline and performance. When there are a large number of equipment pieces, these manufacturer's drawings and accompanying data are put together in books known as *data books*. These are referred to by the owner for maintenance, repair, and replacement parts. In litigation involving the performance of specific equipment, these documents become vital evidence for all parties.

Preparation of as-built drawings is an extra cost to the architect/engineer or contractor. Therefore, compensation for the cost of preparing as-built drawings must be stipulated in the design or construction documents; otherwise they will not be provided.

For projects which the owner does not intend to maintain afterwards and where the objective is resale only, it is unlikely that as-built drawings will be made.

For many commercial and residential projects, there are no records kept of plumbing, electrical, or mechanical work, since most building departments require only formal architectural and, occasionally, structural plans. No plans are prepared other than the rough sketches made by the subcontractors to obtain their respective permits.

Only plans for major buildings are kept on file by building departments. All others are destroyed after a few months. Building departments normally do not require submittal of specifications with the plans.

---

[18] §§3.16, 4.08, 4.22.

[19] §§3.16, 4.07.

§4.09 2. Specifications

Specifications are one of the most important of the main contract documents. They are, therefore, necessary evidence in construction disputes.

In the days of the early master builders, it was relatively easy to instruct and direct craftsmen on a day-to-day basis as to quality of material and workmanship. The master builder not only designed the building, but also executed the design. The mason, joiner, and slater were employees of the master builder.

As construction became more complex and more specialized crafts developed, administration of building construction became diversified. The builder contracted to construct what the architect/engineer had designed. Since the designer was more remote from the actual construction, a demand developed for detailed instructions, or *specifications.*[20]

Specifications must be considered together with the plans. The plans illustrate the specifications, and the specifications describe the plans. Specifications break down into the following main divisions:

Special Conditions[21]

These include circumstances unique to the particular job.

Legal Provisions

These include documents in advertisement for bids, instructions to bidders, bond requirements, and owner/contractor agreements.

General Conditions[22]

Such conditions would encompass the following:

1. Definitions
2. Work to be performed
3. Contracts
4. Proposals
5. Examination of premises
6. Drawings
7. Shop drawings
8. Record drawings
9. Contractor
10. Subcontractors
11. Prosecution of work
12. Lines and grades

---

[20] **§3.17.**

[21] **§4.64.**

[22] *Id.*

13. Permits
14. Utilities for construction
15. Materials and workmanship
16. Superintendent and workers
17. Inspection
18. Compliance
19. Safety protection
20. Compensation insurance
21. Indemnity to owner
22. Public liability and damage

Technical Provisions

These describe the kinds of materials and methods to be used in construction. They may include architectural, civil, structural, plumbing, electrical, heating/cooling, and mechanical phases of a project, and can be divided into the following headings:

1. General scope of work
2. Description of work
3. Materials to be used
4. Time of installation
5. Installation procedure
6. Testing and measurement

Addenda[23] or amendments to specifications.

Design professionals use different forms when they amend specifications. One is a letter in duplicate, with space for acknowledgment by the contractor. Another is a formal bulletin.[24] Each bulletin carries an identifying number and date, and indicates the purpose, cost estimate, time extension, and approval of the change by the owner.

Specifications are rarely custom-written for a particular job. For many years, architects and engineers have followed a cut-and-paste method of writing specifications, relying on previously issued specifications.

When this cut-and-paste method is done as a matter of routine specifications may contain data not applicable to the job or may lack certain necessary data. Many design firms have master specifications which contain most of the language required for their contracts. Specifications for any given job are derived by selecting appropriate portions of the master specifications. By cutting, pasting, and photocopying, complete specifications are compiled.

Many firms have upgraded the cut-and-paste method using electronic data processing equipment. The key to computer-assisted specifications writing is still the master specifications. These are stored in the computer by chapter, section, paragraph,

---

[23] **§4.21.**

[24] *Id.*

and line. Phrases or options within a line are coded so that they can be recalled simply by referencing the code. As operation of sophisticated equipment is handled by specialists, this method gives the designer of the project less control over the final product.

The use made of and respect given to specifications vary from one extreme to the other with different types of jobs. For example, specifications are strictly enforced in most government-financed jobs but are frequently ignored in owner builder speculative construction.

The format and organization of specifications usually follow the recommendations of both the American Institute of Architects[25] and the Construction Standards Institute. They are a legal document, written and organized to meet evidentiary standards for litigation. Specifications are written by architects and engineers and interpreted by contractors or, when disagreements occur, defined by the court.

§4.10 3. Parcel and Tract Maps

Some projects begin with raw land. There are many required stages of engineering and preparation of documents before land can be subdivided and improved. Necessary maps, plans, and documents include (see Figures 4-3 and 4-4):

1. Preliminary tract map
2. Topographic map[26]
3. Final tract map
4. Street plans
5. Sewerage plans
6. Water distribution plans
7. Grading plans
8. Tract restrictions
9. Covenants
10. Metes and bounds
11. Electric distribution plans
12. Storm drainage plans

The purpose of the plans and documents is to allow review and approval by the governing agencies. Most cases of land development involve the following agencies:

1. Storm drain or flood control department
2. Sanitation and health department
3. Parks and recreation department
4. Regional planning commission
5. Road departments of the city, county, or state

---

[25] **App A.**
[26] **§§5.04-.05.**

Figure 4-3 Portions of typical (a) Base Map, (b) Zone Map and (c) Tract Map

From *Civil Engineering for the Plant Engineer* by Max Schwartz. Copyright © 1972 by McGraw-Hill, Inc. Used with the permission of McGraw-Hill Book Company.

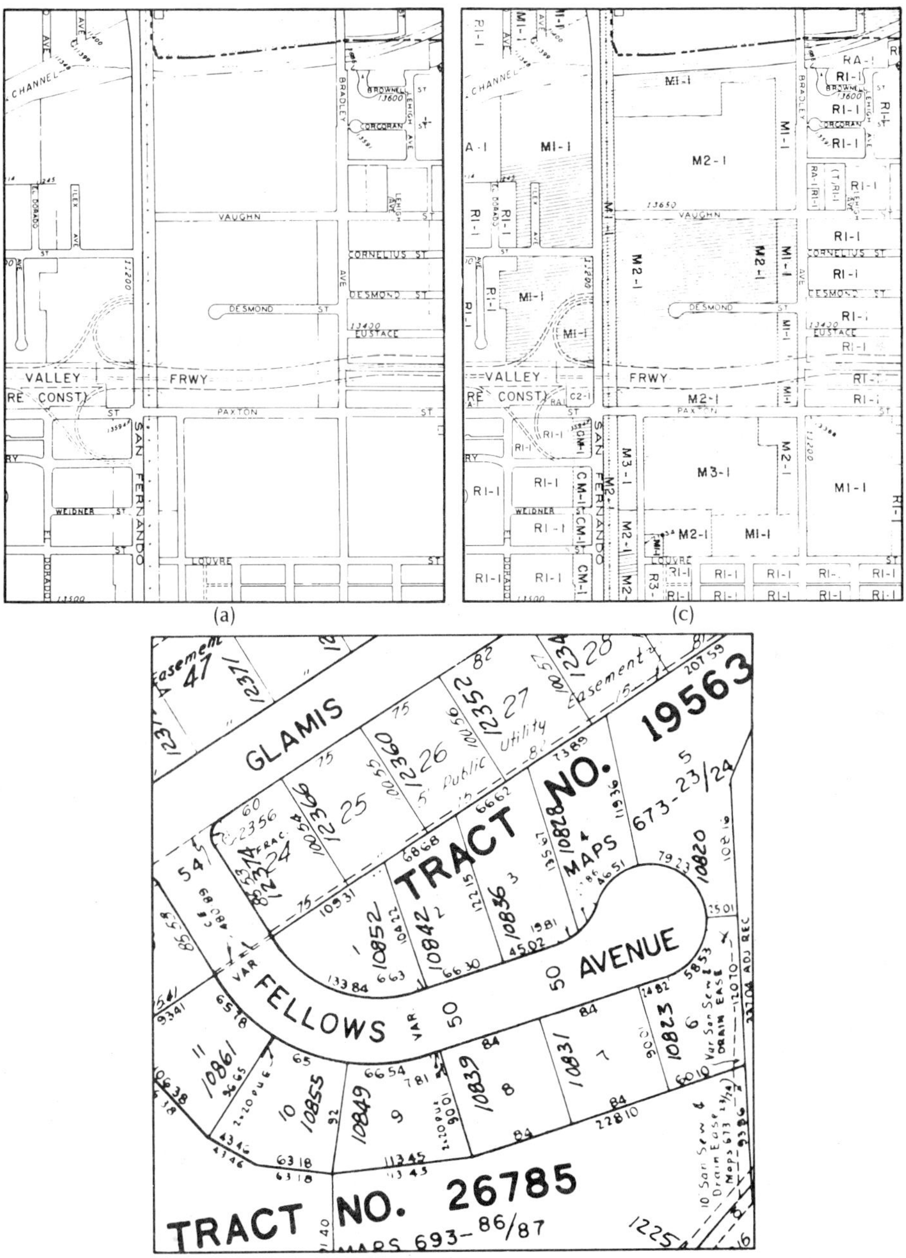

(a) (c)

(b)

Figure 4-4 Data Shown on Plat Maps

From *Civil Engineering for the Plant Engineer* by Max Schwartz. Copyright © 1972 by McGraw-Hill, Inc. Used with the permission of McGraw-Hill Book Company.

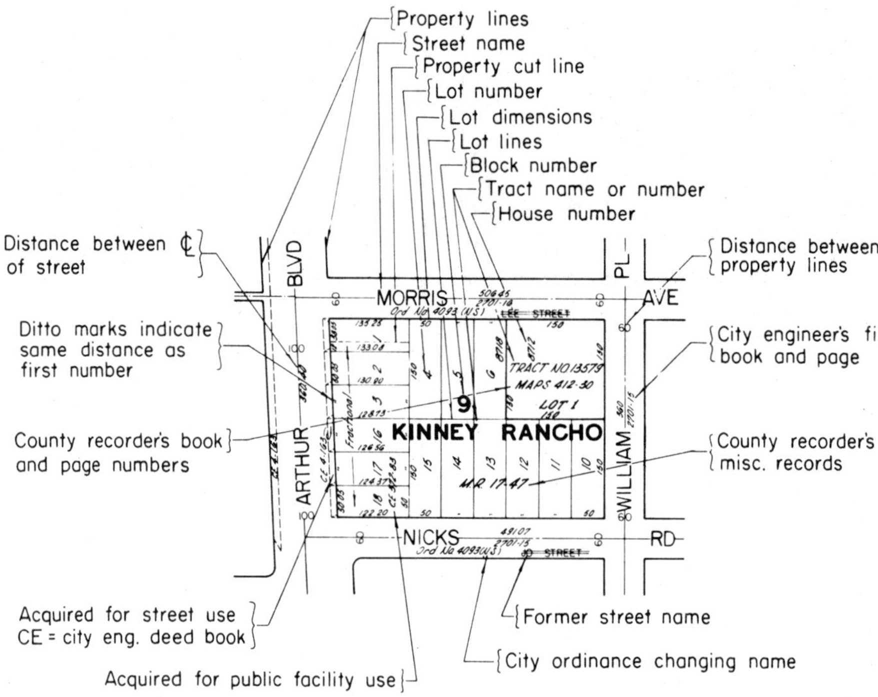

6. School district
7. Survey department

A flow diagram for approval of a typical land subdivision is shown at Figure 4-5.

§4.11 a. History of Land Subdivision

The United States government authorized on May 20, 1785, the United States rectangular system[27] for surveying public lands. This congressional authorization was known as the Land Ordinance of 1785. The surveying system established townships of six miles square. Each township was divided into 36 one-mile-square sections. Each

[27]United States Rectangular System of May 20, 1785. Data can be obtained from Manual of Instructions for the Survey of the Public lands of the United States, prepared and published by the Bureau of Land Management, US Dept of the Interior, Superintendent of Documents (1947).

Figure 4-5 The Subdivision Trail

Association of Land Surveyors of Los Angeles County, *The Subdivider's Guide* (1936)

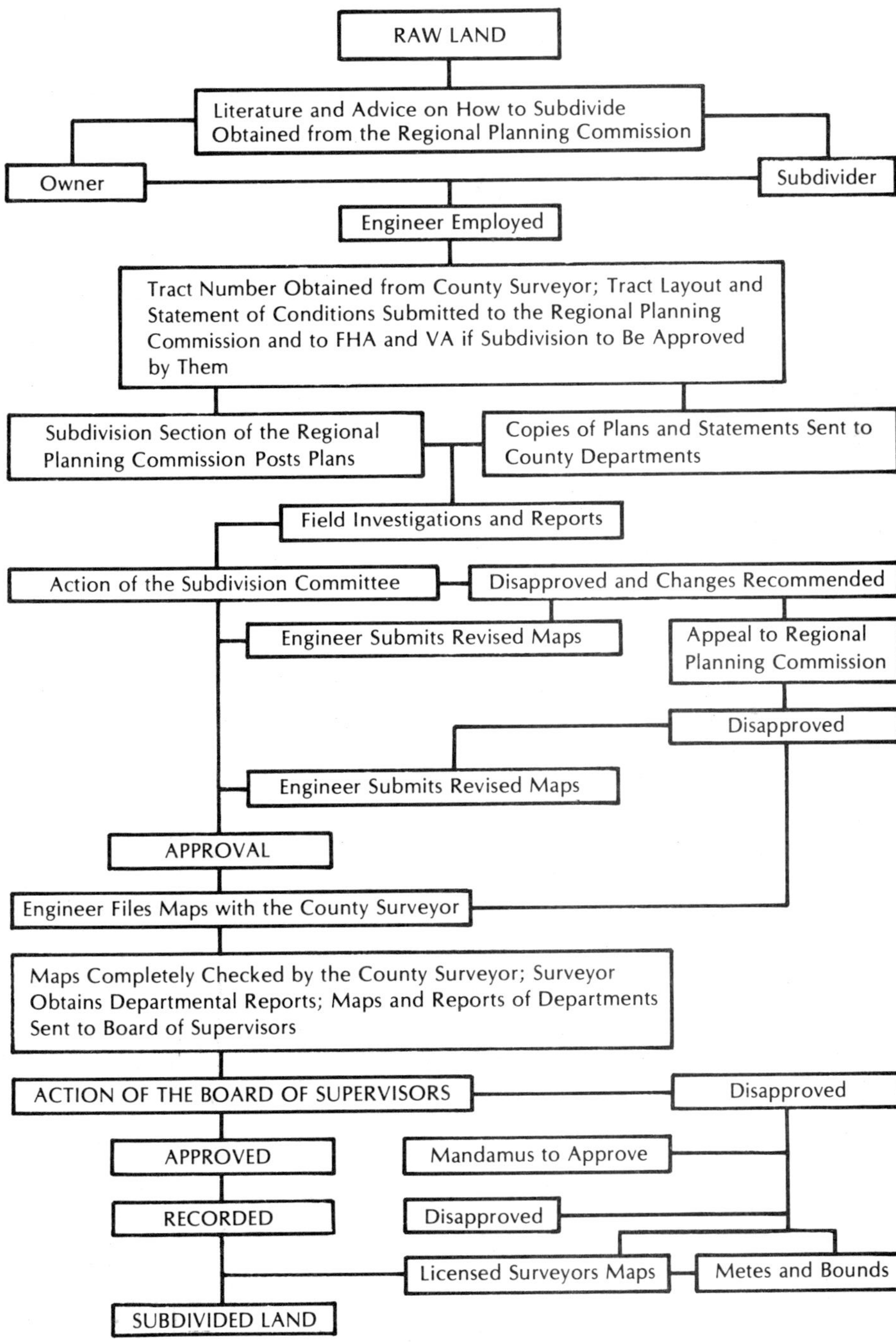

group of townships is measured with reference to a north-south axis called the *principal meridian*, and an east-west axis called the *base line*. The principal meridian and base line were established as reference lines throughout the United States. In California, for example, there are three principal meridians and base lines known, respectively, as the Humboldt meridian and base line in the north, Mt. Diablo meridian and base line in the center, and San Bernardino meridian and base line in the south. (See Figure 4-6.)

As people began purchasing smaller pieces of land, sections were further subdivided, most commonly into fractions of a section. This division was in direct proportion to the true area of the original section, nominally a mile square containing 640 acres. For example, when locating a 160-acre parcel within a specified section, such parcel may be designated as a quarter of that section in a particular geographical location (Figure 4-6—NW¼ of Section 14). Similarly, when locating a smaller parcel of 40 acres, it is necessary to go back even further in dividing the 160-acre quarter into another quarter at a designated location (Figure 4-6—NW¼ of NW¼ of Section 14). Finally, a particular section may be subdivided into a 5-acre parcel by designating the location of that parcel in relation to the total section. This subdivision can be illustrated by the following designation: N¼ of the NW¼ of the NW¼ of the NW¼ of Section 14.

When public land came to be held by private land developers, civil engineers were retained to make careful subdivisions of the land into commercial developments by preparing tract maps. The tract maps legally subdivided the land within their boundaries into blocks, lots, and streets. This division of property was recorded onto maps and permanently marked on the land by monuments set by surveyors.

§4.12 b. Procedure for Tract Subdivision

The procedure followed by the land developer in subdividing a property is complex, tending to follow the diagram shown in Figure 4-5.

Generally, the landowner or the subdivider will confer with the regional planning commission to reach agreement on the best use of the land in conformity with the master plan for the area. The tract is identified by a number obtained from the county surveyor. A civil engineer must then prepare a tentative tract map and statement of conditions to be submitted to and approved by the regional planning commission.

The planning commission distributes copies of the tentative tract map to other county or city departments, including the survey, road, building and safety, sanitation, fire, and health departments, as well as the real estate commission. All these departments review and comment on the proposed tract and return the map to the subdivider. If the basic plan is approved by all necessary departments, the civil engineer, in conjunction with the subdivider, completes the final tract maps,[28] street plans, water and sewage plans, and survey of the site. This work is then rechecked by each concerned department and submitted to the board of supervisors for final approval. On approval, the information is recorded and the land is considered legally subdivided.[29] The various

---

[28]**§4.10.**

[29]**§4.11.**

Figure 4-6 Government Survey System of Public Land

(a) starting points of land surveys in California, (b) standard parallels and guide meridians, (c) typical township subdivided into 36 sections, (d) typical section showing fractional sections

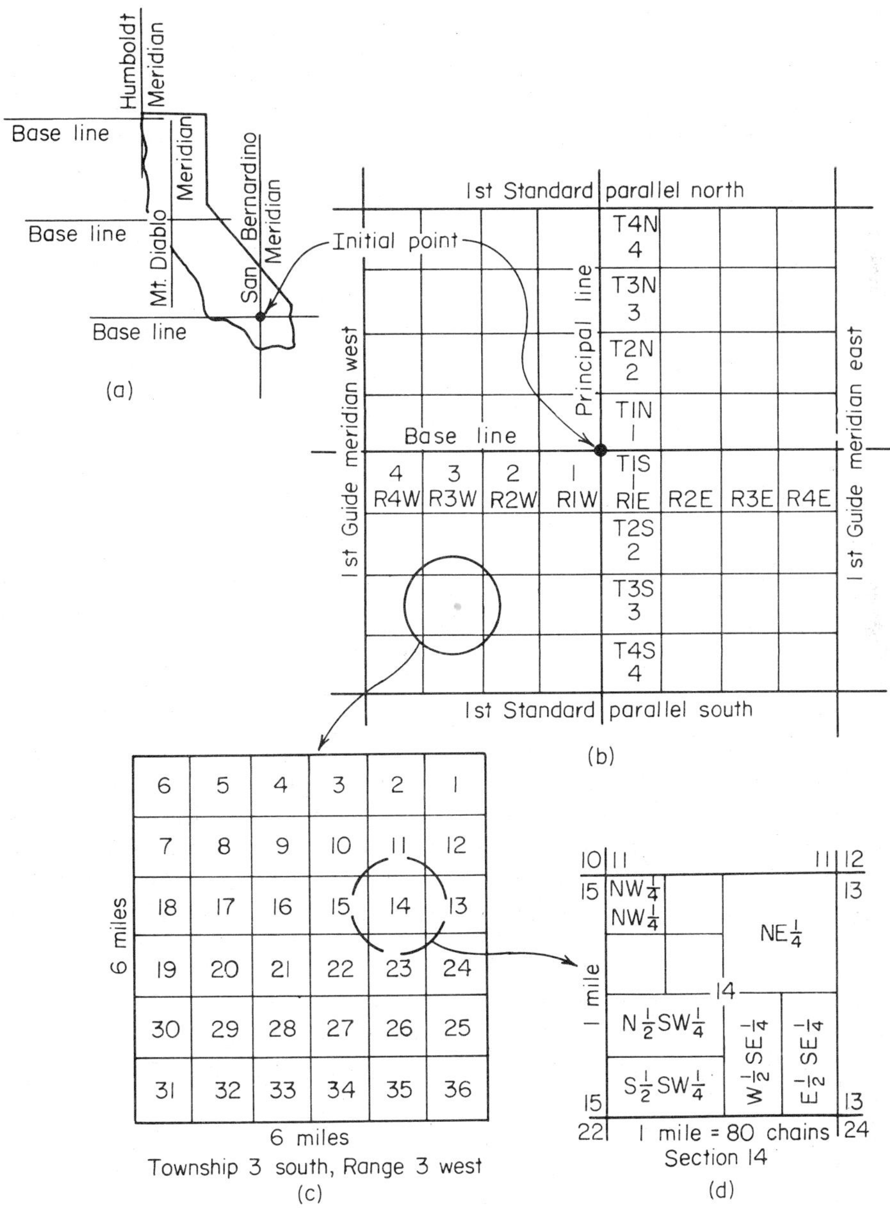

department names may vary with the community, but this process occurs similarly throughout the country.

Besides preparing the tract map, the subdivider may create another set of restrictions to protect and control the character of the tract. The declaration of restrictions is executed and recorded when the subdivision map is recorded. Such restrictions or covenants usually run for at least 25 years and provide for:

1. Regulation of land use
2. Architectural control
3. Side-yard and setback regulations
4. Regulation of lot sizes.
5. Restriction of temporary dwellings
6. Limitation of minimum cost and area of buildings
7. Reservation of utility easements
8. Suitable enforcement of provisions
9. Regulation of nuisance

§4.13 4. Calculations

The traditional method of preparing calculations is to use handwritten, verifiable computations. Sketches appear within the mathematical data where they help clarify the computations. Most engineers have an accepted format in which the computations are arranged. The symbols they use are also standardized. Most follow the American National Standards Abbreviations and Symbols, as shown in Appendix E of this book.

It is generally easy for one engineer to follow the work of another. Constants, variables, assumptions, and formulas are usually identified. Where unusual formulas are used, the references are given.

A basic fact to keep in mind about engineering calculations is that precision does not necessarily mean accuracy. Although one part of the calculations may be extended to three decimal points, another may be approximated only to the nearest whole number. Therefore, the accuracy of the overall answer is governed by the whole number.

§4.14 a. Conventional

Usually, calculations which are part of the contract documents are structural calculations. When a building's supporting elements exceed the limits of arbitrary (traditional or empirical) construction, a civil or structural engineer must design the structural components. This is done by computing the magnitude of forces to which that building's components may be subjected, and selecting the proper size, shape, and strength of members to resist those forces. Mathematical evidence verifying these selections is generally referred to as engineering calculations, or simply as calculations, or *calcs*.

In some cases, calculations prepared by a soils engineer are part of the contract documents. The ground on which a building rests is as important a structural component as the building superstructure itself. The soil must resist forces applied to it in order for a building to be stable and safe.

On larger or more complex buildings, calculations are required by the mechanical engineer for heating and cooling load, duct and pipe sizing, and energy use. Electrical engineers must submit calculations for feeder sizing and lighting intensity.

Engineering calculations are a very important item of evidence in making the determination whether faulty design or construction occurred. The trail of a building structure begins with the engineer's calculations and sketches, and these are followed by the drawings, specifications, and actual construction.

§4.15 b. Computer

Use of computers has changed many aspects of calculations. The credibility of a computerized calculation is based as much on the programmer's skill as on the designer's input. Many computer engineering programs are not only complex, but are also proprietary to the programmer. Checking a program is difficult. If a program is not confirmed, the answers cannot be accepted.

Programming for computer usage is an art which does not necessarily follow the accepted sequence of handwritten calculations. Each programmer can use an individual style, set of factors, and sequence of steps.

There are three primary types of computer facilities used in engineering offices:

1. The walk-in service bureau
2. A time-sharing computer terminal
3. An in-house computer

The walk-in service bureau is an installation located at some remote point, to which the input must be delivered and from which the output must be retrieved. This is essentially a computer utility, renting time on a job basis. This is the type of service in which the program is most likely to be proprietary, since such service bureaus have a series of *canned* programs.

The second type of facility is one in which input and output are made available within the design engineer's office by means of a computer terminal. The computer terminal is usually connected by telephone lines to the central computer, which may be in the same city or in another state. In the case of such a system, the programs may also be proprietary to the organization controlling the central computer.

The third type of facility is the in-house computer. The computer itself, as well as its input and output devices, is in the user's office. Depending on the size of the design organization and the workload, one or more programmers may be needed to work with the design engineers.

There may be major difficulties with the use of computers in engineering evidence. The programming, or software, must be comprehensible so that the answers can be used by the design engineer. There should be methods of verifying answers by conventional computation.

In using computer output as evidence, issues of credibility and confidence arise, since interpretation of computerized calculations by the expert relates directly to understanding of the program.

§4.16 c. Design Disputes Regarding Use of Computers

As use of computers[30] becomes more popular with design engineers, a new and complicating element has been added to the process of determining negligence in design.

Until recently, calculations were prepared according to a commonly understandable method. Engineering design manuals, handbooks, and governmental regulations included acceptable formulas and procedures. An engineer could read and follow another engineer's analysis or calculations as applied to a problem. Plan checkers at building departments could check calculations.

With use of computers and to achieve economy in design costs, proprietary programs for problem solution became popular. Since development of a program is an expensive task, performed by relatively few programmers, the designer may subcontract a major portion of the design work to a computer firm. Despite controlling input such as building configurations, loadings, and parameters, the designer relies on answers from the computer. It must be assumed that the programs are correct, and applicable to the designer's particular problem.

Few programmers design a program the same way. Each has an individual technique, but all programs are designed to reach a correct mathematical answer. Most computer manufacturers provide software or programs for specific engineering problems. Here, too, the designer must assume the program purchased is correct.

A problem could arise if an owner were to retain a second engineer to check the work of the original engineer, and each engineer were to obtain a different result by the use of a different computer program. When this is the case, one of the programs must be in error. A difficulty occurs in determining which of the programs is wrong, due to their proprietary nature.

Building departments will approve certain programs by testing the program results with a known design.

§4.17 d. Surveyors' Notes

Another important source of evidence in construction litigation is surveyors' field notes, sketches, and drawings. Surveyors' work includes the setting out of property lines, building lines, depth and location of underground drains and sewers, finish grades, and street improvements. Surveyors are also instrumental in keeping buildings and structures vertical and square. They check accuracy of the alignment of a steel structure before the building is closed up with walls and floors.

Throughout the surveyor's work, notes are maintained in field books. These notes are valuable in determining the accuracy of construction during its early phases.

Previous settlement, cracking, or other defects in adjoining property also can be recorded by survey. Public agencies and engineering contractors often mark with yellow paint all cracks in pavements and walls which exist before the beginning of construction.

---

[30] §4.15.

§4.18 D. Owner/Contractor Documents

The documents which pass between the owner and the contractor may vary from the most sophisticated and detailed construction contracts to the simple standard form contracts available at office supply stores. The former type would be similar to those recommended by the American Institute of Architects.[31] The latter is represented by the preprinted contracts published by certain stationery printers. Simple preprinted contracts between the subcontractor and general contractor also are available at many stationery stores.

Highly legalistic contract forms have been prepared by governmental agencies and large corporations. There are no limits to the numbers of conditions and refinements which can be added to construction contracts when the writer borrows from the various available contract documents.

§4.19 1. Construction Documents

A recommended authority on construction contracts is *Construction Industry Formbook*,[32] which is divided into three parts:

1. "The Construction Documents I Advocate Using When Representing the Prime Contractor"
2. "The Construction Documents I Advocate Using When Representing the Subcontractor"
3. "Documents to Secure and Obtain Payment"

The written contract sometimes can be far more explicit than the drawings and details. However, a written contract also can be vague, as when it contains phrases such as, "all work shall be done in a workmanlike manner."

Frequently, construction contracts or specifications will refer to other documents, such as governmental codes, industrial standards, or manufacturer's recommendations as being part of the contract or specifications. Examples of such phrases would be, "all plumbing shall be in accordance with the National Plumbing Code,"[33] or "all electrical work shall be in accordance with the National Electrical Code."[34] Some construction documents may incorporate by reference as many as 30 different codes covering every conceivable discipline.

Some designers of buildings or industrial facilities will refer generally to "all relevant published codes and standards" rather than preparing detailed designs or material specifications as part of their work. Such phrases make supervision or inspection of a job difficult, since the job superintendent may not be familiar with the contents of all these codes. In addition, the building department inspectors may not necessarily

---

[31]**App A.**

[32]Robert F. Cushman, Michael S. Simon & McNeil Stokes, Construction Industry Formbook (Shepard's/McGraw-Hill, Colorado Springs, Colo, 1979).

[33]**§4.39.**

[34]**§4.40.**

enforce every provision of the various codes specified. This results in a vacuum in which the contractors, subcontractors, and materialmen are free to furnish any material and use any method of construction. Contractors and subcontractors do not usually spend the time necessary to research all the codes referred to in the plans and specifications.

The meaning of the word *boilerplate*[35] is important in the interpretation of construction documents. Sometimes, frequent reference to standard codes and regulations is a self-protection device on the part of the designer who has insufficient time or knowledge to prepare plans and specifications adequate for the job. It is obvious in such cases that the designer wishes to avoid making design decisions and wants to transfer that burden onto the contractor. In other cases, a designer may merely copy phrases from previously drawn plans without having personally determined whether these phrases actually apply to the particular job.

Another consideration is that most construction documents are prepared by engineering professionals rather than by lawyers. Provisions may be included to protect the designer and the owner. However, such provisions may be legally vague, or not applicable.

This whole situation is particularly likely to arise when the fee is not adequate to allow sufficient study and preparation of plans and specifications. It is also common when the designer is retained by the builder, who demands freedom in selection of material and workmanship. It can occur when the owner of the project is interested merely in a quick sale. In such a case, it is mutually understood among the designer, owner, and builder that the plans and specifications are only a guide to the subcontractors, a document necessary in order to obtain a building permit and a construction loan. Unfortunately, parties to a project often show little concern for the contents of construction documents. It is only when litigation commences that the parties become aware of the significance of those printed words and plans for purposes of establishing liability.

§4.20 a. Construction Contracts

Following is a check list for documentary evidence that may be useful in litigation in which a general contractor is a party:

1. Plans and specifications contract
   a. American Institute of Architects (AIA)[36] Document A101—standard form, stipulated sum agreement between owner and contractor
   b. American Institute of Architects (AIA) Document A201—standard form, general conditions
2. Construction management contracts
   a. Associated General Contractors of America, Inc. (AGC)[37] Document No. 8—standard form of agreement between owner and construction manager

---

[35] **§3.17.**

[36] 1785 Massachusetts Avenue, NW, Washington, DC 20036.

[37] 1957 E St, NW, Washington, DC 20006.

   b. Associated General Contractors (AGC) Document Nos. 8a and 8b—amendment to owner-construction manager agreement, guaranteed maximum price
3. Turnkey and design-build contracts
   a. Associated General Contractors (AGC) Document Nos. 6 and 6a—Preliminary design-build agreement between owner and contractor
4. Subcontractors and suppliers
   a. Sub-bid proposals
   b. Subcontract agreements
   c. Subcontractor's application for payment, waivers, releases, and discharges
5. Contractor's daily reports
6. Joint venture documents

Next is a check list for documentary evidence that may be useful in litigation involving the subcontractor:

1. Subcontractors and general contractors
   a. Subcontractors' proposals
   b. Subcontract AIA Document A401—authorization for extra or changed work
2. Suppliers
   a. Purchase orders
3. Joint venture agreements

The last check list deals with documents recommended for use as evidence when securing or obtaining payment:

1. Assignments, joint checks, and guarantees
   a. Assignment
   b. Notice of assignment
   c. Agreement by general contractor to issue check to joint order of subcontractor and supplier of labor and/or materials to subcontractor
   d. Agreement by owner to issue check to joint order of general contractor and supplier of labor and/or materials to general contractor
   e. Guarantee of payment to building materials supplier
   f. Bank guarantees
2. Mechanics' liens
3. Bonds

§4.21 b. Addenda and Change Orders

Changes in construction contracts can be implemented by addenda, bulletins, or change orders. Generally, bulletins are issued in numerical sequence and are channeled to the various parties involved in the project. Bulletins may be initiated by the owner, contractor, or architect/engineer. Before such bulletins can be made into change orders, all parties must agree to the extra cost, credit, extension of time, and reasons for the change. On computer-controlled critical path method scheduling, the impact of change orders continually reflects revisions in the critical path[38] of the project.

Change orders are as vital an item of evidence as the original construction documents.

§4.22 2. Suggested Check List for Construction Documents

The list which follows encompasses a whole range of useful documents:

1. Plans[39] (architectural, civil, structural, mechanical, and electrical)
   a. Preliminary plans
   b. Plan check corrections
2. Specifications[40]
   a. Preliminary specifications
3. Contracts and agreements[41]
   a. Contract between owner and architect/engineer
   b. Contract between architect and consultants
   c. Construction contracts[42]
   d. Subcontract agreements
4. Contractor's Bid or Proposal
   a. Subcontractor's proposal
5. Permits
   a. Building permit application
   b. Building, grading, plumbing, electrical, sewer, mechanical, etc.
6. Addenda[43]
   a. Bulletins[44]
   b. Change orders[45]
   c. Authorizations for extra work
7. Daily reports
   a. Contractor's

---

[38] **§4.25.**

[39] **§4.04.**

[40] **§§3.17, 4.09.**

[41] **§4.18.**

[42] **§4.20.**

[43] **§4.21.**

[44] *Id.*

[45] *Id.*

   b. Clerk of the works'
   c. Field engineer's
   d. Inspector's
8. Payment certificates
   a. Job estimates
   b. Purchase orders
   c. Bonds (payment, performance)
   d. Receipts of building materials
9. Warranties of equipment
10. Drawings
   a. Shop[46]
   b. Certified[47]
11. Reports
   a. Material testing (concrete, steel, soil compaction)
   b. Steel mill testing
   c. Concrete mix
   d. Pile driving
   e. Weather records
12. Engineer's calculations[48]
13. Surveyor's plats
14. Construction schedule
   a. Bar[49]
   b. Charts
   c. Critical path method[50]
15. Notice of completion
16. Waivers, releases, and discharge forms
17. Certificate of occupancy
18. Job inspection card

E. Construction Chronology

§4.23 1. Construction Schedules

Litigation where the issues are delayed completion, extended overhead, and loss of productivity will require a chronology of the job from beginning to end.

---

[46]§§4.03, 4.06.
[47]§§3.17, 4.07-.08.
[48]§§4.14-.15.
[49]§4.24.
[50]§4.25.

Construction scheduling is usually the responsibility of the contractor, although the owner approves the final completion target date. Job schedule charts indicate the manner in which the contractor and subcontractor will use their work force as well as availability of equipment and materials. One purpose of a schedule is to facilitate efficient performance of the work outlined in the plans and specifications. Another purpose of scheduling is to insure that materials and labor necessary to complete a particular job are at the site when required. Almost every phase of a project depends on the completion of other phases of work.

Scheduling a project can only be accomplished with an understanding of all the individual units of work required. Most construction projects include the following major activities:

1. Excavation or earthwork
2. Foundations
3. Erection of structural frames
4. Installation of exterior walls
5. Roofing
6. Electrical
7. Mechanical
8. Finishing of interiors

Construction schedules can be organized according to one of the following methods:

1. Bar chart[51]
2. Progressive chart
3. Critical path method[52]

§4.24 a. Bar Chart

A *bar chart* is made up of rows and columns. Each horizontal row stands for a separate construction activity. The vertical columns indicate dates and time periods (days, weeks, or months). The expected duration of each activity is shown in its respective row or column. This is accomplished by shading the particular row to form a bar. The length of the bar corresponds to the projected time from start to completion of activity.

§4.25 b. Critical Path Method

A common cause of construction litigation is delay in completion which results in financial damages to both the owner and the contractor. A tool becoming more popular

---

[51] **§4.24.**

[52] **§4.25.**

to both the plaintiff and defendant is the CPM, or *critical path method*, and the PERT, or *progress evaluation review technique*.[53]

These systems were devised to maintain an optimum construction schedule, but they are equally useful to illustrate how changes or delays on any specific activity can cause an overall delay in the project. A brief description of a CPM chart is presented in Figures 4-7 and 4-8.

The encircled letter represents a specific element of an operation, such as the completion of foundation or final testing of an elevator. The number between the circled tasks or the lines or arrows indicates the estimated time in days or weeks to complete each unit of operation. Another way of identifying the symbols is to refer to the circles, or nodes, as *events* and the lines, or arrows, as *activities*.

By adding the total of all elapsed time of activities from event A to event N along all possible paths, the longest path is described as the *critical path*, hence the term, *critical path method*. Any delay on this specific path will delay the entire project. Changes or delays on other paths may not cause an overall delay in the project if the delay does not exceed the total slack time. If it does exceed that total, a new critical path may have been created.

On large, complex jobs, the entire CPM network is programmed into a computer. Progress of the job is checked periodically and changes are automatically computed, giving a revised completion date, if needed. In this manner, any change or delay can be identified and it can be determined if such change will cause a delay in the overall schedule.

When a job goes beyond its scheduled completion time, the contractor suffers what is called *extended overhead*,[54] general job and main office overhead expenses that are in addition to the original estimate. These include maintenance of a field office, personnel, vehicles, etc.

The printout of the CPM computer has been used in evidence in disputes of this type.

§4.26 2. Inspection Reports and Material Records

Most large construction projects have a number of persons inspecting or supervising phases of work. Daily and weekly reports are made by superintendents, field engineers, clerks of the works, building department inspectors, deputy inspectors, project architects, and consulting engineers.

There are also delivery tickets on concrete, steel, and other building materials. These delivery tickets are supported, in turn, by the material manufacturer's analysis and test results. Examples are concrete mixes, steel mill tests, and chemical analysis for each run or batch of building materials. Lumber is grade-inspected and marked. Plasterboards carry a coded production number identifying the day and shift of manufacture. By means of such records, it is possible to trace back a particular building material to its source.

---

[53]PERT is primarily a method of estimating, research and development programs based on *optimistic*, *pessimistic*, and *most likely* dates of completion. It involves a probability approach.

[54]**§4.66.**

Figure 4-7 Simplified Network Diagram of a Critical Path Method

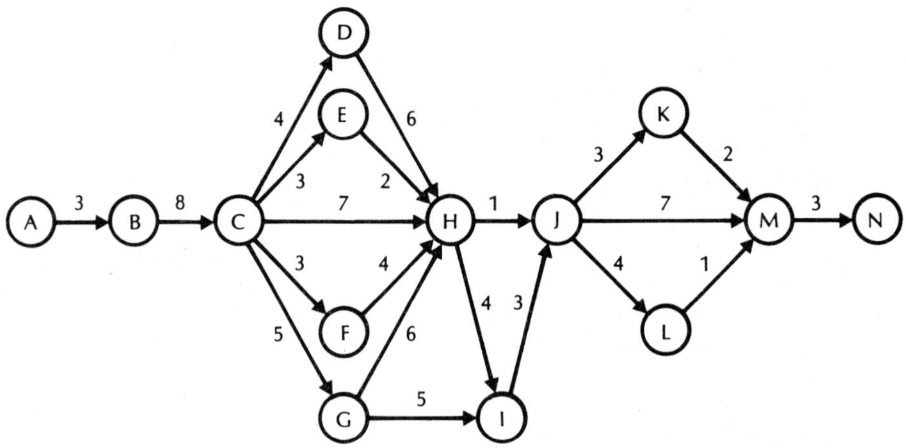

Circled letters represent events of completion of activity. Numbers between circles are estimated time periods for the completion of the activities.

Figure 4-8 Critical Path Method Network Showing Typical Activities

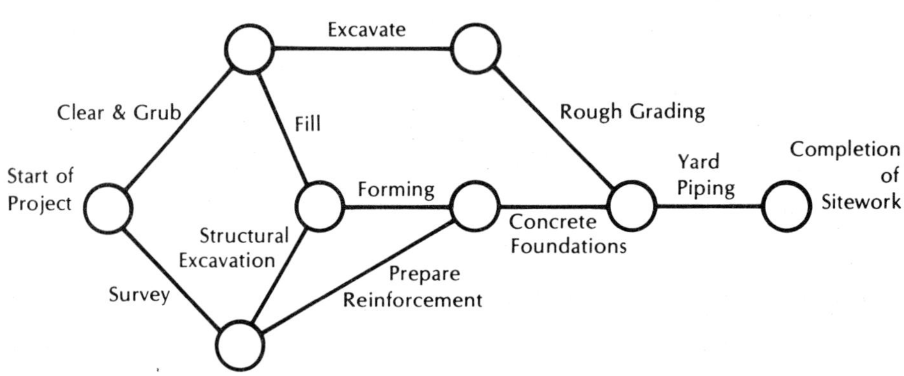

§4.27 F. Cast of Characters

In any construction dispute, the attorney should identify and understand the roles of the various parties. The relationships among members of the cast of characters on construction projects are in a continuous state of change. In addition, the parties often work as antagonists rather than as a team.

The main characters are:

1. owner
2. architect/engineer
3. consulting engineers
4. contractor
5. subcontractors
6. sub-subcontractors
7. material and equipment suppliers

In addition, some of those listed have representatives, such as the clerk of the works (who represents the architect), field engineer (who represents the consulting engineers), inspectors (who represent the building department), quality control personnel, timekeepers, and laboratory technicians.

Removed from the actual work, but involved in design and construction, is another class of persons. These include estimators, schedulers, purchasing agents, draftspersons, specifications writers, computer programmers, plan checkers, and sales representatives who handle the various materials and equipment used on the job.

§4.28 1. Organization Charts

The following sections discuss simplified organizational charts of typical construction projects. These are distinguished by different relationships of the architect/engineer to the other parties of a construction project.

Case 1—architect/engineer retained by owner

Case 2—architect/engineer retained by contractor or contractor with in-house design capability

Case 3—owner with in-house architect/engineer

Case 4—owner/builder with in-house architect/engineer

§4.29 a. Architect/Engineer Retained by Owner

This is the classic case in which the architect/engineer represents the owner and is also the judge of all conflicts between the owner and the builder regarding the contract documents. In such a case, the contract documents become very important and are rigorously enforced by the architect/engineer. See Figure 4-9.

§4.30 b. Architect/Engineer Retained by Contractor

The situation illustrated in Figure 4-10 is that of a construction company with an in-house capability for design. The usual job of such a company is the so-called *turn-key contract.* In this case, the builder is responsible not only for construction, but also for design. The builder's contract with the owner is usually based on preliminary design and specifications.

Figure 4-9 Commercial Project Classic Organization

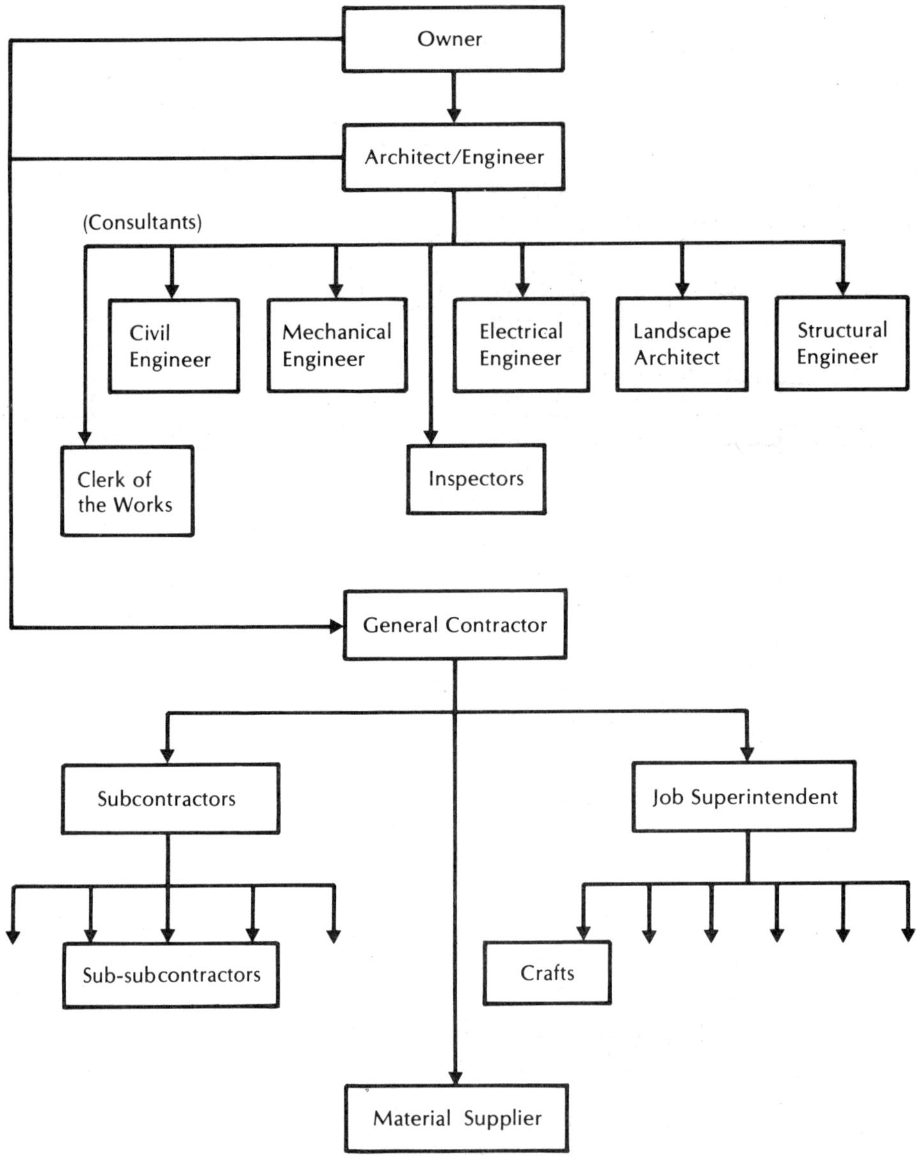

A variation of this situation occurs when a builder retains an architect/engineer but remains responsible to the owner for the design. The design firm would have relatively little control over the builder since the designer would be employed by the builder. In addition, the plans and specifications would be likely to be only a guide, not strictly enforced.

Generally, in this type of case, the plans and specification[55] use generic terms rather than specific brand names. This allows the contractor more freedom in selection of materials.

§4.31 c. Owner with In-House Architect/Engineer

In the case depicted in Figure 4-11, the owner is a large industrial firm with an in-house design capability. The owner may also be a developer of a housing tract or an industrial park.

Here the designer has the strongest influence over the builder because it is the owner who is the designer. In this situation the contract documents would be rigorously enforced.

§4.32 d. Owner/Builder with In-House Architect/ Engineer

The situation represented in Figure 4-12 will cover the case where a large industrial corporation may have an in-house capability for design, contract administration, and supervision. Another example may be a developer who designs and constructs for lease or sale portions of the completed project, such as housing developments or industrial parks.

In this case, the builder has maximum flexibility since all parties are part of the same company. In addition, the plans and specifications are only a guide and are loosely enforced.

§4.33 2. Prime Professional

The prime professional may be an architect or an engineer, depending on the type of project. On building facilities for human occupancy, the architect is normally the prime professional. On fixed works, industrial complexes, and projects where human shelter is negligible, the prime professional is normally the engineer. The term *architect/engineer* identifies the prime professional.

The prime professional is the designer of the plans and specifications. This person usually does not provide field supervision of the contract work, but is the agent for the owner and serves as the liaison between the owner and the contractor.

Due to the complexity of modern-day construction, engineering specialists from various disciplines are often retained by the prime professional as consultants. The architect/engineer coordinates the efforts of all the consultants to come up with a single set of plans and specifications.

Contacts between the engineering specialists and the owner or contractor are usually

[55] §3.17.

Figure 4-10 Turnkey Job

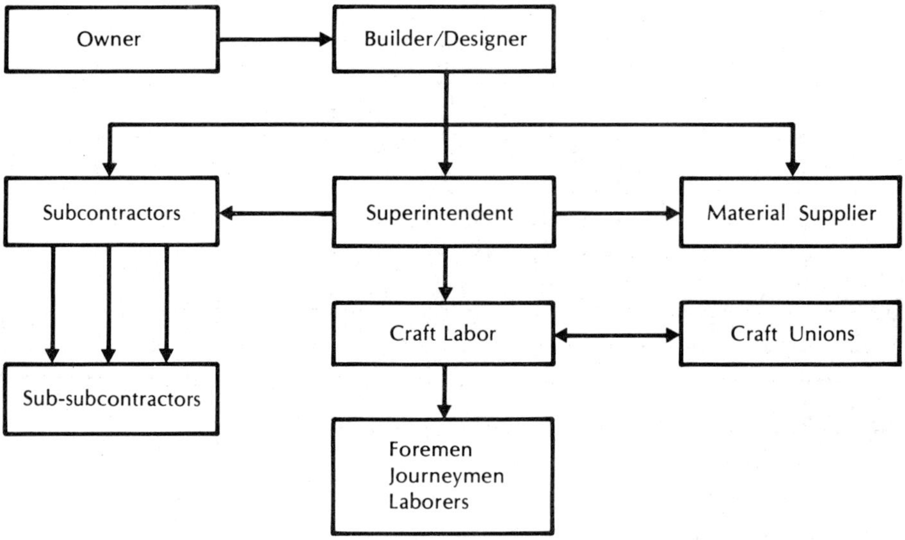

Figure 4-11 Owner with In-House Design Capabilities

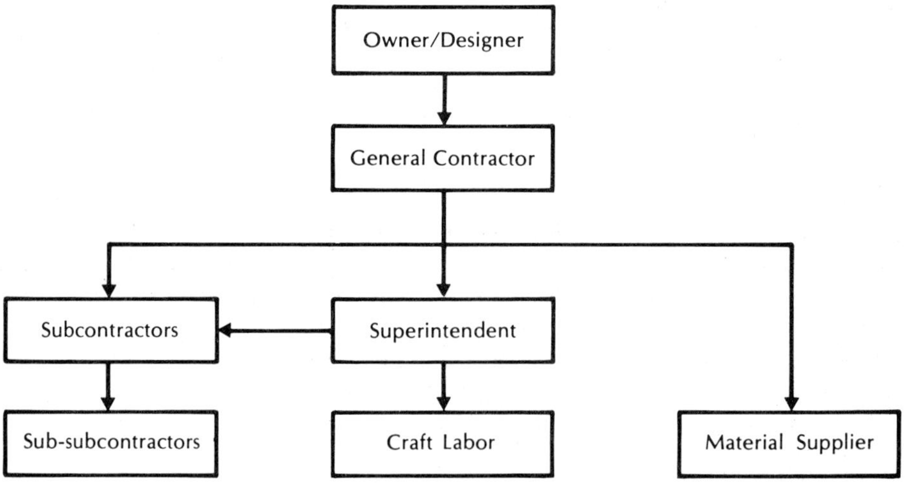

Figure 4-12 Owner/Builder with In-House Design Capabilities

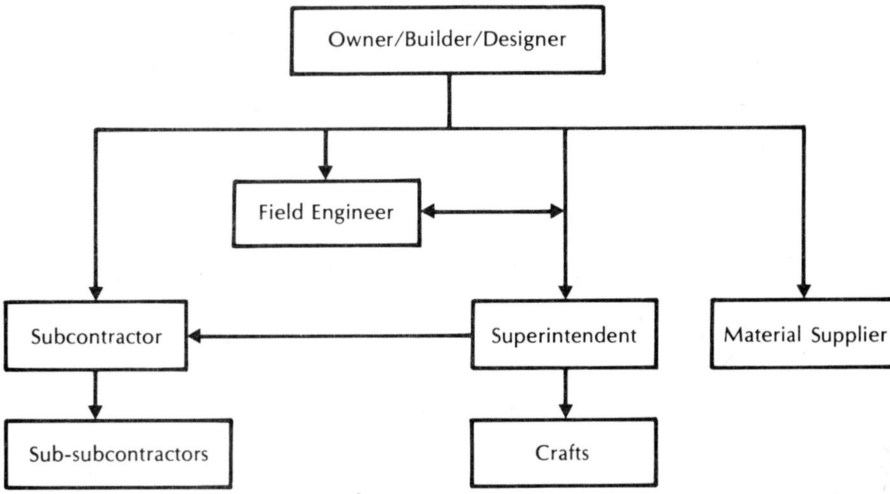

through the prime professional. In some architectural/engineering offices, the various engineering specialists are members of the same firm. However, they are more often independent professional engineers, practicing as consulting engineers in their particular specialties.

Figure 4-13 is a typical organization chart for a hospital construction project indicating the interrelationships between the parties.

§4.34 3. Nonprime Professionals

When the prime professional is an architect, the disciplines of structural, mechanical, and electrical engineering are beyond the prime professional's expertise. Consequently, the architect resorts to use of consultants. These consultants are professional engineers, and are referred to as *nonprime professionals* for the project.

On most commercial building projects, nonprime professionals include the following engineers:

1. Civil engineers[56]
2. Structural engineers[57]
3. Electrical engineers[58]

---

[56]§2.03.
[57]§2.05.
[58]§2.08.

Figure 4-13 Typical Organization Chart

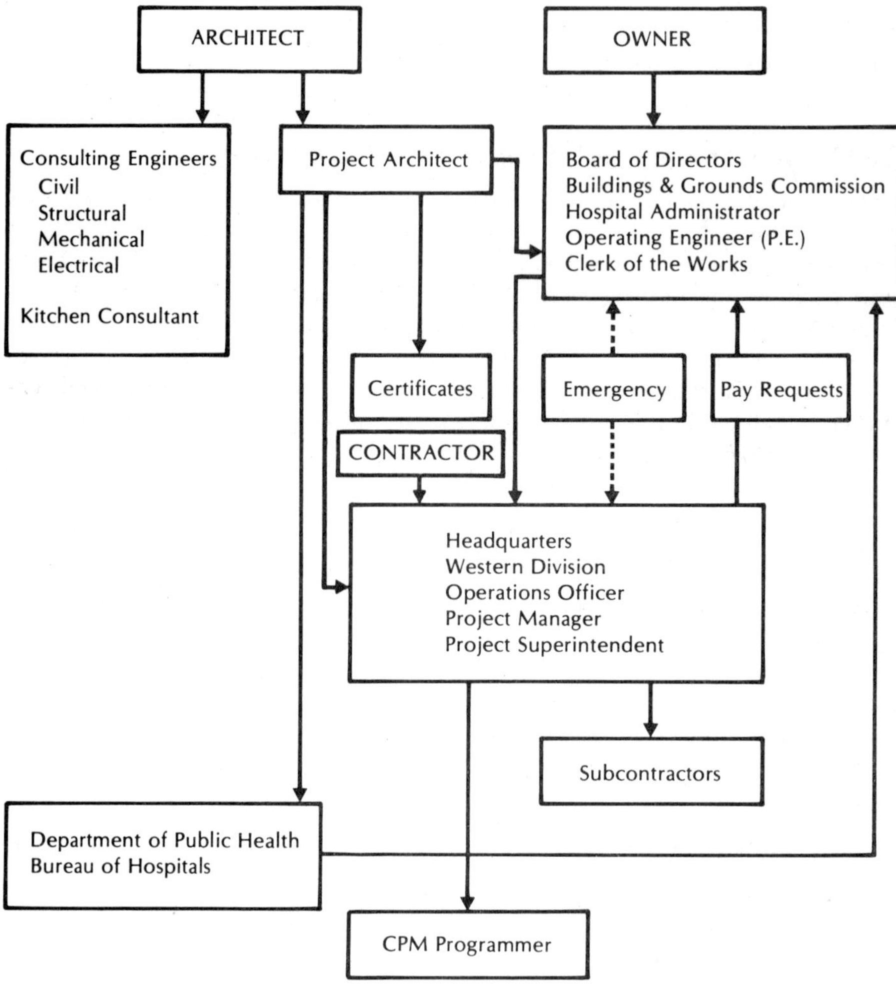

4. Mechanical engineers[59]
5. Soils engineers[60]

In some cases, other specialists, not considered professional engineers, are retained as consultants. These may include:

---

[59] **§2.07.**
[60] **§2.04.**

1. Interior decorators
2. Landscape architects
3. Scheduling programmers
4. Specifications writers

§4.35 4. General Contractor or Prime Contractor

The general contractor converts plans and specifications to physical reality. In the past, the general contractor performed virtually all of the work with a personal labor force. However, with the complexity of today's modern construction, the general contractor has become a conglomerate of subcontractors, material suppliers, union affiliations, accountants, engineers, technicians, and estimators.

Today, the general contractor may do all or some part of the work using hired craftsworkers. In some cases only a superintendent is employed by the general contractor and all work is done by subcontractors;[61] the general contractor is said to be *brokering* or *subbing out* the job.

The main responsibilities of the general contractor are: planning and execution of a sequence of work; selection of subcontractors; coordination of subcontractors' work with the general contractor's work forces; providing centralized authority; maintenance of the quality of work.

Where the general contractor is not affiliated with the designer, the basis of the contract is the plans and specifications.

§4.36 5. Subcontractors and Sub-Subcontractors

Today, most work on a job is done by subcontractors and sub-subcontractors. Usually, only overall administration is performed by the general contractor.

Subcontractors have become the main contracting force because of their ability to specialize and keep the work force and equipment constantly employed. There are subcontractors for almost every phase of construction. They are usually required to be licensed, and are limited by statute to practice in a particular specialty. These specialty subcontractors are described in the subsections which follow.

Electric Contractors

The electric contractor is a subcontractor within the general scheme of construction. This specialty involves placing, installing, erecting, and connecting electric wire, fixtures, applicances, or any apparatus which generates, transforms, or utilizes electrical energy.

Plumbing Contractors

This subcontractor's expertise includes the creating and maintenance of sanitary conditions in buildings and structures where humans or animals live. This involves

---

[61] §4.36.

the assembling and supplying of a safe and ample source of water for drinking, cooking, bathing, washing, and cleaning. In addition, the subcontractor's responsibilities include construction of devices for receiving and removing fluid and semifluid organic waste and other impurities incidental to the occupation of the premises.

Painting Contractors

The painting subcontractor is responsible for preparing surfaces for application of foreign materials. This is the specialist who ultimately applies such materials as paints, oils, turpentines, driers, thinners, varnishes, shellacs, stains, fillers, and waxes.

Plastering Contractors

The specialty of the plastering subcontractor involves the coating of surfaces with a mixture of sand, gypsum plaster, and quicklime or sand, cement, and water.

Roofing Contractors

The roofing subcontractor is in charge of examining surfaces, such as roofs, and applying to them materials necessary for sealing, waterproofing, and weatherproofing in order to prevent, hold, and stop water from penetrating the roof surface. This subcontractor must be knowledgeable about the methods of using asphaltum, pitch, tar, felt, flax, shingles, tiles, or slate in surfacing a roof.

Tile Contractors

The specialty of this subcontractor is the preparation and surfacing of structures with ceramic, semivitreous and other tile work, in cases in which the tile will be adhered by suction or adhesives.

Cement and Concrete Contractors

The cement subcontractor specializes in batching and mixing aggregates of sand, gravel, crushed rock, cement, and water. This subcontractor mixes these materials in a specified manner and mass.

Masonry Contractors

The masonry subcontractor is certified in selecting, cutting, and laying brick, as well as baked clay and stone products. This subcontractor may precast blocks and use structural glass bricks laid with or without mortar.

Wood Flooring Contractors

The wood flooring subcontractor is licensed to select, cut, lay, finish, and repair wood floors in structures previously built or presently under construction. This subcontractor's work includes scraping, sanding, filling, staining, shellacking, and waxing wood floors.

Sheet Metal Contractors

The sheet metal subcontractor cuts, shapes, fabricates, and installs sheet-metal such as cornices, flashings, gutters, leaders, rainwater downspouts, kitchen equipment, patented chimneys, and metal flues.

Lathing Contractors

The lathing subcontractor examines surfaces and specifies, selects, and applies wood and metal lath to provide key or suction bases for support of plaster coatings. In addition, this subcontractor installs channel ironwork to support metal or other fireproof lathwork for solid plaster partitions.

Cabinet and Millwork Contractors

This specialist is skilled in cutting, surfacing, joining, sticking, glueing, and framing wood and wood products for cabinets, cases, sashes, doors, trims, and nonbearing partitions.

Excavating, Grading, Trenching, Paving, and Surfacing Contractors

This subcontractor uses hand and power tools and machines to dig, move, and place earth materials, and is responsible for all excavation work, grading, trenching, tunneling, and backfilling operations. In addition, this subcontractor is authorized to use explosives and may mix, fabricate, and place pavement and surfacing consisting of graded mineral aggregates.

Warm-Air Heating, Ventilating, and Air Conditioning Contractors

This specialty subcontractor installs warm-air heating systems and appliances, ducts, registers, and flues with or without air filter, and humidity and thermostatic controls. This subcontractor also installs ventilating and air conditioning systems.

Landscaping Contractors

The landscaping subcontractor grades and prepares plots and areas of land for architectural horticulture, and is responsible for decorative treatment, arrangement, planting, and maintenance of gardens, lawns, shrubs, bushes, and trees. This subcontractor may construct pools, tanks, fountains, pavilions, fences, walks, drains, and sprinkler systems. The landscaping subcontractor usually carries out work in conformity with agreed landscaping project specifications.

Building, Moving, and Wrecking Contractors

The skill of such a subcontractor is to raise, crib, underpin, and move buildings so that alterations, additions, and new structures may be built under the existing portions of such structures. The functions of this subcontractor may also include wrecking and demolition of buildings and structures.

Boiler, Hot-Water Heating, and Steam Fitting Contractors

This subcontractor installs fire-tube and water-tube power boilers and low pressure boilers, including steam fitting and piping, hot-water piping, valves, gauges, pumps, radiators, convectors, chimney flues, and heat insulation.

Elevator Installation Contractors

The subcontractor must be skilled in the fabrication, erection, and installation of elevators, sheave beams, motors, sheaves, wire ropes, guides, cabs, counterweights, doors, automatic and manual controls signal systems, and all other apparatus pertinent to safe and efficient installation and operation of hydraulic and manually operated elevators.

Reinforcing Steel Contractors

The specialty of this subcontractor is fabrication and placing of steel reinforcing bars which may be used to reinforce concrete buildings and structures.

Structural Steel Contractors

As distinguished from the reinforcing steel subcontractor, this subcontractor erects the steel shapes and plates that are used as members for structures. This includes bolting, welding, and rigging for erection of structural steel work.

G. Governing Codes

§4.37 1. Building Codes

Construction in most urban areas and in some rural areas of the United States is governed by building and safety codes. The major building codes are the Uniform Building Code, the Southern Building Code, and the Basic Building Code. Looked at geographically: the Uniform Building Code is recognized in the western and midwestern states; the Southern Building Code is a guide for construction in the southern states; and the Basic Building Code is the code for the eastern and central states.

In addition to these major building codes, there are numerous state, county, and city building and safety codes. These are usually modeled after one of the major codes, with special conditions added to suit local needs. The codes are written by committees of experts on engineering, construction, fire prevention, safety, and building materials. Their purpose is to establish minimum standards to safeguard life, property, and the public welfare by regulating design, construction, quality of materials, use and occupancy, location, and maintenance of buildings and structures.[62]

The codes apply not only to new construction, but also to alteration, moving, demolition, repair, and use of buildings, and are in a continuous state of change. When there are practical difficulties in implementing the code provisions, there may be variance granted in individual cases or code modification. The use of new materials is a common reason for changes in the code.

Although the building departments have to inspect plans, approve applications for construction, issue permits, and inspect and approve construction, there are limits to the liability of the building department. An excerpt from the Uniform Building Code says the following about liability:

> The building official or his authorized representative charged with the enforcement of this code, acting in good faith and without malice in discharge of his duties, shall not thereby render himself personally liable for any damage that

[62] §10.38.

> may accrue to persons or property as result of any act or by reason of any act or omission in the discharge of his duties. Any suit brought against the building official or employee because of such act or omission performed by him in the enforcement of any provision of this code shall be defended by legal counsel provided by this jurisdiction until final termination of such proceedings.
>
> This code shall not be construed to relieve from or lessen the responsibility of any person owning, operating or controlling a building or structure for any damages to persons or property caused by defects, nor shall the code enforcement agency or its parent jurisdiction be held as assuming any such liability by reason of the inspections authorized by this code or any certificates of inspection issued under this code.

In essence, the above statement implies that conformity with the code is the responsibility of the designer and the builder. Approval of the plans and construction does not mean that the code has been complied with.

The authors of the three major codes are:

1. Uniform Building Code: International Conference of Building Officials, 5360 South Workman Mill Road, Whittier, CA 90601
2. BOCA Basic Building Code: Building Officials & Code Administrators International, Inc., 1313 East 60th Street, Chicago, IL 60637
3. Southern Building Code: Southern Building Code Congress International, Inc., 900 Montclair Road, Birmingham, AL 35213

A typical building code generally includes the following provisions:

1. Administrative
   a. Title, scope, and general application
   b. Organization and enforcement
   c. Permits and inspection
2. Definitions and abbreviations
3. Requirements based on occupancy
   a. Classification by use or occupancy
   b. General requirements for all occupancies
   c. Requirements for assembly buildings
   d. Requirements for commercial buildings and industrial buildings
   e. Requirements for educational buildings
   f. Requirements for hazardous buildings
   g. Requirements for hospitals
   h. Requirements for dwellings
4. Requirements based on types of construction
   a. Classification of all buildings by types of construction
5. Engineering regulations—quality and design of materials of construction
   a. General design requirements

   b. Masonry construction
   c. Wood construction
   d. Concrete construction
   e. Steel construction
6. Detailed regulations
   a. Excavation, foundations, and retaining walls
   b. Veneer
   c. Roof construction and covering
   d. Stairs, exits, and occupant loads
   e. Skylights
   f. Fire extinguishing systems
7. Fire resistance standards for fire protection
8. Regulations for use of public streets and projections over public property

§4.38 2. Zoning Codes

The purpose of zoning codes, also known as planning codes, is to provide a general scheme for development of a community. Consideration is given to such elements as:

1. Land use, such as industrial, commercial and residential
2. Density of buildings and populations
3. Circulation, including major thoroughfares and streets
4. Service systems, such as utilities and fire protection

These codes put various uses of land into general groups, such as agricultural, residential, commercial, and industrial. In addition, the codes define special zones for such purposes as airports, cemeteries, educational institutions, and the keeping of horses.

Before any building permit is issued for new construction, zoning department approval is generally required. Zoning approval is also a prerequisite for a business license.

The zoning code contains requirements for parking facilities, both for public and private parking. These regulations describe the required number, size, and access to parking stalls. It also deals with landscaping, fencing, and illumination criteria.

Other regulated areas include minimum side yards, rear yards and setbacks for all buildings within a zone, as well as maximum building height and type of construction.

Another important code aspect deals with division of land. Regulations cover matters such as lot sizes, street widths, slopes, curbs, and gutters. Other requirements relate to easements for utilities and access, storm drains, and sewers. Procedures for division and development of land are described in detail in the zoning code. Such description will include the information required on the tentative[63] and final tract maps.[64] The

---

[63]§4.12.
[64]§4.10.

code also sets forth the requirements for surveying, establishment of monuments, and preparation of drawings legally describing the subdivision.

A building's construction type is closely related to the zoning of the area and occupancy. Local government establishes these zones and occupancies by the following general criteria:

1. Land Use
   a. Residential—habitation of population
   b. Commercial—centers of trade, commerce, and service
   c. Industrial—production of goods
   d. Agricultural—production of food
2. Fire Considerations
   a. Fire Zone No. 1—high land value, extreme density of land development, potential traffic problems, and multistory buildings
   b. Fire Zone No. 2—buildings seldom exceeding two stories, low density of development, and light vehicular traffic
3. Building Occupancy
   a. Use to which the building is put; degree of hazard housed in building; and building's capacity to resist fire
   b. Some occupancy groups include assembly, hospital, residential, commercial, and manufacturing. These are usually subdivided according to relative densities and effect on the environment

Generally, the following definitions apply:

1. *Zone* refers to land use
2. *Group* refers to occupancy
3. *Type* refers to construction

For example, zone R-1 designates single-family residences, group A-1 designates assembly buildings, and type I designates concrete building construction.

§4.39 3. Plumbing Codes

Plumbing codes are written and published by local entities as well as by plumbing industry associations. In addition, there is a National Plumbing Code.[65]

The National Plumbing Code was written by a committee which included representatives of the following organizations:

1. American Public Health Association
2. American Society of Mechanical Engineers

---

[65]Vincent T. Manas, National Plumbing Code Handbook (McGraw-Hill Book Co, New York, NY, 1st ed 1957).

3. American Society of Sanitary Engineers
4. Building Officials Conference of America
5. Conference of State Sanitary Engineers
6. National Association of Plumbing Contractors
7. Western Plumbing Officials Association

The basic goal of plumbing codes is environmental sanitation, effected through properly designed, acceptably installed, and adequately maintained plumbing systems. The major items covered in the codes are supply of pure and wholesome water, plumbing fixtures with proper protective devices to prevent contamination of water, systems for heating and storing water, safe and effective means of removal of human and other wastes, and design of piping and equipment for ease of maintenance.

The subject matters covered in a typical plumbing code are:

1. Administration
    a. General
    b. Permits
    c. Definitions
2. Quality and weights of materials
3. Drainage systems
4. Vents and venting
5. Indirect waste piping
6. Traps and interceptors
7. Joints and connections
8. Plumbing fixtures
9. Water distribution
10. House sewers and private sewage disposal systems
11. Fuel gas piping
12. Water heaters and vents
13. Backflow protection
14. Fire sprinklers and standpipes
15. Foot establishment requirements
16. Trailer parks
17. Swimming pools
18. Rain and surface water drainage

A plumbing permit is required for installation, alteration, reconstruction, removal, or repair of any water piping, fire sprinkler system, swimming pool piping, and plumbing appurtenances. Permits are not required for minor repair or maintenance.

Issuance of a plumbing permit by a building and safety department is not an approval or authorization of the work specified, but is merely an application for inspection. As in the case of the building permit, issuance of a plumbing permit or approval of plans does not constitute approval of any violation of the plumbing code.

In litigation regarding plumbing, items of evidence would include the application for the plumbing permit, the record of the inspector's approval of a plumbing installation, and receipts for fees paid for permits and inspections.

§4.40 4. Electrical Codes

All electrical systems used in buildings and other facilities are in accordance with the recommendations of the 1978 National Electrical Code.[66] This code was adopted by the National Fire Protection Association in 1962, and was adopted as an American standard following the procedures established by the American Standards Association. The original code was drawn in 1897, a product of the united efforts of various insurance, electrical, architectural, and allied interests.

The purpose of the National Electrical Code is to practically safeguard persons as well as buildings and their contents against hazards arising from the use of electricity for lighting, heat, power, radio, signaling, and other purposes.

The code contains the minimum provisions considered necessary for safety. Compliance with the code and proper maintenance generally would result in a hazard-free installation. However, compliance does not necessarily mean efficient, convenient, or adequate services. Proper design is the responsibility of the qualified and trained professional electrical engineer.

Many cities and counties have written their own electrical codes. These are normally based on the National Electrical Code with modifications as required by local conditions.

The major subject areas in the electrical code are:

1. Administration
2. Wiring design and protection
3. Wiring methods and materials
4. Electrical equipment for general use
5. Special hazardous occupancies
6. Special equipment
7. Special conditions
8. Communication conditions

Documentary evidence related to electrical work may include: electrical plans prepared by the electrical engineer or electrical contractor; electrical specifications; application for an electrical permit; records of inspection; certificates for approval; records of work rejected or corrected; and all notices by the electrical inspector.

The National Electrical Code, Article 500, covers design of wiring and equipment for occupancies in hazardous locations. These hazardous locations are identified by

---

[66]National Fire Protection Association International, 60 Batterymarch Street, Boston, Mass 02110.

classes, groups, and divisions, and are interpreted as explained in the four sections which follow.

§4.41 a. Hazardous Locations Groups

For purposes of testing and approval, the following atmospheric mixture groups have been established for Class I and II locations:[67]

Class I	*Maximum Surface Temperature	**Chemical Atmosphere
Group A	280°C	acetylene
Group B	280°C	acrolein, butadiene, ethylene and propylene oxide, hydrogen, manufactured gases
***Group C	180°C	a cetaldehyde, ally alcohol, carbon monoxide, cyclopropane, diethyl ether, diethylamine, ethylene, hydrogen sulfide, morpholine, tetrahydrofuran
***Group D	280°C	acetic acid, ammonia, benzene, butane, alcohol, gasoline, hexanes, natural gas, naphtha, octanes, propane, styrene

Class II	*Maximum Surface Temperature	**Dust Atmosphere
Group E	200°C	metal dust, including aluminum, magnesium, and their commercial alloys
Group F	150°C	carbon black, coal, coke dust
Group G	120°C	flour, starch, grain dust

*Temperature based on normal operation of equipment that may be overloaded.

**Certain chemical and dust atmospheres may have characteristics that require safeguards beyond those required in any of the above groups. For a complete list noting properties, see NFPA No. 325M-1969.[68]

***For complete list of chemical atmospheres, refer to National Electric Code 1978, Pages 70-350.

§4.42 b. Hazardous Locations Class I

Class I encompasses locations where flammable gases or vapors are or may be present in the air, in quantities sufficient to produce explosive or ignitable mixtures.

[67]Process Plant Construction Estimating Standards (Richardson Engineering Services, Inc, San Marcos, Cal, 1979). Paraphrased with permission of Richardson Engineering Services, Inc.

[68]National Fire Codes, vol 1, NFPA No 325M (National Fire Protection Association International, 470 Atlantic Avenue, Boston, Mass 02210, 1969).

Class I, Division 1

1. Hazardous concentrations exist continuously, intermittently, or periodically, under normal operating conditions
2. Where vapors or gases frequently are present because of repair, maintenance operations, or leakage
3. Where breakdown or faulty operation of equipment or processes might release hazardous concentrations of flammable gases or vapors which could also cause simultaneous failure of electrical equipment.

   Examples: Loading racks for liquids or liquefied gases
   Transfer of liquids or liquefied gases from one container to another
   Spray booths and vicinity
   Areas containing open tanks or vats of volatile flammable liquids
   Solvent handling
   Gas generator rooms
   Gas manufacturing plants
   Pump rooms, etc.

Class I, Division 2

1. Where flammable gases or volatile liquids are handled, processed, or used, but where hazardous liquids, vapors, or gases will normally be confined within closed containers or closed systems from which they can escape only in case of accidental rupture or breakdown of such containers or systems, or in case of abnormal operation of equipment
2. Where hazardous concentrations of gases or vapors are normally prevented by positive mechanical ventilation, but which might become hazardous through failure or abnormal operation of ventilating equipment
3. Areas adjacent to Class I, Division 1 areas, to which hazardous concentrations of gases or vapors might occasionally be communicated unless this is prevented by adequate positive pressure ventilation from a source of clean air and unless effective safeguards against ventilation failure are provided.

   Examples: Where volatile liquids, flammable gases, or vapors are used but where such use, in the judgment of the code enforcing authority, would be hazardous only in case of accident or some unusual operating condition
   The record of the business with respect to explosions or fires
   Piping without valves, checks, meters, or similar devices
   Storage in sealed containers

§4.43 c. Hazardous Locations Class II

Class II takes in areas of combustible dust.

Class II, Division 1

1. Locations which are hazardous because combustible dust is, or may be, in suspension in the air continuously, intermittently, or periodically, under normal operating conditions, in quantities sufficient to produce explosive or ignitable mixtures
2. Where mechanical failure or abnormal operating might cause such mixtures to be produced, and might provide a source of ignition through simultaneous failure of electrical equipment
3. Areas where dusts of an electrical conducting nature may be present.

   Examples: Areas of grain handling, and storage and processing plants

   Similar dust-producing machinery and equipment in pulverizing plants, except where all equipment is essentially dust-tight

   Processing of coal, coke, charcoal, magnesium, aluminum, organic materials

Note that, for example, solvent extraction plants—preparation process would be Class II, Group G, Division 1.

Class II, Division 2

1. Locations where combustible dust will not normally be in suspension in the air, but where deposits or accumulations of such dust may be sufficient to interfere with safe dissipation of heat from electrical equipment or apparatus
2. Where such deposits or accumulations of dust on, in, or in the vicinity of electrical equipment might be ignited by arcs, sparks, or burning material from such equipment

§4.44 d. Hazardous Locations Class III

Class III refers to areas which are hazardous because of the presence of fibers or flyings which are easily ignitable but which are not likely to be in suspension in air.

Class III, Division 1

These are locations where easily ignitable fibers or flyings are handled, manufactured, or used, such as the following:

1. Textile mills
2. Rayon, cotton plants
3. Cotton seed and flax processing plants
4. Woodworking plants

Class III, Division 2

This division encompasses locations in which easily ignitable or combustible flyings such as the following are stored or handled: rayon; cotton; jute; hemp; cocoa; oakum; kapok; spanish moss; or excelsior.

For detailed information and specific code requirements for equipment used in hazardous locations, refer to Article 500 of the National Electric Code 1978 Edition.[69]

§4.45 5. Fire Codes

The principal regulation for fire protection is the National Fire Code, written and published by the National Fire Protection Association, International.[70] This association was organized in 1896 to promote the science and improve methods of fire protection and prevention.

The National Fire Code has now expanded to fill 10 volumes, and is the basis for laws, ordinances, and other regulatory measures. Each volume of the code contains standards, recommended practices, and manuals relating to a particular fire hazard.

Fire hazards dealt with in the 10 volumes include the following:

1. Flammable liquids, boiler-furnaces, and ovens
2. Gases
3. Combustible solids, dusts, and explosives
4. Building construction and facilities
5. Electrical
6. Sprinklers, fire pumps, and water tanks
7. Alarm and special extinguishing systems
8. Portable and manual fire control equipment
9. Occupancy standards and process hazards
10. Transportation

The specific subject matters covered in the fourth volume, which deals with building construction and facilities, are:

1. Lightning protection
2. Fire doors and windows
3. Protection from exposure fires
4. Air conditioning and ventilation systems
5. Warm-air heating and air conditioning
6. Roof coverings
7. Fire tests, building construction, and materials

Many of the standards and regulations of the National Fire Code are incorporated into the building and safety codes as well as the fire codes.

---

[69]National Fire Protection Association International, 60 Batterymarch Street, Boston, Mass 02110.

[70]470 Atlantic Avenue, Boston, Mass 02210.

§4.46 6. Safety Codes

The principal national code dealing with industrial safety is the Occupational and Safety Act of the Occupational Safety and Health Administration, Department of Labor (OSHA).[71] This act was enacted in 1970 and borrows heavily from previously existing safety codes, such as the National Electrical Code and other consensus standards. OSHA standards cover six major categories, which include:

1. Workplace standards
2. Machine and equipment standards
3. Materials standards
4. Employee standards
5. Power source standards
6. Process source standards

A more detailed description of the OSHA regulations appears at Appendix D. The importance of this code in construction litigation is to establish a standard of safe practice. In addition, it provides the basis for other codes accepted in the industry as of the time of writing the OSHA regulations.

Safety codes which specifically cover the construction industry are usually written by that agency in each state which controls industrial safety. For example, the State of California Department of Industrial Relations has published *Construction Safety Orders*.[72] This is part of the California Administrative Code, and covers the following major subjects:

1. Dusts, fumes, mists, vapors, and gases
2. Rock drilling
3. Excavations, trenches, and earthwork
4. Bins, bunkers, hoppers, and material storage
5. Explosives
6. Derricks, cranes, boom-type excavators, and loading or lifting devices
7. Haulage and earth moving
8. Traffic control flagmen, barricades, and warning devices
9. Pile driving
10. Workover water
11. Construction elevators
12. Hoisting
13. Standard railings
14. Ramps, runways, stairwells, and stairs
15. Access

---

[71] 29 USC §651 *et seq*, 29 CFR §1910; see **App C.**

[72] 16 Cal Adm Code §14.

16. Floor, roof, and wall openings
17. Temporary floors
18. Scaffolds
19. Safety belts and nets
20. Ladders
21. Power saws
22. Power-actuated tools
23. Miscellaneous construction equipment
24. Erection and construction
25. Roofing operations
26. Demolition
27. Oxygen, acetylene, and fuel gas
28. Electrical requirements for construction

In addition to federal and state published safety codes, various industrial associations have prepared their own recommendations and manuals. One such industrial association is the Associated General Contractors of America, Inc. Its publication is the *Manual of Accident Prevention in Construction*.[73]

The *Manual of Accident Prevention in Construction* generally covers all the subjects listed above. In addition, it contains recommendations for creating an accident prevention organization for each construction project. These recommendations deal with:

1. Planning the accident prevention program
2. Developing the program
3. Assignment of responsibility
4. Prejob meetings
5. Start-of-job meetings
6. Supervisory meetings
7. Toolbox meetings
8. Mass meetings

In cases of accidents during construction, the manual notes that an effort must be made to reconstruct the events, building materials, and type of work in progress. The first step in discovery is to obtain the following items:

1. Construction plans
2. Construction specifications
3. Daily log of contractor's superintendent or clerk of the works
4. Minutes of safety and tailgate meetings

---

[73]Associated General Contractors of America, Inc, Washington, DC.

5. Inspection reports
6. Laboratory test reports

In order to understand the organizations of the general contractor and subcontractors who may have been connected with the incident, the names and addresses of persons holding the following positions should be obtained:

1. President
2. Vice presidents
3. General manager
4. General superintendent
5. Director of safety
6. Job or field superintendent
7. Trade foremen
8. Trade journeymen

§4.47 a. Accident Prevention in Erection of Structural Steel

Erection of structural steel is one of the most dangerous aspects of building or bridge construction. Federal, state, and local governments have established safety procedures for this type of work. In addition, the Associated General Contractors of America, Inc.[74] has published recommendations with special emphasis on steel erection.

Some of the general requirements are:

1. Persons working aloft on hanging scaffolds or open-steel frames should wear safety belts tied to permanent structures, except where safety nets are hung directly below
2. No one should work on open-steel frames during high winds or when steel is slippery from ice, snow, or rain
3. In setting steel, each piece should be secured in place before the line is taken off
4. When setting steel trusses, sides or cross braces should be secured until permanent braces are in place. Trusses and beams should be braced laterally or progressively during construction
5. All workers should wear hard hats
6. Care should be used in carrying, hanging, and working from floating scaffolds. Scaffold platforms should be kept clear of debris, bolts, and nuts
7. Scaffolds should be inspected before use
8. Unless necessary, material should not be hoisted to a structure until it is ready to be put into position and fastened

---

[74]Manual of Accident Prevention (Associated General Contractors of America, Inc, Washington, DC).

Figure 4-14 Components of a Steel-Framed Building

From *Civil Engineering for the Plant Engineer* by Max Schwartz. Copyright © 1972 by McGraw-Hill, Inc. Used with the permission of McGraw-Hill Book Company.

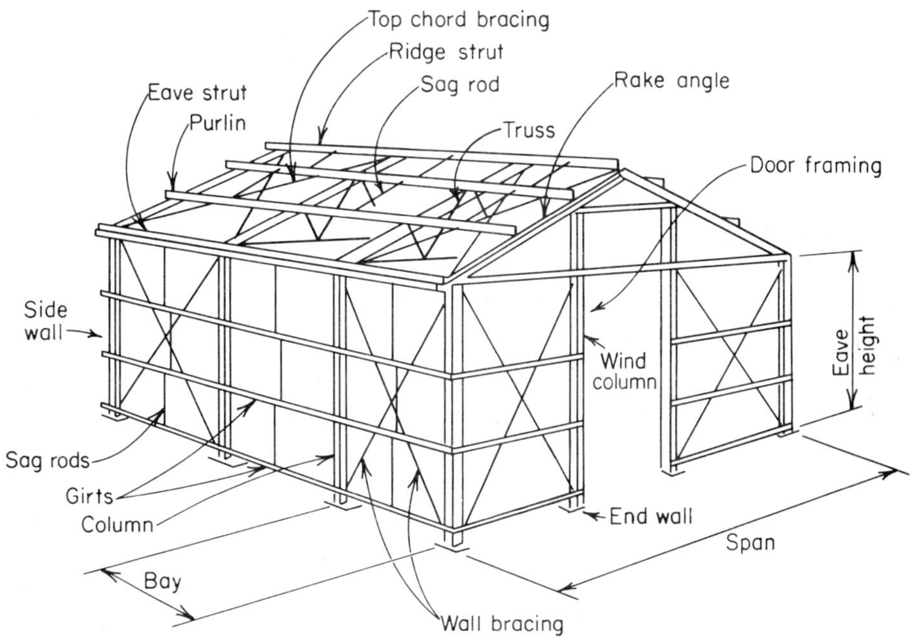

Figure 4-14 illustrates the principal components of a steel-framed building. As occurs in every type of construction, the names for parts of a building vary from discipline to discipline. This is further indicated in Figure 4-15, where each steel member is given its own specific name based on its shape.

§4.48 b. Accident Prevention in Hoisting

The Associated General Contractors of America, Inc.,[75] has published recommendations for accident prevention in hoisting. Some of the general requirements follow:

1. Cranes, derricks, and other equipment should not be operated less than 10 feet from electric power lines
2. Hoisting should be carried out so that loads do not pass over the heads of workers, except where there is suitable overhead protection

[75]Manual of Accident Prevention (Associated General Contractors of America, Inc, Washington DC).

Figure 4-15 Typical Hot-Rolled Structural Shapes

(a) Bar 1-1/4 ∅ = round bar, (b) Bar 1 = square bar, (c) Bar 2-1/2 x 1/2 = flat bar, (d) L 6 x 6 x 1/4 = equal leg angle, (e) C 12 x 20.7 = American standard channel, (f) S 24 x 100 = S shape, (g) W 24 x 76 = W shape, (h) WT 12 x 38 = structural tee cut from a W shape, (i) Pipe 4 Std = pipe, (j) TS 4 x 4 x .375 = structural tubing, square

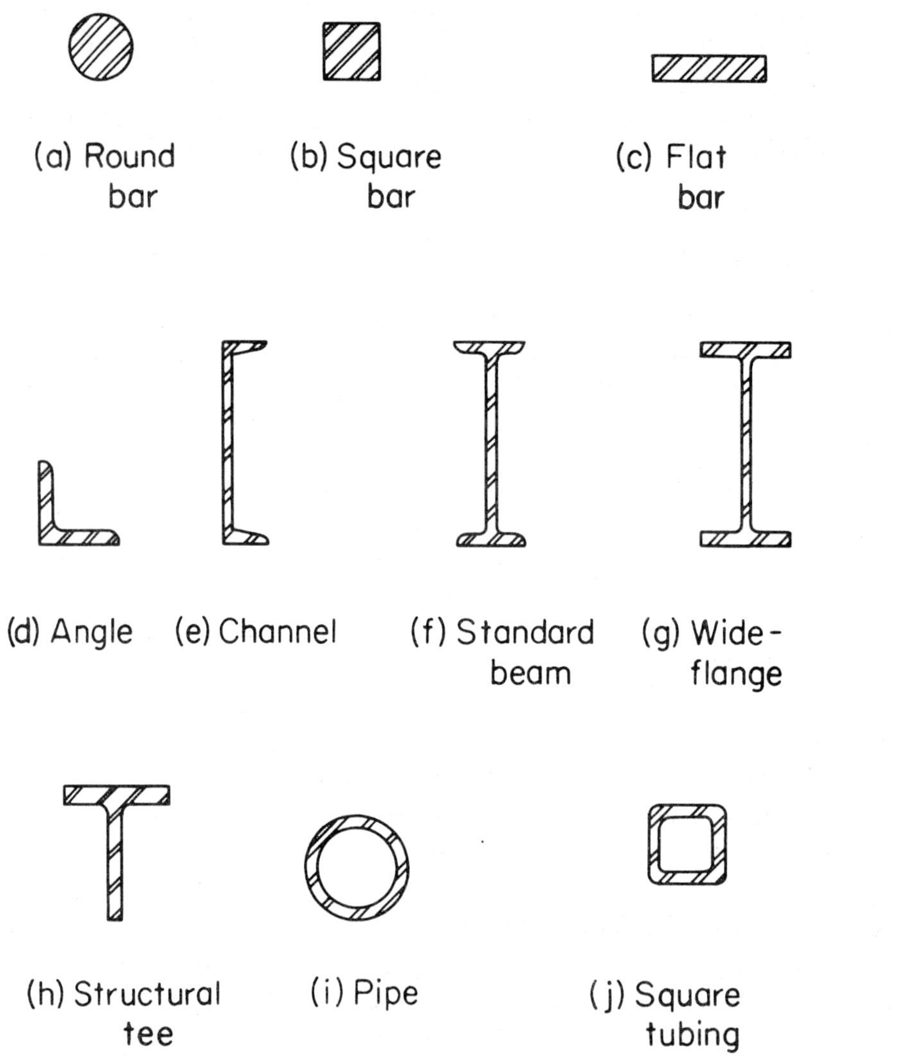

3. Hoisting of steel bundles should be avoided, except where each piece is secured to prevent it from slipping out of the bundle. Only safety hooks should be used
4. Tag lines should be used to control loads when hoisting materials

§4.49 c. Accident Prevention in Use of Platforms

The Associated General Contractors of America, Inc., has published recommendations in the area of prevention in the use of platforms.[76] Some of the general requirements are:

1. In buildings and other structures of skeleton construction, the entire tier of beams on which the structural steel work is being erected (called the working floor) should be thorougly planked over, except for openings required for erection work. Permanent floors should be installed as soon as possible
2. Where more than two stories of open-steel frames are being erected, and where bolting, welding, or other work is being done, the floor two stories below the working floor should be planked over
3. Workers should be prohibited from working under areas where bolting or welding is taking place unless they are protected by a planked floor between them and the overhead work
4. Safety nets should be used in areas where temporary floors cannot be readily installed. Safety nets should be installed where workers are likely to fall, especially where safety belts and life lines, guarded platforms, and scaffolds or temporary floors are not feasible
5. Safety nets should be installed as close under the working level as practicable, and in no case lower than 25 feet below working level
6. When persons must work below safety nets, the net should be faced with wire or fiber meshing. Safety belts, bosun's chains or scaffolding should be used, where necessary, when installing nets
7. Perimeter nets should follow the work upward. Such nets should not be less than 10 feet wide when the possible fall distance is 25 feet or less
8. The net suspension system should be tested after installation
9. There should be frequent and careful inspections of all rigging, falsework, derricks, travelers, erection cars, and other equipment
10. Employees should not be hoisted or lowered in tackle and runner lines or on the load

§4.50 7. Construction Standards

In establishing construction standards for a particular job, many factors must be considered. Some of these factors are geography, state of the art, occupancy or usage, nature of ownership, and existing market for that particular type of building.

---

[76]Manual of Accident Prevention (Associated General Contractors of America, Inc, Washington, DC).

Differences in construction quality are pronounced. Quality level may be reflected in the architectural and engineering fees paid to designers. These fees are related to the amount of time and detail spent in preparation of plans and specifications and in follow-up. Life expectancy of construction materials, quality and experience of crafts workers, and effectiveness of supervision and inspection all directly affect the overall standard of construction.

Each of these factors should be understood before one establishes a basis of construction standards. Some types of evidence used to establish construction standards are similar to the evidence used by a real estate appraiser in arriving at a sale price. These include the following:

1. Survey of the quality of construction in the neighborhood
2. Survey of buildings of similar occupancy
3. Review of the published costs of construction for low-quality, average, and high-quality construction of similar types of buildings
4. Comparison of components of construction of the subject building, such as roofing, plumbing and electrical work, wall finishes, ceilings, and floor finishes to establish their level of quality. Foundations and structural frame are usually governed by code and structural requirements, and do not affect the relative cost of the building
5. Determination of fees paid to the designers as compared to fees generally paid to designers of low-quality, average, and high-quality buildings
6. Determination of number of consultants used in the design. Many buildings can be designed without using structural, civil, mechanical, and electrical engineers. In these cases, the design is generally left up to the subcontractors

There are different standards of construction. Low-cost housing does not receive the same degree of quality control as a high-cost institutional facility. Degree of quality control can be determined from the tone and content of the plans and specifications. The cost of the job reflects this difference in quality standards.

Controversies in construction often arise out of the application of high quality standards to low-cost buildings.

§4.51 H. Evidence of Damages

Failures in construction should be classified by definable portions of a project. Some major areas are:

1. Soils and foundations
2. Structural
3. Masonry
4. Roofs
5. Piping
6. Electrical

The sections which follow will briefly discuss common failures and types of evidence for the above areas of construction.

§4.52 1. Soil and Foundation Failures

There are essentially five major soil types. These are, in order of stability:

1. Massive crystalline bedrock
2. Sedimentary and foliated rock
3. Sandy gravel and/or gravel
4. Sand, silty sand, clayey sand, silty gravel, or clayey gravel
5. Clay, sandy clay, silty clay, and clayey silt
6. Manmade fill

Each type of soil requires specific consideration in construction design. Inappropriate design of structures for the underlying soil type can result in differential settling.

Excessive or differential settlement can cause the following conditions: cracks in slabs and foundations; leaks in pipelines, which can result in further settlement and flooding; failures in columns, beams, and other supporting members; cracked walls and windows; and jammed doors and equipment, such as elevators and process equipment.

Some soils have a tendency to expand when wet or frozen. This can cause an uplift of foundations and concrete slabs.

The objective of the science of soil mechanics is to anticipate expected settlement, displacement, or upheaval. This is why documents relating to the investigation, analysis, and recommendations of the soil engineer are important evidence.

The foundation engineer looks on the structure and the soil supporting it as an integrated working unit. In the design of a foundation, two questions must be answered: (1) whether the earth under the proposed building will support the structure and the superimposed loads; and (2) what is the amount of resulting settlement.

The answers to these two questions define the two major parts of soils mechanics. The first issue is stability of the soil; the second is its elasticity.

Accidents occur when there is a cave-in in the course of trench excavation. This can happen in pipeline or foundation construction. Figure 4-16 illustrates common methods for preventing cave-ins.

Common causes of building foundation failure are shown in Figure 4-17.

§4.53 2. Structural Failures

There are many minor structural failures; however, unless the failure involves a loss of life or has some other newsworthy feature, the public usually does not hear about it. Usually, only the owner and the repairman are aware that there has been any type of failure. At times, an owner may request that no publicity be given to the failure.

Most structural failures are due to improper detailing of connections. It is common for *handbook engineers* to select structural members of ample size and then to ignore

Figure 4-16 Protection of Trench Excavation

A major cause of cave-in accidents is associated with the shoring system of the trench. This figure illustrates the two commonest shoring systems and indicates the principal components.

(a) Trenches in hard, compact material

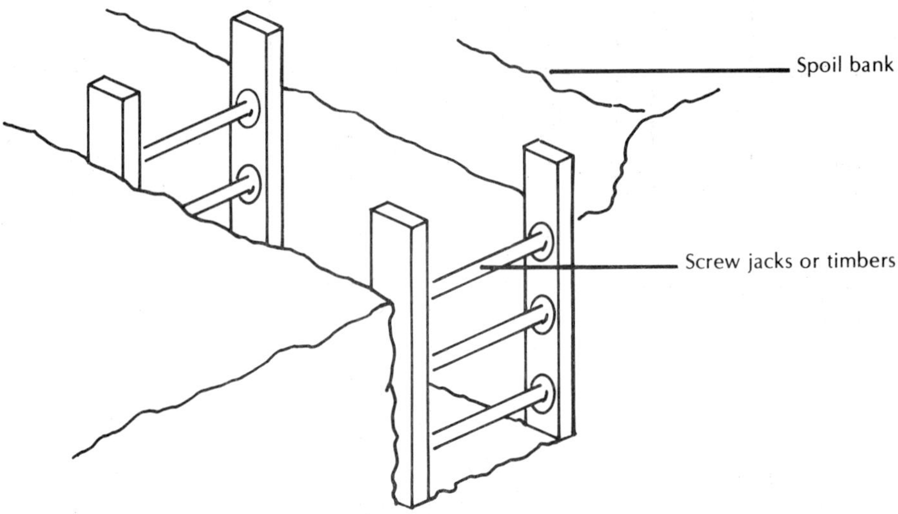

(b) Trenches in running material

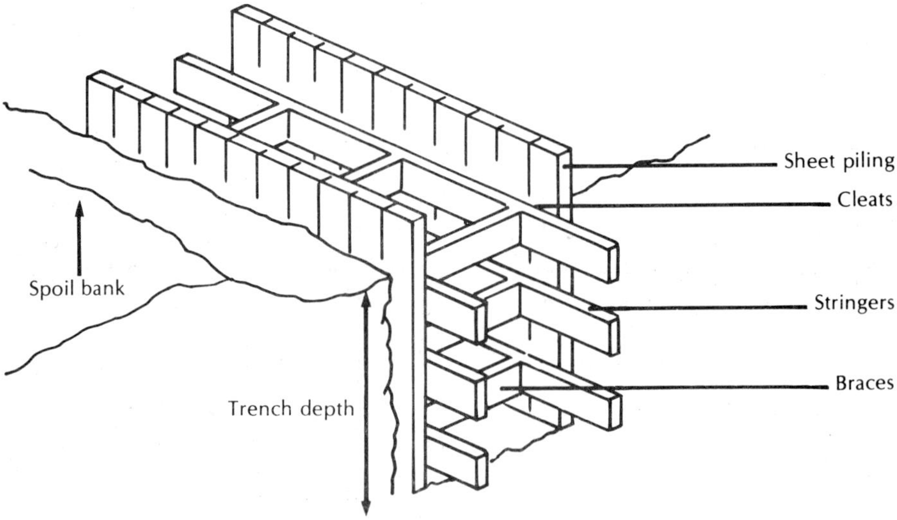

Figure 4-17 Common Failures of Foundations

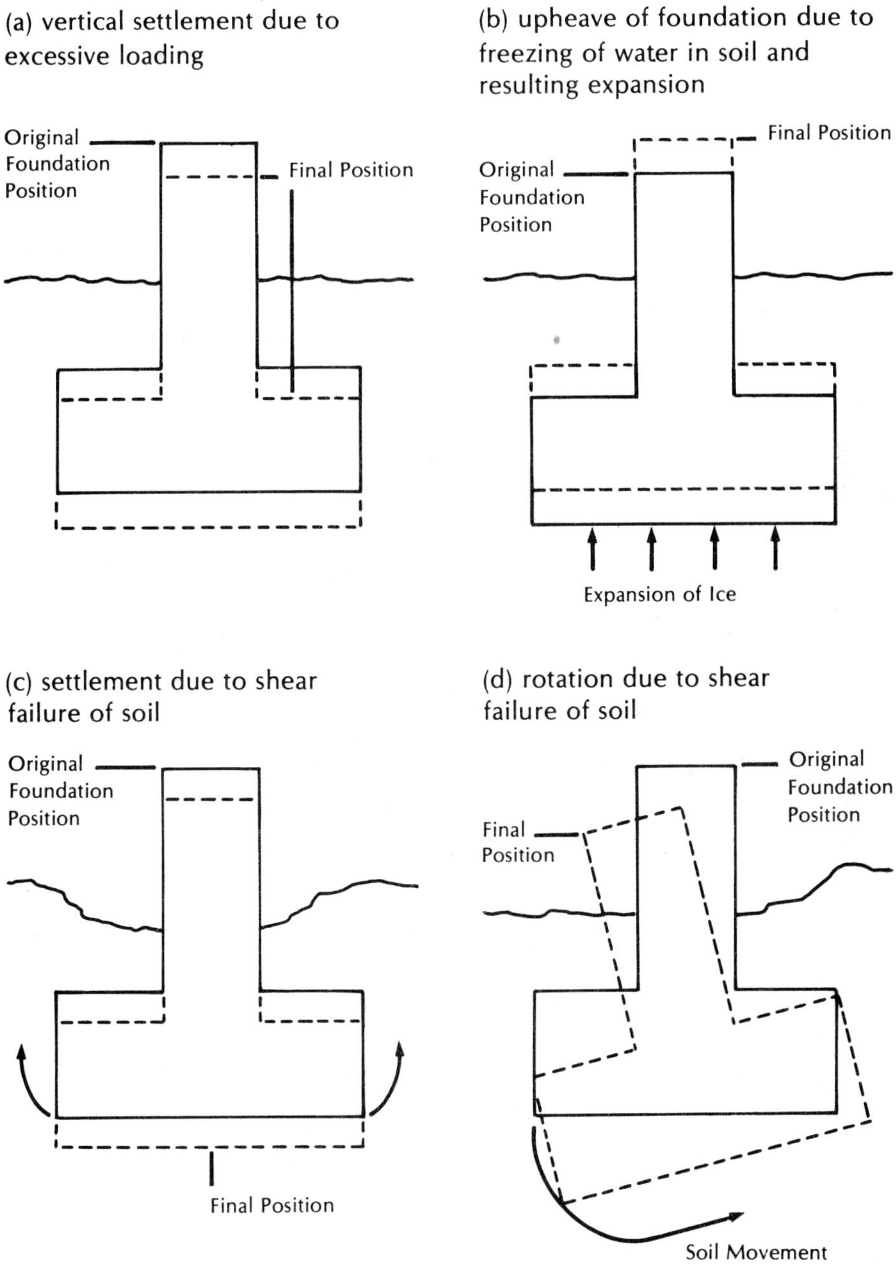

their connections. One reason for this is that design and detailing of connections take up more time than does selection of a beam from a table in the handbook.

Failures from overloading due to occupancy, wind, or earthquake forces can often be traced to the framing connections. For this reason, it is important for the expert to concentrate investigation on how the connections were designed, fabricated, and constructed.

Another common subject of complaint is excessive deflection of structural members. Damage from deflection of structural framing relates to properties of walls and floors.

Deflection of beams which does not adversely affect flexible or ductile materials may result in serious damage when brittle materials are involved. Examples of brittle material are masonry walls, plastered surfaces, or plate glass. Amount of deflection can be determined mathematically or by using surveying instruments. Building codes and structural design standards do provide for maximum allowable deflection for roofs, floors, walls, and beams for brittle and flexible materials.

Figure 4-18 illustrates the sequences of failure of a cantilever beam connection. The entire episode shown occurred within several seconds after buckling of the column web.

Every connection must resist one or more of the following forces: shear; tension; bearing; compression; flexure; and torque.[77] Connections may be stressed in combinations of two or more stresses.

Connections may fail in many ways. Merely unscrewing a nut from a bolt holding a monorail can cause the monorail, trolley, and load to collapse. By failing in shear, a bolt can actually be cut in two by excessive loading. A gusset plate can fail in tension, shear, or bearing. A column anchor bolt can fail in bond when pulled out of concrete. Although the bolt could resist the load, the bond between steel and concrete has not been able to sustain the pull of the anchor bolt. A weld can fail by cracking in shear.

The following are suggested checkpoints in the area of potential failure of connections in steel.:

1. Loose bolts in friction-type, high-strength bolts
2. Oversize holes
3. Unequal stressing of bolts due to poor bolt arrangement
4. Unequal stressing of plate due to poor layout
5. Fatigue of bolt or plate
6. Bolt flexure
7. Tension in bolt
8. Reversal of stresses of connection
9. Secondary stresses due to eccentricity of connection

The loss of a single bolt in a group can cause a moment or twisting action on the remaining bolts through induced eccentricity in the connection. This eccentricity can create additional secondary loads on the remaining bolts which can cause failure. Therefore, it is not necessarily true that when two bolts out of ten fail, the connection

[77]**§3.31**; also **App E.**

Figure 4-18 Sequence of Failure of Cantilever Beam

Fabricator neglected stiffener plates in column adjacent to seat angle required to resist compressive forces. Cantilever beam when loaded causes both shear and compressive force on column web.

1. Unstiffened web of column buckles due to high compressive stresses
2. Because of loss of seat-angle effectiveness, the entire beam moment is taken by bolts in web of beam to flange of column, which causes failure in top bolts due to tension, causing further increased tension in the second set of bolts until they also fail
3. Remaining bolts fail in tension and shear
4. Beam collapses

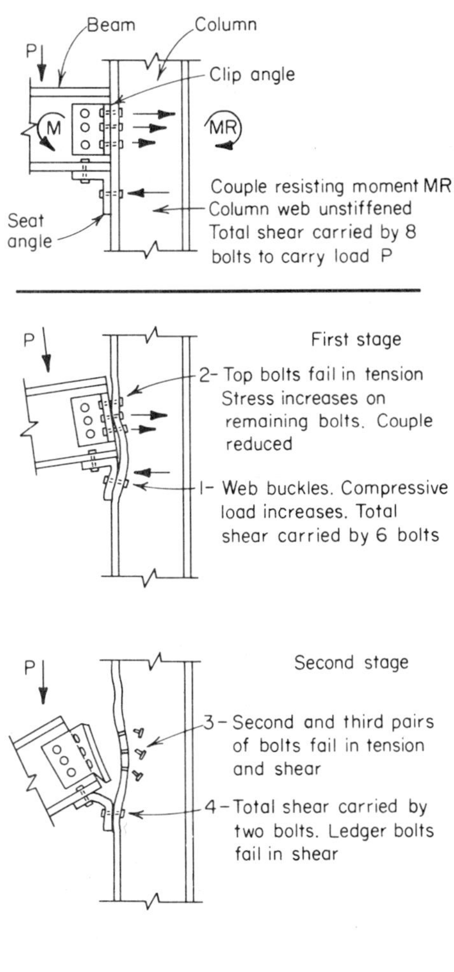

Figure 4-19 Typical Wood-Framed Building, or Stick Framing

From *Civil Engineering for the Plant Engineer* by Max Schwartz. Copyright © 1972 by McGraw-Hill, Inc. Used with the permission of McGraw-Hill Book Company.

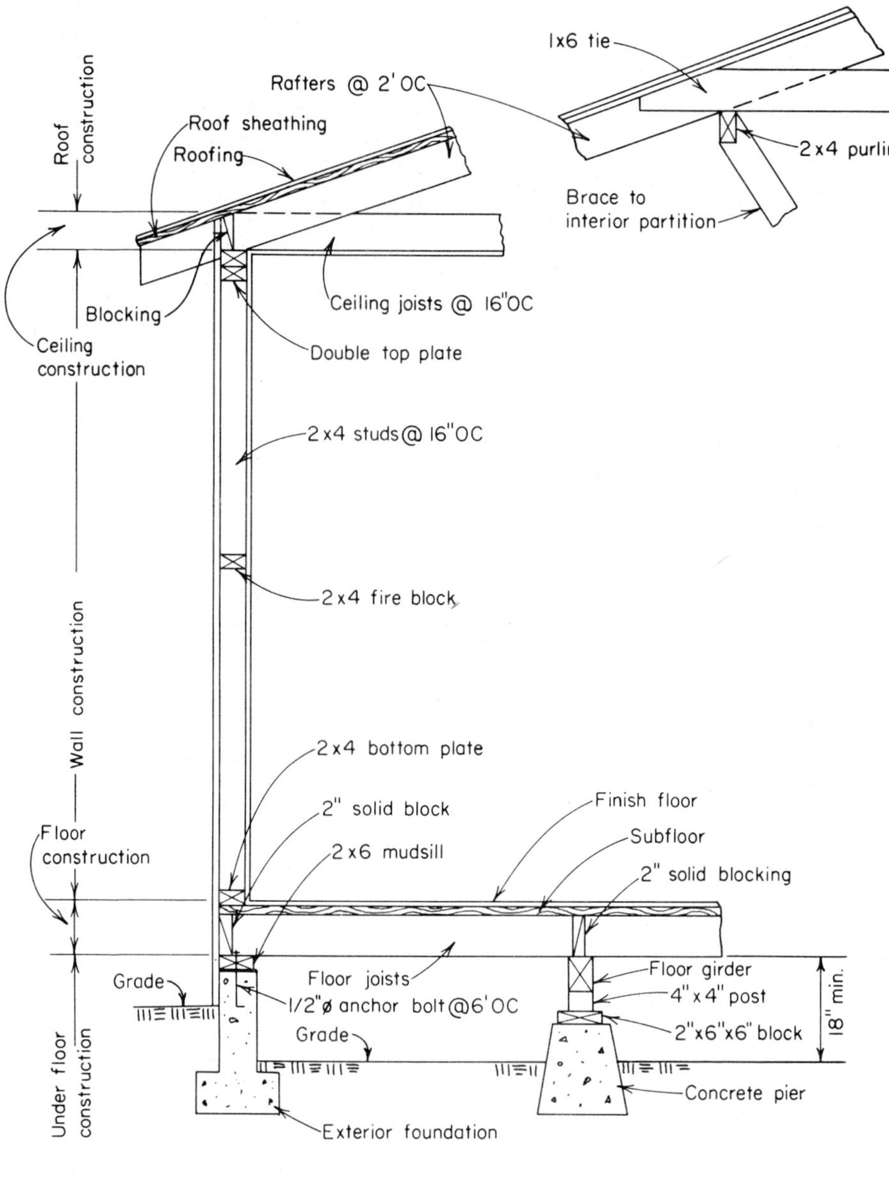

still retains 80 per cent of its initial strength. The failure of two bolts can cause new secondary stresses which may reduce the strength of the connection by as much as 50 per cent or even more.

Figure 4-20 Typical Reinforced Concrete Beam (Top, Bottom and Column Reinforcement)

From *Civil Engineering for the Plant Engineer* by Max Schwartz. Copyright © 1972 by McGraw-Hill, Inc. Used with the permission of McGraw-Hill Book Company.

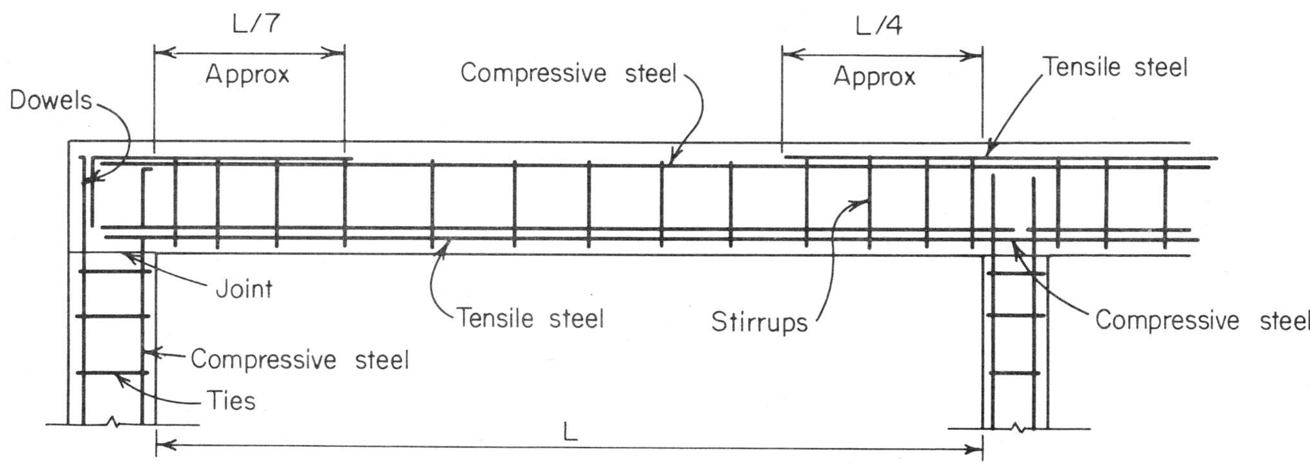

Figure 4-21 Failures in Concrete Beams

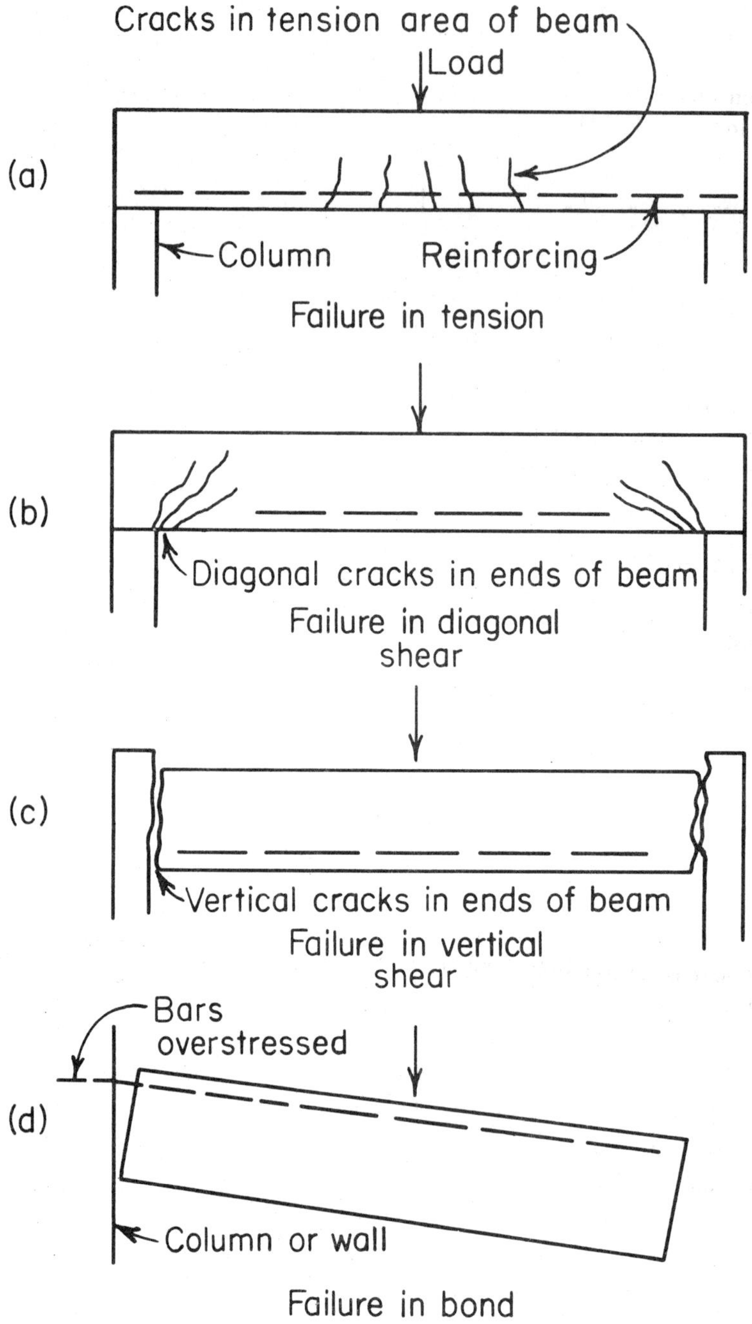

In order to better understand structural failures in other types of construction, the attorney should have a basic knowledge of the terms used in each type. Figure 4-19 illustrates a section through wood-framed building with the major components identified. Figure 4-20 indicates the parts of a reinforced concrete beam and column which may be involved in a failure. Four common types of failure of reinforced concrete beams are shown in Figure 4-21.

§4.54 3. Masonry Failures

Generally, the term *masonry* encompasses clay brick, concrete block, clay tile, building stones, and adobe. Masonry units are joined together with mortar, a mixture of cement, sand, lime, and water.

Most failures in masonry structures involve cracking, penetration of water, discoloration, loose masonry units, and occasionally complete structural collapse.

Masonry quality and workmanship can be tested. When testing occurs during construction, the testing records constitute essential evidence. Other tests can be made after the signs of failure have been noted. These may be *core tests* or *prism tests.*

In the core test, a cylindrical section of masonry is cut out of the wall and tested in compression in a laboratory. The stress at the point of compressive failure can then be compared to the design specifications and code requirements.

The prism test is similar to the core test but involves a cubical-shaped specimen. This sample is also tested to determine bond and shear strength between the masonry unit and the mortar.

Some questions that should be answered as to masonry failure follow:

1. Was the material used the same material called for in the plans?
2. Did the plans specify the proper choice of materials?

   Check manufacturer's specifications for recommended usage

   Check with Masonry Institute of America
3. Was the design structurally sound?
4. Were the design details shown on the plans?
5. Was the material *manufacturer-approved*?

§4.55 4. Defective Roofs

The commonest defect in building construction is probably the leaky roof. Rainwater is most unforgiving of faulty construction. A single error in an otherwise perfect roof can cause expensive damages to the building and its contents.

It helps in understanding roofing to briefly describe the types and features of a roof which commonly affect its weathertightness.

Flat and nearly flat roofs are usually covered by some type of built-up roofing, consisting of layers of asphalt and asphalt-saturated felt, covered with a mineral topping. The number of layers, or plies, as well as the thickness of each layer will depend on the slope of the roof, the nature of the surface under the roofing, and the desired useful life of the roofing.

Another important factor in the watertightness of a roof is the treatment of terminations and the interface between building components. These may be the parapets, expansion joints, and penetration by stacks, pipes, and chimneys through the roof interfaces. This portion of the roofing job is called the flashing. Flashing is a sheet-metal water seal.

The useful life of a roof is usually described by designation as a 10-, 15-, or 20-year bondable roof. This means that when the roofing is installed in accordance with the roofing manufacturer's specifications by a manufacturer-approved contractor, inspected by the manufacturer's agent, and not modified in any way except with the manufacturer's approval, the roof will be guaranteed for watertightness by the manufacturer for a period of 10, 15, or 20 years. The period of warranty would depend on the roofing specifications.

The factors which affect proper selection of roofing are:

1. Material of the deck (concrete, insulation or wood)
2. Slope of the deck (0 inches to 1/2-inch per foot, 1/2-inch to 3 inches per foot, 3 inches to 6 inches per foot, or 6 inches to 9 inches per foot)
3. Period of warranty desired (10, 15, or 20 years)

The mineral surfacing over a built-up roof can be either crushed rock or slag spread over a bed of asphalt. An alternate method is to put a factory-impregnated mineral surface over the top layer of felt.

The number of plies in a built-up roof can vary from three to five. The gravel topping can be in either one or two layers. The greater the number of layers, the longer the roof will last.

Residential and similar types of buildings with sloping roofs use more traditional roofing materials such as wood shingles, shakes, composition shingles, clay tiles, concrete tiles, or slates.

Failures in roofing are due most commonly to the effects of temperature, moisture, time, and solar radiation. Expansion and contraction caused by temperature changes can tear the membrane, open metal flashing, and break solder joints in metalwork. Moisture penetrating between layers of roofing will vaporize and expand from the sun, causing blisters which tear the membrane.

In addition, oxidation and solar radiation can deteriorate the asphaltic base of the membrane, thereby weakening and reducing the flexibility of the built-up roofing. Gravel surface can loosen, thereby eliminating the protection of the felt.

Other points of failures are in the metal capping, expansion joints, roof penetrations of pipes and stacks, and ponding due to excessive roof deflection. Vegetation growing on flat roofs can also destroy roofing by root action.

§4.56 a. Suggested Check List for Roof Investigations

Following is a list of procedures suggested for the expert who is investigating roof failure:

1. Determine cause of failure
   a. Age of roof
   b. Corrective measures taken in past
2. Examine flashing
   a. Parapets, penetrations, and equipment supports
3. Erosion of top surface
   a. Gravel, final surface asphalt
4. Laboratory tests of underlying materials
   a. Deteriorating wood roof deck, insulation, or concrete
   b. Wet insulation
   c. Wet fill
   d. Splits at joints
5. Test cuts
   a. Cut and remove 12-inch by 36-inch sections from center and all four edges of roofing, including flashing
   b. Freeze in 0-degree Fahrenheit freezing compartment until gravel surface can be removed and membrane plies peel apart
   c. Check ply structure for full uniform mopping
   d. Determine weight of material per square foot

§4.57 5. Piping Failure

Common piping failures include leaks, inadequate flow, valve failure, corrosion, and structural collapse. Some recommended investigation procedures are:

1. Hydrostatic testing
2. Metallurgical testing
3. Weld testing by nondestructive means
4. Calculations of deflection, expansion, contraction, and compressive stresses
5. Comparison to design plans and specifications
6. Comparison to requirements of
   National Plumbing Code[78]
   American Society of Testing and Materials,[79] Specifications on Materials
   American Society of Mechanical Engineers,[80] Specifications on Design

---

[78]Vincent T. Manas, National Plumbing Code Handbook (McGraw-Hill Book Co, New York, NY, 1st ed 1957).

[79]1916 Race Street, Philadelphia, Pa 19103.

[80]345 East 47th Street, New York, NY 10017.

§4.58 6. Electrical Failures

Many suits have been based on damages caused by electrical mishaps. Such mishaps have included electrocutions, burns, fires, explosions, damages to equipment, and faulty operation of electrical controls and equipment.

Most people fear electricity because of their ignorance about the equipment, materials, and crafts involved in the electrical installation. A brief description of a typical electrical installation seems appropriate for this reason.

Electrical installations in a residence, public building, commercial building, or industrial building are generally similar but will vary in size and complexity. An electrical system has the following major elements:

1. Conduit system. This can be compared to a piping system
2. Wires and cables. These can be compared to the liquid or gases flowing in pipes
3. Enclosures and junction boxes. These house the control devices or splices in wires
4. Transformers. These increase or decrease voltages
5. Switches
6. Switch gears and switchboards. These may be likened to valves which open or close the flow of current through wires
7. Circuit breakers. These are used to interrupt the flow of electricity when such flow is unintentionally increased
8. Motor starter. These devices control the amount of current needed to start an electric motor
9. Control station, push buttons and motor control centers. These are single or multiple devices to open or close the flow of current to various motors
10. Convenience outlets. These are electrical receptacles used for plug-in, movable appliances or tools
11. Lighting fixtures

§4.59 a. Electrical Short Circuits

Electrical currents will follow the path of least resistance. This statement has been proven over the years, in incidents which have resulted in death and destruction. Every electrical system has a maximum output rated in kilovolt-amperes (KVA) which can be converted into amperes at a rate dependent on the voltage. A system supplied by one generator of 20,000 KVA has the capacity to deliver 24,000 amperes at 480 volts or 55,000 amperes at 208 volts. A single lighting circuit can deliver 20 amperes of a circuit to a five-horsepower motor which could deliver 15 amperes. Each circuit must have a protective device which can interrupt the current to which it may be subjected.

The basic purpose of each protective device is to protect downstream circuits against overcurrent. Within any such downstream circuit, there will usually be secondary protective devices with their secondary circuits. These should be coordinated to allow the secondary devices to operate (under a fault or overload condition in the secondary circuit) before the upstream protective device does.

There are three types of protective devices:

1. Fuse-melting metal
2. Molded case circuit breaker-thermal magnetic response
3. Relay-integrating response

§4.60 b. Electrical Fires and Explosions

The most serious industrial fires and explosions tend to be due to existence of one of three conditions in an area:

1. A flammable liquid, vapor, or combustible dust is present in sufficient quantity.
2. A flammable liquid, vapor, or combustible dust is mixed with air or oxygen in the proportions required to produce an explosive mixture
3. A source of energy is applied to the explosive mixture

For this reason, any ignition occurring within such an area would cause an explosion. An electric conduit from this area could spread the fire into adjacent, hazardous areas if the electric system were improperly installed. In addition, improper electrical devices within the hazardous area can be the source of ignition which starts the conflagration.

Because of this danger the 1978 National Electrical Code[81] requires special consideration for each classification of hazard. Each requires particular electrical devices.

A review of electrical equipment after a fire or explosion may provide evidence regarding the cause of the disaster.

§4.61 c. Suggested Check List for Electrical Failures

Following is a list of matters to be looked into by the expert who is investigating an electrical failure:

A. Electrical Fault
   1. Water in junction box
   2. Explosion in junction box
   3. Explosive dusts
   4. Explosive gases
   5. Explosion in switchboard
   6. Explosion in motor
   7. Explosion in lamp
   8. Explosion in switch

---

[81]National Fire Protection Association International, 60 Batterymarch Street, Boston, Mass 02110.

B. Evidence
   1. Seals on gasket
   2. Explosion-proof equipment
   3. National Electrical Manufacturers Association and Underwriters' Laboratories, Inc., standards
   4. National Electrical Code
   5. Air samples—type concentration limits
   6. Use of improper hand tools
   7. Ignition temperature
   8. Ground joints and threaded joints
   9. Isolation of arcing devices

§4.62 7. Experts in Specific Building Components

Because of the enormous range of engineering specialties, possible sources of experts are extremely varied. Figure 4-1 provides a rapid method for identifying experts for various areas of building construction.

§4.63 8. Suggested Check List for Testing of Construction Materials

This section presents a more general check list for the expert in the overall area of construction materials testing:

A. Soil testing
   1. Field tests
      a. Compaction, proctor
      b. Maximum density—optimum moisture tests
   2. Foundation and fill investigation (bearing capacity, stability, settlement)
      a. Drilling and core sampling
      b. Laboratory tests
   3. Moisture content
   4. Permeability
   5. Shear testing

B. Asphalt testing
   1. Compressive strength
   2. Penetration
   3. Specific gravity
   4. Swell test

C. Concrete testing (aggregates, abrasion)
   1. Absorption

2. Petrographic analysis
3. Specific gravity
4. Sieve analysis
5. Sulfate soundness
6. Cement
    a. Physical tests
    b. Chemical tests
7. Compressive strength
8. Flexural beam test
9. Modulus of elasticity
10. Tensile test

D. Masonry testing
1. Absorption
2. Chemical resistance
3. Compressive strength
4. Efflorescence
5. Imperviousness
6. Modulus of rupture
7. Moisture
8. Mortar
    a. Compressive test

E. Reinforcing steel testing
1. Bend test
2. Tensile test

§4.64 I. Estimate of Costs

Among the most frequently occurring causes of disputes in construction practices are the contractor's claims for extra costs and extensions of time. Other common sources of disputes are changed conditions on the site, delays due to acts of the owner and other contractors, delays due to events beyond the contractor's control, and conflicting and ambiguous statements in the contract documents.

Damages, or extra costs, may take the form of loss of productivity, repair of defective work, replacement of improper material, or extended overhead due to the job extending beyond its planned period.

An accurate determination of damages is usually difficult. Another difficulty is the impossibility of foreseeing all the conditions that might lead to disputes in construction work.

In evaluating a damages claim, it is worthwhile to begin by reviewing the original estimate of the job. Based on this summation of material, labor costs, overhead, and profit, the impact of changed conditions on the construction can be evaluated. Construction is usually divided into major phases of work.

Its principal phases are:

1. Site preparation
2. Earthwork
3. Foundations
4. Site utilities
5. Masonry
6. Structural steel
7. Carpentry
8. Concrete
9. Thermal and moisture protection
10. Doors and windows
11. Finishes
12. Specialties
13. Air conditioning, heating, and ventilation
14. Plumbing
15. Electrical
16. Equipment

The items above listed are referred to as *main accounts* and reference to them is the standard method of estimating in accordance with the Uniform Construction Index.

Here is a brief description of the method used to determine the total cost of a job.

A material takeoff is made for each item, whether it is cubic yards of concrete, pounds of reinforcing steel, or board feet of lumber. Cost of the material is then determined for each account.

Based on the amount of material and the nature of the work, a given number of manhours per unit of material is established for installation of that portion of work. The manhours represent a composite of manhours which include work of the foreman, journeyman, and laborers associated with each type of work. The total manhours to perform each phase of construction work is then calculated.

Using the existing hourly rate for the composite work crew, a total labor cost is then figured. At that point, a figure representing the total direct cost of labor and material for all of the accounts for the particular job can be reached.

Added to the material cost is the sales tax. Added to the direct cost is the overhead, the indirect cost of the job. This figure includes costs of the superintendent, rented equipment, expendable materials, and office expenses.

Each subcontracted account is then totalled to determine the total subcontracted cost of the job. An administrative cost is added to the sum of the subcontracted cost representing an overhead expense to the general contractor.

Now all the costs to the general contractor have been accounted for. The cost of required bonds is then added. Finally, the profit to the contractor is calculated.

A major problem in dealing with construction claims and interpreting their backup materials is understanding the many terms as the contractor intended them. Some critical terms in estimating damages are:

1. Overhead
2. Main office overhead
3. Labor
4. Supervisory labor
5. Craft labor
6. General conditions
7. Direct labor charge
8. Loss of productivity
9. Extended overhead

It is commonly understood in the construction industry that there are two types of overhead. There is *main office overhead* and *job overhead.* Job overhead and *general conditions* are often used interchangably and are referred to accasionally as job overhead/general conditions.

Main office overhead includes: salaries of officers, estimators, and engineers; office rent; furniture; stationery; utilities; insurance; taxes; legal and consulting fees; sales expense; equipment purchases; and similar costs that relate to the main office and the construction yard.

Job overhead and general conditions are usually divided into two groups of costs: (1) overhead/general conditions; and (2) special conditions. The former includes: supervision, temporary offices, payroll taxes, insurance, and normal charges. Specifically, these last include the job office personnel, project manager, superintendent, timekeeping secretary and field engineer, sometimes known as indirect labor. Special conditions include extraordinary charges like testings and field inspections.

It is important at the outset that terms used be fully defined before calculations of costs are made.

§4.65 1. Loss of Productivity

Loss of productivity can have various causes, including the following:

1. Changes in design during midconstruction
2. Delay in approval of shop drawings
3. Delay in clarification of plans and specifications
4. Weather conditions
5. Labor disputes
6. Unforeseen conditions of the job

Evidence proving these causes for loss of productivity can be records of changes, addenda, verbal hold orders confirmed by memos, and revision sketches provided by the architect. Each such document which refers to changes must be dated and compared to the job progress records. It may be possible to note the time of change on the critical path method chart, and determine impact graphically and mathematically.

Loss of productivity is generally given as a percentage of normal productivity. It does not apply to extended time of completion or extra material costs. Rather, this loss factor is an intangible element, taking in confusion on the part of superintendents, foremen, and craftsworkers. It can mean relocating construction equipment and scaffolding, loss of work continuity, and loss of worker morale. More seriously, it can require the layoff of an experienced crew and its replacement in the future with a new and untried crew. Subcontractors who have been instructed to delay starting or completing their work will assign their workers and material to other jobs; such subcontractors will not be available immediately at the call of the superintendent.

There is a long, interconnected chain of cause and effect linking most of the personnel and equipment connected with the job and its planned schedule. The key item of evidence in calculating loss of productivity is the detailed job schedule. This should be backed up by memos, letters, and the daily construction log.

Loss of productivity occurs when the subcontractors and the superintendent hold workers on the job with little to do while waiting for a decision on a change order. Manhours per unit work figures would indicate a slowdown in productivity.

Loss of productivity is especially serious in jobs involving remodeling or additions to existing facilities. A typical case was that of an addition to an existing hospital. The contractor blamed the loss of productivity on the many changes in scheduling, excessive bulletins, and lack of cooperation from the owner. Although the hospital agreed at the beginning of the job to a schedule which would allow the contractor access to certain work areas, the hospital management changed this schedule because of internal operating problems. A continuing conflict between the hospital management and the contractor resulted over who should suffer the greatest inconvenience during the construction period. In addition, the contractor was not able to complete work in certain areas as scheduled which would have allowed the hospital to move into such completed areas and vacate other areas of the hospital needed by the contractor.

Evidence used by both sides included the original schedule, letters, and memos from the contractor and the hospital relating to the completion dates for certain areas and vacation dates for other areas.

Another effect of productivity loss is the necessity to make up for time lost due to delays. This problem is solved by assigning more workers and equipment than is efficient. Loading a job with a surplus of workers and equipment for a short period of time, in order to complete the project before the deadline date, may reduce productivity by 20 per cent because of interference caused by the situation. These periods of inefficiency can be documented by the job log, personnel list, and production records from the particular period.

Loss of productivity can be documented by preparation of the following:

1. Charts showing effects of change bulletins on schedule
2. Curves showing actual and estimated labor costs
3. Critical path method chart
4. Tabulation of bulletins
5. Chart showing estimated total project cost versus time
6. Chart showing estimated labor cost versus time
7. Indication of period of effect

§4.66 2. Extended Overhead

Extended overhead is the cost of maintaining supervisory personnel, support, and other expenses beyond the date by which the job was to have been completed. An extension of completion time would automatically increase the overhead of the job for the extended period.

Extra costs for changes and additions to a job do not necessarily cover the extended overhead resulting from these changes. There must be clarification when granting additional time for changes, including a percentage for overhead and profit, as to whether this figure will cover extended overhead.

A review should be made of every request for extra cost by the contractor which does not include a request for time extension. All bulletins should be analyzed to determine whether they caused delay or extended time for the job.

A search should be made of all records of notices by the contractor or the architect that the job was being delayed by change orders which required approval. These materials should be backed up with drawings, sketches, changes in schedule, or other documents.

Extended overhead can be described as all costs except direct labor which contribute to the contractor's overhead for the period beyond the original date of completion. This overhead includes equipment, temporary offices, tools, and supervisory and administrative personnel. Also included are services such as telephone, electricity, fuel, and that part of the contractor's home office expense that relates directly to the subject project.

§4.67 3. Costs of Labor

In disputes relating to construction change orders or unexpected difficulties, it may be necessary to compute the amount of extra construction labor costs.

Prevailing rates and fringe benefits for each craft at the time of an event can be determined. The United States Department of Labor, Bureau of Labor Statistics publishes data listing the prevailing minimum wages payable in federal and federally assisted construction projects to laborers and mechanics engaged in contract work pursuant to the provisions of the Davis-Bacon Act. This minimum rate is listed for all major cities in the continental United States.

Tabulations of rates are subdivided into:

1. Basic hourly rate
2. Fringe benefit payments, which include health and welfare, pensions, vacations, and education and/or apprentice training
3. Total hourly rate

An index is included after the listing for each location to indicate percentage of increase or decrease in total hourly rate over the previous month.

§4.68 4. Costs of Material

In addition to labor costs, the principal construction material costs are also published by the United States Department of Labor, Bureau of Labor Statistics. These costs are recorded for the years 1967 to the present. Construction materials covered include:

1. Softwood lumber
2. Hardwood
3. Plywood
4. Building paper and board
5. Steel products
6. Nonferrous metal material
7. Plumbing fixtures
8. Heating equipment
9. Concrete ingredients
10. Clay products
11. Plastic materials
12. Gypsum wallboard
13. Glass
14. Insulation

The above list of selected construction material prices uses information from the following sources:

1. *Boeckh Indexes*, The American Appraisal Co., Inc. (residences, apartments, hotel/office buildings, commercial and industrial)
2. *Engineering News-Record* (buildings and construction)
3. Environmental Protection Agency (sewers and plants)
4. Federal Highway Administration (structures, composite)
5. Bureau of Census (new one-family houses)
6. Bureau of Reclamation
7. Turner Construction Company
8. Handy-Whitman Public Utility (buildings and electrical light and power)

§4.69 5. Professional Organizations for Construction Cost Appraisals

Where there is need for accurate estimation or appraisals of replacement costs or confirmation of extra work, the following associations are recommended sources of experts:

American Society of Professional Estimators
7989 Othella Street, Suite A
San Diego, CA 92111

American Association of Cost Engineers
308 Monongahela Building
Morgantown, WV 26505

§4.70 J. Determining Liability for Damages

The legal standard for determining professional negligence, or malpractice, requires proof that a person who is considered to be a professional (as determined by education, training, licensing, and/or experience) has failed in the rendering of services to meet the standards of ordinary care and skill expected of the average practitioner in the class to which the professional belongs, who is acting in similar circumstances.[82]

The main areas of malpractice are: incomplete design analysis; failures in communication with clients, contractors and others; use of ill-prepared documents; and unsound management procedures.

§4.71 1. Errors and Omissions

From the viewpoint of the engineer, *error* means a mathematical mistake, such as a decimal point located in the wrong place, an improper function such as plus instead of minus, or incorrect use of a factor in a formula. Incorrect dimensions on a drawing would also be considered an error. These are all similar to the typographical errors made by a typist; however, their consequences are far more serious. Mathematical errors tend to compound when extended through the calculations and may end in grossly erroneous answers which cannot always be detected. A result of this type of error might include selection of undersized shaft or building column.

An *omission* is a different type of mistake. An example would be neglecting to specify number or size of bolts. This type of mistake usually occurs because of a rushed job and lack of checking.

Errors and omissions are usually associated with the design and detailing function of a professional engineer. Many items are constructed without any design involvement. These items are conceived out of experience or as copies of existing items with some variation. Some products which become subjects of litigation receive their only engineering analysis from the expert witness assigned to the case.

Use of computers in mathematical analysis has changed the whole picture in the area of assigning design responsibility. When the professional engineer prepared the entire analysis, personally or using supervised subordinates, and recorded calculations in a universally accepted manner, the accuracy of the analysis could be checked. However, at present, many problems can only be analyzed by a computer. Since programming a computer to solve specific problems is a specialty in itself, the engineer relies on another party for accurate programming and solution to the problem. These programs are often proprietary, and are not divulged for inspection. The engineer may make spot checks; however, generally the engineer must rely on answers provided by the computer operator.

§4.72 2. Suggested Evidence to Establish Liability

The check list below suggests particular types of evidence which may be helpful in determining liability arising out of the following kinds of cases:

---

[82]Cowles v Minneapolis, 128 Minn 452, 151 NW 184 (1915).

1. Negligence Cases
   a. Plans
   b. Specifications
   c. Contracts
   d. Soil tests
   e. Engineering standards
2. Fraud Cases
   a. Bid proposals
   b. Soil report
   c. Payment certificates
   d. State licenses
3. Statutory Liability Cases
   a. Building codes
   b. Zoning codes
   c. Inspection reports
   d. Licensing reports
   e. Safety codes
   f. Scaffolding act
   g. Job photos
4. Contract Cases
   a. Inspection records
   b. Plans and specifications
   c. Construction contract
   d. Design contract
5. Estimate Liability Cases
   a. Preliminary cost estimate
   b. Change orders
   c. Construction contract
   d. Subcontractors' bids
   e. Records of delays
   f. Weather records
   g. Records of average building costs
   h. Payroll records
6. Warranty Cases
   a. Survey records
   b. Plans and specifications
   c. Soil compaction report
   d. Equipment brochures and manuals

e. Subcontracts
f. Pile driving records
g. Inspection reports
h. Construction contract

§4.73 3. Preventive Law

Preventive law, in the area of malpractice claims, can take in the following procedures:

1. Internal quality control methods and procedures to minimize chance of errors and assure excellence
2. Specific contract language and conduct during the engagement that accepts only necessary liability risks
3. Insurance against risks which the firm cannot handle by itself

Internal quality control demands the minimum of human error. Independent review is the best way to catch and correct errors. Each major decision or analysis should be reviewed by a second person who can exercise independent judgment. Depending on the complexity and importance of the decision, a third or fourth review may be needed to assure that discipline interfaces and overall project concerns are adequately taken into account.

Another important quality control element is complete and documented client communication. First and foremost, the professional needs to understand the client's needs and objectives.

In order to achieve risk control there must be a thorough understanding with the client as to the scope of services and the responsibility of the design professional. The professional should avoid any unplanned risk assumption. The client should be involved in decisions relating to the client's use of the project, project cost, and potential risks. In addition, the client's understanding in these areas should be documented.

K. Typical Construction Cases

§4.74 1. Case of the Defective Condominium

This case contains examples of malpractice, misrepresentation, and negligence on part of the building designers. The contractor failed to supervise the project, accepted defective work from the subcontractors, and refused to make corrections or to repair damages caused by defective work.

To briefly recount the facts, the owner-client purchased a parcel of land. Included as part of the sale was a set of plans and specifications for a condominium designed for this parcel. The plans had been prepared by a building designer rather than an architect. The building designer retained a registered civil engineer to design the structural elements of the building. A building permit was issued on these plans.

A contractor offered to construct this project on a *cost-plus-fee* basis, on the condition that a licensed architect of the contractor's choice be retained by the owner to correct and modify the plans. The owner-client retained the recommended architect, who modified the plans and, in turn, retained a structural engineer to review the structural design. All changes to the plans were described as revisions so as to avoid initiating a new permit. A cost-plus-fee contract was executed by the owner-client and the contractor. During construction, the architect provided inspection services.

On completion of the building and after all units had been sold and occupied, many defects became obvious. When corrections of the defects were demanded from the contractor, the contractor denied responsibility on the grounds that the plans had been followed. The architect also denied responsibility, insisting that such architect was a consultant and not the architect of record. The original building designer disclaimed any responsibility, arguing that the plans had been changed by others. The subcontractors who did most of the work denied responsibility, claiming that although the plans were incomplete, the building had cleared building inspection.

Briefly, the damages and defects in the buildings were that: balconies and roofs leaked; concrete columns supporting the building cracked; metal caps on all chimneys corroded and leaked water into the building; and exhaust gases from basement garages leaked into the first-floor living quarters.

An engineering expert was retained by the owner-client to determine the causes of the leaks in the building and cracks in the concrete columns and to ascertain who was responsible for the defects. The expert inspected the buildings, prepared notes and sketches of observations, photographed all visible defects, reviewed the original and modified plans and specifications, and conferred with the building designer, civil engineer, architect, and contractor. The expert also got in touch with the manufacturers of various building components used on this job to find out about the properties of those materials.

The causes of the defects were found to be:

1. Improper use of unprotected, lightweight concrete decks on the balconies
2. Lack of drainage slope
3. Lack of expansion joints
4. Inadequate flashing

The cracked concrete columns were improperly placed directly under expansion joints in the floor slab. The expansion joints in the first-floor slab did not have an adequate seal to prevent gases from passing into the living quarters. Sheet-metal caps on the fireplace stacks were too thin and did not have proper slope for drainage.

It was easier to determine the causes of leaks and failures than to identify parties responsible for the defects. The engineering expert reported on the cast of characters in this job as follows:

1. The building designer stamped the plans with a seal which stated that he was a certified architectural designer. There was no such title in the state code governing licensing of architects. However, since a registered civil engineer was involved, the local building and safety department disregarded the non-licensed status of the designer and considered the civil engineer as the engineer of record

and as responsible for the entire design of the building. A building permit was granted after a cursory check of the plans

2. The building department, in relying on the skill of the design professional (licensed architect or registered professional engineer) to properly prepare plans and specifications, only checks for major safety features. Waterproofing and appearance are not concerns of the building department. Even in the area of safety, the building department does not make a comprehensive check. In this case, the department missed the improper column design
3. The building department inspector's function is also directed towards safety compliance in the approved plans. Acceptance by the inspector does not mean there has been compliance with good design or the building code. The workload of the plans checker and inspector very much influences the extent of any plans check and construction inspection. In this case, such inspection was minimal
4. The licensed architect had a dual position. One role was to provide responsible professional services in upgrading the plans and specifications; the other was to provide architectural consulting services only, in the exercise of which role responsibility remains with the original designer. There was a conflict of professional ethics. The licensed architect became subservient to a non-licensed designer. This would be similar to a lawyer providing consulting services to a law clerk performing legal services and thereby relinquishing responsibility. The plans and specifications on this project were so poor that many errors were not corrected by the architect. In addition, to avoid possible delay from initiation of a new building permit, changes were kept to a minimum. All changes were noted to be revisions. Another factor which influenced the architect was the standard of work at that time in construction of speculative buildings, which was to use loose plans and specifications, allowing the general contractor flexibility in slecting the lowest bid from all subcontractors. The lowest bid means the absolute minimum in quality and workmanship acceptable to the building department. As noted above, many areas of construction are not controlled by the building department. The result of all these factors is a marginal-quality building
5. The general contractor is also influenced by the current standard used in speculative buildings of this type
6. The contractor who subcontracted the major portion of the work relied on the subcontractors to interpret the plans. The fact that the plans and specifications were so ill-defined allowed the subcontractors to install the minimum of quality and workmanship. Ironically, the minimum has become the standard in this type of project
7. The building department, understaffed for the construction boom and with little jurisdiction over the quality of material or workmanship, did not police the job

In summary, the owners of individual units discovered water leaks throughout the walls and ceilings as well as ponding of the balcony decks. In addition, driving rain passed through their double-entrance doors. Interior finishes and carpets were ruined.

The engineering expert had little difficulty documenting the defects but found apportioning liability more complex. The principal culprit was a faulty set of plans and specifications which gave very little control over material and workmanship. As each materialman and subcontractor shaved quality to be competitive, the end result was a flimsily constructed, $4.5 million project which had many angry owners and was a source of complex lawsuits.

§4.75 2. Case of the Cracking Concrete Walls

Soon after completion of a 12-foot by 120-foot concrete tank which was to be used for an oil/water separator, and before the tank was filled with water, vertical cracks about four feet apart appeared in both walls. The owner became concerned, withheld final payment to the contractor, and retained an attorney who in turn hired an expert to investigate and report on the causes and severity of the cracks.

After a visual inspection, the expert determined that there were several possible causes:

1. Uncompacted soil causing excessive settlement
2. Clayey soil losing strength due to penetration of water
3. Insufficient reinforcement in the wall
4. Incorrect wall design
5. Weak concrete mix
6. Improper curing of concrete

The expert checked each point by the following actions:

1. Obtaining a copy of the soil compaction report, made by a soil engineer, which was found to be adequate
2. Reviewing the soil analysis report, and determining that the soil was sandy and not affected by moisture
3. Requesting a recheck of the number of bars placed in the wall. Records showed that the bars were according to plans
4. Requesting a recheck on design and plans which were found to be correct, except that no control joints were called for
5. Checking the records of the concrete mix delivered to the job. This was found to be better than specified
6. Checking whether the concrete work was kept continuously moist for seven days after pouring. Here it was discovered that no effort had been made to wet down the concrete following the pour, and that the week following had been unusually hot

The above investigation found that cracking was due to shrinkage of concrete during curing. The number of cracks would have been much smaller if proper curing procedures had been followed. If control joints had been installed, the cracks would have occurred in the joints and would have been less noticeable. The conclusion was that although the cracks were unsightly, they would not increase but would instead decrease in size from the moisture of the contained water.

To understand the properties of reinforced concrete structures, the expert should analyze each type of failure. Failure results from exceeding the ultimate strength of a particular stress, whether compression, shear, bond, or bearing. The expert should develop a mental picture of each type of failure and review all stresses created under expected loads.

An example of failure in compression would be a concrete pedestal crushing under a heavily loaded steel column. Figure 4-21(a) illustrates a failure in tension of a concrete beam with inadequate reinforcing steel. The bottom of the beam cracks open in failure of tension. Figure 4-21(b) shows a concrete beam failing in a diagonal shear. These cracks appear diagonally from the point of support, sloping in toward the center of the beam. Figure 4-21(c) illustrates a concrete beam failing in vertical shear. The shear is perpendicular to the beam. Figure 4-21(d) shows a concrete cantilever beam failing due to the overstress in bond of the reinforcing bars which have pulled loose in the concrete.

§4.76 L. Additional Readings

James Acret, *Architects and Engineers, Their Professional Responsibilities*, Shepard's/McGraw-Hill, Colorado Springs, Colo, 1977.

James Acret, *California Construction Law Manual*, Shepard's/McGraw-Hill, Colorado Springs, Colo, 1975.

Charles J. Allen, The Use of the Computer in the Design Office, *Consulting Engineer*, 55, February 1977.

James M. Antill & Ronald W. Woodhead, *Critical Path Methods in Construction Practice*, Wiley-Interscience, New York, NY, 2d ed 1970.

BOCA Basic Building Code, Building Officials & Code Administrators International, Inc, Chicago, Ill, 1970.

Brown & Eldridge, *Evidence and Procedures for Boundary Locations*, John Wiley & Sons, New York, NY, 1962.

Cushman, Simon & Stokes, *Construction Industry Formbook*, Shepard's/McGraw-Hill, Colorado Springs, Colo, 1979.

Max Feldman, A Contractor Looks at the Causes of Construction Contract Disputes, *Arbitration Journal*, September 1972.

Fire Code, County of Los Angeles, 1968.

Edwin H. Gaylord & Charles D. Gaylord, *Structural Engineers Handbook*, McGraw-Hill Book Co, New York, NY, 1968.

General Conditions of the Contract for Construction, AIA Document A201, The American Institute of Architects, Washington, DC, 1970.

John R. Groves, Jr., Building Code Officials and Design Professionals: The Need for Cooperation Has Never Been Greater, *Building Safety*, March, April 1979.

Havers & Stubbs, *Handbook of Heavy Construction*, McGraw-Hill Book Co, New York, NY, 1971.

Jack M. Landers, *Construction Materials, Methods, Careers*, The Good Heart-Wilcox Co, South Holland, Ill, 1976.

Letter Symbols for Units Used in Science and Technology, American National Standards, 1972.

Bernard T. Lewis, *Management Handbook for Plant Engineers*, McGraw-Hill Book Co, New York, NY, 1977.

Manual of Steel Construction, American Institute of Steel Construction, Inc, Chicago, Ill, 8th ed 1980.

National Electrical Code, National Fire Protection Association International, 470 Atlantic Ave, Boston, Mass 02210, 1978.

Plan Review Manual, International Conference of Building Officials, Pasadena, Cal, 1971.

Planning and Zoning Code, City of Los Angeles, 1975.

Process Plant Construction Estimating Standards, Richardson Engineering Services, Inc, San Marcos, Cal, 1979.

Joseph C. Rodgers, CEPA Members Keep Pace with Computer Advances, *Consulting Engineer*, 85, July 1979.

Dwight C. Schroeder, Quality Control in Design, *Consulting Engineer*, September 1976.

Max Schwartz, *Civil Engineering for Plant Engineers*, McGraw-Hill Book Co, New York, NY, 1972.

Uniform Building Code, International Conference of Building Officials, Whittier, Cal, 1979.

Leonard Church Urquhart, *Civil Engineering Handbook*, McGraw-Hill Book Co, New York, NY, 4th ed 1959.

5 Discovering Evidence in Catastrophic, Natural Disasters

§5.01 A. Types of Disasters

Common types of natural disasters include earthquakes,[1] floods,[2] mudslides,[3] and windstorms. In most litigation arising out of these catastrophic events, the damaged plaintiff is seeking to recover compensation from building contractors, federal, state, and local agencies, or architects and engineers.

§5.02 1. Earthquakes

Since most destructive earthquakes result from movements along faults, the locations and characteristics of faults in an earthquake belt are of particular interest. This is especially true of active faults, that is, those that either have a history of earthquake foci along their courses or show evidence of geological movement within the last few thousand years. A fault is considered active if it has displaced recent alluvium deposit and its surface effects have not been modified significantly by erosion.

Faulting may occur in all kinds of rock. In addition, displacement at any particular time may extend from a fraction of an inch to several feet in distance.

All along the course of a major fault, repeated small displacements with resulting earthquakes may take place at irregular intervals over long periods of geologic time. The cumulative relative displacement length may amount to several miles.

In such situations the fault becomes a fault zone of shattered and broken rocks; such a zone may be more than a mile wide. This fault zone may be characterized by rock formations of widely different type, structure, and age which are brought into contact.

The surface along which the movement takes place may approach a plane. However, it is usually highly irregular, marked by the development of slickensides, breccia (broken rock), and gouge (clay-like powdered rock). The fault surface may dip (incline) at any angle from the horizontal to vertical, but most faults approach the vertical. Relative displacement of the opposite sides of the fault may be horizontal, vertical, or a combination. (See Figure 5-1 for movement along fault.)

---

[1] **§5.02.**
[2] **§5.03.**
[3] **§5.04.**

Figure 5-1 Causes of Earthquakes

(a) Adjacent blocks of earth's crust begin to move in opposite directions

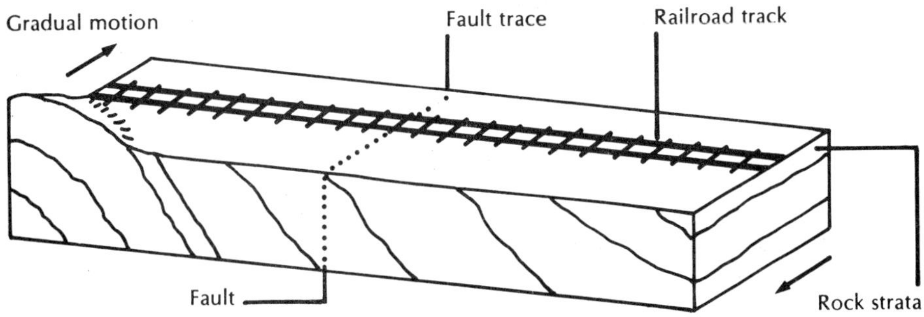

(b) This motion stores strain energy in the crust until finally the elastic limit is reached

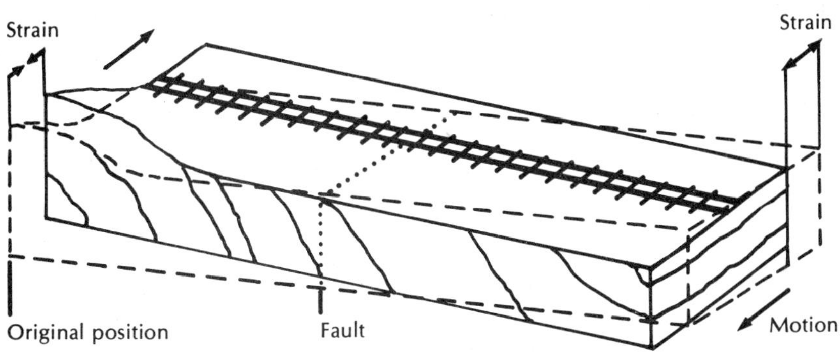

(c) Fracture of the rock allows sudden movement at the fault and releases stored energy causing an earthquake

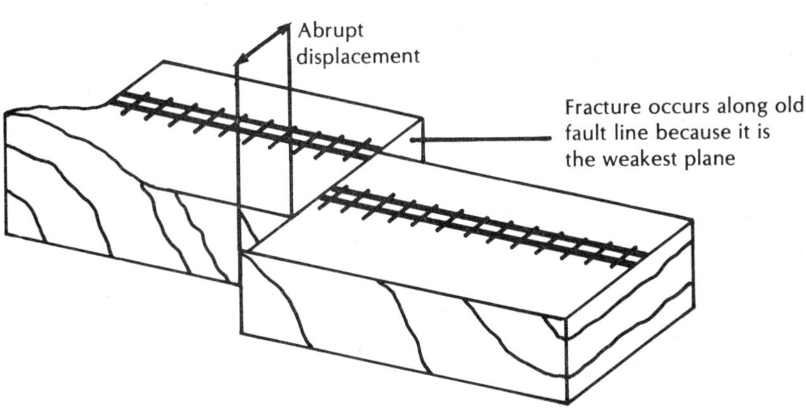

§5.03 2. Floods

Potential defendants in a case of flood damage may be the civil engineer, contractor, or public agency responsible for the design and construction of flood control devices.

A characteristic common to claims resulting from floods is that they are often brought by a class of plaintiffs. This is a frequent occurrence because such catastrophic events usually affect more than one person at a time.

Land developments, roadways, and other facilities which are exposed to the flood hazard must meet minimum design standards. Many governmental agencies and professional associations have established design criteria. Special consideration is given to land subject to overflow, ponding, or high ground water by regional planning commissions and real estate commissions.

Storms are usually classified as *frequent*, *infrequent*, or *remote*. A frequent storm, or other dangerous condition, is one that can occur at intervals of ten years or less when averaged over a long period of time. For example, over a 500-year period, a frequent storm may be expected to occur at least 50 times. Several of these conditions may occur in a single decade, or there may be no so such occurrence for several decades.

An infrequent condition is one with an average interval between occurrences of longer than ten years. A remote flood depends on conditions which do not lend themselves to frequency analysis. This would include situations such as a stream's diversion from its present bed due to a breach of the channel bank, a deposit of debris, or other channel obstructions.

§5.04 3. Landslides and Subsidence

In mountainous areas which have been developed into residential zones, there are frequent mudslides, landslides, subsidence, and various earth movements. Occasionally, entire housing tracts and apartment structures will be damaged in a single rainy season. Some structures are damaged beyond repair, while others require expensive reconstruction. Plaintiffs in such cases are usually the property owners. The defendants may be prior owners, building contractors,[4] architects[5] and engineers,[6] the building department, the grading department, soils engineers,[7] geologists, and grading contractors.[8]

The evidence required in such a controversy may include geological reports[9] based on surface structures of the soil and rocks, and core borings reports which sample the earth at various depth levels.

In addition, topographic maps[10] showing the original as compared to final topography after development of the area often may be important evidence. In many in-

---

[4]§2.38.

[5]§2.06.

[6]§2.03.

[7]§2.04.

[8]§2.39.

[9]§5.18.

[10]§5.05.

stances, these maps show storm drainage devices which may identify the possible causes of landslides and subsidence.

B. Acquisition of Historic Documents

§5.05 1. Topographic Maps

A topographic map is a drawing of a portion of land in which the surface is illustrated by a series of contour lines. Each contour line represents a level of equal elevation. These contour lines are identified by numbers indicating the elevations they represent above some basic datum. The datum may be sea level or an arbitrarily assumed elevation.

Topographic maps showing both contour lines and spot elevations appear in Figures 5-2 and 5-3. A steep gradient causes the contour lines to group closer together, while a flattening makes them spread out. Shading often indicates a sudden embankment, and hachure marks mean a depression. The slope or grade between two points is determined by the vertical distance divided by the horizontal distance stated as a ratio or a percentage.

The ridge, or crest line, divides two drainage areas. The region from which the rainfall will drain to a particular channel or area is referred to as the watershed of that area. The natural watercourse can be a gully, valley, or ditch.

Every change of the land surface made by a grading contractor requires a survey of the existing ground surface to establish the topography prior to the grading operation. Finish grades are then determined above or below existing grades, and these are indicated on a grading plan. This represents the final topography. If the earthwork is under the control of a governmental agency, these topographic maps are retained as records by the local grading department, the department of building and safety, or the road department.

Topographic maps are made using aerial photography and land surveying, by the highway department, flood control agencies, and land developers.

§5.06 2. Weather Records

Weather records are obtainable from the federal, state, and county departments responsible for gathering and recording rainfall, runoff, temperature, and storm records. Rainfall records are measured at each weather monitoring station. They are given in terms of precipitation in inches per periods of time. Such periods may be per season, per storm, per 24-hour day, per hour or per 10-minute interval. Records may extend as far back as 100 years depending on the development of a particular area. State and county agencies involved in the design of structures affected by flooding generally maintain their own records of runoff and flooding conditions in their respective areas.

Runoff is measured as the volume of water per units of time flowing in creeks, streams, and rivers throughout the nation. Runoff is usually stated in acre-feet per second. This refers to a volume of water one foot deep covering one acre which flows past a point in one second. At critical points along most streams and rivers in the

Figure 5-2 Typical Topographic Map

From *Civil Engineering for the Plant Engineer* by Max Schwartz. Copyright © 1972 by McGraw-Hill, Inc. Used with the permission of McGraw-Hill Book Company.

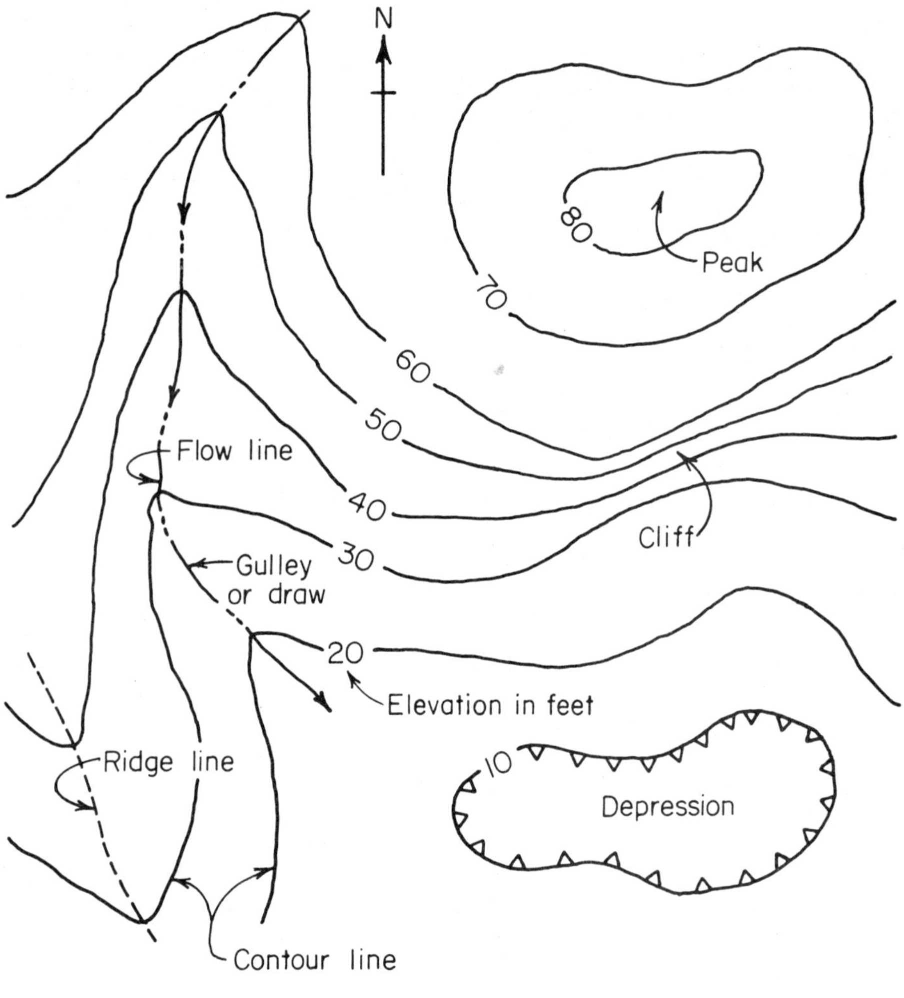

nation, there are gauging stations where the depth flow is measured and recorded at selected times. By determining the cross section of the riverbed, volume of water passing that point can be ascertained with the help of flow meters. This process is known as *stream gauging*.

Many piers and bridge abutments carry markings which indicate the depth of water.

Figure 5-3 Topographic Map by Spot Elevations

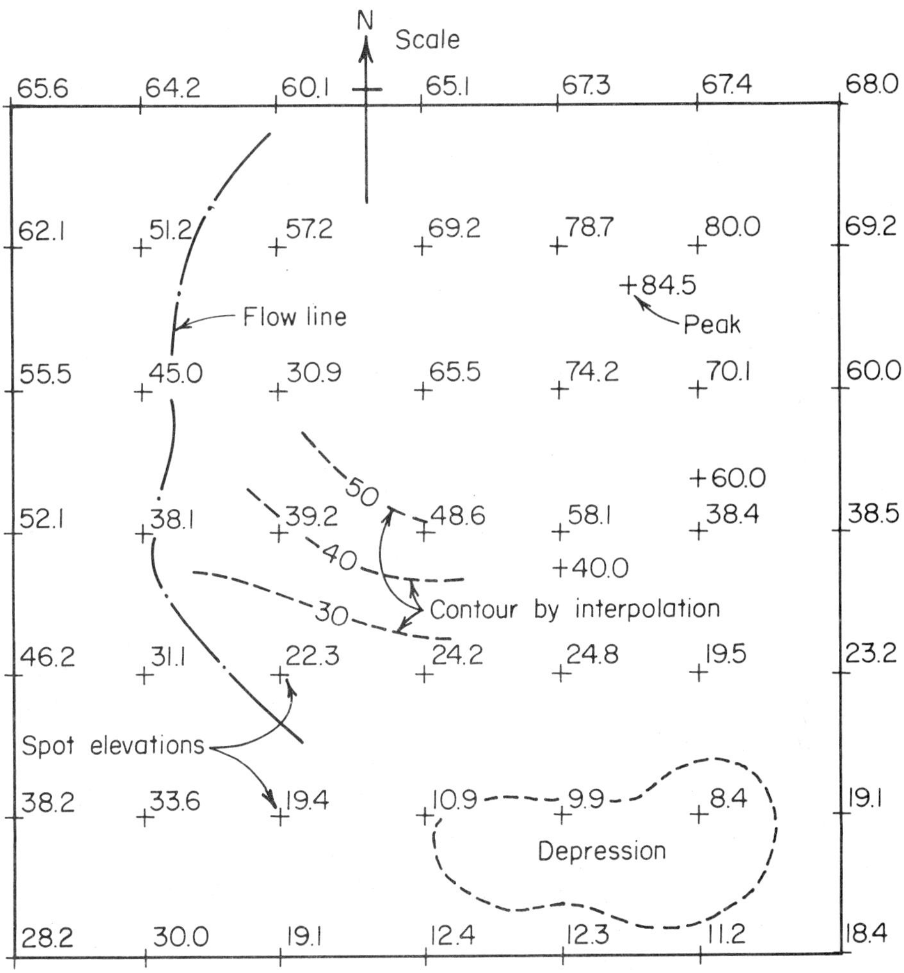

Monitoring of flow can be done by reading the depth of water at various points in time. By these means runoff over most of the country can be determined at any specific point. The runoff from any watershed or tributary area can be estimated by means of the history of runoff.

Flood records are compiled in a similar manner. Gauges may be installed at critical points to measure water level during various flood conditions.

Newspaper publications of weather reports and storm forecasts furnished by the National Weather Service sometimes can provide useful information. Those involved with the design and construction of projects exposed to flooding and flash storms should be aware of the warnings given by the National Weather Service.

The following illustrates a typical runoff tabulation by a county hydrology department:

RUNOFF RECORDING STATION NO. 5
ARROYO SECO AT CAMINO REAL NEAR SAN JUAN

LOCATION: LAT. 33°34′41″, LONG. 117°30′25″, approximately 300 feet downstream of freeway bridge, 1.8 miles north of San Juan.

DRAINAGE AREA: 45.6 square miles.

GAUGE: Float-operated, dual-pen water stage recorder on the downstream side of the Camino Real Bridge on the center wall of a double rectangular channel. Communication to float well by siphon pipe from silt box in each channel. Altitude of gauge is 153 feet (from channel plans).

RECORDS AVAILABLE: October 1930 to present.

EXTREMES: Maximum discharge, 9240 cfs on February 6, 1937 gauge height 6.80); no flow at times each year.

AVERAGE DISCHARGE: 44 years (1932-1975): 5.41 cfs (3920 acre-feet per year); median of yearly mean discharges, 0.56 cfs (406 acre-feet (AF) per year).

REMARKS: Most low flows conserved in several small reservoirs or retarded in areas of gravel excavation above gauge. Maximum measurement for period of record, 3200 cfs on December 6, 1966. Station rating curve derived from Mannings equation.

A typical example of general weather records is the national and local weather forecast as published in a daily newspaper. Data includes: a national, regional, and local weather map in which high and low pressure areas are shown; the movement of cold and warm fronts, stationary and occluded fronts; areas of rain and snowfall; low and high temperatures; wind direction; and the anticipated cloud condition at various cities. Also, there are weather reports and three, to five-day forecasts for geographical regions which describe cloud conditions, temperatures, rain and snow, and wind velocity.

§5.07 a. Records of National Oceanic and Atmospheric Administration Weather Service

Climatological data is also available from the United States Department of Commerce, National Oceanic and Atmospheric Administration National Weather Service. This information includes the following:

1. Location of each recording station by name, latitude, longitude, and ground elevation
2. Daily record of each month for

a. Temperature
    (1) Maximum
    (2) Minimum
    (3) Average
    (4) Departure from normal
b. Precipitation
    (1) Total water equivalent
    (2) Snowfall, ice pellets
c. Wind
    (1) Average speed (mph)
    (2) Fastest speed
    (3) Direction

3. Maximum recorded rainfall in inches, per month and per year
    a. 5-minute duration
    b. 10-minute duration
    c. 15-minute duration
    d. 30-minute duration
    e. 1 hour
    f. 2 hours
    g. 24-hour period
    h. Calendar day
    i. Month
    j. Seasonal
    k. Storm
4. Minimum recorded rainfall in inches, per month and per year
    a. Season
5. Longest period of consecutive days of rain
6. Longest period of consecutive days without measurable rain
7. Greatest snowfall in 24-hour period

Based on the above data, it is possible to view a storm which results in litigation against the history of storms for that particular area.

§5.08 3. Flood and Runoff Records

The case history now discussed will outline the evidence needed in litigation resulting from a flood.

A housing developer, whose project included construction of a recreational lake, retained an engineering firm to design a 5-mile long, 21-inch diameter pipeline to supply water from deep well pumps to the recreational lake. The plans and specifications were completed, and were submitted to the local water company for approval. The water company was to be given ownership and maintenance responsibility for the pipeline on completion. After approval by the water company, the plans were offered for competitive bidding by contractors. The contractor who submitted the lowest bid was awarded the contract.

The pipeline was to be constructed mainly on the side of a hill, except for a one-mile portion which was located in a dry creek bed. The job was nearly complete when a heavy rainstorm struck the area. The creek bed became a raging torrent, and the one-mile length of pipeline was washed out.

The contractor, who had obtained a flood damage insurance policy at the outset of the project, demanded payment for reconstruction of the pipeline. The estimated cost of reinstallation of the pipe was $300,000. The insurance company retained an engineering expert to find out two things: first, to verify whether the cost claimed by the contractor was realistic; second, to determine whether any person was responsible for the destruction of the pipeline.

In carrying out the first assigned task, the engineering expert conferred with the pipeline contractor, the engineers who designed the project, the land developer, and the water company. The expert also obtained a number of documents which would ultimately be used as engineering evidence if there turned out to be litigation. These documents were the plans and profiles of the five-mile pipeline over its entire length. Also included were details of the concrete anchorage devices, relief valves, elbows, concrete encasement of the pipeline under certain water crossings (locations where pipes cross streams or rivers), and the general notes which described the materials to be used on the pipeline. Attached to the plans, profiles, and details was a set of standard specifications printed by the local water company. The specifications contained general conditions and a description of the excavation, backfill, pipeline material, and the various appurtenances to the pipeline. Additional documents included the request for bids prepared by the developer, the proposal made by the subject engineering contractor, and an alternative to the material of the pipeline.

In this case, the plans and specifications called for a steel pipe with welded joints. But the alternate proposal was for a ductile iron pipe with bell and spigot joints. The substitution was approved by both the developer and the water company. The reason for substitution of material was earlier delivery time as well as a lower installation cost. The engineering expert also obtained from the contractor a breakdown of the cost of reinstalling the pipe which included equipment, material, and labor.

Since the first task was to verify the cost of replacing the pipeline, there was no need to investigate the cause of destruction at this point. The expert's functions focused on confirming the manhours involved, as well as the costs of labor, equipment, and materials. Investigative activities included x-ray testing of the salvaged pipe and purchase of new pipe. The engineering expert completed verification of the estimates and then reported his opinion to the insurance company.

An alternative to replacing the pipe in its original location was another plan prepared by the contractor and land developer, which proposed installation of the pipeline in a different location. The alternate location was along the side of the hill as opposed to the old location in the creek bed. The plan required acquisition of additional lands and easements. However, its ultimate cost was estimated to be less than the cost of reinstalling the pipeline back in the creek bed. The new plan would also carry a prediction of no future risk of washout. The cost of the alternate pipeline plan was reviewed and confirmed by the expert.

The insurance company agreed to finance the change in location since it was proved to cost less than reinstallation of the pipe in the creek bed. The new location was determined to be a safer one as well.

The expert was then instructed to go on to ascertain causes of initial damages, and to determine whether there was any possibility of subrogating, so that the insurance company might recover its losses from another source. The engineering expert commenced his inquiries with a search for new documents. His investigation included several visits to the county flood control district and county department of hydrology.

The expert found that the subject creek bed had a history of major floods over the preceding 50 years. The intensity of these floods and the resulting damages were documented in the records of the county offices. Data on rainfall intensity for the preceding 50 years was obtained from the National Weather Service and compared with figures from the recent storm. In the flood control office, the expert reviewed information which clearly indicated existence of flood control improvements downstream of the area in which the pipeline was destroyed. The expert determined that these improvements were designed and documented prior to the design and construction of the subject pipeline. Thus, pertinent flooding information was available to the engineers responsible for design and approval of the water pipeline. In addition, the expert noted on the pipeline drawings that a sanitary sewer existed adjacent and parallel to the water pipeline, yet the sanitary sewer was at least eight feet deeper than the subject pipeline, which was at a four-foot depth.

The expert went to the sanitation district for copies of the original plans for that particular sanitary sewer. These designs had been prepared and documented prior to the design of the subject pipeline, hence they were accessible to pipeline engineers. From these documents, the expert determined that designers of the sanitary sewers had been aware of the flooding conditions and had designed the sanitary sewer, which did not wash out, at a depth adequate to prevent destruction by flooding. Various protecting devices were incorporated into the sanitary sewer to prevent the manholes from being undermined by flood waters. The engineering expert concluded from a review of the sanitary sewer plans that the designers of the water lines should have taken notice of the unusual depth of the sewer line.

From the local newspapers, the expert obtained photographs showing the raging water of the river. From the hydrology department, the expert obtained photographs showing prior damage to bridges, roadways, and structures along the creek bed.

Finally, the engineering expert looked into the characteristics of the alternate pipe that was installed. Whereas the original plans called for a steel pipe with all joints welded, the alternate was a ductile iron pipe with bell and spigot joints. The latter type of joint was flexible, and under outside twisting action was prone to separate. The expert determined that this pipe could not withstand the disturbances caused by rapidly flowing water.

In summary, the expert reported that the design engineers of the pipeline had been negligent in the following respects:

1. Failing to review the history of that creek bed

2. Failing to set the pipe at an adequate depth since the sanitary sewer was at 12 feet while the water pipe was only at a 4-foot depth
3. Approving an alternate bell and spigot pipe which was not as rigid as the welded pipe and which was susceptible to damage from turbulence

The expert also questioned the water company's approval of the substitution of bell and spigot pipe for the welded pipe. The expert referred to standards of other authorities, including the Corps of Engineers, the State Department of Water Resources, the American Water Works Association and the American Society of Civil Engineers. Relying on the expert's report, the insurance company decided to subrogate in an attempt to recover its losses.

§5.09 a. Documents Used

As demonstrated in the previous section, the evidence used by experts in floods or washout conditions may consist of the following types of documents: plans and profile of the subject structure; original topography prior to the flood; topography subsequent to the flood; and photographs of earlier floods and their impact. Also of value are hydrology records showing rainfall over the entire watershed which contributed to the flow in the subject area, the plans and specifications of similar structures which sustained the flood impact without damage, and all data made available by the National Weather Service, appropriate professional associations, and the manufacturers of the subject product.

Where there is ample historical evidence of potential danger to a particular area, a conscientious engineer will research all available information and incorporate that data into the design of any new project. Most documents relating to natural catastrophic events are generated by public agencies, and as a result are available to the investigating expert at a minimum cost. The engineering expert should be aware that many governmental agencies are responsible for recording all historical events within their subject areas. Therefore, it becomes a question of determining what types of documents are required in the case of the specific structure under investigation.

§5.10 b. Determination of Runoff

The most accepted method for determining *runoff* [11] from areas subject to rainfall uses the *Rational Runoff Formula*[12]

$$Q = C\,i\,A$$

Where:

Q = The flow or peak discharge of watershed in cubic feet per second (cfs). Due to maximum storm assumed

---

[11]The part of precipitation which appears in streams and rivers.

[12]1 Elwyn E. Seelye, Data Book for Design Engineers 18-02 (John Wiley & Sons, London 1960).

i = Intensity of rainfall in inches per hour based on the concentration time, which is the time required for rain falling at the most remote point of the watershed to reach the discharge point

C = Coefficient of runoff which is the ratio of runoff to rainfall. The value is a function of the earth surface, such as degree of saturation, compaction, irregularity, slope, character of subsoil, and presence of frost, glazed snow, or ice.

A = Area of the watershed in acres

Rainfall intensity figures are based on a frequency of 10 to 50 years. Agencies regulating design and construction projects will impose a particular type of rainfall requirement depending on the work involved.

A typical hydrological report describing the historic runoff at a particular recording station might read as shown on the chart at **§5.06.**

§5.11 4. Earthquake Records

There has been a great deal of study all over the world of the nature of earthquakes and their potential recurrence. This study has taken on a greater interest since the volcanic eruption of Mt. St. Helens in Washington. Unlike runoff and flooding, the earthquake phenomenon is more abstract, and is difficult to measure and record.

Various scientific and engineering associations and governmental agencies have assigned particular zones of probability to seismic activity. The United States has been divided into zones of seismic probability ranging from 0 to 4.

Earthquakes generally have been measured by two primary methods. One method is the *Richter Magnitude Scale.* The other is the *Modified Mercalli Intensity Scale of 1931.* Structural engineers, however, use a factor equivalent to a percentage of the force of gravity to calculate the amount of earthquake force a structure sustains.

Earthquakes have been described as a wave action over the earth's surface resulting in a horizontal as well as a vertical movement. This wave action has a period, a frequency, and an amplitude. The waves may come from any direction, since their source may be anywhere within the seismic area.

Inasmuch as earthquakes and the designs needed to withstand earthquakes are continuously studied, the building codes of those states affected by frequent seismic activity have been subject to constant modification. Methods of design to protect from earthquakes are demonstrably different under present codes than under earlier versions. Consequently, a problem of standards arises when the issue in litigation is whether a structure was adequately designed to withstand earthquake activity. Inquiry should focus on the code that applied at the time of construction to that specific location.

In some metropolitan areas on the west coast where earthquakes are considered a normal occurrence, three different building codes may govern a single square-mile area. State, county, and municipal regulations on seismic design differ. Each code requires compliance with a different approach to earthquake design. In addition to regulations and formulas dictated by the building codes, the military services have their own methods of designing to protect against the effects of earthquake forces.

Some professional federal and state committees dedicated to research in the area of earthquake-resistant structures make recommendations which are more conservative than the requirements of prevailing building codes. Eventually, these recommendations are adopted by the various building departments in each governmental agency. The governing regulations tend to compromise in taking into account such factors as safety, the law of probability, economic considerations, and foreseeability of damages.

Earthquake design of buildings relates not only to seismic zone intensity, which is rated from 0 to 4, but also to other factors affecting a particular building or structure. These factors include the following:

1. Ratio of a building's height to its width
2. Type of framing used in the building, affecting the flexibility or rigidity of the structure
3. Soil condition beneath the building, whether resilient or rigid
4. Policy considerations of the importance of the building and how critical it is to the benefit of the community

§5.12 a. Sample Case

The following description of a case involving earthquake design illustrates the difficulty of making positive determinations about proper earthquake construction and design. Although no actual earthquake occurred in this particular case, consideration of a potential earthquake precipitated the litigation.

This was the case of a building contractor who offered to design and build a four-story office structure for a specified sum. The contractor retained an engineer to design the building. The final plans and calculations were approved by the city building department. Consequently, the building was constructed according to plans. Soon after the building was occupied by many tenants, the owner noted some apparent deflection of several beams. After the original design engineer assured the owner that the beam deflection was not serious, the owner retained another engineer to review the design of the beams. The second engineer's investigation expanded on the owner's request to take in full review of the building's entire structural design. The reviewing engineer reported that the building did not conform to the earthquake resistance requirements in effect at the time of construction. A disagreement developed between the original design engineer and the reviewing engineer. As a result, the owner retained the reviewing engineer to design remedial work. The concerned owner reported the findings of the reviewing engineer to the building department, and the reviewing engineer then became the engineer of record for the building. Subsequently, the building department ordered that the building be either reinforced or condemned.

The contractor was advised of this order, and the owner had the building reinforced by another contractor according to the design of the new engineer. The cost of the remedial work was $250,000, a figure approximately equal to the withheld portion due the original contractor. A lawsuit followed in which the first contractor sued for final payment for the initial construction. The owner cross-complained for the cost of remedial work. The issue in controversy was how to interpret regulations governing correct design for earthquake resistance. Each engineer approached the factors affecting earthquake design differently. The building department maintained that the ultimate responsibility for the building design was with the engineer of record. The dispute continued for years, in an attempt to establish a positive interpretation of the earthquake design. This included a comprehensive understanding of the facts and principal compromises on which the code provisions were based.

As knowledge of earthquakes and the properties of building materials exposed to violent shaking increases, the earthquake provisions of building codes will come closer to the optimum. It is not now possible to write a simple building code that will satisfactorily cover all possible types of buildings. This is why the earthquake resistant provisions of the building codes are geared for *typical* uniform building.

§5.13 b. Accelerograph Records

Accelerographs, which are instruments for detecting and measuring accelerations or vibrations, and are located in earthquake-prone areas, provide valuable engineering data on the seismic motions of the ground and structures. This data is the basis for improved methods of designing earthquake-resistant structures. Research on earthquakes and their effects is continuous. Only through research can the understanding of earthquakes be increased together with the ability to minimize their hazards. All public authorities are encouraged to cooperate with private and public agencies in collecting and publishing information on future earthquake probabilities. These authorities support field work and studies in geology, geophysics, soil dynamics, and physical response to earthquakes.

§5.14 c. Earthquake Fault Records

Strong shaking during an earthquake typically extends over many square miles, while permanent fault dislocation is a very localized phenomenon. For this reason, more structures are affected by shaking than by faulting. Accordingly, avoidance of faults is not, in itself, protection from earthquake damage, and fault locations are often unknown or poorly defined. Nevertheless, the building of structures directly across known active fault traces should be avoided whenever possible. Communication, transportation, and utility lines should not be run along major active faults for long distances if there are feasible alternatives.

§5.15 d. Seismograph Records

Ground vibrations caused by earthquakes are detected on instruments called *seismographs*. These instruments can record waves from earthquakes a great distance away.

The first waves of an earthquake recorded by seismographs appear to originate from a single point, called the *hypocenter*. This is believed to be the location of initial fracture of the rocks. The point on the earth's surface directly above the hypocenter is called the *epicenter*.

Formerly, earthquakes were rated solely on scales based on effects commonly observed during an earthquake. In such scales, degrees of damage were assigned numerical designations, so that intensity of an earthquake at a given location might be defined as the amount of disturbance felt.

The intensity scale most commonly used today is the *Modified Mercalli Scale of*

1931. Scales like this one are useful to seismologists, who summarize the effects data from a single earthquake as an *isoseismal map* which shows areas of equal intensity. A given earthquake will have a higher intensity at locations near the epicenter than at locations farther away. Comparison of earthquakes is better made using the *Richter Magnitude Scale*. The Richter Magnitude Scale is based on the amplitude of seismic waves which are recorded on a standard seismograph. This method takes into consideration the distance of the instrument from the epicenter.

The scale is logarithmic rather than arithmetic. Each graduation represents ground motion 10 times greater than the motion represented by the next lower graduation. An earthquake of magnitude 4 has ground motions 100 times greater than the ground motions of an earthquake of magnitude 2.

Earthquakes are vibrations transmitted as waves in the earth's crust. The wave transmission is similar to the waves generated when a pebble is dropped into a pond. Earthquakes may have a variety of causes, including landslides, explosive volcanic activity, movement of molten rock beneath the earth's crust, natural and artificial explosions, and abrupt movements of masses of rock along faults in the earth's crust.

Seismograph records show that there are deep-focus earthquakes originating at depths as great as 400 miles, shocks of intermediate origin at depths of 27 to 150 miles, and shallow earthquakes whose foci are at depths of less than 27 miles. All destructive earthquakes fall into the last group, and nearly all of these have been the result of sudden movements of blocks of the earth's crust along faults. Rock, which makes up the crust of the earth, is elastic, and yields to stresses by slow creep over periods of time. Records of the San Andreas Fault in California show that the block on the east side of that fault is moving southward with respect to the west block at a rate of about two inches per year.

When the elastic limit of the rock material is exceeded at any point or the friction along an old fault surface is overcome, there will be an abrupt movement. A 21-foot horizontal displacement took place along the San Andreas Fault to cause the San Francisco earthquake in 1906.

The exact causes of such stresses are not thoroughly understood; however, they are known to be common at the margins of continental platforms and ocean deeps. The number of variables involved, the lack of recorded data covering a long period, and the incomplete measurements of all observed phenomena make predictions of specific earthquakes for a particular time and place impossible at this time.

§5.16 e. Richter Magnitude Scale

The Richter Magnitude Scale represents measurement of ground motion. The various magnitudes are expressed by ordinary numbers and decimals. This scale is intended to rate an earthquake as a whole, rather than in terms of effects at any particular point. This is done by determining the reading of the seismogram at some station and then taking into account distance of that station from the epicenter.

Magnitude can be estimated roughly from the records of a single station. Magnitudes recorded at different stations usually vary by a few tenths of a unit. As a result, final assignments of magnitude are based on an average of all the independent determinations.

The Richter magnitude is defined as the logarithm (base 10) of the maximum motion amplitude, expressed in units of thousandths of a millimeter, of the seismogram which would be recorded on a standard seismograph instrument located 100 kilometers from the epicenter.

For example, if at 100 kilometers from the epicenter the deflection of the seismogram is one millimeter, the magnitude is the logarithm of 1000, or 3. These units were chosen purposely to give the smallest recorded earthquakes magnitudes between 0 and 1.

For every upward step of one unit on the scale, the amount of motion as recorded on the seismogram increases tenfold. The table which ends this section gives the deflection of the seismograms for various magnitudes as multiples of the deflection of the seismogram for magnitude 3.

It should be noted that many different types of seismographs are in use, recording earth movements with varying magnification factors. In order to determine the Richter magnitude of any earthquake from the record of a given instrument, it is necessary to apply a correction factor. This correction factor will vary with the characteristics of the particular instrument and the distance to the epicenter of the recorded earthquake.

Earthquake statistics must be based on a magnitude scale or some equivalent. Early writers on earthquake frequency commonly allowed their findings to be distorted by large numbers of small earthquakes which happened to be felt in populated areas, while unfelt but greater earthquakes originating under the sea or in the remote parts of the continents went unnoticed.

In the year 1954 every earthquake of magnitude 7 was recorded at seismological stations all over the world. In addition, no shock of magnitude 6 or over could escape being recorded and eventually noted in the international catalogs.

Following is a comparison of Richter magnitude with ground motion and intensity:

Richter Magnitude	Deflection of Seismogram in Terms of That for Magnitude 3	Approximate Maximum Intensity at Epicenter Modified Mercalli
1	0.01	–
2	0.1	I–II
3	1	III
4	10	V
5	100	VI–VII
6	1000	VII–VIII
7	10000	IX–X
8	100000	XI

§5.17 f. Modified Mercalli Intensity Scale of 1931 (Abridged)

Following is a description of physical effects of 12 types of earthquake activities as defined in the modified Mercalli intensity scale of 1931:[13]

1. Type I, not felt except by a very few, under especially favorable circumstances (I Rossi-Forel Scale)

[13]Earthquake Effect on Buildings, Costly Damage Can Be Reduced (Structural Engineers Association of California).

2. Type II, felt only by a few persons at rest, especially on upper floors of buildings. Delicately suspended objects may swing (I to II Rossi-Forel Scale)
3. Type III, felt quite noticeably indoors, especially on upper floors of buildings, but many people do not recognize it as an earthquake. Standing motorcars may rock slightly. Vibration like passing truck. Duration estimated (III Rossi-Forel Scale)
4. Type IV, during the day felt indoors by many, outdoors by few. At night, some awakened. Dishes, windows, doors distrubed; walls make creaking sound. Sensation like heavy truck striking building. Standing motorcars rocked noticeably (IV to V Rossi-Forel Scale)
5. Type V, felt by nearly everyone; many awakened. Some dishes, windows, etc., broken; a few instances of cracked plaster; unstable objects overturned. Distrubances of trees, poles, and other tall objects sometimes noticed. Pendulum clocks may stop (V to VI Rossi-Forel Scale)
6. Type VI, felt by all; many frightened and run outdoors. Some heavy furniture moved; a few instances of fallen plaster or damaged chimneys. Damage slight (VI to VII Rossi-Forel Scale)
7. Type VII, everybody runs outdoors. Damage negligible in buildings of good design and construction; slight to moderate in well-built ordinary structures; considerable in poorly built or badly designed structures; some chimneys broken. Noticed by persons driving motorcars (VIII Rossi-Forel Scale)
8. Type VIII, damage slight in specially designed structures; considerable in ordinary substantial buildings, with partial collapse; great in poorly built structures. Panel walls thrown out of frame structures. Fall of chimneys, factory stacks, columns, monuments, walls. Heavy furniture overturned. Sand and mud ejected in small amounts. Changes in well water. Disturbance felt by persons driving motorcars (VIII+ to IX Rossi-Forel Scale)
9. Type IX, damage considerable in specially designed structures; well-designed frame structures thrown out of plumb; great in substantial buildings, with partial collapse. Building shifted off foundations. Ground cracked conspicuously. Underground pipes broken (IX+ Rossi-Forel Scale)
10. Type X, some well-built wooden structures destroyed; most masonry and frame structures destroyed with foundations; ground badly cracked. Rails bent. Landslides considerable from river banks and steep slopes. Shifted sand and mud. Water splashed (slopped) over banks (X Rossi-Forel Scale)
11. Type XI, few, if any, (masonry) structures remain standing. Bridges destroyed. Broad fissures in ground. Underground pipelines completely out of service. Earth slumps and land slips in soft ground. Rails bent greatly
12. Type XII, damage total. Waves seen on ground surfaces. Lines of sight and level distorted. Objects thrown upward into the air

§5.18 5. Soil and Geological Reports

The history and characteristics of the soil conditions surrounding a damaged structure are as important to the expert as is the legal definition of the site. Type of soil can have a great effect on the stability of all structures built on a site.

Figure 5-4 Boring Log Report

R. T. Frankian & Associates, Inc

(a) boring number, (b) depth at which undisturbed samples were taken, (c) strength of soil at various depths as indicated by the number of blows per foot of penetration, (d) moisture content of soil at various depths, (e) dry density of various samples taken, (f) depth of boring, (g) description of soil type at various depths

LOG OF BORINGS (a) BORING NUMBER 1

(b) Sample depth	(c) Blows per foot	(d) Moisture content, %	(e) Dry unit weight, lb/cu ft	(f) Depth, ft		(g) DESCRIPTION Surface conditions: Level asphaltic concrete parking
				0	SM-SP	Sand: Brown-gray, fine to medium, silty, damp, mederately dense
2	Push	9	98			
4	11	7	95			grades dense
				5		
8	44	5	98			grades very dense
				10		
12	3	4	99			grades no silt and fine to coarse
						grades gravel
				15		
17	2	8	104		ML-SM	Silt: Gray-brown, sandy, damp to moist, firm
						(8" sand layer)
						(cobble)
				20	ML-SM	
22	2	11	108			
						End of boring at 25 1/2', no water

No caving, much caving at 4' to 8'

In understanding soil conditions, the expert must look not only to the site itself but also at conditions in adjoining areas and the whole community to obtain a proper perspective of the situation. The property may be located in an alluvial plain, at a river's edge, in an excavated section of a hill, on a manmade fill, or in the gravel wash of an old riverbed. The subject building may be on or adjacent to a manmade flood control device such as a levee or dike. All these facts significantly affect the stability of the building.

Knowledge of the surface soil alone is not sufficient. The history of the earth beneath the surface is in many cases more important than the history of the exposed material. An area's strength is in its subsoil.

All soil material comes originally from igneous rock. Over the centuries, particles of rock have been broken free from their original material by freezing, chemical reactions, or contact with other rocks. The rocks were washed down by wind, rain, or force of gravity. Layer on layer of the decomposed rock came to form what is now known as soil.

The term *soil* as used by soil engineers generally means the earth material lying in its original, undisturbed state. Soil is usually found in layers. The surface material is called *topsoil*, and contains mineral composition and organic material derived from decomposed vegetation. Beneath the topsoil lies another layer, commonly known as *subsoil.* Below the subsoil is the *substratum,* where the water table is usually found. This stratification is caused by continual erosion from higher ground.

Most industrial plants are on level sites, and therefore lie on deep beds of mineral and organic sediment, transported over long periods of time by wind and rain.

In general, soil strength is determined by age of sedimentation, history of freezing and thawing, degrees of chemical cementation of particles, water content, and density of particles.

§5.19 a. Content of Report

In evaluating the soil condition of a site in a case of foundation failure, the expert should obtain a soils report before coming to final conclusions. The report on a soils test should contain the following basic information:

1. Site description, topography, existing vegetation, drainage, general geology
2. Soils condition, moisture content, water table
3. Graphs showing cross sections of borings taken, listing various depths of color, moisture content, and density of soils (Figure 5-4)
4. Recommendations for method of backfill for structural excavations and trenches
5. Suitability of local soil for use as compact fill
6. Charts showing results of shearing tests and expected settlements under various loads and at various moisture contents (Figure 5-5)
7. Treatment of soils under roads and paved areas
8. Statement of anticipated plant structures and types and amount of loadings
9. Recommendations for types of footings or foundation including sizes, depths, allowable loading, and expected settlement
10. Recommendations for treatment of soil including reworking, rolling, compacting, and removal

Figure 5-5 Pressure versus Consolidation

R. T. Frankian & Associates, Inc

Chart shows typical consolidation test data illustrating pressure in pounds per square foot versus consolidation in inches per inch. Three samples are charted (B1, B2 and B3) which were taken at 1.5-, 5-, and 8-foot depths.

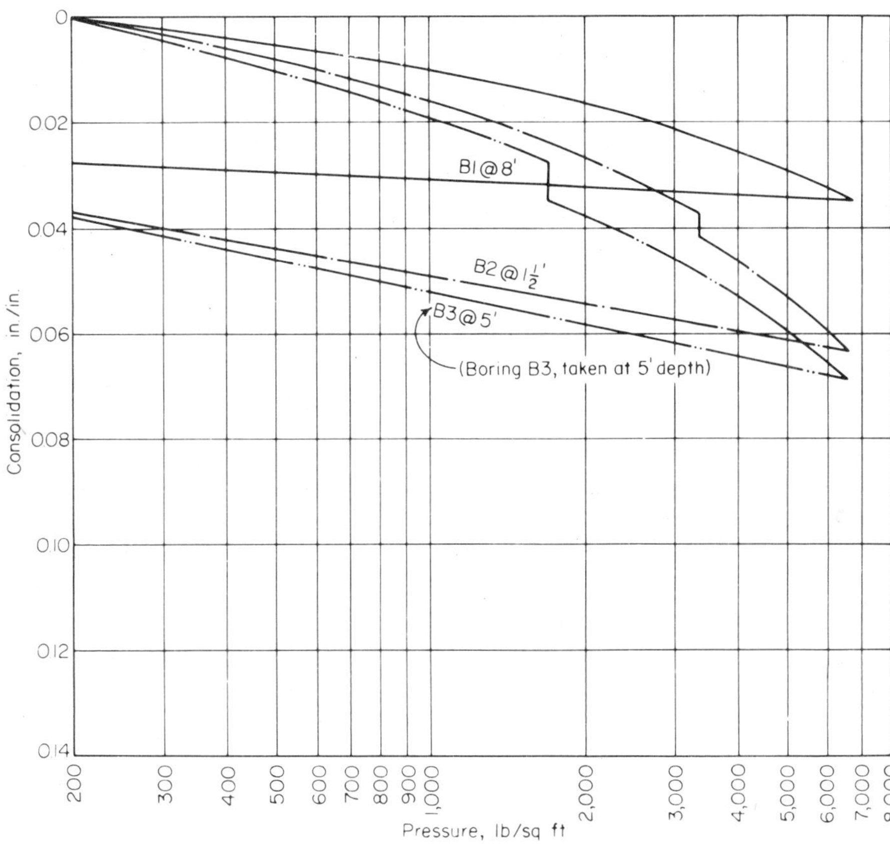

Another method of accurately classifying soil is by its grain size and the percentage of each grain size within the mixture. This is illustrated in the textural-classification chart shown in Figure 5-6.

Generally, grain size of the particles defines the soil. Grains of sand, for example, are between 2.0 and 0.05 millimeters in diameter, while silt is between 0.05 and 0.002

Figure 5-6 Soil Types

From *Civil Engineering for the Plant Engineer* by Max Schwartz. Copyright © 1972 by McGraw-Hill, Inc. Used with the permission of McGraw-Hill Book Company.

This graphic description is based on the United States Department of Agriculture textural classification chart.

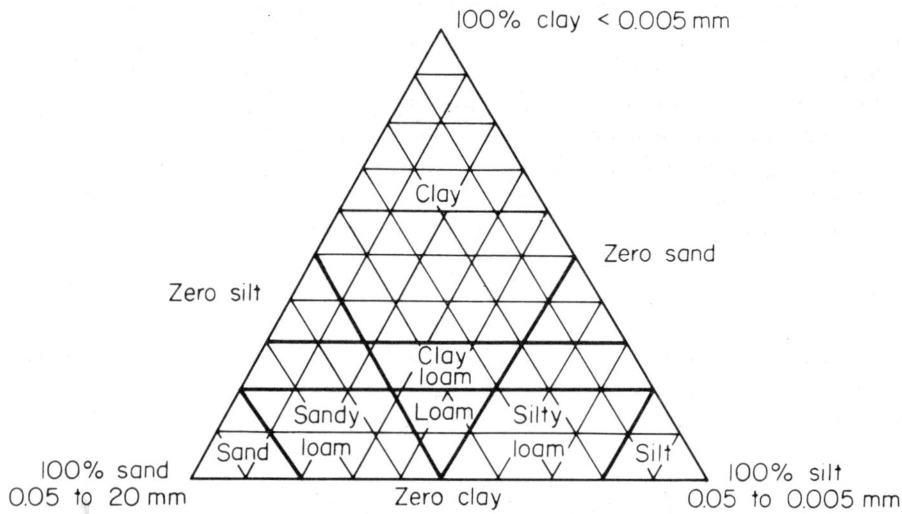

millimeters in diameter. Clay is soil with grains under 0.002 millimeters in diameter. A variety of laboratory testing procedures have been developed to determine specific gravity, grain size and shape, liquid limit, water content, ratio of voids, unconfined compressibility, and other important soil properties.

§5.20 b. Determining Soil Strength

The strength of any soil depends on its primary properties, which are internal friction (or resistance to sliding), cohesion (or mutual attraction of its particles), compressibility (reduction of volume under pressure), capillarity (attraction of moisture), elasticity (or ability to rebound), and permeability (the property that permits water to flow through a material). Internal resistance, which is a combination of internal friction and cohesion, is the most important of all soil properties. Internal friction is characteristic of granular soil; cohesion is typical of clay. Granular-soil classifications include gravel, sand, coarse sand, compact gravel, compact sand, loose gravel, and loose sand.

Cohesive soil consists of hardpan, a compact mixture of clay with sand, hard clay, medium clay, soft clay, and inorganic soil. Granular soils are very low in cohesion but high in internal friction; they have a high shearing strength that increases with pressure. Clay soils are highly cohesive because of molecular attraction but are very low in internal friction. The shearing strength of clay soil depends only on its cohesion and is independent of the foundation pressures, but its strength is greatly reduced by water.

For this reason, an ideal soil is a mixture of granular and cohesive soils. Such a foundation soil would maximize the benefits of each type of soil, since the weaknesses of one would be canceled out by the strengths of the other. The measure of good soil is its degree of shearing strength and resistance to settlement. The ability of soil to support heavy foundations or to remain stable on a steep slope is directly proportional to its shearing strength. Friction is a resistance that exists independently of the area loaded; it is a function of the intensity of the load and the surface of the contact.

Other important properties of soil are its capillarity, plasticity, liquid limit, and permeability. In the case of clay soils which become highly plastic with the addition of moisture, excessive settlement or plastic flow could endanger a structure. High permeability is dangerous when there is water within the soil. Water changing to ice will tend to expand and raise not only the surface of the soil, but also any foundations or paved surfaces in the area. This is known as frost heave.

Capillary action by the soil causes water to be drawn into a building through basement walls and floor slabs. This moisture can damage the interior finishes of the building. Another term used by the soil engineer is the plastic limit, defined as the lease amount of moisture a soil sample can hold and still be rolled into an 1/8-inch diameter thread. This indicates the soil's type of plasticity. The liquid limit is the maximum amount of liquid a soil can absorb before it fails in shear.

§5.21 C. Governing Agencies

Agencies of the federal, state, county, and municipal governments are responsible for record-keeping, monitoring and establishing design criteria to prevent major catastrophic damage. Many of these agencies have overlapping responsibilities and rely on the same sources of information in setting their respective standards.

§5.22 1. Federal

On the federal level, the agencies described in the following paragraphs are the most active, and information may be obtained from them in the form of historic records of natural, catastrophic phenomena.

The Federal Meteorological Agency has monitoring stations throughout the country, situated in every major airport, city and suburb. These stations measure and continuously report temperature, wind velocity, precipitation, snowfall and other data regarding storms.

The United States Geological Survey, Department of the Interior, provides data on land topography, and issues maps showing the topographic features of the entire country. These maps are known as *quadrangle sheets*, and are available from the United States Geological Survey, Denver, Colorado 80225, or Reston, Virginia 22092. Establishment and maintenance of benchmarks and monuments for triangulation and surveys is also controlled by this agency.

The United States Corps of Engineers conducts studies of all navigable waters, harbors, and coastlines. In addition, it provides data on the condition of the sea bottoms in coastal areas. This agency is also responsible for construction of many flood control dams, channels, and other preventive devices funded by the federal government.

The Departments of Defense and the Interior have parallel responsibilities with reference to flood control. They undertake the design of dams to protect national forests from potential flood damage.

§5.23 2. State

Most states have real estate commissions which control the development of new subdivisions for purposes of preventing damage from floods, subsidence, wind, and storms.

Specifically, the state may require that each city, county, and regional or area planning commission develop a general plan for the conservation, development, and utilization of natural resources. This includes water and its hydraulic force, forests, soils, rivers, harbors, and other natural resources. Also, this plan may cover flood control regulations relating to use of land in stream channels, and the prevention, control, and correction of the erosion of soils, beaches, and shores.

§5.24 3. County

County governmental agencies generally have direct control over flood prevention programs and the design and construction of housing developments. The county has hydrology departments, flood control departments, and grading departments which are part of the building and safety department, as are the geological and engineering departments. Within the building and safety department are engineers who review construction plans to confirm a plan's ability to withstand wind forces and seismic forces. Building department inspectors attempt to verify the adequacy of the soil in a given location to support the weight of the proposed structures. County governmental agencies will normally control all earthworks, whether matters of excavation or fill, when the volume of earthwork is in excess of 50 cubic yards, or over 3 feet in depth of cut or fill.

To prevent placement of a fill which later may be found to be unconsolidated and unsupportive of the structures built on it, the county grading departments subject such activities to the control of a grading permit. To obtain these permits, there must be an advance topographic survey of the existing site along with a final grading plan. A soils engineer must report on existing soil conditions, and a geological report must be prepared as well. The fill operation must be supervised by a licensed soils or grading engineer who certifies that a proper compaction has been made on the fill. It is common for the contractor or owner responsible for that fill to obtain a performance bond to insure that, should work remain uncompleted, the county government will receive sufficient funds for another contractor to complete the work. Similar requirements govern work on hillsides in which land is excavated and pads created.

§5.25 4. Municipal

Municipal agencies are usually the local city building departments. Each city generally has its own building and safety department which encompasses a grading department, a storm drainage department, a flood control department, and geological and engineering departments. All proposed construction projects within a city must meet the approval of the city planning department and its enumerated subdivisions.

Some earthquake-prone cities have seismic analysis agencies. Such an agency determines the proximity of the nearest earthquake fault to a proposed area and project.

§5.26 D. Professional Associations and Governmental Agencies

Professional associations and governmental agencies are another source of evidence in cases of catastrophic occurrences. Most of the professional associations have committees dedicated to researching and recommending means to prevent damages due to catastrophes such as windstorms, floods, earthquakes, and fires.

The major associations and agencies are:

1. American Society of Civil Engineers
2. American Water Works Association
3. American Society of Military Engineers
4. National Fire Protection Association
5. Structural Engineers Association of California Seismology Committee
6. Seismological Society of America
7. Earthquake Engineering Research Institute
8. International Conference of Building Officials
9. United States Department of Commerce, Environmental Science Services Administration, Coast and Geodetic Survey
10. California Legislature Joint Committee on Seismic Safety
11. California Institute of Technology—Seismological Laboratory

E. Check List for Discovery

§5.27 1. Interrogatories

With respect to litigation involving the design engineer of a project which has suffered damages from flood or subsidence, some suggested areas of inquiry are listed in the sections following this one.[14]

§5.28 a. In Case of Flood

The following interrogatories are suggested for use in cases arising out of floods:

1. What rainfall intensity did you project when you designed the subject project?
2. What is the recorded frequency of a rainfall of such intensity?

---

[14] §§7.26-.29, 10.14-.18.

3. What quantity of water runoff was designed for at the project point?
4. Prior to construction of the project, what was the historic runoff at that point over a 50-year period?
5. What was the water mark height for the subject storm at the particular project location?
6. What had been the historic high-water mark over the preceding 50 years?
7. What was the tributary area for the watershed, or area contributing water to the subject location?
8. Do any control devices exist to reduce runoff upstream of the subject project?
9. Are there any debris control devices?
10. If draining devices do exist, what is their capacity? (Specify in acre-feet or cubic feet per second.)
    a. What is the criterion of the local planning department as to runoff or drainage design?
11. Has the structure of the watershed changed since the time of design?
12. Has the surface been paved or in any way changed to reduce the amount of water penetration into the soil?
13. What was the historic water drainage line through this area prior to development of the project?
14. Has any adjacent construction work reverted the direction of water runoff?

§5.29 b. In Case of Subsidence

The following interrogatories may be helpful where the litigation has arised out of an incident of subsidence:

1. Was the earthwork performed on virgin (untouched) land?
2. Is a topographic map of the original land site available?
3. Is the grading plan of the final graded land available?
4. Were any soil borings made on the land prior to the excavation or grading operation?
5. Did a laboratory perform soil and compaction tests?
6. Was the land disturbed in any manner by the adjoining property owners by cuts or fills, or by construction of heavy structures?
7. Was the fill certified by a soils engineer and recorded in the local city or county grading department?

§5.30 2. Depositions

When the adverse engineers were responsible for the design in question, all the engineers' notes, plans, sketches, calculations, and specifications should be produced at the time of deposition.[15]

---

[15]§§7.30-.31.

The person being deposed should be questioned as to the meaning of each item presented. For instance, with regard to soil testing and borings, each item in the test results should be examined to determine the engineer's understanding of all elements of the soil test report. The purpose of such a line of questioning is to determine whether the engineer was aware of the input and importance of all data obtained. If there is no evidence that the engineer utilized available data in conjunction with government records of rainfall, runoff, and general soil conditions, the validity of the design may be discredited.

In the event that the witness brings in calculations prepared by subordinates, such witness still should be required to explain the calculations or admit a lack of knowledge.

§5.31 3. Request for the Production of Documents

A request for production of documents directed to a design engineer should include: all plans, soils reports, geological reports, calculations, applications for permits, corrections made by the governing agencies, construction permits, laboratory reports on compaction, original topographic map, final grading plans, details of erosion control, flood control devices, construction photographs made during earthwork, field engineer's daily log, inspection reports, survey notes of the original topography, and survey notes for the final topography.[16]

F. Evidence of Damages

§5.32 1. Photographs

In gathering evidence of damage from storms, floods, or earthquakes, any available photograph relating to damages incurred will be useful. Photographs can be taken by professional photographers to insure that the site will be represented without exaggeration or diminution of the effects of the catastrophic event.

In addition to obtaining the services of a professional photographer, a search may be conducted for photographs taken by laypersons, insurance investigators, newspaper reporters, and television camera operators, who might have covered the incident in question. Of course, photographs taken by the interested parties or their agents may be useful as well.

A very useful type of photograph in ascertaining rainstorm or flood damages is the aerial photograph. The value of such a photograph is enhanced when it can be compared to photographs taken prior to the storm. See **§§7.33-7.35, 8.08-8.18, 8.21** and **8.26** for additional data on photographic evidence.

§5.33 2. Cost Estimate of Damage

An important item of evidence is the estimated cost of remedial work or reconstruction of the damaged property. The cost estimate may include demolition work, hauling away of debris, excavation, backfill, concrete work, pipelines, grading, paving, curbs,

---

[16] **§§7.26-.29.**

and gutters. These estimates cover the costs of reconstructing buildings which have cracked due to subsidence and refinishing interiors damaged by flooding.

The estimated cost of remedial work should be calculated in a format governed by recognized estimating procedures. These procedures involve a takeoff of all materials, an estimation of manhours required to perform certain tasks, the rate of manhour labor based on a composite crew including laborers, crafts workers, and foremen, and the cost of equipment and materials. In addition, the contractor's overhead and profit should be taken into account.

§5.34 G. Evidence of Negligence

In establishing evidence of negligence, plans and specifications may be used to demonstrate either that the work was not designed in accordance with good engineering practice, or that the construction was not completed in accordance with the plans and specifications.

In addition, plans and specifications required for remedial work to correct the conditions caused by the catastrophic event may be used to prove improper design and damages.

§5.35 H. Determining Liability for Damage

The design of facilities exposed to dangers of catastrophic events is one of the more difficult tasks undertaken by the design engineer. This difficulty arises not only out of the element of chance but also out of economic considerations.

An oversimplified but clear example would be the design of a bomb shelter. Should the shelter be designed to protect against a bomb explosion 5, 50, or 100 yards away? A bomb shelter could be designed to protect adequately against any one of these possibilities. However, it becomes a matter of economics measured against the probability that a bomb would strike close to the shelter.

A similar situation arises in the areas of design to resist earthquake,[17] tornado, hurricane, and flood damage.[18] Governmental agencies and professional associations recommend criteria which weigh economics and probabilities. These criteria serve as a guideline in allowing the engineer to design in accordance with the standard professional practice for a particular location. Consequently, one issue to be determined by engineering evidence is whether the engineer followed the recommended design standards. A second area of inquiry is whether the design engineer conducted an adequate search for historical records[19] on rainfall, earthquake conditions, or windstorm activity for a particular location.

A potential defense for the design engineer would be to shift the blame to either the governmental agency which reviewed the plans or set the standards used, or the construction contractor who failed to follow plans and specifications, substituted materials, or displayed inadequate workmanship. Additional targets may be the geologist

[17] §5.02.
[18] §5.03.
[19] §5.08.

who made the exploration and reported the soil condition or the owner of adjacent land who may have changed the direction of runoff flow or removed the support of the soil, causing a subsidence or landslide.

§5.36 I. Check List of Evidence

Following is a check list of useful items of evidence in particular types of cases:

1. Storm
   a. Historic records of wind
   b. Wind velocity at various heights above ground
   c. Pressure on windward side of building
   d. Suction on leeward side of building
   e. Duration of storm
2. Earthquakes
   a. Probability zone
   b. Intensity in accordance with Richter scale
   c. Amplitude
   d. Proximity of epicenter area damaged
   e. Existence of active or inactive faults
3. Rainstorms
   a. Historical records of rainfall intensity in
      (1) Inches per hour
      (2) Inches per day
      (3) Inches per storm
   b. Intensity for the entire watershed contributing to runoff
   c. Records of historic runoff through the channel affecting subject property, recorded in cubic feet per second, and acre-feet per second
   d. Degree of erosion and debris carried by storm waters
   e. Terrain of subject site and vulnerability to erosion and dislocation of the soil
4. Subsidence and Mudslides
   a. Geological studies as to borings
   b. Topographic maps of original terrain
   c. Topographic maps of altered terrain
   d. Water tables, springs, and any type of underground water conditions
   e. History of brush and forest fires in the area

§5.37 J. Additional Readings

H. Babbit & J. Doland, *Water Supply Engineering,* McGraw-Hill Book Co, New York, NY, 3d ed 1939.

H. Barrows, *Water Power Engineering,* McGraw-Hill Book Co, New York, NY, 3d ed 1943.

Coast and Geology Survey, United States Department of Commerce, 1963.

C. Davis, *Handbook of Applied Hydraulics,* McGraw-Hill Book Co, New York, NY, 2d ed 1952.

Design Manual Debris, Dams and Basins, Los Angeles County Flood Control District.

Design Manual Hydraulic, Los Angeles County Flood Control District, 1973.

Design Manual Hydrology, Los Angeles County Flood Control District, 1977.

Design Manual Standard Drawings, Los Angeles County Flood Control District, 1978.

Handbook of Drainage Construction Products, ARMCO Drainage & Metal Products, Inc, Middleton, Ohio, 1955.

Handbook of Water Control, ARMCO Drainage & Metal Products, Inc, Berkeley, California, 1949.

Arthur Holmes, *Principles of Physical Geology,* The Ronald Press Co, New York, NY, 1945.

Hydraulic Data Report, Orange County Environmental Management Agency, 1974-1975.

Dimitri P. Krinine, *Soil Mechanics,* McGraw-Hill Book Co, New York, NY, 2d ed 1947.

Thaddeus Merriman & Thomas H. Wiggin, *American Civil Engineers Handbook,* McGraw-Hill Book Co, New York, NY, 1959.

Seismic Design for Buildings, United States Department of the Army, Navy & Air Force, 1973.

Soil Mechanics, Foundations and Earth Structures, United States Department of the Navy, Naval Facilities Engineering Command, 1971.

E. Steel, *Water Supply and Sewerage,* McGraw-Hill Book Co, New York, NY, 4th ed 1960.

Structural Engineering, United States Department of the Navy, Naval Facilities Engineering Command, 1970.

Subdivision Manual, Los Angeles County Flood Control District, 1964.

Leonard Church Urquhart, *Civil Engineering Handbook,* McGraw-Hill Book Co, New York, NY, 4th ed 1959.

Codes

California Business & Professions Code §4478.

County of Los Angeles Building Code.

Uniform Building Code, International Conference of Building Officials, Whittier, Cal, 1979.

Earthquakes

The Behavior of Reinforced Concrete Structures in the Caracas, Venezuela Earthquake of July 29, 1967, Portland Cement Association.

G. Berg & J. Stratta, *Anchorage and the Alaska Earthquake of March 27, 1964,* American Iron and Steel Institute, New York, NY, 1964.

Bulletin of the Seismological Society of America, Vol 53, No 2, February 1963.

Henry J. Degenkolb, *Earthquake Forces on Tall Structures,* Bethlehem Steel, 1970.

Earthquake Effect on Buildings, Costly Damage Can Be Reduced, Structural Engineers Association of California.

Meeting the Earthquake Challenge, California State Legislature Joint Committee on Seismic Safety, January 1974. Part One: A Comprehensive Approach to Seismic Safety submitted pursuant to the Provisions of Senate Concurrent Resolution 128 (1969).

Recommended Lateral Force Requirements and Commentary, Structural Engineers Association of California, 1974.

The San Fernando Earthquake, February 9, 1971, Report of the Los Angeles County Earthquake Commission, November 1971.

Seismic Design for Buildings, TM5-809-10, NAV FAC P-355, AFM 88-3, Ch 13, Departments of the Army, Navy and Air Force, Washington, DC, April 1973.

Edward J. Teal, *Seismic Design Practice for Steel Buildings,* Structural Steel Educational Council, 1975.

6 Discovering Evidence in Transportation Accidents

§6.01 A. Generally

Discovery of evidence in transportation accidents concentrates on the physical aspects of an incident. Relevant evidence relates not only to the vehicles involved, but also to the condition of the roadway or railway, any traffic and safety control devices, and regulations pertaining to design of these modes of transportation.

This chapter covers three major areas in the reconstruction of transportation accidents, road transportation, rail transportation, and the laws of physics which relate to such accidents. Road transportation includes passenger vehicles,[1] trucks, and trailers. Rail transportation includes locomotives, passenger cars, and various types of freight cars.

The components of both roadways and railways are explained to familiarize the reader with engineering terminology[2] and the functional purposes of the design of these transportation modes. Knowledge of the physical components of the roadway or railway is crucial because these factors can affect safety.

Another important safety aspect relates to the traffic control devices incorporated in the design and construction of roadways and railways. Governmental regulations pertaining to these devices are dealt with in detail.

The chapter also discusses physical characteristics of moving vehicles as related to their weight, velocity, impact, and construction, so that the reader may look on the moving vehicle objectively and recognize the forces which are part of an accident.

A recommended check list for discovery is presented at the end of the chapter.

B. Road Transportation

§6.02 1. Trucks and Trailers

Generally, there are two types of trucks, the truck and the truck-tractor.[3] The term *truck* describes any self-propelled motor vehicle used to transport property.

---

[1]A passenger vehicle is any motor vehicle other than a motor truck or truck-tractor, designed to carry not more than 10 persons including the driver. California Motor Vehicle Code.

[2]**App E.**

[3]A truck-tractor is a self-propelled vehicle designed and used primarily for drawing other vehicles and not constructed so as to carry a load other than a part of the weight of the vehicle and load so drawn.

A *full trailer* means any vehicle designed to be drawn by another vehicle, and constructed so that only the towing device rests on the towing vehicle. A combination can be a truck-tractor and a semitrailer, either with or without a full trailer, or a truck with one or more full trailers. The term *semitrailer* refers to any vehicle designed to be drawn by another motor vehicle and so constructed that some part of its weight rests on the towing vehicle. A semitrailer equipped with an auxiliary front axle (dolly) is considered a full trailer. (Figure 6-1)

A *pole trailer* is a vehicle without motive power, possibly of variable wheel base, designed to be drawn by another vehicle, and attached to the towing vehicle by means of a *reach* or *pole* which is *boomed* or otherwise secured to the towing vehicle. This type of vehicle is used to transport long or irregularly-shaped loads such as poles, pipes, or structural members generally capable of sustaining themselves as beams between the supporting connections.

§6.03 a. Truck Weights

The weight of trucks is designated by an H-loading classification, given in tons per vehicle. For example, an H20 classification means a 20-ton vehicle, H15 is a 15-ton vehicle, and H10 is a 10-ton vehicle. The weight of the vehicle is distributed with 20 per cent of the total load on the front axle and 80 per cent of the total load on the rear axle. With single wheels at each axle, the axle loads are equally divided between the two wheels. For instance, a H20 truck has 8,000 pounds on the front axle and 32,000 on the rear axle. The front wheels will each carry 4,000 pounds while the rear wheels carry 16,000 pounds each. The number after the H represents the gross weight in tons of the truck or truck-tractor. For HS loadings, the number after S represents gross weight in tons of the rear axle load of the semitrailer.

The weight carried by each axle load of a H20/S16 truck-trailer is 8,000 pounds on the front axle, 32,000 pounds on the middle axle, and 32,000 pounds on the rear axle. See Figures 6-1 and 6-3 for various combinations of H and HS loadings.

Common terms relating to weight of trucks include:

1. Curb weight, the weight of the truck empty, without a payload or driver, but including fuel, cooling system and crankcase filled, tools, spare wheel, and all other equipment
2. Gross vehicle weight, the total sum of the weights of the chassis, complete with fuel, oil, water, cab, body, equipment, and payload or, in other words, the total weight of the loaded truck on tires
3. Gross combination weight, the total sum of weights of a truck-tractor with cab, including oil, fuel and water, and a fifth wheel, plus the semitrailer, its body, and payload. Gross combination weight may also be used to indicate total loaded weight of a straight truck chassis pulling any type of full trailer
4. Pay load, the weight of the actual cargo and occupants carried by the vehicle or combination

The weight of a motor vehicle is distributed throughout its components, but can be considered concentrated at the center of gravity for purposes of analyzing forces. If

Figure 6-1 Semitrailer Conventional Dimensions and Components

From *Civil Engineering for the Plant Engineer* by Max Schwartz. Copyright © 1972 by McGraw-Hill, Inc. Used with the permission of McGraw-Hill Book Company.

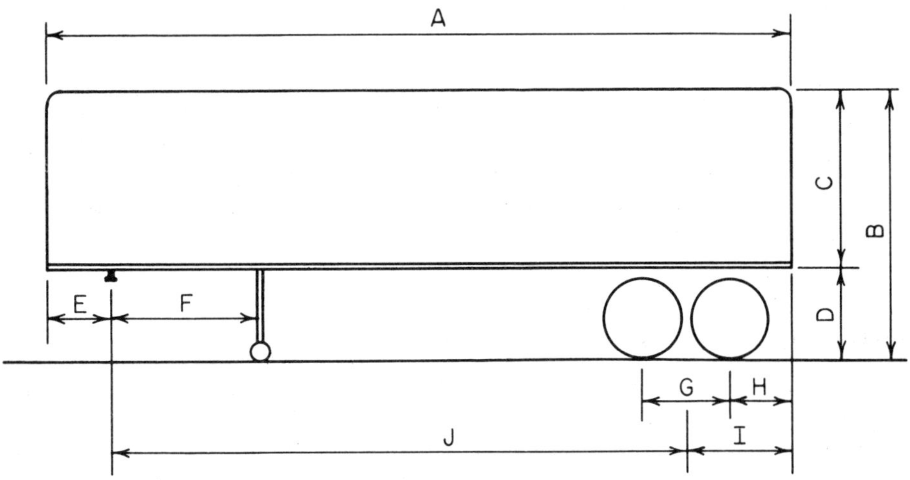

CONVENTIONAL DIMENSIONS

A	Overall length	22' - 40'
B	Overall height	12'-6" - 14'
C	Body height	7' - 10' (more for drop frame)
D	Floor height	4' - 4'-6"
E	Front to C/L kingpin	2' - 3'-6"
F	C/L kingpin to landing gear	82" (SAE)*
G	Tandem axle spacing c to c	4' - 4'-4"
H	C/L rear axle to rear end	2' - 7'
I	C/L tandem assembly to rear end	4' - 10'
J	C/L kingpin to C/L of tandem assembly	14' - 34'

*Minimum dimension with three axle tractors

The weight of a motor vehicle is distributed throughout its components, but can be considered concentrated at the center of gravity for purposes of analyzing forces. If the vehicle is suspended or supported at this theoretical center of gravity, it will remain in equilibrium, provided no outside forces act on the vehicle.

The weight on each wheel is distributed in proportion to the distance between the center of gravity and that wheel.

Figure 6-2 Maximum Axle Loading for H20, H15, and H10 Trucks

(a) Truck with single rear drive axle

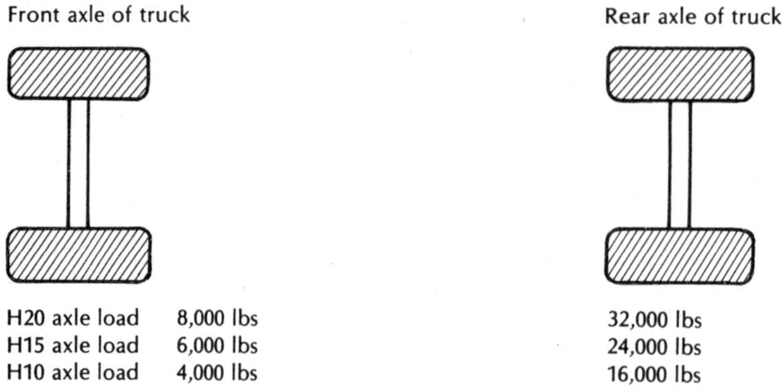

(b) Truck with tandem rear drive axles

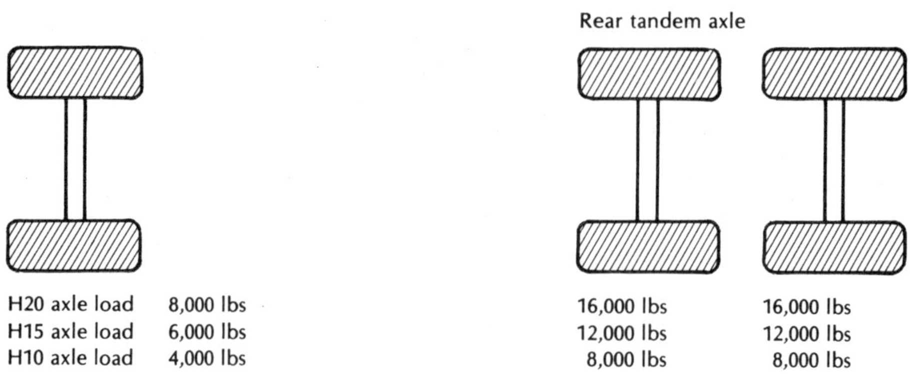

2. Components of Roadways and Facilities

a. Streets and Highways

§6.04 (1) Design

Some important factors to be taken into account in cases involving the design of streets include the elements affecting geometric design of the roadway, data on traffic flow in the area, and physical design and characteristics of typical vehicles.

Figure 6-3 Maximum Axle Loads for H20-S16 and H-15-S12 Truck Tractor with Semitrailer

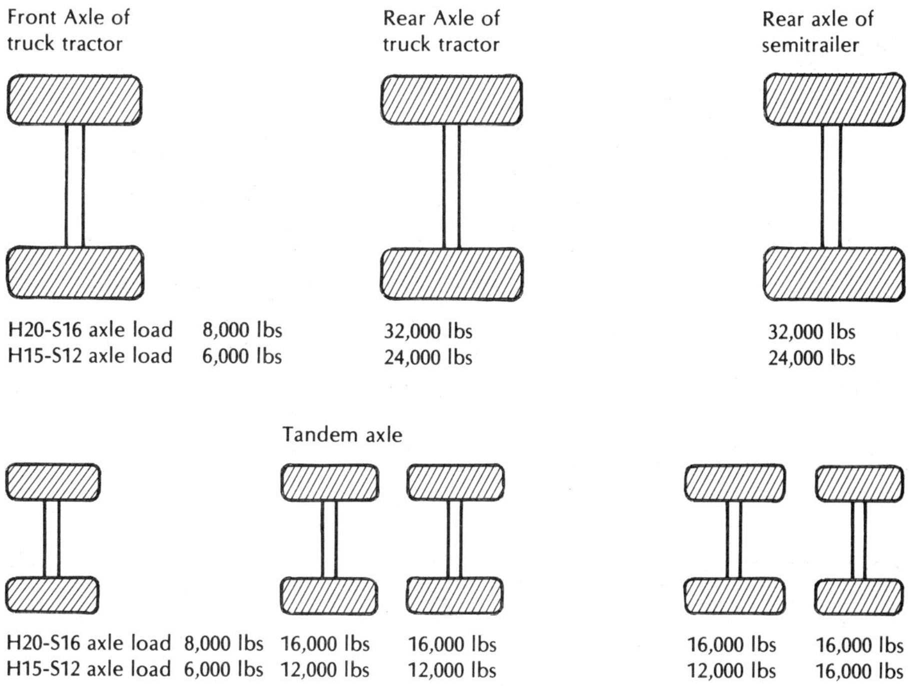

Geometric design of a roadway is influenced by considerations such as vehicular capacity, need for drainage control,[4] and physical and topographic[5] conditions prevailing in the particular area.

The major components of a roadway are the pavement, curbs, gutters, medians, bulkheads, and traffic guides. See Figure 6-4 for typical highway and street sections. Figure 6-5 and 6-6 illustrate structures relating to highway construction.

The height of a vehicle directly affects the vertical clearance between the vehicle and the roadway structures, the sight distance, and the driveway clearance. The maximum height of vehicles permitted on highways is usually 13.5 feet. However, each state sets its own limitations.

Gross weights of vehicles affect design of roadways and bridges. Some state regulations permit a maximum wheel load of 9,500 pounds on any one wheel supporting one end of an axle, and a maximum of 18,000 pounds per axle on a given roadway.[6]

---

[4]**§5.06.**

[5]**§5.05.**

[6]California Motor Vehicle Code.

In addition to the physical characteristics of a vehicle, the designer of roadways must take into account the element of speed. The large majority of drivers, about 85 per cent,[7] does not constantly adjust speed to the highway, but rather chooses some approximately uniform speed that seems to be safe for a given set of existing conditions. The other 15 per cent will drive at either a higher or lower rate.

It is impractical to design a highway to accommodate this 15 per cent, since it is economically unfeasible to design at the higher standard required for the faster drivers, which would mean larger radius of curves, wider traffic lanes, and steeper banking. Designing for the slower driver may be more economical with respect to construction costs. However, this would probably result in higher vehicular operating costs due to steeper grades, dissatisfaction on the part of the majority of drivers, and danger to the faster driver when adverse traffic conditions prevail.

The following list indicates typical design speeds for various classes of roadways:[8]

Roadway Type	Design Speed (mi/h)
Major highways	55
Secondary highways	50
Collector streets	40
Local (flat) streets	30
Local (hillside) streets	25

Roadway design looks toward these enumerated design speeds for a given roadway type, as well as maximum superelevation or banking, minimum sight distances, and horizontal curvatures.

There have been numerous comprehensive studies of highway accidents and their causes. These studies have identified safety measures necessary for prevention of most accidents. Some of these safety measures are subject to the control of the highway designer, and are taken into account in designing a proposed highway or improving an existing street.

The following factors are considered safety design:

1. Volume—to provide adequate facilities, increase vehicular capacity, and reduce vehicular density
2. Pavement and lane width—to provide lane widths of at least 10 feet and pavement widths of at least 20 feet
3. Lateral clearances—to provide adequate lateral clearances to structures and other roadside features
4. Sight distances—to provide adequate vertical and horizontal sight distances for stopping and passing maneuvers[9]
5. Alignment—to provide good alignment by not incorporating constrictions, jogs, and excessive curvatures in the design of a proposed street, and by eliminating them in existing streets

---

[7]City of Los Angeles Dept of Public Works, Bureau of Engineering Manual—Street Design, pt E (1970).

[8]*Id.*

[9]**§§6.10-.11.**

Figure 6-4 Section through Typical Rural Road

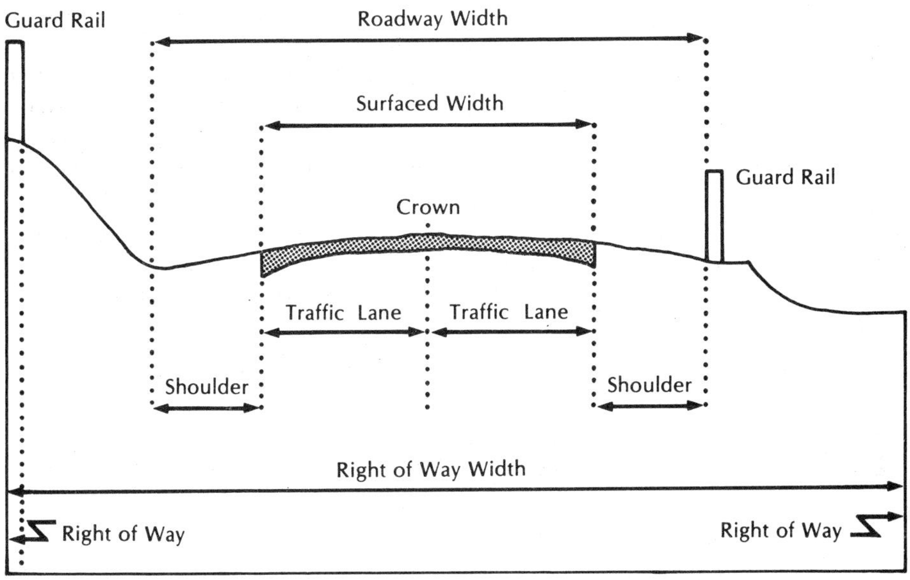

6. Elimination of cross traffic—by providing grade separation
7. Minimizing conflict areas—by means of channeling and right-angle crossings

Additional safety factors in highway design include prohibiting parking, providing signals and traffic signs, and marking crosswalks.

§6.05 (2) Design Drawings as Evidence

In building the legal foundation for descriptions at trial of transportation accidents occurring on streets, one vital source of evidence is the design drawings for the street in question. These drawings consist of plans and profile sheets.[10] They show the alignments, both in vertical and horizontal planes. In addition, detail sheets and specifications may be found which describe various appurtenances of the roadway.

An important source of standards in roadway design include those published by the following agencies:

1. American Association of State Highway Officials

---

[10]§4.10.

Figure 6-5 Typical Highway Structures

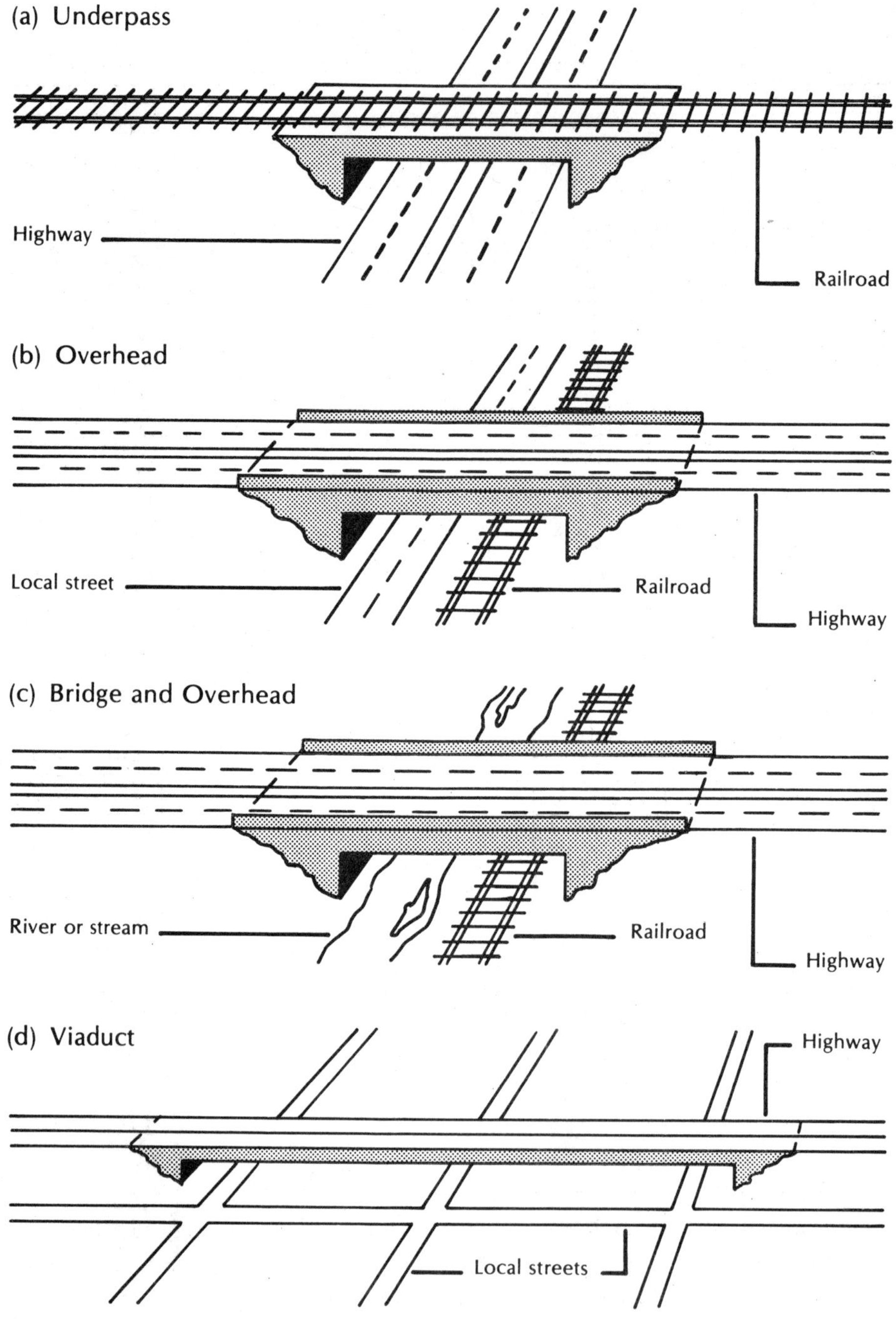

Figure 6-6 Typical Highway Structures

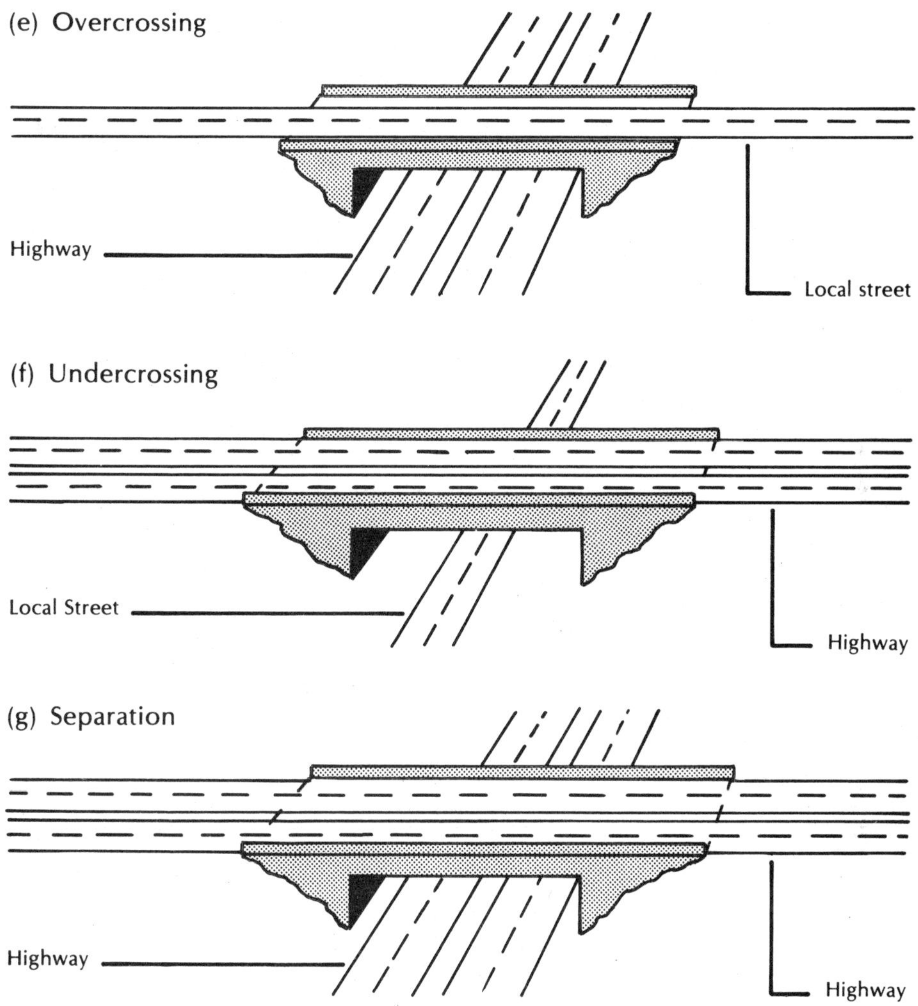

2. United States Department of Transportation, Bureau of Public Works
3. National Academy of Sciences, National Research Council, Highway Research Board
4. Various state and county highway and road departments

Design of roadways looks first to physical characteristics and minimum clearances of the vehicles utilizing the roadway. Sizes of vehicles affect the radius of curves, lane widths, and horizontal and vertical clearances.

The various cross-section elements of a highway are illustrated in Figure 6-8, and are briefly described as follows:

1. Roadway—the portion of a highway, including the shoulders, used for vehicular traffic. A divided highway has two or more roadways
2. Parking lane—an auxiliary lane, primarily for parking of vehicles
3. Speed-change lane—an auxiliary lane, including tapered areas, used primarily for acceleration and deceleration of vehicles entering or leaving the through-traffic lanes.
4. Median lane—a speed-change lane within the median to accommodate left-turning vehicles.

§6.06 (3) Maintenance

Commonly, the property owner and the public entity assume responsibility for maintenance of specific improvements lying within public and private streets. The public entity is primarily responsible for maintenance of existing street improvements located between the curbs,[11] alleys, pedestrian walks, that portion of the curb sidewalk lying within the returns of the street, and the alley intersections. See Figure 6-7, a section through a highway and streets.

Typically, street maintenance includes resurfacing or replacing asphalt pavements which are in poor condition by removing areas of insufficient thickness. This can be effected by burning off the high spots and high-crown areas, providing the entire area with new pavement and gutters,[12] or reconstructing the crown surface where it is considerably higher than the standard section.

The property owner's maintenance responsibilities within a publicly dedicated area are generally limited to those portions of the existing improvements extending from the edge of the pavement to the property lines, with certain exclusions such as the curb return area. The property owner or the city may be held responsible for private improvements extending into such an area in case of a defective condition.

§6.07 (4) Right of Way

There are standard right-of-way widths for many classifications of streets and highways. Major highways usually require a 100-foot right-of-way, while secondary highways have an 86-foot right-of-way. Local streets have a 64-foot right-of-way. Collector streets and continuous streets have a 60-foot right-of-way. Noncontinuous streets have a 54-foot right-of-way, and frontage roads along freeways require 50 feet, as do hillside streets and access roadways.

Figure 6-8 illustrates some of these types of roadways. Included in the illustrations are the paved roadway, shoulders, medians,[13] and parkway.

---

[11] **§6.04.**

[12] *Id.*

[13] **§6.05.**

Figure 6-7 Section through Typical Street

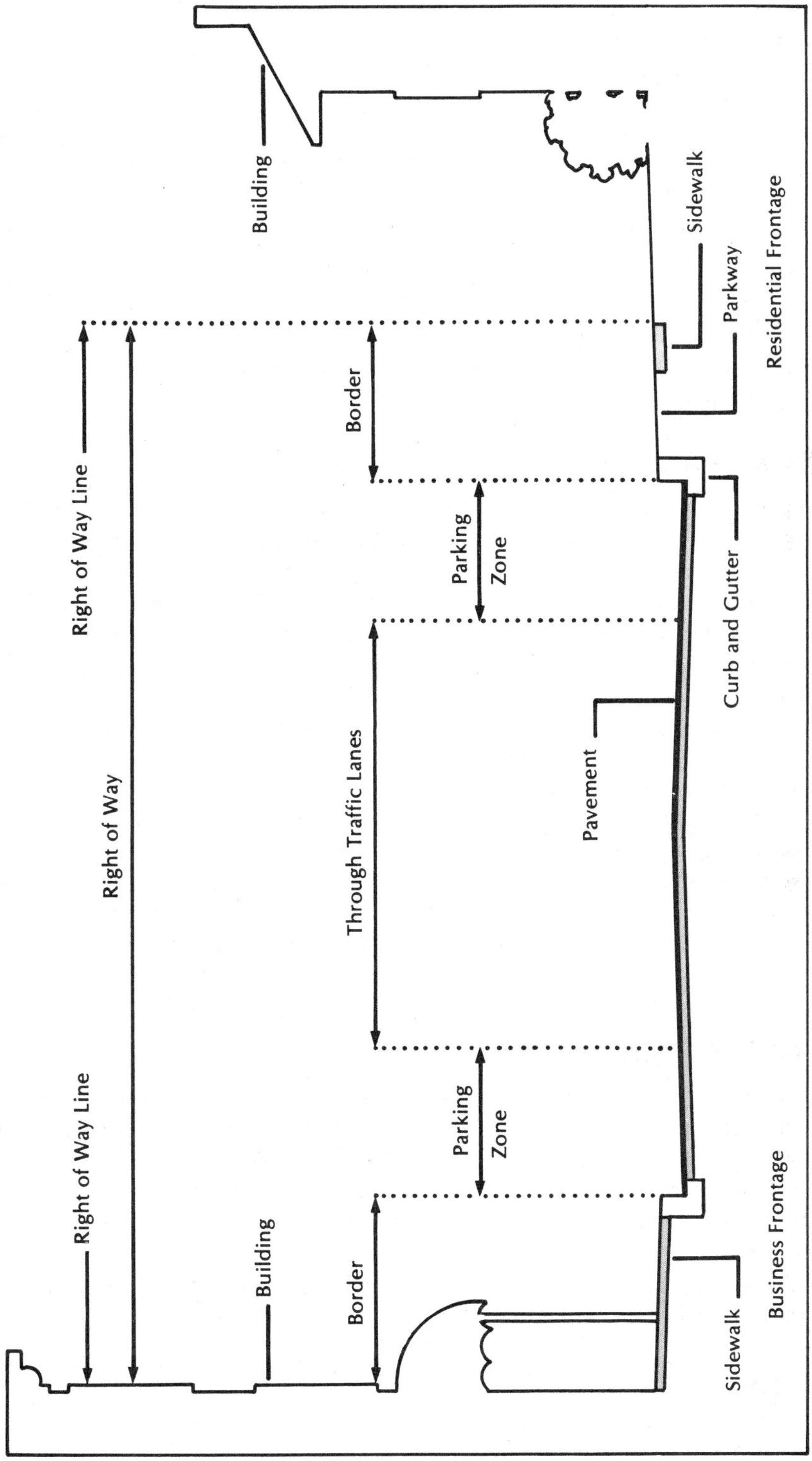

Figure 6-8 Section through Half of Divided Highway

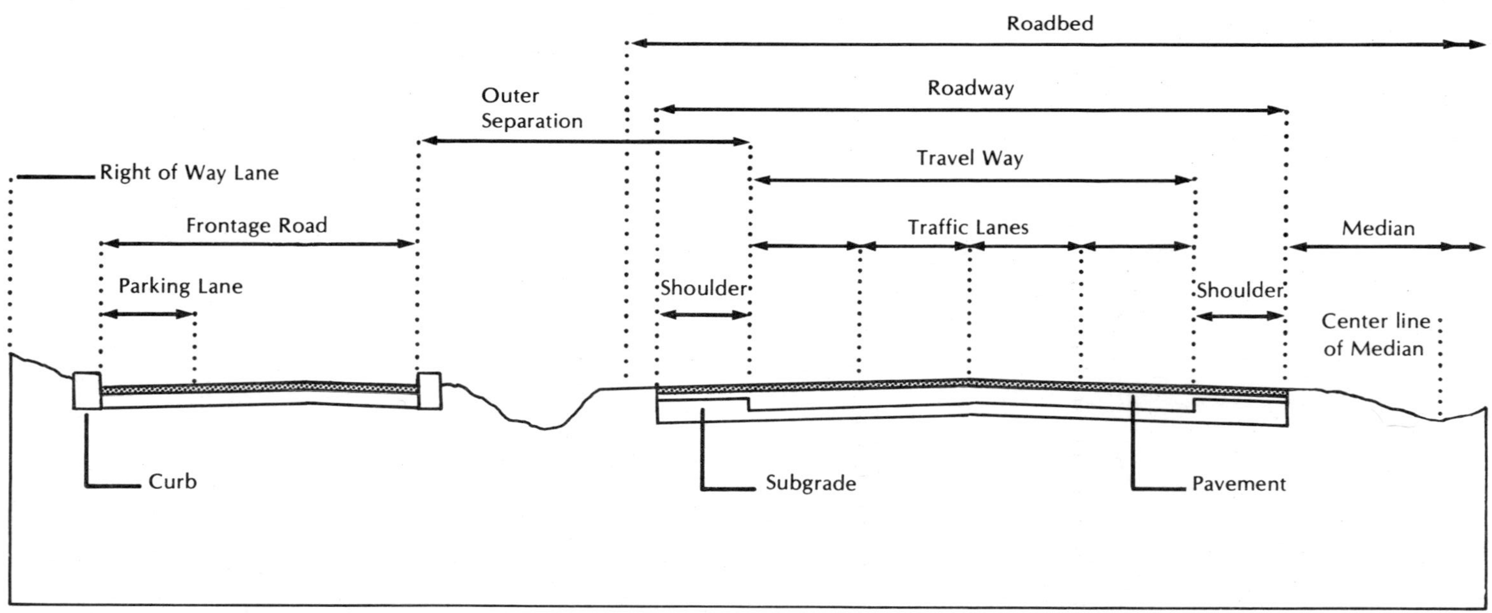

§6.08 3. Traffic Control Devices

In investigating any transportation accident involving moving vehicles, it is necessary to find out about the roadway and its traffic control devices.[14]

Two important factors in analyzing traffic safety designs are volume of traffic in a given area and presence of effective signaling devices. Additional factors are illumination of streets and highways, existence of obstructions such as barricades, barriers, or flagmen, and delineation of traffic flow.

Traffic safety devices are subject to the regulations of such agencies as the American Association of State Highway Officials, the Department of Transportation, the Federal Highway Administration, and various governing state highway commissions and departments.

§6.09 a. Traffic Signs

There are four basic types of traffic signs:

1. Warning signs
2. Regulatory signs
3. Guide signs
4. Construction signs

Warning signs caution the driver about road conditions which may require extraordinary care in the operation of the vehicle. *Regulatory signs* inform motorists about regulations which govern movement, speed, and weight. *Guide signs* provide information concernng distance and location. *Construction signs,* which are usually temporary, advise the traffic in advance of those areas which are undergoing construction or road maintenance.

The location of a particular sign is governed by federal and state regulations which determine its height and lateral position. Lateral position is the horizontal distance between a sign and the edge of the roadway. The orientation of a sign relative to the centerline of the roadway is also governed by these standards.

The size, symbols, lettering, and configurations of a sign are set by the *Manual on Uniform Traffic Control Devices For Streets and Highways.*[15]

A typical regulatory sign is a speed sign used in conjunction with a curve warning sign. The appropriate advisory speed is determined by experimentation, trial runs made in both directions by a vehicle equipped with an airplane ball-bank indicator.[16] An indicator reading of 15 degrees at speeds of 20 miles per hour or less, 12.5 degrees for speeds of 25 to 30 miles per hour, and 10 degrees for speeds of 35 miles per hour or more is generally taken as the limiting value for comfort and safety. The advisory speed may also be determined or checked by calculations based on the radius of

---

[14]**§7.40.**

[15]US Dept of Transportation, Federal Highway Administration, Manual on Uniform Traffic Control Devices For Streets and Highways (1971).

[16]The angle the suspended ball swings off of vertical is proportional to the centrifugal force caused by the vehicle traversing a curve.

Figure 6-9 Pavement Markings at Railroad-Highway Grade Crossing

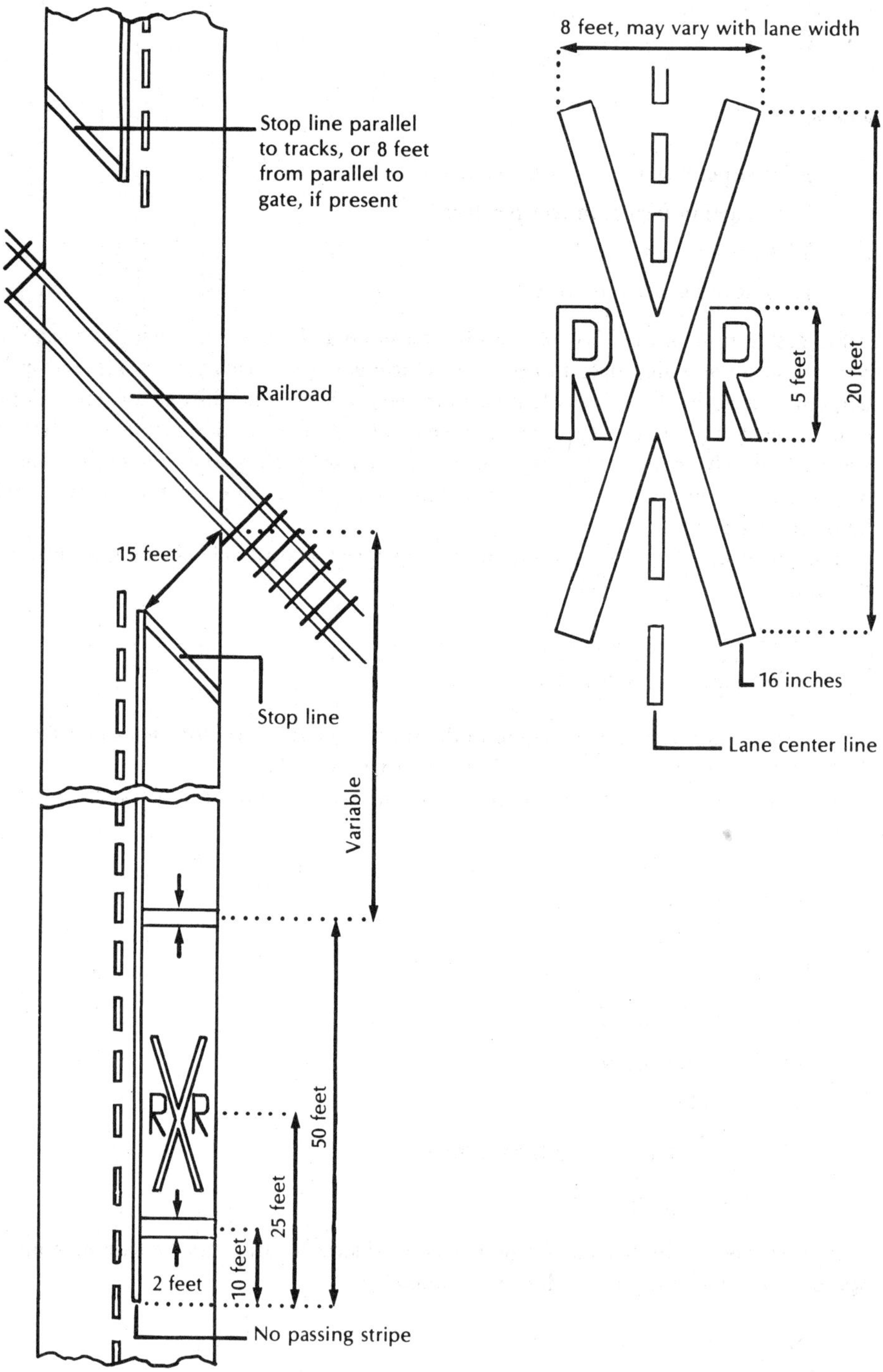

curvature, superelevation, and friction factor of the subject roadway. The formula used to equate superelevation, friction, velocity, and radius of curve is as follows:

$$E + F = \frac{.067V^2}{R} = \frac{V^2}{15R}$$

where:

E = superelevation, in feet per feet
F = friction factor, in feet per feet
V = speed, in mi/h
R = Radius of curve in feet

Superelevation, or *banking*, of a roadway around a curve is constructed to resist the centrifugal force which tries to keep the vehicle going in straight line. The factor E is given as a decimal part of a foot rise per foot of horizontal distance. A cross slope of a roadway of 1/10-foot per foot is noted as 0.10. The friction factor F is that of side friction. This depends on the condition of the road surface and the tire. The units of F are also given in feet per feet, indicating a maximum slope at which there would be no sliding sideways.

The factor of safety for F at maximum safe speed against side skidding is given as the ratio:

$$\frac{\text{F at impending side skid}}{\text{F for maximum safe speed}}$$

The factor of safety varies according to the speed. For instance, the factor of safety at 100 miles per hour is 3.33, and at 20 miles per hour is 1.67.

For example, to determine maximum safe speed, the same formula is rearranged as follows:

$$V^2 = \frac{R}{.067} \times (E + F)$$

given:

E = .05 feet per feet
F = .20 feet per feet
R = 500 feet

$$V^2 = \frac{500}{.067} \times (.05 + .20) = 1865.67$$

V = 43.19 mi/h

As seen above, the friction factor F has considerable effect on the safe maximum speed. Conditions that will reduce the value of F are:

1. Smooth tires
2. Wet roadway surface

3. Bumpy roadway surface
4. Loose sand

§6.10 b. Delineation

In addition to signs, markings on pavement are an effective means of traffic control. Some common pavement makings are pedestrian crossing, indication of school zone, railroad crossing (see Figure 6-9), stop ahead, signal ahead, limit lines, cattle guards, divided highways, and bicycle lanes. Other markings signal preferential lanes for high-occupancy vehicles. The commonest pavement marking is traffic striping for a no-passing zone on verticle and horizontal curves. This is figured on the basis of what is considered a safe sight distance.

§6.11 c. Sight Distance

The *safe sight distance* is determined according to the prevalent speed of vehicles. The takes into consideration all the factors of stopping.

The determination of sight distance involves three factors:

1. Distance required for stopping
2. Distance required for overtaking and passing vehicles applicable on two- and three-lane roads
3. Criteria for measuring these distances in the design of vertical and horizontal curves.

The equations used for determination of this data incorporate the following factors and symbols (see Figures 6-10, 6-11, 6-12):

S = sight distance, stopping distance, *or* stopping-sight distance in feet

V = design speed in mi/h

L = length of vertical curve in feet

a = vertical acceleration in feet per second per second (ft/s^2)

A = algebraic difference in grade in per cent of both sides of vertical curve

$R = \frac{L}{A}$ = minimum radius of vertical curve in ft

The sight distance considered is measured from the driver's eyes to an object on the roadway. The measurement for safe stopping distance is different from safe-passing sight distance. Also, sight distance on a vertical curve involves different elements than sight distance on a horizontal curve.

The average height of the driver's eyes is assumed to be 3.75 feet above the road surface. The average height of an object viewed by the driver on a crest of a vertical curve is assumed to be 0.5 feet. The average height of an object for passing sight distance is 4.0 feet, equivalent to the height of another motor vehicle. The average height of a truck driver's eyes above the pavement is 6.0 feet.

Figure 6-10 Vertical Sight Distance Calculation

To determine sight distance on vertical curves, the basic formulas for length of parabolic curve in terms of the algebraic difference in grade and sight distance are:

When S is less than L,
$L = A\,S^2/100\,(\sqrt{2h_1} + \sqrt{2h_2})^2$
When S is greater than L.
$L = 2\,S - (200\,(\sqrt{h_1} + \sqrt{h_2})^2)/A$

Where: L = length of vertical curve in feet; S = sight distance in feet; A = algebraic difference in grades, in per cent; h_1 = height of eye above the roadway surface, in feet; and h_2 = height of object above the roadway surface, in feet

PROFILE

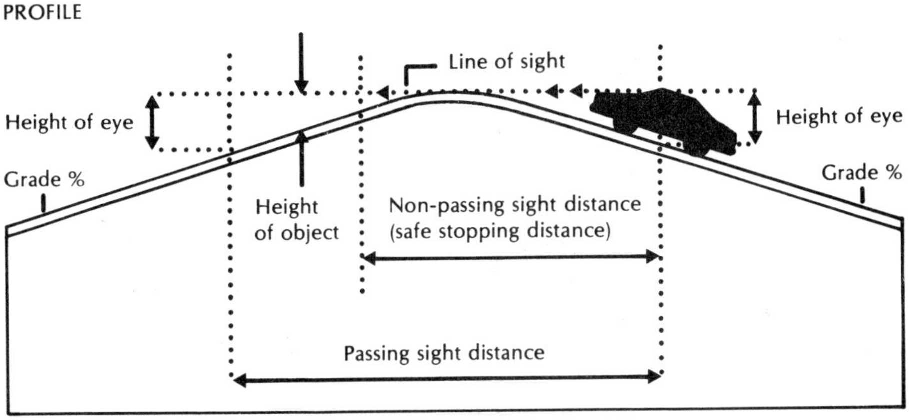

PLAN

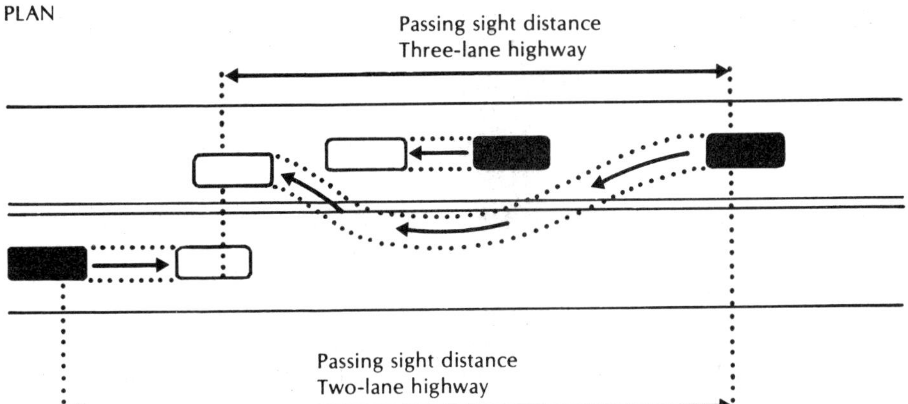

Figure 6-11 Sight Distance of Horizontal Curves

M = middle ordinate, S = sight distance in feet from sight obstruction to center line of inside lane measured perpendicular to line of sight, D = degree of curve = 5729.58 ÷ R, R = radius of center line of inside lane, in feet

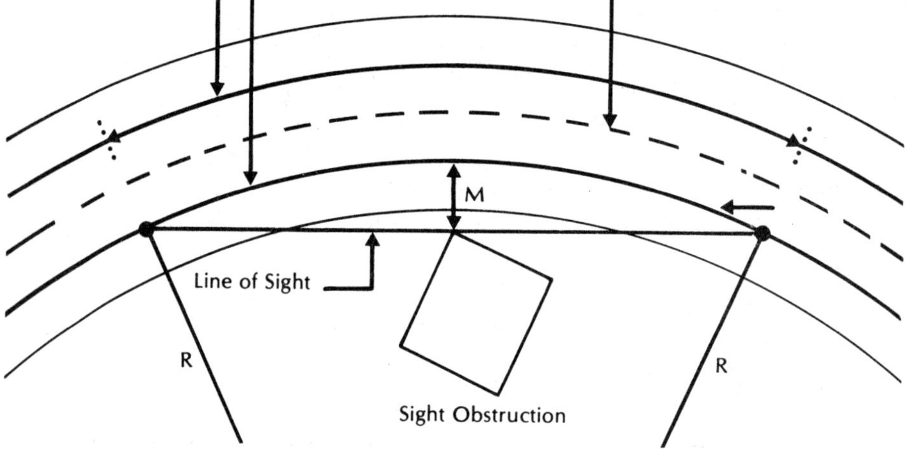

The minimum stopping sight distance is equal to the safe stopping distance, which is the sum of: (1) the distance covered by the vehicle from the instant the driver sights an object to the instant the brakes are applied. This is given as D_1; and (2) the distance required to stop the vehicle from the instant the brakes are applied, or D_2.

D_1 is the perception time and the total amount of time between seeing the object and realization that a stop must be made. An average perception time is 1.5 seconds. However, this varies with the individual driver.

The D_2 time is known as brake reaction time and is the time required to actually apply the brakes. The American Association of State Highway Officials (AASHO) recommends the usage of 1.0 seconds[17] for perception time or a total of 2.5 seconds for perception and brake reaction time. At 60 miles per hour a vehicle travels 220 feet in 2.5 seconds.

The AASHO formulas for safe stopping distances are:

$$S = \text{Safe stopping distance in feet}$$
$$= D_1 + D_2$$

[17] §§6.05, 6.08.

Figure 6-12 Middle Ordinate Stopping Sight Distance on Horizontal Curves (Open-Road Condition)

From *Data Book for Civil Engineers—Design, Third Edition,* Volume 1, by Elwyne E. Seelye.

$$m = \frac{5730}{D} \text{ vers } \frac{50}{200}$$

$$m = R\left(\text{vers } \frac{28.65\,S}{R}\right)$$

$$S = \frac{R}{28.65} \cos^{-1} \frac{R-M}{R}$$

D = degree of curve-centerline of inside lane
m = middle ordinate: centerline inside lane to sight obstruction-feet
R = radius-centerline of inside lane-feet
● = maximum D when e = 0.10
V = design speed, MPH
e = rate of superelevation, ft per ft.

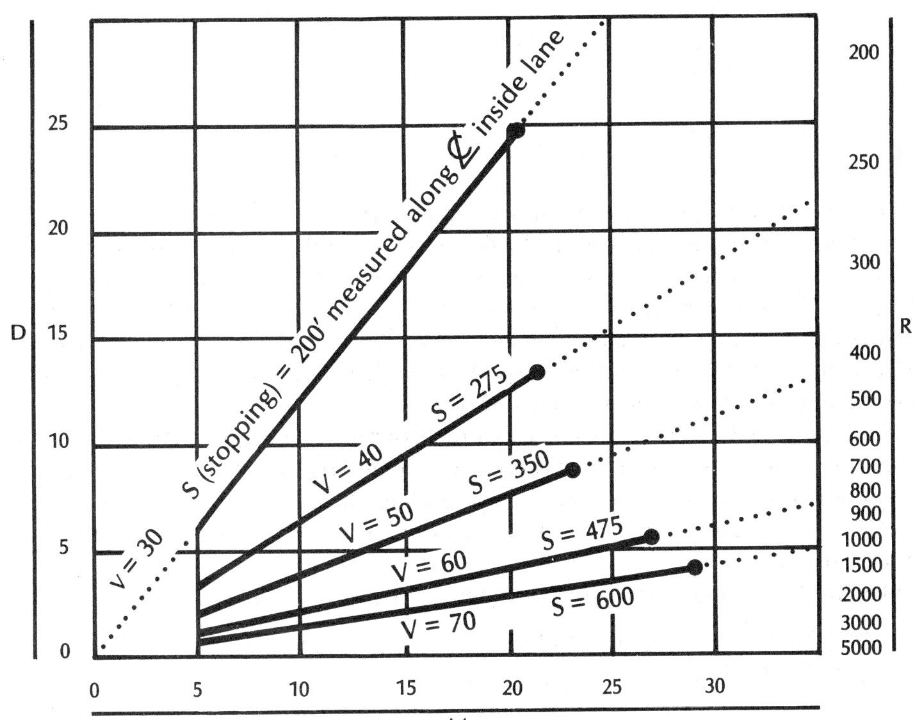

where:

$$D_1 = \text{reaction distance in feet}$$
$$= 1.47\ V\ (3.75 - 0.025\ V)$$

and:

$$D_2 = \text{braking distance in feet}$$
$$= (0.0334\ V^2) \div [(.575 - .0025\ V) \pm (G \div 100)]$$
$$V = \text{velocity in mi/h}$$
$$G = \text{grade in per cent}$$

For example, assuming a vehicle travels at 60 miles per hour on a level road, the safe stopping distance is calculated as follows:

$$D_1 = (1.47 \times 60) \times [(3.75) - (.025 \times 60)]$$
$$= 198.45 \text{ ft}$$
$$D_2 = (.0334 \times 60^2) \div [(.575) - (.0025 \times 60)]$$
$$= 282.92 \text{ ft}$$
$$D_1 + D_2 = 481.37 \text{ ft}$$

A downhill slope of the roadway would increase the safe stopping distance, while an uphill grade would decrease the safe stopping distance.

These distances will increase according to the relative factors of safety, type of vehicle, road, and lighting conditions.

§6.12 d. Guardrails

Guardrails are installed as a means of traffic control. They are usually placed along highway embankments and around fixed objects, and are aimed at reducing the frequency and severity of runoff road accidents. They do this by deflecting the vehicle away from the embankment, slope, or fixed object, which reduces the energy of the moving vehicle.

Serving a purpose similar to that of the guardrails are the *impact energy attenuators.* These devices are intended to protect a motorist from the consequences of a collision with a fixed object that cannot be removed or in situations where other protective systems are not suitable. Guardrails are designed to handle glancing impact and are not effective in case of head-on or near head-on impacts. The commonest types of impact energy attenuators now in use are steel drums, water-filled tubes, lightweight concrete, and sand-filled plastic drums.

§6.13 e. Traffic Light Signals

The most familiar traffic control devices are traffic light signals. These signals are power-operated devices which alternately direct traffic to stop or proceed at highway and street intersections. They make an orderly assignment of right of way to various traffic movements. A warranted and properly designed traffic signal installation may effectively reduce the frequency of certain types of accidents. Properly coordinated, signals can insure continuous or nearly continuous traffic flow at definite speeds along a given route. They allow other vehicles or pedestrians to cross a continuous traffic stream, and they control traffic more economically than manual methods do.

However, an improperly designed or maintained traffic signal may increase accident frequency and create excessive delays. It may promote disregard of signals and lead to circuitous travel as it becomes necessary to divert travel to alternate routes. Experience has shown that although the number of right-angle collisions may decrease after installation of signals, numbers of rear-end collisions often tend to increase. Thus, many considerations must be taken into account before deciding whether to install a traffic signal.

The authorized minimum requirements for traffic control signals rely on the analysis of data covering a large number of factors coupled with the judgment of experienced traffic engineers. The data to be analyzed is to include such factors as minimum vehicle volume, frequency of interruption of continuous traffic, minimum pedestrian volume, and location of school crossings. In addition, progressive movement of traffic and accident experience in the area must be considered.

The accident experience factor may warrant experimentation with various methods of traffic control. Where certain methods have been observed and put into effect, but have failed to reduce accident frequency, more restrictive methods of traffic control may be employed.

§6.14 C. Rail Transportation

The Association of American Railroads (AAR) is an organization established in 1934 by the merger of a group of railroad associations. The purpose of this organization is to coordinate railroad activity in areas such as operations and maintenance, law, research, traffic, finance, accounting, taxation, and valuation. Information regarding the organization and operation of the AAR may be obtained from its headquarters in Washington, D.C.

The Interstate Commerce Commission (ICC) regulates *interstate* traffic of railroads in such matters as service, rates, safety, issuance of securities, and construction and abandonment of railroad lines. The ICC also regulates other transportation agencies including motor carriers, water carriers, freight forwarders, and pipelines for petroleum products.

Various state departments of public utilities, railroad commissions, and similar agencies also take part in the regulation of railroads' *intrastate* activities.

1. Rail Vehicles

§6.15 a. Locomotives

The vehicles which serve as the motive power for railways are locomotives, multiple-unit electric cars, and rail diesel cars.

There are three major groups of locomotives:

1. Reciprocating steam engines which are mechanically connected to driving axles
2. Diesel electric and gas (or steam) turbine electric
3. Electric

The first two groups are similar in that the locomotive carries its own power plant, whereas electric locomotives have an unlimited source of power available in the electrical distribution system. The second and third groups are similar in that the final drive is electric.

Locomotive capacity, or the final output of a locomotive, is the combination of speed (usually expressed in miles per hour) and tractive effort (expressed as TE or pull). The power of a locomotive is expressed as horsepower available at the driving axles. The capacity of the locomotive is limited by the amount of power it can develop and the amount of power it can use. At starting or low speeds, it is limited by the friction between the driving wheels and the rail; the amount of friction also depends on the type of rail, weather conditions, and uniformity of the torque of the wheel. Available adhesion between the wheel and the rail may vary from 5 per cent of the weight of the drivers under extremely poor rail conditions to 40 per cent under exceptionally good conditions. The usual adhesive limit is taken at 25 per cent of the weight of the drivers for steam locomotives and 30 per cent for locomotives with electric drives.

The power capacity depends on various design factors of the locomotive. In steam engines, these include size and stroke of the piston, number of cylinders, boiler pressure, diameter of driver wheels, and diameter of cylinder. The rated TE of the locomotive can be developed only at starting or very low speeds. However, for running speeds, it must be reduced by a speed factor. There are various formulas to determine TE.

The average dimensions of the three types of locomotives are:

Type	Height	Width	Length
Steam	16′-0″	11′-2″	100′-0″ to 130′-0″
Diesel electric	15′-0″	10′-8″	50′-0″ to 70′-0″
Electric	16′-0″	10′-10″	60′-0″ to 75′-0″

§6.16 b. Railroad Cars

Among the various types of railroad freight cars are tank cars, flatcars, gondola cars, hopper cars, boxcars, automobile cars, refrigerator cars, stock cars, container cars, and other specially designed cars.

The average dimensions, weights, and capacities of typical freight cars are:

Type of Car	Length	Width	Height	Maximum Capacity (cubic feet)	Tare Weight
Flat	53′-0″	10′-3″	—	—	48,700#
Gondola	43′-0 1/2″	10′-3 3/4″	8′-7 3/16″	2241	42,800
Hopper	35′-10″	10′-5 5/16″	10′-8″	2605	30,000
Box	41′-9 1/2″	10′-8 8/8″	14′-09/16″	3468	48,200
Automobile	52′-2 1/2″	10′-8″	15′-0 15/16″	4860	53,000

Included in the many types of passenger cars are lounge cars, club cars, and observation cars equipped with reclining chairs and couches.

2. Railroad Roadbeds and Structures

§6.17 a. Railroad Tracks

A typical railroad track has three basic components, *rails, ties,* and *ballast.*

The rails of a railroad track are made of extremely hard steel and include accessories such as splice plates and spikes. The rails are manufactured in a wide range of weights and configurations to suit the type of traffic to be carried. High-speed main line tracks require a heavier weight rail, while spur tracks on private industrial sidings utilize a lighter rail. Rails are identified by weight per linear yard. For instance, a 90-pound rail weighs 90 pounds per yard. The three common designations of rails are: (1) ASCE (American Society of Civil Engineers); (2) USS (United States Steel); and (3) Bethlehem.

Ties are normally made of wood, and are spaced at intervals of about 21 inches to 24 inches on center. The rails are attached to the ties by spikes. Precast concrete ties are also used.

Ballast is the granular material which fills space between and under the ties in order to make the track firm and solid. This is usually 3/4-inch crushed rock. The ballast holds the tracks in line and grade, provides drainage, and distributes the load from the wheels uniformly to the subgrade.

The subgrade is the earth directly under the ballast. This is also called the roadbed. See Figures 6-13 and 6-14 for illustrations of the components of a railroad track.

§6.18 3. Traffic Control Devices

Railway traffic is guided by railway signals, which are used to direct and control the operation of trains on main tracks, at crossings, at junctions, and at terminals.

Signaling relates to traffic uses. Therefore, there are all kinds of signal and traffic control devices. The many traffic control mechanisms include crossover switches, car retarders, interlocking block signals, centralized traffic control devices, automatic train control, and train communication systems.

The Interstate Commerce Commission is the federal agency which prescribes the rules and regulations for installation and maintenance of signaling systems and related equipment.

A signaling device has two important characteristics, *aspect* and *indication.* The aspect of a signal is the actual sign observed by the engineer. The indication is the subject matter of the sign, or what the engineer is required or instructed to do.

Semaphore signals are used for daylight aspects and have one or more blades operated in three distinct positions in the upper-right quadrant. The horizontal position indicates *stop,* an angle of 45 degrees, indicates *caution,* and the vertical position indicates *clear.*

Figure 6-13 Section through Railroad Track

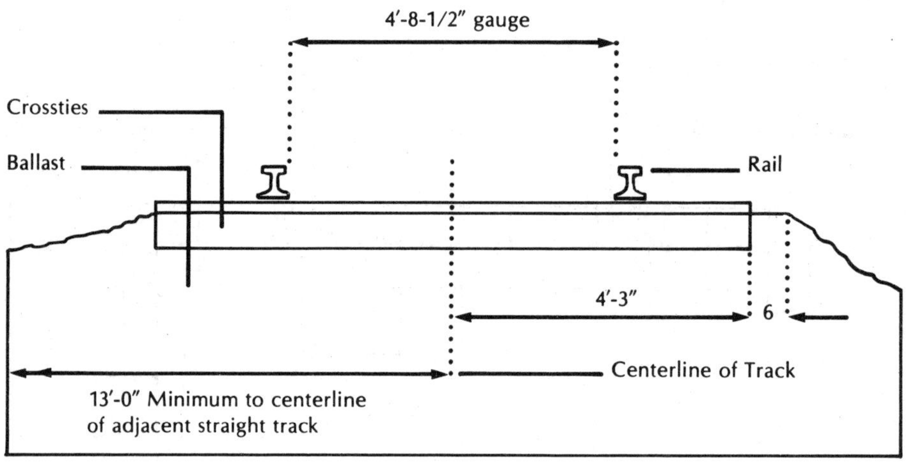

The night aspects of semaphore signals take the form of colored lights, *red, yellow* and *green,* with the same respective indications.

State public utility commissions require that minimum clearances be maintained adjacent to and above all tracks as shown on Figure 6-15. On a straight track, a minimum clearance distance of 8 feet 6 inches is required, while on a curve the clearance should be 1 foot greater. The minimum overhead clearance above the rail should be 22 feet 6 inches. Many telephone and power companies prefer to maintain as much as 26 to 27 feet vertical clearance.

The clearances required for tracks within a building may be an exception. Generally, the overhead clearance above a rail located inside a building may be reduced to 18 feet provided that the track terminates within the building and that all railroad cars are brought to a stop before they enter the building.

For parallel tracks, the minimum distance between centerlines of adjacent tracks should be 14 feet. Side clearance of railroad tracks should be as follows: a side clearance to a pole is 8 feet 3 inches; for switchboxes, switch-operating mechanisms, and accessories necessary for the control and operation of the signals projecting 4 inches or less above the top of the rail, the clearance is 3 feet; for signals and switches projecting more than 4 inches and less than 3 feet above the top of the rail, the clearance should be 6 feet. For other detailed regulations, reference should be made to the public utility commission orders.

§6.19 4. Railroad Terms

Following is a short glossary of common railroad terms:

Figure 6-14 Sections through Grade Crossings

(a) wood planking

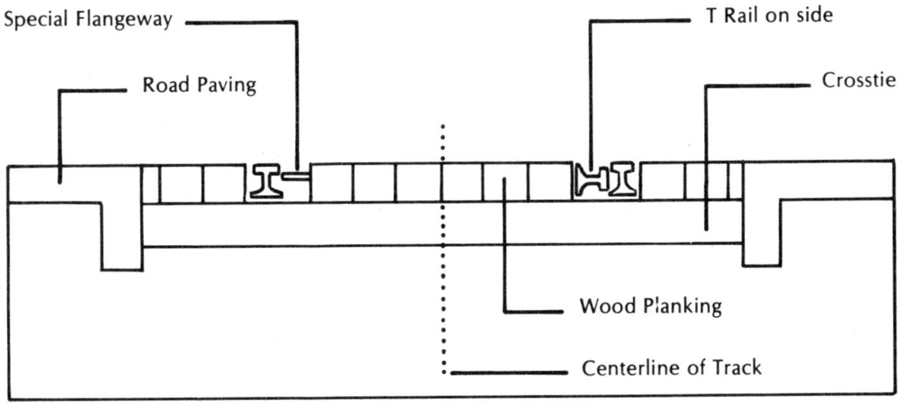

(b) asphaltic concrete

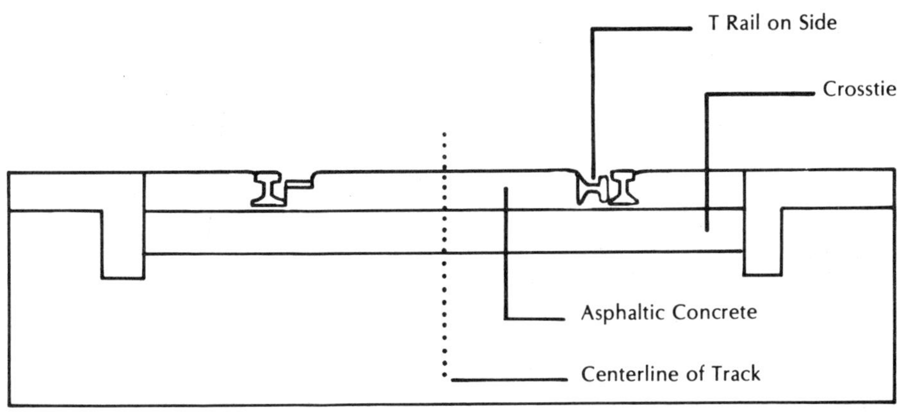

Back shop: shop for heavy repairs to locomotives

Bad order: car or locomotive needing repair, also called *cripple*

Bend the iron: change the position of the switch

Captain: conductor

Car knocker: car inspector

Clock: steam or air gauge on locomotive

Figure 6-15 Clearance of Structures from Standard Railroad Track

California General Industrial Safety Orders, tit 8, art 24, §3428, "Industrial Railroads," 432.61 (Mar 1, 1969)

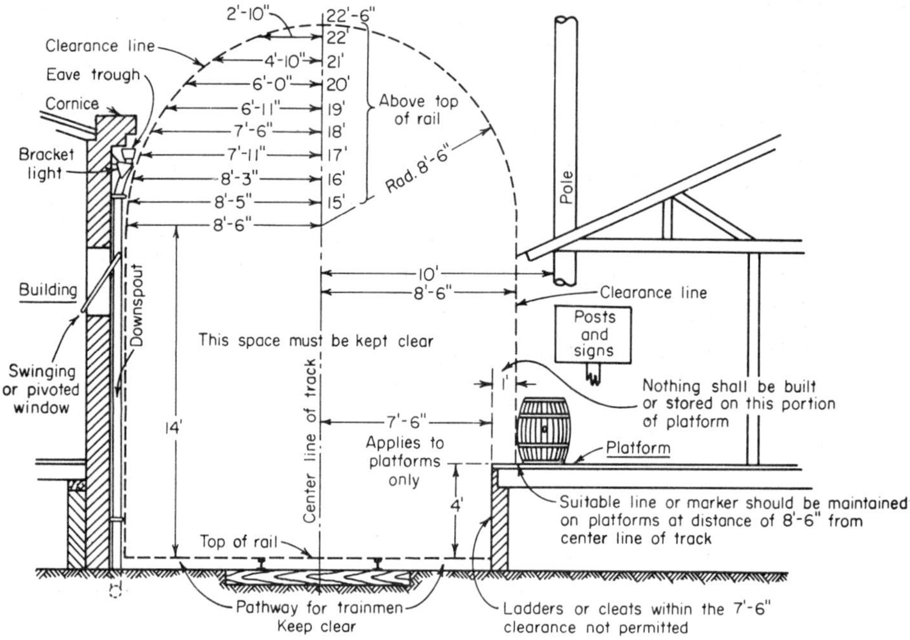

Notes

Overhead wire clearances shall conform to commission's general order No. 95 or amendments thereof

Posts, poles, signs, and similar facilities may have minimum clearance of 8'-6", but clearance of 10' is recommended where practicable

All side clearance dimensions are for tangent track. In general, side clearance for curve track to be 1' greater than that for tangent track

When track is used principally for loading or unloading refrigerator cars, platform with height of 4'-6" above top of rail may be maintained, provided that minimum side clearance to center line of track shall be 8'

Platforms 4' or less in height with minimum clearance of 7'-3" may be extended at existing clearances if such extension is not in connection with reconstruction of original platform

Icing platforms and supports shall have minimum clearance of 7'-8"

Crummy: caboose

Drag: slow freight train

Drop: switching movement, e.g., "drop cars on track 2"

Frog: X-shaped device to enable wheels running on one track to cross the rails of another track

Fusee: red flare used for signaling purposes

Gandy dancers: Section workers on rail beds

Goat: yard or switch engine

Green eye: Clear signal

Highball: signal to come ahead or pick up speed

High iron: main line track

Hog: locomotive, also called *jack*

Hotshot: see *Redball*

In the Color: train in the signal block, waiting for a clear board, or sign to proceed

Jack: see *hog*

Main line: principal line of the railroad

Manifest: see *Redball*

Paddle: semaphore signal, also called *board*

Piggyback train: flatcars carrying truck trailers

Redball: fast freight train, also called *manifest* or *hotshot*

Red board: stop signal

Reefer: refrigerated car

Shoofly: temporary track built around flooded area, wreck, or some other obstacle

Switch: connection between two lines of track to permit cars or trains to pass from one track to another

Timetable: authority for the movement of regular trains, or schedules of such movement of trains

Wiping the gauge: stopping suddenly

Wye: tracks running off the main line, forming a huge Y—used for turning cars or engines where no turntable is available

D. Laws of Physics Affecting Vehicles

1. Motion

§6.20 a. Linear

Investigation of vehicular accidents often concentrates on *linear motion*. When a vehicle travels along a straight line, its motion is said to be linear.

A body has *uniform linear motion* if it traverses equal distances during equal intervals of time no matter how brief those intervals may be. Very often motion that is linear is not uniform. A falling body travels faster and faster as it approaches the earth. Similarly, a motor vehicle starting from rest, or stopping after having been in motion, does not have uniform motion.

The *speed* of a body with uniform linear motion is defined as the distance which the body traverses divided by the time required to traverse this distance. In equation form, this formula appears as:

$$V = \frac{S}{t}$$

where:

V = speed of the body
S = space or distance traveled
t = time required to travel that distance

Units in which linear speed is expressed depend on the systems of units used to designate distances and time. If the distance is stated in miles and the time in hours, the speed is given in miles per hour. However, this speed expressed in miles per hour may be converted into feet per second by multiplying it by the suitable conversion factors. It is a useful rule of thumb to remember that a speed of 30 miles per hour is equal to 44 feet per second.

In the metric system the speed of vehicles is expressed in kilometers per hour or meters per second. The conversion factors are:

1 mile = 1.60935 kilometers; *or*
30 mi/h = 48.28 km/h

1 kilometer = 0.62137 miles, *or*
30 km/h = 18.64 mi/h

§6.21 (1) Velocity

Engineers distinguish between speed and velocity. *Speed* of a body only refers to the time required to traverse a distance but makes no reference to the direction in which the body moves.

The *velocity* of a body is a vector quantity having the same magnitude as its speed, but it includes the direction of motion. The term *vector* is applied to quantities which have both magnitude and direction. Thus, in stating a velocity of a body, both speed and direction of motion must be indicated. If either speed or direction changes, the velocity of the body must be altered.

§6.22 (2) Acceleration and Deceleration

An important mechanical property of a vehicle is its *pickup* , or the rapidity with which the vehicle gains velocity. If a vehicle starting from rest acquires a velocity along a straight road of 4 feet per second at the end of one second, then increases its velocity by another 4 feet per second at the end of the next second, and so on, the vehicle is said to have an acceleration of 4 feet per second per second (4 ft/s^2). By the end of five seconds, the vehicle will have a velocity of 20 feet per second.

The *acceleration* of a body is defined as its change of velocity during any interval of time divided by the duration of that interval. This is illustrated in the following equation form:

$$a = \frac{V_f - V_o}{t}$$

where:

a = acceleration
V_f = final velocity
V_o = original velocity
t = time interval

By rearranging this formula, a final velocity, V_f, can be determined for a vehicle starting from rest at a known acceleration and time interval.

$$V_f - V_o = a\ t$$

If:

V_f = final velocity
$V_o = 0$
t = 5 seconds
a = 4 ft/s^2

then:

$$V_f = 4 \times 5 = 20 \text{ ft/s}$$

The acceleration of a vehicle can also be expressed as the difference between the traction available from a vehicle's engine and that required to achieve a steady speed at a given grade. This can be expressed as the acceleration in miles per hour per second:

$$a = 21.9 \times \frac{\text{surplus traction force}}{\text{total effective car weight}}$$

The maximum acceleration rate possible is limited by the weight on the driving wheels and the coefficient of friction[18] between the wheels and the road. If half of the car's weight is on the driver wheels and the coefficient of tire friction is 0.8, the limiting traction force for a 4000-pound vehicle will be (4000 × .5 × .8) 1600 pounds, and the maximum acceleration rate will be calculated as follows:

$$a = 21.9 \times \frac{(.8 \text{ x } 2000)}{4000} = 8.8 \text{ mi/h per second}$$

[18] §6.28.

This is equivalent to an acceleration from 0 to 60 miles per hour in 6.82 seconds.

Deceleration is defined as the time rate of decrease in velocity. A common example would be a vehicle slowing down or stopping.

Modern motor vehicles have the ability to accelerate at a great rate. The maximum acceleration is usually used for ascending steep grades or to overtake other vehicles. Maximum rates of acceleration for passing vehicles vary from 4 to 6 miles per hour per second and rates for trucks from 1.5 to 2 miles per hour per second. The rate of deceleration determines the safe stopping distance and the safe sight distance.

The equation used to determine distance traveled by a body accelerating or decelerating over a known period of time is expressed as follows:

$$S = V_{av}\, t = \frac{(V_o + V_f)}{2}\, t$$

where:

S = distance traveled, in feet

V_{av} = average velocity, in feet per second (ft/s)

t = time interval, in seconds

V_o = initial velocity, in ft/s

V_f = final velocity, in ft/s

This formula can be used to determine relative positions of vehicles involved in collisions at specific points in time.

§6.23 b. Angular Motion

A wheel spinning about its axle is an example of *angular* as opposed to linear motion. The radius of any point of the wheel to the axis sweeps through an angle of 360 degrees for every revolution of the wheel. For this reason, a rotating body is said to have angular motion.

The angular speed of a body which has uniform angular motion is defined as the angle through which the body sweeps divided by the time required to sweep through this angle. This can be illustrated by the following formula:

$$\text{Angular speed} = \frac{\text{angle swept through}}{\text{time}}$$

Angular speed can be expressed in several different ways, in degrees per second, revolutions per minute, or other similar increments.

When a wheel is set into rotation from a standstill, it gains angular velocity and ultimately assumes some desired speed. If this final speed is reached in a short time, the wheel is said to have a high angular acceleration. If it takes the wheel a longer time to reach the same final speed, the wheel is said to have a lower angular acceleration. In short, angular acceleration of a body is that body's time rate of change of angular velocity.

In accordance with Newton's first law of motion, a body in motion left to itself will

Figure 6-16 Forces Acting on Vehicle Rounding Curve on Level Road

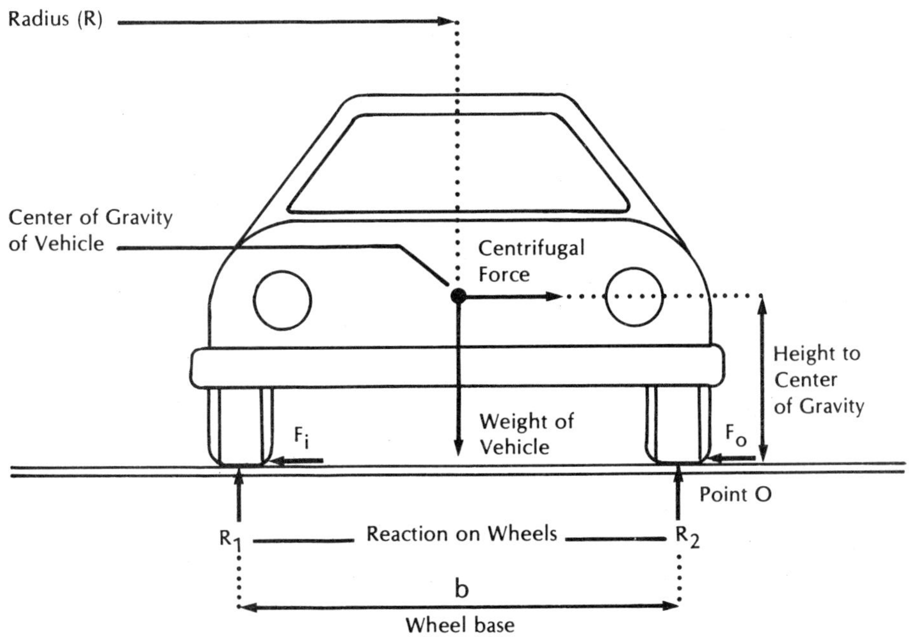

travel in a straight line; a body will not move around a curve unless a lateral force is exerted on it.

When a locomotive encounters a curve, its forward motion causes the flanges on the wheels to press outwardly against the edges of the outer rail. Consequently, the rail presses inward against the flanges. The locomotive, under the action of this inward force, undergoes a change in direction and continues to follow the track.

An automobile's traveling around a curve at a constant speed will cause the tires to act on the roadway surface with a constant force directed radially outward from the center of the curve. This outward push or pull is called the *centrifugal force*. See Figures 6-16 and 6-17.

Since for any action there is always an equal and opposite reaction, the restraining reaction exerts an equal inward force on the moving object which is called the *centripetal force*. In all motion on curves the centrifugal and centripetal forces are equal and opposite, and each is exerted in the plane of rotation. Although equal, these forces cannot balance each other because they are not exerted on the same object. An unbalanced force always produces acceleration, and thus the centripetal force acting on a body in circular motion continually accelerates it toward the center of the circle. In fact, it is this inward motion combined with the forward motion that makes the body move in a circle.

Figure 6-17 Forces Acting on Automobile Transversing Superelevated, Curved Roadway

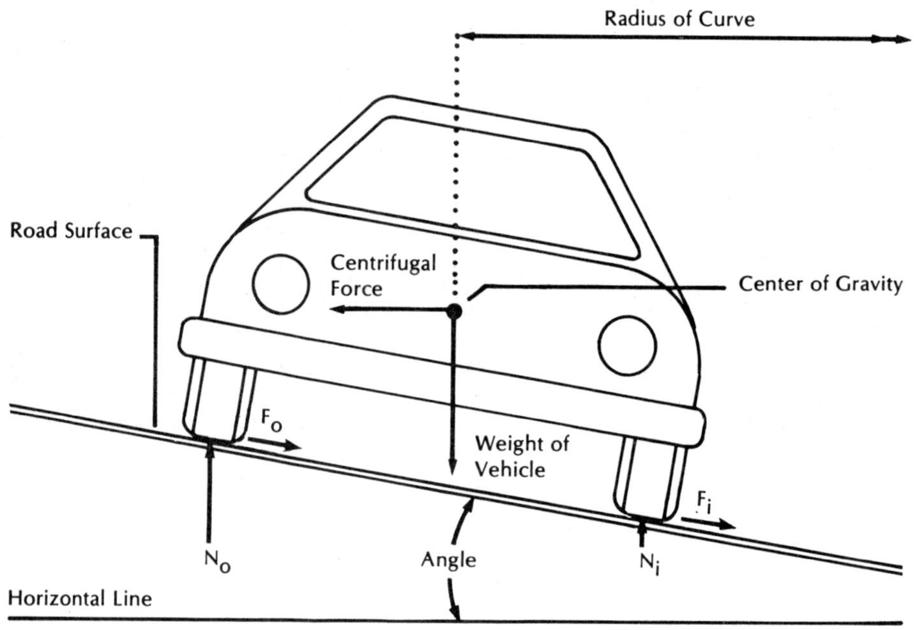

Following are the laws of angular motion:

1. First Law—a body in rotation will continue to turn about a fixed axis with undiminished angular speed unless acted on by some unbalanced torque
2. Second Law—a body that is subjected to an unbalanced torque will be accelerated angularly, and the acceleration produced will be proportional to and in the same direction as the torque, and furthermore, the acceleration will be inversely proportional to the moment of inertia of the body about its axis of rotation
3. Third Law—when a body exerts a torque on another body, the second exerts an equal torque upon the first in the opposite direction and about the same axis of rotation

§6.24 2. Forces

Acceleration[19] is always produced by a force. Whenever a body is accelerating, a force must be acting on it to cause that acceleration. See Figure 6-18.

[19]§6.22.

Figure 6-18 Forces Acting on Vehicle Moving on Level Road

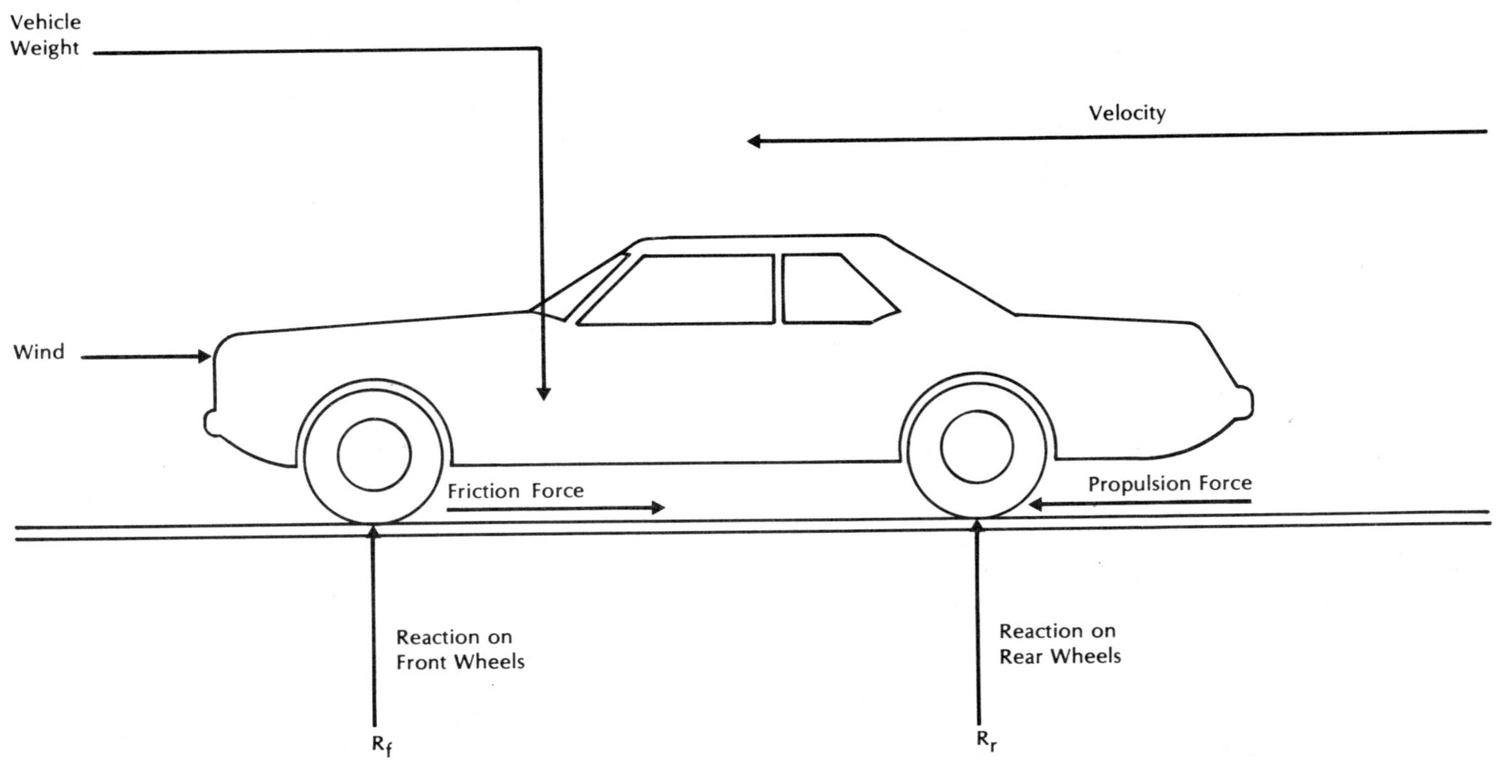

A *force* can be described as a push or pull acting on a body. A locomotive pulling a train exerts a force on that train. Although a body which is accelerating must have a force acting on it, the reverse is not true. A force exerted on a body will not necessarily cause that body to accelerate if there is a force, for example, on a rock, while at the same time friction or some other agent exerts an equal force on the rock in the opposite direction. The two forces balance each other, and the rock will not accelerate.

In almost every case of a transportation accident involving a collision, the relationship of force to motion as set forth by Newton's Laws prevails.

Newton's Laws of Motion are as follows:

1. First Law—a body at rest remains at rest, and a body in motion continues to move at a constant speed along a straight line unless the body is acted upon in either case by an unbalanced force
2. Second Law—an unbalanced force acting on a body causes the body to accelerate in the direction of the force, and the acceleration is directly proportional to the unbalanced force and inversely proportional to the mass of the body
3. Third Law—for every action, there is an equal and opposite reaction

Action refers to the force which the first body exerts on a second body. *Reaction* refers to the force which the second body exerts on the first body.

Newton's Second Law states that the acceleration of a body is directly proportional to the unbalanced force producing it. When a body is released so that it falls freely, the unbalanced force acting on it would be its weight and the acceleration due to gravity, that is, 32.2 feet per second per second.

a. Linear

§6.25 (1) Momentum and Impact

The *momentum* of a body is defined as the product of its mass and velocity, or symbolically:

$$M = mv$$

where:

M = momentum

m = mass

v = velocity

Momentum is a vector quantity which has the same direction as the velocity. This is an important consideration in analyzing collisions[20] between vehicles.

---

[20]§6.30.

Newton's Second Law of motion states that when an unbalanced force, F, acts for a time, t, on a body of mass, m, changing the velocity of that body from V_o to V_f, the relationship between these terms is expressed:

$$F = ma = m\frac{(V_f - V_o)}{t}$$

where:

F = force

m = mass

V_o = initial velocity

V_f = final velocity

t = time

a = acceleration

On rearrangement of these terms, this expression becomes:

$$Ft = mV_f - mV_o$$

When a force acts for a very short time, it is referred to as an *impact,* and the change in momentum is called an *impulse.* Although impact between bodies occurs in a very short interval of time, it is during this time that energy is consumed to deform these bodies. If the bodies are elastic, they will restore this energy when they spring back to their original shape. Otherwise, they will remain deformed. The energy used in deforming the bodies will not be recovered.

In any impact, or collision, between two bodies, elastic or not, Newton's Third Law of motion dictates that the colliding bodies exert equal and opposite forces on each other for a short interval of time. Hence, the impulses received by the two bodies are equal and opposite. One of the bodies will gain as much momentum as the other body loses. The total momentum of the two bodies is not changed by the impact. This notion is demonstrated by the law of conservation of momentum, which states that, for any collision, the vector sum of the momenta of the colliding bodies after collision equals the vector sum of their momenta before collision. Consequently, in a collision between a small car and a large truck, a major portion of the momentum of the truck is transferred to the small vehicle.

There is a close analogy between linear and angular momentum. An unbalanced angular impulse will cause a change in angular momentum of a body, and these two quantities will be numerically equal. The angular momentum of a body is defined as the product of the moment of inertia of a body and its angular velocity. The moment of inertia is equal to the mass of one particle of the body multiplied by the square of its distance from the axis of rotation, plus the mass of another particle of the body multiplied by the square of its distance from the axis of rotation, and so forth, until all the particles of the body are included. In symbols, this relationship is described as:

$$I = \Sigma mr^2$$

where:

I = moment of inertia
Σ = summation
m = mass of each particle
r = radius of gyration of each particle

§6.26 3. Power

The time rate of doing work is called power. *One horsepower* is defined as the power delivered by an agent while doing work at the rate of 550 feet-pounds per second, or 33,000 feet-pounds per minute.

Watt and kilowatt are power units used in rating electrical machines. Relationships between some power units are:

1 foot-pound/second = 1.356 watts
1 kilowatt = 1000 watts = 1.34 horsepower

When considering the horsepower rating of a motor vehicle, a number of horsepower classifications are commonly used. The *gross horsepower* of an engine is the amount of power the engine delivers after it has been stripped of accessories such as muffler, fan, generator, pump, compressor, and other devices. *Net horsepower* is the power remaining and actually available to the flywheel to drive the vehicle after power consumption of the accessories has been subtracted from the *gross horsepower.*

Indicated horsepower is the power actually developed inside the engine cylinders. This is always greater than the gross horsepower, because power is consumed through friction and heat loss.

§6.27 4. Energy of Work

In scientific and engineering terminology, *work* has a technical meaning derived from two factors, force and distance. The amount of work is the product of force and distance.

If an agent is able to do work, it is said to possess *energy*. The amount of energy which an agent has equals the amount of work it can do.

There are many different forms of energy. For instance, coal has chemical energy, steam has thermal energy, a stretched spring has mechanical energy, and a battery has electrical energy.

Mechanical energy encompasses both kinetic and potential energy. *Kinetic energy* is energy that a body has by virtue of its motion. *Potential energy* is energy that a body has by virtue of its position.

The law of conservation of energy[21] states that energy can neither be created nor destroyed, and that, therefore, the total amount of energy in the universe remains

[21] §6.25.

Figure 6-19 Forces and Reactions on Accelerating Motor Vehicle

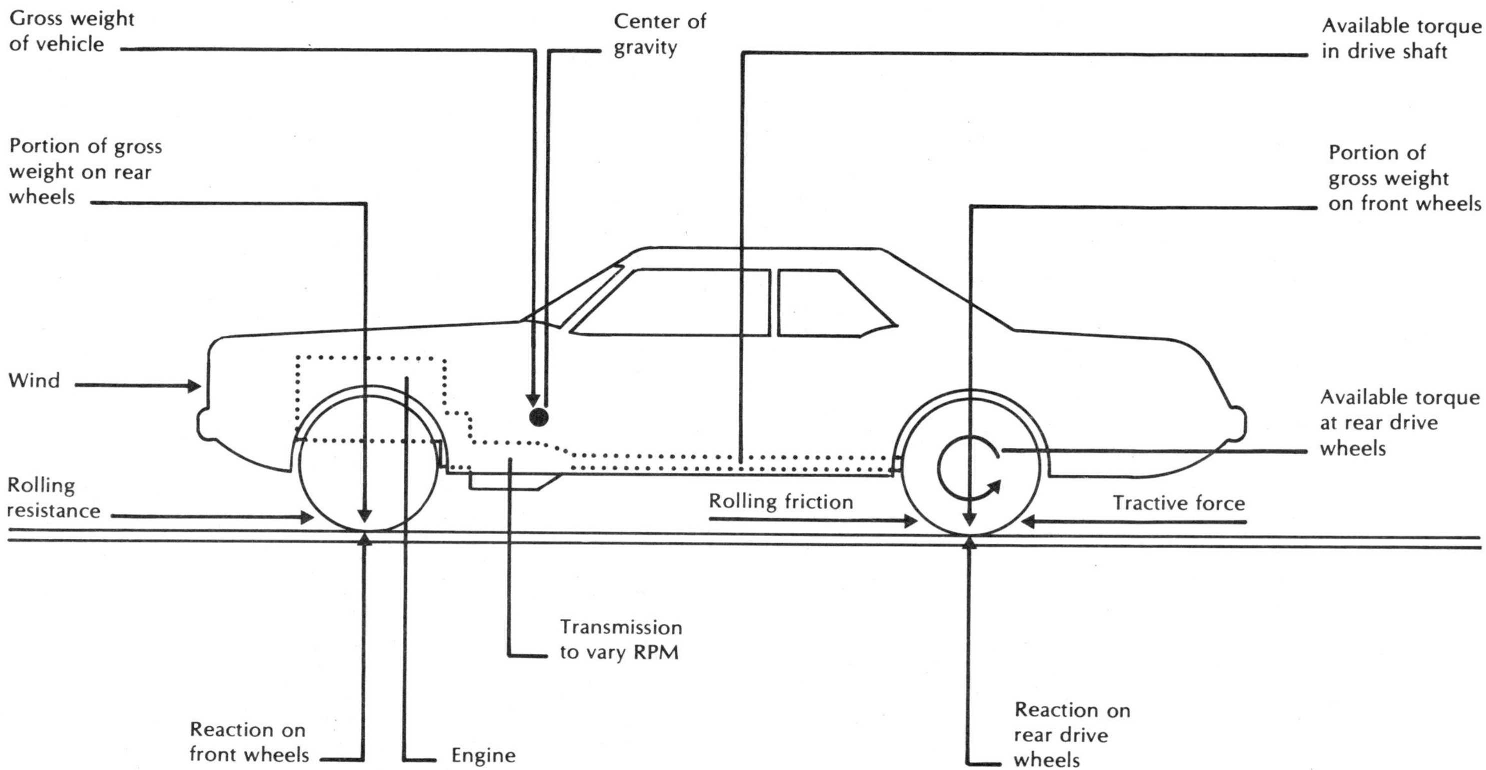

Figure 6-20 Forces and Reactions Acting on Braking Motor Vehicle

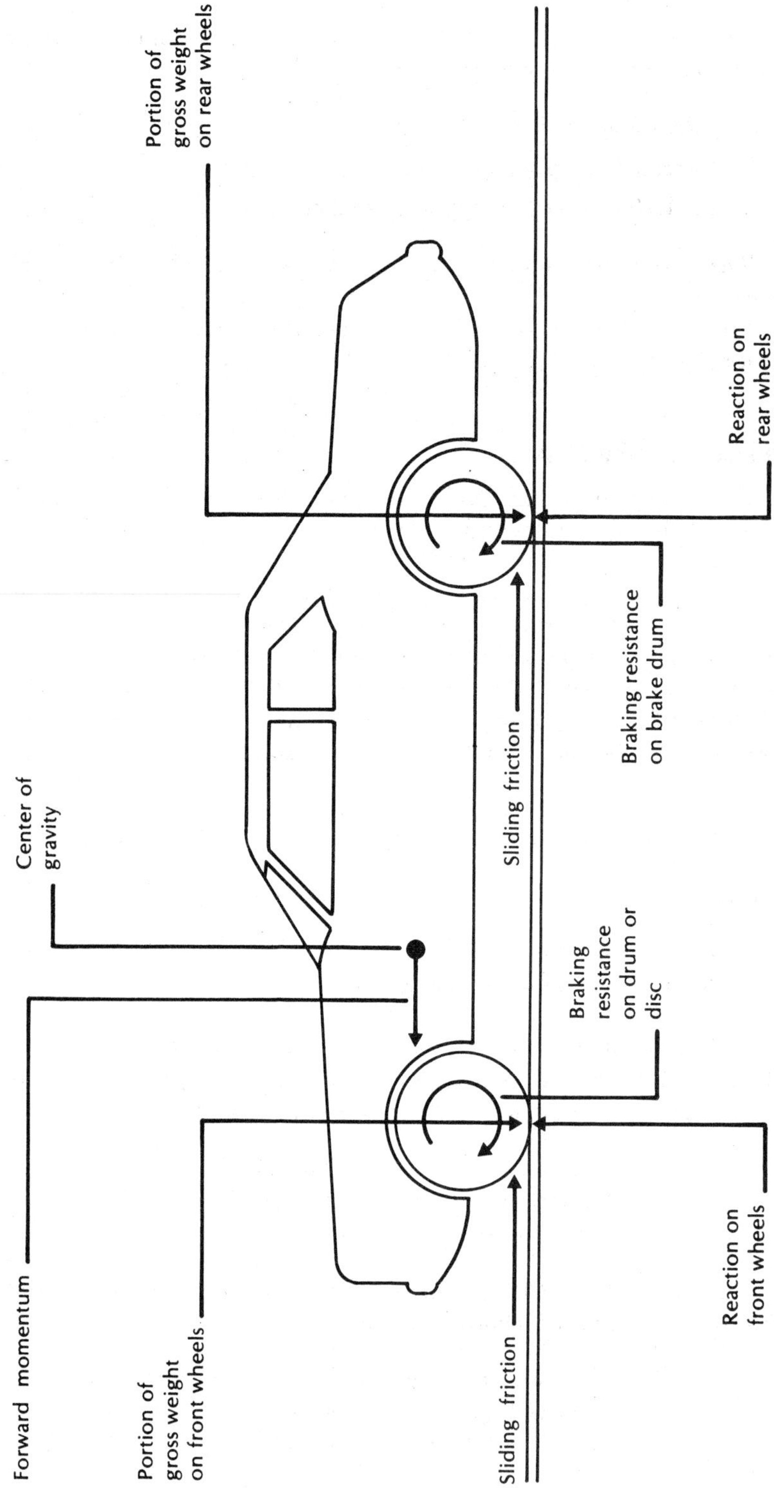

constant. When mechanical work is done on a body, it can be accounted for entirely by one or more of the following effects:

1. Increase in kinetic energy of the body
2. Increase in its potential energy
3. Production of heat in opposing friction

The law of conservation of energy is a basic principle utilized in reconstruction accidents.

Figures 6-19 and 6-20 illustrate the forces and reactions on motor vehicles accelerating or braking.

§6.28 5. Friction

If the surface of any solid object were magnified, it would be found to be rough and uneven. These irregularities resist the sliding of one surface over another. This resistance is called *sliding friction*.

The amount of friction which one body is capable of exerting on another is directly proportional to the normal or perpendicular force with which their surfaces are pressed together. For example, the friction, or tractive force, of a wheel is the product of the weight on that wheel and the coefficient of friction between tire and pavement.

The coefficient of friction μ is defined as the ratio of the force of friction between two bodies to the normal force pressing their surfaces together.

$$\mu = \frac{F}{N}$$

where:

F = friction, in pounds
N = normal force, in pounds

The coefficient of sliding friction may be taken as a constant for any two surfaces. This will vary with the materials involved and the conditions of the surfaces in contact. Some representative values of coefficient of sliding friction are as follows:

Wood on wood	.25 to .50
Metal on wood	.20 to .60
Metal on metal	.15 to .20

The coefficient of rolling friction is much smaller than the coefficient of sliding friction as given in the following lists:

Cast iron wheels on rails	.004
Ball bearings in rolling contact	.001 to .003
Roller bearings in rolling contact	.002 to .007

Figure 6-21 illustrates the relationship between speed of a vehicle and the coefficient

Figure 6-21 Relationship of Coefficient of Friction to Vehicle Speed

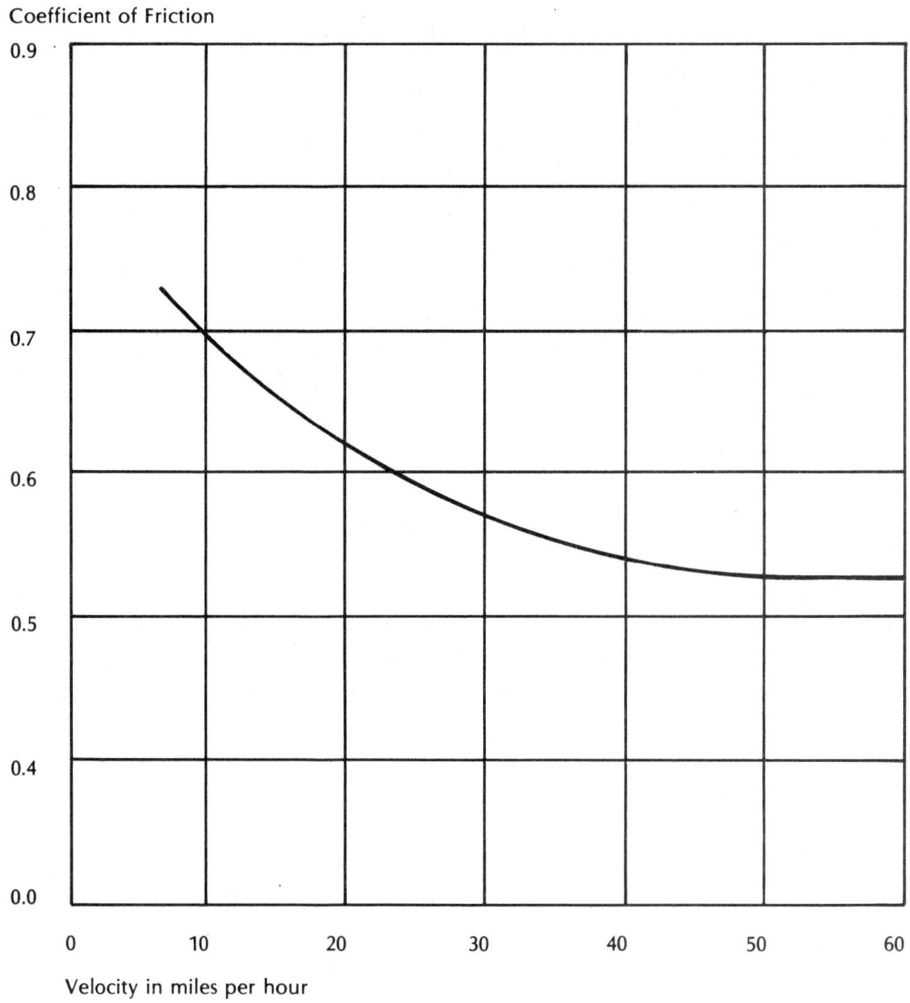

of friction. Because of its road-adhesion capabilities, the motor vehicle tire develops substantial traction, steering, and braking reactions. It also provides lateral and directional stability, by exerting side thrust when the direction of travel is changed, which causes the vehicle to turn. The total slipping resistance of a tire is the basic frictional resistance between the tread and the ground plus a mechanical interlocking between these two surfaces.

Train resistance of locomotives and cars is a combination of *inherent level tangent* resistance and *incidental* resistance due to grade, curvature of track, and wind pressure.

The *level tangent* resistance is often called *tractive*, *frictional*, or *rolling* resistance, and varies with speed, axle load, cross-sectional area, streamlining, types of journals, condition of track, temperature, and winds.

Grade resistance is usually equivalent to 20 pounds per ton for each percentage point of grade. Curve resistance amounts to 0.8 pounds per ton per degree of curvature. The total resistance of a locomotive includes the level tangent resistance together with the grade and curve resistance.

§6.29 6. Unit Systems

In determination of forces and acceleration of moving bodies, whether motor vehicles or trains, specific units of measurement must be used. The units form a consistent system of kinetic units.

There are five consistent systems of kinetic units. The *absolute system*, also known as the *mks* system, is generally used by physicists. The units of length, mass,[22] and time are respectively designated by the meter (m), the kilogram (kg), and the second (sec). All three are arbitrarily defined. In the *mks* system, the unit of force is called a *newton*, defined as a force which gives an acceleration of 1 m/s^2 to a mass of 1 kg.

$$1 \text{ newton} = (1 \text{ kg}) \times (1 \text{ m/s}^2)$$

The mks system is said to be an absolute system of units because the three types of units, meter, kilogram, and second, are independent of the location where the measurements are made. That is, they may be made on earth or in space and the formulas remain valid.

Other absolute systems of units are the *cgs* system and the *British absolute* system. In the cgs system, the units of length, mass, and time are respectively designated by the centimeter (cm), the gram (g), and the second. The centimeter is .01m and the gram is .001 kg. The unit of force is the dyne. In the British absolute system the units of length, mass, and time are the foot (ft), the pound (lb), and the second (sec). The unit of force in this system is the *poundal*, defined as the force which gives an acceleration of 1 ft/s^2 to a mass of 1 lb.

Most engineers do not use absolute systems of units. They normally use as fundamental units the units of length, force, and time, called the *gravitational system*. This is particularly true in English-speaking countries. In this system, the pound is used as a unit of force rather than a unit of mass. Force is defined as a mass of one pound, or the force exerted by the earth on a mass of 1 lb at sea level and at latitude 45 degrees. Also, a force of 1 lb gives an acceleration of freely falling bodies at the rate of 32.2 ft/s^2[23] to a mass of 1 lb.

§6.30 E. Elements of Vehicular Accidents

In the discovery of evidence relating to vehicular collisions, many physical factors must be considered. The basic laws of mechanics, physics, and mathematics form the

---

[22] §6.25.

[23] §6.24.

framework for interpreting this type of evidence. Newton's laws of dynamics[24] and Einstein's theories of conservation of energy[25] are the foundation of these basic laws. One needs an understanding of the definitions of force,[26] inertia,[27] velocity,[28] energy impact,[29] and momentum.[30] As to impact, it is necessary to know the direction of the forces involved, their relative momenta, and the dissipation of energy of the vehicles.

Rarely will any two accidents be exactly the same. Consequently, there is no standard method of analyzing an accident. This section will briefly go over some of the important types of evidence required for an approximate reconstruction of a vehicular accident.

One important factor is the original speed[31] of each vehicle involved in the accident. In addition, it is necessary to be familiar with the physical laws governing bodies in motion[32] and on impact.[33] The incident must be broken down into separate, calculable sequences of action. The sum of all these individual phases will represent the translation of all the energy[34] contained by each vehicle prior to and after the accident. The energy consumption will occur because of separate events absorbing a determinable proportion of the kinetic energy[35] contained in each moving vehicle prior to the incident. The initial kinetic energy of a moving body is a factor of its mass and speed. Hence, this is a valuable starting point for determining speed.

$$KE = \frac{mV^2}{2}$$

where:

KE = kinetic energy[36]

$m = \text{mass} = \frac{w}{g}$

g = gravitation acceleration[37] = 32.2 ft/s^2

V = velocity, ft/s[38]

w = weight, pounds

---

[24] §6.24.

[25] §6.25.

[26] §§3.04-.05, 6.24.

[27] §6.25.

[28] §6.21.

[29] §6.25.

[30] *Id.*

[31] §6.21.

[32] §6.22.

[33] §6.25.

[34] §6.27.

[35] *Id.*

[36] §6.27.

[37] §6.24.

[38] §6.21.

Example: What is the kinetic energy of a 4000-pound vehicle traveling at 60 miles per hour?

$$w = 4000 \text{ pounds}$$
$$V = 88 \text{ ft/s } (60 \text{ mi/h} = 88 \text{ ft/s})$$
$$KE = \frac{4000}{32.2} \times \frac{88^2}{2} = 480{,}993.4 \text{ feet-pounds}$$

The sequence of events in the collision of two motor vehicles includes some of the following separate and distinct actions (See Figure 6-22):

1. Braking, with or without skidding
2. Impact[39] between the vehicles, with resulting bending and breaking of metal and other materials
3. Pushing aside of one or both vehicles following impact
4. Final skidding or sliding of vehicles until they come to a rest

Each of these phases will consume a portion of the total original kinetic energy. By calculating the amount of energy used in each phase, total energy can be determined. The total energy will represent the kinetic energy of each vehicle prior to the accident.

In the reconstruction of an accident, the evidence must be sufficient to permit calculation of the energy consumed in each phase of the accident. Therefore, it is necessary to investigate:

1. Braking system
2. Weight of each vehicle
3. Nature of the skid marks
4. Amount of damage to each vehicle
5. Relative positions of the points of contact and stopping

Another source of evidence is available through comparison with controlled test collision results.

Other sources of energy consumption are metal parts gouging and/or rubbing on the pavement, rolling to a final stop, or striking a curb. Any of these elements or any combination of them may result in an erroneous estimate of the original speed.

Internal elements of a vehicle's braking system also affect the rate of retardation. Some of these factors are:

1. Pressure exerted on the braking surfaces (lining and drum)
2. Weight carried on the wheel[40]
3. Overall radius of the wheel (distance from the center of the wheel to the outer tread of the tire)

---

[39] §6.25.

[40] §6.04.

Figure 6-22 Elements of Vehicle Stop

A = sum of perception and reaction time, B = braking effort, C = distance covered while brakes applied

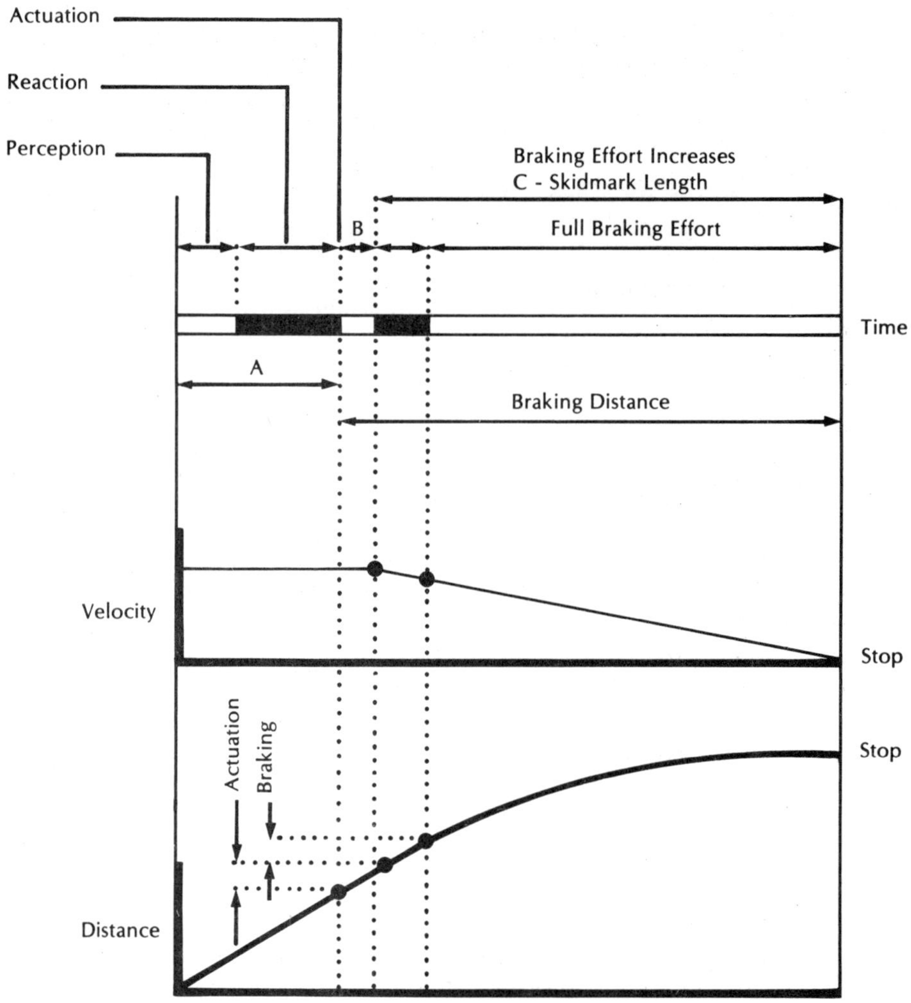

4. Radius of the brake drum
5. Coefficient of friction between tire and road[41]

---

[41]§6.28.

Standardized braking systems are best explained by the following excerpts from Federal Motor Carrier Safety Regulations[42] concerning performance of brakes:

1. The vehicle must develop a braking force at least equal to the percentage of its gross weight specified
2. Deceleration[43] to a stop from 20 miles per hour at not less than the rate specified
3. Stopping from 20 miles per hour in a distance, measured from the point at which movement of the service brake or control begins, that is not greater than the distance specified

§6.31 1. Skid Marks

Properly analyzed skid marks are effective evidence. However, when skid marks are misunderstood by the expert witness, misrepresentation can result.

Many factors can be responsible for making a tire skid mark. A skid mark is a mark on the surface of the pavement caused by a tire sliding or skidding on that surface. This may occur when brakes are applied. However, it also may occur when there has been no attempt to brake the vehicle, as in a side skid perpendicular to the path of travel.

Skid marks can be produced by the transfer of tire material to the road surface. In addition, they can be produced from road surface material.

A skidding tire may generate extreme heat. This is frequently evidenced by smoke. The tire temperature may rise high enough to cause the tire material to soften and transfer onto the pavement. Not all skid marks result from tire transfer onto pavement. For example, dust and debris may be wiped clear in the path of the skidding tire. The nature and length of skid marks are influenced by such factors as speed of the vehicle at the time of skidding, material and surface of the tire, and surface conditions and composition of the pavement (See Figure 6-23). Additional factors may include temperature of the road surface, distribution of the weight of the vehicle between all wheels, amount of contact surface of the tires, number of wheels locked by the brakes and condition and effectiveness of the brakes.

Overlapping skid marks can occur when the skid marks of the rear wheels pass directly over the skid marks of the front wheels. These make it difficult to determine the beginning of skid for the rear wheels or the end of skid for the front wheels.

2. Check List of Evidence

§6.32 a. Roadway Accidents

The following items can be important evidence in a roadway accident case:

A. Driver reaction time
   1. Reaction time distance[44]

---

[42] 49 CFR §393.52 (1979).

[43] **§6.22.**

[44] **§6.04.**

Figure 6-23 Ranges of Friction Factors for Different Types of Road Surfaces

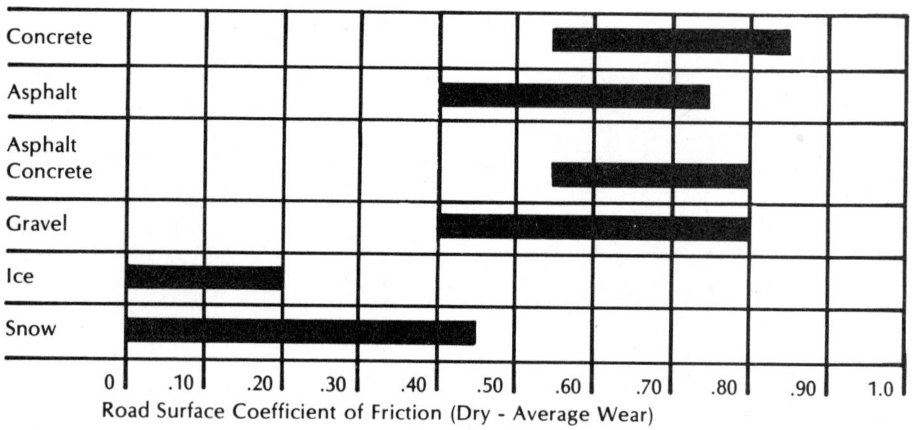

2. Stopping distance[45]
3. Point of perception
4. Decision phase
5. Duration of reaction time
6. Eye-to-foot reaction
7. Braking reaction

B. Skid marks[46]
1. Tire skid marks[47]
2. Metal skid marks
3. Gouge marks
4. Drag marks
5. Tire material
6. Melted rubber
7. Melted asphalt
8. Polish marks

[45]**§6.11.**

[46]**§6.31.**

[47]*Id.*

9. Speed from inclined skid marks
10. Speed from level surfaces[48]
11. Coefficient of friction[49] determined by test drive
12. Skid marks on combination level and inclined road surface

C. Tire Imprints
   1. Impending skid marks
   2. Deceleration scuff marks
   3. Skips on skid marks
   4. Side scuff marks
   5. Tire condition of skid marks
   6. Effect of heat on tires
   7. Effect of tire tread
   8. Flexibility of tire
   9. Quantity of rubber in contact with ground

D. Effect of road gradient[50]
   1. Level road
   2. Uphill inclines
   3. Downhill declines
   4. Determination of grade
   5. Survey
   6. Maps
   7. Sight distance[51]

E. Effect of road curves
   1. Degree and radius curve[52]
   2. Determination of degree of curve[53]
      a. Centrifugal force[54]
      b. Critical speed
      c. Frictional resistance[55]
   3. Survey
   4. Street plans[56]

---

[48]§6.21.
[49]§6.28.
[50]§4.10.
[51]§§6.04, 6.10.
[52]§6.04.
[53]§6.10.
[54]§§6.09, 6.23.
[55]§6.28.
[56]§6.10.

5. Sight distance[57]
6. Banking or superelevation[58]
7. Overturning and skidding speed on curved roadway
8. Critical speed on superelevated curve
9. Speed of a vehicle slipping sideways[59]
10. Rotational speed and spin time
11. Maximum speed on banked curve without slippage or overturning

F. Brakes and braking[60]
   1. Type of brake system
      a. Hydraulic
      b. Air
      c. Air and oil

G. Speed[61] and collision[62]
   1. Impact energy[63]
   2. Skidding energy
   3. Pushing energy
   4. Angular collision
   5. Head-on collision
   6. Rear-end collision

H. Intersections
   1. Speed from stop position
   2. Distance vehicle traveled from stop position
   3. Time required for acceleration
   4. Acceleration after stop
   5. Initial speed at stop sign
   6. Safe speed of vehicle approaching blind, uncontrolled intersection
   7. Speed determined by energy to push another vehicle aside

I. Head-on collision

J. Rear-end collision
   1. With brakes application by leading vehicle only
   2. With both vehicles moving

---

[57] **§6.04.**
[58] **§6.09.**
[59] **§6.30.**
[60] *Id.*
[61] **§6.21.**
[62] **§6.30.**
[63] **§6.25.**

3. When one vehicle accelerates from a stop, making a right-angle turn
4. Skidding and sliding speed of vehicle striking parked vehicle

§6.33 b. Railroad Accidents

Railroad accidents generally fall under one of the following four categories:

1. Grade-crossing collisions between motor vehicles and trains
2. Derailment resulting from defective trackage,[64] overturning at curves, and obstructions on track
3. Cattle being hit by trains
4. Train–train collisions involving one train overtaking another or collisions at switches and crossovers

A suggested check list for discovery of evidence relating to railroad accidents might take in the following subjects:

A. Identification
   1. Name and address of owner of train and track
   2. Names and addresses of engineers, firemen, brakemen, and conductors
   3. Name, number, or other designation of train
   4. Location of incident
   5. Direction of travel
   6. Type of train (passenger, freight)
   7. Type and number of locomotives[65]
   8. Number of railroad cars[66]
   9. Speed of train
      a. One mile from location of incident
      b. One-half mile from location of incident
      c. One-fourth mile from location of incident
      d. At location of incident
   10. Speed recorder in locomotive
      a. Location of tape or other record
   11. Speed limit regulations on subject track
   12. Locomotive whistle
      a. Sound frequency
      b. Decibel rating

---

[64] §6.17.
[65] §6.15.
[66] §6.16.

6-24 Grade of Track

Recommended maximum grades: Road engines, 1-1/2%; Diesel electric engines, 2%; Main line service on heavy trains, 2%; Sidings, 4%

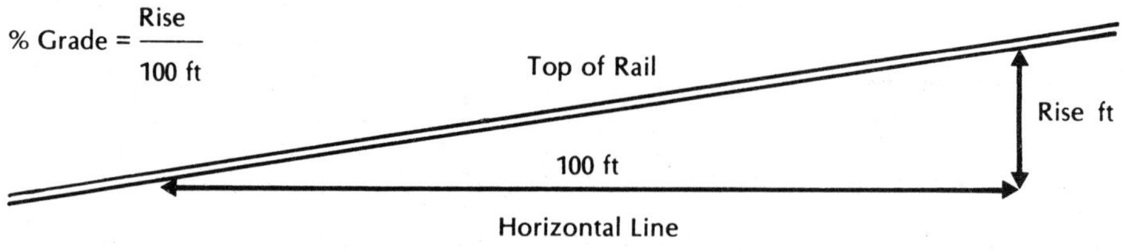

Figure 6-25 Horizontal Railroad Curve

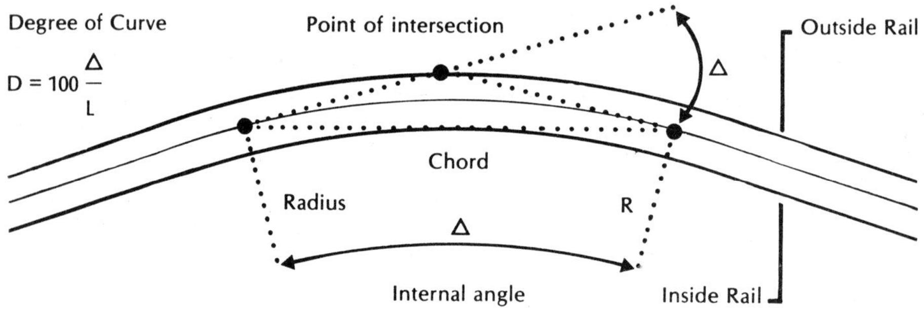

Figure 6-26 Superelevation of Railroad Track

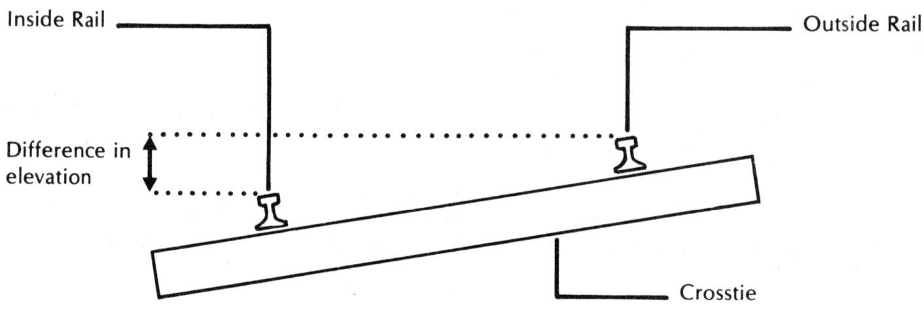

Figure 6-27 Section of Railroad Rail

A = width of head, B = height of rail, C = web, D = fishing distance, E = width of base

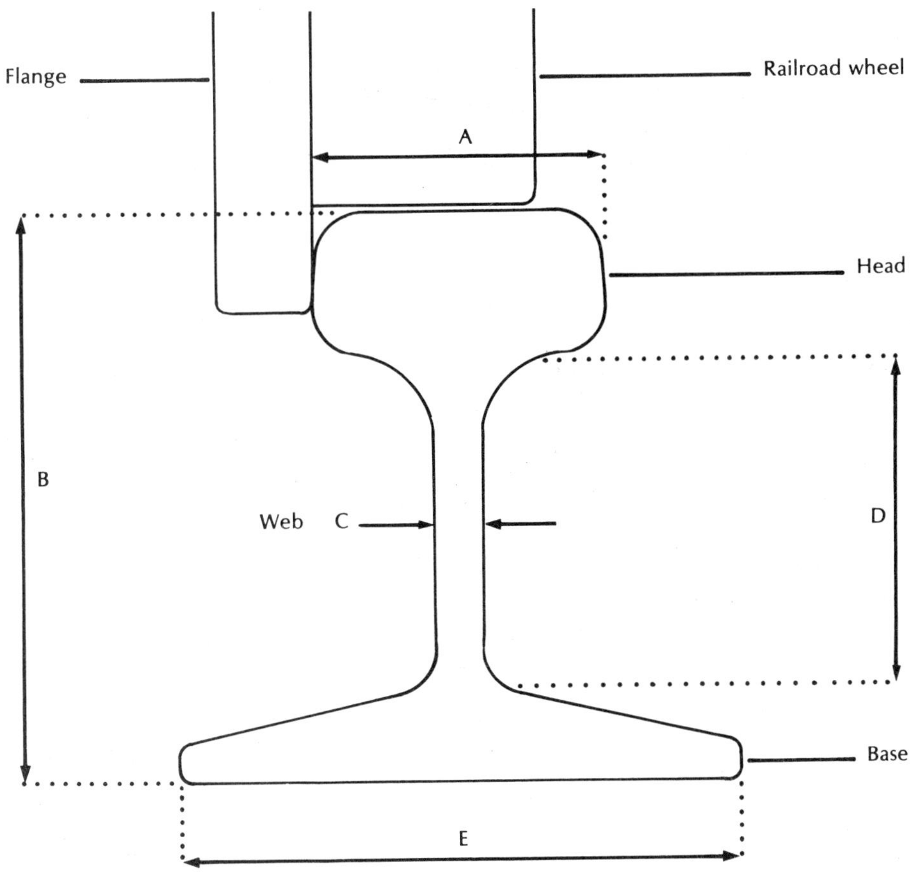

B. Train braking system
   1. Type of system
   2. Sanding device
   3. Distance required to reduce speed to 15 miles per hour, to full stop
   4. Location of locomotive when brakes applied

C. Railroad signal devices
   1. Type of device

Figure 6-28 Railroad switch

The distance from the point of frog to the point of switch is called the *lead.* The distance from the point of switch to the pivot point of the switch rail is called the *length of the switch rail.* The angle of the frog is called the *frog angle.* The length of frog is divided into two distances, the *toe* and the *heel.* The sketch also shows point of intersection (PI), point of curve (PC), point of tangent (PT), radius point (RP), radius (R) and centerline of track.

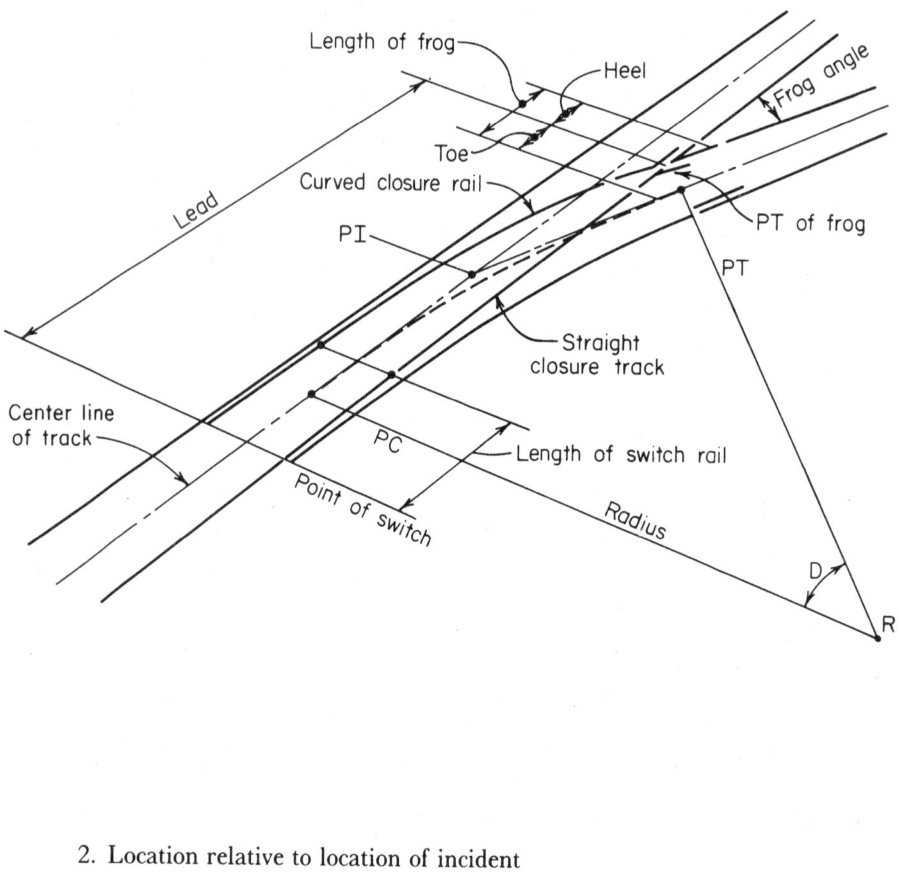

2. Location relative to location of incident

D. Description of accident site

1. Number of railroad tracks
2. Per cent of grade of track (Figure 6-24)
3. Degree of curve of track superelevation (Figure 6-25 and 6-26)
4. Sight distance of train engineer
5. Sight distance of motor vehicle driver or pedestrian

6. Width of street at crossing
7. Grade of street
8. Angle of crossing
9. Point of impact on the train

E. Conditions at time of incident
1. Lighting
2. Weather conditions at time of incident

F. Description of railroad track[67]
1. Size of rails and crossties (See Figure 6-27)
2. Type and depth of ballast
3. Last time track was maintained
4. Frequency of track inspection
5. Frequency of rail testing
6. Description of switch (see Figure 6-28)
   a. Type of operation
   b. Position at time of incident
   c. Description of signal at switch
7. Description of crossover
8. Central traffic control
   a. Location of console
   b. Limits of operation
9. Automatic traffic control
   a. Extent of control
   b. Location of each automatic signal transmitter that train passed between last stop and location of incident
   c. Engineer override of automatic control

§6.34 F. Additional Readings

John H. Batemen, *Introduction to Highway Engineering*, John Wiley & Sons, New York, NY, 4th ed 1942.

Ferdinand P. Beer & E. Russell Johnston, *Vector Mechanics For Engineers: Statics and Dynamics*, McGraw-Hill Book Co, New York, NY 1962.

City of Los Angeles Dept of Public Works, *Bureau of Engineering Manual—Street Design*, pt E, 1970.

Code of Federal Regulations, tit 49 ch III, pt 390, subpart B, 1978.

Code of Federal Regulations, tit 49, ch I, pt 179, §179.2(a)(4), 1974.

[67]§6.17.

County of Los Angeles Road Dept, *Standard Plans* 1975.

Ford Motor Co, *Ford Truck Data Book*, Ford Division Advertising Office, Dearborn, Mich 1976.

E. Hausmann & E. Slack, *Physics*, McGraw-Hill Book Co, New York, NY, 2d ed 1939.

George W. Lacy, *Automobile Accident Reconstruction*, Mathew Bender & Co, New York, NY 1979.

Thaddeus Merriman & Thomas H. Wiggin, *American Civil Engineers Handbook*, McGraw-Hill Book Co, New York, NY, 4th ed 1959.

William H. Searles & Howard Chapin Ives, *Field Engineering*, John Wiley & Sons, London, 22d ed 1950.

1 Elwyn E. Seelye, *Data Book For Civil Engineers*, John Wiley & Sons, New York, NY, 3d ed 1960.

Leonard Church Urquhart, *Civil Engineering Handbook*, McGraw-Hill Book Co, New York, NY, 4th ed 1959.

State of California Business and Transportation Agency, Dept of Transportation, *Standard Plans* 1975.

State of California Dept of Transportation, *Standard Specifications* 1975.

State of California Public Utilities Commission, *General Orders*, California Office of State Printing 1967.

US Depts of the Army and the Air Force, *Principles of Automotive Vehicles* 1956.

US Dept of Transportation, Federal Highway Administration, *Manual on Uniform Traffic Control Devices For Streets and Highways*, Superintendent of Documents, US Government Printing Office, Washington, DC 1970.

7 Preparation of Expert and Evidence for Trial

A. Preparing the Expert

§7.01 1. Identifying the Expert's Function

The primary purpose for retaining an expert is to better enable counsel to successfully prosecute or defend a case. Generally, this assistance takes three forms. First, the expert can be used as a witness, offering an opinion on a technical or scientific matter which is considered beyond the common understanding of the average layperson. Second, the expert can be used in preparing the case, for and through litigation. Third, the expert can be used to counter the other side's expert. Each function must be discussed with the prospective expert so that requirements, obligations, and responsibilities are understood early in the relationship.

Timing in retaining an expert can be crucial. It is common for attorneys to seek an expert late in the litigation process. Usually, such delay is motivated by counsel's desire to save on costs of the expert's time. Unfortunately, since many experts would hesitate or refuse to become involved in eleventh-hour litigation, the procrastinating attorney has inadvertently elimated a wide range of qualified experts.

An expert who is timely retained is able to help counsel develop liability or damage issues, prepare discovery, evaluate the strengths and weaknesses of the case, determine equity of settlement, and carry out research and other preparation to avoid surprises at trial. The dual role of the expert as a consultant and witness manifests itself in that the expert first educates the attorney and then educates the trier of fact.

Many attorneys believe that an expert's ability to perform as a witness on direct and cross-examimation is of greater value than the fact of being a knowledgeable consulting expert. The basic characteristics commonly sought in such a performing expert witness are credibility, communication and presentation skills, knowledge of litigation, flexibility, and ability to establish the reasoning process on which the case is based. On the other hand, the basic characteristics commonly sought in an expert consultant are knowledge of the subject, capacity to educate counsel and play devil's advocate, and ability to assist in discovery.

One legal author has defined the seven basic qualifications of an expert witness as:

Honesty

Good character and reputation

Quick intelligence and attentive ears

Courage—the determination not to be browbeaten into retreat from what the expert knows to be the truth

Appealing personality and presentable appearance

Good manners and tact

Terseness—the quality of answering briefly and not volunteering [1]

§7.02 2. Alerting the Expert

An expert witness will usually have to endure extensive pretrial and trial demands. Some experts consider subjection to cross-examination at depositions and trials an unpleasant and trying experience. Since a witness is frequently vulnerable to vigorous and potentially embarrassing attacks, counsel should be discreet, yet honest, in warning a new expert about what is entailed in testifying as an expert witness.

Before any engineering expert testifies, counsel should make sure that such expert has carefully reviewed and studied all available, relevant documents, records, and tangible evidence. In addition, when appropriate, the expert should have visited the location of the litigated incident. The expert who intends to rely to some extent on information or reports submitted by associates, subordinates, or investigators should review and study these materials so as to be capable of understanding, explaining, supporting, and adopting the data as such expert's own.

B. Initial Conference with the Expert

§7.03 1. Generally

When a particular expert in a field is being considered as a potential witness, the most expeditious beginning is for counsel to communicate with the expert directly. Initial contact may be by telephone. After introductory amenities, counsel should describe briefly the case and area of expertise where assistance is needed. Assuming that the expert being considered has adequate qualifications, is competent, and is

---

[1] Lloyd Paul Stryker, Courts & Doctors (MacMillan Co, New York, NY 1932).

willing to testify in court, counsel must weigh the assets which the expert would bring to the case.

Depending on the nature of the case, counsel may want more than merely an expert who will testify at trial. Frequently, an expert is also needed to help counsel prepare the complaint, draft interrogatories, direct investigations, review documents, interpret facts, and translate and explain technical data to counsel.

In deciding which competent expert to select, it is necessary to consider not only which expert will be available and accessible to the attorney, but also which expert will make the best appearance in front of the jury. Sometimes both an expert witness and an expert consultant will be retained. One reason for this type of arrangement may be that the expert consultant would lack dynamic appeal as a witness. However, where counsel is looking for an all-in-one expert, there must be an evaluation of the expert's ability to preform before the trier of fact. This decision, as well as other observations and inquiries, should be made on the basis of a preliminary interview where counsel and the expert can meet face to face.

§7.04 2. Expertise in Particular Trial Issues

Although an expert may possess extraordinary credentials in the relevant field of engineering, there should be a detailed inquiry about the expert's experience and expertise in the subject matter of the specific trial issues. For example, a civil engineer[2] may be well qualified to offer testimony on transportation structures, such as highways,[3] bridges, railroads,[4] and airports, yet that same expert may have little knowledge or experience of the condominium construction[5] which is the subject of the lawsuit.

§7.05 3. Knowledge of Litigation

Of particular importance to counsel is an expert's general knowledge of the legal process. Attention should focus on the expert's familiarity with and interest in the art of litigation. An expert must appreciate what is required and what happens in legal proceedings, because the demands and responsibilities often prove too burdensome for some experts as the time of trial draws closer.

Counsel should advise and discuss with the expert who accepts these obligations the evidentiary and procedural characteristics of the tribunal which will hear the case. For example, rules of evidence and procedures will differ substantially depending on whether the trier of fact is a judge, jury, arbitrator, or administrative agency. The expert should know what to expect in order to be fully prepared.

§7.06 4. Articulateness

An expert witness's most important service is testifying before the trier of fact. Such testimony will be most likely to involve a subject matter that is not easily understood

---

[2] §2.03.

[3] §6.04.

[4] §6.14.

[5] §4.74.

by the judge or jury. Therefore, a major task of the expert witness is to explain to the trier of fact, in a comprehensible manner, certain evidentiary matters. For this reason, counsel should look for an expert who will be articulate and professional.

§7.07 5. Background Qualifications

It is always helpful to have the expert prepare, verify, and submit to counsel a complete résumé of such expert's background, education, training, and experience. Such information will make it easier to evaluate the expert's actual qualifications and confirm whether the expert is a proper witness on the subject matter in issue.[6]

In addition, the résumé will provide a convenient source of information which counsel may use to: (1) respond to interrogatories regarding the particular expert; and (2) qualify that expert as a witness at trial.

§7.08 6. Prior Statements

Inasmuch as an expert's prior statements, such as books, articles, letters, publications, lectures, speeches, depositions, and trial testimony, can be discovered by the adverse party, counsel should be advised of all such prior statements. This information is especially crucial where the expert is being retained to offer an opinion which is in conflict with prior statements of that same expert. In this situation, counsel may wish to find another expert. On the other hand, counsel and the expert might use their knowledge of the apparent inconsistency as a basis for a rational explanation reconciling the differing statements.

In addition, reviewing the expert's prior deposition or trial transcripts will enable counsel to evaluate the expert's prior litigation performance.

§7.09 7. Identifying Litigants

The process of familiarizing an expert with a case does not stop with an explanation of factual contentions. There should be a meticulous description of all interested persons connected with the litigation, covering names, employment relationships, and background material of all litigants, expert witnesses, lay witnesses, investigators, and attorneys. When this information is provided, the expert can find out about any potential conflicts or prejudices. Additionally, the expert who is aware of such data is better able to take in and identify with the facts of the case. This results in a better, more compatible witness.

§7.10 8. Ascertaining Additional Evidence

After the decision to retain the expert, it is necessary to review the facts of the case with such expert. The review should cover all pleadings, depositions, interrogatories, and evidence that may exist at that point. This is also the proper time to ascertain from the expert which additional data, documents, and other evidence must be con-

---

[6]See §§7.27, 9.03, 9.12.

sidered or inspected for the expert to be able to render an opinion on the subject matter in issue.

§7.11 9. Obtaining Reading Material

One important request counsel may make of the expert at, or soon after, the first meeting is for a recommended reading list. In any technical field, the expert retained should know what source materials are available for counsel's self-education on the litigated topic. Whether the case concerns a geographical survey error, an improperly closed septic tank, a high-water-level intrusion into a condominium basement, or an earthquake settlement problem,[7] the expert should be able to refer counsel to or provide general reading material on the subject.

Such a reading list will help counsel understand the subject and communicate with the expert. Less time will be wasted by the expert in explaining simple concepts if counsel has a basic understanding of the technical matter involved. Needless to say, this general background information also provides the initial foundation for counsel's eventual cross-examination of the adverse expert.

C. Pretestimony Guidelines for the Expert

§7.12 1. Generally

If an expert witness will be called to testify at trial, and particularly where the trier of fact is a jury, certain basic guidelines should be reviewed and discussed by counsel and the expert prior to the expert's actual testimony. These fundamental points aim at maximizing the effect of the expert's testimony.

The impact of an expert witness on the trier of fact is, like other things in life, influenced by psychological considerations. Counsel's main task is to show that the witness is a person whose opinion should be accepted by the judge or jury.

§7.13 2. Objectivity

It should go without saying that an expert must appear to be an objective witness who is honestly applying the facts in the case in arriving at a particular conclusion. Subjective favoritism, bias, or overzealous advocacy should not characterize an expert witness's demeanor.

This impartial manner should be maintained by the expert not only when testifying in court, but also outside the courtroom, in the halls, at deposition, and in contact with any public media. Aggressive exhortation by an expert witness, observed by the trier of fact, frequently creates a negative and lasting impression. There is no reason to retain an expert whom the trier of fact will not believe, or one whose conclusion the trier of fact is not willing to accept.

---

[7] §5.02.

§7.14 3. Tenacity

If an expert witness is to help at all, the opinion stated by such expert on direct examination must stand reasonably firm. An expert with impeccable qualifications and experience is a catastrophic liability if opposing counsel can make that expert substantially modify the opinion testimony elicited on direct examination. Therefore, prior to hearing, counsel should anticipate all areas of potential cross-examination and conduct a vigorous rehearsal. This should reinforce the expert's tenacity to the opinion elicited on direct examination.

§7.15 4. Self-Restraint

An expert is often called on to exercise enormous self-restraint during a tough cross-examination; all aspects of the expert's personal and professional background may be subject to inquiry and scrutiny. Notwithstanding any questions on cross-examination, the expert should respond calmly, confidently, and succinctly. The expert must not allow the cross-examiner's attack to divert attention away from the issues in the case by provoking a battle of the egos. In other words, the expert should avoid engaging in argument with the cross-examiner or referring to the adverse attorney or party in a disrespectful manner.

§7.16 5. Skeleton in Expert's Past

Since a cross-examiner has great latitude in disqualifying and discrediting the testimony of an expert witness,[8] old skeletons hidden in the expert's past may be a fertile source of impeachment material. Therefore, the expert should reveal to counsel any such matters including professional disciplinary action and peer criticism. Such notice lets counsel appreciate more accurately the strengths and weaknesses of the case. In addition, this enables counsel to intentionally restrict the scope of cross-examination by limiting direct examination to a narrow set of issues. In the course of the inquiry for skeletons, counsel should find out about all names or pseudonyms used by the expert.

§7.17 6. Humility

In seeking and preparing an effective expert witness, humility is another trait to be emphasized. Lack of arrogance is important not only in building a rapport with the trier of fact but also in establishing a flexible position from which the expert is to operate. In other words, an intemperately proud and assertive witness may find it difficult to back down or to concede even a minor collateral issue on cross-examination. If an expert shows appropriate humility, the ego does not interfere with the witness admitting a lack of knowledge. The paramount concern is to present a witness that the trier of fact will honestly believe.

---

[8]Youngblood v Austin, 102 Ariz 74, 424 P2d 824 (1967); Arkansas State Highway Commn v Dean, 247 Ark 717, 447 SW2d 334 (1969); Northern Ind Pub Serv Co v Otis, 145 Ind App 159, 250 NE2d 378 (1969).

Humility should not, however, be confused with excessive modesty. A competent expert, retained to render a particular opinion based on specific skills, education, or experience, should not demur on cross-examination and disclaim expertise because there may be or are other persons somewhere in the world who are more qualified. Counsel should explain to the expert the legal effect and necessity of being qualified as an expert. In addition, counsel should advise the expert to admit expertise on the witness stand.

§7.18 7. Motivation

A question commonly asked of an expert witness on cross-examination is that expert's reason for testifying in court. This line of inquiry is proper, since it goes to the issues of credibility, interest, and bias. The expert should not be intimidated by such a question, but rather, should summarily explain the relationship with the party and counsel. This explanation should mention that the expert was requested, because of unique qualifications, to review, investigate, and evaluate certain events or conditions, and that after performing such work, the expert was requested to discuss his or her findings in court.

As to compensation for services rendered, the expert should be forthright in admitting the fee arrangements. As long as the compensation is reasonable in light of the complexity of the case and consistent with time and energy spent, it will be difficult for the cross-examiner to demonstrate bias. In addition, it is important for the expert to point out that payment is not being made for testifying. Rather, the expert is being reimbursed for loss of time from such expert's own business.

No one, especially the trier of fact, would expect an expert to work gratis. In fact, it may appear more suspect for an expert to perform services without charge. Therefore, it is normally advisable for the expert to be paid at least a nominal fee.

D. Trial Preparation Considerations

§7.19 1. Explaining Theory to Laypersons

It is axiomatic that communication between expert and counsel must be total. Each must understand the technical facts, theories, and language used by the other. For this reason, both counsel and expert must completely review questions and responses which will be covered on direct examination. Any uncertainties, weaknesses, or ambiguities must be recognized and resolved at this juncture.

A frequent problem in preparing for direct examination is that counsel and the expert realize that the technical matter and vocabulary may be too esoteric for the trier of fact. If the judge or jury is unable to understand the questions propounded or the expert's responses, counsel has failed in presenting the case. Therefore, during preparation for examination, there should be particular emphasis on using comprehensible language and concepts at trial.

Simple analogies supported by demonstrations are often effective to communicate difficult ideas. For example, in explaining electrical current, one expert analogized it to water flowing through a pipe. In another situation, an expert demonstrated the concept of force by means of a rubber band which impacted against a small, stationary object.

The trial attorney who has worked adequately with an expert on using understandable concepts and terminology will usually be successful in educating the trier of fact to reach a proper verdict.

A concurrent consideration in expert testimony is placement or timing for offering expert evidence. Counsel must prepare for trial by scheduling not only for efficiency and convenience, but also with an eye to maximizing the dramatic highlights. In other words, it is essential that a trial commence and conclude with strong testimony.

§7.20 2. Disputing Factual Theories

The expert always should be encouraged to criticize and dispute any weaknesses in the factual theories which counsel is advancing. This criticism serves a twofold purpose. First, counsel may be able to adopt a new theory to support liability. Second, the criticism may be able to be resolved if openly discussed. In identifying and discussing potential weaknesses before trial, both expert and counsel are provided with anticipative exposure to likely subjects for cross-examination.

§7.21 3. Anticipation of Scrutiny by Adverse Experts

Counsel must stress, especially to an expert with little or no trial experience, that the expert's opinion will be scrutinized not only by the adverse attorney, but also by the adverse experts, and that therefore, the expert must investigate and prepare thoroughly.

The materials relied on by the expert must be verified as current. Calculations should be triple-checked to assure that no error has been made. Erroneous conversion factors and decimal points, not to mention minor mathematical mistakes, often lead to enormous miscalculations when they are carried over a series of steps. In addition, if tests are performed by the expert, the propriety of the procedures must be well documented and religiously followed.

§7.22 4. Expert's Relationship with Authoritative Publications

Generally, an expert may not be cross-examined about the contents of a particular technical or scientific publication unless such publication is accepted as authoritative or unless the expert has relied on, referred to, or considered it in forming an opinion.[9]

This principle reflects two basic policies. First, the true expert should know whether there are standard publications in the field which may be considered authoritative on the subject matter in question. If such official or scholarly publications do exist, the expert should appreciate the extent to which these publications support or conflict with the expert's position. A complete understanding of the basis for an authoritative publication's espousal of a theory contrary to that of the expert is essential to preserve

---

[9] See **§§10.35, 10.38.**

the expert's credibility. Second, the expert should not be so absolutely opinionated, ego-inflated, or insecure in defending an opinion as to deny the authoritativeness of well-known and reliable publications which may support a conflicting view. The obvious problem with such a one-sided approach is that the credibility of the expert's testimony suffers.

When the expert believes in good faith that certain publications are not authoritative, and where the expert has not relied on, considered, or referred to such publications in forming an opinion, even the most humble of experts should disclaim such publications if offered. Where this is the case, some courts hold that use of such publications during cross-examination is improper.[10] However, other courts have permitted use of such publications where other experts testify and acknowledge the publication as authoritative,[11] or where the court itself takes judicial notice that the work is authoritative.[12]

Where there are authoritative publications in conflict with the expert's opinion or where the expert has at least referred to or considered such conflicting publications in forming an opinion, such expert should openly acknowledge that more than one school of thought exists on the subject within the professional community. In addition, the expert should not hesitate to explain, limit, or distinguish the statements contained in those publications from the expert's own conclusions.

Rule 803(18), Federal Rules of Evidence provides:

> Hearsay Exceptions; Availability of Declarant Immaterial.
>
> The following are not excluded by the hearsay rule, even though the declarant is available as a witness:
>
> (18) Learned treatises. To the extent called to the attention of an expert witness upon cross-examination or relied upon by him in direct examination, statements contained in published treatises, periodicals, or pamphlets on a subject of history, medicine, or other science or art, established as a reliable authority by the testimony or admission of the witness or by other expert testimony or by judicial notice. If admitted, the statements may be read into evidence but may not be received as exhibits.

§7.23 5. Drafting Hypothetical Questions

When counsel intends to obtain an expert's opinion in the form of a response to a hypothetical question, it is often expedient for counsel to draft the question in advance. Such drafting may be done with the expert's assistance to insure inclusion of all material facts. Irrespective of who actually drafts the hypothetical, the question should be studied and discussed by counsel and the expert prior to trial.

On direct examination of the expert it should be mentioned that the expert has considered the prepared question prior to trial. Such an admission will serve a double purpose. First, it will negate any inference that the expert has merely memorized the particular opinion. Second, it will emphasize to the trier of fact that the expert has

---

[10]Ross v Colorado Natl Bank of Denver, 170 Colo 436, 463 P2d 882 (1969).

[11]Ravenis v Detroit Gen Hosp, 63 Mich App 79, 234 NW2d 411 (1975).

[12]Howell v Outer Drive Hosp, 66 Mich App 142, 238 NW2d 553 (1975).

spent substantial time in arriving at the opinion rather than merely responding on impulse when questioned on the witness stand.[13]

§7.24 6. Presence at Counsel Table

Irrespective of whether counsel's expert has been retained as a consultant or a witness, it is advantegeous to arrange for the expert to be present with counsel at the counsel table during cross-examination of the adverse expert at trial. This not only insures that counsel will understand all the technical testimony of the adverse expert, but also keeps the adverse expert from overstating or exaggerating certain opinions.

An expert who is present at the counsel table should have sufficient writing materials so that any comments, suggestions, or points developed during testimony can be brought to the attention of counsel. Generally, written rather than oral communication between counsel and the expert during the direct or cross-examination of the adverse expert is preferable. Thus, counsel is able to direct primary attention to the testimony of the adverse expert without dangerous distractions. Even a minor spoken interruption may cause counsel to miss an important admission by the witness.

§7.25 7. Pitfalls

Counsel must take special care about any written communications with the expert. The general rule is that any writing used to refresh a witness's recollection is subject to inspection and introduction into evidence by the adverse party.[14] It does not matter whether the particular writing is used by the witness while actually testifying or at some time prior to trial testimony.

One situation in which a detrimental impact may be clear is where counsel writes an introductory letter to the prospective expert which refers to the specific opinion that counsel desires to be offered at trial. This act by the attorney may enable the adverse party not only to introduce the letter at trial, but also to attack the expert's opinion and credibility, by arguing that the expert is merely mirroring counsel's original opinion rather than objectively analyzing relevant facts and events.

In addition, counsel may subject otherwise privileged writings to the inspection of the adverse party if such writings are reviewed or considered by the expert prior to testifying. In other words, if counsel allows the expert to review written confidential reports, witness's statements, or counsel's legal theories or strategies, production of such writings could be requested by the adverse party and ordered by the court. In such a situation, failure to produce the writing may preclude testimony by the expert.[15]

E. Discovery Involving Adverse Experts

§7.26 1. Generally

If a case merits one party's retaining an expert, it will usually merit the adverse party's retention of an expert as well. The adverse expert is a serious factor in the

---

[13]See **§§10.11-.13, 10.33.**

[14]Patchogue Oil Terminal Corp v Sambach, 15 Misc 2d 266, 178 NYS2d 659 (1958); People v Schepps, 217 Mich 406, 186 NW 508 (1922).

[15]Cal Evid Code §771(a) (West).

preparation of a case for trial. The adverse expert's qualifications must be subjected to rigorous scrutiny. In addition, the factual basis for the expert's opinion, as well as the opinion and factual findings themselves, are subject to exhaustive pretrial discovery.

Therefore, counsel and expert should prepare a complete set of interrogatories to be served on the adverse party, to gather advance information on the adverse expert. Data received from responses to interrogatories will be reviewed by counsel and expert in preparation for subsequent deposition and trial testimony of the adverse expert. Information obtained from the adverse expert also may be used to help counsel's expert anticipate various adverse contentions and areas of potential cross-examination.

Timing of discovery will vary with the nature of the case and the procedural statutes of the different jurisdictions. Discovery about adverse experts should be conducted as soon as counsel becomes aware that the adverse party has retained an expert. Certainly, such discovery should not take place any later than the date of the trial-setting conference or 90 days before the date set for trial, whichever is earlier.

Discovery of an adverse expert at deposition should go into the nature of all information and reports gathered or prepared by the adverse expert. This includes disclosure of the strong and weak points developed by the adverse expert's investigation. Production of all data and reports relied on or prepared by the adverse expert should be demanded by the cross-examiner prior to deposition so that there can be detailed inquiry at deposition into such matter. Finally, in order to limit adverse expert testimony at trial, the cross-examiner should find out from the adverse expert whether or not the expert intends to or needs to conduct further investigation, and if so, elicit a description of such work.

§7.27 2. Illustrative Interrogatories on Adverse Expert's Qualifications

The following interrogatories illustrate the types of questions which will elicit relevant qualifications of an adverse party's expert:

1. Have you employed any expert to test, analyze, or examine the condition or product which is involved in this action?
2. If you have, for each expert, state:
   a. Your expert's name, address and telephone number
   b. Your expert's profession or occupation, and the field in which your expert purportedly has expertise
3. Has your expert had a formal education in the subject field?
4. If so, state:
   a. The name and address of each school or university where your expert received special education or training in this field
   b. The dates when your expert attended each such school or university
   c. The name or desciption of each degree your expert received, including the date when each was received, and the name of the school or university from which it was received
5. Did your expert have other specialized training in the subject field?

6. If so, give:
   a. A description of the training received by your expert
   b. The name, address, and location of the school where training was received
   c. The dates when your expert received this training
7. Is your expert a member of any professional or trade association in the subject field?
8. If so, supply:
   a. The name and address of each professional or trade association
   b. The date your expert became a member
   c. A description of the nature of the association
   d. A description of each office held by your expert in each association
9. Has your expert written any books, papers, articles, or other publications on the subject field, individually or with others?
10. If so, for each book, paper, article, or other publication, state:
    a. The title and author(s)
    b. A description of the subject matter
    c. The name and address of the publisher
    d. The date of publication
11. Is your expert licensed by any governmental authority or regulatory agency to practice in the subject field?
12. If so, indicate
    a. The name and address of the authority or agency which licensed your expert
    b. The date when your expert was licensed
    c. A description of the general requirements that your expert had to meet to obtain such license
    d. How and when your expert fulfilled these requirements
13. Was your expert's license to practice in the subject field ever revoked or suspended?
14. If so, for each revocation or suspension, give:
    a. The name and address of the authority or agency which revoked or suspended the license
    b. The reason given for such revocation or suspension
    c. The dates in question
    d. A description of any disciplinary action taken by such authority or agency
15. Has your expert practiced or worked in the subject field during the past 15 years?
16. If so, state:
    a. Whether your expert was self-employed, employed by someone else, or associated as a partner
    b. Identity by name and address of where your expert practiced or was employed

c. The dates your expert was with each employer or employment

d. The type of duty your expert performed with each employer or employment

17. If your expert has not practiced or worked in the subject field during the past 15 years, describe your expert's employment during that period.

18. What experience, other than that stated above, has your expert had in the subject field?

19. Has your expert had any previous experience in the subject field with problems similar or related to those involved in this action?

20. If so, state:

    a. A description of each similar problem with which your expert has had experience

    b. Whether a lawsuit arose out of such problem

    c. The caption and case number of each such lawsuit in which your expert has testified by deposition or in trial

21. With respect to your expert's present employment, provide:

    a. Your expert's present address

    b. The dates your expert has been so employed

    c. A description of your experts' present responsibilities

22. Is your expert to be compensated for work and efforts in connection with this action?

23. If so, what is the expert's compensation arrangement?

24. Is your expert to receive any additional compensation if you are successful in this action?

25. If so, what are the terms of this additional compensation?

26. Has your expert already been paid?

27. If not, when will your expert be paid?

§7.28 3. Illustrative Interrogatories on Adverse Expert's Analyses and Findings

The following interrogatories illustrate types of questions which will elicit from the adverse party descriptions of tests,[16] analyses, and examinations conducted by the adverse expert and the results of such procedures:

1. Did your expert test, analyze, or examine the subject condition or product in reference to this action?

2. If so, state:

    a. The dates of each test, analysis, or examination

    b. The address where each test, analysis or examination was conducted

---

[16]§3.30.

c. The facts or information sought in conducting this test, analysis, or examination

d. The steps followed in each test, analysis, or examination

e. The total time spent on such testing, analysis, and examination[17]

3. Did anyone assist your expert in conducting the test, analysis, or examination?
4. If so, give:

   a. The name, address, and telephone number of each person who assisted your expert

   b. A description of the assistance rendered

   c. The dates of such assistance

5. Were any results or conclusions reached by means of your expert's test, analysis, or examination?
6. If so, what were these results or conclusions?
7. Did any results or conclusions reached through your expert's test, analysis, or examination relate to whether the subject condition or product is the same as it was at the time of the subject incident?
8. If so, what were these results or conclusions?
9. On what facts were the results or conclusions based?
10. Were any results or conclusions reached through your expert's test, analysis, or examination on the question of whether the subject condition or product was defectively designed or constructed?
11. If so, what were these results or conclusions?
12. On what facts were the results or conclusions based?
13. Did any results or conclusions reached by your expert's test, analysis, or examination relate to whether the subject condition or product was negligently maintained?
14. If so, what were such results or conclusions?
15. On what facts were the results or conclusions based?
16. Identify each and every source of information your expert has relied on or will rely on in supporting the opinions or conclusions described in this interrogatory.
17. Did your expert submit a report of the objective findings?
18. If so, state:

   a. The date the report was submitted

   b. The name, or other identification, of the person to whom this report was submitted

   c. The name and address of the person with present custody of this report

19. Did your expert submit a report setting forth opinions or conclusions based on the test, analysis, or examination that your expert conducted?

---

[17] §9.14.

20. If so, give:
    a. The date this report was submitted
    b. The name, or other identification, of the person to whom this report was submitted
    c. The name and address of the person who has present custody of this report
21. Did your expert submit any other reports based on the tests, analyses, or examinations conducted?
22. If so, provide:
    a. A description of each report made
    b. The date that each report was made
    c. The name, or other identification, of the person to whom each report was submitted
    d. The name and address of the person with present custody of each report
23. If you will do so without a motion to produce, attach a copy of any reports made by your expert on the basis of your expert's tests, analyses, or examinations to your answers to these interrogatories.

§7.29 4. Utilizing Discovered Information

Once information has been obtained on discovery about the adverse expert's qualifications and opinions, counsel is ready to submit the collected evidence to counsel's own expert for review. Thereafter, the expert has the task of helping counsel prepare for cross-examination of the adverse expert at trial. In the couse of considering the discovered materials, the expert may explain technical data or point out errors or weaknesses in the findings or conclusions of the adverse expert. Such facts would have a significant impact at trial.

F. Preparing Expert for Deposition

§7.30 1. Generally

Before counsel's expert is deposed by the adverse party, counsel should meet with the witness and discuss the significance, purpose, and procedures involved in a deposition. Counsel must of course, stress that preparing for desposition testimony is as important as preparing for a trial itself.

In addition to reviewing and rehearsing with the expert anticipated areas of examination, counsel may wish to give the expert the following basic caveats:

1. Listen attentively to each question asked and pause for a couple of seconds before responding. This will serve two functions. First, this will give counsel time to object to the form or substance of a question if it is improper. Second, it will force the expert to think about the question asked and, consequently, the expert will be less likely to respond impulsively

2. Give complete, yet concise, responses to each question. The expert should never volunteer information beyond that which is directly requested by the cross-examiner. In addition, the expert should respond only to questions which are clearly understandable and unambiguous. Any question asked that is not perfectly clear should meet with an objection by counsel or a request to rephrase the question by the witness
3. Honesty, objectivity, sincerity, and confidence should be displayed by the expert. The expert must not allow the cross-examiner's ruse or tactics to precipitate anger or discourtesy. Hostile or partisan responses usually only detract from the expert's concentration and from the personal impression made
4. The expert should refrain from guessing or speculating. Only information personally known to the expert or statements based on reasonable certainty are relevant. The expert also must have sufficient humility to admit lack of knowledge on a particular subject if that is the case

§7.31 2. Deposition Outline

As part of preparing an expert for deposition, counsel should compose a deposition outline. The outline should encompass a diverse range of subjects on which cross-examination of the expert by the adverse party may be anticipated. Counsel may refer to this same outline in cross-examining the adverse party.

Generally, the deposition outline can include the following subjects;

I. Expert
   A. Identification and background
      1. Name, address, telephone number, age
      2. Specialty and areas of expertise
      3. General and special education in areas of expertise
      4. General and special professional experience in areas of expertise (when, where, in what capacity)
      5. General and special training in areas of expertise (when, where, what)
      6. Identity of other persons considered experts in area of expertise
      7. Standard publications, texts, and journals considered, relied on, used, referred to, or subscribed to in area of expertise
      8. Professional memberships, governmental licenses (when, where, what)[18]
      9. Membership or governmental license revocation or suspension (when, where, by whom, why)
      10. Professional or governmental standards in area of expertise
      11. General and special areas in which published (when, where, what)[19]
      12. Instructing, teaching, and lecturing experience in area of expertise (when, where, what)[20]

---

[18]§§2.02, 2.46.

[19]§2.49.

[20]§2.50.

13. Prior expert experience (when, where, on what subjects, for whom)
14. Prior experience with subject condition or product (when, where, what)
15. Interest in litigation or in party (fees, charges, and expenses incurred or anticipated)
16. Date expert was retained

II. Product or condition

A. Identification and history

1. Designer (who, when, what)
2. Existence of plans, specifications, records, contract documents
3. Identity of custodian of documents and materials
4. Relevant national, state, local, or industrial standards
5. Identity of all persons involved with or responsible for product or condition (manufacturer, distributor, retailer, contractor, subcontractor)
6. Prior problems, complaints, notices, failures
7. Governmental regulations, permits, inspection, licensing

B. Extent of knowledge of product or condition

1. Inspection (when, where, how, what, why, with whom, how long)
2. Sources of all information considered or used (including other experts, witnesses, reports, documents, books, publications, photographs, records, plans, specifications, depositions, statements, letters, and communications)
3. Tests (when, where, what, how, why, with whom)
4. Total time spent in inspecting, reviewing, researching, and arriving at opinion[21]

C. Conclusions

1. Conclusions, opinions, and findings
2. Factual basis
3. Facts relied on
4. Culpability
5. Reports, drawings, models (prepared or anticipated)
6. Additional tests, examinations, or information (anticipated or required)

G. Exhibit Preparation

§7.32 1. Generally

In the course of preparing exhibits for trial, counsel should compose an exhibit list which describes all documents, real evidence, graphic devices, and photographs which

---

[21]**§9.14.**

counsel intends to offer in evidence. This list will aid counsel in organizing the evidence, and insure that all evidence will be accounted for at trial. In addition, a copy of the exhibit list should be exchanged with opposing counsel shortly before trial to avoid disruption or delay during the actual proceedings. Of course, those exhibits which counsel intends to use for impeachment purposes or tactical surprise should not be disclosed to the adverse party.

In the case of important documentary evidence, counsel should prepare prior to trial a sufficient number of copies to distribute to the opposing parties and to the court along with the exhibit list. This makes trial easier for all concerned.

§7.33 2. Photographs

Photography is the process of producing images on a sensitized surface by exposure to light. One sensitized surface is the film, from which negatives are processed and developed. Negatives can then be printed on a second type of sensitized surface. This printing of the negative results in a positive print, in essence, a negative of a negative.[22]

For litigation purposes, it is desirable to have:

1. Photographs conforming to the same physical dimensions. This facilitates organization and handling of the exhibits
2. Prints with a glossy rather than a mat finish, since the former provides a greater degree of detail
3. Photographs printed on a heavy paper to prevent cracking and tearing
4. Black and white prints when perspective definition and distance are at issue
5. Color prints when sight contrast is at issue

§7.34 a. Sources

In cases based on industrial and construction accidents, a viable source of photographs may be the client's photographic department. Many companies have come to realize the importance of photographs in industry-related litigation, and have created in-plant photography departments. Their industrial photographers take pictures for advertising campaigns, promotion, publicity, and accident prevention instructions to personnel.

In cases of catastrophic accidents,[23] newspaper and television photographers may be good sources of information. Such photographers will usually arrive at the scene of an accident, flood, fire, or collapse of a building as soon as or even before police or fire department photographers. These press photographers usually tend to take more snapshots than are actually used by their employers; therefore, the attorney may be able to obtain the extra photographs from them.

Many claims adjusters carry cameras and take photographs to illustrate and substantiate their reports. These snapshots may be another useful source of evidence.

---

[22]See **§§7.34-.35, 7.39, 8.08-.18, 8.21, 8.26.**

[23]**Ch 5.**

§7.35 b. Misrepresentations

Inasmuch as many types of photographs, cameras, and reproduction techniques are available, there is also great potential for misrepresentation in the use of photographic evidence. Photographs may exaggerate some situations and minimize others. They may emphasize or omit certain significant and controversial aspects of a scene. A simple procedure by the photographer, like reversal of the negative, may reverse the scene depicted from left to right and thus completely change the existing set of conditions. In addition, photographs may create optical illusions intentionally or unintentionally. Consequently, a photograph is not necessarily an accurate representation of a scene.

On the other hand, a photograph has a better memory than most eyewitnesses. It overcomes the limitations of language, and eliminates problems arising out of changed conditions. On balancing the merits of photographic evidence, a good photograph remains a valuable piece of evidence.

§7.36 3. Models, Diagrams, Maps, and Plans

Since it is usually impossible for a witness to compose an accurate and detailed graphic representation of a particular condition or product while undergoing the rigors of testifying, counsel should have prepared prior to trial any models, diagrams, maps, or plans that will be offered into evidence or used for illustration in argument. Such pretrial exhibit preparation insures that the effectiveness of the evidence is not lost through omission or inaccuracy. In addition, it should be specified whether any such exhibit is to scale.[24]

§7.37 4. Casting

When casting is chosen as a method of reproducing a tangible object for presentation at trial, several procedures may be considered. One inexpensive procedure uses modeling or potter's clay and some plaster of Paris.

The complexity of the casting procedure depends on the physical shape of the item to be reproduced. Where the item is a pipe connection, rope, tool, foot, or hand, the item should be rubbed with vaseline or grease, pressed deeply into the clay, and then removed. Next, the plaster of Paris should be mixed with water until it is as thick as pancake batter. When a sufficient quantity has been made, the mixture should be poured into the clay impression. After about 30 minutes to an hour, the plaster should be hard and the plaster replica can be removed.

Depending on what item is being reproduced, the casting can be carefully painted to resemble the original object.[25]

§7.38 5. Special Exhibits

Where it is anticipated that a voluminous or even a moderate number of exhibits will be offered, all parties should meet shortly before the trial to classify and tentatively premark the various items of evidence.

---

[24] See **§§8.05-.07.**

[25] See **§8.30.**

In addition, in cases where there are exhibits of evidence representing items actually involved in the litigated matter, special arrangements may have to be made. This is likely to happen where the evidence is bulky, burdensome, or potentially dangerous. For instance, if an overhead crane,[26] tunnel-boring mole,[27] gasoline engine, electric oven, or acidic chemical is the subject of litigation there may be substitution of exhibits utilizing photographs, models, or diagrams.

6. Reviewing Exhibits

§7.39 a. Photographs

When demonstrative evidence such as photographs, models, maps, or samples is relevant to a case, it is essential to review such evidence at an early stage to verify its accuracy. For example, a photograph which depicts a certain defective condition of a sidewalk should be checked to assure its relevance.

It is not uncommon for counsel on either side, early in litigation, to send out a photographer to a location described with particularity, to photograph a certain condition. In one case, after completion of extensive discovery by the defendant, it should have been realized that the defective sidewalk where plaintiff tripped was actually more than 20 feet away from the defective condition photographed by the defendant. Plaintiff's photographs were of poor quality, and the sidewalk had been repaved long before the defendant responded to a request for production of photographic evidence. Unfortunately for the defendant, defendant's photographs depicted a condition in which the difference in elevation between the two slabs of the cracked sidewalk was approximately two inches, whereas at the location specifically described by the plaintiff the difference in elevation in the sidewalk was actually approximately only one-half inch.

Failure to collate demonstrative evidence with discovered facts can result in a grossly inaccurate evaluation of a case.[28]

§7.40 b. Traffic Signal Plans

A common and useful item of evidence in intersection motor vehicle accident cases is the city's traffic signal plan.[29] Such a plan can usually be obtained for a nominal charge by writing a letter to the traffic engineering department in the city or municipality with jurisdiction over the particular intersection. Such a plan is useful in many ways. First, it provides an accurate diagram with precise dimensions. Second, placement of the traffic signals and other landmarks is given, which together with other facts may make it possible to calculate the speed of the vehicles. Third, it enables testing of credibility of testimony.

In one case, a plaintiff who had been involved in an intersection accident claimed

---

[26]**§3.47.**

[27]**§3.29.**

[28]See **§§7.33-.35, 8.08-.18, 8.21, 8.26.**

[29]**§6.08.**

to have been struck by defendant's automobile which turned left in front of the plaintiff. The defendant claimed that the plaintiff ran the red light. The particular intersection where the accident occurred was an offset intersection, with two sets of traffic signals 100 feet apart, the distance of the offset. The testimony of the plaintiff was that the first traffic signal was yellow as she drove past it, and that the second traffic signal was green as she drove past it. The accident occurred after the plaintiff passed the second signal.

When the defense presented its case, a city engineer testified about the traffic signal plans of that intersection. The engineer testified that the plans indicated that the two signals were phased together, and changed colors simultaneously. For this reason, it would have been impossible for the sequence to have been as the plaintiff testified.

In another case, a plaintiff was driving an automobile which was hit while making a left-hand turn from a parking lot onto a steep and hilly street that formed the top of a T-intersection. The plaintiff testified that she turned left (east) after the signal which controlled east-west traffic had turned red, and that she was hit by the defendant's automobile proceeding west which had run the red light. Plaintiff also testified that since this was very early in the morning, she observed no other automobiles or pedestrians traveling north along the T-post portion of the intersection.

The defense called a city engineer who brought in a set of traffic signal plans which covered not only the location of the traffic signals[30] controlling the T-intersection, but also the means by which the signals were activated. The expert testified that the street at the top of the T-intersection which ran east-west and which carried the heavy traffic was set with an open-ended green light. The green light would not change phases unless a loop device, situated in the street pavement, was triggered by an automobile traveling north on the T-post towards the main street. Since the plaintiff testified that she was certain that no automobile or pedestrian was traveling north on the T-post, it seemed to be impossible for her to have turned left on a red east-west light.

As can be seen, a review of demonstrative evidence is essential to early preparation of litigation. In addition, it is important to corroborate any such information at first hand. The interesting thing about the testimony of the city engineer in the latter case was that the engineer was wrong. For whatever reason, practical observation, as opposed to the theoretical application, revealed that the traffic signals went through continuous full cycles without being triggered by automobile or pedestrian traffic traveling north as indicated on the current traffic signal plans.

Effective use of pretrial discovery procedures should enable counsel to determine prior to trial the identity, contents, subject matter, and location of all relevant documents, papers, photographs, and objects. In addition, request for inspection procedures permit counsel to actually examine, observe, and review all tangible evidence in advance of trial. Theoretically, counsel should go to trial familiar with all relevant evidence that may be introduced not only by counsel but also by the adverse party.

---

[30] §6.05.

8 Presenting Demonstrative Engineering Evidence for Trial

A. Demonstrative Evidence

§8.01 1. Generally

Presentation of tangible or demonstrative engineering evidence at trial culminates the investigation and preparation stages of litigation. Demonstrative evidence may take the form of an item that is the same or similar to those at issue in the case, or it may be a photograph which helps the trier of fact to better understand certain facts in issue.

Aside from providing necessary information on relevant issues, tangible evidence tends to expedite trial proceedings by eliminating extensive oral testimony and argument on some issues. This form of evidence also has collateral benefits in that demonstrative evidence is often a welcome relief to the judge or jurors, who can supplement their senses of hearing with their senses of sight, touch, and smell as they work to comprehend and absorb frequently monotone, oral testimony. Without some form of tangible evidence to put before and capture the attention of the jury, the eyes of jurors may roam the courtroom, focusing on distracting and irrelevant matter.

§8.02 2. Admissibility of Exhibits

Generally speaking, an exhibit is a paper, photograph, object, or other thing that is produced and exhibited to the trier of fact during the hearing. The exhibit is offered in proof of certain facts which are probative to the subject matter of the action. The admissibility of exhibits, like that of other evidence, is within the trial court's discretion. The court will reject an exhibit where it finds it to be of little probative value or incompetent to prove a matter in issue.[1] On being accepted, the exhibit is marked for identification and becomes a part of the case.

Prior to trial counsel should have determined which evidence will be introduced through exhibits and by whom. All exhibits will have to be qualified by the laying of a foundation prior to their admission into evidence unless both parties stipulate in advance of trial to the admission of an exhibit without foundation.[2] Where there has been no such stipulation, counsel must plan and prepare a method for the introduction of each exhibit.[3] Counsel's own witnesses may be able to identify and authenticate all

---

[1]Laff v Chapman Performance Prods, Inc, 63 Ill App 3d 297, 379 NE2d 773 (1978).

[2]Davies v Lynch, 4 AD2d 1008, 167 NYS2d 849 (1957).

[3]Camden v City of New York, 119 AD 84, 103 NYS 971 (1907).

exhibits. However, where this is not possible, there must be advance planning to properly secure subpoenas on any person or custodian of records who may possess essential papers, documents, photographs, or other things unavailable to counsel.

Exhibits usually are introduced into evidence during direct examination of a party's case-in-chief. However, since counsel on cross-examination has the right to elicit all facts within the knowledge of an adverse witness relating to matters testified to on direct examination, it is also proper for counsel to introduce certain exhibits during cross-examination.[4]

§8.03 3. Exhibit List

One helpful method of organizing exhibits for trial is to prepare an exhibit list. Basically, such a list gives counsel a means of insuring that all evidence offered by counsel and opposing counsel is accounted for. Such a list facilitates expeditious reference to various exhibits after they have been received into evidence.

An example of an exhibit list appears in Figure 8-1. It should be noted that *Pltf. Ten. I.D.* means plaintiff's tentative identification number which counsel marks on an exhibit for personal use before the court clerk or court reporter marks an exhibit for identification. *Deft. Ten. I.D.* refers to defendant's tentative identification number. The column *description* refers to a description of the exhibit itself. *Witness* means the identity of the witness who will identify and authenticate the exhibit with foundation testimony. *Marked for I.D.* is the number the court clerk or court reporter gives to the exhibit. The column *accepted* refers to the court's acceptance or receiving of the exhibit into evidence so that it can be considered by the trier of fact in evaluating the merits of the case.

§8.04 4. Making a Good Record

Whether being examined on direct or cross-examination, it is necessary for the expert witness to keep in mind the importance of making a good record.

To insure such a record, the expert should speak slowly and distinctly. This not only will enable the trier of fact to follow the testimony, but also will allow the court reporter to transcribe an intelligible record. The expert who refers to an exhibit should make the effort to orally describe for the record the context in which the exhibit is being discussed. In addition, where the expert's terminology becomes esoteric or includes unusual terms of art, the expert should not hesitate to spell out such terms for the court reporter.

B. Models

§8.05 1. Duplicate Models

Models, to an even greater extent than photographic evidence,[5] leave the trier of fact with a more durable impression and a greater understanding of the facts than

---

[4] Eddy v Gallaway, 11 Cal App 3d 185, 89 Cal Rptr 491 (1970).

[5] **§8.08.**

Figure 8-1 Exhibit List

EXHIBIT LIST

Court: ______________________________

Date: ______________________________

Case No.: ______________________________

______________ vs. ______________

Plaintiff(s) Defendant(s)

Dept.: ______________________________

Plaintiff Ten. I.D.	Defendant Ten. I.D.	Description	Witness	Marked for I.D.	Accepted

oral testimony does. Photographs, being two-dimensional and subject to various distortions, often do not present the subject condition or object in a truly objective and comprehensible manner. Models do not have these shortcomings. Because of their three-dimensional existence, models can communicate spatial relationships to the trier of fact clearly and expeditiously. Models also allow the expert or attorney to easily explain conditions, objects, mechanical processes, or other subjects at issue.

Whether a model must be to scale depends on the purpose for which it is being used. In a geographical model where distances, grading, curves, or embankments are essential factors, scale accuracy would probably be required. Otherwise, as long as a model gives some benefit to the trier of fact without distorting important conditions, it need not be to scale.

In defective products cases, models may be very useful where it would be inappropriate or difficult to bring the object itself into the courtroom. Models have the advantage of being able to be made in a convenient size, smaller or larger than the object or condition in issue. In addition, models may be made with clear exterior parts, to reveal interior components.

The usual purpose of exhibiting a model of a product is to help the trier of fact visualize an unfamiliar and complex device or machine. One example would be a small-scale model of a machine used to excavate a canal. Most components of the actual machine could be presented in the model. Such a model would be of great help in explaining the use of the machine and identifying various machine parts.

A model tends to have a greater effect on the viewer than drawings or photographs, since it can be observed from various angles, thereby depicting the product or condition more realistically.[6]

§8.06 2. Block-Type Models

Another type of exhibit is a block-type model. For instance, a broom handle can represent a shaft.[7] Similarly, a yardstick can represent a wood beam.[8] When the block-type model is damaged in court in the same manner as the original product, various features of failure may be identified and shown to the trier of fact. The use of the block-type model may more effectively represent the actual occurrence than drawings and photographs would.

One advantage in the use of a model is the possibility of illustrating otherwise intangible properties such as stress and strain.[9] For example, a rubber rod that is marked at equal increments can demonstrate the effects of compression and tension as the markings on the rod spread or converge. Longitudinal lines can show the effect of torsional stresses as these lines move into a spiral.

A good guide to effective use of models is the classroom instructor. An instructor's methods may be incorporated into an expert's courtroom presentation. Models should always be used with the trier of fact in mind. The model itself should be large enough

---

[6]See §§7.36, 8.06-.07.

[7]§3.24.

[8]§3.27.

[9]§3.32.

to be seen from a distance. Bright colors setting off different parts of the product can help identify each part. The model can also be augmented by illustrations on a chalkboard or drawing pad.

§8.07 3. Admissibility

A model, like other demonstrative evidence, is admissible if:

1. It is a true and accurate representation of the condition or object which it purports to model
2. It would assist the witness in presenting testimony
3. It would aid the trier of fact in understanding the evidence[10]

The model's maker usually need not qualify the model. Rather, any competent witness who is familiar with the condition or object depicted can provide a sufficient foundation for admissibility.[11]

Where a model is scaled and its accuracy is important to some issue in the case, a civil engineer or surveyor, after being qualified, should offer testimony that the model not only would help the witness testify, but also would aid the trier of fact in understanding the testimony. In addition, the witness should verify and explain:

1. How the original measurements for the model were taken
2. What was done with the original measurements
3. Whether the original measurements were compared against the model
4. How the measurements were compared
5. Whether the measurements compared accurately
6. What scale has been utilized
7. Whether the witness has an opinion as to whether the model truly and accurately represents the object or condition which it purports to represent
8. What that opinion is

C. Photographs

§8.08 1. Generally

Photographs are an inexpensive means of memorializing events, acts, or conditions. Consequently, when trial approaches, witnesses testimony may be refreshed, explained, or rebutted with the help of such evidence. In addition, if the photographs are well qualified, their educative and persuasive impact on the trier of fact will be substantially greater than the impact of conflicting oral testimony on the same matter.

---

[10]Arkansas State Highway Commn v Rhodes, 240 Ark 565, 401 SW2d 558 (1966).

[11]Kooyumjian v Stevens, 10 Ill App 2d 378, 135 NE2d 146, 151 (1956).

In order to effectively use them, counsel must assure that photographs accurately and objectively represent the subject event, act, or condition.[12]

In taking photographs it is not necessary to retain professional photographers in every instance. The subject matter to be photographed often dictates whether a professional photographer is required. Obviously, there is rarely a chance to engage a professional for on-the-scene photographs depicting spontaneous or exciting events.

Where the taking of a photograph can be planned in advance, care should be taken to avoid including in the photograph irrelevant background or foreground material that may detract from the significance of the subject. Similarly, printing should be done on paper which modestly and objectively conveys the substance sought to be presented. Excessively elaborate prints may have an adverse effect on the trier of fact, while simple prints will communicate the same information without risk.[13]

§8.09 2. Locating Sources

Depending on the subject to be photographed, counsel may have to decide the best way to obtain an item of photographic evidence. Where a condition continues to exist, counsel has the option of retaining a professional legal photographer, a commercial photographer, or an amateur (including the client).

Legal photographers are in the business of providing photographic evidence for use in litigation. By reason of their experience, the attorney needs to spend less time explaining the relevant evidentiary issues and subjects of inquiry to them. The professional legal photographer is trained to understand reasons and purposes behind such photographs and is familiar with effective courtroom presentation.

Amateurs are a source of photographers, but where the photograph has technical significance, it is doubtful whether an amateur could qualify. Testimony about camera position, shutter speed, film speed, aperture opening, and the developing and printing process generally would be beyond the understanding of an amateur.

Generally counsel should not participate directly in the taking of photographs where there is a possibility that counsel actually might have to testify as to the photograph's identity and authenticity. It is a wise policy to have an independent person, professional or amateur, take photographs, since recent case law indicates that the fact that an attorney may have to testify on some issue in the case may be sufficient grounds for disqualification.[14]

§8.10 3. Changed Conditions

Where a certain condition has changed so substantially as to no longer be similar to the condition existing at the time of the incident, counsel must employ other methods of searching for potential photographic evidence. In one case, counsel was eager to locate photographs depicting the condition of a tract of homes as it existed prior to extensive flooding which washed away numerous roads and structures. Counsel's search consisted of getting in touch with the following:

---

[12]State v Smith, 27 NJ 433, 142 A2d 890, 899 (1958).

[13]See §§**7.33-.35, 7.39, 8.09-.18, 8.21-.26.**

[14] Comden v Superior Court, 20 Cal 3d 906, 576 P2d 971, 145 Cal Rptr 9 (1978).

1. Local residents, to determine whether they had taken photographs of their tract prior to the flooding
2. Developers, contractors, and real estate brokers, to determine whether they had taken photographs of the tract for any advertisement campaign
3. Designers, architects, or engineers responsible for the planning and design of the tract
4. Local magazines, newspapers, and free-lance photographers who might have photographed the tract prior to the flood
5. Local newspapers or other media, to advertise a reward for persons with photographs or film depicting the prior condition of the tract
6. Public and private entities which used aerial photographs for mapping and other purposes
7. Insurance companies which provided coverage for the tract development

§8.11 4. Special Conditions

Where illumination or weather conditions are factors in the case in controversy, there must be a decision whether reproduction of such condition should be attempted on film. Assuming that photographic evidence cannot be obtained at the time of occurrence of the original condition itself, reproduction of such a condition is usually most difficult.

Variables affecting a condition itself, such as indoor lighting or positioning of the sun or other light sources, are burdensome to reproduce. In addition, even if photographic evidence is available at the time of the original condition, the developing and printing processes involve too many variables to exactly duplicate conditions. However, by providing a series of photographs with a range of exposures, it would be possible for a witness to testify which photograph most closely resembled the lighting condition at the time of the incident.

Another approach would be simply to have a photograph taken of the condition without attempting to duplicate the illumination factors, and then have the witness qualify and explain the lighting conditions with reference to the photographs.

§8.12 5. Panoramic Views

Photographs fastened edge to edge to form a panoramic view, introduced as a true representation of the locality, are admissible in evidence at trial. In an Oklahoma case,[15] the plaintiff alleged that motorists on the road approaching certain railroad tracks were unable to see defendant's trains because of trees, high weeds, telephone poles, and frame buildings. Defendant alleged that an approaching train was clearly visible.

To support its position, the defendant sent a professional photographer with a camera and a normal lens to the scene one day after the incident. The defendant's

[15]St Louis-San Francisco Ry v Davis, 399 P2d 463 (Okla 1965).

photographer later testified that he had made a series of eye-level photographic exposures with the camera fixed to a tripod at a certain point in the road east of the tracks. The first photograph was the subject intersection, and the others were made by turning the camera at intervals to the right to record consecutive views, with the last picture facing practically due north. Later the photos were placed edge to edge, so that details of trees, houses, rails, and objects coincided with those of adjoining photos, and the edges were held together with flexible tape. The photographer testified that the panoramic exhibit showed the view that a person standing at the subject position would have. The court held that absent any showing of deception, distortion, or inaccuracy as between the actual scene and the panoramic view, the exhibits should have been admitted.

§8.13 6. Aerial Photographs

Aerial photographs are subject to the same authentication requirements that apply to photographic evidence in general. That is, the photograph must be qualified as a true and accurate representation of the scene at the time in issue and as an aid to the trier of fact in understanding the evidence. In addition, aerial photographs, as well as telescopic photographs, chance photographs, or automatic photographs, may be probative in themselves in a proper case, since the memory of a photograph is significantly more accurate and reliable than that of a human witness.[16] Nevertheless, admissibility of aerial photographic evidence is within the discretion of the trial court.

In a Virginia case,[17] the court held inadmissible an aerial photograph depicting certain lots of land involved in litigation, reasoning that aerial photographs taken seven years before the events in litigation were too remote in time. The court also pointed out that the aerial photos failed to accurately portray conditions existing at the time in controversy which were disclosed by other evidence as that some lots were low, marshy, and irregular in shape.

However, the fact that photographic evidence may depict certain conditions which are not precisely the same as those at the time of the controversy does not necessarily render evidence inadmissible. Rather, the crucial determination is whether the jury will be misled.[18]

§8.14 7. Magnified Photographs

The mere fact that a photograph has been enlarged is not a basis for an objection to its admissibility where the magnification does not tend to mislead. Photographs of objects already in evidence, enlarged to clarify details and to illustrate testimony of witnesses, may go to the jury as would a magnifying glass or microscope.[19]

§8.15 D. Photographic Distortion

There are numerous ways of distorting conditions, acts, or events as depicted by photographic evidence. This is an important consideration, since for photographs

---

[16]People v Bowley, 59 Cal 2d 855, 382 P2d 591, 31 Cal Rptr 471 (1963).

[17]Chandler v Russell, 164 Va 318, 180 SE 313 (1935).

[18]Saldana v Wirtz Cartage Co, 74 Ill 2d 379, 385 NE2d 664 (1978).

[19]Sim v Weeks, 7 Cal App 2d 28, 45 P2d 350 (1935).

to be admissible they must accurately and objectively represent the subject matter in issue. Notwithstanding admissibility requirements, photographic misrepresentations, intentional or unintentional, are common. It would not be difficult to find a plaintiff's attorney who would discard a photograph which minimized settling cracks in a building foundation, property damage to a motor vehicle, or potholes in the street. Similarly, a defense attorney would generally reject photographs which maximized those same conditions.

Where the accuracy and probative value of photographic evidence is in issue, an objection to the admissibility of such evidence is proper. Where the court finds that the foundational facts on admissibility are close, and exercises its discretion by admitting such evidence, counsel may still discredit the probative value of such photographs by conducting a vigorous cross-examination of the photographer aimed at revealing any distortion methods employed.

§8.16 1. Lens Distortion

Type of camera lens substantially affects photographic representation. The lens is a specially shaped piece of transparent material, either or both of the opposite surfaces of which are curved. The particular shape of a lens causes light rays to be reflected so that they converge to form an image on the film.

Since the image exposed on film is the result of light passing through the specially shaped lens, any lens defect or aberration would cause a photographic distortion.

In addition, use of wide-angle lenses, zoom lenses, and telephoto lenses can lead to significant perspective distortion. Generally, however, perspective distortion will not occur where the photograph is viewed at the proper distance from the observer's eyes. The proper distance is governed by the following formula:

$$D = F \times E$$

where:

D = the proper distance between the observer's eye and the photograph

F = the focal length, or the distance between lens and film

E = the enlargement multiple factor between the negative size and the actual photograph

The problem with maintaining the proper distance is that the observer or trier of fact is often uncomfortable, incapable, or unfamiliar with observing photographs from an exceptionally close or far distance. Also, certain basic information would have to be provided regarding the different variables needed to determine proper distance.

§8.17 2. Filter Distortion

Filters are another source of photographic distortion. Since the purpose of a filter is to remove certain wavelengths of light, the actual subject matter photographed often is not being objectively represented. Some filters are used either to correct film defects as suggested by the manufacturer or to increase contrast on black and white film where two separate colors otherwise would produce the same shade. Others are used to remove glare from the subject matter. The paramount concern when considering potential photographic distortions remains the issue of whether the photograph is accurate and probative or distorted and prejudicial.

§8.18 3. Size Distortion

Photographs can effectively deceive when used to illustrate essential size or dimensional characteristics. Width of a street, difference in elevation between two slabs of a cracked sidewalk, an undersized ceiling joist, or consistency of soil and rock formations on a mountainside can be misrepresented in photographs unless certain precautions are taken. Such precautions entail the use of some sort of measuring device to which the viewer can relate in evaluating the size of the street, crack, joist, rocks, or any other object. Use of a ruler, meterstick, person, automobile, or other common reference standard in photographs themselves can often counteract size distortions.

Of course, a witness would still have to qualify the photograph by testifying, for example, that the object in the photograph standing adjacent to the crack in the sidewalk and purportedly measuring the difference in elevation between the two slabs, is in fact a 12-inch ruler and not merely a miniature or other facsimile. When possible, it is helpful for the witness to actually bring the measuring or reference device to court for display during examination.

E. Presentation Procedures

§8.19 1. Papers and Documents

When certain types of papers and documents are admitted into evidence, counsel may desire that the jury examine and understand those particular pieces of evidence as soon as the witness has identified and authenticated them. For example, in a case where an expert witness is testifying and pointing out improper engineering features of certain design plans,[20] there are several methods by which counsel can share the contents of the plans with the members of the jury at the same time. First, counsel may simply allow the expert to remain seated with the plans on the witness stand and have the expert review and discuss those plans. Second, counsel may have the plans posted on the exhibit board near the jury box and request that the expert approach the board and review and explain the plans. Third, the plans may be projected using an overhead projector or some other form of photographic enlargement, and displayed on a wall, screen, or exhibit board while the expert reviews and discusses them. The concept underlying this method of presentation is that the jury is better able to understand the significance of an exhibit if it can see the exhibit while it hears the witness's testimony.

§8.20 2. Diagrams, Charts, and Maps

When testimony is to be elicited concerning geographic placements, an adequate foundation must be laid by a qualified witness for any diagram, chart, or map which

---

[20]§4.04.

will be used to illustrate or explain testimony. Whether the witness actually prepared the exhibit in question is not essential. However, it is important that the witness be qualified to testify to having inspected, measured, and either prepared the exhibit or checked that the exhibit is a true and accurate representation of the geographic condition when examined.[21]

Often both sides in litigation will stipulate that a diagram, chart, or map is a true and accurate representation of the subject geographic location. Although the preliminary foundation is unnecessary in such a case, testimony is still required to make the exhibit comprehensible.

§8.21 3. Photographs

Before referring to photographs at trial, counsel should know which photographs will be offered into evidence, and when, how, and why they will be offered into evidence.

In deciding which photographs to offer into evidence, counsel should assiduously review all available photographs and select those which illustrate the issues without unnecessary repetition. Once photographs have been selected for offering into evidence, counsel should develop some method of simple identification so that the sequence of locating, referring, and offering each photograph will be smooth and efficient at trial. One effective method of organization is to maintain an exhibit check list as part of counsel's trial notebook.

The point at which the photographs will be offered into evidence depends on the progress of the case. Plainly, for the photographs to be relevant to the issues, a foundation must already have been laid.

The manner of introducing photographs into evidence is a two-part process. First, counsel must consider procedural requirements, and second, admissibility requirements. Procedurally, counsel who intends to offer a photograph or series of photographs into evidence should, in most jurisdictions, have the clerk or court reporter mark each photograph as an *exhibit* or an *exhibit for identification only*, and then show each photograph to opposing counsel.

The admissibility of photographic exhibits then turns on their identification and authentication. A qualified witness must offer testimony that each particular exhibit is a true and accurate representation of the act, event, or condition depicted.[22] In most situations, the photographer is not a necessary witness to the identification and authentication of a photograph. Any percipient witness is qualified.[23] However, where a photograph contains information which must be interpreted in a technical manner, the photographer may be required to testify not only about the camera, film, and lenses used, but also the exposing, developing, and printing process.

Once the photographic exhibit has been sufficiently identified and authenticated, the foundation has been properly laid for the exhibit to be admitted into evidence. Where the photograph depicts a condition which has changed significantly because of

---

[21]Zube v Weber, 67 Mich 52, 34 NW 264 (1887); Merkel v Consumers Power Co, 220 Mich 128, 189 NW 997 (1922).

[22]Perri v Tassie, 293 Mich 464, 292 NW 370 (1940).

[23]Finch v WR Roach Co, 295 Mich 589, 295 NW 324 (1940).

construction, demolition, weather, or sun position, the witness must acknowledge any discrepancy between the photograph and the actual condition in issue. For example, in a case where counsel was attempting to demonstrate that a guardrail and warning sign were improperly located in the vicinity of a particular mountain road, and where there were physical variations between conditions at the time the photographs were taken and the time of the incident, counsel qualified the exhibit as follows:

> Omitting the repaving of the street surface, the presence of snow on the shoulder of the road and the construction of the condominiums in the background, does this photograph truly and accurately represent the position of the guardrail and warning signs as they existed on the date of the incident.

Where the degree of variation between the photographs and the actual condition is substantial, the court may preclude introduction of any such exhibits into evidence. The rationale for such a ruling would be that the probative value of such photographs would be minimal, and that their admission into evidence would tend to mislead or confuse the jury. Such a determination is solely within the descretion of the trial judge. Where accuracy of a photograph presents an open question, a court may well rule that impeachment would go to the weight and not the admissibility of the evidence.[24]

§8.22 4. Markings on Photographs

Placement of markings on photographs to call attention to some particular feature of evidence is proper where: 1) the expert identifies and explains the markings; and 2) they help the trier of fact to understand the testimony of the witness. However, where an identifying mark relates only to hearsay testimony, the mark or the photograph itself should be excluded.[25]

§8.23 5. Samples

Demonstrative evidence consisting of a sample of an object or substance is admissible in evidence if properly qualified.[26] The sample must:

1. Be identified as to its source
2. Reflect the condition of the object or substance at the time of the incident
3. Be fairly representative of the subject matter in issue.[27]

In an Oregon case,[28] plaintiff sued defendant contractor for failing to properly join sewer pipes with the specified cement mortar. The defendants offered expert evidence on the lasting quality of the specified cement mortar: that such mortar would disintegrate in a very short time; that it was porous; that water would percolate through

---

[24]See **§§7.33-.35, 7.39, 8.08-.18, 8.26.**

[25]Moore v Crowe, 117 Ga App 213, 160 SE2d 406 (1968).

[26]**§3.23.**

[27]Kunzman v Cherokee Silo Co, 253 Iowa 885, 114 NW2d 534 (1962).

[28]City of Seaside v Randles, 92 Or 650, 180 P 319 (1919).

the pores; and that sand would also work its way through. In rebuttal, the plaintiff excavated two samples of sewer pipe joints from an adjacent line which had been laid for six years in the sand, within six feet of the sewer pipe laid by the defendants. The cement joints were produced, offered, and received in evidence. The court held the samples competent to rebut the theory of defendant's experts.

§8.24 6. Demonstrations

Demonstrations frequently provide helpful information to the trier of fact in determining disputed issues. However, demonstrations, like experiments or other forms of demonstrative evidence, must be sufficiently qualified to be admissible. For instance, it would be improper for an expert to demonstrate before the trier of fact the respective movements and reactions of two model cars after impact in the absence of foundational evidence connecting such a demonstration with conditions and circumstances at the time of the subject collision.[29] On the other hand, such a demonstration would probably be proper if done merely to illustrate a general principle, like a physics principle, rather than to confirm a specific conclusion.[30]

§8.25 7. Chalkboards and Drawing Pads

Sometimes an expert may wish to illustrate a particular conditon or event with a two-dimensional representation. In such a case, where the expert does not have any charts, diagrams, or illustrations already prepared for jury presentation, use of chalkboards or drawing pads can be an effective tactic if properly rehearsed prior to testifying. That is, the expert should appear spontaneous in front of the jury, but should, in truth, know well in advance the general format of any graphic presentation.

In a situation where an expert is explaining the concept of centrifugal force, describing the moving parts of a defective gin pole derrick, or discussing deficiencies in a critical path method, a rehearsed, contemporaneous, and animated diagram using colorful and contrasting chalk, crayons, grease pencils, or felt tip pens is certain to engage the jury. In fact, when the subject to be discussed is not so complicated as to demand use of a previously prepared illustration, the expert should take such a spontaneous approach. Previously prepared illustrations often go unheeded, and have about as much appeal and interest for the jury as a typical outdoor advertisement has for a passing motorist.

§8.26 8. Photographing the Chalkboard

Trials occur in which counsel or the expert have not anticipated use of particular diagrams, calculations, or illustrations. In these situations, depending on the circumstances, counsel or the expert may resort to use of the chalkboard. Adverse counsel or the adverse expert may also use a chalkboard. Where this is the case, vital illustrative information may be erased to make room for the diagrams or calculations of other counsel or witnesses.

---

[29]Fort Worth & Denver Ry v Williams, 375 SW2d 279 (Tex 1964).

[30]Millers' Natl Ins Co v Wichita Flour Mills Co, 257 F2d 93 (10th Cir 1958).

One method of preserving chalkboard data is to photograph it with a Polaroid or other instant-printing camera. Usually, there should be no objection to this procedure, and the photographs depicting the chalkboard may be marked as exhibits. Some courts, however, may object to counsel photographing the chalkboard in front of the jury on the grounds that it may unduly emphasize the information appearing on the chalkboard. Where this is the case, photographs should be taken during a recess. Any such procedural matters should be discussed with the court in chambers prior to trial.

§8.27 9. Magnetic Blackboard

Another method of presenting evidence by way of visual aid is to use a magnetic blackboard as a visual or graphic means of giving testimony. These devices are commonly used in describing vehicular accidents. This method also can be helpful to an expert in explaining certain aspects of a construction or products liability case to the trier of fact.

§8.28 10. Overlays

One helpful method of presenting charts, diagrams, and maps is to use a transparent overlay. Each plastic sheet may be placed over the original chart, diagram, or map, and marked accordingly. This facilitates comparisons among witnesses' testimony. In addition, it provides a system of compiling the simple testimony of numerous witnesses into an intricate and complete picture of a particular condition, process, or geographic location.

§8.29 11. Illustrations Based on Photographs

Frequently, photographs deal with complex subjects which are understandable to a trained expert but not to a layperson. In such a situation where, for example, the photograph may reflect an aerial view of a washed-out storm drain system, an intricate tunnel-boring mole, or an elaborate structural framing on a condominium, it may be helpful to represent the photograph by illustration. In other words, the photograph can be used as model, being either traced or copied so that the end result will be an illustration of the photograph. The obvious advantage of this technique is that it becomes possible to stress significant details or to remove nonessential ones. Where a photograph may fail to clearly differentiate various conditions because of contrast or other problems, illustrations can easily remedy such deficiencies by controlling color contrast and outlining. Such a method of presentation will often prove to better aid the trier of fact in understanding the issues than the photograph itself.

In qualifying the illustration, it is good practice for the witness to refer to the photograph from which the illustration was prepared. This would serve to increase the witness's credibility.

§8.30 12. Molding and Casting

Another method of representing an item of real evidence is by use of a casting procedure, a method which often provides excellent results. The mold of a machine part or tire tread can exactly duplicate a relevant product or condition. In addition, the molding and casting procedure is relatively inexpensive, can be carried out utilizing plaster and clay, and produces a permanent record of the item of evidence for presentation to the trier of fact.[31]

§8.31 13. Taking the Jury Outside the Courtroom

In a West Virginia case,[32] the plaintiff sued the defendant, a manufacturer of an 11-inch power-driven circular saw, for injuries received. The plaintiff contended that the saw should have been protected with a guard. The defendant contended that it was not reasonably possible to enclose or guard the saw. On the representation of plaintiff's counsel that it would be unhandy to bring the guard and saw into the courtroom, and on plaintiff's motion, the court took the jury to a shop that had a power-driven saw similar to defendant's saw, but which employed an effective and satisfactory saw guard. The court held that a practical demonstration of machinery to the jury outside the courtroom is proper where such action places the jury in a position to satisy itself on a question of fact. In addition, demonstrations enable the jury to determine issues on firsthand information, and not based merely on the opinions or theories of experts.

§8.32 14. Tactics

Where photographic exhibits are admitted into evidence, the jury has the right to study, examine, and consider them. Prior to jury deliberation, when exhibits may be taken into the jury room at the discretion of the court,[33] exhibits can be displayed to the jury in the courtroom after the court has received them into evidence.

Method of display will frequently depend on the size of photographs. Counsel may choose to personally hold up a large photograph in front of the jury box, to attach the photographs to the exhibit board, to utilize an overhead projector, or to pass the photographs among the jurors. Where a number of small photographs are involved and sequence of viewing is unimportant, counsel may expedite display procedures by starting half of the photographs at juror number one and the other half at juror number twelve.

Another strategy concerns timing of the display. Generally, counsel should not pass around or exhibit photographs during actual direct examination of the expert witness, since jurors might tend to divide their attention between the exhibits and the oral testimony. Rather, counsel should either wait until jurors have completed their perusal of the exhibits before continuing the examination, or display the exhibits after completing the examination of the witness. This latter timing of display can help divert the jury's attention from opposing counsel's cross-examination.

---

[31]See §7.37.

[32]Tarr v Keller Lumber & Constr Co, 106 W VA 99, 144 SE 881 (1928).

[33]People v De Frenn, 247 Mich 698, 226 NW 710 (1929).

§8.33 15. Problems

While the effective use of demonstrative evidence is often a key to success in litigation, use of such evidence can also be a severe disadvantage for the party presenting such evidence.

One source of trouble in the use of demonstrative evidence is that the trier of fact may become so engrossed in a piece of tangible evidence presented as to divert concern from other relevant issues. In addition, excessive use of demonstrative evidence can complicate the evidence to be considered by the trier of fact, with the result that the trier of fact may either disregard all such evidence or give undue weight to inconsequential matters. Obviously, the solution is moderation in the use of demonstrative evidence.

9 Examining Experts in Trial

§9.01 A. Direct Examination of Experts

Direct examination of an expert is a crucial point in the trial. The expert has been retained by the party, at a respectable fee, to testify on a certain matter. Such testimony will relate to facts, opinions, or conclusions which lie beyond the common experience of a layperson. Such testimony calls on the expert's unique experience, training, knowledge, skill, or education. The expert's testimony may be solicited to rebut or impeach adverse lay or expert testimony. It also may be used to corroborate the party's own lay testimony or to impress the trier of fact with the magnitude of the controversy.

An obvious characteristic of successful witness examination is witness control on both direct and cross-examination. Where a witness who supports counsel's theory of the case has a history of being difficult, argumentative, hot-tempered, verbose, unlikable, and generally uncontrollable, it may be necessary to forfeit that witness's testimony. Where such a witness's favorable testimony is essential to a case, examination time should be kept to an absolute minimum.

One method of maintaining witness control is to conduct a vigorous prehearing rehearsal with the witness, emphasizing all areas of examination. A tape recorder may be used to record the witness's testimony during the rehearsal. Sometimes an uncontrollable witness will be shocked and/or educated by listening to the playback.

§9.02 1. Subjects of Expert Testimony

An expert witness plays a valuable role in drawing inferences from facts which would be beyond the understanding of the average layperson. Implicit in this role is that the expert testimony should help the trier of fact understand the issues. If the issues relate to a matter of common knowledge from which the average layperson is capable of drawing a correct inference, there is no need for expert testimony.[1]

In one case, the court precluded a mechanical engineering expert from testifying as to the results of tests which the expert had performed on the slipperiness of a particular surface. The court reasoned that the physical facts could be perceived by the average layperson and did not require proof by expert testimony.[2]

In all cases, the trial judge has wide discretion to decide what is a proper subject of expert testimony.[3]

§9.03 2. Qualifying the Expert

Before expert testimony can be elicited, it is essential that the witness be qualified as an expert. This can be done by presenting evidence tending to show that the expert possesses special training, knowledge, experience, skill, or education.[4] This type of presentation serves a twofold purpose. First, it lays the necessary foundation to demonstrate the witness's competence to testify. Second, it gives the trier of fact an opportunity to hear the expert's qualifications, making it easier to give the expert's opinions or findings appropriate weight.[5]

---

[1] Swartley v Seattle School Dist No 1, 70 Wash 2d 17, 421 P2d 1009 (1966); Collins v Zediker, 421 Pa 52, 218 A2d 776 (1966); Walter v England, 133 Cal App 676, 680, 24 P2d 930 (1933).

[2] Peters v Shortt, 214 Va 399, 200 SE2d 547 (1973).

[3] Allen Morris Co v McNally, 305 So 2d 79 (Fla 1974).

[4] Dunwoody v Royal Indem Co, 218 Mich 358, 188 NW 498 (1922).

[5] See **§§7.07, 7.27, 9.12.**

In establishing an engineering expert's qualifications, the following subjects should be covered:

Education

Testimony should be elicited regarding the expert's higher education, i.e., the names of undergraduate and postgraduate schools at which the expert received instruction.[6] The major course of study at each such school, a description of relevant classes taken, the title of each degree received, and the respective dates of any noted activities should also be covered.

Professional Experience

This area includes a description of the expert's professional employments, including self-employments, positions, titles, responsibilities, number of persons under expert's supervision in case of each employment, chronology of employments, and respective duration of each.[7]

Publications

Testimony on publications should include any and all books, articles, chapters, papers, or letters written or contributed by the expert relating to the expert's field.[8]

Certification and Registration

There should be discussion of whether the expert is a professional or nonprofessional engineer.[9] Inquiry should be made about the expert's compliance with state requirements, including any state examination or grandfather clause.[10]

Teaching Experience

Testimony should deal with subjects taught, dates of instruction, names of institutions, and nature of expert's status, i.e., professor, associate professor, lecturer, teacher, etc.[11]

Professional Membership

There should be inquiry about the expert's past and present membership and participation in any local, state, national, or international society or organization related to the expert's field of specialty. This is important in establishing the expert's professionalism.[12]

---

[6]**§2.47.**

[7]**§2.46.**

[8]**§2.49.**

[9]See **ch 2** for a more detailed discussion.

[10]A *grandfather clause* permits registration of an engineer without such engineer having passed a state examination. This may occur where the engineer has demonstrated a certain minimal experience in a particular discipline and state law provides for it. See **§2.46.**

[11]**§2.50.**

[12]**§2.51.**

Prior Expert Witness Experience

Testimony should include the number of times and subject matters on which the expert has previously testified in trial, arbitration, or administrative or investigative hearings.

Miscellaneous

This catchall classification covers other special factors which qualify an expert to testify, and include the following: attendance at conferences, seminars, or symposia, participation in governmental hearings, and being a recipient of awards or other professional recognitions.

§9.04 3. Stipulating to Expertise

Opposing counsel may offer to stipulate to the expertise of the witness. This will eliminate the need to lay a foundation regarding the expert's qualifications. However, such an offer is usually only made when opposing counsel knows that the witness is a reputable expert whose qualifications might tend to unduly impress the trier of fact.

Unless counsel's expert lacks favorable qualifications, there is no advantage for counsel in entering into such a stipulation. The offer should be refused with a response that the trier of fact will be interested in hearing the basis of the witness's expertise.

However, a stipulation including a detailed list of the expert's qualifications is generally acceptable. This allows counsel to score points with the trier of fact by saving court time while still preserving counsel's right to emphasize the expert's qualifications during argument.

Where counsel's own expert does not have favorable qualifications, a stipulation by opposing counsel might be viewed as a confirmation of the witness's expertise.

§9.05 4. Challenging the Expert—Voir Dire

An expert witness must be properly qualified before offering expert opinion testimony. Whether the witness qualifies as an expert is a preliminary fact, determined by and within the sole discretion of the trial judge.[13] Opposing counsel may challenge the expert's qualifications and, by that means, seek to preclude the expert's testimony by showing that the expert is not competent. Opposing counsel also may question whether the proffered evidence is properly the subject of expert testimony. This is accomplished through *voir dire* examination, which refers generally to the court's preliminary examination of the expert's qualifications or the subject matter of testimony as to which the expert's competence to testify is challenged.

Opposing counsel may interrupt direct examination of the expert by requesting voir dire after the expert has testified regarding qualifications and before the expert has offered opinion testimony.[14] In addition, opposing counsel may interpose an objection

---

[13]Pfingsten v Westenhaver, 39 Cal 2d 12, 244 P2d 395 (1952).

[14]Davis v Pennsylvania RR, 215 Pa 581, 64 A 774 (1906); State v McRae, 200 NC 149, 156 SE 800, 803 (1931); People v Hawes, 98 Cal 648, 33 P 791 (1893).

to the expert's opinion testimony on direct examination, subject to a motion to strike after opposing counsel completes cross-examination of the expert.

If opposing counsel establishes to the court's satisfaction that the expert is not competent or that the testimony does not deal with a proper subject of expert testimony, the expert is precluded from testifying about any opinion or finding relative to such witness's purported expertise.

If opposing counsel is unable to establish to the court's satisfaction that the expert is not competent or that the testimony does not relate to a proper subject of expert testimony, the expert is deemed qualified to render an opinion. However, the trier of fact still may scrutinize the expert's qualifications as part of determining what weight, if any, to give to the expert testimony.[15]

§9.06 a. Tactics

Several tactical factors must be considered in challenging an expert.

First, where objection to an expert's qualification is made subject to a motion to strike after cross-examination, there may be undue prejudice even if counsel's motion to strike is subsequently granted, since the expert's opinion testimony has already been heard by the trier of fact on direct examination. To avoid this possible prejudice, especially where the trier of fact is a jury, counsel should attempt to challenge an expert by voir dire examination during the expert's direct examination instead of merely objecting subject to a motion to strike during subsequent examination.

Second, where the expert is obviously qualified, or the issue sought to be proved by the expert is not very significant, counsel should consider concentrating on cross-examination rather than on voir dire. A futile voir dire examination may cause the jury to give undue weight to the expert and to the subject matter on which the expert testifies.

Third, where voir dire examination is conducted in a jury trial, counsel may request that the jury be excluded or that the parties convene in chambers, to prevent possible prejudice should the expert ultimately be deemed unqualified.

Finally, counsel sometimes may attempt to use voir dire as a discovery device and rehearsal for subsequent cross-examination of the adverse expert. Where voir dire occurs out of the presence of the jury, there is an opportunity for counsel to explore much of the adverse party's case. Even if counsel is not successful in disqualifying the expert, this still leaves counsel in a better position to cross-examine the expert when the trial resumes before the jury. In addition, experienced counsel sometimes intentionally time voir dire so that the trial cannot continue until the following morning. In this way, counsel and counsel's own expert can spend the evening searching for impeachment material based on facts obtained from the adverse expert during voir dire examination. This time-consuming tactic will probably not be successful in cases where the expert and the subject matter are well recognized.

§9.07 5. Expert Opinion Testimony

An expert who has been qualified is competent to state an opinion on the relevant issue. As a general rule, even though a foundation has been laid as to the expert's

---

[15]In re Heart River Irrigation Dist, 78 ND 302, 49 NW2d 217 (1951).

qualifications, it is still necessary to lay a foundation for the factual basis as to which the expert is going to render an opinion.[16]

Such a factual basis may be established through testimony, records, or documents that are in evidence or that will be introduced into evidence. The latter situation would require an offer of proof and would be subject to a motion to strike. In addition, the expert's personal observations and materials reasonably relied on by the expert in forming an opinion may be the basis for such an opinion.

Various considerations in eliciting expert opinion testimony are illustrated by a case in which the expert was retained to render an opinion on a defectively designed tunnel-boring machine.[17] After qualifying the expert, counsel proceeded to develop testimony as to:

1. How, when, and why the expert was retained.
2. A description of the expert's examination, review, and inspection of the subject product.
3. A discussion of all relevant data, including descriptions of: the component parts of the machine; the nature of its design, manufacture, and operation; condition of the soil at the time of failure; and similar tunnel-boring machines
4. Photographs, diagrams, plans, models, reports, and industry standards and specifications
5. Whether the expert had an opinion as to whether the tunnel-boring machine was defectively designed
6. What that opinion was
7. The reasons for the expert's opinion and the matter on which it was based

In addition to having the expert state an opinion that the tunnel-boring machine was defectively designed, counsel also elicited testimony which precluded attacks that could have undermined the expert's conclusions. This was accomplished by having the expert methodically eliminate all other major factors which arguably could have caused the tunnel-boring machine to malfunction. In this particular case, the expert testified as to why improper maintenance and operation were ruled out as possible causes of malfunction.

§9.08 6. Costs of Services

It is important, especially when the trier of fact is a jury, to elicit from the expert on direct examination the fact that the expert has been retained and compensated by the examining party for the specific purpose of testifying in court about certain disputed issues.

This voluntary disclosure emphasizes the forthright nature of the expert's testimony. In addition, it obviates the potential drawing of adverse inferences on cross-examination. It is a fair assumption that opposing counsel will inquire into any financial

---

[16] O'Connor v Plotkins, Inc, 32 Md App 329, 362 A2d 95 (1976).

[17] §3.29.

relationship between the expert and the party. With this in mind, somethought must be given to the expert's fee and its impact, if any, on the trier of fact.[18]

§9.09 B. Cross-Examination of Experts

The cross-examination of an expert witness is a pivotal point in any trial. The witness is testifying because an expert opinion is essential to an ultimate issue in the case. Since the success of the litigation relates directly to the weight given by the trier of fact to the expert's testimony, the triumphant attorney carefully plans cross-examination strategy. Counsel has wide latitude during cross-examination of an expert since the scope of inquiry takes in the expert's qualifications, the subject to which the expert's testimony relates, the matter on which the expert's opinion is based, and reasons for the expert's opinions. In addition to scope of cross-examination, counsel should recognize the psychological tendency of a jury to identify more closely with witnesses than with attorneys, and more closely with lay witnesses than with expert witnesses.

With all this in mind, the major goals of cross-examination can be enumerated as follows:

1. To abstain from questioning when the adverse expert's testimony on direct examination is favorable to the cross-examiner
2. To abstain from needless questioning when the adverse expert's testimony cannot be effectively attacked and cross-examination may only serve to reinforce certain adverse testimony
3. To discredit the adverse expert's testimony with respect to that expert's own qualifications
4. To impeach the adverse expert by examining the nature of that expert's relations with the adverse party or attorney
5. To discredit the adverse expert in the area of the basis or validity of that expert's opinions or conclusions
6. To effect a change in the adverse expert's stated opinions or conclusions as compared with that expert's testimony on direct examination
7. To discredit the adverse expert's testimony on collateral issues
8. To elicit from the adverse expert favorable testimony on collateral issues
9. To elicit admissions from the adverse expert which make the cross-examination appear successful

One legal writer has suggested that three cardinal principles of cross-examination are: (1) keeping your objective hidden; (2) making a mountain out of a molehill; and (3) utilizing a bit-by-bit examination technique rather than rushing in with only a couple of questions.[19]

---

[18]See **§§9.13, 10.26-.31.**

[19]See I. Goldstein & F. Lane, Trial Technique chs 14 & 19 (Callaghan & Co 2d ed 1969).

The reasoning behind these principles is quite sound. First, when the cross-examiner hides the ultimate goal of the examination from a partisan witness, the witness is more likely to tell the truth and not to resist the direction of the examination. Second, the testimony most favorable to the cross-examiner's theory of the case should be emphasized, even if it is only on a minor collateral issue. Third, where certain facts are emphasized in the course of a detailed, crescendo-like examination, the whole subject matter will generally appear more important.

Other basic principles include using leading questions, asking short, simple questions, maintaining an air of confidence, knowing the facts and authority, and resisting the impulse to ask that one extra question which allows the witness to explain why.

Leading questions are an appropriate and effective method of maintaining witness control. However, they are not always required. For instance, when the witness does not need to be controlled or where the answer is unimportant, nonleading questions may create a comfortable change of pace.

§9.10 1. Abstaining—Favorable Testimony

Cross-examination of an adverse expert is generally essential to prevent the expert's testimony from being given devastating weight by the trier of fact. However, on some occasions it is the best policy to abstain from cross-examination of the adverse expert, as when the adverse expert actually provides testimony which appears favorable to the cross-examiner. Abstention from cross-examination precludes that expert from varying, correcting, or explaining such apparently favorable testimony.

In addition, it is important that the cross-examiner not elicit testimony that is inconsistent with the cross-examiner's theory of the case. For instance, in a case involving a settled building foundation, an expert testified on direct examination at trial that the defendant engineer had erroneously designed a certain support foundation for a depth of three feet rather than three-and-one-half feet. On vigorous cross-examination, the young attorney badly impeached the expert with prior inconsistent deposition testimony. The problem, however, was that in the deposition the expert had testified that the proper foundation depth would have been four feet. The end result was that even though the expert had been impeached, the trier of fact came to believe after cross-examination that the cross-examiner's client, the engineer, had committed a more culpable design error than the one it may have believed in before such examination commenced.

§9.11 2. Abstaining—No Effective Attack

Another limited situation in which a cross-examiner may decide to abstain from conducting lengthy cross-examination is where the adverse expert's testimony is consistent with other evidence and cannot be undermined. For instance, in a construction case alleging overstressed materials, the adverse expert testified that certain steel beams in issue had been overstressed. Where the cross-examier's view coincides with the opinion propounded, the cross-examiner may be reluctant to delve into the reasons for the adverse expert's opinion on the cause or responsibility for the construction defect. This is true where the cross-examiner knows that such testimony would tend to buttress the adverse party's conclusion.

Similarly, cross-examination of an expert is necessary only to the extent required to support the cross-examiner's theory of the case. One legal writer[20] has said that the mark of a master trial attorney is to do as little as possible. This includes having the courage to say, "no questions," where nothing will be gained by cross-examining a witness.

§9.12 3. Discrediting Qualifications

An expert qualifies when it is shown that the witness has some specialized knowledge which will help the trier of fact understand the evidence or determine a fact in issue. Once the expert has qualified, the magnitude and depth of the witness's expertise are subject to careful consideration by the trier of fact, which usually compares the expert's qualifications to those of the opposing expert in determing the weight to be given such testimony.

Therefore, in any case in which the qualifications of an adverse expert are not impeccable, cross-examination may be an effective means of emphasizing that fact. The adverse expert's background and experience will usually have been documented prior to trial through the various methods of discovery. The areas of cross-examination about the adverse expert's qualifications run parallel to the relevant subject matter for establishing counsel's expert's qualifications. In deciding what qualifications to emphasize on cross-examination, there must be consideration of the particular subject matter in issue and the respective qualifications of counsel's own expert. Obviously, it would be poor strategy to emphasize deficiencies in the adverse expert's qualifications which counsel's expert shares.

These categories may be considered in challenging an expert's qualifications:

1. Education
2. Work history
3. Professional experience
4. Publications
5. Certification and registration
6. Teaching experience
7. Professional membership
8. Prior expert witness experience
9. Miscellaneous

A more detailed outline suggesting five areas for examining an adverse expert about such follows.[21]

1. Education
    a. Where, when, degrees received, accreditation of school

---

[20] I. Younger, The Art of Cross-Examination (ABA Section of Litigation No 1, 1976).

[21] See **§§7.07, 7.27, 9.03.**

   b. Classes offered, classes taken, classes passed, classes failed, relevant to subject matter of testimony
   c. Thesis written, when and where
   d. Names of professors recognized in the field, and publications of such professors
   e. Formal education in specific subject matter. If any, what, when, where, and whether there have been major changes in field
   f. Continuing education in specific subject matter. If so, what, when, where
2. Work history and experience
   a. When, where, and what
   b. Whether witness held responsible decision-making position. Whether witness worked under another person's supervision
   c. Discussion of any of witness's other experiences that are similar to the subject incident
3. Publications
   a. Names, dates, and subjects of witness's own publications
   b. Publications and writings which witness considers authoritative in the field
4. Registration
   a. Examination versus grandfather clause
5. Prior expert testimony
   a. Prior testimony of the witness, statements made in trials, depositions, writings, etc.

Cross-examining an expert about such expert's qualifications must be done tactfully. The trier of fact, especially a jury, is often psychologically sensitive to one professional criticizing another. For this reason, effective cross-examination may well take the line that the expert is well qualified in general but not in the particular specialty which the case at bar involves. Also, an effective method of cross-examination is to show that the adverse expert has not kept up with the state of the art. After eliciting names of publications and sources of information that the adverse expert considers authoritative, the cross-examiner can produce an expert to testify as to recent significant changes in the engineering field of which the adverse expert was unaware.

§9.13 4. Emphasizing Bias

If true bias can be shown in the testimony of the adverse expert, the credibility and weight given to that expert's testimony will be somewhat affected. Bias can be caused by a number of factors. However, the commonest method of displaying an expert's bias is to show that expert's financial interest in the outcome of the case or that expert's long-term relationship with the party or counsel.[22]

In cross-examining the adverse expert, any financial bias may be shown by eliciting responses to the following questions:

---

[22]See **§§9.08, 10.26-.31.**

1. Who is paying for your testimony?
2. Who paid for your report?
3. Who paid for your research?
4. How much were you paid?
5. What is your rate of compensation?
6. How many times have you worked previously with the party or the attorney?
7. On how many occasions have you testified on behalf of the party and attorney?
8. What percentage of your yearly income do you make from performing such services?

§9.14 5. Discrediting Basis of Opinions

One of the goals of cross-examination is to discredit the adverse expert's conclusions. This can be accomplished by showing the trier of fact that the expert's conclusions are:

1. Incompatible with other trial testimony
2. Incompatible with recognized authoritative books, articles, and writings
3. Incompatible with prior testimony, statements, or publications of the expert
4. Based on erroneous computation of information including opinions or statements of a third person
5. Reached in reliance on certain omissions of relevant data known to the adverse counsel or party but not disclosed to the adverse expert
6. Based on certain limited facts of questionable accuracy

In one case, a structural engineer testified that a ladder in issue was not defective and could not have broken as the plaintiff was ascending.[23] The expert offered stress calculations of the wood component parts to show that instead the ladder must have broken only after the plaintiff had fallen with it to the ground. On cross-examination, the cross-examiner discredited the expert by showing that the expert's calculations were based on an erroneous assumption that the ladder was fixed at a 60-degree angle at the time of use and pointing out that the testimony of the plaintiff had been that the ladder had been placed at a much smaller angle. Therefore, the expert was forced to admit that his conclusions did not address these essential facts.

An adverse expert may also be discredited on the basis of a conclusion which is in conflict with authoritative scientific, technical, or professional texts, treatises, journals, or similar publications. Generally, the jurisdictions vary as to their requirements that:

1. The expert consider the publication authoritative[24]

---

[23]**§§3.27, 3.49.**

[24]Ithier v Solomon, 59 AD2d 935, 399 NYS2d 450 (1977); Jones v Bloom, 388 Mich 98, 200 NW2d 196 (1972).

2. The expert refer to, consider, or rely on the publication[25]
3. The publicaton be considered authoritative for some other reason[26]

The primary purpose of referring to such authoritative publications on cross-examination is to find out whether the adverse expert properly read, interpreted, and applied such materials. If the expert did not rely on them, the purpose of referring to authoritative publications is to test the expert's professional knowledge and conclusions by confrontation with impartially established treatises on the subject.

In either event, many experienced cross-examiners find it impresses the jury if they stack a number of such authoritative publications on the cross-examiner's table during the testimony of the adverse expert. Such a practice creates, the appearance, at least, that the cross-examiner is well versed and qualified in the particular field. Similarly, it makes it easier for counsel to maintain control during cross-examination. On the other hand, some counsel prefer not to reveal their comprehension of the subject matter too early during cross-examination, so that they can offer a comfortable forum in which the adverse expert may offer careless testimony.

In those jurisdictions which require an expert to consider authoritative or rely on a particlar publication before the cross-examiner may discuss it, an expert's refusal to admit that any of the various publications are authoritative creates the impression that the expert is either not that knowledgeable on the subject, unreasonable, or a biased advocate.

The most devastating method of discrediting an adverse expert is to use prior testimony, depositions, admissions, or publications of that expert in conflict with the expert's present testimony. Thorough pretrial discovery of the adverse expert will put the cross-examiner in touch with prior statements made by the expert on the subject in question. Various legal associations and publications maintain lists of experts used in trials. Copies of trial transcripts or depositions could then be obtained through the associations or court services.

In addition, names of articles, books, theses, and other publications, as well as transcribed speeches given by the expert at lectures and seminars may be obtained through pretrial discovery or by searching periodicals indexes and university libraries. It is, of course, essential to learn through pretrial discovery all names ever used by the expert.

Another way of discrediting the basis of an expert opinion is to inquire whether the expert has actually visited the subject site or is familiar with the component parts of and method of manufacturing the product. It is also a fertile area of cross-examination for counsel to look into whether the adverse expert is knowledgeable about the operation and maintenance of the product, since there is a significant difference between the design of a product and its operation and maintenance.

An adverse expert frequently has no firsthand knowledge of the facts in issue but merely bases an opinion on a review of materials provided by the adverse attorney. For example, in one case an expert testified that a particular road curve was improperly

---

[25]Darling II v Charleston Community Memorial Hosp, 50 Ill App 2d 253, 200 NE2d 149 (1964).

[26]Ravenis v Detroit Gen Hosp, 63 Mich App 79, 234 NW2d 411 (1975).

banked and that the recommended speed limit was in excess of the allowable safe speed. On cross-examination the expert admitted that her opinion was based solely on a review of plan and profile sheets[27] and a general description of the plaintiff's vehicle. She admitted that she had made no attempt to negotiate the curve prior to appearing in court and that her opinion was purely theoretical. Of course, on rebuttal, the defendant produced an expert who not only testified as to the safe street design, but also testified that he visited the particular site and successfully negotiated the curve while traveling in a vehicle similar to the plaintiff's vehicle and at a speed 10 miles per hour over the subject speed limit. Theoretical testimony usually runs a poor second to direct experience.

In some cases, a relevant cross-examination area is the total amount of time that the adverse expert spent in inspecting, researching, reviewing, analyzing, and preparing in order to arrive at the desired opinion. Where an engineer or architect is being sued for negligent design, a significant point may be the amount of time that the defendant engineer or architect probably spent on the particular design compared to the time that the adverse expert actually spent in analyzing, testing, researching, and reviewing prior to determining a better design.

§9.15 6. Attempting to Change Opinions

Effective cross-examination can be based on attacking any link in the chain of foundational facts on which the adverse expert's conclusion is based.

For example, in one situation, an accident reconstruction expert testified about a rear-end traffic collision. Based on observations three weeks after the accident that there was no substantial bumper damage to the automobile and that there were no scrapings on the shock-absorbing bumper rods of plaintiff's automobile, the expert concluded that the force of impact between the two vehicles had been minimal. On cross-examination the expert conceded that: (1) movement on the bumper rods would be inversely proportional to the forward movement of plaintiff's automobile on impact;[28] and (2) if plaintiff's automobile freely jumped forward on impact, damage to the bumper as well as movement of the bumper rods could be minimal irrespective of any significant force of impact.

The expert also conceded that if plaintiff's automobile had traveled through mud or experienced extensive rusting during the three-week period before inspection, the conclusions based on absence of scrapings on the bumper rod would have been erroneous. As a result, the cross-examiner was able to elicit from the adverse expert a change in testimony to admit that a significant impact could have occurred and that such an impact, even if it produced movement in the bumper rods, could have gone undetected due to subsequent accumulation of dirt and rust.

As indicated, a thorough cross-examination should inquire into every link in the chain of foundational facts. The basis of each link must be established. Once the substantive basis of each link has been ascertained, the cross-examiner should ask the expert whether the expert's opinion might change if any particular foundational link, or series of links, were modified, omitted, or added. By following this technique and

---

[27] §6.04.

[28] §6.25.

examining each crucial link, the cross-examiner may find an opening to discredit the adverse expert's conclusions. The adage that a chain is as strong as its weakest link appropriately illustrates the giving of weight to an expert's opinion.

Where any foundational link does not depend on verifiable facts, but rather on the experienced value judgment of the expert, the cross-examiner should ask the expert whether that judgment could be wrong.[29] Either response would help the cross-examiner, since an affirmative answer would emphasize fallibility, while a negative answer would indicate an overinflated ego.

§9.16 7. Discrediting on Collateral Issues

An expert witness testifying on the witness stand often appears and acts with the extreme confidence of presumed infallibility. This can work to the cross-examiner's advantage where an expert's arrogance prevents the admission of lack of knowledge on collateral matters.

In one case, an expert testified forcefully that a particular tractor-trailer landing gear was defectively designed in that there was: (1) no safety latch to prevent tipping from an oversetting gear position; and (2) no safety jack to prevent the trailer from tipping from improper loading. On cross-examination, the cross-examiner asked if the expert was familiar with other makes of trailers utilizing safety jacks and oversetting locks. The expert responded in the affirmative. After eliciting details of how these other trailers differed from the subject trailer, the expert was asked to name the manufacturers of these other trailers. After some procrastination, the expert admitted that he could not immediately recall the names of other manufacturers. By his own refusal to back down or to admit limitations in knowledge, the expert's bold opinions were successfully discredited and shown to be unreliable. An expert's arrogance in itself will also tend to have an adverse effect on the trier of fact.

Another method of discrediting an adverse expert on a collateral issue is to point out some act or omission inconsistent with the expert's conclusions. For example, in an injury case, an expert testified on direct examination that a particular tailgate lift of a truck, currently in use, was unsafe because of its propensity to drop due to a defective locking device. The cross-examiner elicited from this expert that although the tailgate lift allegedly posed a substantial danger to users, the expert had not warned or advised the users to discontinue use of operation of the tailgate.

In another injury case, an expert testified for the city that a particular manufactured chair was defectively designed in that its stem was too thin to support the required loads. Here again, the expert never advised the city to discontinue use of other similar chairs. In fact, it was elicited that the city continued to order the same chair model for its employees.

§9.17 8. Emphasizing Collateral Issues

It is usually possible to elicit testimony from an adverse expert which will benefit the cross-examiner's case-in-chief. In one case, a well-qualified civil engineer testified

---

[29] I. Younger, Trial Techniques With Irving Younger (Natl Prac Inst, Minneapolis & Los Angeles, R. Oliphant ed 1978).

on direct examination that the subject warehouse which utilized wood columns for interior supports had been negligently designed and constructed. The warehouse was frequented by forklifts which constantly moved loads throughout the warehouse area. During one such move, a forklift impacted an unprotected, undersized wood column. As a result, the column was severed, the portion of the roof being supported by the column collapsed, and a contractor who happened to be working on that portion of the roof fell to the ground sustaining serious injuries.

The cross-examiner was able to elicit from the expert that although the wood columns were undersized and unprotected from such foreseeable warehouse occurrences, the cost of substituting properly sized and protected columns would be prohibitive. Eventually, in response to repeated questioning the expert reluctantly testified that had he been retained to design and engineer the subject warehouse, he would have specified similar columns.

In addition, the cross-examiner developed testimony that emphasized negligent operation of the forklifts as the primary cause of the incident.

By carefully considering the major and collateral issues relevant to a case, the cross-examiner can often elicit significant testimony from the adverse expert which will prove or buttress the cross-examiner's case-in-chief.

§9.18 9. Appearing Successful

When a qualified expert completes devastating testimony on direct examination, there are often few substantive benefits to be derived from vigorous cross-examination. Notwithstanding, cross-examination should not be waived because of the strong impact on the jury when an expert's conclusions go unchallenged.

One appropriate response to such testimony is for the cross-examiner to ask a series of concise, leading questions to elicit short, affirmative responses from the adverse expert. Limiting and narrowing the scope of responses will prevent the expert from getting into long-winded and flower oratory. Additionally, the jury will get the impression that the adverse expert's testimony has not been totally unfavorable to the cross-examiner's case.

There was one situation in which the adverse expert testified on direct examination that the subject cement mixer was not defective in design, notwithstanding its failure to have a barrel lock or a protective shield covering a cement mixer's intermeshing gears. On cross-examination, the cross-examiner elicited a series of admissions favorable to the cross-examiner's position relating to general principles of design safety, economics in design change, and testing procedures.

By preparing in advance, counsel may be able to insure that the cross-examination of an adverse expert will conclude with the appearance of success. The attorney who carefully forms questions and commits them to writing will be in a position to save the best for last and end the cross-examination on a confident note.

C. Examination of an Expert Regarding Demonstrative Evidence

§9.19 1. Generally

Demonstrative evidence is evidence which directly addresses the senses. This term covers two types. First, it refers to real evidence, or those items which have actually played a part in the case. Included in this category would be design plans, a fractured bolt, or the remains of a tire blowout. The second type of demonstrative evidence is photographs, maps, models, and diagrams. This kind of evidence is offered to illustrate and clarify other evidence, usually oral testimony.

The foundation for demonstrative evidence depends on the particular type of evidence at issue. Where real evidence is being offered, the primary consideration is whether the item being offered can be authenticated as being in substantially the same condition it was in at the time of the subject event.

Where evidence is being offered for illustrative purposes, the primary consideration is whether the item accurately and substantially represents the evidence so that it will assist the trier of fact.

§9.20 2. Direct Examination—Real Engineering Evidence

Before real engineering evidence may be admitted, a proper foundation must be laid. For example, where counsel desires to offer into evidence a defective coupler, it is necessary to establish on direct examination that the particular item proffered is: (1) the same item which was involved in the litigated incident; and (2) in substantially the same condition that it was in at the time of the litigated incident.[30] The latter element of proof can often be verified by establishing the history or chain of control of the item of proffered evidence from the date of the incident to the present. Where counsel is attempting to demonstrate the defective nature of a coupler which failed to function several years earlier, the fact that the coupler has since undergone rusting, substitution of parts, or other changes is relevant to the admissibility and/or weight of such evidence.

§9.21 3. Direct Examination—Illustrative Engineering Evidence

Photographs, diagrams, models, and maps are all examples of demonstrative evidence that may be used to clarify or explain testimony to the trier of fact. For demonstrative evidence to be illustrative, it must be relevant to an issue in the case. Therefore, even though an item of demonstrative evidence may be referred to and marked as an exhibit or an exhibit for identification only, counsel must still lay a foundation to properly show the item's relevance.

Relevance may be established by having a witness testify that the particular exhibit is a true and accurate representation of certain relevant factual matters. In most situations, the witness must be able to identify the item or exhibit from personal knowledge. However, the witness usually need not have actually prepared the exhibit.[31]

Accordingly, in a construction case involving misplacement of a building structure 10 feet west of the property line, counsel had a survey map admitted into evidence by establishing the following:

---

[30]Gutman v Industrial Commn, 71 Ohio App 383, 50 NE2d 187 (1942).

[31]People v Fish, 125 NY 136, 26 NE 319 (1891); Stiasny v Metropolitan St Ry, 58 AD 172, 68 NYS 694, *affd*, 172 NY 656 (1901).

1. That the witness was qualified as a surveyor, or civil engineer
2. The manner by which the survey map was prepared
3. That the survey map was a true and accurate representation of the relevant condition of the property

There is also a prerequisite that the court determine that the probative value of the evidence is not substantially outweighed by any undue prejudice, confusion, or waste of time which the evidence might cause if admitted.[32]

In the same construction case, the court refused to accept into evidence photographs which purportedly illustrated aesthetic depreciation of the property due to proximity of the misplaced structure to other existing monuments. The court reasoned that to admit such two-dimensional photographs might well mislead the jury and cause undue prejudice, since such aesthetic considerations are actually part of a three-dimensional, spatial environment and should be evaluated in that perspective. Accordingly, the court allowed the jury to visit the subject site.

§9.22 4. Cross-Examination—Illustrative Engineering Evidence

Effective cross-examination of a witness with respect to certain items of demonstrative evidence should focus on the same admissibility considerations discussed in **§8.02.** The primary difference is that once the foundation has been sufficiently laid for an exhibit, it is admitted into evidence. The cross-examiner's purpose in cross-examination is to elicit testimony that will diminish the weight given to the evidence by the trier of fact.

Of course, the cross-examiner may be able to exclude the demonstrative evidence where it is possible to challenge successfully:

1. The qualifications of the witness to testify
2. The competency of the witness (lack of personal knowledge)
3. The accuracy and correctness of the evidence
4. The probative value of the evidence

In almost all cases involving engineering evidence, photographs are one type of demonstrative evidence. Yet, photographs often pose admissibility problems because of distortion. Significantly distorted photographs cannot truly and accurately represent the subject condition. Common forms of photographic distortion include color distortion, angle distortion, enlargement distortion, lense distortion, and emulsion deterioration.

---

[32]Bertram v Harris, 423 P2d 909 (Alaska 1967).

10 Statutory and Case Law on Expert Evidence

§10.01 A. What Expert Evidence Is

All evidence is offered to try to prove or disprove certain issues in controversy. The procedure which regulates offers of proof is stringent in demanding that facts admitted into evidence be trustworthy and reliable. Accordingly, a witness generally may not testify on a subject unless it appears that the evidence offered is competent to support a finding that the person has personal or firsthand knowledge of the matter.[1]

Opinion evidence is to be distinguished from personal or firsthand knowledge of a matter in that an opinion is no fact. In essence, an opinion is merely what someone thinks about something. That thought may be correct or incorrect, and still represent the genuine, deep-rooted belief of the person expressing it. While separating mere opinion from fact may be difficult, since fact often develops out of inference, observation, and reflection, the distinction is significant. Under normal circumstances a witness's opinions, as opposed to facts within the witness's knowledge, are irrelevant and inadmissible.[2]

An exception to the rule excluding opinion evidence is expert opinion. Expert

---

[1]Fed R Evid 602.

[2]Schwartz v Peoples Gas Light & Coke Co, 35 Ill App 2d 25, 181 NE2d 826 (1962); Hartley v Szadkowski, 32 AD2d 550, 300 NYS2d 82 (1969).

evidence is generally opinion testimony given by a witness who qualifies as an expert by special knowledge, skill, experience, training, or education, distinctly related to some scientific, technical, or other specialized knowledge which will assist the trier of fact in understanding, evaluating, and deciding complex evidentiary issues.[3] An expert witness is in the unique position of being capable of rendering an opinion (*opinion* is used broadly and includes inferences, conclusions, and other subjective statements made by the witness[4]) or drawing an inference from facts which the layperson would not be competent to evaluate. Further, the expert is in a position to explain and discuss technical, scientific, or other specialized knowledge material to the case, leaving the trier of fact to apply such knowledge to the facts.[5] Experts are not required to be professionals with university degrees, certificates, or memberships. They need only be sufficiently skilled in their fields of specialty.

§10.02 1. How Expert Testimony Is Used

When a subject matter in issue is considered sufficiently beyond the knowledge of a layperson, expert testimony must be used to assist the trier of fact in resolving disputed issues. Expert testimony is particularily common in engineering-related cases, which deal with construction,[6] transportation,[7] catastrophic,[8] and manufacturing problems.[9] Some specific cases in which expert engineering evidence has been used include the following: consulting engineer[10] establishing construction, safety, and characteristics of terrazzo steps;[11] licensed architect[12] used to establish condition of stair tread;[13] chemical engineer[14] proving that hole in pavement had been in existence not less than four weeks prior to automobile accident;[15] consulting engineer establishing time it took for vehicle to traverse certain distance;[16] electrical engineer[17] showing that machine was not safely designed;[18] mechanical engineer establishing that design of a snap-tie was unsuitable for supporting scaffolding;[19] civil engineer[20] indicating effect of certain

---

[3]Fed R Evid 702; United States v RJ Reynolds Tobacco Co, 416 F Supp 313 (D NJ 1976).

[4]Cal Evid Code §800, Comment-Law Revision Comm.

[5]Fed R Evid 702, Advisory Comm's Notes.

[6]See **ch 4.**

[7]See **ch 6.**

[8]See **ch 5.**

[9]**Ch 3.**

[10]**§2.02.**

[11]Associated Dry Goods Corp v Drake, 394 F2d 637 (8th Cir 1968).

[12]**§2.06.**

[13]Naney v Lane, 247 Or 367, 428 P2d 722 (1967).

[14]**§2.09.**

[15]Chambers v Kansas City, 446 SW2d 833 (Mo 1969).

[16]Forney v Calvin, 35 Ill App 3d 32, 340 NE2d 603 (1975).

[17]**§2.08.**

[18]Grant v National Acme Co, 351 F Supp 972 (WD Mich 1972).

[19]Gates & Sons, Inc v Brock, 199 So 2d 291 (Fla 1967).

[20]**§2.03.**

land development on flooding;[21] hydraulic engineer[22] determining cost of constructing lateral ditch for irrigation purposes;[23] and civil engineer showing whether certain construction work was consistent with plans and specifications.[24]

§10.03 2. Admissibility of Expert Testimony—Subject Matter

Generally, expert testimony is not admissible where the subject at issue is a matter of common knowledge. When this is the case, the matter should be decided by the trier of fact without the assistance of expert evidence.

Some courts are reluctant to permit expert testimony, believing that it usurps the function of the jury.[25] Nevertheless, the modern trend is to permit expert witnesses to testify not only where the subject matter is complicated and outside the knowledge and understanding of the common layperson, but also where the subject matter is within such common knowledge and understanding but is difficult to explain and comprehend.

Accordingly, in a New York case,[26] an expert builder testified that the weakness of certain notched building joists rendered a grandstand structure unable to bear the strain put on it, and that this resulted in its collapse. The court received the expert testimony on the theory that the jury, not being made up of builders who would be acquainted with the means of securing strength and security to a grandstand structure, could be enlightened by the judgment and experience of an expert familiar with such structures.

On the other hand, in an Illinois case,[27] the court held that an expert's testimony, that a plaintiff's fall off a scaffold could have been prevented if guardrails had been installed, was inadmissible since there was nothing complicated or difficult to comprehend about the fact situation.

With respect to expert testimony on interpreting safety codes, a New Jersey court[28] held that the interpretation of the National Electrical Code,[29] as it applied to the situation of an overhead power line which caused severe injuries when it came in contact with the boom of a crane, was not a proper subject of expert testimony. Rather, such interpretation was for the trial court.

At the same time, the mere fact that expert testimony is not required in a particular case does not make it reversible error for the court to permit an expert to testify.[30]

---

[21]Kuklinska v Maplewood Homes, Inc, 336 Mass 489, 146 NE2d 523 (1957).

[22]**§2.20.**

[23]Morrison v Cottonwood Dev Co, 38 Wyo 190, 266 P 117 (1928).

[24]Sioux City v Western Asphalt Paving Corp, 223 Iowa 279, 271 NW 624 (1937).

[25]Baptiste v Boatmen's Natl Bank, 148 SW2d 743 (Mo 1941); Stillwell v Schmoker, 175 Neb 595, 122 NW2d 538 (1963), but note that *Stillwell* was superseded by state statute §27-704 RRS 1943 as discussed in State v Rotella, 196 Neb 741, 246 NW2d 74 (1976).

[26]Fox v Buffalo Park, 163 NY 559, 57 NE 1109 (1900).

[27]Hernandez v Power Constr Co, 73 Ill 2d 90, 382 NE2d 1201, 22 Ill Dec 503 (1978).

[28]Gallas v Public Serv Elec & Gas Co, 106 NJ Super 527, 256 A2d 289 (1969).

[29]**§4.40, App A.**

[30]Naney v Lane, 247 Or 367, 428 P2d 722 (1967).

It should also be noted that admissibility of expert evidence is at all times dependent on the court finding that the state of the art of the particular type of testimony has gained general acceptance in the field to which it relates[31]

§10.04 3. Qualifying the Expert

Generally, an expert witness is qualified[32] to offer an opinion if the court finds that the expert, because of certain skill, experience, education, or training, is better able to form an accurate opinion on the matter under consideration than is a layperson. Determination of the expert's qualification is a preliminary question for the trial court, and will not be reversed unless clearly in error.[33]

In considering the expert's qualifications, the court does not require that a party produce the most qualified expert available. Rather, the court's inquiry focuses on whether the expert's knowledge of the subject matter probably will help the jury ascertain the truth.

§10.05 4. Two Classes of Experts

There are two classes of cases in which expert testimony is admissible. The first includes those cases in which the conclusions to be drawn by the trier of fact depend on facts which are not common knowledge. Instead, these facts are within the knowledge of certain persons whose skill, experience, or education enables them to speak with authority on the subject. In this first class, the trier of fact, if provided with all the evidence, can form its own conclusions. In fact, it is the trier of fact's sole province to do so.[34]

The second class takes in cases in which the conclusions to be drawn from the facts, as well as knowledge of the facts, depend on technical or scientific skill, experience, or study which are not within common knowledge. In this class, the facts as well as the conclusions to which those facts lead are proper subjects of expert testimony. The practical result is that, in one instance, the facts are stated by the expert and the conclusions are drawn by the trier of fact. In the other, the expert states the facts and gives the conclusions in the form of an opinion which is accepted or rejected by the trier of fact.[35]

§10.06 5. Weight of Expert Evidence

The weight and probative value which is given to expert testimony is a matter which is exclusively within the domain of the trier of fact. Such testimony is not necessarily

---

[31]Tonkovich v Department of Labor & Indus of State, 31 Wash 2d 220, 195 P2d 638 (1948); United States v Kilgus, 571 F2d 508 (9th Cir 1978).

[32]**§§2.45-.52, 7.27, 9.03, 9.12.**

[33]Hagen v Swenson, 306 Minn 527, 236 NW2d 161 (1975).

[34]Dougherty v Milliken, 163 NY 527, 533, 57 NE 757 (1900).

[35]*Id.*

conclusive or controlling even when uncontradicted by testimony of other experts.[36] The factors which determine the weight and bear on the value accorded to expert testimony are similar to those which govern the weight given to nonexpert testimony. In other words, bias, prejudice, character weakness, discrepancies in testimony, qualifications, care taken, and basis for the witness's reasoning are elements considered by the trier of fact in the overall context of common sense and the surrounding facts and circumstances of the case.[37]

The trier of fact is not required to accept an expert's opinion on the relevant issues where it finds such opinion to be in conflict with other evidence or in contradiction with common sense. In addition, in resolving any conflicts in the testimony of expert witnesses, the trier of fact is to weigh the opinion of one expert against that of another, taking into consideration the qualifications and credibility of the respective expert witnesses.

Justice Drew of the Pennsylvania Supreme Court wrote the following on the weight to be afforded to expert opinion:

> An opinion is only that: it creates no fact. It is what someone thinks about something, and the thought may be precisely accurate or totally inaccurate, and yet represent the absolutely honest conviction of the person who expresses it. Because of this, opinion evidence is generally considered of a low grade, and not entitled to much weight against positive testimony of actual facts. There is a great difference between factual and opinion testimony. In the one the witness testifies to the fact and certifies that what he says of it is true. In the other, he only testifies to his opinion that such a thing is true, and certifies only to his integrity of belief. He says he believes his opinion to be correct, but he does not warrant it to be true, and does not pretend that he cannot be mistaken. The world is mad with opinions upon every imaginable subject, but fortunately we only have to take those we approve. And so it is with juries; they may reject in toto the opinion of any witness they disbelieve, and this whether that opinion is contradicted or not.[38]

However, where expert testimony covers matters actually perceived by the expert and the expert's testimony stands unimpeached, it cannot be ignored. In addition, where the subject of testimony is not a matter of general knowledge, but rather falls under an area of expertise of which a layperson could have no understanding or knowledge, the trier of fact must rely to a great extent on the testimony of a qualified expert.[39]

§10.07 6. Limitation and Weight on Number of Experts

Since all matters relating to the conduct of a trial are within the sound discretion of the court, the court may impose reasonable limitations on the number of expert

---

[36]Buckhanon v State, 151 Ga 827, 108 SE 209 (1921); Sloan v Baird, 162 NY 327, 56 NE 752 (1900).

[37]Cohn v City & Town of Hartford, 130 Conn 699, 37 A2d 237 (1944); Windham v City of Florence, 221 SC 350, 70 SE2d 553 (1952).

[38]Ray v City of Philadelphia, 344 Pa 439, 441-42, 25 A2d 145 (1942).

[39]Mims v United States, 375 F2d 135, 143 (5th Cir 1967).

witnesses to be called on any subject. However, the facts of a particular case determine what a reasonable number is.[40]

In addition, it is well established that the weight to be given to expert testimony is not simply a matter of the number of expert witnesses who testify.[41] Rather, the number of experts who testify is merely a factor which may be considered by the trier of fact along with other matters in evaluating the weight it gives to certain testimony.

B. Basis of Expert Testimony

§10.08 1. Generally

An expert may testify as to an opinion based on personal observation,[42] facts in the record at the time the expert testifies,[43] a hypothetical question given to the expert by the attorney in court,[44] or material reasonably relied on by the expert in forming an opinion on the subject to which the testimony relates.[45]

§10.09 2. Personal Knowledge

An expert who has had an opportunity to personally observe the pertinent facts may describe those observations and offer an opinion based on them. In a typical case, the court held that a mechanical engineer who was familiar with a particular type of machine and the kind of work it performed could offer an opinion on whether the machine was completed in conformity with the controlling specifications.[46]

Some courts require the expert to disclose on direct examination the underlying facts or data on which the opinion is based.[47] Other courts follow the rule that the expert need not state the underlying facts and data since such expert may be required to disclose the grounds for an opinion on cross-examination.[48]

§10.10 3. Nonpersonal Data

Some courts allow an expert to base an opinion on facts and data presented to the expert outside of court and by other means than the expert's own observations. These

---

[40]Hill v Meister, 133 Ill App 2d 678, 273 NE2d 643 (1971); Fuhrman v Fuhrman, 254 NW2d 97 (ND 1977); Commonwealth ex rel Amorso v Amorso, 212 Pa Super Ct 94, 239 A2d 878 (1968).

[41]Motion Picture Appeal Bd of Chicago v SK Films, 65 Ill App 3d 217, 382 NE2d 103, 21 Ill Dec 809 (1978).

[42]Holecek v Janke, 171 NW2d 94 (ND 1969).

[43]Fed R Evid 703.

[44]Barnett v State Workmen's Compensation Commr, 153 W Va 796, 172 SE2d 698 (1970).

[45]Cal Evid Code §801(b) (West).

[46]Fernholtz Mach Co v Wilson, 118 Cal App 573, 5 P2d 679 (1931).

[47]State Highway Commn v Barnes, 151 Mont 300, 443 P2d 16 (1968).

[48]Fed R Evid 705; Cal Evid Code §802 (West); NJ Evid R 57, 58, NJ Stat Ann §2A:84A-32 (West).

facts and data need not be admissible into evidence if they are reasonably relied on by experts in the particular field in forming opinions or inferences on the subject. This procedure of admitting opinion testimony, based in part on reports of others which are not in evidence but which the expert customarily relies on in professional practice, is aimed at bringing judicial practice into line with practices of experts when not in court.[49]

However, the majority view is that an expert's opinion is improper if it is based on reports, statements, or textbook material that is not in evidence or which is inadmissible as substantive evidence because it is considered hearsay.[50] (For our purposes, *Hearsay* is defined as a statement, other than one made by the declarant while testifying at trial, offered in evidence to prove the truth of the matter asserted.[51]) One major exception is where materials refer to subjects in the exact sciences, as opposed to matters of current scientific opinion.[52]

§10.11 4. Hypothetical Questions

An expert without personal knowledge of the relevant factual issues in a dispute may still give an expert opinion if the expert attends the court trial and hears the testimony making the record, or if the expert is asked to assume certain facts and render an opinion based on them. The latter method involves a hypothetical question.

Even though a hypothetical question to an expert must be based on facts in evidence, considerable latitude is allowed in framing it. In addition, the expert may not only assume facts which the evidence justifies, but the hypothetical may be based on any reasonable inference from the evidence.[53]

Obviously, where the question propounded to the expert is based on voluminous records and documents, counsel will be unable to construct an intelligible hypothetical covering every factual detail appearing in the record. The courts are not concerned with omissions or errors in the propounded hypotheticals as long as they are inconsequential. Where any fact assumed in the hypothetical question has not been established by the evidence, the trier of fact must determine the effect of that omission on the value of the opinion.[54] However, an expert opinion based on a hypothetical question not supported by the evidence is not evidence, and has no probative value.[55] The opinion of the expert must fall with the hypothesis.

Where the expert's opinion conflicts with lay testimony, the trier of fact is not required to give such expert testimony preference. Rather, it must be considered along with all other evidence.[56]

---

[49]Fed R Evid 703, Advisory Comm's Notes.

[50]Sykes v Norfolk & West Ry, 200 Va 559, 106 SE2d 746 (1959).

[51]Fed R Evid 801(c).

[52]*See* 29 Am Jur Evidence 2d (*Printed Matter*) §889 (1967).

[53]Rosenberg v Goldstein, 247 Cal App 2d 25, 55 Cal Rptr 306 (1966).

[54]California Book of Approved Jury Instructions (BAJI) 2.42 (6th rev ed 1977).

[55]Heard v United States, 348 F2d 43 (DC Cir 1964).

[56]Shapiro v Wendell Packing Co, 366 Mich 289, 115 NW2d 87 (1962).

§10.12 a. Necessity for Hypothetical Questions

An expert generally can offer an opinion on a matter as to which the expert is acquainted with the facts by personal perception or observation, or by assuming facts not personally known. Therefore, an expert need not be asked a hypothetical question before such expert states an opinion.[57] However, the value of framing a hypothetical question, especially in complicated matters, is that it not only provides a chance for counsel to argue the case, but it also enables counsel to present a clear statement of the facts on which the expert will base an opinion. Finally, an effectively prepared hypothetical question will often emphasize some important factual matter not fully appreciated by the jury during the initial testimony.

§10.13 b. Objections to Hypothetical Questions

Counsel may object to a hypothetical question propounded by opposing counsel which omits or misstates a significant fact. Procedurally, where counsel points out errors contained in a proposed hypothetical question, opposing counsel has an opportunity to rephrase the question. However, where counsel fails to raise a timely objection, and where opposing counsel is deprived of the opportunity to correct any errors, counsel may not raise the issue for the first time on appeal.[58]

A properly raised objection based on assumption of facts not in evidence or omission of material facts in evidence should be sustained. It is proper as well to object to a hypothetical question where the witness is not qualified or where no foundation for the question was established. In any event, a hypothetical question which seeks an opinion on a matter of common knowledge is objectionable on the grounds that it is not a proper subject of expert opinion testimony.

C. Disclosure of Expert Evidence

§10.14 1. Attorney-Client Privilege

Full disclosure of information between attorney and client is essential to insure that the client will freely confer with and confide in the attorney, and not be deprived of adequate advice and proper defense.[59] To promote this policy, most communications between an attorney and client are privileged, and an attorney is ethically obligated to preserve the confidences and secrets of a client.[60]

This traditional privilege of attorney-client communication exempts from discovery relevant written communications between the attorney and client which are in the attorney's file.[61] However, where the client is in possession of relevant writings between

---

[57]Cal Evid Code §801(b) (West); Crawford v Rogers, 406 P2d 189 (Alaska 1965).

[58]Strickland v Perruccio, 5 Conn Cir Ct 142, 246 A2d 810 (1968).

[59]Baird v Koerner, 279 F2d 623 (9th Cir 1960).

[60]ABA Canons of Professional Responsibility No 4.

[61]Wise v Western Union Tel Co, 178 A 640 (Del Super Ct 1935).

the client and an expert, merely forwarding those writings to the attorney for placement in the attorney's file will not evoke the privilege.[62]

§10.15 2. Work Product Doctrine

Similar to the attorney-client privilege in its policy of encouraging maximum disclosure is the attorney's work product doctrine. This doctrine generally enables the attorney to retain an expert to help with an extensive and thorough investigation of the case for trial. In addition, this doctrine lets the attorney and the expert analyze the unfavorable aspects of a case as well as the favorable ones without allowing the adversary to take undue advantage of the attorney's industry and efforts.[63]

Under the Federal Rules of Civil Procedure, a model for provisions in several states, the work product of the attorney, that is, documents and tangible evidence prepared in anticipation of litigation, or in preparation for trial, by or for a party or any representative acting on the party's behalf, is discoverable only on a special showing. Such a special showing would be that the other party seeking discovery has a substantial need for the material and is unable without undue hardship to obtain the substantial equivalent of the material by other means.[64] Notwithstanding that a party has made the requisite showing, courts have generally protected against disclosure of documents containing mental impressions, conclusions, opinions, or legal theories of an attorney or other representative of a party, concerning litigation. Thus, a court may order that certain portions of disclosed materials be deleted.

In a case concerning allegedly inaccurate soil borings made by the defendant, the court held that reports and photographs submitted to the plaintiff by the plaintiff's independent soil expert 19 months prior to the actual filing of the lawsuit were subject to disclosure to the defendant on the ground that the time lag created a prima facie assumption that the reports were not materials prepared in anticipation of litigation.[65]

In another case, the court held that laboratory test reports on certain machinery which had been damaged while being tested were subject to discovery. The court reasoned that since the machinery was no longer available for inspection by the adverse party, withholding such reports would result in an injustice to the demanding party.[66]

On the other hand, in a case where defendant's metallurgist expert inspected and analyzed certain broken machine parts, and the plaintiff's attorney was advised that plaintiff could have his own expert inspect and analyze the relevant parts, the report of the defendant's expert's conclusions and opinions was not discoverable.[67]

§10.16 3. Expert Witness-Expert Consultant

Rule 26(b)(4) of the Federal Rules of Civil Procedure, which is followed in the rules of other states,[68] deals with discovery of facts and opinions obtained by a party from an expert retained by that party in relation to litigation or trial.

---

[62] Palatini v Sarian, 15 NJ Super 34, 83 A2d 24 (1951).

[63] Cal Civ Proc Code §2016(g) (West); NY Civ Prac Law §3101(c) (McKinney).

[64] Fed R Civ P 26(b)(3); NY Civ Prac Law §3101(d) (McKinney).

[65] Board of Educ v Ace Test Boring, Inc, 47 Misc 2d 864, 263 NYS2d 193 (1965).

[66] Haywood v Willard Mountain, Inc, 48 Misc 2d 1032, 266 NYS2d 453 (1966).

[67] Hoagland v TVA, 34 FRD 458 (ED Tenn 1963).

[68] *See* Ark Stat Ann §28-348; Willet v General Elec Co, 113 NH 358, 306 A2d 789 (1973).

Subsection (b)(4)(A) provides for discovery of facts and opinions held by an expert who is to testify at trial. Under this provision, a requesting party must first serve interrogatories on a party who intends to use an expert at trial. These interrogatories may require the other party to:

1. Identify each person the party expects to call as an expert witness at trial
2. Indicate the subject matter about which the expert is expected to testify
3. State the substance of the facts and opinions to which the expert is expected to testify
4. Summarize the grounds for each opinion

The court may order further discovery to be carried out by means other than interrogatories. The court also may regulate the timing and scope of discovery to prevent abuse by the requesting party. Generally, when further discovery is ordered, the court also will order that the expert be reasonably compensated.

Subsection (b)(4)(B) of Rule 26 deals with the case of an expert who has been retained by the party in anticipation of litigation or in preparation for trial (as distinguished from a general employee) in a consulting capacity, and who is not expected to be called as a witness. Under this subsection, discovery of any facts or opinions held by such consulting expert is permissible only on a showing of exceptional circumstances, that is, that it would be impracticable for the party seeking discovery to obtain facts or opinions on the same subject by other means.[69] However, names and addresses of retained or specially employed consultants are discoverable.[70] It should be pointed out that this subsection appears to preclude discovery against experts who were informally consulted but not retained or specially employed.[71]

Where discovery is allowed, the court is to require the party seeking discovery to: (1) pay the expert a reasonable fee for time spent in responding to discovery; and (2) pay the other party a fair portion of the fees and expenses incurred in originally obtaining facts and opinions from the expert.[72]

Courts generally encourage the use of consulting experts to bring a greater understanding of the merits into the attorney's file. Engaging a consulting expert to assist in evaluating a case is a necessary part of the efficient and accurate determination of liability and settlement prospects. In addition, an attorney often finds it expedient to seek a consulting expert long before making any decision about litigation. Such an expert will be in a position to obtain evidence and perform tests while events and recollections are fresh, and while the physical evidence is available in its original form and condition. To encourage such diligence, the courts tend to protect facts and opinions obtained by consultants absent a showing of special need or hardship on the part of the adverse party.

On the other hand, if the consultant becomes a designated prospective witness, the facts and opinions obtained by the expert are then discoverable.[73] An expert is con-

---

[69]Crenna v Ford Motor Co, 12 Wash App 824, 532 P2d 290 (1975).

[70]Sea Colony, Inc v Continental Ins Co, 63 FRD 113 (D Del 1974).

[71]Baki v BF Diamond Constr, 71 FRD 179 (D Md 1976).

[72]Fed R Civ P 26(b)(4)(C)(ii).

[73]Williamson v Superior Court, 21 Cal 3d 829, 582 P2d 126, 148 Cal Rptr 39 (1978).

sidered as *expected to testify* if and when it becomes reasonably probable that the expert will be called as a witness.[74]

The distinction between expert consultant and expert witness is an important consideration in the preparation and structuring of successful litigation. Each role must be carefully thought out by the attorney in light of the consequences of each. In the first role, the expert is employed in a *consulting* capacity. This means that the expert is employed not as a prospective witness to be used at trial, but rather to aid the attorney in the preparation of the case.

As noted, when an expert has been retained by an attorney on a consulting basis, the work product doctrine generally protects from disclosure of the expert's knowledge, opinions, and reports except under certain conditions. One condition is where denial of disclosure of the expert's information would unfairly prejudice the party seeking disclosure or would result in an injustice.[75]

A second condition which limits the work product doctrine in the case of consulting experts is *waiver*. Since full disclosure is a preferred policy and privilege tends to greatly inhibit such desired expedience, the attorney must vigorously claim work product at every stage where disclosure is sought. If the holder fails to raise it in response to interrogatories, depositions, requests for production of documents, or at hearing, work product will be deemed waived and discovery will be allowed.[76]

A third exceptional condition, in some jurisdictions, arises in situations where the expert is employed long before retention of the attorney. This might happen in construction—design settings where a party retains an engineering consultant to study or report on a certain disputed situation before having any thoughts of litigation.[77]

As noted, the attorney work product doctrine may not apply to a consulting expert who submits studies or reports to a client at a time when such client is not preparing for litigation. When this is the case, eventual transmittal of a consultant's findings to a client's subsequently retained attorney will not affect the result if the material was not obtained or produced in preparation for litigation.[78]

§10.17 4. Exchange of Expert Lists

In light of the tactical advantage that could be gained by limiting the period of time during which a party's expert witness would be exposed or subjected to discovery, some attorneys would intentionally delay naming their expert witnesses.

In response to such practices and with the intent of codifying a full disclosure policy, California has enacted legislation on discovery of expert witnesses. The California law provides that not later than the sixteenth day after a trial date is selected or 70 days before the trial date, any party may file and serve on any other party a demand to exchange lists of expert witnesses. The failure of a party to timely respond constitutes a waiver of that party's right to call an expert witness at trial.[79]

---

[74]Workman v Public Serv Co, 113 NH 422, 308 A2d 540 (1973).

[75]Mack v Superior Court, 259 Cal App 2d 7, 66 Cal Rptr 280 (1968).

[76]Hurley v McMillan, 268 SW2d 229 (Tex Civ App 1954).

[77]Thomas Organ Co v Jadranska Slobodna Plovidba, 54 FRD 367 (ND Ill 1972), *contra,* State ex rel Shelby Mut Ins Co v Circuit Court, 67 Wis 2d 469, 228 NW2d 161 (1975).

[78]Bank of the Orient v Superior Court, 67 Cal App 3d 588, 136 Cal Rptr 741 (1977).

[79]See Cal Civ Proc Code §§2037-.9 (West).

The intent behind such provisions is to promote the mutual and equitable exchange of data between parties. However, a demand for the disclosure of adverse expert witnesses who might be called to testify made while the trial date is still unscheduled, is premature.[80]

§10.18 5. Suppression Agreement

A recent California case[81] concerned a plaintiff who was attempting to discover a report prepared by an expert who had been engaged by one of the defendants.

The defendant in question had originally intended to call the expert as a witness at trial. However, in return for a codefendant's promise of indemnification, the defendant who employed the expert subsequently withdrew the expert as a witness. The issue considered by the court was whether withdrawal of the expert witness because of such an indemnification agreement re-established the privilege against disclosure which defendant's report had originally enjoyed.

In reviewing the facts, the court said that such an agreement between codefendants showed a very real potential for "subtle but deliberate attempts to suppress relevant evidence," which is void or against public policy in California and in most common law jurisdictions.[82]

The opinion also pointed out that if such suppression agreements were condoned by the trial court, one party in a multiparty case might be encouraged to auction off an expert witness's testimony to the highest bidder.[83]

D. Court-Appointed Experts

§10.19 1. Generally

A primary criticism of the use of experts in the judicial process is that they have become professional advocates. The search for the best expert is in fact a search for the best witness, not the most knowledgeable one. Expert shopping is prevalent. It is not uncommon for a party to consult with four different experts and request the honest opinion of each on the particular factual situation. The result often will be that two experts support the party and two do not. The two that support the party will be asked to give evidence based on a partisan hypothetical. The other two will be thanked and dismissed. Needless to say, this is the practice of both sides. Unfortunately, such carefully chosen and biased expert testimony often has diminished worth since it complicates and prolongs litigation to such an extent that it is often impossible for the trier of fact to resolve the issues on the merits. In addition, the propensity of some experts to respond to monetary influence stains the credibility of the reputable experts.

One remedy to the problem of the battle of the experts is to have the court appoint

---

[80]South Tahoe Pub Util Dist v Superior Court, 90 Cal App 3d 135, 154 Cal Rptr 1 (1979).

[81]Williamson v Superior Court, 21 Cal 3d 829, 582 P2d 126, 148 Cal Rptr 39 (1978).

[82]Williamson v Superior Court of Los Angeles County, 21 Cal 3d 829, 836-37, 582 P2d 126, 148 Cal Rptr 39, 44 (1978).

[83]*Id* at 838, 148 Cal Rptr at 45.

or summons expert witnesses on its own motion. The disinterested court-appointed expert will be able to review the entire case history, and render and substantiate an opinion to the trier of fact without having an allegiance to any of the parties. Generally, court appointment of an expert is most appreciated where there is great diversity among the opinions of the partisan experts. In such a case an impartial opinion would aid the trier of fact. These procedures are by no means limited to modern times. Cases were noted in the fourteenth century in which judges would summon experts to aid them in determining scientific issues.[84]

The court has inherent power to appoint disinterested expert witnesses on its own motion.[85] There is statutory authority in many jurisdictions for the appointment of experts by the court. Some of these statutes are broad and apply to any type of expert evidence.[86] Other statutes limit court appointments of experts to criminal cases only.[87]

Nevertheless, it is unlikely that court-appointed experts would ever take the place of partisan experts for the reason that the neutral expert is unable to help the attorney review the file, participate in settlement discussions, or prepare for litigation. In addition, the court-appointed expert is almost always appointed late in the prelitigation stage of a lawsuit.[88]

§10.20 2. Modern Trend

Typical of the modern trend is Rule 706 of the Federal Rules of Evidence. This rule covers all types of experts in all types of cases, and provides:

> (a) Appointment. The court may on its own motion or on the motion of any party enter an order to show cause why expert witnesses should not be appointed, and may request the parties to submit nominations. The court may appoint any expert witnesses agreed upon by the parties, and may appoint witnesses of its own selection. An expert witness shall not be appointed by the court unless he consents to act. A witness so appointed shall be informed of his duties by the court in writing, a copy of which shall be filed with the clerk, or at a conference in which the parties shall have opportunity to participate. A witness so appointed shall advise the parties of his findings, if any; his deposition may be taken by any party; and he may be called to testify by the court or any party. He shall be subject to cross-examination by each party, including a party calling him as a witness.
>
> (b) Compensation. Expert witnesses so appointed are entitled to reasonable compensation in whatever sum the court may allow. The compensation thus fixed is payable from funds which may be provided by law in criminal cases

[84]McCormick on Evidence 38 n 18 (2d ed 1972), *citing* Rosenthal, *The Development of the Use of Expert Testimony,* Law & Contemp Prob 403, 406-11 (1935).

[85]Kennedy v Parrott, 243 NC 355, 90 SE2d 754 (1956).

[86]Fed R Evid 706; Cal Evid Code §730 (West); Sup Ct R 215, Ill Rev Stat, ch 110A, §215(d) (1967); Neb R Evid 706, Neb Rev Stat §27-706; Nev Rev Stat §27-706; NM R Evid 706, NM Stat Ann vol 1 (1978); Wis Stat Ann §907.06 (West).

[87]Wis Stat Ann §957.27 (West).

[88]Notes, *Contingent Fees for Expert Witnesses in Civil Litigation,* 86 Yale LJ 1680 (1977).

and civil actions and proceedings involving just compensation under the Fifth Amendment. In other civil actions and proceedings the compensation shall be paid by the parties in such proportion and at such time as the court directs, and thereafter charged in like manner as other costs.

(c) Disclosure of appointment. In the exercise of its discretion, the court may authorize disclosure to the jury of the fact that the court appointed the expert witness.

(d) Parties' experts of own selection. Nothing in this rule limits the parties in calling expert witnesses of their own selection.

It is apparent that one of the benefits resulting from court appointment of an expert is improved administration of objective fact-finding and evaluation. In addition, the trial itself generally will proceed at a faster rate, since cross-examination on collateral matters is limited.

Irrespective of these benefits, however, some attorneys still resist or resent court appointment of an expert, since it may not necessarily be in the client's best interests. Cross-examination of a court-appointed expert with respect to that expert's own personal prejudices on the basis of the expert's opinions may be more difficult. This is true where the witness has disclosed to the jury the fact of being court-appointed, and the jury is unduly impressed to the point of endowing the witness's testimony with judicial approval.

One method of reducing this problem, provided for under Federal Rule 706(a) is for the parties jointly to agree on a competent and objective expert. Another is for the court not to disclose to the jury that the expert is court-appointed. While this might prevent the jury from giving too much weight to the expert's testimony, it would also substantially reduce furtherance of the policy behind the rule. The better procedure would seem to be for such disclosure to be discretionary. Where special circumstances would make disclosure unfair, the court could prohibit it. Otherwise, disclosure should be allowed as long as there is an admonition in the jury instructions that testimony from a court-appointed expert is not entitled to greater credence and weight than other evidence.

§10.21 3. Waiver of Right

Appointment of an expert may be made by the court on its own motion or on the motion of any party. However, a party who fails to request court appointment of an expert waives any right to object to the court's failure to act on its own initiative.[89] A court is under no duty to call a court-appointed expert unless request is made by a party.[90] In addition, a party's request that the court appoint an expert is generally subject to the court's discretion.[91] In one New York case, the court held that in the absence of a showing of financial necessity it would not appoint an expert, even if the

[89] Daly City v Smith, 110 Cal App 2d 524, 533, 243 P2d 46 (1952).

[90] Vey v State, 35 Ohio App 324, 172 NE 434 (1929).

[91] Laguna Salada Union Elementary School Dist v Pacific Dev Co, 119 Cal App 2d 470, 473, 259 P2d 498 (1953).

parties had agreed on one, since the policy behind the rule was not that the state should provide gratuitous expert witness services.[92]

§10.22 4. Practical Considerations

Even though existence of procedures for court appointment of experts is common, the practice is not readily followed at present.

There are several reasons for this situation. There may be more than one school of thought on the matter of which expert evidence is required. If an expert is selected who represents only one school of thought, the trier of fact's function has been usurped and a party may be denied the right to present opposing views. Second, the court-appointed expert may have excessive influence over the trier of fact since the expert is colored with judicial approval. Third, even court-appointed experts have latent, if not patent, personal prejudices. Notwithstanding such prejudices, counsel is significantly limited in successful cross-examination because of the expert's status in the eyes of the trier of fact.

A remedy for one of the above problems would be for the court also to appoint an expert from an opposing school of thought, so that the trier of fact would have an opportunity to fully evaluate and consider the matter. Alternatively, the court-appointed expert could be required to testify with respect to differing schools of thought and authorities. Some courts provide that even though there may be a court-appointed expert, a party may still produce other expert evidence on the same fact or matter.[93]

It has been said that availability of a procedure by which the court is entitled to call and disclose to the jury that it appointed the expert witness actually decreases the need to resort to that procedure.[94] This is because the readily accessible mechanism by which a court may appoint an expert in a given situation encourages realistic and effective selection of a reputable expert by the party utilizing expert services.[95]

§10.23 5. Compensation of Court-Appointed Experts

Compensation of court-appointed experts, like compensation of experts in general, is of particular interest to the parties as well as to the experts themselves. In several states the courts are empowered to determine the fee for court-appointed expert services at any amount which appears to be reasonable to such court.[96] Rules of evidence in these states also provide that in most civil action, the fee initially fixed by the court is to be apportioned and charged to the several parties proportionately as the court may determine. Thereafter, the fee may be taxed and allowed in the same manner as other costs.[97]

---

[92]Pedi v Phillips, 1 Misc 2d 1061, 149 NYS2d 753 (1956).

[93]Cal Evid Code §733 (West).

[94]Fed R Evid 706(c); Cal Evid Code §722(a) (West).

[95]Fed R Evid 706, Advisory Comm's Notes.

[96]Cal Evid Code §730 (West); NM R Evid 706(b), NM Stat Ann, vol 1 (1978); RI Gen Laws §9-17-19; Wis Sup Ct R 907.06(2), Wis Stat Ann §907.06(2) (West).

[97]Cal Evid Code §731(c) (West).

§10.24 6. Right to Call Own Experts

The fact that the court appoints an expert does not necessarily preclude parties from calling their own experts. However, an interesting feature designed to discourage partisan selection of experts where there has already been a court appointment appears in statutory restrictions which entitle the party calling such a partisan expert to tax as costs only ordinary witness fees, rather than the actual amount of expert witness fees paid.[98]

§10.25 7. Cross-Examination

An expert appointed by the court is subject to cross-examination by each party, including the party calling the expert as a witness. In addition, where the court calls an expert witness and interrogates that witness, the parties may object to the questions asked and the testimony given just as if the expert witness had been called and were being examined by an adverse party.[99]

E. Compensation of Party Experts

§10.26 1. As Expert Witness

An expert witness who is not a party to the action and who is required to testify in a civil action solely as to an expert opinion held by such witness is generally entitled to receive a reasonable compensation. This compensation would cover the time required to travel to and from the place where the court is located and the time the witness is required to remain at such place pursuant to subpoena.[100] Rules governing compensation of experts apply not only to court testimony, but may also apply to testimony before other types of tribunals[101] and the taking of depositions.[102]

Two essential considerations regarding the compensation for expert witness services are that the expert: (1) qualify as an expert; and (2) testify solely as to an expert opinion held because of special knowledge, skill, expertise, training, or education.

In one recent case,[103] the court held that where an expert was called on to testify both as to general knowledge of specific facts and as to such expert's special opinion in a particular field, the court was without authority to grant compensation. The court reasoned that the expert was not testifying solely as to an expert opinion.

The expert or any party to the action generally may motion the court for an order

---

[98]Cal Evid Code §733 (West).

[99]Fed R Evid 706(a); Cal Evid Code §732 (West); NM R Evid 706(a), NM Stat Ann, vol 1 (1978).

[100]Cal Govt Code §68092.5(a) (West).

[101]Cal Civ Proc Code §1283.2 (West); Cal Govt Code §68092.5(a) (West); Notes of decision to Iowa Code Civ Prac & Proc §622.72, 1943 Op Atty Gen 483.

[102]Fed R Civ P 26(b)(4)(C)(i); Congrove v St Louis-San Francisco Ry, 77 FRD 503 (WD Mo 1978); Cal Govt Code §68092.5(a) (West).

[103]Bureau of Medical Economics v Cossette, 44 Cal App 3d Supp 1, 118 Cal Rptr 242 (1974).

fixing the compensation for an appearance. The compensation plus statutory witness fees is to be paid by the party requiring the witness to attend. However, such fees usually are not allowable as costs.[104]

§10.27 2. As Percipient Witness

With increasing frequency, partly because of the high fees demanded by experts, parties are subpoenaing experts to testify on percipient information only. Percipient information means knowledge of particular facts as opposed to expert opinions. If the attorney elicits from the expert any percipient information, the party calling the expert is required only to pay ordinary witness fees. Such an expert is then actually like any other lay witness with knowledge of certain facts. Therefore, it can be argued that it is irrelevant that the witness may have discovered such facts by reason of such witness's expertise. When testifying as a nonexpert, the witness is simply testifying to certain information relevant to an issue, as if a witness to the particular event leading to the litigation.[105]

In California the legislature attempted to clarify the distinction between percipient and expert testimony elicited from a witness on deposition by providing, in part, as follows:

> Any party desiring to take the deposition of a person retained as an expert by another party to a case, shall pay the expert a reasonable fee not exceeding his customary hourly or daily fee for the time reasonably and necessarily spent in connection with such deposition including time spent in travel to and from the deposition, but excluding time spent in preparation. A fee based upon the anticipated length of the deposition shall be tendered to the expert. In the event the examination and necessary cross-examination of the expert takes longer than originally anticipated, the balance of the fee due the expert shall be paid by the party who noticed the deposition within five days of receipt of an itemized statement from the expert.[106]

It appears that the two prerequisites to payment of expert's fees are that: (1) the witness be already *retained* as an expert by another party to the case; and (2) the deposing party treat the witness as an *expert.*

For the sake of expediency, an engineer or other expert who becomes aware of the likelihood of being deposed on a matter that has been investigated, should insist on being retained as an expert by the attorney requesting the investigation. A letter to that effect would appear to create expert witness status, and entitle the witness to demand expert witness fees from the deposing party.

Should a dispute develop between a party and the expert witness over the amount of compensation that the expert is entitled to receive, the court may issue protective orders. Such orders may be made on motion of the expert witness or any party. The

---

[104]Cal Govt Code §68092.5(a) (West); *contra,* Commission of Conservation v Connor, 321 Mich 648, 32 NW2d 907 (1948).

[105]City & County of San Francisco v Superior Court, 37 Cal 2d 227, 231 P2d 26 (1951).

[106]Cal Civ Proc Code §2037.7 (West).

purpose is to protect the witness or party from annoyance, embarrassment, or oppression, and to determine reasonableness of fees claimed.[107]

Generally, where statutory authority relating to expert witnesses makes no provision for expert witness fees, only ordinary witness fees are compensable.[108]

In addition, courts in some jurisdictions make no distinction between an ordinary witness and an expert. Both are considered under a duty to appear, and both are entitled to ordinary witness fees.[109] While it would seem improper to compel an expert to engage in technical research or investigation in preparation for testimony without adequate compensation,[110] an expert may well be compelled to testify to an already formed opinion without receiving special compensation.[111]

§10.28 3. Canceled Proceedings without Adequate Notice

Where a proceeding to which an expert has been subpoenaed is continued or canceled, the party who subpoenaed the expert is required to give notice of such continuance or cancellation to the expert by the quickest and most reliable means under the circumstances. Where the subpoenaing party fails to give such notice, the expert witness is entitled to compensation for travel and appearance time, notwithstanding the fact that the expert gives no testimony.[112]

§10.29 4. Contracts for Compensation

An express contract relating to compensation, entered into between an expert and the party requesting the expert to testify, is enforceable.[113] In addition, where a party requests an expert witness to perform special work in anticipation of and preparation for testifying, and there is no express agreement relating to fees, compensation is governed by an implied contract for the reasonable value of the expert's services.[114]

§10.30 5. Contingent Fee Arrangement

It has long been the general rule that an agreement to pay expert witness fees contingent on the outcome of the litigation is void as against public policy. In a typical case,[115] the court held that a contingent fee contract between a party and the party's

---

[107]*Id* at §2037.8(a); Fed R Civ P 26(c).

[108]Ulaski v Morris & Co, 106 Neb 782, 184 NW 946 (1921); *contra,* Stanton v Rushmore, 112 NJL 115, 169 A 721 (1934).

[109]State v Teipner, 36 Minn 535, 32 NW 678 (1887).

[110]Nielsen v Brown, 232 Or 426, 374 P2d 896 (1962).

[111]Philler v Waukesha County, 139 Wis 211, 120 NW 829 (1909).

[112]Cal Govt Code §68092.5(b) (West).

[113]Cal Govt Code §68092.5(c); Barrus v Phaneuf, 166 Mass 123, 44 NE 141 (1896); Philler v Waukesha County, 139 Wis 211, 120 NW 829 (1909).

[114]Barrus v Phaneuf, 166 Mass 123, 44 NE 141 (1896).

[115]Van Norden v Metson, 75 Cal App 2d 595, 599, 171 P2d 485 (1946).

expert, a civil engineer, was void. However, such a fee arrangement would affect credibility, not competency to testify.[116]

American Bar Association Disciplinary Rule 7-109 (c) states in part, "A lawyer shall not pay, offer to pay, or acquiesce in the payment of compensation to a witness contingent upon the content of his testimony or the outcome of the case."[117]

The policy behind such a rule is: (1) to discourage attorneys from "buying" lawsuits; and (2) to insure that judicial proceedings are free of false testimony which might occur if payment of expert witnesses depended on the litigation's outcome. In addition, since expert testimony by definition deals with matters beyond the knowledge of common laypersons, the trier of fact is usually unable to detect perjured expert testimony.

Interestingly enough, prior to reversal by the Second Circuit, the United States District Court for the Eastern District of New York declared that ABA Disciplinary Rule 7-109 (c), in effect in all 50 states, was unconstitutional. The court stated, among other things:

> The interests involved are *first,* the interest of plaintiff and every other lawyer in being able freely to seek out and, on his clients' behalf, contract on a contingent fee basis with qualified experts where that is the only way in which the client can afford to engage the expert's services or the way which is otherwise appropriate, and, *second,* the client litigant's interest in having genuine access to the courts. . . . In comforting theory the lawyer can turn his back on such clients and seek other work. But the client has no alternative to seeking justice except the courts established to dispense it. . . . In the case where one party is of limited means the "discrimination" in treatment is individual, pointed and specific as well as general in its tendency to handicap the less affluent and the indigent classes of litigants in their efforts to vindicate their rights.

Nothwithstanding the district court's reasoning, the court of appeals reversed, holding that the rule had sufficient rational basis to withstand the constitutional challenge. The court did, however, agree that legislative change would be desirable, since:

1. Cross-examination would reveal whatever financial stake a witness might have in the outcome of litigation
2. Experts often have ongoing business relationships with the parties who retain them and, therefore, have a stake in the outcome of litigation even though their fee is not contingent and thus not covered by the rule
3. Other experts, although retained on a fixed fee basis, often do not expect to receive payment unless the party for whom they testify is successful[118]

One suggested method of safeguarding the veracity of contingent expert testimony

---

[116]In re Shore, 93 Misc 2d 933, 403 NYS2d 990 (1978).

[117]*See also* In re O'Keefe, 49 Mont 369, 142 P 638 (1914).

[118]Person v Association of Bar of City of NY, 414 F Supp 144, 145-46 (1976), *revd,* 554 F2d 534 (2d Cir 1977).

is to have judicial scrutiny of contingent fee arrangements which would limit compensation to a reasonable amount.[119]

§10.31 6. Expert's Liability

Once an expert has been retained by a party to testify at trial, there is a legal relationship between that expert and the party. In a New Jersey case,[120] a party sued an expert in the field of glass fractures who had failed to appear and testify at a prior trial. The theory of the lawsuit, based on a cause of action for breach of contract and negligence, was that the expert's failure to appear at the prior trial forced the plaintiff to settle the case. The value of the forced settlement was allegedly lower than settlement or recovery would have been with the help of the expert's testimony.

F. Examination of Experts

§10.32 1. Generally

A witness who testifies as an expert may be cross-examined as any other witness may be.[121] However, an expert is exposed to a much broader cross-examination than an ordinary witness. An expert witness invites exploration of the extent of the expert's knowledge and reasons for the expert's opinion. This includes examination of the facts and other matters on which the expert's opinions are based and which the expert took into consideration. In addition, the expert may be subjected to vigorous cross-examination concerning the expert's qualifications[122] and prior opinions given in other proceedings or to other persons.[123]

The obvious purpose in cross-examining the expert is to demonstrate that such expert's testimony on direct examination was not trustworthy, reliable, or accurate.

§10.33 2. Hypothetical Questions

It is proper to cross-examine an expert witness by hypothetical question.[124] This method is utilized to test the expert's knowledge,[125] refute the expert's direct testimony,[126] or show that the expert's opinion is consistent with the adverse party's.[127]

---

[119] Notes, *Contingent Fees for Expert Witnesses in Civil Litigation*, 86 Yale LJ 1680 (1977).

[120] Lapham v Ding Wall, No L-20697-75 (Morris County, NJ, Super Ct, filed Nov 19, 1976); ATLA Law Rptr, vol 20, no 2, 52 (Mar 1977).

[121] **§§7.26-.31, 9.09-.18, 9.22.**

[122] Hope v Arrowhead & Puritas Waters, Inc, 174 Cal App 2d 222, 230, 344 P2d 428, 433 (1959); Shurpit v Brah, 30 Wis 2d 388, 141 NW2d 266 (1966); Clark V State, 12 Ohio 483 (1843).

[123] McGrath v Fash, 244 Mass 327, 139 NE 303 (1923); Young v Group Health Coop of Puget Sound, 85 Wash 2d 332, 534 P2d 1349 (1975).

[124] People v Tallman, 27 Cal 2d 209, 214, 163 P2d 857 (1945); Shuffield v Taylor, 125 Tex 601, 83 SW2d 955 (1935).

[125] Kansas City v Marsh Oil Co, 140 Mo 458, 41 SW 943 (1897).

[126] State v Eidsvold Creamery Co, 156 Minn 27, 194 NW 17 (1923).

[127] Louisville, NA & C Ry v Wood, 113 Ind 544, 14 NE 572 (1887).

§10.34 3. Compensation

It is generally believed that a jury is in a better position to appraise the extent to which feelings of obligation have affected an expert's testimony if it is informed of the amount of compensation and expenses the expert has received or expects to receive for testifying.

This inquiry is considered relevant in establishing credibility and weight to be given testimony.[128] On the other hand, amount of compensation paid to an expert in previous cases with no connection to the case in which the expert is currently testifying is considered irrelevant and not a proper subject of cross-examination.[129]

§10.35 4. Use of Texts or Treatises

An expert witness generally may not be cross-examined on the content of any scientific, technical, or professional text, treatise, or journal unless: (1) the expert has referred to, considered, or relied on such publication in forming an opinion; or (2) the publication has been admitted in evidence. This is consistent with the hearsay rule and the philosophy behind cross-examination, that is, that the ultimate goal in cross-examination of an expert is to discredit the expert's testimony, not to have the material admitted into evidence as proof of the truth of its content.

The jurisdictions show a diverse range of standards governing cross-examination of experts on texts, treatises, and other material. Some states allow cross-examination on material generally similar to that which the expert relied on,[130] or on materials the expert concedes to be authoritative,[131] or on judicially noticed materials.[132]

G. Expert Testimony on Special Subjects

§10.36 1. Ultimate Issue

Older cases held that it was improper to offer expert opinion testimony on an ultimate issue because doing so usurps the province of the trier of fact.[133] The modern trend is to the contrary.[134] In one case, the issue was whether failure to insulate a 7200-volt power wire with 10.64 inches of polyethylene was the proximate cause of injury. The court approved permitting an expert to express an opinion on that ultimate issue, reasoning that, since the trier of fact would not be required to accept that expert's opinion, such evidence would not usurp the province of the jury.[135] Instead, proper

---

[128] Cal Evid Code §722(b)(West).

[129] Zamsky v Public Parking Auth, 378 Pa 38, 105 A2d 335 (1954).

[130] Ruud v Hendrickson, 176 Minn 138, 222 NW 904 (1929).

[131] Ruth v Fenchel, 21 NJ 171, 121 A2d 373 (1956).

[132] Ravenis v Detroit Gen Hosp, 63 Mich App 79, 234 NW2d 411 (1975).

[133] People v Creasy, 236 NY 205, 140 NE 563 (1923).

[134] NJ Evid R 56(3), NJ Stat Ann §2A:84A-32 (West).

[135] Spence v Commonwealth Edison Co, 34 Ill App 3d 1059, 340 NE2d 550 (1975).

weight must be accorded to the underlying facts and opinions of the expert, and to the qualifications, trustworthiness, and reasonableness of the expert.

Even though the modern trend and Rule 704 of the Federal Rules of Evidence indicate that opinion testimony will not be objectionable simply because it embraces an ultimate issue in the case, the trial judge has wide discretion to exclude such testimony. Where a civil engineer was asked on direct examination whether a certain condition constituted an "extra hazardous" crossing under Ohio law, the court held that it was a proper exercise of discretion to exclude the expert's opinion since such opinion would amount to a legal conclusion on an ultimate issue.[136]

Other courts still insist that an expert witness may not testify at all on an ultimate issue in a case.[137]

Of course, an opinion on an ultimate issue may always be objectionable on other grounds, for example, that the witness is unqualified, that the opinion is not a proper subject for expert testimony, or that the probative value of the testimony is outweighed by the risk of misleading the trier of fact.

§10.37 2. Experiments

Conduct of experiments, either in or out of court, to substantiate or rebut the truth of certain disputed facts is a proper basis for expert testimony. Generally, evidence relating to an experiment is admissible if the following foundational requirements are met:

1. The experiment was conducted by a qualified expert
2. The evidence was relevant and probative as to some issue in the case
3. The expert conducted the experiment under conditions substantially similar to those of the actual incident under consideration
4. The experimental evidence will not consume undue time, confuse the issues, or mislead the jury
5. The results will aid the trier of fact in its consideration of the evidence and issues[138]

The court also must find that the scientific principle on which the experiment is based is established sufficiently to have gained general acceptance in the particular field to which it belongs.[139]

Where the court finds that the experiment is substantially similar to the occurrence to which it is supposed to relate, minor variations between the conditions existing at the time of the experiment and those at the time of the original incident go to the weight of the evidence rather than to its admissibility.[140]

One court has stated that test results should not be admissible as evidence unless

[136]Stoler v Penn Central Transp Co, 583 F2d 896 (6th Cir 1978).

[137]Laff v John O Butler Co, 64 Ill App 3d 603, 381 NE2d 423 (1978).

[138]Culpepper v Volkswagen of America, Inc, 33 Cal App 3d 510, 109 Cal Rptr 110 (1973).

[139]Frye v United States, 293 F 1013 (DC Cir 1923).

[140]Larson v Meyer, 161 NW2d 165 (ND 1968).

the test was made by a qualified independent expert or unless the opposing party has had the opportunity to participate in the testing.[141] Another court has held that absence of notice and opportunity for a party to be present is not a valid basis for objection to the admissibility of such evidence, but may be argued on the issue of the weight to be afforded such evidence.[142]

A common objection to admissibility of experimental evidence concerns the problem of assuming conditions or facts not reasonably inferable from the evidence. For instance, one court held that it was improper for an expert to testify about results of various experiments performed on a chair similar in design and construction to the lost subject chair, since it was not reasonable to infer that the subject chair was actually sound to begin with.[143]

Some examples of experimental engineering evidence have covered the following subjects: reconstruction of an automobile accident;[144] determination of the slipperiness of a floor;[145] identifying the cause of an explosion;[146] finding out whether a vehicle could be maneuvered at 65 miles per hour with the right tie rod end removed;[147] determining the chemical composition of a certain substance;[148] examining lighting conditions at a particular time;[149] testing the effectiveness of a bus interlock mechanism;[150] gauging the capability of steering and brakes systems;[151] determining stopping distance;[152] evaluating flammability of certain materials;[153] and testing visibility and illumination of objects at a given distance.[154]

When experimental evidence is offered, counsel should realize that whether it will be admitted is peculiarly within the discretion of the trial judge.[155] Therefore, any objection to admissibility of experimental evidence for failure to establish a foundation must be timely raised or it will be waived.[156]

§10.38 3. Safety Codes vs Learned Treatises

Reference is often made to safety codes as objective standards of safe construction, recognized and accepted in the type of construction industry involved in a case. Gen-

---

[141]Fortunato v Ford Motor Co, 464 F2d 962 (2d Cir), *cert denied,* 409 US 1038 (1972).

[142]Burg v Chicago, RI & P Ry, 90 Iowa 106, 57 NW 680, 683 (1894); Larson v Meyer, 161 NW2d 165 (ND 1968).

[143]Andrews v Barker Bros, 267 Cal App 2d 530, 73 Cal Rptr 284 (1968).

[144]Nanda v Ford Motor Co, 509 F2d 213 (7th Cir 1974).

[145]Dritt v Morris, 235 Ark 40, 357 SW2d 13 (1962).

[146]Kotiadis v Gristede Bros, 20 AD2d 689, 246 NYS2d 662 (1964).

[147]Shover v General Motors Corp, 198 Neb 470, 253 NW2d 299 (1977).

[148]Davidson v Wee, 5 Ariz App 187, 424 P2d 835 (1967).

[149]McKnight v Wire Properties, Inc, 288 A2d 405 (DC 1972).

[150]Thomas v Chicago Transit Auth, 115 Ill App 2d 476, 253 NE2d 492 (1969).

[151]Mack v Davis, 76 Ill App 2d 88, 221 NE2d 121 (1966).

[152]Hanson v NH Pre-Mix Concrete, Inc, 110 NH 377, 268 A2d 841 (1970).

[153]CF Church Div of AM Radiator & Standard Sanitary Corp v Golden, 429 P2d 771 (Okla 1967).

[154]Habers v Madigan, 213 Va 485, 193 SE2d 653 (1973).

[155]Lynch v Missouri-Kan-Tex Ry, 333 Mo 89, 61 SW2d 918 (1933).

[156]People v Modell, 143 Cal App 2d 724, 300 P2d 204 (1956).

erally, safety codes represent a consensus of opinion, carrying the approval of a significant segment of an industry. Such codes are not introduced as substantive law, as proof of regulations or absolute standards with the force of law or of scientific truth. Rather, they are offered together with expert testimony which identifies the codes as illustrative evidence of safety practices or rules generally prevailing in the industry. As such, they provide support for opinions of experts about the proper standard of care.[157]

A treatise, on the other hand, is basically a single expert's opinion on a particular factual or legal situation. For this reason, where contents of a treatise are offered as substantive evidence in a case, the general rule has been to deny admission. The reasoning behind this rule is that such evidence is merely an out-of-court statement by a person not subject to cross-examination.[158]

However, it is proper for an expert to rely on an authoritative or specialized text as the basis for an opinion. In such a situation, the expert already possesses professional experience and knowledge of the general subject. This uniquely enables the expert to evaluate and ascertain the trustworthiness of the authority, the propriety of the sources of information, and the plausibility of the views expressed.[159] Obviously, a layperson would not have the expert's qualifications and would be unable to evaluate independently the trustworthiness of certain materials. It is for this reason that a layperson, or nonexpert, may not rely on an authoritative text as the basis for an opinion.

§10.39 4. Custom and Common Practice

Expert testimony as to common practice or custom is important in engineering cases. However, its admissibility depends on having the witness display adequate knowledge of the custom or practice as a matter of fact,[160] not as an opinion. Specifically, the expert's testimony must be based on general custom rather than on an individual instance.[161]

In addition, admissibility depends on whether such evidence will be sufficiently helpful on the ultimate issue of culpability. Generally, a qualified expert is permitted to testify whether a particular condition, product, or construction project did or did not conform with custom and common practice in the particular subject area. After this testimony and all other evidence has been received, the trier of fact is still free to determine the ultimate issue of negligence.[162]

On the relationship between the issue of negligence and proof of custom and common practice, it is appropriate to cite the court in *Pauly v King*[163] which quoted from *Owen v Rheem Mfg Co*:[164]

---

[157]McComish v DeSoi, 42 NJ 274, 200 A2d 116 (1964).

[158]Ruth v Fenchel, 21 NJ 171, 121 A2d 373, 375 (1956).

[159]Brown v Colm, 11 Cal 3d 639, 522 P2d 688, 114 Cal Rptr 128 (1974).

[160]Davenport v White Mountain Power Co, 92 NH 20, 24 A2d 274 (1942).

[161]Asbury v Fidelity Natl Bank & Trust Co, 231 Mo App 437, 100 SW2d 946 (1936).

[162]Clark v Iceland Steamship Co, 6 AD2d 544, 179 NYS2d 708 (1958).

[163]44 Cal 2d 649, 655, 284 P2d 487, 490 (1955).

[164]83 Cal App 2d 42, 45, 187 P2d 785, 786 (1947).

Failure to observe custom may be evidence of negligence, but the standard is not fixed by custom. The standard is always due care. The presence or absence of custom does not alter that standard. Custom may assist in the determination of what constitutes due care. What others do is some evidence of what should be done, but custom is never a substitute for due care.

§10.40 5. Computer Printout

Properly authenticated computer printouts[165] are admissible as business records.[166] The general foundation requirements applicable to business records must be satisfied in the case of computer documents. That is, a qualified witness must testify that:

1. The original data has been put into computer language and transferred into the computer
2. The business uses the computer system in the regular course of its business
3. The business relies on the accuracy of the computer system in conducting its business
4. The computer system is a standard and reputable one

In one case,[167] a contractor brought an action against the owner and architect to recover for increased costs incurred on a construction project. One exhibit offered by the contractor was a computer readout consisting of paper measuring approximately 11 inches by 15 inches which in the aggregate was three inches thick. Each page had various columns containing words or figures. The court in reviewing the computer readout concluded that such readout would be unintelligible to the jury without expert testimony to explain how it related to the issues in the case. In addition, the court said that an expert might testify from the readout, but that the readout itself should not be admitted into evidence or go to the jury. The reasoning was that if such a complex exhibit were considered by the jury, the jury might misinterpret the document.[168]

H. Experts in Arbitration Proceedings

§10.41 1. Generally

Since arbitration offers parties a relatively expeditious and economical forum in which to resolve disputes, there is a strong public policy in its favor.

The extensive use and misuse of discovery which prevails in civil litigation is generally restricted in arbitration. As discovery procedures require close scrutiny and

---

[165]**§4.15.**

[166]People v Cohen, 59 Cal App 3d 241, 130 Cal Rptr 656 (1976); Union Elec Co v Mansion House Center N Redevelopment Co, 494 SW2d 309 (1973); State v Loehmer, 159 Ind App 156, 304 NE2d 835 (1973).

[167]Huber, Hunt & Nichols, Inc v Moore, 67 Cal App 3d 278, 136 Cal Rptr 603 (1977).

[168]*Id* at 294, 136 Cal Rptr at 612 n 13, 613.

enforcement of which the arbitration tribunals are often incapable, most formal pretrial discovery is prohibited as contrary to the policies behind arbitration. Nevertheless, the parties are free to stipulate to exchange information, propound interrogatories, or take depositions.

§10.42 2. Uniform Arbitration Act

More than half of the states have enacted statutory arbitration procedures based on[169] or similar[170] to the Uniform Arbitration Act.[171]

In states with arbitration statutes, the right to conduct discovery is limited, if not nonexistent.[172] Under the Uniform Arbitration Act, depositions of witnesses who cannot be subpoenaed or who are unable to attend the hearing may be taken on prior application to the arbitrator. Such procedure is for use as evidence, not discovery.[173]

In some states, not only is prior authorization of the arbitrator necessary to take the deposition of an unavailable witness, but a court order also is required.[174]

In addition, under the Uniform Arbitration Act, arbitrators may issue subpoenas for the attendance of witnesses, including experts, and for the production of books, records, documents, and other evidence. Enforcement of a subpoena is accomplished through a court having jurisdiction and on application of a party or arbitrator.[175]

Other states under their own arbitration statutes provide for depositions for discovery where the dispute is one involving injury or death of a person caused by the wrongful act or negligence of another[176] or where the arbitrator grants leave to do so.[177] The

---

[169]The jurisdictions which have adopted the Uniform Arbitration Acts and their corresponding statutory citations are as follows: Alaska (Alaska Stat §§09.43.010-.180); Arizona (Ariz Rev Stat Ann §§12-1501 to 12-1518); Arkansas (Ark Stat Ann §§34-511 to 34-532); Colorado (Colo Rev Stat §§13-22-201 to 13-22-223); Delaware (Del Code Ann, tit 10, §§5701-5725); District of Columbia (DC Code Ann §§1-21); Idaho (Idaho Code §§7-901 to 7-922); Illinois (Ill Rev Stat, ch 10, §§101-123); Indiana (Ind Code §§34-4-2-1 to 34-4-2-22); Kansas (Kan Stat Ann §§5-401 to 5-422); Maine (Me Rev Stat Ann, tit 14, §§5927-5949); Maryland (Md Cts & Jud Proc Code Ann §§3-201 to 3-234); Massachusetts (Mass Gen Laws Ann, ch 251, §§1-19 (West)); Michigan (Mich Comp Laws §§600.5001-.5035); Minnesota (Minn Stat Ann §§572.08-.30 (West)); Nevada (Nev Rev Stat §§38.015-.045); New Mexico (NM Stat Ann §§22-3-9 to 22-3-31); North Carolina (NC Gen Stat §§1-567.1-.20); Oklahoma (Okla Stat, tit 15, §§801-818 (West)); South Dakota (SD Codified Laws Ann §§21-25A-1 to 21-25A-38); Texas (Tex Civ Code Ann, tit 10, §§224-238.6 (Vernon); Wyoming (Wyo Stat §§1-36-101 to 1-36-119).

[170]California (Civ Proc Code §§1280-1289 (West)); Connecticut (Conn Gen Stat Ann §§52-408 to 52-424 (West)); Florida (Fla Stat §§682.01-.22); Hawaii (Hawaii Rev Stat §§658-1 to 658-14); Louisiana (La Rev Stat Ann §§9:4201-:4217 (West)); New Hampshire (NH Rev Stat §§542:1-:10); New Jersey (NJ Stat Ann §§2A:24-1 to 2A:24-11 (West)); New York (NY Civ Prac Law §§7501-7514 (McKinney)); Pennsylvania (Pa Cons Stat Ann §§161-209).

[171]Uniform Arbitration Act §§1-20.

[172]NY Civ Prac Law §§7501-7514 (McKinney).

[173]Uniform Arbitration Act §7(b).

[174]Ohio Rev Code Ann §2711.07 (Page); RI Gen Laws §10-3-9.

[175]Uniform Arbitration Act §7(a).

[176]Cal Civ Proc Code §1283.1 (West).

[177]*Id* at §1283.05(e).

arbitration law in Massachusetts was recently expanded to add a discovery device whereby a party may request production of documents and things as well as entry on land for inspection.[178]

It is thus apparent that even though the general rule is that discovery is greatly restricted in arbitration, each jurisdiction has specific exceptions and procedures which control.

§10.43 3. American Arbitration Association

The American Arbitration Association has established distinct sets of arbitration rules[179] which vary with the particular subject matter of the claim. Generally, these rules provide that the arbitrator may, when authorized by law, subpoena expert witnesses or documents on such arbitrator's own initiative or the request of any party.

The same rules permit the arbitrator to receive and consider evidence of experts by mere affidavit. However, the arbitrator is to give the affidavit only such weight as the arbitrator deems it entitled to after considering any objections to its admission. Obviously, the fact that in this situation the expert would not be subject to cross-examination is a reason to significantly discount the weight of such testimony.

Generally, discovery is not allowed under the American Arbitration Association rules except under accident claims rules where statutory authority permits it.[180]

§10.44 4. Uninsured Motorist Arbitration

Almost no states allow discovery under uninsured motorist arbitration. However, the California statute[181] permits full discovery, including discovery about experts, in uninsured motorist arbitration. The discovery rights exist between the parties, i.e., the insurance company and the insured.

Where discovery is not allowed in arbitration, counsel may attempt to circumvent the problem by concurrently filing a civil action against the uninsured driver and utilizing the available civil discovery procedures.

§10.45 5. Mandatory Arbitration

In California a new mandatory arbitration program went into effect on July 1, 1979.[182] Significant in this program is the authorization of use of affidavits or decla-

---

[178]Mass Gen Laws Ann, ch 251, §7 (West).

[179]These rules can be obtained by contacting one of the Regional Offices of The American Arbitration Association located throughout the United States: Ariz (Phoenix); Cal (Los Angeles, San Diego, San Francisco); Conn (Hartford); DC; Fla (Miami); Ill (Chicago); Mass (Boston); Mich (Detroit); Minn (Minneapolis); NC (Charlotte); NJ (New Brunswick); NY (New York City, Rochester, Syracuse, Garden City); Ohio (Cincinnati, Cleveland); Pa (Philadelphia, Pittsburgh),. Tex (Dallas); Wash (Seattle). In addition, most law libraries would contain copies of these rules.

[180]McRae v Superior Court, 221 Cal App 2d 166, 34 Cal Rptr 346 (1963); Cavanaugh v McDonnell & Co, 357 Mass 452, 258 NE2d 561 (1970).

[181]Cal Ins Code §11580.2(f) (West).

[182]Cal Civ Proc Code §§1141.10-.32 (West); West's California Rules of Court 1979 (Supplementary Pamphlet), Rules 1600-1617.

rations of witnesses. The rules provide that written statements of witnesses, including written reports of expert witnesses and statements of opinions which the witness would be qualified to express if personally testifying at hearing, may be offered and received in evidence.[183] There are certain notice requirements, however, as well as procedures for objections by the adverse party. Other states also have various compulsory arbitration statutes aimed at expediting litigation.[184]

In a district court case in Pennsylvania,[185] the court held that an experimental local rule which provided for compulsory, nonbinding arbitration as a prerequisite to a civil jury trial was proper where the amount in controversy was under $50,000.

---

[183]*Id* at Rule 1613(b)(2).

[184]42 Pa Cons Stat Ann §7361 (Purdon).

[185]Kimbrough v Holiday Inn, 478 F Supp 566 (ED Pa 1979).

Appendix A
Sources of Experts

Architects

National

American Institute of Architects
1785 Massachusetts Avenue NW
Washington, DC 20036

Arkansas

American Institute of Architects—
Arkansas Chapter
Gazette Building, 118 West Third
Street
Little Rock 72201

Arkansas State Board of Architects
Gazette Building, 118 West Third
Street
Little Rock 72201

California

American Institute of Architects—
California Council
1736 Stockton Street
San Francisco 94133

American Institute of Architects—
Northern California Chapter
254 Sutter Street
San Francisco 94108

American Institute of Architects—
Southern California Chapter
304 South Broadway
Los Angeles 90013

American Institute of Building Design
839 Mitten Road, Suite 128
Burlingame 94010

Engineers and Architects Association
417 South Hill Street
Los Angeles 90013

Engineers and Architects Institute
1052 West Sixth Street
Los Angeles 90017

Florida

Florida Association of Architects of the
American
Institute of Architects
1815 Ponce de Leon Boulevard
Miami 33134

Georgia

American Institute of Architects—
Georgia Chapter
Peachtree Center Building
Atlanta 30303

American Registered Architects
Carnegie Building
Atlanta 30303

Illinois

American Institute of Architects—
Chicago Chapter
221 North LaSalle Street
Chicago 60601

Architects Association of Illinois
405½ South Sixth Street
Springfield 62701

Illinois Architects Association
221 North LaSalle Street
Chicago 60601

Illinois Society of Architects
134 North LaSalle
Chicago 60602

Kentucky

Engineers and Architects Club of Louisville
Henry Clay Hotel
Louisville

Louisiana

Louisiana Architects Association
1925 North Riverside
Baton Rouge 70815

Mississippi

American Institute of Architects—Mississippi Chapter
204 South State Street
Jackson 39201

Missouri

American Institute of Architects—Kansas City Chapter
922 Walnut Street
Kansas City 64106

New York

American Institute of Architects—New York Chapter
20 West 40th Street
New York 10018

Architects League of New York
41 East 65th Street
New York 10021

Ohio

American Institute of Architects—Cleveland Chapter
The Arcade, 401 Euclid Street
Cleveland 44114

Architects Society of Ohio
37 West Broad Street
Columbus 43215

Oregon

American Institute of Architects—Oregon Chapter
519 SW Third Street
Portland 97204

Virginia

American Institute of Architects—Virginia Chapter
513 East Main Street
Richmond 23219

Automotive Engineers

National

Society of Automotive Engineers, Inc.
2 Pennsylvania Plaza
New York, NY 10001

Society of Automotive Engineers, Inc.
18121 East Eight Mile Road
East Detroit, MI 48021

Regional

Society of Automotive Engineers, Inc.—California Section
1335 South Flower Street
Los Angeles, CA 90015

Society of Automotive Engineers, Inc.
343 South Dearborn Street
Chicago, IL 60604

Chemical Engineers and Chemists

National

American Chemical Society
1155 16th Street NW
Washington, DC 20036

American Institute of Chemical Engineers, Inc.
345 East 47th Street
New York, NY 10017

Association of Consulting Chemists and Chemical Engineers
50 East 41st Street
New York, NY 10017

Chemistry

National

American Chemical Society
1155 16th Street NW
Washington, DC 20036

American Chemical Society
1540 North Hudson Avenue
Los Angeles, CA 90028

American Chemical Society
86 Randolph Street
Chicago, IL 60601

American Chemical Society
2082 Center Street
Berkeley, CA 94704

American Chemical Society—Philadelphia Section
34 Spruce Street
Philadelphia, PA 19106

American Institute of Chemists
79 Madison Avenue
New York, NY 10016

American Oil Chemists Society
1250 South Boyle Street
Los Angeles, CA 90023

Chemists Club
52 East 41st Street
New York, NY 10017

The Electrochemical Society, Inc.
30 East 41st Street
New York, NY 10017

Geochemical Society, Department of Chemistry
University of Wisconsin
Madison, WI 53706

Louisiana Chemical Association
Carondelet Building
New Orleans, LA 70130

Civil Engineers

National

American Society of Civil Engineers
345 East 47th Street
New York, NY 10017

Regional

California Council of Civil Engineers and Land Surveyors
1107 Ninth Street
Sacramento, CA 95814

Civil Engineers and Land Surveyors Association of California
608 South Hill Street
Los Angeles CA 90014

Connecticut Society of Civil Engineers, Inc.
P.O. Box 5176
Hamden, CT 06514

Boston Society of Civil Engineers
47 Winter Street
Boston, MA 02108

American Society of Civil Engineers—Philadelphia Section
1317 Spruce Street
Philadelphia, PA 19107

Consulting Engineers

National

American Institute of Consulting Engineers
345 East 47th Street
New York, NY 10017

Association of Consulting Management Engineers
347 Madison Avenue
New York, NY 10017

Consulting Engineers Council
1155 15th Street NW
Washington, DC 20005

Regional

Arizona Consulting Engineers Association, Inc.
3625 North 16th Street
Phoenix, AZ 85016

Consulting Engineers Association of California
555 East Walnut Street
Pasadena, CA 91101

Consulting Engineers Association of New Mexico
13130 Central Street East
Albuquerque, NM 87123

New York Association of Consulting Engineers, Inc.
101 Park Avenue
New York, NY 10017

Consulting Engineers of Ohio
294 East North Broadway
Columbus, OH 43214

Consulting Engineers Council of Oregon
4475 SW Scholls Ferry Road
Portland, OR 97225

Electrical and Electronic Engineers

National

American Institute of Electrical Engineers
345 East 47th Street
New York, NY 10017

The Institute of Electrical and Electronic Engineers, Inc.
345 East 47th Street
New York, NY 10017

Regional

Aerospace Electrical Society
4201 Long Beach Avenue
Los Angeles, CA 90058

American Institute of Electrical Engineers—Los Angeles Chapter
520 West Seventh Street
Los Angeles, CA 90014

Electrical Maintenance Engineers Association of California
1052 West Sixth Street
Los Angeles, CA 90017

American Institute of Electrical Engineers—Philadelphia Chapter
1317 Spruce Street
Philadelphia, PA 19107

Engineering

National

American Association of Engineers
8 South Michigan Boulevard
Chicago, IL 60603

Engineers' Council for Professional Development
345 East 47th Street
New York, NY 10017

Engineers' Joint Council
345 47th Street
New York, NY 10017

National Society of Professional Engineers
2029 K Street NW
Washington, DC 20006

National Society of Professional Engineers
354 South Spring Street
Los Angeles, Ca 90013

Midwest

Western Society of Engineers
314 South Federal Street
Chicago, IL 60604

New England

Engineering Societies of New England
61 Exeter Street
Boston, MA 02116

Alabama

Alabama Society of Professional Engineers
P.O. Box 1325
Birmingham 35201

Alaska

Alaska Society of Professional Engineers
2508 Eide Street
Anchorage 99503

California

California Society of Professional Engineers
2707 K Street
Sacramento 95816

Engineers and Scientists of California
4383 Piedmont Avenue
Oakland 94611

Engineers Club of San Francisco
160 Sansome Street
San Francisco 94104

Los Angeles Council of Engineering Societies
626 North Garfield Avenue
Alhambra 91801

Los Angeles Professional Engineers
354 South Spring Street
Los Angeles 90013

Southern California Professional Engineers Association
7315 South Western Avenue
Los Angeles 90047

Colorado

Colorado Engineering Council
1380 South Santa Fe Drive
Denver 80204

Colorado Society of Engineers
1380 South Santa Fe Drive
Denver 80204

Connecticut

Connecticut Society of Professional Engineers
P.O. Box B
Devon 06460

Connecticut Technical Council, Inc.
P.O. Box 265
New Haven 06502

Hartford Engineers Club, Inc.
P.O. Box 1913
Hartford 06101

Delaware

Delaware Council of Engineering Societies
P.O. Box 1212
Wilmington 19899

Delaware Society of Professional Engineers, Inc.
P.O. Box 1848
Wilmington 19899

Sussex Engineering Society
P.O. Box 154
Seaford 19973

Georgia

Georgia Engineering Society, Inc.
230 Spring Street NW
Atlanta 30303

Illinois

Chief Engineers Association of Chicago
22 West Madison Avenue
Chicago 60602

Engineering Societies Personnel Service, Inc.
29 East Madison Street
Chicago 60602

Illinois Society of Professional Engineers
55 East Washington Street
Chicago 60602

Illinois Society of Professional Engineers
612 South Second Street
Springfield 62704

Indiana

Fort Wayne Engineers Club
Chamber of Commerce Building
Fort Wayne 46802

Indiana Society of Professional Engineers
1224 North Capitol Avenue
Indianapolis 46202

Iowa

Iowa Engineering Society
4931 Douglas Avenue
Des Moines 50310

Kansas

Kansas Engineering Society Inc.
4125 Gage Center Drive
Topeka 66604

Kentucky

Engineers and Architects Club of Louisville
Henry Clay Hotel
Louisville

Kentucky Society of Professional Engineers
120 Graham Avenue
Lexington 40506

Louisiana

Louisiana Engineering Society
404 Baronne Street
New Orleans 70112

Maryland

Engineers Club of Baltimore
6 West Fayette Street
Baltimore 21201

Maryland Association of Engineers, Inc.
1274 Neridene Drive
Baltimore

Maryland Society of Professional Engineers, Inc.
908 Rappaix Court Towson
Baltimore 21204

Massachusetts

Engineering Society of Western Massachussetts
P.O. Box 149
Springfield 01101

Massachusetts Society of Professional Engineers
27 School Street
Boston 02108

Massachusetts State Engineers Association, Inc.
100 Nashua Street
Boston 02114

Michigan

Engineering Society of Detroit
100 Farnsworth Avenue
Detroit 48202

Engineering Society of Midland
P.O. Box 347
Midland 48640

Michigan Society of Professional Engineers
533 South Washington Street
Lansing 48933

Minnesota

Engineering Club of Minneapolis
1821 University Avenue
St. Paul 55101

Minnesota Society of Professional Engineers
Griggs-Midway Building
St. Paul 55104

Minnesota Federation of Engineering Societies
1821 University Avenue
St. Paul 55101

Mississippi

Mississippi Society of Professional Engineers
3100 Old Canton Road
Jackson 39208

Missouri

Engineers Club of Kansas City
President Hotel, 13th and Baltimore Streets
Kansas City

Engineers Club of St. Louis
4359 Lindell Boulevard
St. Louis 63108

Missouri Society of Professional Engineers
210 Monroe Street
Jefferson City 65101

New Jersey

Engineers Club of Trenton
Hotel Stacy-Trent
Trenton

New York

Albany Society of Engineers
25 South Allen Street
Albany 12208

Brooklyn Engineers Club
117 Remsen Street
Brooklyn 11201

Engineering Society of Buffalo, Inc.
Hotel Statler Hilton
Buffalo 14202

Engineers Association
2044 Hillside Avenue
New Hyde Park, Queens 11423

New York State Society of Professional Engineers
500 Fifth Avenue
New York 10036

Rochester Engineering Society
55 St. Paul Street
Rochester 14604

Scientists and Engineers Technological Institute
176 East 75th Street
New York 10021

North Carolina

North Carolina Society of Engineers
Hart Building, Raleigh Engineering Club
P.O. Box 1268
Raleigh 27602

Ohio

Cleveland Engineering Society
3100 Chester Avenue
Cleveland 44114

Engineering Club of Dayton
112 East Monument Avenue
Dayton 45402

Engineering Society of Cincinnati
1349 East McMillan Street
Cincinnati 45206

Ohio Society of Professional Engineers
445 King Avenue
Columbus 43201

Oklahoma

Oklahoma Society of Professional Engineers
200 Classen Center Building
112 Arcade Building
Oklahoma City

Engineers Club of Bartlesville
P.O. Box 1335
Bartlesville 74003

Engineers Society of Tulsa, Inc.
1131 South Norwood Avenue
Tulsa 74112

Oregon

Professional Engineers of Oregon
309 SW Fourth Street
Portland 97204

Pennsylvania

Engineers Club of Philadelphia
1317 Spruce Street
Philadelphia 19107

Engineers' Society of Western Pennsylvania
William Penn Hotel
Pittsburgh 15221

Pennsylvania Society of Professional Engineers
2121 North Second Street
Harrisburg 17110

Engineering and Technical Societies Council of the Delaware Valley
1317 Spruce Street
Philadelphia 19107

Engineering Society of York
26 South Beaver Street
York 17401

Rhode Island

Providence Engineering Society
615 Turks Head Building
76 Westminster Street
Providence 02903

South Carolina

South Carolina Society of Engineers, Inc.
210 Creason Building
Columbia

Texas

Houston Engineering and Scientific Society
2615 Fannin Street
Houston 77002

Texas Society of Professional Engineers
503 San Jacinto Boulevard
Austin 78701

Texas Society of Professional Engineers
3116 Commerce Street
Dallas 75226

Utah

Utah Society of Professional Engineers
3563 Monte Verde Drive
Salt Lake City 84109

Vermont

Vermont Society of Engineers
80 Pleasant Street
Barre 05641

Virginia

Engineers Club of Hampton Roads
P.O. Box 946
Norfolk 23501

Virginia Society of Professional Engineers, Inc.
609 Shirley Avenue
Norfolk 23517

Washington

Associated Engineers of Spokane
East 1411 Mission Street
P.O. Box 1445
Spokane 99210

Engineers Club
Northern Life Tower
1218 Third Avenue
Seattle 98101

Wisconsin

Engineers and Scientists of Milwaukee, Inc.
1545 South 108th Street
Milwaukee 53214

Engineers Society of Milwaukee
3112 West Highland Boulevard
Milwaukee 53208

Wyoming

Wyoming Engineering Society
P.O. Box 2285
Airport Station, Cheyenne 82001

Geology

National

American Association of Petroleum Geologists
1444 South Boulder Avenue
Tulsa, OK 74119

American Geological Institute
2201 M Street NW
Washington, DC 20037

Colorado

Rocky Mountain Association of Geologists
Johnson Building
Denver

Texas

West Texas Geological Society
Wilkinson Foster Building
Midland 79701

Heating, Refrigeration and Air Conditioning Engineers

National

American Society of Heating, Refrigeration and Air Conditioning Engineers, Inc.
345 East 47th Street
New York, NY 10017

Regional

American Society of Heating, Refrigeration and Air Conditioning Engineers, Inc.—Philadelphia Chapter
1317 Spruce Street
Philadelphia, PA 19107

Industrial Engineers

National

American Institute of Industrial Engineers
345 East 47th Street
New York, NY 10017

American Institute of Industrial Engineers
25 Technology Park, Norcross
Atlanta, GA 30071

Industrial Research Institute
100 Park Avenue, Suite 2209
New York, NY 10017

Regional

American Institute of Industrial Engineers—Los Angeles
Technical Safety Council
520 West Seventh Street
Los Angeles, CA 90014

Mechanical Engineers

National

American Society of Mechanical Engineers
345 East 47th Street
New York, NY 10017

Regional

American Society of Mechanical Engineers—California Section
626 North Garfield Street
Alhambra, CA 91801

American Society of Mechanical Engineers—District of Columbia Section
2029 K Street NW
Washington, DC 20006

American Society of Mechanical Engineers—Chicago Section
312 South Federal Street
Chicago, IL 60604

American Society of Mechanical Engineers—Missouri Section
5109 Cherry Street
Kansas City, MO 64110

American Society of Mechanical Engineers—Milwaukee Section
1545 South 108th Street
Milwaukee, WI 53214

Military Engineers

American Society of Naval Engineers
1012 14th Street NW
Washington, DC 20006

Society of American Military Engineers
800 18th Street NW
Washington, DC 20006

Society of Naval Architects and Marine Engineers
74 Trinity Place
New York, NY 10016

Structural Engineers

Regional

Structural Engineers Association of Northern California
171 Second Street
San Francisco, CA 94105

Structural Engineers Association of Southern California
2503 Beverly Boulevard
Los Angeles, CA 90057

Structural Engineers Association of Oregon
717 Board of Trade Building
Portland, OR

Surveying

National

American Congress of Surveying and Mapping
Woodward Building
Washington, DC 20005

Society of Professional Land Surveyors
127 North Dearborn Avenue
Chicago, IL 60602

California

California Council of Civil Engineers and Land Surveyors
1107 Ninth Street
Sacramento, CA 95814

Civil Engineers and Land Surveyors Association of California
608 South Hill Street
Los Angeles, CA 90014

Transportation Engineers

National

American Association of State Highway Officials
341 National Press Building
Washington, DC 20045

American Railway Engineering Association
59 East Van Buren Street
Chicago, IL 60605

Institute of Traffic Engineers
1815 Fort Myer Drive #905
Arlington, VA 22209

Miscellaneous Engineering Disciplines

American Association of Cost Engineers
160 Sansome Street
San Francisco, CA 94104

American Association of Cost Engineers
P.O. Box 5199
University of Alabama, Alabama 34586

American Society of Plant Engineers
1056 Delta Avenue, Suite 11
Cincinnati, OH 45208

American Society of Lubrication Engineers
838 Busse Highway
Park Ridge, IL 60068

American Society of Safety Engineers
850 Busse Highway
Park Ridge, IL 60068

American Society of Safety Engineers
417 East 13th Street
Kansas City, MO 64106

American Society of Sanitary Engineering
1028 Connecticut Avenue NW
Washington, DC 20036

American Society of Sanitary Engineering
Standard Building
Cleveland, OH 44113

National Association of Corrision Engineers
P.O. Box 510
Spencer, IA 51301

National Institute of Ceramic Engineers
4055 North High Street
Columbus, OH 43214

Society of Aerospace Material and
Process Engineers
P.O. Box 613
Azusa, CA 91702

Society of Manufacturing Engineers
20501 Ford Road
Dearborn, MI 48128

Society of Plastic Engineers
656 West Putnam Avenue
Greenwich, CT 06830

American Nuclear Society
244 East Ogden Avenue
Hinsdale, IL 60521

American Society of Quality Control
161 West Wisconsin Avenue
Milwaukee, WI 53203

Appendix B
Authors of Regulations and Standards

A continuous flow of regulations and standards is published by governmental agencies, professional and trade associations, and materials and manufacturing associations.

A number of these publications are outlined in this appendix and the two which follow to acquaint the reader with their contents. Publications mentioned are not necessarily the latest editions, but reference should be made to the particular publication which was current at the time of the incident.

These publications relate to the following major areas: construction and buildings; industry and machinery; transportation; and national consensus standards.

Building codes rely heavily on these standards to serve as criteria for acceptable safe practice, for materials, products, and construction methods and uses. The codes also indicate whether conformance with these standards is mandatory or permissive.

The following outline lists the authors of some of the principal regulations and standards used in the areas of construction, industry, transportation, and general safety:

I. Construction and buildings
   - A. Regulations
      - 1. Federal government
         - a. Civilian
            - (1) United States Department of Labor
            - (2) United States Department of Agriculture
            - (3) National Bureau of Standards
         - b. Military
            - (1) United States Department of the Navy
            - (2) United States Department of the Army
            - (3) United States Department of the Air Force
            - (4) United States Department of Defense
      - 2. State government
      - 3. County government
         - a. Building and safety department

4. Municipal government
    a. Building and safety department
    b. Department of engineering

B. Standards
1. Contractors' associations
    a. Associated General Contractors of America
    b. Engineering and Grading Contractors Association
    c. Mason Contractors Association of America
    d. National Electrical Contractors Association
    e. American Road Builders Association
    f. American Federation of Labor—Congress of Industrial Organizations
2. Materials associations
    a. American Concrete Institute
    b. American Institute of Steel Construction
    c. American Welding Society
    d. Portland Cement Association
    e. American Aluminum Manufacturers Association
    f. Gypsum Association
    g. National Concrete Masonry Association
    h. National Lime Association
3. Professional and standard-developing associations
    a. American Society of Civil Engineers
    b. American Society of Mechanical Engineers
    c. National Bureau of Standards
    d. American National Standards Institute, Inc.
    e. American Society for Testing and Materials
    f. American Society of Heating, Refrigeration and Air Conditioning Engineers
    g. American Water Works Association
    h. International Conference of Building Officials
    i. International Association of Plumbing and Mechanical Officials
    j. Building Officials and Code Administrators International, Inc.

II. Industry and machinery

A. Regulations
1. Federal
    a. United States Nuclear Regulatory Commission
    b. United States Department of Interior, Bureau of Mines

c. United States Department of Labor
d. United States Health Service
e. United States Department of the Navy
f. United States Department of the Army
g. United States Coast Guard
h. United States Department of Agriculture

2. State
3. County
4. Municipality

B. Standards

1. Manufacturers' associations
a. American Foundrymen's Association
b. Electronic Industries Association
c. National Electric Manufacturers' Association
d. Industrial Safety Equipment Association
e. National Association of Chain Manufacturers
f. Foundry Equipment Manufacturers' Association
g. National Foundry Association
h. Woodworking Machinery Manufacturers' Association
i. Crane Manufacturers' Association of America, Inc.

2. Materials associations
a. American Gas Association
b. American Petroleum Institute
c. National Paint, Varnish and Lacquer Association
d. American Iron and Steel Institute
e. Cast Iron Pipe Institute

3. Professional associations
a. American Society of Mechanical Engineers
b. American Conference of Governmental Industrial Hygienists
c. American Nuclear Society
d. American Society of Quality Engineers

III. Transportation

A. Regulations

1. Federal
a. United States Department of Transportation, Federal Highway Administration
b. National Academy of Sciences, National Research Council, Highway Research Board

2. State
   a. Division of highways
   b. Department of highways
   c. Highway commissions
   d. Department of transportation
   e. Public utilities commission
   f. Department of public works
3. County
   a. Department of roads
   b. Department of engineering
4. Municipality
   a. Department of streets and traffic
   b. Department of public works

B. Standards
1. Manufacturing associations
   a. Association of American Railroads
2. Professional associations
   a. American Association of Highway Officials
   b. Society of Automotive Engineers, Inc.
   c. Institute of Traffic Engineers
   d. National Highway Safety Bureau
   e. National Safety Council
   f. National Committee of Uniform Traffic Laws and Ordinances

IV. National consensus standards
A. American National Standards Institute, Inc. (formerly American Standards Association)
B. American Society for Testing and Materials
C. National Fire Protection Association
D. American Insurance Association
E. American Mutual Insurance Alliance
F. Factory Mutual Engineering Corporation
G. National Safety Council
H. National Bureau of Standards
I. Underwriters' Laboratories, Inc.
J. International Conference of Building Officials
K. Building Officials Conference Association
L. Southern Building Code Congress

Appendix C
Outlines of Typical Regulations and Standards

1. Construction and Buildings

a. Construction Safety and Health Regulations, Part 126

Author: Department of Labor, OSHA—2207, Washington, DC
Publisher: Department of Labor, OSHA—2207, Washington, DC
Edition: June 24, 1974
Scope:

General safety in the working place is sought by reducing safety and health hazards. Regulations are to encourage employers and employees to meet safety and health standards in all places of business and commerce and to enforce these standards.

Major subjects:

1) Working hours
2) Environmental controls
3) Personal protective and lifesaving equipment
4) Fire protection and prevention
5) Signs, signals, and barricades
6) Materials handling, storage, use, and disposal
7) Equipment used in construction
8) Demolition
9) Blasting

Potential issues for litigation:

1) Personal injury due to exposure to:
   a) Radiation

b) Excessive noise

c) Contaminated air

2) Failure of personal safety devices
3) Negligent use of flammable and combustible liquids
4) Failure to properly dispose of hazardous waste materials
5) Personal injury caused by failure to provide guardrails

b. Code Manual for the State Building and Construction Code, State of New York

Author: State Building Code Council, Housing and Building Codes Bureau, 393 Seventh Avenue, New York, NY 10001

Scope:

The Code Manual is an advisory guide interpreting the New York State Building Construction Code. The manual contains standards which are acceptable methods of compliance with the code. The manual pertains to the construction of one- and two-family dwellings and multiple dwellings.

Major subjects:

1) Space requirements
2) Structural regulations
3) Fire safety regulations
4) Equipment requirements

Potential issues for litigation:

1) Improper provision for snowload
2) Improper fire protection
3) Defective safety devices in coal-burning equipment
4) Fire caused by failure to provide separation walls

c. County of Los Angeles Building Code

Authors: Building and Safety Division, Department of County Engineer

Publisher: Building News, Inc., 3O55 Overland Avenue, Los Angeles, CA 90034, (213) 870-9871

Edition: 1975

Scope:

This volume of building laws includes four ordinances:

1) The County of Los Angeles Building Code—Ordinance 2225 amended to 11,095, adopting the Uniform Building Code Standards (1973 edition) prepared by the International Conference of Building Officials
2) The Plumbing Code—Ordinance 2269, adopting the Uniform Plumbing Code (1973 edition) prepared by the International Association of Plumbing and Mechanical Officials
3) The Mechanical Code—Ordinance 9544, adopting the Uniform Mechanical Code (1973) as promulgated by the International Association of Plumbing and Mechanical Officials and the International Conference of Building Officials
4) The Electrical Code—Ordinance 11,096, adopting the National Electric Code (1978 edition) published by the National Fire Protection Association.

The fundamental purposes of these codes are to protect the public health, safety, and welfare within the area in which the codes apply by determining minimum acceptable standards of building design and construction, and establishing procedural safeguards in administration through plan review and inspection.

These building laws apply directly to construction in all unincorporated portions of Los Angeles County, and, by the governing bodies, in the 31 cities which contract with the county for building inspection and related services.

Major Subjects:

1) Building codes
    a) Administrative
        (1) Organization and enforcement
        (2) Permits and inspection
    b) Requirements based on occupancy
    c) Fire zones
    d) Types of construction
    e) Engineering regulations-quality and design of materials for construction
    f) Regulations for use of public streets and projections over public property
2) Plumbing code
    a) Administration
        (1) Inspection
        (2) Licensing
    b) Installation requirements
3) Mechanical code
    a) Administrative
        (1) Inspection
        (2) Alternate materials and methods of construction
        (3) Violations and penalties
        (4) Permits

   b) Heating, ventilation and comfort cooling
   c) Refrigeration
4) Electrical code
   a) Duties and liability of electrical inspector
   b) Installation methods
   c) Violations and penalties

Potential issues for litigation:

1) Breach of duty by inspectors
2) Damage caused by re-use of previously used industrial apparatus and processing equipment
3) Damage from use of unapproved equipment
4) Injury caused by malfunction of pressure limiting device on heating equipment
5) Trespass—failure to obtain easement for sewers
6) Damage to drainage and sewer systems
7) Dangerous or unsanitary construction
8) Malfunction of fire extinguishing systems
9) Hazardous buildings
10) Damage to adjoining property in construction of foundation—soil excavation
11) Fire caused by careless wiring
12) Building defects from improper construction
13) Building repairs—cost of repairing defects caused by poor workmanship

d. Manual of Accident Prevention in Construction

Author and Publisher: Associated General Contractors of America, 1957 E Street NW, Washington, DC 20006
Edition: Sixth Edition, 1971
Scope:

The manual's primary objective since first publication in 1927 has been to insure effective control of accidents in the construction industry. It outlines techniques and procedures which are essential for that protection.

The manual states that it is not compiled for legislative or mandatory uses; however, numerous provisions promulgated by the Associated General Contractors have been formally adopted by the Department of Labor in its Occupational Safety and Health Act.

Major subjects:

1) Accident prevention organization
2) Occupational diseases
3) Safety nets

4) Fire hazards and prevention
5) Power tools
6) Ladders
7) Scaffolding
8) Mobile cranes, derricks, and tower cranes
9) Handling and storage of materials

Potential issues for litigation:

1) Damage caused by defective material hoists
2) Explosion due to improper use or storage of explosives or flammable gases
3) Accidents caused by failure to post visible signs in highway construction
4) Personal injury due to defective equipment
5) Accidents caused by failure to provide adequate training to operators of heavy earthmoving equipment

e. Construction Safety Orders

Author: Division of Industrial Safety, Department of Industrial Relations, State of California, California Administrative Code, Title 8, Industrial Relations
Publisher: Document Section, P.O. Box 20191, Sacramento, CA
Scope:

This publication lists the regulations which provide for construction work and construction sites to be safe. The requirements parallel those of the general industrial safety orders but aim specifically at safety during construction.

Major subjects:

1) Accident prevention programs
2) Sanitary conditions
3) Protection against dust, mists, fumes, and gases
4) Rock drilling
5) Excavation and earthwork
6) Explosives
7) Cranes, derricks, and other lifting devices
8) Pile driving
9) Construction elevators
10) Hand and guardrails, ramps, stairs, and ladders
11) Temporary floors
12) Scaffolding and shoring
13) Demolition

Potential issues of litigation:

1) Collapse of crane
2) Failure of hoisting cable
3) Falls from high places
4) Damage due to wall collapse during demolition
5) Collapse of shoring

f. The BOCA Basic Building Code

Author: Buiding Officials and Code Administrators International, Inc., 17926 South Halsted Street, Homewood, IL 60430
Edition: Seventh Edition, 1978
Scope:

The BOCA Basic Building Code states regulations in terms of measured performance rather than rigid specification of materials. It presents the purposes to be accomplished and does not specify methods, so as to allow a wide range of discretion to building designers and engineers. The code accepts nationally recognized standards as the criteria for evaluation of minimum safe practices or performance of materials and systems of construction.

The code is published in a convenient form to facilitate adoption by local governments. The regulations are aimed at controlling all matters of construction, alteration, addition, repair, removal, demolition, location, use, and occupancy of buildings and structures.

Major subjects:

1) Administration and enforcement
   a) Department of building inspection
   b) Duties and powers of building officials
   c) Permits
   d) Unsafe buildings
   e) Emergency measures
2) Defects and classifications of building types
3) Building limitations
4) Light and ventilation
5) Means of egress
6) Structural and foundational loads and stresses
7) Materials and tests
8) Fire resistive construction requirements
9) Heating equipment and appliances—mounting, clearances and connections
10) Prefabricated construction
11) Light-transmitting plastic construction

Potential issues for litigation:

1) Damage from failure to follow accepted engineering practice
2) Fire damage caused by inferior fire alarms
3) Damage due to collapse of columns caused by insufficient reinforcement
4) Unsafe storage of combustible dust, grain, and construction materials
5) Flooding damages caused by failure to protect against corrosion
6) Sanctions for deviation from code
7) Fire caused by unsafe electrical wiring
8) Damage to adjoining property because of failure to provide protection during excavation
9) Damage during fire caused by:
   a) Defective sprinklers
   b) Locked exits
10) Personal injury due to insufficient lighting in stairways and exit ways
11) Personal injury to passersby caused by negligent storage of hazardous materials and equipment

g. Uniform Plumbing Code

Authors: International Association of Plumbing and Mechanical Officials (formerly Western Plumbing Officials Association), 5032 Alhambra Avenue, Los Angeles, CA 90032
Edition: 1973
Scope:

The International Association of Plumbing and Mechanical Officials Code is an attempt to unify plumbing standards. The association formed a committee composed of plumbing inspectors, master and journeymen plumbers, and sanitary and mechanical engineers which compiled the first edition of the Uniform Plumbing Code in 1945.

The 1973 publication is an amended edition which is subject to adoption by the various jurisdictions.

Major subjects:

1) Installation requirements
2) Materials used
3) Drainage systems
4) Vents and venting
5) Water distribution
6) Indirect and special wastes
7) Traps and interceptors
8) Fuel gas piping
9) Rules for sizing water systems

10) Minimum plumbing facilities
11) Rainwater systems
12) Trailer park plumbing standards
13) Swimming pools

Potential issues for litigation:

1) Damage resulting from abandoned cesspools
2) Damage due to unauthorized gas service
3) Nuisance cause of action based on unsanitary conditions or industrial waste
4) Damage due to defective materials
5) Damage due to defective drainage system
6) Damage from undetected gas leaks resulting in fire

h. Uniform Building Code Standards

Authors: National associations, societies, and federal agencies
Publishers: International Conference of Building Officials, 5360 South Workman Mill Road, Whittier, CA 90601
Edition: 1976
Scope:

This publication provides various specifications and requirements for materials and processes, while citing the source materials for any such requirement in the heading of each standard. The publication omits materials which deal with subjects extraneous to the Uniform Building Codes. For this reason, the author organizations assume no responsibility for rewriting and re-editing their respective codes.

The conference does this editing because the standards are not originally written with the building official or legal requirements of a building code in mind. Hence, revisions aim at making the language of a standard compatible with enforcement requirements. These revisions are necessary to legally translate a standard from permissive to mandatory.

The standards present, compactly and concisely, all the national tests, materials, and special design standards referred to in the Uniform Building Code.

Major subjects:

1) Testing of noncombustible materials
2) Storage and handling of flammable and combustible liquids
3) Fire alarm systems for high-rise buildings
4) Load-bearing of concrete masonry units
5) Classification, defects, and methods of grading for all species of lumber
6) Field tests for grout and mortar concrete tests
7) Specifications for structural steel
8) Material and methods in construction of roofing
9) Moisture-density relations of soils

Potential issues for litigation:

1) Personal injury in construction due to mishandling or negligent storage of flammable materials
2) Fire damage due to malfunction or negligent installation or construction of fire alarm system
3) Cracking and structural failure in construction due to overloading structural units
4) Construction failure due to misuse of lumber species
5) Damage from collapse of defective roofing
6) Damage due to flooding

i. Manual of Steel Construction

Author: American Institute of Steel Construction, Inc.
Publisher: American Institute of Steel Construction, Inc., 400 North Michigan Avenue, Chicago, IL 60611
Edition: Eighth Edition, 1980
Scope:

The purpose of this manual is to: (1) improve and advance the use of fabricated structural steel for buildings and bridges; (2) provide the most economical and efficient methods of design and construction; and (3) be the source of standard method of design, fabrication, and construction of steel structures.

Major subjects:

1) Standard methods of design, symbols, abbreviations, and detailing of steel structures
2) Standard sizes and configurations of steel members manufactured by steel mills
3) Standard steel mill practice
4) Allowable stresses in columns and beams
5) Camber and deflection of beams
6) Standard steel connections
7) Bolts, rivets, and welding
8) Specifications for design, fabrication, and erection of structural steel
9) Code of standard practice

Potential issues for litigation:

1) Failure of connections
2) Excessive deflection
3) Distortion of steel members
4) Building collapse due to fire
5) Conflict as to design methods
6) Misfit of steel
7) Backcharges to fabricator or designer

j. Douglas Fir Use Book

Author: West Coast Lumbermen's Association
Publisher: *Daily Journal of Commerce,* Portland, OR
Edition: First Edition
Scope:

Physical and mechanical properties of Douglas fir lumber.

Major subjects:

Grades of Douglas fir lumber and their properties, including the following:

1) Design data including description of loads and stresses
2) Glued laminated lumber
3) Preservation of wood
4) Joists, beams, columns, planks, and rafters
5) Connections, including nails, bolts, lag screws, dowels, and anchors
6) Wind and earthquake design
7) Fire protection

Potential issues for litigation:

1) Excessive deflection of beams under load
2) Splitting and failure of girders
3) Nonstandard lumber quality
4) Excessive drying and warping of lumber
5) Failure of connections

k. Concrete Reinforcing Steel Handbook

Author: Engineering Practice Committee of the Concrete Reinforcing Steel Institute
Publisher: Concrete Reinforcing Steel Institute, 228 North LaSalle Street, Chicago, IL 60601
Edition: First Edition, 1974
Scope:

Provides basic design data and standard construction methods for reinforced concrete construction. All data is based on the 1971 American Concrete Institute (ACI) Building Code. Most building and safety codes published by public entities incorporate the ACI Building Code.

Major subjects:

1) Computer programs for design
2) Grades of steel and strength of concrete
3) Standard design of concrete columns, beams, slabs, and joists

4) Methods of splicing reinforcing bars
5) Alternate methods of design

Potential issues for litigation:

1) Cracking of concrete walls
2) Cracking of concrete beams
3) Substandard concrete test results
4) Improper concrete mixes
5) Misplacement of reinforcing bars
6) Improper grade of steel reinforcement
7) Excessive deflection of slabs and beams
8) Conflict in design methods
9) Deterioration of concrete

2. Industry and Machinery

a. Code of Federal Regulations—Labor

Publisher: *Federal Register*, National Archives and Records Service, General Services Administration, Washington, DC 20408
Edition: January 1, 1972
Scope:

Parts 900 to the end, chapters 9 to 20, of the Code of Federal Regulations, Title 29, Subtitle B, deal with regulations relating to labor practices, safety, and administration.

Major subjects:

1) Construction Industry Collective Bargaining Commission
2) National Mediation Board
3) Occupational Safety and Health Administration, Department of Labor
   a) Regulations for ship repairing
   b) Regulations for shipbuilding
   c) Regulations for ship breaking
   d) Regulations for longshoring
   e) Enforcement of §41 of the Longshoremen's and Harbor Workers' Compensation Act
4) Construction Industry Stabilization Committee

Potential issues for litigation:

1) Personal injury due to failure to provide personal protective equipment
2) Injury to employee because of malfunction or defects in respiratory protection devices

3) Personal injury caused by failure to warn of hazardous condition
4) Personal injury from failure to instruct
5) Damage caused by negligent failure to lock brakes while loading or unloading trucks, trailers, or railway cars
6) Injury due to defective ladders

b. Industrial Ventilation—A Manual of Recommended Practice

Author: Committee on Industrial Ventilation, P.O. Box 453, Lansing, MI 48902
Publisher: American Conference of Governmental Industrial Hygienists
Edition: 13th Edition, 1974
Scope:

The manual, which goes back to an original publication of 1951, is based in part on a field manual of the Division of Occupational Health, Michigan Department of Health.

Showing an awareness of the importance of clean, uncontaminated air in the industrial work environment, the manual sets use standards in the design of ventilation systems. Proper ventilation is essential in work environments where chemical compounds are used, which cause the dissemination of fumes, gases, vapors, and mists into the workplace atmosphere.

Major subjects:

1) Principles of ventilation
2) Design procedure
3) Air cleaning devices

Potential issues for litigation:

1) Contamination due to improper ventilation
2) Intoxication due to defective ventilation system
3) Personal injury due to defective fans, i.e., improper location, improper installation, or improper maintenance

c. Recommended Good Practice for Safeguarding Flammable Liquid Storage and Processing

Publisher: Factory Insurance Association, Chicago, IL
Edition: 1953
Scope:

The standards promulgated by the Factory Insurance Association are intended to supplement federal, state, and local regulations. They describe the facilities and techniques required to safeguard flammable liquid storage and processing in factory insurance association plants.

Major subjects:

1) Inside storage and handling of flammable liquids drums and smaller containers
2) Outside storage
    a) Buried tanks
    b) Above ground tanks

Potential issues for litigation:

1) Intoxication caused by improperly stored flammable vapors
2) Explosions

3. Transportation

a. Manual of Uniform Traffic Control Devices for Streets and Highways

Author: American Association of State Highway Officials and National Joint Committee on Uniform Traffic Control Devices
Publisher: United States Department of Transportation, Federal Highway Administration, Washington, DC 20591
Edition: 1971, supersedes 1961 publication
Scope:

The necessity for coordination of standards applicable to different road and street systems prompted publication of the original edition of this manual in 1935. The standards developed and revised since the original publication date have been adopted by the Federal Highway Administration as national requirements for application to all classes of highways.

The manual sets standards for installation of traffic control devices on all federally aided highway systems. Implementation is expected to be governed by federal directives. It is a manual which can also be a source of suggestions, however, for local jurisdictions.

Major subjects:

1) Signs
2) Markings
3) Signals
4) Traffic controls for street and highway construction and maintenance operations
5) Traffic controls for school areas

Potential issues for litigation:

1) Transportation accidents due to faulty installation of traffic control devices
2) Transportation accidents caused by malfunctioning of devices
3) Accidents caused by improper signaling

4) Accidents due to lack of signs
5) Accidents due to negligent maintenance

4. National Consensus Standards

a. Catalog of American National Standards

Publisher: American National Standards Institute, 1430 Broadway, New York, NY 10018
Edition: 1980
Scope:

American National Standards Institute administers a federated national standards system. It has been recognized nationally as a standards-producing organization under the Department of Labor.

This catalog lists standards by subject and by designation, facilitating location of pertinent standards in a desired field of inquiry.

American National Standards Institute-approved American National Standards are identified by the sponsor's designation (where there is one), preceded by the organization's acronym, and ANSI's—for example, ANSI/ASTM A134-74. This refers to the standard for electric-fusion welded, steel plate pipe.

Major Subjects:

The catalog of the ANSI Standards is arranged under alphabetically arranged headings. Some examples are:

1) Access control
2) Accidents
3) Acids
4) Acoustics
5) Aerospace equipment
6) Aerospace material
7) Building construction
8) Chemicals, industrial
9) Ducts, air
10) Elevators
11) Exhaust systems
12) Explosions
13) Fire doors
14) Fire fighting equipment
15) Flammable liquids
16) Glazing materials

17) Head protection
18) Hydrocarbons
19) Inspection
20) Lifting devices
21) Metal products
22) Nuclear fuels
23) Petroleum
24) Plastics
25) Shipping containers
26) Timber
27) Tires
28) Vehicles, motor
29) Wood working machinery

Potential Issues for Litigation:

1) Conflict in construction plans
2) Improper construction
3) Defective materials
4) Delay in completion
5) Malpractice in design
6) Errors and omissions
7) Defective installation
8) Building collapse
9) Conflict in cost of construction
10) Explosion
11) Fire

b. National Fire Codes

Author: National Fire Protection Association Technical Committees
Publisher: National Fire Protection Association International, 470 Atlantic Avenue, Boston, MA 02210
Edition: Revised Edition Volume 1, 1973-74
Scope:

The National Fire Codes are a set of 10 volumes of codes, standards, recommended practices, and manuals developed by the National Fire Protection Association (NFPA).

The NFPA codes serve as a basis for laws, ordinances, and other regulatory measures in the interest of public safety.

Each volume contains a group of codes arranged to relate to one broad subject as indicated by the volume title. Each text within a volume deals with a single subject or feature.

The NFPA is an international, nonprofit, technical and educational association functioning in an advisory capacity to provide a high standard of care for public safety.

Its recommendations are often adopted by formal legislation.

Major subjects (Volume #1 on flammable liquids, boiler furnaces, and ovens):

1) Flammable and combustible liquids code
2) Oil-burning equipment
3) Dry cleaning plants
4) Solvent extraction plants
5) Tank vehicles for flammable and combustible liquids
6) Portable shipping tanks
7) Flammable and combustible liquids on farms and isolated construction projects
8) Natural gas, fuel oil, and gas-fired boiler furnaces

Volumes in set:

#2 Gases
#3 Combustible solids, dusts, and explosives
#4 Building construction and facilities
#5 Electrical
#6 Sprinklers, fire pumps, and water tanks
#7 Alarm and special extinguishing systems
#8 Portable and manual fire control equipment
#9 Occupancy standards and process hazards
#10 Transportation

Potential issues for litigation:

1) Fires
2) Explosions
3) Defective fire protection
4) Unsafe electrical equipment
5) Defective fire alarm systems
6) Unsafe storage facilities
7) Unsafe dwellings

c. National Electric Code, 1978

Author: National Fire Protection Association
Publisher: National Fire Protection Association International, 470 Atlantic Avenue, Boston, MA 02210
Scope:

This code contains minimum provisions for safety in the use of electricity for light, heat, power, radio, signaling, and other purposes.

Major subjects:

1) Wiring, design, and protection
2) Appliances, motors, generators, and transformers
3) Hazardous occupancies and locations
4) Special equipment, including electric signs, crances, elevators, welding, x-ray, and machinery
5) High and low voltage
6) communication

Potential issues for litigation:

1) Electrocution
2) Electrical fires
3) Errors in design
4) Improper installation
5) Substandard material

Appendix D
OSHA Regulations as a Reference Source

One of the best sources of information regarding safe design, installation, and operation of industrial facilities, machinery, materials, and processes is the Occupational Safety and Health Administration (OSHA) standards. Since these regulations incorporate many of the national consensus standards, this information is a convenient, single-source reference for the attorney and the engineering expert in establishing a basis for standard practice.

The applicability of the OSHA regulations to the issue of negligence in construction injury cases has been considered by numerous courts.

In an Arkansas case,[1] a general contractor's employee sued a subcontractor for personal injuries received when the employee stepped from scaffolding to an unfastened portable ladder, which shifted its position, causing the employee to fall upon debris on the ground. OSHA regulations provided that portable ladders should be fastened and the area below them kept clean. The court held violation of the OSHA regulation to be evidence of negligence, to be considered with the other facts and circumstances.

Similarly, in a Washington case,[2] an employee of a subcontractor sued the general contractor for injuries received from a fall. The employee claimed that OSHA regulation 29 CFR §1926.105 required use of a safety net and that the general contractor's failure to provide such a safety device was negligence. The court agreed holding that not only was the OSHA regulation relevant to the appropriate standard of care, but also, since OSHA regulations were specifically authorized for the purpose of making safe the employee's place of work, and since employers and workman alike had full and adequate notice of the existence of the regulations, violation of the OSHA regulations in these circumstances was negligence per se, or negligence as a matter of law, rather than a question of fact.

However, a federal district court[3] has reasoned in a minority rule case, that since OSHA does not create a cause of action for which a civil remedy exists, a violation of its standards should not be considered evidence of negligence in a civil action.

The following is a check list based on the references given in the OSHA standards, and subdivided into a presentation of the workplace, machinery and equipment, employee, process, and administration standards. Each of these subdivisions is further subdivided.

---

[1]Dunn v Brimer, 259 Ark 855, 537 SW2d 164 (1976).

[2]Kelly v Howard S Wright Constr Co, 90 Wash 2d 323, 582 P2d 500 (1978).

[3]Otto v Specialties, Inc. 386 F Supp 1240 (ND Miss 1974).

Potential Issues of Litigation Relating to the Workplace	29 CFR 1910 Sub-part	29 CFR 1910 Section
A. Electrical wiring, fixtures, and controls		
1. General—National Electrical Code (NEC)	S	309
2. Grounding		309
3. Hazardous locations (Classes I-III)		309(a)
4. Lighting fixtures		309
5. Overcurrent protection (NFPA Article 240)		309
B. Exits and Access		
1. Access to exits, exterior	E	37(g)
2. Access to exits, interior		37(f)
3. Application and general requirements		36(a)
4. Arrangement		37(e)
5. Capacity, occupancy loads		37(d)
6. Fundamental requirements		36(b)
7. Maintenance, path of travel		37(k)
8. Markings, locations and illumination		37(g)
9. Obstructions and decorations		37(1)
10. Permissible exit components		37(a)
11. Protection during construction and repair		36(c)
12. Special buildings, rooms, and operations		
a. Acetylene generator houses	G	252(a)(6)
b. Bulk plant storage, flammable and combustible liquids	H	106(f)(2)
c. Gaseous hydrogen systems	H	103(b)(3)
d. Liquefied hydrogen systems	H	103(c)(2)&(3)
e. Sawmills, emergency exits, doors, and fire escapes	R	265(c)(6)
f. Sawmills, fuel hoses, and bins	R	265(c)(23)
C. Fire protection		
1. Automatic sprinklers, fixed systems	L	159
a. Fire department connections		159(b)
b. General requirements		159(a)
c. Maintenance		159(d)
d. Sprinkler alarm systems		159(c)
e. Sprinkler head clearances		159(e)
2. Carbon dioxide extinguishing systems	L	161
a. General requirements		161(a)
b. Inspection and maintenance		161(b)
3. Dry chemical extinguishing systems, fixed	L	160
a. Alarms and indicators		160(b)

Potential Issues of Litigation Relating to the Workplace	29 CFR 1910 Subpart	29 CFR 1910 Section
b. General requirements		160(a)
c. Inspection and maintenance		160(c)
4. Fire alarm signaling systems	L	163
a. Fire alarm boxes		163(b)
b. General requirements		163(a)
c. Maintenance		163(h)
5. Fire extinguishers, portable	L	157
a. General requirements		157(a)&(c)
b. Inspection, maintenance, and testing		157(d)
c. Location and placements		157(a)(2)
d. Marking of location and extinguishers		157(a)(3)&(4)
e. Mounting		157(a)(5)-(10)
f. Numbers and distribution		157(c)(1)
g. Selection and distribution		157(b)(1)
–By anticipated type fires and occupancy		157(b)(1)
–By classes of hazards		157(b)(2)
–All classes of hazards (Tables L-1 and L-2)		157(c)
h. Size and placement		158
6. Hazardous locations, electrical	S	308(c)
a. Electrical fixtures, wiring, locations (Classes I-III)		309
b. New electrical installations		309(b)
7. Standpipe and hose systems	L	158
a. General requirements		158(a)
b. Hoses and connections		158(b)
c. Maintenance and testing		158(d)
d. Water supply		158(c)
D. Housekeeping and general work environment		
1. Asbestos	G	93a(h)
2. Crane cabs	N	179(o)(2)
3. Pulpwood logging	R	266(e)(3&4)
4. Sanitation	J	141(a)(1),(2),(3)&(4)
5. Storage areas, indoor	N	176(c)
6. Work areas	D	22(a)
E. Illumination (lighting)		
1. Crane cabs	N	179(c)(4)
2. Emergency lighting, pulp and paper mills	R	261(b)(7)
3. Exits and exit signs	E	37(9)

Potential Issues of Litigation Relating to the Workplace	29 CFR 1910 Sub-part	Section
4. Floor landings, manlifts	F	68(b)(14)
5. Other		
a. Labor camps	J	142(g)
b. Laundry operations	R	264(f)(2)
c. Loading and unloading areas, pulp and paper mills	R	261(c)(10)
d. Machine rooms	R	261(k)(21)
e. Machinery, basement areas	O	219(c)(5)
f. Operating areas, industrial trucks	N	178(h)
g. Pulpwood harvesting, roads and trails	R	266(e)(15)
h. Sawmills, work areas, buildings, and rooms	R	265(c)(9)
i. Spray booths	H	107(b)(10)
j. Storage areas, indoor	N	177(f)(1)
F. Sanitation and Health		
1. Application and general requirement	J	241(a)
a. Laundry operations	R	264(f)(2)
b. Pulp, paper, and paperboard mills	R	261(g)(15)
c. Sawmills	R	265(k)
2. Change rooms	J	141(e)(1)
a. Asbestos workers	G	93a(d)(4)
- Clothes lockers		93a(d)(4)
- Contaminated clothes, laundering		93a(d)(4)
3. Laundries	R	264(f)(2)
4. Lunchrooms	J	141(g)
5. Retiring rooms		141(f)
6. Temporary labor camps		142
7. Toilet facilities		141(c)
8. Washing facilities		141(d)
9. Waste disposal systems		141(a)(3)
a. Nonwater carriage		143
10. Water supply		
a. Nonpotable		141(b)(2)
b. Potable		141(b)(1)
c. Standpipe and hose systems		141(g)
G. Signs, labels, markings, and tabs		
1. Application and design	J	145
2. Labels		
a. Acceptable certifications, electrical equipment	S	308(d)
b. Asbestos	G	93a(g)
c. Electrical equipment (NFPA/NEC)	S	309

Potential Issues of Litigation Relating to the Workplace	29 CFR 1910 Sub-part	Section
d. Respiratory protection equipment	I	134
- Breathing gas containers, air quality		134(d)(4)
- Canisters, gas mask identification		134(g)
e. Welding rods, fillers, and coatings	Q	252(f)
3. Markings		
a. Compressed gas cylinders	Q	252(a)(2)
b. Explosive beads, power-actuated hand tools	P	243(d)(3)
c. Load ratings, markings, and charts		
- Crawler, locomotive, and truck cranes	N	180(c)(2)
- Derricks	N	181(c)
- Powered industrial trucks	N	178(a)(3)
- Powered platforms	F	66(c)(7),(21)
d. Standpipes, hose connections	L	158(b)(7),(c)(4)
4. Physical hazards, color coding	J	144(a)
a. Sawmills	R	265(c)(11)
5. Signs		
a. Asbestos caution signs and labels	G	93a(g)
b. Exit signs and markings	E	37(q)
c. Exits, emergency—sawmills	R	265(c)(6)
d. Extinguishers, locations	L	175(a)(3)
e. Extinguisher systems, carbon dioxide	L	161(a)(2)
f. Fuel gas systems, cylinder storage	Q	252(a)(2)
g. Lawn mowers, caution signs	P	243(2)(1)(v)
h. Manlifts, warning signs	F	68(c)(7)
i. Manifold systems, oxygen	Q	252(a)(3)
j. Radiation signs, signals and labels		
- Ionizing	G	96(e)
- Nonionizing		97(a)(3)
k. Storage areas, sawmills	R	262(l)(2)
l. Sprinkler systems, automatic	L	159(b)(4)
m. Standpipes, hose connections		158(b)(7)&(c)(4)
n. Traffic, in-plant	J	145(d)(8)
o. Vehicles, slow-moving		145(d)(10)
p. Water, nonpotable		141(b)(2)
6. Tags		
a. Biohazard	J	145(f)(8)
b. Caution		145(f)(5)
c. Danger		145(f)(4)
d. Defective equipment		145(f)(1)

Potential Issues of Litigation Relating to the Workplace	29 CFR 1910 Subpart	29 CFR 1910 Section
e. Defective ladders, metal	D	26(c)(2)
f. Defective ladders, wood		25(d)(1)
g. Do not start	J	145(f)(3)
h. Out of order		145(f)(6)
i. Radiation		145(f)(7)
j. Scope and purpose		145(f)(1)
H. Ventilation		
1. Air requirements, sawmills	R	265(c)(7)
2. Maintaining comfortable working conditions, laundries	R	264(d)
I. Walking and Working Surfaces		
1. Application and general requirements	D	22
a. Aisles and passageways		22(b)
b. Covers and guardrails, pits, tanks, and ditches		22(c)
c. Floors		
- General requirements		22(a)&23(a)
- Loading protection		22(d)
d. Housekeeping	D	22(a)&(b)
- General	J	141(a)
- Storage	N	176(c)
e. Safety factors, sawmills	R	265(c)(1)
2. Floors		
a. Crane access, footwalks and catwalks	N	179(c)&(d)
b. Guarding openings and holes	D	23(a)
- Chutes, hatchways, ladderways	R	261(k)
- Manholes, pits, trap doors, and skylights	R	265(i)
c. Loading protection	D	22(d)
d. Open-sided floors, ramps, runways, walkways		
- Bakery operations	R	263(d)(1)
- General requirements	D	23(c)
- Pulp, paper, and paperboard mills	R	261(b),(i),(j),&(k)
- Sawmills	R	265(c)(3),(4)
e. Sanitation, maintenance, and construction		
- General requirements	D	22(a)&(b)
	J	141(a)(1),(2)&(c)(2)
- Laundry operations	R	264(d)(1)
- Sawmills, nonslip floors	R	265(c)(2)&(3)
- Temporary labor camps	J	142(b)(4)&(f)(2)
- Washrooms and washing facilities	J	141(d)(1)

Potential Issues of Litigation Relating to the Workplace	29 CFR 1910 Sub-part	Section
3. Ladders		
a. Access ladders and platform guards	D	23(a)(2)
b. Crane access, ladders, and footwalks	N	179(c)&(d)
c. Fixed ladders, sawmills	R	265(c)(10)
d. Fixed ladders, design, construction, and installation	D	27
e. Mobil ladder stands and scaffolds	D	29
f. Portable metal ladders		
- Care, maintenance, and use	D	26(c)
- Design and construction		26(a)(1)
- Platform		26(a)(5)
- Step		26(a)(3)
- Straight and extension		26(a)(2)
- Testing		26(b)
- Trestles and extension trestle ladders		26(a)(4)
g. Portable wood ladders		
- Applicable requirements	D	25(a)
- Care and use		25(d)
- Construction and materials		25(c)&(b)
- Rung ladders		25(c)(3)
. . Extension ladders, two-sections		25(c)(3)(iii)
. . Sectional ladders		24(c)(3)(iv)
. . Single ladders		24(c)(3)(ii)
. . Trestles and extension trestle ladders		25(c)(3)(v)
h. Special-purpose ladders		
- Applicable requirements	D	25(c)(4)
- Masons' ladders		25(c)(4)(iii)
- Painters' stepladders		25(c)(4)(ii)
- Platform stepladders		25(c)(4)(i)
i. Trolley and side-rolling ladders	D	25(c)(5)
4. Other working and walking surfaces		
a. Bridge plates and dockboards	D	30(a)
	R	261(c)(11)
b. Forging machine areas	D	30(b)
c. Veneer machine areas	D	30(c)
d. Log dumps, booms, and ponds, sawmills	R	265(d)
e. Rail cars and ships, pulp, paper, and paperboard mills	R	261(c) (3), (4),&(11)
f. Roads and trails, pulpwood logging	R	266(e)(15)

Potential Issues of Litigation Relating to the Workplace	29 CFR 1910 Sub-part	Section
g. Roof areas	D	28(s)
h. Roof loading	D	28(d)
5. Scaffolding		
a. Application and scope	D	28(v)
b. General requirements and specifications		28(a)
- Anchorage		28(a)(2)
- Guardrails		28(a)(3)
- Midrails		28(a)(3)
- Overhead protection		28(a)(16)
- Planking		28(a)(8)(9)(11)&(13)
- Safe workloads		28(a)(4)
- Toeboards		28(a)(3)
c. Types of scaffolds		
- Boatswain's chair		28(j)
- Bricklayers' square		28(l)
- Carpenters' bracket		28(k)
- Crawling boards and chicken ladders		28(t)
- Float or ship		28(u)
- Horse		28(m)
- Interior hung		28(p)
- Ladder jack		28(q)
- Masons' adjustable multipoint suspension		28(f)
- Needle beam		28(n)
- Outrigger		28(e)
- Plasterers' and decorators' large area		28(o)
- Roofing brackets		28(s)
- Single-point adjustable suspension		28(i)
- Stonesetters' adjustable multipoint suspension		28(h)
- Tube and coupler		28(c)
- Two-point suspension swinging		28(g)
- Window jack		28(r)
- Wood pole		28(b)
6. Specifications		
a. Floor opening cover guards	D	23(e)(7)
b. Railings		23(e)(1),(2)&(3)
c. Skylight screens		23(e)(8)
d. Stairway railings and guards		23(d)(1)&(2)
e. Toeboards		23(e)(4)

Potential Issues of Litigation Relating to the Workplace	29 CFR 1910 Sub-part	29 CFR 1910 Section
7. Stairs, fixed industrial		
a. Application of requirements and limitations	D	24(a)&(b)
b. Design, construction, and installations	D	24(c)-(k)
c. Stair requirements, sawmills	R	265(c)(5)
d. Stairway railings and handrails	D	24(h)
8. Stairway railings and guards		
a. Access to different structures	D	24(b)
b. General specifications		23(d)&(e)
c. Sawmills	R	265(c)
d. Winding stairs	D	23(d)(2)
9. Wall openings and holes, guarding		
a. Dough chutes, bakeries	R	263(i)(9)
b. General requirements	D	23

Potential Issues of Litigation Relating to Machines and Equipment	29 CFR 1910 Sub-part	29 CFR 1910 Section
A. Appliances, electrical utilization	S	309
B. Compressed gas and compressed air equipment		
1. Air receivers	M	169
2. Compressed gas cylinders, inspection	M	166
3. Safety relief devices		
a. Cargo and portable tanks	M	168
b. Cylinders		167
C. Conveyers		
1. Bakeries	R	263(d)(7)&(i)(7)
2. Pulp, paper, and paperboard mills	R	261(f)(4) 261(c)(15)
3. Sawmills	R	265(c)(18)
4. Spray booths, spray finishing		107(h)(7)
D. Cranes—crawler, locomotive, and truck		
1. Application and general requirements	N	180(b)
a. Crane mounting, load tipping, and posting load rating charts		180(c)
b. Design, construction, and modification specifications, effective dates		180(b)(2)
c. Load rating, stability and lifting performance		180(c)
2. Crane testing	N	180(e)
a. Operational tests		180(e)(1)
b. Rated load tests		180(e)(2)
3. Inspection	N	180(d)
a. Records		180(d)(6)
b. Types		180(d)
4. Load handling	N	180(h)
a. Attaching loads		180(h)(2)
b. Holding and controlling loads		180(h)(4)
c. Moving loads		180(h)(3)
d. Restrictions on load size		180(h)(1)
5. Maintenance, repair procedures, and operational restrictions	N	180(f)
6. Operating near electric power lines and overhead wires	N	180(i)
7. Other		
a. Ballast and counterweights	N	180(i)(2)
b. Crane cabs, housekeeping		180(i)(3)
c. Fire protection and extinguishers		180(i)(5)
d. Rail clamps		180(i)(1)

Potential Issues of Litigation Relating to Machines and Equipment	29 CFR 1910 Sub-part	Section
e. Refueling		180(i)(4)
f. Swinging locomotive cranes		180(i)(6)
8. Rope inspections	N	180(g)
a. Other ropes		180(g)(2)
b. Reports		180(g)(2)
c. Running ropes		180(g)(1)
E. Cranes, overhead and gantry		
1. Application and general requirements	N	179(b)
a. Clearances from obstructions and parallel cranes		179(b)(6),(7)
b. Design construction and modification		179(b)
c. Guarding moving parts and hoisting ropes		179(e)(5),(6)
d. Rail clamps and wind indicator devices		179(b)(4)
e. Rated load markings		179(b)(5)
f. Warning devices		179(i)
2. Bumpers—bridge and trolley, rail sweeps, and other guards	N	179(e)
3. Brakes and braking system		
a. Hoists and hoist motors	N	179(f)(1)-(3)
b. Trolleys and bridges		179(f)(4)-(16)
4. Crane cabs and access to cranes		
a. Footwalks, ladders, stairways, toeboards, and handrails	N	179(d)
b. Location, fire protection and lighting		179 (c)
5. Electrical equipment	N	179(g)
6. Hoisting equipment, sheaves, ropes, fittings, hooks, and equalizers	N	179(h)
7. Inspection, testing, and maintenance		
a. Cranes and equipment	N	179(j)(k)&(l)
b. Hoist limit switch		179(n)(4)
c. Rope inspection reports		179(m)(2)
d. Running ropes and other ropes		179(m)
8. Load handling, attaching, and moving	N	179(n)
F. Derricks		
1. Application and general requirements	N	181(b)(1)
a. Design, construction, and modification		181(b)(1)&(2)
b. Load ratings and markings		181(c)
2. Inspection	N	181(d)

Potential Issues of Litigation Relating to Machines and Equipment	29 CFR 1910 Sub-part	Section
a. Derricks		181(d)
b. Ropes		181(g)
3. Load handling	N	181(i)
a. Attaching load		181(i)(2)
b. Boom securing		181(i)(6)
c. Load restriction and size		181(i)(1)
d. Moving and holding load		181(i)(3)&(4)
e. Winch heads		181(i)(5)
4. Maintenance and repair	N	181(f)
a. Adjustment and repairs		181(f)(3)
b. Maintenance procedures		181(f)(2)
c. Preventive maintenance		181(f)(1)
5. Operating near electric power lines	N	181(j)(5)
6. Operating of derricks	N	181(h)
7. Other requirements	N	181(j)
a. Cabs or operating enclosures, maintenance		181(j)(6)
b. Fire extinguishers		181(j)(3)
c. Guarding exposed machinery		181(j)(1)
d. Hook specifications		181(j)(2)
e. Refueling		181(j)(4)
8. Testing		
a. Anchorage	N	181(e)(2)
b. Operational tests		181(e)(1)
G. Hand and portable powered tools		
1. Abrasive wheels, portable	P	243(c)
2. Explosive-actuated fastening tools		243(d)
3. General requirements		242(a)
a. Signs, markings, and color codes		
- Explosive-actuated fastening tools		243(d)
- Lawn mowers		243(e)
4. Lawn mowers, powered		243(e)
5. Other portable equipment		244
a. Abrasive blast cleaning nozzles		244(b)
b. Electrode holders, welding	Q	252(b)(4)
c. Gas torches and valves		252(d)(4)
d. Hand tools, logging	R	266(c)(2)
e. Jacks	P	244(a)
f. Miscellaneous electrical equipment	S	309(a)
6. Pneumatic-powered hand tools and hoses	P	243(b)
7. Woodworking, portable powered tools		243(a)
H. Machinery and machine guarding		
1. Abrasive wheel machinery	0	215

Potential Issues of Litigation Relating to Machines and Equipment	29 CFR 1910 Sub-part	Section
2. Anchoring fixed machinery		212(b)
3. Cooperage machinery		214
4. Forging machines		218
5. General requirements		212
6. Guarding machines		212(a)
7. Mechanical power presses		217
8. Mechanical power transmission apparatus		219
9. Mills and calenders, rubber and plastics industries		216
10. Other machinery and equipment		
a. Alligator shears		212(a)(3)(iv)
b. Bakery equipment	R	263
c. Forming rolls	O	212(a)
d. Guilloting cutters		212(a)
e. Laundry equipment	R	264
f. Milling machines	O	212(a)
g. Revolving drums, barrels, and containers		212(a)
h. Shears, power		212(a)
i. Textile equipment	R	262
11. Woodworking machinery	O	213(l)
a. Boring and mortising machines		217
b. General requirements		213(a)&(b)
- Guarding		212(a) 213(r)(4)
- Inspection and maintenance		213 (s)
- Ventilation, exhaust hoods		213(r)(4)
c. Jointers	O	213 (j)
d. Other woodworking machines		
- Miscellaneous woodworking machines		213(r)
- Pulp, paper, and paperboard mills	R	261
- Pulpwood logging		266
- Sawmills		265
e. Planing, molding, sticking, and matching	O	213(n)
f. Profile, swinghead lathes		213(o)
g. Sanding machines		213(p)
h. Saws		
- Bandsaws and band resaws		213(i)
- Circular resaws		213(e)
- Hand-fed crosscut table saws		213(d)
- Hand-fed ripsaws		213(c)

Potential Issues of Litigation Relating to Machines and Equipment	29 CFR 1910 Sub-part	Section
- Radial saws		213(h)
- Self-feed circular saws		213(f)
- Swing cutoff saws		213(g)
- Veneer cutters and wringers		213(q)
I. Miscellaneous equipment used in general industry		
1. Manlifts	F	68
2. Manually propelled mobile ladder stands and scaffolds	D	29
3. Portable metal ladders	D	26
4. Portable wood ladders	D	25
5. Powered platforms for exterior building maintenance	F	66
6. Vehicle-mounted work platforms	F	67
J. Miscellaneous equipment used in special industries		
1. Bakery equipment	R	263
2. Laundry machine operations		264
3. Pulp, paper, and paperboard mills		261
4. Pulpwood logging		266
5. Sawmills		265
6. Textiles		262
K. Trucks		
1. Powered industrial trucks	N	178
a. Application and general requirements		178(a)
b. Converted powered industrial trucks and operating locations		178(d)
c. Environmental controls		
- Lighting operating areas	N	178(h)
- Noxious gases and fumes	N	178(i)
	G	93
d. Maintenance	N	178(q)
- Fueling, fuel handling, and storage		178(f)&(p)
- Storage batteries, charging and changing		178(g)
e. Operation, traveling, and loading		178(k),(m),(n)(o)&(p)
f. Operator training and authorized operators		178(l)
g. Overhead guards for high-lift rider trucks		178(e)&(m)(9)
h. Restricted use in designated locations and hazardous atmospheres		178(b)&(c)

Potential Issues of Litigation Relating to Machines and Equipment	29 CFR 1910 Subpart	Section
2. Trucks, other types		
a. Ammonia systems mounted on farm vehicles	H	111(g)
b. Ammonia-transporting tank motor vehicles		111(f)
c. Explosives transport		109(d)
d. Flammable liquids, tank vehicles		106(e)(4)&(g)(1)
e. LP-gas systems mounted on commercial vehicles		110(g)
f. LP-gas transport trucks		110(b)(15)
g. Personnel transport	R	266(e)(8)

Potential Issues of Litigation Relating to Materials	29 CFR 1910 Subpart	Section
A. Hazardous materials		
1. Air contaminants	G	93
a. Acceptable ceiling concentrations and 8-hour time-weighted averages (Table G-2)		93(h)
b. Ceiling values and 8-hour time-weighted averages (Table G-1)		93(a)
c. Mineral dusts 8-hour time-weighted averages (Table G-3)		93(c)
d. Requirements and specifications		93
2. Anhydrous ammonia, storage and handling	H	111
a. Basic rules		111(b)
b. General requirements		111(a)
c. Refrigerated storage systems		111(d)
d. Systems mounted on farm vehicles, ammonia		111(h)
e. Systems mounted on farm vehicles, other than ammonia		111(g)
f. Systems utilizing portable DOT containers		111(e)
g. Systems utilizing stationary, nonrefrigerated storage containers		111(c)
h. Tank motor vehicles for ammonia transport		111(f)
3. Compressed gases		
a. Acetylene	H	102
b. General requirements		101
c. Hydrogen		103
d. Nitrous oxide		105
e. Oxygen		104
4. Explosives and blasting agents	H	109
a. Blasting agents		109(g)
b. General requirements		109(b)
c. Small arms ammunition, primers, propellants		109(j)
d. Storage of ammonium nitrate		109(i)
e. Storage of explosives		109(c)
f. Transportation of explosives		109(d)
g. Use		109(e)
5. Flammable and combustible liquids	H	106
a. Bulk plants		106(f)
b. Container and portable tank storage		106(d)

Potential Issues of Litigation Relating to Materials	29 CFR 1910 Subpart	29 CFR 1910 Section
c. Definitions		106(a)
d. Industrial plants		106(e)
e. Piping, valves, and fittings		106(c)
f. Processing plants		106(h)
g. Refineries, chemical plants, and distilleries		106(i)
h. Service stations		106(g)
i. Tank storage		106(b)
6. Ionizing radiation	G	96
7. Storage and handling of liquefied petroleum (LP) gases	H	110
a. Basic rules		110(b)
b. Cylinder systems		110(c)
c. Motor fuel		110(e)
d. Service stations		110(h)
e. Storage of containers awaiting use or resale		110(f)
f. System installations on commercial vehicles		110(g)
g. Systems using other than DOT containers		110(d)
B. Hazardous locations due to materials		
1. Class I installations—presence of flammable gases, vapors, or liquids	S	309
2. Class II installations—presence of combustible dusts		309
3. Class III installations—presence of easily ignitable fibers or flyings		309
4. General		309
C. Materials handling and storage		
1. General	N	176
a. Clearances, mechanical equipment		176(a)
b. Clearance limits and signs		176(e)
c. Drainage, storage areas		176(d)
d. Guarding open pits, vats, and ditches		176(g)
e. Housekeeping, storage areas		176(c)
f. Rolling railroad cars		176(f)
g. Secure storage, materials		176(b)
2. Indoor storage	N	177
a. Application and general requirements		177(b)
b. Building service equipment		177(f)

Potential Issues of Litigation Relating to Materials	29 CFR 1910 Subpart	29 CFR 1910 Section
c. Fire protection		177(d)
d. Mechanical handling equipment		177(e)
e. Piling procedures and precautions		177(c)
f. Smoking restriction and signs		177(g)
3. Storage and handling		
a. Ammonium nitrate	H	109(i)
b. Anhydrous ammonia	H	111(a)(1)
c. Batteries, industrial trucks	N	178(g)
d. Blasting agents	H	109(g)
e. Compressed gases		101(b)
f. Explosives		109(c)
g. Flammable and combustible liquids		106(d)
h. Flammable liquids		107(e)
i. Flammable liquids, dip tanks		108(d)
j. Flour	R	263
- Dumpbins and blenders		263(d)(3)
- Storage bins		263(d)(6)
k. Liquids, Classes I-III	H	106(f)
l. LP-gas containers		110(f)
m. Pulpwood and pulp chips	R	261(c)
- Chemicals, tagged or drummed		261(h)(4)
- Chocking rolls		261(d)(4)
- Liquid chlorine		261(h)(3)
n. Radioactive materials	G	96(j)
o. Refrigerated storage	H	lll(d)
p. Sawmills		
- Bins, bunkers, and hoppers	R	265(c)(23)
- Log handling, sorting, and storage		265(d)
- Lumber piling and storage		265(c)(27)
q. Tanks		
- Acid storage	R	261(g)(3)
- Flammable and combustible liquids	H	106(b)
D. Materials-handling machines and equipment		
1. Bakery flour-handling equipment		
a. Bag chutes and bag lifts	R	263(d)(2)
b. Chain tackles		263(i)(12)
c. Conveyers		263(i)(7)
d. Flour elevators		263(d)(4)
e. Hand trucks		263(i)(4)
f. Overhead rail systems		263(i)(8)
g. Racks		263(i)(6)

Potential Issues of Litigation Relating to Materials	29 CFR 1910 Sub-part	29 CFR 1910 Section
j. Screw conveyers		263(d)(7)
k. Troughs and other hoists		263(i)(13)
2. Crawler, locomotive, and truck cranes	N	180
3. Derricks		181
4. Overhead and gantry cranes		179
5. Powered industrial trucks		178
6. Pulpwood and pulp chips	R	261(c)
a. Banding of skids, cartons, cases		261(m)(3),(4)
b. Conveyer belts		261(c)(15)
c. Cranes		261(c)(8)
d. Powered hand trucks		261(m)(2)
e. Trucks and trailers		261(c)(7)
7. Pulpwood logging	R	266
a. Skidding and prehauling		266(e)(6),(7)
8. Sawmills, log-handling equipment	R	265
a. Blowers, collecting and exhaust systems		265(c)(20)
b. Mechanical stackers and unstackers		265(d)(26)
c. Mobile equipment for sawmills, planing mills, storage, and yard operations		265(c)(30)

Potential Issues of Litigation Relating to Employee Safety	29 CFR 1910 Subpart	29 CFR 1910 Section
A. Ionizing radiation protection		
1. Employee exposure and controls	G	96(b)
2. Evacuation warning signals		96(f)
3. Exposure to airborne radioactive materials		96(c)
4. Exposure to radiation in restricted areas		96(b)
5. Personnel monitoring and precautionary procedures		96(d)
6. Personnel monitoring equipment		96(d)
7. Posting		96(g)
8. Records		
a. Disclosure		96(o)
b. Employee radiation exposure		96(n)
9. Reporting requirements		
a. Notification of incidents		96(l)
b. Overexposure, excessive levels and concentrations		96(m)
B. Medical and first aid		
1. First aid	K	151
a. Open-surface tank operations	G	94(d)(9)
b. Pulpwood logging	R	266(c)(1)
c. Temporary labor camps	J	142(k)
d. Textiles	R	262(pp)
e. Welding	Q	252(f)(13)
2. General requirements	K	151
3. Medical examinations, asbestos	G	93a(j)
4. Medical records, asbestos	G	93a(j)
5. Medical restrictions	G	94(d)(9)
6. Radiation exposure records	G	96(n)
C. Personnel protection in tanks and confined spaces	G	94(d)(11)
1. Acid tanks—pulp, paper, and paperboard mills	R	261(g)(4)
2. Open surface tanks	G	94(d)(9)
3. Vessel entry, tanks and ship bins	R	261(b)(5)
4. Welding and burning in confined spaces	Q	252(e)(4)
D. Personal protective equipment		
1. Application and general requirements	I	132
2. Electrical (personal) protective devices, sawmills	I	137
3. Eye and face protection		

Potential Issues of Litigation Relating to Employee Safety	29 CFR 1910 Subpart	Section
a. Application and general requirements	I	133
b. Explosive-actuated fastening tools	P	243(d)(1)
c. Pulp, paper, and paperboard mills	R	261(b)(2)
- Chemical processes, pulp making		261(g)(5),(14),(15)
d. Pulpwood logging		266(c)(1)
e. Sawmills		265(c)(17)&(g)
4. Foot protection		
a. General	I	136
b. Pulp, paper, and paperboard mills	R	261(b)(2)
c. Pulpwood logging		266(c)(1)
d. Sawmills		265(g)
5. Head protection		
a. General	I	135
b. Pulp, paper, and paperboard mills	R	261(b)(2)
c. Pulpwood logging		266(c)(1)
d. Sawmills		265(g)
6. Noise exposure		
a. General	G	95(b)(1)
b. Pulpwood logging	R	266(c)(1)
7. Protective clothing and equipment		
a. Acids, alkalis, caustics, and heat	I	132(a)
b. Emergency showers, bubblers, and eye fountains		
- Open-surface tank operations	G	94(d)(9)
- Pulp, paper, and paperboard mills	R	261(g)(5)(15)
c. Open-surface tank inspection and maintenance	G	94(d)(9)
d. Pulp, paper, and paperboard mills	R	261(b)(2)
e. Pulpwood logging		266(c)(1)
f. Sawmills		265(g)
g. Textiles		266(qq)
h. Welding and burning	Q	252(e)(3)
8. Respiratory protection		
a. Abrasive blasting	G	94(a)(5)
b. Air quality	I	134(d)
c. Application, general and engineering controls	I	134(a)(1)
d. Asbestos	G	93a(d)
e. Gas mask canister identification	I	134(g)
f. Open-surface tank operations	G	94(d)(11)
g. Pulp, paper, and paperboard mills	R	261(b)(2)
- Bleaching, liquid chlorine		261(h)
- Chemical processes		261(g)(2),(4),(10),(15)

Potential Issues of Litigation Relating to Employee Safety	29 CFR 1910 Sub-part	Section
- Lead burning		261(g)(6)
h. Pulpwood logging		266(c)(1)
i. Respiratory protective programs	I	134(b)
j. Sawmills	R	265(g)
- Chemicals handling, use, and storage		265(c)(17)
k. Welding, brazing, and cutting	Q	252(f)(2),(4),(5),(7)-(10)
9. Safety belts and lifelines		
a. Power platforms, exterior building maintenance	F	66(d)(8)
b. Pulp, paper, and paperboard mills	R	261(b)(5)&(g)(4),(15)
c. Scaffolding		
- Boatswain's chairs	D	28(j)(4)
- Floats and ship scaffolds		28(u)(6)
- Needle beam scaffolds		28(n)(8)
- Roof work		
· ·Crawling boards and chicken ladders		28(t)(2)
· ·Sloping roofs		28(s)(3)
d. Tank maintenance and repairs	G	94(d)(11)
e. Welding	Q	252(e)(4)(iv)
E. Skills and knowledge		
1. Explosives	H	109(d)(3)
a. Pulpwood logging	R	266(c)(7)
2. Power presses	O	217(E)(3)&(f)(1),(2)
3. Powered industrial trucks	N	178(1)
4. Welding	Q	252(b)(1)&(c)(1)

Potential Issues of Litigation Relating to Power Sources	29 CFR 1910 Sub-part	Section
A. Electrical power		
1. National Electrical Code adopted	S	309
B. Explosive-actuated power		
1. Explosive-actuated fastening tools	P	243(d)
C. Hydraulic power		
1. Forging presses	O	218(f)(2)
2. Jacks	P	244 (a)
3. Mechanical power presses	O	217(b)(11),(12)
4. Sawmills	R	265(c)(13)
D. Pneumatic power		
1. Air lift gravity hammers	O	218(e)(1)
2. Air receivers	M	169
3. Compressed air used for cleaning	P	242(b)
4. General	P	243(b)
5. Mechanical power presses	O	217(b)(9),(10),(12)
6. Pneumatic-powered tools and equipment	P	243(b)
7. Spray finishing and spraying containers	H	107(e)(5)
E. Steam power		
1. Steam control valves, textiles	R	262(h)(1),(p)(1),(q)
2. Steam hammers	O	218(d)
3. Steam pipes		
a. Laundry operations	R	264(c)(4),(d)(2)
b. Textiles		262(c)(9)
c. Pulp, paper, and paperboard mills		261(k)(11)
F. Miscellaneous power sources used in special industries		
1. Bakery equipment	R	263
2. Laundry machinery operations		264
3. Pulpwood logging		266
4. Pulp, paper, and paperboard mills		261
5. Sawmills		265
6. Textiles		262

Potential Issues of Litigation Relating to Processes	29 CFR 1910 Sub-part	29 CFR 1910 Section
A. Abrasive blasting		
1. Air supply and air compressors	G	94(a)(6)
2. Blast cleaning enclosures, construction		94(a)(3)
3. Dust hazards—allowable levels of concentration, limited use of combustible abrasives, and fire-explosion requirements		94(a)(2)
4. Exhaust ventilation systems, construction, maintenance, and inspection		93(a)(4)
5. General requirements		94(a)
6. Operational procedures and general safety		94(a)(7)
7. Personal protective equipment		94(a)(5)
	I	132
a. Eye and face protection	G	94(a)(5)
	I	133
b. Protective clothing, shoes and gloves	G	94(a)(5)
c. Respirators, need, approvals, and types	G	94(a)(5)
d. Respiratory protection	I	134(a)&(b)
8. Standard	G	94(a)(8)
B. Dry grinding, polishing and buffing, exhaust systems		
1. Abrasive wheel machinery	O	215
2. Application and requirements	G	94(b)(2)
3. Exhaust system design	G	94(b)(4)
4. Exhaust ventilation	G	94(b)
a. Buffing and polishing wheels (Table G-5)		
b. Grinding and abrasive cutoff wheels (Table G-4)		
c. Grinding and polishing belts (Table G-9)		
d. Horizontal double-spindle disk grinders (Table G-7)		
e. Horizontal single-spindle disk grinders (Table G-6)		
f. Vertical spindle disk grinders (Table G-8)		
5. Hood enclosure design	G	94(b)(5)
6. Standards		94(b)(6)

Potential Issues of Litigation Relating to Processes	29 CFR 1910 Sub-part	Section
C. Process, dip and open-surface tanks		
1. Application and general requirements	G	94(d)
a. Washing, degreasing, pickling, quenching, dyeing, dipping, bleaching, stripping, rinsing, electroplating, anodizing, tanning, and coating	H	108
2. Classification of open-surface tanks	G	94(d)(2)
a. Fire and explosion determination		94(d)(2)
b. Hazard potential determination		94(d)(2)
c. Toxic gas, fumes, and mists, allowable concentrations (TLV)		93
3. Controls other than ventilation		94(d)(6)
4. Dip tanks containing flammable or combustible liquids	H	108
a. Construction and design		108(c)
b. Fire extinguishing facilities		108(c)(15),(16)&(d)&(g)
c. Storage of flammable liquids		108(d)&(g)
d. Ventilation		108(b)
5. Dip tanks, special applications		108(h)
a. Electrostatic coatings		108(h)(3)
b. Flow coatings		108(h)(2)
c. Hardening and tempering tanks		108(h)(1)
d. Roll coatings		108(h)(4)
6. Exhaust systems design	G	94(d)(7)
7. Exhaust systems operation and maintenance		94(d)(8)
8. Fire prevention and protection	H	108(g)
a. Extinguishing facilities (automatic)		108(c)(5)
b. Ignition sources		108(e)
9. Installation, maintenance, and inspection of open tanks	G	94(d)(11)
10. Open-surface tank operations	G	94(d)(13)
11. Operation, maintenance, and inspection of dip tanks	H	108(f)
12. Other special process tanks		
a. Acid tanks—pulp, paper, and paperboard mills	R	261(g)(4)
b. Dissolving tanks—smelting		261(g)(18)
c. Open-mixing tanks—textiles		262(11)
13. Personal protection against acids, corrosives, and irritating contaminants	G	94(d)(9)

Potential Issues of Litigation Relating to Processes	29 CFR 1910 Sub-part	Section
a. Chemical splashes, water flushing		94(d)(9)
b. Clothing, coats, jackets, sleeves, aprons		94(d)(9)
c. Cyanide, special precautions		94(d)(10)
d. Emergency showers and bubblers	R	261(g)(18)
e. Emergency situations	G	94(d)(9)
- Hazardous concentration contaminants, respirators		94(d)(9)
- Oxygen-deficient atmospheres, respirators		94(d)(9)
- Personal protective equipment	I	134
f. Eye and face protection	G	94(d)(9)
g. Foot protection, impervious types		94(d)(9)
h. Hand protection, impervious types		94(d)(9)
i. Hazard instruction, employee		94(d)(9)
j. Locker space or change rooms		
- Asbestos workers	G	93a(d)(4)
- General requirements	J	141(e)
- Open-tank workers	G	94(d)(9)
k. Medical examinations		
- Asbestos workers	G	93a(j)
- Chromic acid workers		94(d)(9)
l. Medical restrictions and treatment		94(d)(9)
m. Pulp, paper, and paperboard mill processes	R	261(g)(2),(4),(5)
- Personal protective equipment	I	133
n. Pulpwood logging processes	R	266(c)(17)
o. Rescue work, respirators	G	94(d)(11)
p. Washing facilities, general	J	141(d)
q. Washing facilities, open-tank workers	G	94 (d)(9)
- General environmental controls	J	141(d)
14. Storage and handling flammable liquids	H	106
a. Tanks	H	108(d)
15. Vapor degreasing tanks	G	94(d)(12)
a. Welding precautions	Q	252(f)(11)
16. Ventilation	G	94(d)(3)
a. General potential exposure control	G	94(a)(4)
b. Tanks for flammable and combustible liquids	H	108(b)
D. Processing plants and operations		
1. Chemical processing operations	H	106(h)

Potential Issues of Litigation Relating to Processes	29 CFR 1910 Subpart	Section
2. Refineries, chemical plants, and distilleries		106(i),(j)
E. Special industries and related processes		
1. Agricultural operations	R	267
2. Bakery equipment and operations		263
3. Laundry machinery and operations		264
4. Pulp, paper, and paperboard mills		261
5. Pulpwood logging operations		266
6. Sawmills		265
7. Textiles		262
F. Spray finishing		
1. Application, location, and general requirements	G	94(c)
	H	107
2. Drying, curing, and fusion apparatus	H	107(j)
3. Electrical equipment	G	94(c)(3)
4. Electrostatic hand spraying equipment	H	107(i)
a. General requirements		107(i)(6),(7)
b. Grounding and maintenance		107(i)(1)
c. Specifications and approvals		107(i)(3)
d. Ventilation		107(i)(9)
5. Electrostatic spraying apparatus, mechanical		107(h)
a. Conveyers and fail-safe controls		107(h)(7),(9)
b. Fire protection		107(h)(12)
c. Grounding high voltage, insulators		107(h)(5)
d. Guarding and grounding of equipment		107(h)(10)
e. Location, type, and approvals		107(h)(z)
f. Ventilation		107(h)(11)
6. Fire protection		107(f)&(g)
a. Electrostatic apparatus		107(h)(12)
b. Fire extinguishers, portable		107(f)(4)
c. Sprinkler systems		107(f)
7. Ignition sources	G	94(c)
	H	107
8. Liquids, flammable and combustible	H	107(e)
a. Containers, spraying containers		107(e)(3),(4),(5)
b. Storage and handling		107(e)(1)
c. Transferring liquids—pumps, pipes, hoses, and grounding		107(e)(4),(6)&(9)
9. Operation and maintenance	H	107(g)

Potential Issues of Litigation Relating to Processes	29 CFR 1910 Sub-part	Section
a. Cleaning solvents		107(g)(5)
b. Clothing storage		107(g)(4)
c. Hazardous material combinations		107(g)(6)
d. Housekeeping, cleaning, and waste disposal		107(g)(2),(3)
10. Other spraying techniques		
a. Asbestos	G	93a
b. Automobile undercoating	H	107(k)
c. Organic peroxides and dual-component coatings		107(m)
d. Powder coating		107(l)
11. Spray booths and spray rooms	G	94(c)(8)
a. Flammable and combustible materials	H	107(n)
12. Spray booths, design and construction	G	94(c)(3)
13. Spray rooms, design and construction	G	94(c)(4)
14. Ventilation and atmospheric controls	G	94(c)(5)
a. Automobile undercoating	H	107(k)
b. Electrostatic spraying, hand		107(i)
c. Electrostatic spraying, mechanical		107(h)
d. Spray finishing		107(d)
G. Welding, cutting, and brazing		
1. Arc welding and cutting		
a. Equipment installation	Q	252(b)(3)
- Conductors and supply connectors		252(b)(3)
- Grounding of welding machines		252(b)(3)
b. Equipment installation and operation		252(b)
- Employee qualifications and instructions		252(b)(1)
- Equipment selection, atmospheric and environmental considerations		252(b)(2)
- Voltage and design		252(b)(2)
c. Equipment operation and maintenance		252(b)(4)
2. Fire prevention and protection		252(d)
a. Confined spaces, care of idle equipment		252(d)(4)
b. Containers, welding and cutting		252(d)(3)
c. Hazards, guards and restrictions		252(d)(1)
d. Special precautions		252(d)(2)
3. Fuel-gas systems installation and operation		252(a)

Potential Issues of Litigation Relating to Processes	29 CFR 1910 Sub-part	Section
a. Acetylene generators		252(a)(6)
b. Calcium carbide storage		252(a)(7)
c. Cylinders and containers, approval and identification		252(a)(2)
d. General requirements		252(a)(1)
e. Manifolding cylinders		252(a)(3)
f. Oxygen-fuel gas systems		252(a)
g. Public exhibitions and demonstrations		252(a)(8)
h. Regulators, hoses, piping, and protective devices		252(a)(5)
i. Service piping systems		252(a)(4)
j. Storage and operating prcedures		252(a)(2)
k. Storage of cylinders		252(a)(2)
4. Health protection and ventilation		252(f)
a. Application and general requirements for atmospheric contamination, ventilation, maximum allowable concentrations, warning labels, shielding, and screening		252(f)(1)
b. Confined spaces	Q	252(f)(4)
- Air line respirators		252(f)(4)
- Air replacement		252(f)(4)
- Respiratory protection	I	134
- Self-contained respirators	Q	252(f)(4)
c. Exhaust hoods and booths		252(f)(3)
d. First aid equipment requirements		252(f)(13)
- Medical and first aid	K	151
e. Ventilation	Q	252(f)(2)
f. Welding and cutting		252(f)
- Air contaminants	G	93
- Beryllium	Q	252(f)(8)
- Cadmium		252(f)(9)
- Cleaning compounds		252(f)(11)
- Fluorine compounds		252(f)(5)
- Lead		252(f)(7)
- Mercury		252(f)(10)
- Stainless steel		252(f)(12)
- Zinc		252(f)(6)
5. Protection of personnel		
a. Eye, head, and face protection	Q	252(e)(2)
- Eye and face protection	I	133

Potential Issues of Litigation Relating to Processes	29 CFR 1910 Sub-part	Section
- Head protection	I	135
- Selection and specifications	Q	252(e)(2)
- Welding booths, screens, and shields	Q	252(e)(2)
b. Noise exposure	G	95
c. Protection against falls	Q	252(e)(1)
d. Protective clothing, types and specifications	Q	252(e)(3)
e. Respirators	Q	252(f)(4)
- Respiratory protection	I	134(2),(4),(5),(7)-(10)
f. Welding cables and hoses	Q	252(e)(1)
g. Work in confined spaces		252(e)(4)
- Ventilation, lifelines, warning signs, securing equipment		
h. Radiation		
- Ionizing	G	96
- Nonionizing		97
6. Resistance welding	Q	252(c)
a. Equipment installation, operation, guarding, and employee		252(c)(1)
b. Flash welding equipment		252(c)(4)
- Flash guards, fire curtains, and ventilation		
c. Hazards evaluation		252(c)(5)
d. Maintenance, inspection, and records		252(c)(6)
e. Portable welding machines		252(c)(3)
- Counterbalance, safety chains, switch guards, holders, and grounding		
f. Spot and seam welding equipment, nonportable		252(c)(2)
- Guarding, interlocks, shielding, emergency stop buttons, and grounding		
7. Special industrial applications	Q	252(g)
a. Mechanical piping		252(g)(2)
b. Transmission pipelines		252(g)(1)
c. X-ray inspections		252(g)(1)&(2)
- ionizing radiation	G	96

Potential Issues of Litigation Relating to Administrative Safety Procedures	29 CFR Part	29 CFR Section
A. Advisory committees on standards	1912	
1. Construction Safety Advisory Committee		.20
2. National Advisory Committee on Occupational Safety and Health		.3
3. Participation by interested persons		.29
4. Standing and temporary committees		.10
5. Subcommittees, experts, and consultants		.28
B. Inspections, citations, and proposed penalties	1903	
1. Advance notice of inspections		.6
2. Authority for OSHA inspections		.3
3. Citations		.14
4. Complaints by employees		.7
5. Conduct of inspections		.7
6. Employer and employee contests before OSHA Review Commission		.17
7. Failure to correct cited violation		.18
8. Informal conferences with OSHA regional administrators to discuss citations		.19
9. Posting of citations at or near site of violation		.16
10. Posting of notices, availability of OSH Act, regulations, and applicable standards		.2
11. Proposed penalties		.15
12. Representatives of employers and employees		.8
C. Promulgating, modifying, or revoking Occupational Safety and Health Standards	1911	
1. Construction standards		.10
2. Emergency standards		.12
3. Hearings		.15
4. Other standards		.11
5. Petition for the promulgation, modification, or revocation of a standard		.3
D. Recording and reporting occupational injuries and illnesses	1904	
1. Annual summary, injuries and illnesses posting		.5
2. Employer completion of survey form		.21

Potential Issues of Litigation Relating to Administrative Safety Procedures	29 CFR Part	29 CFR Section
3. Falsification and failure to keep records or reports		.9
4. Log of occupational injuries and illnesses		.2
5. Reporting fatalities or multiple hospitalization accidents within 48 hours		.8
6. Retention of records		.6
7. Supplementary records		.4
E. Records—employee exposure to hazardous substances or conditions	1910	
1. Asbestos	G	93a
a. Medical records		93a(f)
b. Monitoring		93a(j)(6)
2. Ionizing radiation		
a. Notification of incidents	G	96(l)
b. Personnel monitoring		96(d)
c. Records		96(n)
d. Reports of overexposure		96(m)
F. Variances, limitations, variations, tolerances, and exemptions	1905	
1. Limitations, variations, tolerances, or exemptions under §16 of OSH Act (national defense)		.12
2. Modification, revocation, and renewal of rules or orders		.13
3. Requests for hearings		.15
4. Variances and other relief under §6(b)(6)(A) of OSH Act		.10
5. Variances and other relief under §6(d) of OSH Act		.11

Appendix E
Engineering Terminology

One of the main problems that an attorney may have in conversing with an engineering expert or in questioning an opposing expert is understanding engineering terminology. Such terminology is a necessary part not only of communications between the expert and attorney, but also of communications between the expert and attorney on one hand and the trier of fact on the other.

In cases involving structural and machinery failures, a number of engineering terms of art are used to describe the properties of materials and their reactions to outside forces. *Modulus of elasticity, shear modulus, flexural stiffness, density, ultimate strength in compression, tension,* and *shear* are frequently used engineering terms which relate to mechanical properties of materials. These and many other terms are defined and discussed in the glossary.

Symbols used in engineering calculations and drawings are important in determining intent. In order to establish standard symbols, American National Standards, Inc., in conjunction with most professional engineering societies, has published *Letter Symbols for Units Used in Science and Technology.* This publication is also known as ANSI Y10.19. Another helpful publication is ANSI Y1.1-1972, American National Standards, Inc.'s *Abbreviations for Use on Drawings and in Text,* which can be obtained from the American Society of Mechanical Engineers, 345 East 45th Street, New York, NY 10017.

This appendix lists some of the most commonly used terms and symbols in the various engineering disciplines discussed in this book.

Standard Letter Symbols

Term	Symbol
acceleration	a
acceleration of gravity	g
aggregate	AGG
air conditioning	A.C. or AIR COND
algebraic difference in grades	A
alternating current	ac
aluminum	ALUM or AL
American Society for testing Materials	ASTM
American Welding society	AWS
ampere	A
anchor bolt	AB
angle	L
angular speed	N
architect(ural)	ARCH
area	A, a
at	@
beam	bm
bending moment	M
block	blk
blocking	blkg
board	brd
bottom	bot
British thermal unit	btu
building	bldg
cantilever	cant
cased opening	c.o.
cast iron	c.i.
catch basin	c.b.
ceiling	clg
centerline	℄
centimeter	cm
channel	c
clean out	c.o.
clear	clr
column	col
company	co
concrete	conc
connection	conn
construction	const
continue(ous)	cont
contract(or)	contr
corridor	corr
cubic foot	ft^3
cubic foot per minute	ft^3/min
cubic foot per second	ft^3/s
cubic inch	in^3
cubic meter	c^3
cubic meter per second	m^3/s
cubic yard	yd^3
current	I
cycle	c
cycle per second	Hz, c/s
degree	deg or °
degree Celsius	°C
degree Fahrenheit	°F
department	dept
detail	det
diagonal	diag
diameter	dia or ⌀
dimension	dim
direct current	dc
distance	S
door	dr
door opening	d.o.
double	dbl
downspout	d.s.
drawing	dwg or drwg
drinking fountain	d.f.
each	ea
each way	e.w.
electric	elec

Term	Symbol
electric welded wire mesh	e.w.w.m.
elevation	elev
energy	E
equal	eq
equipment	equip
exhaust	exh
existing	exstg or exist
expansion	exp
expansion joint	e.j.
exterior	ext
face of masonry	f.o.m.
face of stud	f.o.s.
finish	fin
finish floor	f.f.
finish grade	f.g.
fire extinguisher	f.e.
fire hose cabinet	f.h.c.
flashing	flash
floor	flr or fl
flow line	f.l.
foot	ft
footing	ftg
foot per minute	ft/min
foot per second	ft/s
foot per second squared	ft/s^2
foot pound-force	ft-lb
foot-pounds	ft-lbs
force	F
foundation	fdn
frequency	f
gallon	gal
galvanized	galv
galvanized iron	g.i.
gauge	ga
glass	gl
grade	grd
gypsum	gyp
gypsum board	gyp brd

Term	Symbol
hardware	hwd
height	hgt
horizontal	horiz
hose bib	h.b.
hertz	Hz
horsepower	hp
hour	h
inch	in
inch per second	in/s
insulation	insul
interior	int
joint	jt
kilometer	km
kilometer per hour	km/h
kilovolt-amperes	KVA
kinetic energy	KE
lavatory	lav
length	l, L
length of vertical curve	L
load	P
manhours	mh
manufacturer	mfg or manfr
masonry opening	m.o.
maximum	max
mechanical	mech
metal	met or mtl
mile	mi
miles per hour	mi/h
minimum	min
minute	min
modulus of elasticity	E
natural	nat
not in contract	N.I.C.
not to scale	n.t.s.
number	No., N$\underline{\text{o}}$, or #
ohms	Ω
on center	o.c.

Term	Symbol
opening	opng
outside diameter	o.d.
penny	d
per cent	%
period	T
plate	⅊
plywood	plywd
potential energy	PE
radius	R
reaction	R
required	req'd
resistance	R
revolutions per minute	rpm
revolutions per second	r/s
ridge line	r.l.
right of way	R/W
roof drain	r.d.
room	rm
rough opening	r.o.
schedule	sched
section	sect
service sink	s.s.
shear	V
side friction factor	F
sight distance	S
similar	sim
specifications	specs
speed	V
square	sq
standard	std
steel	stl

Term	Symbol
stress	S
structural	struct
summation	Σ
superelevation	E
symmetrical	sym
temperature, degree F	t
temperature, degree R	t
thick(ness)	thk
time	t
tongue and groove	t & g
tooled joint	t.j.
top of concrete slab	t.s.
top of curb	t.c.
top of curve	t.c.
top of drain	t.d.
top of wall	t.w.
torque	T
tread	tr
typical	typ
velocity	V
vent thru roof	vtr
vertical	vert
vestibule	vest
volt	V
volume	v
waterproof	w.p.
watts	W
weight	wt
with	w/
wood	wd
wrought iron	w.i.
year	y

Typical Electrical Symbols

Reproduced by Permission of Richardson Engineering Services

SYMBOL	LEGEND	
O_1	Ceiling fixture outlet.	
 2	Wall fixture outlet.	Numerical denotes Fixture type
 3	Fluorescent fixture outlet.	
S	Single pole switch.	
S_2	Double pole switch.	w/pilot light where superscript "P" appears adjacent to symbol
S_3	Three way switch.	
	Junction box 4″ sq. cast metal w/threaded hubs and gasketed blank cover unless otherwise indicated.	
	Duplex receptacle outlet.	
 WP	Duplex receptacle outlet, weatherproof.	
	Branch circuit panel.	
	Disconnect switch. Type & rating as noted.	
S^{P}_{TE}	Manual motor starter w/overload device & w/pilot light where subscript "P" appears.	
	Start-stop push button control station.	
	Jog push button control station.	
	Hand-off-auto control selector switch.	
 HA	Two position hand-auto control selector switch.	

SYMBOL	LEGEND
	Thermostat.
	Motor. A-C induction type. Encircled numeral denote horsepower.
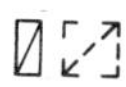	Control panel integral part of or furnished w/mechanical equipment.
	Branch circuit or feeder, two wire circuits unless indicated as follows: 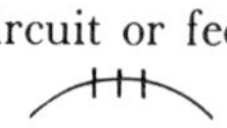 3 wires, 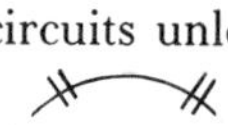 4 wires, etc.
	Conduit turning up. Solid circle indicates conduit turning down.
	Home run to panel. Number of arrows indicates no. of circuits.
	Telephone conduit.
	Telephone outlet.
	Molded case circuit breaker rating & no. of poles indicated.
	Combination magnetic motor starter, circuit breaker type. Breaker rating & no. of poles indicated. Size 1 full voltage non-reversing starter unless otherwise indicated.
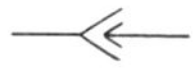	Disconnecting device for draw out equipment.
	Potential transformer. Ratio as indicated.
	Current transformer. Ratio as indicated.
	Phase selector switch. Enclosed letters indicate function as follows: AS - Ammeter VS - voltmeter WS - Wattmeter "on-off" switch.
	Meter or relay-enclosed letters indicate function as follows: VM - AC voltmeter AM - AC ammeter FM - frequency meter WM - wattmeter

SYMBOL	LEGEND
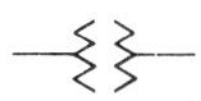	Transformer. Type & rating as noted.
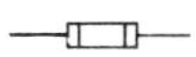	Fuse. Size & quantity as indicated.

Glossary

A

AAA: American Arbitration Association.

Absorption (masonry): amount of water, by weight, absorbed by a masonry unit when totally immersed in water, expressed as a percentage of its dry weight; usually determined by immersion in cold water for 24 hours, or in boiling water for five hours.

Absorption rate (initial rate of absorption, rate of suction): amount of water, by weight, absorbed by masonry unit in one minute when held in 1/8-inch of water of the lower surface, (expressed in grams or ounces per square inch).

Acceleration: (a) where a contractor is required to complete at an earlier date than that originally scheduled; (b) change in velocity over a specific interval of time.

Accelerograph: instrument for measuring seismic accelerations or for detecting and measuring vibrations, installed in critical installations and tall structures to record potentially destructive motion.

Accessory: secondary part of assembly or parts which contribute to the overall function and usefulness of a machine.

Accretion: act of growing to a thing, usually applied to the gradual and imperceptible accumulation of land by natural causes, as out the sea or a river.

Acre-foot (AF): volume unit of water equal to an area of one acre of one foot depth.

Activity (CPM): each separate operation or process which consumes time.

Act of God: natural and inevitable necessity, implying entire exclusion of human agency.

Activity (CPM): each separate operation or process which consumes time.

Adhesion contract: standardized contract form offered to consumers of goods and services on a "take it or leave it" basis which fails to offer the consumer a true opportunity to consent.

Adjoining owners: persons who own land touching the subject land and who, as a result, have the right to notice of proceedings concerning the subject property.

Admixture: materials added to mortar or grout to retard or speed up setting.

Aftershock: part of the release of accumulated elastic strain along faults; when an earthquake occurs, it not only relieves the pressure along its particular section of fault but it also changes the stress patterns in the immediate area.

Aggregate: one of the two components of concrete, generally 60 per cent to 75 per cent of the concrete mixture.

Aggregate, coarse: particle sizes greater than 1/4-inch.

Aggregate, fine: natural or manufactured sand with particle sizes smaller than 1/4-inch.

Agreement: written agreement between the owner and the contractor covering the work to be performed; contract documents are usually attached to and made a part of it.

AIA: American Institute of Architects.

Allowable stress (safe working stress): (a) stress permitted by the governing code; (b) stress which is standard or good practice and is less than a damaging stress (the margin between the allowable stress and the damaging stress is the factor of safety); (c) stress which will safely support a given load under given conditions.

Alloy: material with metallic properties composed of two or more elements, of which at least one is a metal.

Amperes: unit of intensity of electrical current being produced in a conductor by the applied voltage.

Angle indicator (boom): accessory which measures and indicates the angle of a crane's boom to the horizontal.

Appliance: electrical utilization equipment, generally other than industrial equipment, normally built in standardized sizes or types; examples include units for clothes washing, air conditioning, food mixing, or deep frying.

Appliance, portable: electrical appliance which can be moved from one place to another in normal use.

Appliance, stationary: electrical appliance which cannot easily be moved from one place to another in normal use.

Application for payment: form furnished by the architect/engineer, to be used by the contractor in requesting progress payments.

Appraisal: expert opinion on the market value of property, including damages, as of a specified date, based on an analysis of facts.

Arbitration: arrangement through agreement for taking and abiding by the judgment of an impartial (third) person chosen by the parties to a disputed matter.

Architect's lien: lien on real estate created by statute in favor of the architect who drew the plans and supervised the construction, for purposes of insuring payment of fees.

Arrow diagrams: diagrams drawn from a CPM (critical path method) printout showing the critical path.

Arterial highway: generally denoting a highway primarily for through traffic, usually on a continuous route.

ASTM: American Society for Testing and Materials.

Automatic: self-acting; operating by its own mechanism when actuated by a change in electric current, pressures, temperature, or mechanical configuration.

Automatic crane: crane which, when activated, operates through a pre-set cycle or cycles.

Auxiliary hoist: supplemental hoisting unit of lighter capacity and usually higher speed than that of the main hoist.

Auxiliary lane: portion of the roadway adjoining the traveled way for weaving, truck climbing, speed change, or other purposes supplementary to through-traffic movement.

Axis of rotation: vertical axis around which the crane superstructure rotates.

Azeotrope: mixture which, on boiling, keeps the same percentage composition in both the liquid and vapor phase.

B

Backing it out: attempt by owner and/or general contractor to recoup on later requisitions by underpaying the amount overpaid on previous requisitions; see *Get ahead of*, definition (b).

Backup: that part of a masonry wall which is generally behind the exterior facing.

Bar chart: time chart consisting of columns representing periods of time and horizontal lines representing construction activities, used for planning and scheduling construction projects; black bars indicate various activities in proper time frame.

Barricade: portable or fixed barrier with object markings, used to close all or a portion of the right of way to vehicular traffic.

Barricade warning light: portable, power-operated, lens-directed, enclosed light used in either the steady burn or flashing mode to mark obstructions or hazards in construction and maintenance work areas.

Barrier curb: curb designed to prevent or discourage vehicles from leaving the pavement.

Base: layer of selected, processed, or treated aggregate material of planned thickness and quality, placed immediately below the pavement and above the subbase of basement soil.

Base course: bottom portion of a pavement where the top and bottom portions are not of the same composition.

Basement soil: material in excavation, embankments, and embankment foundations, immediately below the first layer of the structural section and extending to the depth that affects structural design.

Bat: piece of brick, usually one-half brick or less.

Batter: recessing or sloping a wall or buttress back in successive courses; opposite of corbelling.

Beam: horizontal member, supported at its ends, and subjected to pressure perpendicular to its length.

Bearing partition or wall: wall which supports a vertical load in addition to its own weight.

Bed joint: horizontal layer of mortar on which a masonry unit is laid.

Belled excavation: part of a shaft or footing excavation, usually near the bottom and bell shaped, making the cross-sectional area at that point larger than the area above; also called *belled caisson*.

Bell hole: additional excavation into the sides or bottom of a trench to provide additional work space.

Belly-up: insolvency or inability to perform of one of the parties to a construction contract, i.e., lender, owner, general contractor, subcontractor, or material supplier.

Belt highway: arterial highway for carrying traffic partially or entirely around an urban area or portion thereof; also called *circumferential highway.*

Bending moment: occurs when several forces having different lines of action and different directions act on a member; for example, when a weight rests on the center of a cross beam.

Bid: offer or proposal submitted by a bidder, setting forth the prices for the work to be performed.

Bid bond: type of bond required in public construction projects, which must be filed at the time of the bid, and which protects the public agency in the event that the bidder refuses to enter into a contract after such contract has been awarded to the bidder.

Bidder: any person, firm, or corporation submitting a bid for work; one who offers to perform a certain contract for a specified price.

Blasting cap: shell closed at one end, containing a charge of detonating compound which is ignited from a spark; used for detonating explosives.

Boatswain's chair: seat which may be raised or lowered by means of attached rigging which suspends it and the seated worker from above.

Bond (adhesion): tensile strength between brick and mortar and grout.

Bond beam: course or courses of masonry units reinforced with longitudinal bars, designed to take longitudinal flexural and tensile forces that may be induced in a masonry wall.

Bond, English cross (or Dutch): alternate courses of stretchers and headers offset two inches.

Bond, Flemish: courses of alternating stretcher, header, stretcher, header . . . with headers centered over stretchers in alternate courses; used with standard brick size.

Bonding company: see *Surety.*

Bond, running: brick laid so that the vertical mortar joints are centered over the brick below; sometimes called *center bond* or *half bond.*

Bonds: certificates of evidence of a debt on which the issuing party, usually the contractor and such contractor's surety, promise to pay the bondholder, the bidder, a specified amount for faithful performance of a contract and for all materials and labor costs related to performance.

Bond, stack: vertical mortar joints in continuous vertical alignment; also called *plumb, joint bond, straight stack, jack bond,* and *jack on jack.*

Boom: member section of a crane or derrick, in which the lower end is affixed to a mast, base, carriage, or support, and the upper end supports a hook or other end attachment.

Boom angle: angle between the longitudinal centerline of the boom and the horizontal; the boom longitudinal centerline is a straight line between the boom foot pin (heel pin) centerline and boom point sheave pin centerline.

Boom hoist: hoist drum and rope reeving system used to raise and lower the boom, in which the rope system may be all live reeving or a combination of live reeving and pendants.

Booming, luffing, or topping: raising or lowering the head of a boom.

Boomstop: device used to limit the angle of the boom at the highest position.

Boom-type excavator: power-operated, crane-type excavating machine generally used for digging or moving materials; some excavators of this type are those commonly known as the *dipper stick shovel, back-hoe, trench-hoe shovel, dragline, grab bucket, clamshell,* or *orange peel excavator.*

Borrow: natural soil obtained from sources outside the roadway prism to make up a deficiency in excavation quantities.

Bosun's chair: see *Boatswain's chair.*

Braces for excavation: horizontal members of the shoring system whose ends bear against the uprights or stringers.

Brake: device used to retard or stop motion by friction or power means.

Brake, electric: electric motor acting as a brake by regenerative, counter-torque, or dynamic means.

Brake, electrically-operated: friction brake actuated or controlled by electric means.

Brake holding: brake that automatically prevents motion when all power is cut off from the brake holding mechanism.

Branch circuit: portion of a wiring system that extends beyond the final overcurrent device protecting the circuit.

Branch circuit (appliance): circuit supplying energy to one or more outlets to which appliances are to be connected.

Branch connection: multiple connection between two freeways.

Breach of contract: failure without legal excuse to perform any terms which form the contract.

Breaking strength: see *Ultimate strength.*

Brick (clay or shale): solid masonry unit, formed into a rectangular prism while plastic and burnt or fired in a kiln.

Brick, cored: bricks which have holes (any shape) through them; when the gross cross-sectional area of cores does not exceed 25 per cent of the gross cross-sectional area of a brick, it is classified by ASTM as a solid unit.

Brick, dry-press: brick produced by a process of forming relatively dry clay (5-7 per cent moisture content) in molds at pressures of from 550 to 1500 psi (pounds per square inch.)

Brick, face: solid masonry unit made from a controlled mixture of natural clays or shales only, specially processed during manufacture to produce desired colors and textures, regular in shape and uniformity, and made in modular sizes; also referred to as *facing brick.*

Brick, fire: brick made from refractory clay which resists heat shock and high temperatures.

Brick, paving: very dense and hard face brick.

Brick, salmon: relatively soft, underburned brick, so called because of its color.

Brick, sewer: brick, low in absorption, high in compressive strength, which resists action of sewer gas and abrasion.

Brick, soft-mud: brick produced by forming relatively wet clay (20-30 per cent water content) in molds; when the insides of the molds are sanded, the product is called *sand-struck* or *sand-mold* brick; when molds are wetted with water to prevent clay sticking, the brick is called *water-struck*.

Brick, stiff-mud: brick produced by extruding through a die a plastic clay with a water content of from 12 to 15 per cent.

Bridge: that part of a crane consisting of girders, trucks, end ties, footwalks, and a drive mechanism which carries the trolley or trolleys.

Bridges: structures of a span of more than 20 feet, measured under the copings along the centerline of a road; multiple-span structures are those where the individual spans are in excess of 10 feet, measured from center to center of supports along the centerline of the road.

Bridge travel: crane movement in a direction parallel to the crane runway.

Brinell Hardness Test: test consisting of forcing a ball of standard diameter into the specimen being tested under a stand and pressure, and judging the hardness of the material by the amount of metal displaced.

British thermal unit: unit of heat representing the amount of heat necessary to raise the temperature of one pound of water one degree Fahrenheit; abbreviated BTU or btu.

Buffer: cushioning device at the ends of a trolley, bridge, or other moving part of a crane, operating on rails to minimize shock in the event of a collision.

Building permit: authorization required by local governmental bodies for a new building or major alteration of existing structures, usually required to be displayed on the construction site.

Bulldozer: tractor having a blade in front for moving earth or other materials.

Bumper: device which stops the moving part at the limit of travel of a trolley, bridge, or crane operating on rails, and prevents motion beyond that point.

Burying: see *Covering up*.

Buttering: placing mortar on brick with a trowel before laying.

Bypass: arterial highway that permits traffic to avoid part or all of an urban area.

C

Cab: enclosure for housing the operator and the hoisting mechanism, power plant, or other equipment controlling a crane or boom-type excavator.

Cableway: power-operated system for moving loads in which the loads are conveyed on an overhead cable, track, or carriage.

Cage: open structure for housing the operator and/or equipment which controls the crane or the hoist.

Cantilever: free part of a structural member or beam which projects beyond a support; jutting portions of the member; bracket used in supporting a balcony or heavy shelf.

Capillarity (soil): action by which liquid (water) rises in channel in any direction above the horizontal plane of the supply of free water.

Capillary water (soil): water held in a soil by the capillaries (pores) in the soil, free water, which can be removed from soil only after the water table is lowered or when evaporation takes place faster than the rate of capillary flow.

Capped fuse: length of safety fuse to which blasting cap has been attached.

Carryall: self-loading and unloading vehicle pulled by a tractor or powered attachment, used for movement and placing of earth or other materials.

Catenary or stretch cables: used for the support of staging, secured at each end and extending in a nearly horizontal plane with the staging placed on and supported by these cables.

Cavity wall: wall of masonry units, constructed to provide a continuous center air space, usually two inches wide, within the wall; the withes of masonry are tied together with rigid noncorrosive metal ties at specified intervals.

Cementitious materials: Portland cement plastic or waterproof cement, masonry cement, and lime.

Cement paste: one of the two components of concrete, composed of cement, water, and entrained air (entrapped in air bubbles).

Ceramic veneer: type of architectural terra cotta, characterized by larger face dimensions and thinner sections ranging from 1-1/8 inches to 2-1/2 inches in thickness.

Ceramic veneer, adhesion type: ceramic slabs approximately 1-1/8 inches in thickness, held in place by the adhesion of the mortar to the ceramic veneer and to the backing wall.

Ceramic veneer, anchored type: ceramic slabs approximately 2 to 2-1/2 inches in thickness, held in place by wire anchors and a grout space in which vertical pencil rods are placed; the slabs are anchored to the rods, which, in turn, are anchored to the backing wall.

Certificate of occupancy: document issued by a municipality recognizing that a building meets city codes and ordinances and may be occupied.

cfs-day: amount of liquid resulting from a flow of one cubic foot per second for one day (24 hours), equivalent to 1.9835 acre-feet, 86,400 cubic feet, or 747,317 gallons.

Change order: written order to the contractor, signed by the owner, authorizing an alteration, modification, deletion, or revision in the work, and including an adjustment in the contract price or date of completion.

Channelization: separation or regulation of conflicting traffic movements into definite paths of travel by use of pavement markings, raised islands, or other suitable means to facilitate the safe and orderly movement of both vehicles and pedestrians.

Charpy Impact Test: tests the notched toughness, or impact strength, of a material; measures the energy required to break a standard notched specimen supported at the two ends.

Chase: continuous recess built into a wall to receive pipes or ducts.

Check analysis: analysis of metal after it has been rolled or forged into semifinished or finished forms in which a specimen is struck by a swinging pendulum and the energy absorbed in the fracture is measured, using a striking velocity of 17.5 feet per second.

Chemical analysis: (a) qualitative analysis by separating a substance into its component elements and identifying them; (b) quantitative analysis in which the proportions of all component elements are determined.

Chicago boom derrick: boom used for erecting and transferring material when some convenient structure is available to act as a mast for attaching the topping lift and is capable of supporting the lower end of the boom.

Chord: main horizontal or diagonal top and bottom member of a truss.

Circuit: complete path of an electric current, usually including the generating apparatus.

Circuit breaker: safety device consisting of an automatic or manually controlled switching mechanism for interrupting a circuit, usually activated by abnormal current flow.

Clevis: U-shaped metal strap with a bolt or pin passing through holes in two ends, used for attaching rods or cables.

Closer: last brick laid in a course; it may be a whole unit or one that is shorter, and it usually appears in the field of the wall.

Coffer dam: excavation (generally part of sewer work) where the sides of a cut have been faced with material or wood sheeting.

Cohesion (soil): mutual attraction of particles due to molecular forces and the presence of moisture films.

Collar joint: interior longitudinal vertical joint in a brick masonry wall.

Column: vertical pillar, or post, often used as a supporting member, typically consisting of an upright shaft, base, and cap.

Compression (physics): that which occurs when a member resists a push applied at each end, as when a column supports a roof; act of forcing a substance into a smaller area.

Condemnation: process by which property is acquired for public purposes through legal proceedings under power of eminent domain.

Condominium: single real property parcel as to which all the unit owners have a right to use the common elements with separate ownership confined to the individual units.

Conductor: substance capable of transmitting electricity.

Conductor, bare: conductor without convering or insulation.

Conductor, covered: conductor covered by one or more layers of nonconducting materials.

Construction contract: type of contract in which plans and specifications for construction are made part of the agreement itself; commonly secured by performance and payment bonds to protect both subcontractors and the owner.

Construction contract documents: agreement, bid, bonds, notice of award, specifications, drawings, and change order.

Construction management contract: contract under which the general contractor personally supplies no work on the job, but designs and subcontracts as agent for the owner all the work in return for a fee.

Consumer product: any tangible personal property distributed in commerce normally used for personal, family, or household purposes.

Contract: agreement between two or more parties which creates rights and obligations between the parties.

Contract balance: determined by subtracting the amount paid under the contract from the face amount of the contract; the amount remaining in the hands of the owner or contractor to insure completion of the contract if the contractor or subcontractor, respectively, defaults.

Contract documents: contract and collateral documents signed and furnished by the successful bidder to the owner.

Contractor: any party who for a fixed price undertakes to procure performance of works or services on a large scale; the party with whom the owner has executed the contract agreement.

Contract price: total monies payable to the general contractor under the contract documents.

Contract time: number of calendar days specified in the agreement for completion of the work.

Controller: device, or group of devices, serving to control in a predetermined manner the electric power delivered to the apparatus to which any such device is connected.

Controller, spring return: controller which, when released, will return automatically to a neutral position.

Control of access: circumstance under which the right of owners or occupants of abutting land or other persons to access in connection with a highway is fully or partially controlled by public authority.

Cooking the books: modifying documents subsequent to the occurrence of events to gain a legal advantage; for example, a material supplier may attempt to change the records to apply payments to an unbonded job, thereby leaving open the claim on the bonded job.

Coping: material or units used to form a cap or finish on top of a wall, pier, or pilaster to protect the masonry below from penetration of water from above.

Corbel: (a) shelf or ledge formed by projecting successive courses of masonry out from the face of the wall; (b) an offset in vertical alignment, as in an offset chimney.

Counterweight: weight used to supplement the weight of the machine, to provide stability for lifting working loads.

Course: One of the continuous horizontal layers of masonry bonded together with mortar, forming the masonry structure.

Covering up: sealing up, boarding, or burying work by another trade before it has been completed and tested; can be done inadvertently through lack of coordination of the trades or intentionally on orders of the general contractor.

Crane: machine for lifting or lowering a load and moving it horizontally in which the hoisting mechanism is an integral part of the machine; does not include stackers or lift trucks.

Crane, boom-type mobile: self-propelled crane, equipped with a boom and mounted on a chassis supported on either rubber tires, crawler treads, or railway wheels running on railroad tracks.

Crane, cab-operated: crane controlled by an operator in a cab located on the bridge or trolley.

Crane, cantilever gantry: crane in which the bridge girders or trusses are extended transversely beyond the crane runway on one or both sides; runway may be either on the ground or elevated.

Crane, crawler: consists of a superstructure with power plant, operating machinery, and boom, mounted on a base, equipped with crawler treads for travel.

Crane, floor-operated: crane which is pendant on nonconductive rope, controlled by an operator on the floor or on an independent platform.

Crane, gantry: similar to an overhead traveling crane, except that the bridge for carrying the trolley is rigidly supported on two or more movable legs.

Crane, hammerhead: rotating, counterbalanced cantilever, equipped with one or more trolleys and supported by a pivot or turntable on a traveling or fixed tower.

Crane, jib: fixed crane, consisting of a supported vertical member from which extends a horizontal swinging arm carrying a trolley hoist or other hoisting mechanism.

Crane, locomotive: boom type mobile crane consisting of a self-propelled car operating on a railroad track, on which there is mounted a rotating body supporting the power-operated mechanism together with a boom capable of being raised or lowered its outer end from which is led the wire rope or chain connected to the hoisting mechanism for raising or lowering a load.

Crane, mobile tower: tower crane, mounted on a crawler, truck, or similar carrier for travel or transit.

Crane, motor truck: boom-type mobile crane, mounted on a motor truck frame or rubber-tired chassis; consists of a rotating superstructure with power plant, operating mechanism, and boom.

Crane, overhead (traveling or bridge): crane on a pair of parallel elevated runways adapted to lift and lower a load and carry it horizontally, paralled to, or at right angles to the runway or both; consists of one or more trolleys operating on the bridge, in turn consisting of one or more girders or trusses mounted on trucks operating on the elevated runways; operation limited to area between runways.

Crane, pillar: fixed crane, consisting of vertical member held in position at the base to resist overturning moment, with constant radius-revolving boom supported at the outer end by tension member.

Crane, pillar jib: fixed crane consisting of vertical member held at the base with a horizontal revolving arm carrying a trolley.

Crane, portal: gantry crane without trolley motion with a boom attached to a revolving crane mounted on a ganrty, which boom is capable of being raised or lowered at its head (outer end); may be fixed or mobile.

Crane, power-operated: crane whose mechanism is driven by electric, air, hydraulic, or internal combustion means.

Crane, pulpit-operated: crane operated from a fixed operator station not attached to the crane.

Crane, remote-operated: crane controlled by an operator not in a pulpit or in the cab attached to the crane, but using any method other than pendant or rope control.

Crane runway: structure on which a crane runs; may be: (a) structure consisting of columns, longitudinal bracing, and elevated beams, girders, or trusses for supporting traveling or bridge cranes; (b) elevated beams, girders, or trusses in a building or on the side of a building for supporting traveling cranes; (c) surface tracks or rails; (d) tracks or rails on walls or trestles.

Crane, semigantry or single-leg: gantry crane with the end of the bridge rigidly supported on one or more movable legs running on a fixed rail or runway, with other end of the bridge supported by a truck running on an elevated rail or runway.

Crane, semiportal: portal crane mounted on a semigantry frame instead of on a gantry frame.

Crane, standby: crane which is not in regular service but which is used occasionally or intermittently as required.

Crane, tower: crane in which a boom, swinging jib, or other structural member is mounted on a vertical mast or tower.

Crane, traveling jib: jib crane with its vertical member running on a track and its upper end guided by a parallel overhead track.

Crane, wall: jib crane with or without a trolley, supported from a side wall or line of columns of a building.

Crane, wheel-mounted (wagon crane): consists of a rotating superstructure with power plant, operating machinery, and boom, mounted on a base or platform equipped with axles and rubber-tired wheels for travel; base usually propelled by the engine in the superstructure, but may be equipped with separate engine controlled from the superstructure; function is to hoist and swing loads at various radii.

Creep: (a) plastic deformation or flow of metals held for a long period of time at stresses lower than normal yield strength, important if the temperature of stressing is near the recrystallization temperature of the metal; (b) continuous increase in deformation under constant or decreasing stress, as under high temperatures (700 degrees Fahrenheit or more for steel) metal tends to flow or creep when under stresses which would produce constant strain under normal temperatures.

Creep test: placement of a number of samples, each loaded to a different stress, in heating coils and holding them at a constant predetermined temperature; tests are conducted for periods ranging from 1000 to 2000 hours, during which time the samples stretch, and elongation is measured and recorded at regular intervals; results show the amount of elongation to be expected when steel is subjected to a given stress and temperature within a given time.

Critical path method (CPM): network analysis system used to control job planning and scheduling on large construction projects; this involves identification of known and anticipated activities, approximation of the time and duration of those activities, and determination of the critical path for the shortest possible time to complete the job.

Cross joint: see *Head joint.*

Crosswalk: (a) that part of a roadway at an intersection included within the connections of the lateral lines of the sidewalks on opposite sides of the highway measured from the curbs or, in the absence of curbs, from the edges of the traversable roadway; (b) any portion of a roadway, at an intersection or elsewhere, distinctly indicated as for pedestrian crossing by lines or other markings on the surface.

Cubic feet per second (cfs): expression for rate of flow referring to the number of cubic feet of liquid passing a given point in one second.

Culvert: any structure other than a bridge which provides an opening under the roadway for drainage or other purposes.

Curb: vertical or sloping member, generally along and defining the edge of a roadway.

Curb line: boundary between a roadway and a sidewalk, usually marked by a curb.

Curtain wall: nonbearing wall built between columns or piers for the enclosure of a building which is not supported at each story.

Custom and usage: habitual practice which by common adoption and acquiescence has become a legal measuring standard.

D

Dead load: constant weight and resulting force of a structure to itself, including the weight and force of permanent accessories within but not on the structure.

Dead weight: heavy and constant weight produced by inert forces.

Dedication: appropriation of land, or an easement, by its owner for the use of the public.

Deep etching: etching for examination at low magnification by a reagent that attacks the metal to a much greater than normal extent for microscopic examination; may bring out such features as abnormal grain size, segregation, cracks, or grain flow.

Default: omission or failure to perform a legal or contractual duty, as when a party claims that the other party is in breach of contract; a *material* default entitles the other party to cancel.

Defect: deficiency in something essential to the proper use of something; *latent* defect is one which is not apparent from reasonable observation; *patent* defect is one which is apparent from normal observation.

Deflection: member which curves, buckles, or bends due to strain.

Deformation: changes in dimensions which occur when forces are applied to a body; also called *strain.*

Delay: Anything that delays completion of the job; such delay may be the type which is not the fault of any party and hence result only in the extension of time to finish the job, but if, however, the delay is the fault of any party, damages may be assessed, e.g., a subcontractor who fails to install the work on time may be liable to the general contractor and the other trades for their added expenses caused by holding up the job, and the subcontractor may be *backcharged* by the general and sued by the other subcontractors; an owner who fails to deliver a site to the general contractor on time may be liable to the general for added expenses caused by the late start.

Demand factor: the ratio of the maximum demand of a system, or part of a system, to the total connected load of the system, or of that part of the system under consideration.

Demonstrative evidence: evidence addressed directly to the senses, for example, maps, diagrams, photographs, models, and charts.

Derrick: apparatus consisting of a mast or equivalent member, held at the top by guys or braces with or without a boom, for use with a hoisting mechanism and an operating rope to lift or lower a load and move it horizontally.

Derrick, A-frame: derrick in which the boom is hinged from a cross member between the bottom ends of two upright members spread apart at the lower ends and joined at the top, the boom point is secured to the junction of the side members, and the side members are braced or guyed from this junction point.

Derrick, breast: derrick without a boom; the mast consists of two side members spread farther apart at the base than at the top and tied together at top and bottom by rigid members, and is prevented from tipping forward by guys connected to its top; the load is raised and lowered by ropes through a sheave or block secured to the top crosspiece.

Derrick, gin pole: derrick without a boom, the guys of which are arranged from its top to permit leaning of the mast in any direction; the load is raised and lowered by ropes reeved through sheaves or blocks at the top of the mast.

Derrick, guy: fixed derrick consisting of a mast capable of being rotated, supported in a vertical position by guys, and a boom whose bottom end is hinged or pivoted to move in a vertical plane, with a reeved rope between the head of the mast and the boom point for raising and lowering the boom, and a reeved rope from the boom point for raising and lowering the load.

Derrick, stiffleg: similar to a guy derrick except that the mast is supported or held in place by two or more stiff members, called stifflegs, capable of resisting either tensile or compressive forces; generally has sills to connect the lower ends of the stifflegs to the foot of the mast.

Diamond Pyramid Hardness Test: indentation hardness test employing a 136-degree diamond pyramid indenter and variable loads making it possible to use one hardness scale for all ranges of hardness from soft lead to tungsten carbide.

Discharge, daily mean: tabulation of the average discharge during each day, midnight to midnight.

Discharge (flow): certain volume of liquid passing a given point within a given period of time.

Discharge, mean daily: average of all daily mean discharges within a specified time period, usually one season.

Disclaimer: words or conduct which attempt to limit liability.

Distortion: change in shape (usually refers to those caused by internal stress).

Distress writer: surety company which specializes in writing bonds for principals who do not qualify for bonding by more conservative surety companies; may rely more heavily on security posted by the principal or on collateral indemnities, rather than on character, competence, and credit.

District, business: territory contiguous to and including a highway when within any 600 feet along such highway there are buildings used for business or industrial purposes, including hotels, banks, office buildings, railroad stations, and public buildings which occupy at least 300 feet of frontage on one side or 300 feet collectively on both sides of the highway.

District, residence: territory contiguous to and including a highway not comprising a business district, when the property on such highway for a distance of 300 feet or more is in the main improved with residences or with residences and buildings in use for business.

District, rural: any territory not included in a business or residence district as defined in this glossary, whether or not within the boundaries of a municipality.

District, urban: territory contiguous to and including any street which is built up with structures devoted to business, industry, or dwelling houses situated at intervals of less than 100 feet over a distance of 1/4-mile or more.

Divided highway: highway with separated roadbeds for traffic in opposing directions.

Double-breasted: contractor who operates two companies, one union shop and the other nonunion, to meet union requirements on union jobs and to effect cost savings on nonunion work.

Downside: the worst result which can be reasonably expected from a proposed course of action or inaction.

Drag brake: brake which provides retarding force without external control.

Drainage area: that area, measured in a horizontal plane, from which surface runoff drains by gravity to a specific point on a stream or watercourse.

Draw or line draw: application for payment for work done or services rendered; see *Requisition*.

Dry standpipe: fire protection pipeline for use by fire department only, with no pressure in line until fireman opens the valve at the street; hose connection provided without hose.

Ductility: ability to permit change of shape without fracture; in steel, usually measured by elongation and reduction of area as determined in a tensile test.

Dwarf wall: wall or partition which does not extend to the ceiling.

Dynamic brake: method of controlling crane motor speeds to provide retarding force.

Dynamic forces (earthquake): when structures and contents exert dynamic loads due to their inertia forces when in motion.

Dynamic loading: loads introduced into machine or its components by forces in motion.

Dynamic response (earthquake): vibration of structures in accordance with laws of harmonic motion as determined by their own dynamic characteristics, functions of weight and stiffness.

Dyne: unit of force which gives an acceleration of 1 cm/s^2 to a mass of 1 gram.

E

Earthwork: process of excavating, moving, storing, placing, and working any type of earth materials.

Easement: right to use or control the property of another for designated purposes.

Eddy-current test: nondestructive testing method in which eddy-current flow is induced in the test object and changes in the flow caused by variations in the object are reflected into a nearby coil or coils for subsequent analysis by suitable instrumentation and techniques.

Efflorescence: whitish powder found on the surface of masonry or concrete due to deposits of water-soluble salts contained in Portland cement.

Elastic: capable of sustaining stress without permanent deformation.

Elastic limit: maximum load per unit of area (usually stated as pounds per square inch) that may be applied without producing permanent deformation; common practice is to apply the load at a constant rate of increase, and the measure of the increase of the load is called the proportional limit; elastic limit will usually be equal to or slightly higher than proportional limit.

Elevator, construction: includes any means of hoisting persons or material of any kind on a building under construction when operated within guides by any power other than human power.

Elongation: increase in length of a test specimen after rupture in a tensile test, expressed as a percentage of original length.

Embankment: raised structure, constructed of natural soil from excavation or borrow sources.

Emergency stop switch: manually or automatically operated electric switch able to cut off electric power independently of the regular operating controls.

Eminent domain: power to take private property for public use without the owner's consent on payment of just compensation.

Encroachment: occupancy of highway right of way by nonhighway structures or objects of any kind.

Endurance limit: maximum dynamic stress to which material may be subjected an infinite number of times without causing fatigue failure.

Endurance strength: highest-stress repeated application or reversal which a material can withstand without rupture for a given number of cycles.

Energy, kinetic: energy that a body has by virtue of its motion.

Energy, potential: energy that a body has by virtue of its position.

Epicenter: that part of the earth's surface directly above the point where the fault slip began.

Etch tests: etching to detect inclusions in steel, commonly by dipping a sample into acid, which reacts with the inclusions to disclose their presence.

Evaporation: process when a substance goes from a liquid to a gaseous state.

Event (CPM): completion of an activity, operation, or process.

Excavation: manmade cavity or depression in the earth's surface, including its sides, walls, or faces, formed by earth removal and resulting in unsupported earth conditions; if installed forms or similar structures reduce the depth-to-width relationship, an excavation may become a trench.

Exfoliation: scaling or flaking off of surfaces.

Explosion-proof apparatus: apparatus enclosed in a case which is capable of withstanding an explosion of a specified gas or vapor that may occur inside it; such enclosure must prevent the ignition of gas or vapor surrounding the enclosure by sparks, flashes, or explosion of the gas or vapor within, and the electrical apparatus must operate at such an external temperature that a surrounding flammable atmosphere will not be ignited by it.

Explosive: any mixture or chemical compound capable of producing an explosion by its own energy, including black powder, dynamite, nitroglycerin compounds, fulminate, nitro-carbo nitrates, or explosive substances with explosive power equal to or greater than that of black powder.

Expressway: divided arterial highway for through traffic with partial control of access and generally with grade separations at major intersections.

Extra: work of materials which the owner requests of the general contractor or the subcontractor, not required under the original contract, and supplying of which entitles the party to additional payment.

Extraordinary flood: one so unusual that it could not have been foreseen by persons of ordinary experience and prudence.

Extraordinary risk: lying outside of the sphere of the normal, arising out of conditions not usual in the business, unlike risks which may be obviated by exercise of reasonable care.

F

Facing: any material forming an integral part of a wall, used as a finishing surface, contrasted with veneer which is not integral with the wall.

Factor of safety: ratio of the ultimate unit stress to the allowable unit stress according to the judgment of some competent authority; also called *safety factor*.

Falsework and shoring for concrete construction: temporary formwork and vertical shoring, used to support concrete and placing operations for supported slabs of concrete structures.

Fast track: construction contract that is let without final plans and specifications, which are supplied as the work progresses.

Fatigue: tendency of materials to fracture under repetitions of a stress, considerably lower level than the ultimate static strength.

Fatigue test: process by which highly polished samples are subjected to stress while bending, which results in a reversal of stress for every complete revolution; stress is reduced on each succeeding sample until the maximum stress a sample will sustain for ten million reversals has been reached; experience justifies the assumption that if steel can withstand a stress through ten million reversals, it can withstand such stress indefinitely, and this stress is reported as the fatigue limit.

Fault: fracture in the earth's crust accompanied by a displacement of one side of the fracture with respect to the other, in a direction parallel to the fracture.

Feeder: the circuit conductors between the service, equipment, or the generator switchboard of an isolated plant, and the branch circuit overcurrent device.

Fidelity man: one who works for or on behalf of the surety in the administration of losses on fidelity bonds as opposed to bonds on construction contracts.

Field order: written order issued by the engineer which clarifies or interprets contract documents.

Fire standpipe: lines which provide water source and fire hose connections within buildings.

Fire wall: any fire resistance wall which subdivides a building to restrict the spread of fire and extends continuously from the foundation through all stories to or above the roof.

Flash point: (a) the lowest temperature at which either a flash will appear on the surface of a liquid when tested with a small flame or a liquid will give off flammable vapor; (b) point of flammability in a liquid, as follows:

Class One:	less than 21°F
Class Two:	21° to 70°F
Class Three:	more than 70°F

Flexible pavement: pavement with sufficiently low bending resistance to maintain intimate contact with the underlying structure yet with the required stability from aggregate interlock, internal friction, and cohesion, to support traffic; usually asphaltic concrete.

Flexure: act of bending.

Float or slack: in a critical path method, the extra time allowed for completion of the work, the difference between the latest start time and the earliest start time or between the latest finish time and the earliest finish time.

Force: push or pull acting on a body in motion; a force must be applied to speed it up, slow it down, change its direction, or bring it to rest.

Foreshock: minor movements along faults that sometimes precede, and may even provide part of the triggering device for, a main earthquake shock, sometimes occurring weeks or months in advance; their foci or hypocenters may be somewhat removed from the focus of the main movement.

Fourth tier: subcontractor or material supplier to the third tier.

Free water (soil): refers to both gravitational and capillary water.

Freeway: highway with respect to which owners of abutting lands have no right or easement of access to or from their abutting lands or with respect to which such owners have only a limited or restricted right or easement of access; a full freeway is a divided highway for through traffic, with full control of access and with grade separations at intersections; an expressway is a highway for through traffic with partial control of access, but which may or may not be divided or have grade separations at intersections.

Freeway-to-freeway connection: single or multilane connection between freeways.

Frequency: number of complete cycles per second of alternating current, e.g., 60 cycles.

Frontage road: local street or road auxiliary to and located generally on the side of an arterial highway for service to abutting property and adjacent areas and for control of access.

Front-end loading: practice of overpricing the items to be done at the beginning of a job and underpricing those at the end, entitling the contractor or subcontractor to disproportionately large payments at the beginning of the contract.

Full trailer: any motor vehicle, with or without motive power, other than a pole trailer, designed to be drawn by another motor vehicle and so constructed that no part of its weight other than the towing device rests on the towing vehicle; semitrailer equipped with an auxiliary front axle (dolly) is deemed a full trailer.

G

Galvanizing: applying a coating of zinc to finished cold-rolled sheet or to fabricated parts made from strip products, by hot dip (either hand or continuous) or electrolysis.

Gauge height: position of the water surface in a channel or stream as read on a staff or recorder, and relative to a selected datum (zero) equal to or lower than the invert (bottom).

Gauging station: particular site on a river, channel, or stream where systematic observations of gauge height or discharge are made.

General conditions (job overhead): costs of all permits, temporary work, supervision, payroll taxes, and union fringe benefits on nondistributable labor and bonds.

General conditions (specifications): literally those provisions of the contract which contain the general terms governing contract obligations between the owner and the contractor.

Geometric design: arrangement of the visible elements of a road, such as alignment, grades, sight distances, widths, and slopes.

Get ahead of: refers to two practices: (a) one trade outpacing another trade on the progress of the work; (b) general contractor or subcontractor, because of overstating on requisitions the amount of work completed or materials supplied, being paid more than entitled to based on actual work.

Girder: a main, horizontal supporting member in a structure.

Gore: area immediately beyond the bifurcation of two roadways, bounded by the edges of those roadways.

Grade MW (moderate weather): brick intended for use where exposed to temperatures below freezing, but where unlikely to be permeated with water, or where moderate and somewhat nonuniform degree of resistance to frost action is permissible.

Grade NW (no weather): brick intended for use as backup or interior masonry.

Grade resistance: force of gravity which must be overcome when going uphill, acting against the total weight of the vehicle.

Grade separation: crossing at different levels of two highways or a highway and a railroad.

Grade SW (severe weather): brick intended for use where a high degree of resistance to frost action is desired and where exposure is such that the brick may be frozen when permeated with water.

Gravitational water (soil): water free to move downward from the force of gravity, water that will drain from a soil.

Ground: a conducting connection, whether intentional or accidental, between an electrical circuit or equipment and earth, or some conducting body which serves in place of the earth.

Ground deformation: visible manifestation of earth movement along a fault or earth cracking, vertical, horizontal, or both.

Grounded: connected to earth or to some conducting body which serves in place of earth.

Grout: mixture of Portland cement, sand, and water, with or without the addition of pea gravel or lime, poured into place in structural masonry or slushed into place with a trowel in veneer, fireplace, and chimney work.

Guaranty: in commercial usage, understood to mean a collateral warranty against some default or event in the future, while the term *warranty* is taken as meaning an absolute undertaking against a defect, or for the quality or quantity contemplated by the parties; a promise, entirely collateral to the original contract, and not imposing any primary liability on the guarantor; whereas failure to comply with a warranty provision has the effect of voiding a contract, failure in the case of a guaranty does not.

H

Hard compact: all earth material not classified as running or unstable.

Harsh mortar: a mortar that, due to improper measure of materials, is difficult to spread.

Haulage vehicle: self-propelled vehicle, including its trailer, used to transport materials on construction projects, including trucks, truck and trailer combinations, and all other similar equipment used for haulage.

Header: masonry unit laid flat with its greatest dimension at right angle to the face of the wall, generally used to tie two withes of masonry together; not permitted in reinforced grouted brick masonry construction.

Head joint: vertical mortar joint between ends of masonry units; sometimes called the *cross joint*.

High voltage: sustained voltage of more than 600 volts.

Highway: any main route on land, water, or in the air, with prime essentials being the right of common enjoyment on the one hand and the duty of public maintenance on the other.

Highway, arterial: any United States or state numbered route, controlled-access highway, or other major radial or circumferential street or highway designated by local authorities within their respective jurisdictions as part of a major arterial system of streets or highways.

Highway, controlled access: any highway, street, or roadway with respect to which owners or occupants of abutting lands and other persons have no legal right of access to or from the same, except at such points only and in such manner as may be determined by the public authority with jurisdiction over such highway, street, or roadway.

Highway, divided: highway with separate roadways for traffic in opposite directions.

Highway, major: roadway approach or approaches at an intersection normally carrying the major volume of vehicular traffic.

Highway, minor: roadway approach or approaches at an intersection normally carrying the minor volume of vehicular traffic.

Highway (or street): entire width between the boundary lines of every way, publicly maintained, when any part of such way is open to the public for purposes of vehicular travel.

Highway, through: a highway or portion thereof on which vehicular traffic is given preferential right of way, and at the entrances to which vehicular traffic from intersecting highways is required by law to yield the right of way to vehicles on such through highway in obedience to a stop sign, yield sign, or other official traffic control device.

Hog (in a wall): where for any given height at both ends of a wall, there is a different number of courses, necessitating adjustment of mortar bed joints or use of supplementary height units in the field.

Hoist: any apparatus by which a pulling and releasing action can be transmitted through ropes, wire ropes, or chains to bring about the raising or lowering of loads, an apparatus generally for raising or lowering a load by application of a pulling force not including a car or platform riding in guides.

Hoist, base-mounted electric: similar to an overhead electric hoist, except for having a base or feet, and able to be mounted overhead on a vertical plane, or in any position for which it is designed.

Hoist chain: load-bearing chain in a hoist.

Hoist, clevis suspension: hoist whose upper suspension member is a clevis.

Hoist, hook suspension: hoist whose upper suspension member is a hook.

Hoisting machine: power-operated machine used for lifting or lowering a load, utilizing a drum and wire rope, excluding elevators, and including, but not limited to, a crane, derrick, and cableway.

Hoist, monorail: trolley suspension hoist, the trolley of which is suspended from a single rail.

Hoist motion: motion of a crane which raises and lowers a load.

Hoist, overhead electric: motor-driven hoist, fixed or traveling, with one or more drums or sheaves for rope or chain and supported overhead.

Hoist, simple drum: hoist with one or more drums controlled by manually operated clutches, brakes, or ratchet and pawl on drum and control levers, operated by hand or by power.

> NOTE: This type of hoist is known to the trade as contractor's hoist, and is usually a portable unit: (1) a *double-drum hoist* is a simple drum hoist with two independent hoisting drums; (2) a *single-drum hoist* is a simple drum hoist with only one hoisting drum; and (3) a *single-fixed drum hoist* is a single drum hoist with the drum geared directly to the power unit instead of by means of friction clutches.

Hoist, trolley suspension: hoist, either floor- or cage-operated, whose upper suspension member is a trolley for purposes of running the hoist below a suitable runway.

Hollow tile: masonry units in which the coring exceeds 25 per cent of the gross cross-sectional area of the unit

Horsepower: rate at which work is done, or work done (stated in foot-pounds) divided by the time involved.

HVAC: heating, ventilating, and air conditioning; also, the mechanical subcontractor who does this work.

Hydrated lime: quicklime to which only enough water is added in manufacture to stabilize the lime's chemical affinity for water, used in powdered form; water added to hydrated lime makes lime putty.

Hydrology: science encompassing the distribution and circulation of water as it occurs in the atmosphere, on the ground surface, and underground.

Hypothetical engineering question: question framed in such a manner as to call for an opinion from an engineering expert, based on a series of assumptions claimed to have been established as facts by the evidence in the case.

I

I-J: computerized critical path method arrow diagram is printed out in computer talk as *I-J*, hence, another name for the CPM diagram.

Impact energy attenuators: devices used on highways to protect motorists from consequences of collision by absorbing the energy of the vehicle's impact.

Impact loads: loads applied with sufficient rapidity to cause fluctuating stress and deflection in a member, also known as *dynamic loads*; usually evaluated in terms of energy while static loads are evaluated as a force.

Impact test: determines the energy absorbed in fracturing a test bar at high velocity; may be in tension or bending, or may be a notched bar specimen; the Charpy and Izod tests are used for this purpose.

Impact values: resistance to shock and ability to distribute localized stress as measured by impact test--usually expressed in foot-pounds.

Inclusions: particles of nonmetallic material, usually oxides, sulphides, silicates and such, which are entrapped mechanically or which are formed during solidification or by subsequent reaction within the solid metal.

Indemnify: to restore the victim of a loss in whole or in part by some means of compensation, pecuniary replacement or repair.

Indemnity: collateral assurance by which one person engages to secure another against an anticipated loss, so that liability for loss is shifted from one person held legally responsible to another person.

Indirect job costs: (construction): see *General conditions.*

Inertia: property of physical matter to remain at rest unless acted on by some external force, usually concerning the driven load, and measured in pounds per square foot.

Ingot: mass of metal molded into a convenient shape for shipment, storage, or processing.

Interchange: system of interconnecting roadways in conjunction with a grade separation or grade separations providing for interchange of traffic between two or more intersecting roadways.

Intergranular corrosion: electrochemical corrosion along the grain boundaries of an alloy, usually caused because the boundary regions contain material anodic to the center of the grain.

Internal friction: (soil): resistance to sliding within the soil mass.

Intersection: general area where two or more roadways join or cross, within which are included the roadway and roadside facilities for traffic movements in that area, not including the junction of an alley with a street or highway.

Inverse condemnation: legal process which may be initiated by a property owner to compel payment of compensation where the owner's property has been taken or damaged for a public purpose.

Iron: a metallic element; in the steel industry, the product of a blast furnace containing 92 per cent to 94 per cent iron; blast furnace iron is also called *pig iron* or *hot metal.*

Island: defined area between traffic lanes for control of vehicle movements or pedestrian refuge; within an intersection, includes a median or an outer separation.

Island, approach end: end of an island or area between roadways which faces approaching traffic passing to one or both sides.

Island, buffer: structure at the approach end of a safety zone designed to deflect or stop any vehicle which collides with it.

Island, button: rounded object extending above the normal pavement surface for purposes of channelizing traffic movement.

Island, channelizing: traffic island located in a roadway area to control and direct specific movements of traffic into definite channels.

Island, divisional: traffic island used to separate traffic moving in the same or in opposite directions.

Island, pedestrian refuge: island designed for use and protection of pedestrians.

Island, raised bars: series of bars extending above the normal pavement surface to make any wheel encroachment obvious to a vehicle operator without loss of control of the vehicle.

Island, traffic: area within a roadway from which vehicular traffic is intended to be excluded, together with any part of the approach to such area occupied by warning devices.

Isohyetal line: line drawn on a map joining points that received the same amounts of precipitation during a specified period.

Isolating switch: a switch intended for isolating an electric circuit from the source of power; has no interrupting rating, and is intended to be operated only after the circuit has been opened by some other means.

Izod Impact Test: a test in which a specimen is struck by a swinging pendulum and the energy absorbed in the fracture is measured, using a striking velocity of 11.5 feet per second.

Izod Test: a test to determine the notched toughness of a material, indicating the energy required to break a standard notched specimen supported as a cantilever beam.

J

Jib: (a) horizontal arm, for supporting a trolley or fall block, which does not change its inclination with the horizontal; (b) extension attached to the boom point to provide added boom length for lifting specified loads, either in line with the boom or offset to various angles.

Job payment breakdown: subcontractor's schedule to the general contractor, showing contract items held and ascribing a certain value to each item; percentage of completion is the basis of the subcontractor's requisition to the general contractor for payments as the job progresses; see *Trade payment breakdown* or *Front-end loading*.

Joist: horizontal member which may support the boards of a floor or lath of a ceiling in a parallel position.

K

Kip: shorthand method of designating 1,000 pounds.

L

Ladder: device, other than a ramp or stairway, designed for use in ascending or descending at an angle with the horizontal; intended to be stationary while in service, consisting of two side pieces called side rails, joined at short intervals by crosspieces called steps, rungs, or cleats.

Ladder, extension: consists of two or more sections, with guides or brackets so arranged that the ladder may be adjusted to different lengths by sliding and locking the movable section or sections.

Ladder, extension trestle: combination of an A-frame or trestle ladder with an individual single ladder.

Ladder, fixed: ladder permanently fastened to a structure.

Ladder, portable: ladder, not permanently fixed in place, which may be used at various locations.

Ladder, stepladder: ladder with treads, so constructed as to be self-supporting.

Ladder, steps: rungs, treads, or cleats.

Ladder, trestle or A: two single ladders hinged together at the top to form equal angles with the surface on which they stand.

Lane, median: speed-change lane within the median to accommodate left-turning vehicles.

Lane, numbering: on a multilane roadway, numbering of traffic lanes available for through traffic traveling in the same direction from left to right when facing in the direction of traffic flow.

Lane, separate turning: auxiliary lane for traffic in one direction which has been physically separated from the intersection area by a traffic island.

Lane, speed-change: auxiliary lane, including tapered areas, primarily for acceleration or deceleration of vehicles entering or leaving the through-traffic lanes.

Lane, traffic: portion of the traveled way for movement of a single lane of vehicles.

Latent heat of vaporization: quantity of heat needed to change one pound of liquid at a certain temperature to vapor at the same temperature, given in BTUs per pound.

Laundered money: payment for a phony extra or made as a "consultant's fee" to a certain party who then "kicks back" the bulk of the money to the real parties in interest.

Lay: that distance measured along a rope in which one strand makes a complete revolution around the rope axis.

Ledger: horizontal member of a scaffold that runs at right angles to the wall and directly supports the planking of the platform.

Legal description: description of real property by government survey, metes and bounds, or lot number of recorded plat, complete enough for a particular parcel of land to be located and identified.

Letter of credit: alternative to the furnishing of a performance bond by a surety, by which a bank issues a letter of credit to the owner as security for performance of the contract.

License: permission from a competent authority to do an act which without such permission would be illegal.

Lien: claim or encumbrance on property.

Life line: rope suitable for supporting a worker if one end is fastened to a safety belt and the other end is secured to a substantial object or safety line.

Lift slab: operation whereby a concrete slab is lifted into an elevated position by means of jacks located above the slab on columns or other supporting members.

Lighting outlet: outlet intended for the direct connection of a lampholder, lighting fixture, or pendent cord terminating in a lampholder.

Light well: court within a building to provide light and air to internal rooms.

Limit switch: device designed to cut off power automatically at or near the limit of travel of a crane, trolley, hoist, or similar mechanism.

Line item: category of work shown on a monthly requisition.

Line pull, permissible: line pull, less than available pull, as restricted by rope strength, clutch or brake ability, or other limitation in machinery or equipment.

Lintel: horizontal structure used over openings such as doors or windows which supports the weight above it.

Liquidation: realization on assets and discharge of liabilities.

Live load: variable weight which a structure supports, such as traffic or persons, not including weight of the structure itself.

Load block (lower): assembly of hook or shackle, swivel, sheaves, pins, and frame suspended by the hoisting ropes.

Load block (upper): assembly of sheaves, pins, and frame suspended from the boom.

Loading device: mobile, mechanical-powered machine of the skip-loader type, used for picking up materials and loading or dumping them into haulage vehicles, bins, or hoppers, excluding boom-type excavators and endless belt or chain conveyers.

Load rating: lifting capacity established by the certified agent for various angles and positions.

Load (working): external load in pounds applied on the hoisting line, including the weight of load-attaching equipment such as load blocks, shackles, slings, buckets, and magnets.

M

Machine house: enclosure for housing hoisting mechanism and power plant.

Macroetch Test: deep-etching steel in a hot acid solution to evaluate soundness and homogeneity without magnification.

Magnaflux Test: method of detecting cracks, laps, and other defects by magnetizing the steel and applying fine magnetic particles (dry or suspended in solution); presence of surface or subsurface defects indicated by a particle pattern.

Magnetic-analysis inspection: nondestructive method of inspection to determine existence and extent of possible defects in ferromagnetic materials, by which finely divided magnetic particles applied to the magnetized part are attracted to and outline the pattern of any magnetic leakage fields created by discontinuities.

Main hoist: hoist mechanism provided for lifting the maximum rated load.

Main switch: switch controlling the entire power supply to the crane.

Major street or major highway: arterial highway with intersections at grade and direct access to abutting property, and on which geometric design and traffic control measures are used to expedite safe movement of through traffic.

Malleability: property of metal to deform when subjected to rolling hammering.

Malpractice (engineering): failure of one rendering professional engineering services to exercise that degree of skill and learning commonly applied under all the circumstances by the average prudent, reputable member of the profession in the community, with the result of injury, loss, or damage to the recipient of those services or those entitled to rely on them.

Manufacturer: person who by labor, art, or skill transforms raw material into some kind of a finished good, product, or article of trade.

Manufacturers liability doctrine: liability founded on knowledge of danger attending use of manufactured or assembled product and negligence in failing to give appropriate warning, or on negligence in failure to discover both the danger and the probability that injury will proximately result from use of such product for the purposes for which it was intended.

Markings, barrier line: line which, when placed parallel to a center or lane line or parallel to another barrier line, indicates that traffic must not cross such line for purposes of overtaking and passing.

Markings, center line: line indicating division of roadway between traffic traveling in opposite directions.

Markings, channelizing line: line which directs traffic, indicating that traffic should not cross but may proceed on either side.

Markings, delineator: light-reflecting device mounted at the side of the roadway, in series with others, to indicate alignment of the roadway.

Markings, edge line: line which indicates the edge of the roadway.

Markings, lane line: line separating two lanes of traffic traveling in the same direction.

Markings, object: markings intended for use on obstructions within or adjacent to the roadway.

Markings, pavement: markings set into the surface of, applied on, or attached to the pavement.

Markings, stop line (or limit line): line which indicates where vehicles should stop when directed by a traffic officer or traffic control device.

Markings, traffic (or markings): all lines, patterns, words, colors, or other devices, except signs and power-operated traffic control devices, set into the surface of, applied on, or attached to the pavement or curbing, or to objects within or adjacent to the roadway, placed for the purpose of regulating, warning, or guiding traffic.

Martensite: in case of most steels, cooling as rapidly as possible from quenching temperature develops a distinctive structure called martensite, and in this form the steel is at its maximum hardness.

Master switch: switch which dominates operation of contactors, relays, or other remotely-operated devices.

Matrix: ground mass or principal substance in which a constituent is embedded.

McQuaid-Ehn Test: test for revealing grain size of steel by heating above critical range in a carbonaceous medium, causing grains to be outlined sharply when polished, etched, and viewed under a microscope; grain sizes range from No 8 (finest) to No 1 (coarsest).

Mechanical engineer: professional engineer who designs plumbing and HVAC work.

Mechanic's lien: claim created by statute to secure priority of payment for value of work performed by materialmen, tradesmen, suppliers, and others who furnish services, labor, or materials on construction or improvement of property.

Median: portion of a divided highway separating the traveled ways for traffic in opposite directions.

Merchantable: goods implicitly warranted to be in conformity to ordinary standards of care and of the same quality and value as similar goods sold under similar circumstances.

Miller Act bond or Miller Act-type bond: for work on federal contracts, the government under 40 USC §270(a) requires that the general contractor post a bond for performance and payment; the payment bond recites certain conditions and limitations, such as requiring suit within one year of the date after a party does last work on a project and requiring materialmen and subcontractors to give written notice in a certain form to the general contractor within 90 days after the date they last supplied the job in order to have a valid claim under the bond; this statute has become a model for state legislation called the Little Miller Acts, e.g., NY State Fin Law §137; the form of the bond is adopted in the AIA forms and in many other bonds required by municipal agencies and private owners.

Minimum turning radius: radius of the path of the outer front wheel of a vehicle making its sharpest turn.

Missed hole: drill hole containing an explosive charge that has failed to explode.

Modification: (a) written amendment of the contract documents signed by both parties; (b) change order; (c) written clarification or interpretation issued by the engineer; (d) written order for minor change or alteration in the work issued by the engineer; under any of these definitions, a modification may only be issued after execution of the agreement.

Modified Mercalli Scale: system that describes the effects (intensity) of an earthquake at specified points in terms of a series of levels ranging from I to XII, with these intensities tending to be highest near the epicenter of the earthquake, decreasing with increasing distance from a central area; often this pattern is modified by the nature of the ground.

Modulus of Elasticity: value obtained, within the proportional limit, if the stress (in pounds per square inch) is divided by the strain (stretch in inches per inch); this value for steel is about 30,000,000.

Modulus of Elasticity (Young's modulus): rate of change of unit stress with respect to unit strain, either for unit tensile or compressive stress and strain.

Modulus of resilience: strain energy per unit volume absorbed.

Modulus of rigidity (modulus of elasticity in shear): rate of change of unit shear stress with respect to unit shear strain.

Molten metal handling crane: overhead crane used for transporting or pouring molten material.

Moment of inertia (of an area): sum of the products obtained by multiplying each element of an area by the square of its distance from the neutral axis of the area.

Momentum: product of the mass of body and its velocity.

Motor efficiency: effectiveness with which a motor turns electrical energy into mechanical energy; a motor does not operate at 100 per cent efficiency, but generally lies in the neighborhood of 85 per cent efficiency; the more efficiently a motor operates, the lower the power costs.

Motor vehicle: any vehicle, machine, tractor, trailer, or semitrailer propelled or drawn by mechanical power and used on the highways in the transportation of passengers, property, or any combination of the two.

Mountable curb: curb that can be climbed readily by a moving vehicle.

Multiprimes: some types of owners enter into direct contracts with various trades covering different types of work, e.g., electrical, plumbing, HVAC, and contract the remainder to the general contractors; instead of having one contract with the general contractor for the construction of the building, the owner will have separate contracts with each of those parties covering a portion of the work.

N

Negative float: on a critical path method, where a job is behind schedule; see *Float*.

Negligence per se: conduct, whether of action or omission, which may be declared and treated as negligence without any argument or proof as to the particular surrounding circumstances, either because it is in violation of a statute or valid municipal ordinance, or because it is so palpably opposed to the dictates of common prudence that it can be said without doubt that no careful person would have engaged in it.

NEMA: National Electrical Manufacturers' Association, which establishes certain voluntary industry standards relating to motors, e.g., operating characteristics, terminology, basic dimensions, ratings, and testing.

Network (CPM): diagrammatic representation of a program or plan for a particular project, or part of a project, that shows the correct sequence and relationship of activities and events required to achieve the end objectives.

Network structure: structure in which the crystals of one constituent are partially or entirely surrounded by envelopes of another constituent; an arrangement that gives a network appearance to a polished and etched specimen.

Nickel steel: alloy steel containing nickel as its principal alloying element.

No passing zone: section of highway where overtaking and passing or driving to the left of the roadway would be hazardous.

Normalizing: heating to about 100 degrees Fahrenheit above the critical temperature and cooling to room temperature in still air; provision is often made in normalizing for controlled cooling at a slower rate, but when the cooling is prolonged the term used is *annealing*.

Notice of award: written notice by the owner to the contractor that the contractor is the successful bidder; on compliance with the conditions precedent to be fulfilled by the contractor, the owner will execute and deliver the contract.

Novation (construction): substitution of a new construction contract for an existing one between the same or different parties, the requisite elements of which are: a previous valid construction contract; an agreement of all the parties to a new construction contract; extinguishment of the old construction contract; and validity of the new one.

O

Official traffic control devices (or traffic control devices): all traffic signs, highway traffic signals, traffic markings, and other devices erected or placed on or adjacent to a highway or street by authority of the public body or official having jurisdiction, for purposes of regulating, warning, or guiding traffic.

Operating engineer: operator of cranes, bulldozers, compressors, cement pump, etc., not to be confused with a *professional engineer;* the operating engineer is aided by an *oiler,* who is required to accompany the engineer on the rig and observe hazards; when cranes operate above a certain height, standard practice requires a third assistant, a *safety engineer,* who observes hazards from a vantage point *off the rig*.

Ordinance: permanent rule of action equivalent of a municipal statute, passed by the city council, and governing matters not already covered by federal or state law.

Organic materials: chemical compounds of carbon, excluding carbon monoxide, carbon dioxide, carbonic acid, metallic carbides, metallic carbonates, and ammonium carbonate.

Organic solvents: includes diluents and thinners, organic materials which are liquids at standard conditions and which are used as dissolvers, viscosity reducers, or cleaning agents; however, any material exhibiting a boiling point higher than 104 degrees Celsius (219 degrees Fahrenheit) at 0.5 mm Hg (millimeter mercury) absolute pressure or having an equivalent vapor pressure is not considered to be a solvent unless exposed to temperatures exceeding 104 degrees Celsius (219 degrees Fahrenheit).

Original grade doctrine: doctrine which relieves public body from any liability for property damaged in the reduction of the surface of the street to the grade line the first time it is established.

OSHA: Occupational Safety and Health Act, a recent federal statute which sets forth strict safety controls for the construction industry as well as machinery for its enforcement.

Outer separation: portion of an arterial highway between the traveled ways of a roadway for through traffic and a frontage street or road.

Overhead (construction costs): see *General conditions*.

Overhead loads: loads either passed or suspended directly over workers, occupied workspaces, or passageways.

P

Panelboard: single panel, or group of panel units designed for assembly in the form of a single panel, with or without switches and/or automatic overcurrent protective devices, for the control of light, heat, or power circuits.

Parapet wall: wall extending above roof, usually a continuation of a wall below the roof line.

Parkway: arterial highway for noncommercial traffic, with full or partial control of access, usually located within a park or strip of a parklike development.

Partial taking: acquisition of a portion of a parcel or property.

Particulate matter: any material, except uncombined water, which exists in a finely divided form as a liquid or solid at standard conditions.

Pavement: that part of a roadway with a constructed surface to facilitate vehicular traffic.

Pay line: survey lines within which a party doing excavating or supplying material will be entitled to be paid; an excavator who overshoots the work or overexcavates the hole will only be entitled to payment for materials removed or replaced within the pay lines.

Peddling the depreciation: process of selling the equities in a subsidized building to the investors; see *Final mortgage determination.*

Performance bond: bond given to a public authority, guaranteeing that a contractor will perform a contract once awarded within a fixed period of time.

Perimeter security: cable or double cable strung around the perimeter of a building on open floors to prevent persons from falling during construction.

Period of vibration (earthquake): time necessary to complete one cycle of oscillation, the reciprocal of the natural frequency of vibration.

Permeability (soil): property of soil that allows it to transmit water, the rate at which water is transmitted by soils.

PERT: Program Evaluation Review Techniques, an early form of the critical path method used for scheduling construction work.

Physical properties: properties, exclusive of those listed as mechanical properties, such as density, electrical conductivity, and coefficient of thermal expansion; often used to describe mechanical properties, but such usage is not recommended.

Pillar: vertical shaft, often used as a supporting member, shaped like a post.

Plasticity: property of sustaining appreciable permanent deformation without rupture; also used to denote the property of yielding or flowing under a steady load.

Pointing: repairing and patching cracks in concrete.

Poisson's ratio: ratio of unit deformation at right angles to the direction of the load to unit deformation in the direction of the load.

Pole trailer: any vehicle without motive power, designed to be drawn by another vehicle, and attached to the towing vehicle by means of a reach or pole, or by being boomed or otherwise secured by the towing vehicle; ordinarily used to transport long or irregularly shaped loads such as poles, pipes, or structural members capable generally of sustaining themselves as beams between the supporting connections.

Poured in place: in concrete construction, method of forming and pouring walls and other structures on the job site.

Powder: any explosive other than the detonating agent.

Power: time rate of doing work.

PPM: parts per million by volume.

Precast: forming and pouring concrete components of a building at a factory, and then transporting them to the job site for erection.

Precipitation: water in either a liquid or solid state which falls out of the atmosphere onto the earth's surface.

Primary blasting: blasting operation by which rock or other material that has not previously been disturbed by similar operation is broken into fragments.

Prime coat: initial application of a low viscosity liquid bituminous material to an absorbent surface, preparatory to any subsequent treatment; this is to harden or toughen the surface and promote adhesion between it and the superimposed, constructed layer.

Prime contractor: party to a building contract charged with the total construction, who enters into subcontracts for things like electrical work, plumbing, etc.

Primer: explosive cartridge with a detonator or igniting agent inserted into it.

Procedure diagrams: similar to an I-J diagram but using a different form.

Product liability: tort based on the legal liability of manufacturers and sellers to compensate buyers, users, and even bystanders for damages or injuries suffered because of defects in goods purchased.

Project manager: general contractor's on-site chief, responsible for paper flow, administration, and trade coordination.

Proportional limit: greatest load per square inch of original cross-sectional area for which the elongation is proportional to the load.

Punching out the job: see Punch list; completing punch list items.

Punch list: at the end of a job, the list prepared by the architect showing small, uncompleted items to be taken care of before final acceptance.

Pyrometer: instrument used to measure temperatures.

R

Radial highway: arterial highway leading to or from an urban center.

Radiography: nondestructive method of internal examination in which metal or other objects are exposed to a beam of x-ray or gamma radiation; differences in thickness, density, or absorption caused by internal discontinuities are apparent in the shadow image either on a fluorescent screen or on photographic film placed behind the object.

Radius (load): horizontal distance from the center of rotation of a crane or derrick to the freely suspended hook or load.

Rafter: Generally, sloping timber or member which supports roof sheeting or roof covering.

Railroad ballast: gravel, crushed rock, cinders, slag, and other materials placed on the railbed beneath and around the crossties to increase drainage, strength, and stability of the track, and to lessen dust and weeds.

Railroad crossties: also known as *ties*, *wood sills*, or *cross pieces*, members which support the rails in the track; they are usually spaced 21 inches center to center.

Railroad rails: steel rail designed to carry locomotives and trains weighing between 90 and 155 pounds per yard, and with a standard length of 39 feet, although some railways use rails as long as 78 feet; rails are joined together by two pieces of steel called *angle bars* or *rail joints*, which are held in place by bolts passing through openings in the rails; on some railways, rails are welded together end to end to form continuous rails.

Railroad right of way: strip of land on which the railroad is built, usually between 75 and 200 feet wide.

Railroad roadway: includes the entire structure supporting and forming single or multiple railway tracks, bridges, trestles, culverts, embankments, ballast, crossties, tie plates, and rails.

Railroad tie plates: used to support the rails on the crossties, held in place to the crosstie by spikes.

Ramp: (a) a surfaced sloping passageway connecting two different levels; (b) a connecting roadway between two intersecting roadways at an interchange; (c) an inclined section of way, over which traffic passes for the primary purpose of ascending or descending to make connections with other ways; (d) an interconnecting roadway of traffic interchange, or any connection between highway facilities of different levels on which vehicles may enter or leave a designated highway.

Rated load: maximum load for which a crane or individual hoist is designed and built by the manufacturer, shown on the equipment nameplate(s).

Receptacle (convenience outlet): contact device installed at an outlet for the connection of an attachment plug and flexible cord.

Reeving: rope system in which the rope travels around drums and sheaves.

Regenerative (brake): a form of dynamic braking in which the electrical energy generated is fed back into the power system.

Relinquishment: transfer of the state's right, title, and interest in and to a highway, or portion or highway, to a city or county.

Remote control circuit: any electrical circuit which controls any other circuit through a relay or equivalent device.

Requisition: application of the general contractor to the owner, or of the subcontractor to the general contractor, showing the amount of work done and its claimed value since the previous requisition.

Resident project representative: authorized representative of the engineer assigned to the project site.

Resurfacing: supplemental surface or replacement placed on an existing pavement to restore its riding qualities or increase its strength.

Retainage: under the contract, the amount held back by the owner from the contractor on the otherwise earned progress payment, as security for the contractor's completion on the job; the general contractor withholds a like percentage from the subcontractor, who may withhold it similarly from the material supplier or vendor.

Ribbon: horizontal member in a scaffold which runs from upright to upright, parallel to the building, normally placed directly under the ledger.

Richter Scale: measures the magnitude of an earthquake; earthquake magnitude numbers are used to compare different earthquakes independently of the locations of their epicenters or points of observation, calculated from measurements of seismograph records.

Ridgepole: horizontal member at the top of a roof, to which are fastened the upper ends of the rafters.

Right of access: right of an abutting landowner to entrance to or exit from a public road.

Rigid pavement: pavement with sufficiently high bending resistance to distribute loads over a comparatively large area.

Riley Act: Cal Health & Safety Code, Div 13, pt 3, ch 2 (§§19100-19170), enacted in 1933 following the Long Beach earthquake, establishing minimum standards for construction and exempting farm buildings and dwellings occupied by not more than two families outside the limits of incorporated areas.

Roadbed: portion of roadway extending from curb line to curb line or shoulder line to shoulder line; divided highways are considered to have two roadbeds.

Roadside: generally denotes the area adjoining the outer edge of the roadbed, and may also include extensive areas between the roadbeds of a divided highway.

Roadway: portion of the highway included between the outside lines of the sidewalks, or curbs and gutters, or side ditches including the appurtenant structures, and all slopes, ditches, channels, waterways, and other features necessary for proper drainage and protection.

Rockwell Hardness Test: test in which the hardness of a material is determined by the depth of penetration of an indentor under certain arbitrary conditions, in which the indentor may be either a steel ball of some specified diameter or spherical-tipped, conical diamond.

Rolling resistance: restraining force exerted by the ground against wheels of a vehicle, which must be overcome before the vehicle will move.

Rope: refers to wire rope unless otherwise specified.

RPM: revolutions per minute; in motor terminology, referring to shaft revolutions.

Running: earth material whose angle of repose is approximately zero, as in the case of soil in a nearly liquid state, or dry, unpacked sand which flows freely under slight pressure.

Running around money: generally, large cash payments made to and by the parties to the construction process, such as payments for informal union non-disturbance agreements, for lucrative contracts or subcontracts, or for approval by inspectors of otherwise substandard work or operations.

Running sheave: sheave which rotates as the load block is raised or lowered.

Runoff: that part of precipitation which appears in streams or channels and includes: (a) overflow water from all types of private and commercial irrigation; and (b) discharges from industrial operations.

Run over the plumber, the electrician, etc: see *Covering up*.

S

Safety factor: see *Factor of safety*.

Safety fuse: medium, manufactured especially for firing explosive charges, that conveys a flame at a uniform rate as opposed to a medium that is in itself a detonator or one that operates on some other principle.

Safety hook: hook with a safety latch or arrangement to close the throat of the hook so as to prevent slings on load attachment from accidentally slipping off the hook.

Safety line: line provided to protect a worker from falls caused by failure of scaffolds or working platforms, or by loss of balance, which extends to within four feet of the ground or other stable surface.

Salvage: a surety who completes under the performance bond or pays under the payment bond is subrogated to the principal's rights and to the rights of the party paid or performed for; any securities or rights the party may hold against any person become the property of the surety, who may pursue such persons for salvage to apply against the losses.

Scaffold: includes the platform and all supporting members.

Scaffold, heavy trades: heavily constructed, built to withstand the weight of workers and storage of materials, including bricks, mortar, concrete blocks, etc., intended for use on work where heavy material will accumulate on the scaffold; the load, including workers, is limited to a maximum of 100 pounds per square foot of the scaffold platform.

Scaffold, light trade: used by plasterers, carpenters, sheet-metal workers, or other trades not using heavy tools or storing heavy material on the scaffold; the load, including workers, is limited to a maximum of 30 pounds per square foot of the scaffold platform.

Scaffold, outrigger: not suspended by ropes, but supported by outrigger beams, cantilevered out from the structure to which they are anchored.

Scaffold, suspended: suspended from above by ropes or cables and rigged with pulley blocks, winches, or equivalent, so that the scaffold elevation is easily adjustable.

Scaffold, suspended, power-driven: any suspended scaffold equipped with one or more power units for raising or lowering that are a part of, and travel with, the scaffold.

Scale: iron oxide formed on the surface of hot steel, sometimes in the form of large sheets which fall off when the steel is rolled.

Scenic highway: officially designated portion of a state highway system traversing areas of outstanding scenic beauty which, together with its adjacent scenic corridors, requires special scenic conservation treatment.

Schedule: method of showing the time sequence within which the job is to be built; see *CPM*, *PERT*, and *Bar chart*.

Scleroscope or Shore Hardness Test: dropping a small diamond-tipped hammer from a standard height onto the surface of the specimen being tested; the height to which the hammer rebounds is a measure of the surface hardness of the specimen.

Scraper: machine used to move earth, powered or towed by a track-type, two-axle wheel type, or single-axle wheel type tractor, or by a twin engine unit; primary function is to load, haul, and spread earth in rough grading operation; also known as a *carryall*.

S Curve: chart showing when and how much money must be paid by the owner to the contractor on the anticipated job progress on the contractor's requisitions; base data is taken from the critical path method or bar chart, which shows anticipated rates of progress on the job and is translated into dollars needed by the owner to pay for job progress; a financial tool showing the cash flow to the job.

Seal Coat (Roadway): bituminous coating, with or without aggregate, applied to the surface of a pavement for the purpose of: (a) waterproofing, preserving, or rejuvenating a bituminous surface; or (b) providing increased skid resistance or resistance to abrasion by traffic.

Second tier: subcontractor or material supplier to the general contractor.

Section modulus (section factor): factor used to determine stress, found by dividing the moment of inertia by the distance from the neutral axis of an area to its outermost edge.

Seismic: pertaining to earth movement (earthquake).

Seismic sea waves (tsunami): ocean waves created by submarine earthquakes that travel great distances at high speeds (average 450 miles per hour), with a high destructive potential depending on a number of factors such as shoreline configuration and depth of water.

Seismograph: instrument that writes a continuous record of successive earth waves generated by an earthquake.

Semitrailer: any motor vehicle, other than a pole trailer, with or without motive power, designed to be drawn by another motor vehicle and so constructed that some part of its weight rests on the towing vehicle.

Service: conductors and equipment for delivering energy from the electricity supply system to the wiring system of the premises served.

Service cable: service conductors made up in the form of a cable.

Service conductors: supply conductors which extend from the street main or transformers to the service equipment of the premises supplied.

Service equipment: usually consists of circuit breaker, or switch and fuses and their accessories, located near the point of entrance of supply conductors to a building; intended to constitute the main control and means of cutoff for the supply to that building.

Service factor: allows a motor, when necessary, to deliver greater than rated horsepower; for instance, 5-horsepower, drip-proof induction motor has a service factor of 1.15 per cent greater than rated horsepower; when operated at this overload, the motor will have a higher temperature rise and may have different efficiency, power factor, and speed than at rated load, while the locked-rotor torque will remain unchanged; however, if the service factor of a motor is 1.0, this means the motor is not designed to carry continuous loads greater than rated horsepower.

Severance damages: loss in value to the remainder of a parcel, resulting from a partial taking of real property.

Sewer work: work underground, generally reflected in a contract, part of which is for a fixed price and part of which is for a unit price on items to be excavated or supplied.

Shaft: excavation under the earth's surface the depth of which, either horizontal or vertical, is much greater than its cross-sectional dimensions, as in the case of wells, cesspools, and certain foundation footings.

Shear: (a) type of stress in which adjacent parts of a member tend to slide past each other; (b) fracture where one part of a member or material breaks and slides against the other.

Shearleg derrick: derrick without a boom, similar to a breast derrick; the mast, wide at the bottom and narrow at the top, is hinged at the bottom and has its top secured by a multiple-reeved guy to permit it to handle loads at various radii by means of load tackle suspended from the mast top.

Shooting the bank or sectioning the work: in a unit price contract, a surveyor's final mathematical determination as to how much material was removed or placed within the pay lines.

Shop drawings: drawings prepared by the general or subcontractor showing how such person intends to provide the items required in the architect's working drawings; all drawings, diagrams, illustrations, brochures, schedules, and other data prepared by the contractor, subcontractor, manufacturer, supplier, or distributor, which illustrate the equipment, material, or some portion of the work.

Shore: supporting member that resists a compressive force imposed by a load.

Shoring system: temporary structure for the support of earth that might otherwise move.

Shot rock: rock which has been blasted in order to be excavated; see *Unit price* or *Pay lines.*

Shoulder: portion of the roadway continuous with the traveled way for accommodation of stopped vehicles, for emergency use, and for lateral support of base and surface courses.

Shrinkage limit (soil): as moisture leaves a soil, the soil shrinks and decreases in volume in direct proportion to the loss in moisture until a condition of equilibrium is reached at which shrinkage stops although additional moisture may be removed; this point of moisture content where shrinkage stops is called the shrinkage limit of the soil, and is reported as moisture content by oven-dry weight of soil.

Side pull: that portion of the hoist pull acting horizontally when the hoist lines are not operated vertically.

Side pull or side loading: load applied at any angle to the vertical plane of the boom.

Sides, wall, and faces: vertical or inclined earth surfaces formed as a result of excavation work.

Sidewalk: portion of a street between the curb lines, or the lateral line of a roadway, and the adjacent property lines, intended for the use of pedestrians.

Signal, back-plates: strip of thin material extending outward parallel to the signal face, on all sides of a signal housing, to provide suitable background for the signal indications.

Signal, controller: complete electrical mechanism, mounted in a cabinet, for controlling the operation of a traffic control signal.

Signal, detector: device by which vehicles, streetcars, trolley buses, or pedestrians are enabled to register their presence with a traffic-actuated controller.

Signal, highway traffic: any power-operated traffic control device, except a sign or a barricade warning light or steady burning electric lamps, by which traffic is warned or is directed to take some specific action.

Signal, interval: any one of the several divisions of the time cycle during which signal indications do not change.

Signal, lane-use control: highway traffic signal erected to control the direction of vehicular traffic movement in an individual lane.

Signal, major street: roadway approach or approaches at an intersection normally carrying the major volume of vehicular traffic.

Signal, minor street: roadway approach or approaches at an intersection normally carrying the minor volume of vehicular traffic.

Signal, optical unit: assembly of a lens, reflector, light source, and other components, if required, with necessary supporting parts to be used to provide a signal indication.

Signal, pedestrian: traffic control signal erected for the exclusive purpose of directing pedestrian traffic at signalized locations.

Signal, pedestrian detector: detector, usually push-button type, installed near the roadway, capable of being operated by hand.

Signal, pedestrian signal indication: illumination of a pedestrian signal lens or equivalent device.

Signal, pretimed: type of traffic control signal operating on predetermined, scheduled time cycles and intervals.

Signal, signal face: that part of a traffic control signal provided for controlling one or more traffic movements in a single direction; turning indications may be included in a signal face.

Signal, signal head: assembly containing one or more signal faces.

Signal, signal indication: illumination of a traffic control signal lens or equivalent device.

Signal, signal installation: all equipment and material involved in the control of traffic at a particular intersection by a traffic control signal.

Signal, signal lens: that part of the optical unit which redirects light coming directly from the light source, and its reflector, if any.

Signal, signal support: physical means whereby a signal head is supported in a particular location.

Signal, signal system: two or more signal installations operating in coordination.

Signal, time cycle: time period required for one complete sequence of signal indications.

Signal, traffic-actuated: signal in which the intervals are varied in accordance with the demands of traffic as registered by the actuation of detectors.

Signal, traffic control (traffic signal): type of highway traffic signal, manually, electrically, or mechanically operated, by which traffic alternately directed to stop and permitted to proceed.

Signal, traffic phase: part of the time cycle allocated to any traffic movement receiving the right of way, or to any combination of traffic movements receiving the right of way simultaneously during one or more intervals.

Signal, train approach: indicates to highway traffic the approach and passage of railroad trains at a railroad-highway grade crossing.

Signal, vehicular phase: traffic phase allocated to all traffic except pedestrians.

Sign, guide: used to show route designations, destinations, directions, distances, services, points of interest, and other geographical or cultural information.

Sign, lane-use: indication of regulations governing use of specific lanes.

Sign, legend: word messages or symbols used on signs to convey specific meanings.

Sign, public parking area (or facility): parking facility available for use by the general public, with or without payment of a fee.

Sign, regulatory: used to give notice of traffic laws or regulations.

Sign, traffic (or sign): device mounted on a fixed or portable support, conveying a specific message by means of words or symbols, placed or erected for the purpose of regulating, warning, or guiding traffic.

Sign, warning: used to given notice of conditions on, or adjacent to, a highway or street, that are potentially hazardous to traffic operations.

Skew angle: complement of the acute angle between two lines which cross.

Slab on grade: horizontal deck at ground level which separates the foundation structures from the visible portion of the structure (superstructure).

Sloping of earth: angle with the horizontal at which a particular earth material will stand indefinitely without movement.

Soils engineer: professional engineer who specializes in soil analysis, foundations, design, and drainage.

Spalling: chipping or splitting in layers of concrete, masonry, or stone.

Span: horizontal distance center to center of runway rails.

Specific gravity: ratio of weight of a substance to weight of an equal volume of water.

Specific heat (liquid): quantity of heat (BTUs) needed to raise the temperature of one pound of a substance one degree Fahrenheit at constant pressure.

Spoil: earth material that is removed in the formation of an excavation.

Standing rope (guy): supporting rope which maintains a constant distance between points of attachment to the two components connected by the rope.

Steady burning electric lamps: series of low wattage, yellow electric lamps, used to mark obstructions or hazards in construction and maintenance work areas.

Stemming: material used to conform a charge of explosives in a hole or to cover explosives in mudcapping.

Stick built: construction of a frame structure by cutting and assembling lumber at the job site; opposite of *Systems approach*.

Strain: any forced change in the dimensions of a body; a stretch is *tensile* strain; a shortening is *compressive* strain; a twist is *torsional* strain; an angular distortion is *shear* strain; commonly used to denote unit strain or strain over one square inch.

Stream gauging: process and art of measuring depths, areas, velocities, and rates of flowing water.

Street: generally, see *highway*.

Street, cul-de-sac: local street, open at one end only, with special provisions for turning around.

Street, dead-end: local street, open at one end only, without special provisions for turning around.

Street, frontage (or road): local street or road, auxiliary to and located on the side of an arterial highway, for service to abutting property and adjacent areas and for control of access.

Street, local (or local road): street or road primarily for access to residence, business, or other abutting property.

Stress: (a) internal force exerted by either of two adjacent parts of a body on the other across an imaginary plane of separation; often used to refer to unit stress, most commonly, stress on one square inch area; (b) object's internal response to an applied force; may result in compression, shearing (fracture), tensile (stretching); magnitude measured in pounds per square inch or kips per square inch.

Stress relieving: reducing residual stresses in a metal by heating to a suitable temperature for a certain time; relieves stress caused by casting, quenching, normalizing, machining, cold working, or welding.

Stringers: horizontal members of the shoring system whose sides bear against the uprights or earth.

Structural competence: ability of the machine and its components to withstand stresses imposed by applied loads.

Structural engineer: professional engineer who specializes in the design of bridges, foundations, building structures, and the like.

Structural Section (roadway): planned layers of specified materials, normally consisting of subbase, base, and pavement placed over basement soil.

Stub out: placing plumbing and electrical conduit in wall and floor forms before pouring concrete.

Stud jack: scaffold device of metal with sawlike teeth that grips the stud when the load is applied, with a cantilevered ledger for the support of a working platform.

Subbase: layer of aggregate of planned thickness and quality, placed on the basement soil as the foundation for a base.

Subcontractor: individual, firm, or corporation with a direct contract with the contractor or with any other subcontractor for performance of a part of the work at the site; a party who contracts for a portion of the general contract undertaken by the contractor or another subcontractor; the contractual relation created is between the subcontractor and the general contractor, and not with the owner.

Subgrade: portion of a roadbed surface which has been prepared as specified, on which a subbase, base, base course, or pavement is to be placed.

Substantial completion: date as certified by the engineer at which construction of the project or a specified part thereof is sufficiently completed.

Super: general contractor's site superintendent, responsible for overseeing progress of all trades and the general contractor's own laborers on the site.

Superelevation: banking of a roadway to resist centrifugal forces of a vehicle.

Surety: company which guarantees to an owner that the contractors will complete the contract (performance bond), and which may also guarantee that the contractor will pay all the subs, and that the subs will pay their materialmen (labor and material payment bond); a surety may also issue a mechanic's lien from the premises, to serve as security in lieu of the building or construction fund to which the lien otherwise attaches.

Surety consultant: an engineer, architect, or experienced construction expert hired by a surety to oversee completion of defaulted work, report to it on the cost of completion, and review amounts claimed against it by the owner, subs, and materialmen.

Surety man: a lawyer, engineer, architect, construction consultant, or employee of the surety who usually works for or on the side of the bonding company on construction matters.

Suretyship: contractual obligation whereby one person engages to be answerable for the debt, default, or miscarriage of another who is already bound.

Surface course (roadway): top portion of a pavement where the top and bottom portions are not of the same composition.

Surface tension: property existing in the surface layer of all liquids which, due to molecular forces, causes the layer to pull inward, so that the liquid tends to assume the shape which has the smallest possible surface areas (sphere); given in dynes per centimeter.

Swinging or slewing: act of moving a boom through a horizontal arc.

Switch: device for making, breaking, or changing the connections in an electric circuit.

Switch board: large single panel, frame, or assembly of panels, on the face and/or back of which are mounted switches, overcurrent and protective devices, fuses, and instruments.

Switch gear: central electrical equipment which directs current to the various parts of the building and acts as a fuse.

Synchronous speed and slip: in alternating current (ac) motors, synchronous speed is that speed at which the motor would operate if the rotor turned at the exact speed of the rotating magnetic field; however, in ac induction motors, the rotor actually turns slightly slower, and this difference is defined as slip, expressed in per cent of synchronous speed; most induction motors normally have a slip of 1 to 3 per cent.

Systems approach: construction method whereby component parts of a building are manufactured in a factory and then assembled on the job site; the opposite of stick built (frame construction) and poured in place (concrete construction).

T

T & M: time and materials; work not done for a set price, but where the contractor is paid for time and material plus a percentage or a fixed fee.

Temporary certificate of occupancy: allows occupation of the building, but subject to revocation if certain items required by the city are not supplied; see *Certificate of occupancy.*

Tensile: stretching or rupture resulting from pulling of material in the direction of length.

Thermal protector (as applied to motors): an inherent overheating protective device, responsive to motor current and temperature and which, when properly applied to a motor, protects the motor against dangerous overheating from overload or failure to start.

Third tier: subcontractor or supplier to the subcontractor of the general contract.

Threshold limit value: time-weighed average concentration of solvent vapor in air which should not be exceeded to avoid adverse toxicological effects on workers; set by the American Conference of Governmental Industrial Hygienists, which advises caution in comparing the numbers from one solvent to another because different solvents vary in their toxicological effects and because a solvent with a higher evaporation rate will reach its threshold limit value faster than some other solvent under comparable conditions.

Through street or through highway: every highway or portion of highway on which vehicular traffic is given preferential right of way; vehicular traffic from intersecting highways is required to stop before entering or crossing such a highway.

Thrust-out: beam extending out from a structure to support a suspended scaffold.

Tight site: building site where there is little room to work because the site is hemmed in by other buildings or natural obstacles.

Tinner: also *tin-knocker*; subcontractor doing sheet-metal work.

Toll road, bridge or tunnel: highway, bridge, or tunnel open to traffic only on payment of a direct toll or fee.

Top out: placement of the last piece of framing at the top of the building.

Torque: (a) that force which tends to produce torsion or rotation; in motors, the amount of force produced by a motor to turn the load, measured in pound-feet; (b) a twisting moment; a force which tends to rotate a member about its neutral axis.

Townhouse: dwelling unit normally having at least two stories, usually connected to a similar structure by a common wall, and usually sharing and owning in common the surrounding grounds.

Township: in government survey, a square tract, six miles on each side, containing 36 square miles of land.

Tract: a lot, piece, or parcel of land, of greater or less size, but generally a large piece of land.

Trade: subcontractor who performs a specific item of work in the construction process, e.g., plumber, electrician; when used in the plural (trades), generally refers to all subcontractors on the job.

Trademark: distinctive mark, motto, device, or emblem which a manufacturer stamps, prints, or otherwise affixes to the vendible commodities it produces, so that they may be identified in the market and their origin vouched for.

Trade name: description of a manufacturer or dealer, rather than the commodity; relates to the business and its good will; goal is to secure the advantages of a good reputation.

Trade payment breakdown: a breakdown of the various items in the contract, describing a certain value of each item, submitted by the general contractor to the owner after a job is contracted; this is the basis for the general contractor's requisition for money earned, as the contractor applies the claimed percentage of completion of that item against the total value assigned to it in the trade payment breakdown.

Traffic lane: strip of roadway intended to accommodate the forward movement of a single line of vehicles.

Trailer, full: see *Full trailer.*

Trailer, pole: see *Pole trailer.*

Trailer, semi: see *Semitrailer.*

Transit: moving or transporting a crane from one job site to another.

Travel: function of a machine moving from one location to another on a job site.

Traveled way: that portion of the roadway which is for the movement of vehicles, exclusive of shoulders and auxiliary lanes.

Trench: excavation in which the depth exceeds the average width of its cross-section; excavations more than 15 feet wide at the bottom, such as shafts, tunnels, and mine excavations, are not trenches.

Trolley: truck or carriage supporting the load mounted on an overhead beam, bridge, cableway, or track.

Trolley travel: trolley movement at right angles to the crane runway.

Truck: any self-propelled motor vehicle except a truck tractor, designed and used, or exclusively used whether or not so designed, for transportation of property.

Truck (of an overhead, gantry, or locomotive crane): framework and wheels operating on the runway or rails, and supporting the bridge, trolley, or body of the crane.

Truck tractor: a self-propelled motor vehicle designed and used primarily for drawing other vehicles, and not constructed so as to carry a load other than a part of the weight of the vehicle and load so drawn.

Truss: framework of members, usually including beams, bars, and ties, giving support and rigidity to a structure; usually arranged in a triangular shape or groups of triangles.

Turnkey: method of developing real estate whereby a developer/contractor furnishes all that is necessary to construct the improvements, including architectural and engineering services, under a contract which deeds the property to the developer/contractor and which calls for the property to be deeded back to the owner on completion of the improvements, at which point the owner presumably needs only to "turn the key."

Turnkey contract: contract in which builder agrees to complete building and installation to point of readiness for occupancy.

U

Ultimate strength: the maximum tensile, compressive, or shear stress that a material can sustain before failure; also *breaking strength.*

Unit price: price set for work to be paid per unit for an unknown number of units; work such as sewer work, excavating, foundations, and other underground work is done on unit price contracts since, for example, the type of excavation or the amount of fill to be supplied are unknown and unknowable until such a job is finished; a unit price contract may appear to state a fixed price, but in reality it does not, since numbers of units are based on engineer's estimates at the beginning of the job and are not finally determined until the work has been completed.

Unstable: earth material which cannot be depended on to remain in place without extra support; requires a system of shoring.

Uprights: (a) vertical members of a pole scaffold, such as posts, poles, or columns; (b) vertical members of the shoring systems.

Upset price: contract price which is the maximum the contractor or subcontractor will be paid; if the job comes in at lower cost the savings will be shared in some fashion between the owner and the general.

V

Vapor density: ratio of the weight of a given volume of a vapor to the weight of an equal volume of air.

Vectors: mathematical expressions possessing magnitude and direction.

Vehicle: (a) every device in, on, or by which any person or property is or may be transported or drawn on a highway, except devices moved by human power or used exclusively on stationary rails or tracks; (b) any conveyance, of any type whatsoever, operated on the highways; (c) any conveyance, of any type, operated on the highways.

Viscosity: property of fluids causing them not to flow easily because of the friction of their molecules.

Voltage: unit of electro-motive force, that force which, applied to a conductor, such as wire, will produce a current in the conductor.

W

Waler: structural member in a horizontal or nearly horizontal position used for stiffening or securing other components of concrete forms, excavation sheeting, or similar temporary structures; brace in a coffer dam.

Walking around money: also *coffee money*; usually small cash payments which come to parties in authority in the construction process from a party outside the actual construction contract, e.g., cash payments from junk dealers for scrap from demolition of the old building on the site or payments from neighboring owners for small improvements to their premises or use of materials, machines, etc.

Walk the job: to walk about the job to view progress and performance, generally done with representatives, other parties to the contract, or inspectors.

Want of repair: anything in the state or condition of a highway which renders it unsafe or inconvenient for ordinary travel.

Wet standpipe: in-structure source for fire protection water with constant water pressure in the line; generally intended for small fires and for use by building occupants; requires a connected hose.

Work: (a) agent which works on a body when it exerts force on the body through a distance along the direction of the force; (b) all labor necessary to produce the construction required by the contract documents, and all materials and equipment incorporated or to be incorporated in such construction.

Working drawings: drawings prepared by the architect/engineer showing in detail work to be done.

Y

Yield strength: stress at which a material exhibits a specified permanent deformation or set; for stresses under the yield strength, the material will return to its original dimensions and shape; also called *yield point*, *elastic limit*, *apparent elastic limit*, and *proportional limit*.

Additional Sources of Engineering Terminology

James M. Antill & Ronald W. Woodhead, *Critical Path Methods in Construction Practice*, Wiley Interscience, New York, NY, 2d ed 1970.

Henry Campbell Black, *Black's Law Dictionary*, West Publishing Co, 5th ed 1979.

BOCA Basic Building Code, Building Officials & Code Administrators International, Inc, Harwood, Ill, 1978.

Arthur G. Bowman, *Real Estate Law in California*, Prentice-Hall, Inc, Englewood Cliffs, NJ, 2d ed 1965.

California Business and Transportation Agency, *Standard Specifications*, 1975.

California Dept of Industrial Relation, *Construction Safety* Orders, *reprinted from* Cal Adm Code Title 8, Industrial Relations, Building News, Inc, Los Angeles, Cal, 1972.

City of Los Angeles, *Planning and Zoning Code*, Building News, Inc, Los Angeles, Cal, 1978.

Donald G. Fink, *Standard Handbook for Electrical Engineers*, McGraw-Hill Book Co, New York, NY, 10th ed 1968.

Edwin H. Gaylord, Jr, and Charles N. Gaylord, *Structural Engineering Handbook*, McGraw-Hill Book Co, New York, NY, 1968.

Erich Hausmann & Edgar Slack, *Physics*, D Van Nostrand Co, New York, NY, 1939.

Reno C. King, *Piping Handbook*, McGraw-Hill Book Co, New York, NY, 4th ed 1967.

Manual of Steel Construction, American Institute of Steel Construction, Inc, Chicago, Ill, 8th ed 1980.

John H. Perry, *Chemical Engineers' Handbook*, McGraw-Hill Book Co, New York, NY, 4th ed 1969.

Max Schwartz, *Civil Engineering for Plant Engineers*, McGraw-Hill Book Co, New York, NY, 1972.

Uniform Building Code, International Conference of Building Officials, Whittier, Cal, 1979.

Leonard Church Urquhart, *Civil Engineering Handbook*, McGraw-Hill Book Co, New York, NY, 4th ed 1959.

Table of Cases

A

Allen Morris Co v McNally, 305 So 2d 79 (Fla 1974) **§9.02**

Andrews v Barker Bros, 267 Cal App 2d 530, 73 Cal Rptr 284 (1968) **§10.37**

Arkansas State Highway Commn v Dean, 247 Ark 717, 447 SW2d 334 (1969) **§7.16**

Arkansas State Highway Commn v Rhodes, 240 Ark 565, 401 SW2d 558 (1966) **§8.07**

Asbury v Fidelity Natl Bank & Trust Co, 231 Mo App 437, 100 SW2d 946 (1936) **§10.39**

Associated Dry Goods Corp v Drake, 394 F2d 637 (8th Cir 1968) **§10.02**

B

Baird v Koerner, 279 F2d 623 (9th Cir 1960) **§§10.14, 10.15**

Baki v BF Diamond Constr, 71 FRD 179 (D Md 1976) **§10.16**

Bank of the Orient v Superior Court, 67 Cal App 3d 588, 136 Cal Rptr 741 (1977) **§10.16**

Baptiste v Boatmen's Natl Bank, 148 SW2d 743 (Mo 1941) **§10.03**

Barnett v State Workmen's Compensation Commr, 153 W Va 796, 172 SE2d 698 (1970) **§10.08**

Barrus v Phaneuf, 166 Mass 123, 44 NE 141 (1896) **§10.29**

Bertram v Harris, 423 P2d 909 (Alaska 1967) **§9.21**

Board of Educ v Ace Test Boring, Inc, 47 Misc 2d 864, 263 NYS2d 193 (1965) **§10.15**

Brown v Colm, 11 Cal 3d 639, 522 P2d 688, 114 Cal Rptr 128 (1974) **§10.38**

Buckhanon v State, 151 Ga 827, 108 SE 209 (1921) **§10.06**

Bureau of Medical Economics v Cossette, 44 Cal App 3d Supp 1, 118 Cal Rptr 242 (1974) **§10.26**

Burg v Chicago, RI & P Ry, 90 Iowa 106, 57 NW 680 (1894) **§10.37**

C

Camden v City of New York, 119 AD 84, 103 NYS 971 (1907) **§8.02**

Cavanaugh v McDonnell & Co, 357 Mass 452, 258 NE2d 561 (1970) **§10.43**

D

E

F

G

H

I

J

K

L

M

N

O

P

R

S

Y

Z

Table of Statutes

Maine

Me Rev Stat Ann, tit 14, §§5927-49 **§10.42**

Maryland

Md Cts & Jud Proc Code Ann §§3-201 to 3-234 **§10.42**

Massachusetts

Mass Gen Laws Ann, ch 251, §§1-19 **§10.42**
Mass Gen Laws Ann, ch 251, §7 **§10.42**

Michigan

Registration Act 240, Mich Comp Laws, vol III, §338.552 **§2.06**
Registration Act 240, Mich Comp Laws, vol III, §338.569 **§2.46**
Mich Comp Laws §§600.5001-.5035 **§10.42**

Minnesota

Minn Stat Ann §§572.08-.30 **§10.42**

Nebraska

Neb R Evid 706 **§10.19**
Neb Rev Stat §27-706 **§10.19**

Nevada

Nev Rev Stat §27-706 **§10.19**
Nev Rev Stat §§38.015-.045 **§10.42**

New Hampshire

NH Rev Stat §§542:1 to 542:10 **§10.42**

New Jersey

NJ Evid 56(3) **§10.3**
NJ Evid 57 & 58 **§10.09**
NJ Stat Ann §§2A:24-1 to 2A:24-11 **§10.42**
NJ Stat Ann §2A:84A-32 **§§10.09, 10.36**

New Mexico

NM R Evid 706 **§10.19**
NM R Evid 706(a) **§10.25**
NM R Evid 706(b) **§10.23**
NM Stat Ann §§22-3-9 to 22-3-31 **§10.42**

New York

NY Civ Prac Law §3101(c) **§10.15**
NY Civ Prac Law §3101(d) **§10.15**
NY Civ Prac Law §§7501-14 **§10.42**

North Carolina

NC Gen Stat §§1567.1.20 **§10.42**

Ohio

Ohio Rev Code Ann §2711.07 **§10.42**

Oklahoma

Okla Stat, tit 15, §§801-18 **§10.42**

Pennsylvania

Pa Cons Stat Ann §§161-209 **§10.42**

Rhode Island

RI Gen Laws §9-17-19 **§10.23**
RI Gen Laws §10-3-9 **§10.42**

South Dakota

Texas

Wisconsin

Wyoming

Index

A

B

C

D

E

F

G

H

I

J

K

L

M

N

O

P

S

T

U

V

W

Y

Z